COMMUNIST PARTIES REVISITED

COMMUNIST PARTIES REVISITED

Sociocultural Approaches to Party Rule
in the Soviet Bloc, 1956–1991

Edited by
Rüdiger Bergien and Jens Gieseke

berghahn
NEW YORK · OXFORD
www.berghahnbooks.com

First published in 2018 by
Berghahn Books
www.berghahnbooks.com

© 2018, 2020 Rüdiger Bergien and Jens Gieseke
First paperback edition published in 2020

All rights reserved. Except for the quotation of short passages for the purposes of criticism and review, no part of this book may be reproduced in any form or by any means, electronic or mechanical, including photocopying, recording, or any information storage and retrieval system now known or to be invented, without written permission of the publisher.

Library of Congress Cataloging-in-Publication Data

A C.I.P. cataloging record is available from the Library of Congress

British Library Cataloguing in Publication Data

A catalogue record for this book is available from the British Library

ISBN 978-1-78533-776-5 hardback
ISBN 978-1-78920-845-0 paperback
ISBN 978-1-78533-777-2 ebook

Contents

	List of Illustrations	vii
	Acknowledgments	ix
	Abbreviations	x
Introduction	Communist Parties Revisited: Sociocultural Approaches to Party Rule in the Soviet Bloc, 1956–1991 *Rüdiger Bergien and Jens Gieseke*	1
Chapter 1	The Paradox of Party Discipline in the Khrushchev-Era Communist Party *Edward Cohn*	23
Chapter 2	"It Is Not Possible to Allow Past Mistakes to Come Again": Recruitment Policy in the CPCS in the 1970s and 1980s *Michel Christian*	46
Chapter 3	Behind Closed Doors: The Erosion of SED Party Life in the 1980s *Sabine Pannen*	72
Chapter 4	The Successive Dissolution of the "Uncivil Society": Tracking SED Members in Opinion Polls and Secret Police Reports, 1969–1989 *Jens Gieseke*	95
Chapter 5	On the Way to Party Pluralism? The PZPR and the Reform of the Socialist Party System in 1988–1989 *Frédéric Zalewski*	123
Chapter 6	Communist Party Apparatuses as Steering Organizations: Paths of Development in East Central Europe *Christoph Boyer*	143

Chapter 7	The Central Committee Department of Party Organs under Khrushchev *Alexander Titov*	168
Chapter 8	True Believers Becoming Funded Experts? Personnel Profile and Political Power in the SED Central Committee's Sectoral Apparatus, 1946–1989 *Rüdiger Bergien*	190
Chapter 9	Paternalism in Local Practice: The Logic of Repression, Ideological Hegemony, and the Everyday Management of Society in an SED Local Secretariat *Andrea Bahr*	212
Chapter 10	The SED *Bezirk* Secretaries as Brokers of Territorial Interests in the GDR *Jay Rowell*	237
Chapter 11	The Idea of Social Unity and Its Influence on the Mechanisms of a Totalitarian Regime in the Years 1956–1980 *Krzysztof Dąbek*	259
Chapter 12	Foreign Policymaking and Party-State Relations in the Soviet Union during the Brezhnev Era *Mark Kramer*	281
Chapter 13	Erich Honecker—The "Leading Representative": A Generational Perspective *Martin Sabrow*	313
Chapter 14	Inside the System: The CPSU Central Committee, Mikhail Gorbachev's *Komanda,* and the End of Communist Rule in Russia *Jan C. Behrends*	326
Chapter 15	The Ironies of Membership: The Ruling Communist Party in Comparative Perspective *Padraic Kenney*	352
	Index	364

Illustrations

Figures

1.1.	Communist Party Membership by Year, 1938–1964	27
2.1.	Number of Candidates to the CPCS between 1971 and 1988	50
2.2.	Membership Evolution between 1945 and 1988, according to the Year When Members Joined the Party	51
7.1.	Organizational Chart of the Party Organ Departments of the CPSU, 1954–1964	183

Tables

1.1.	Communist Party Membership, 1938–1964	28
1.2.	The Class Breakdown of Communists, 1945–1953	30
2.1.	Average Rate of Party Membership in the Czechoslovakian Population	52
2.2.	Evolution of the Rate of Party Membership in the Czech and in the Slovakian Regions between 1971 and 1986	52
2.3.	Party Members' Occupation When Joining the Party, according to Social Stratification in Eastern Europe Survey	54
2.4.	Party Members' Occupation When Joining the Party, according to Central Commitee of the CPCS	55
2.5.	Rate of Party Membership in the CPCS in Different Social Groups and Professions in 1981	56
2.6.	Size and Proportion of Post-1968 Membership in Some Primary Party Organizations in the Mělník District in 1979	56

2.7. Organization Rates among Women and among Men in Slovakia, in the Czech Lands, and in Czechoslovakia Overall in 1981 … 57

2.8. People Whose Father Had Ever Been in the CPCS by the End of the 1980s … 62

2.9. People with a Mother or Father Still in the CPCS at the End of the 1980s … 62

2.10. Membership of Mass Organizations among Candidates Recruited in Kutná Hora in 1975 … 64

2.11. Participation of CPCS Candidates in Kutná Hora in 1975 … 64

2.12. Comparable Membership of Mass Organizations among CPCS Recruits in Kutná Hora in 1975 and SED Recruits in Nauen in 1979 … 65

4.1. Demographic Structure of SED Members from Internal SED Statistics and the Infratest Sample … 102

4.2. Social Composition of SED Members … 103

4.3. "Which of these political attitudes apply to person X?" … 104

4.4. "Did X complain about spending too much time on political and societal events or did X express the view that the expenditure of time is acceptable?" … 105

4.5. "Did X complain about political pressure, or did you have the impression that X did not feel under pressure?" … 105

4.6. "Did X occasionally mention the reasons why he/she joined mass organizations or the party (SED, Free German Youth, trade union, Society for Sports and Technology, etc.)? Which ones?" … 106

4.7. "Please tell me what X mentioned as the most important factor in professional success in the GDR" … 106

4.8. "Please tell me for each of these features if it is more a feature of the GDR system or the Federal Republic system" (selected features, 1973) … 108

4.9. Number of Stasi Reports Mentioning Party Members or Specific Groups of Party Cadres, 1960–1987 … 111

5.1. Total Number of Party Members … 127

Acknowledgments

The authors would like to thank the Fritz Thyssen Foundation for their generous support, as well as Dariusz Stola and Bernd Florath for a number of extremely productive comments. Furthermore, we sincerely thank Marion Berghahn, Chris Chappell, Amanda Horn, and the whole staff at Berghahn for their support, and the two anonymous scholars for their extremely helpful reviews. Their comments and recommendations impelled us to improve our ideas and prose.

Our special thanks go to Francesca Bondy, who took the burden of copyediting. At the Centre for Contemporary History, Ute Groß, Stephanie Karmann, Roxanna Noll, Nora Prüfer, Theresa Thaller, and Florian Schikowski accompanied the preparations of this volume with great commitment. We would like to express our gratitude to them, to the whole Communism and Society team and to all other colleagues for the unique warm and inspiring atmosphere at the Centre for Contemporary History.

Abbreviations

CC	Central Committee
Comintern	Communist International
CP	Communist Parties
CPCS	Communist Party of Czechoslovakia
CPSU	Communist Party of the Soviet Union
CV	Curriculum Vitae
ECE	East Central Europe
FDGB	Freier Deutscher Gewerkschaftsbund (East German Trade Union)
FDJ	Freie Deutsche Jugend (East German Youth Mass Organization)
FRG/BRD	Federal Republic of Germany
GDR/DDR	German Democratic Republic (East Germany)
GRU	Glavnoye razvedyvatel'noye upravleniye (Main Intelligence Directorate; foreign military intelligence agency of the USSR)
GST	Gesellschaft für Sport und Technik (East German mass organization for sports and paramilitary training)
ID	International Department (of the CPSU)
KGB	Komitet gosudarstvennoy bezopasnosti (Committee for State Security of the USSR)
KPD	Kommunistische Partei Deutschlands (Communist Party of [West] Germany)
MBA	Master of Business Administration

MID	Ministerstvo Inostrannykh Del' (Ministry of Foreign Affairs)
NATO	North Atlantic Treaty Organization
NKVD	Narodnyi Komissariat Vnutrennikh Del (People's Commissariat for Internal Affairs)
NSDAP	Nationalsozialistische Deutsche Arbeiterpartei (National Socialist German Workers' Party)
OKTI	Ogólnopolska Konferencja Teoretyczno-Ideologiczna (Third Theoretical Ideological National Conference)
PDS	Partei des Demokratischen Sozialismus (Party of Democratic Socialism; successor of the SED)
PPO	Primary Party Organization
PPS	Polska Partia Socjalistyczna (Polish Socialist Party)
PRC	People's Republic of China
PZPR/PUWP	Polska Zjednoczona Partia Robotnicza (Polish United Workers' Party)
RCP	Ruling Communist Party
ROH	Revoluční odborové hnutí (Czechoslovakian Revolutionary Trade Union Movement)
RSFSR	Russian Soviet Federative Socialist Republic
SA	Sturmabteilung (Storm Detachment of the German Nazi Party)
SD	Stronnictwo Demokratyczny (Polish Democratic Party)
SED	Sozialistische Einheitspartei Deutschlands (Socialist Unity Party of Germany)
SPD	Sozialdemokratische Partei Deutschlands (Social Democratic Party of Germany)
SPK	Staatliche Plankommission (State Plan Commission of the GDR)
TASS	Informatsionnoye agentstvo Rossii (Soviet/Russian news agency)
UkrCP	Ukrainian Communist Party

USSR	Union of Soviet Socialist Republics
VLKSM	All-Union Leninist Young Communist League (Komsomol)
VPK	Military-Industrial Commission of the USSR
ZMP	Związek Młodzieży Polskiej (Association of Polish Youth)
ZMW	Związek Młodzieży Wiejskiej (Polish Rural Youth Association)
ZSP	Związek Studentów Polskich (Polish Students' Association)
ZSL	Zjednoczone Stronnictwo Ludowe (Polish United People's Party)

 Introduction

COMMUNIST PARTIES REVISITED
Sociocultural Approaches to Party Rule
in the Soviet Bloc, 1956–1991

Rüdiger Bergien and Jens Gieseke

The communist ruling parties (CPs) of Eastern and East Central Europe after 1945 were among the most powerful political organizations of the twentieth century. They possessed unique political, societal, and cultural shaping powers; for several decades they mobilized significant parts of their particular societies. They drove the socialist transformations forward, and they claimed to put utopian societal models into practice. They efficiently determined millions of their members' biographies and were able to bind them to their basic organizations, despite their erosion and demise in the late 1980s.

However, their treatment by historiography is still remarkably one-sided. Historians have overwhelmingly, if not at all, tended to limit them to their functions of passing on and carrying out the politburos' orders and offering their members career progression in exchange for good conduct. They are seldom recognized as separate organizations and dealt with as elements of an all-encompassing socialist statehood. In addition, their capacities as social and cultural communities have largely remained unnoticed. Their members and functionaries are rarely interpreted as genuine historical actors with their own motives and viewpoints. Rather, they are seen as homogenous masses of "believers" that the party leaderships perceived them to be—or pretended to perceive them to be. Even though the term "party state" has become a historiographical key concept, there are at best vague ideas of what the parties' inner life was like *below* the floors of the supposedly almighty politburos.

This book collects contributions that aim to develop new interpretations of both the inner workings of the parties as well as their political practices. The volume begins by asking about the mutual relationships between the CPs and the particular societies, about the inner life of the parties, and about the scope of action of the medium- and lower-level functionaries. All in all, it strives for a more complex image of the CPs that fits into recent cultural and sociohistorical perspectives. In addition, by collecting contributions about the Communist Party of the Soviet Union (CPSU), the East German Socialist Unity Party of Germany (SED), the Polish United Workers' Party (PZPR), and the Communist Party of Czechoslovakia (CPCS), the book aims to establish comparative viewpoints and, as far as possible, to be a valid base for further research for the whole of the former Eastern bloc.[1]

On the State of Research

The neglect of the CPs in recent historiography has resulted from the way post-socialist societies have attempted to come to terms with their pasts. The protagonists of the former liberation movements—many of whom played a role in their countries' politics after 1989—were particularly interested in identifying "perpetrators," who could be blamed for the crimes and failures of the socialist states. Moreover, they claimed that the liberation movements had overcome totalitarian *power states* (rather than weak, "failing" states), in order to give their own victory more importance.[2] Consequently, research on communism in the 1990s focused on the communist regimes' use of power and repression. Many researchers adhered to top-down perspectives that were developed in the course of the Cold War,[3] even though the now-accessible archives would have enabled them to establish more complex views.

The tendency to perceive the communist regimes primarily as centralized power states became especially strong in the boom of research on Stalinism in the 1990s. Revisionist assumptions of a "Stalinism from below"[4] were re-revised again as Stalin's personal rule and the People's Commissariat for Internal Affairs' (NKVD) practice of persecution came to the fore. The CPSU itself receded more into the background and in the role of a subordinated ideological and organizational frame of reference of the "Stalinist civilization," even though Stalin, as well as his followers (and all those who wanted to survive in Soviet society), had to refer to this "frame" rhetorically.[5] In addition, while the interpretations of Stalinism became realigned, there was a significant need to come to empirically founded insights about the Soviet party rule's classic principles (democratic centralism, nomenclature principle, etc.) and their change over time. Consequently, political practices of power enforcement and securing power came to the fore, as well as the politburo's operational methods and "turf wars" between hardliners and reformers.[6] The research on the CPs concerning Eastern and East Central

Europe after 1945 focused on three relatively stable narrative-analytical patterns.

First, the history of the CPs is interpreted primarily as part of the political system's respective histories (or is even identified with it). Thus, the state party and its ideology often form the narrative center of histories of the Soviet Union, Poland, or the German Democratic Republic (GDR) until 1989–91, by being treated as a kind of impersonal collective actor: "The party" was doing this or that.[7] As far as these narratives differentiate actors within this collective body at all, they stress the power of the party leadership, the interconnections between party and state apparatuses, and they emphasize the fact that anybody with career ambitions was forced to join the party. They leave no room beyond or below the overarching party-state structure that could have given grounds for alternative analytical approaches. There can be no doubt that this pattern has stimulated extensive research about the links between party, state apparatuses, and mass organizations. It has led to quite extensive knowledge about the structures of political rule as well as socioeconomic steering principles in Soviet-style societies. However, it also fostered the disregard of the CPs' inner workings, which were indeed influenced not only by the parties' formal structures—their official rules and procedures—but also by internal dynamics. In addition, the interpretative pattern of the "party states" nurtured the neglect of the continuous, "asymmetric" negotiation processes between the parties and the particular societies. In addition, the "mono-organizational institutional design" blurred the surviving distinctions between party and state.

Second, post-1989 Communist studies wrote the history of the CPs as the history of the politburos and their top officials. The will and convictions of these functionaries alone were seemingly effective in shaping their societies' and nations' histories due to the tight hierarchies.[8] Accordingly, subordinate authorities of party rule—especially the professional employees of the party bureaucracies—were perceived as abstract collective actors and remained hidden within the metaphor "apparatus."[9] Finally, the grassroots-level comrades remained indistinct members of the "party base," who did not have the slightest chance of influencing the party leaders' agendas. Consequently, as they were no more than the insignificant "mass base," the basic organizations' inner life—their regular assemblies, their rituals and social relations—have remained beyond the scope of researchers.[10] *Third*, the period of the socialist "build-up" of the Soviet satellite states have been studied much more closely than the post-Stalinist decades.[11] The former were, and are, considered far more eventful and charged with political and social tensions. Apparently, the course was set for the following post-Stalinist history of decay and erosion during this period. Therefore, these post-Stalinist decades have been much less attractive objects for historical research as they were equated with "ideology loss" and stagnation, and gave grounds for the patterns of interpretation as "defunct societies" (*stillgelegte Gesellschaften*). For these reasons, subcutaneous mental and social transformations in the communist state parties that took place in the post-Stalinist decades have scarcely been noticed in recent research on communism. However, it is obvious that precisely these subcutaneous transformations were crucial to the tightening of the political situation in the late 1980s.[12] Over the past two decades, international research on communism has become highly differentiated and has opened up to new theoretical and methodological propositions. In this process, the separation between political history and history of society (and history of the everyday)—which has marked the research on communism in the 1990s—has been abrogated. In its place, the presence of government institutions in the everyday and, vice versa, *Eigensinn* (stubbornness) and informal processes within the institutions of the communist dictatorships have become objects of research.[13]

In view of the socialist societies (or, more precisely, in view of certain regions, professions, milieus, and gender aspects), recent research has already been able to show how Communist rule was perceived, how it could become willfully (*eigensinnig*) interpreted, and how it was occasionally undermined.[14] Recently, even the social practice of state institutions of physical violence, such as the military and secret police, has been included in such a perspective[15]—yet not the Communist parties themselves. One reason for this could be that they, as intermediate organizations, were positioned between all societal levels, a position that raises the most complex analytical problems.[16] Another reason might lie in the fact that it is more difficult to ascribe the parties' comrades and functionaries to a certain societal (and moral) role. This is especially true if one compares them with the various Communist secret police services as the latter's officers and informers can be dealt with much more easily as "perpetrators." However, is a party functionary a perpetrator per se? Are the millions of rank and file comrades members of Milovan Djilas's "new class" per se?[17]

Perspectives based on history of society and history of the everyday have marked the so-called second wave of research on communism in the 1990s and 2000s (after the first wave of studies in political history).[18] The third wave, in contrast, has become shaped by cultural-historical approaches. The interpretation of political rule as a "rule of discourse"[19] or as "authoritative"[20] or "public discourse" has been particularly influential in this field,[21] although even these discourses could have become mandatory by means of repression. However, they left open the possibility for the individual to acquire and transform prescribed ways of speaking.

Yet again, these cultural-historical approaches have also primarily focused on certain social groups—on Komsomol members, intellectuals, or environmentalists, for instance. Whether and to what extent party members and functionaries also similarly appropriated, changed, or evaded the "authoritative discourse" is still an open question. Similarly, the extent to which the Stalinist party discipline and practices of repression were replaced by more flexible ways of maintaining the parties' coherence—for example, by performative practices or by new offers for collective identities,[22] including references to the nation or regional identities—also remains unanswered.[23] Cultural-historical approaches may be especially fruitful in addressing these problems, and the analysis of the parties' members' "hidden" transcripts and informal patterns of action might contribute to gaining a new, more complex image of the allegedly monolithic parties as well as of the "defunct societies." Moreover, such an analysis might lead to more multidimensional explanations for "1989," which emphasized long-term change more than many of the current political historical studies.[24]

In the last years, the debate about the causes of the decay of the Socialist systems and the CP's dissolution in the 1980s has indeed intensified, stimulated again by cultural-historical and anthropological perspectives. Recent research has particularly begun, controversially, to discuss the role of perceptions of crisis within the socialist functional elites.[25] A systematic analysis of the collective mentalities of party functionaries and party members and how they changed over time, however, is still missing.[26]

New Perspectives on Party Rule

Starting from this view, the state socialist communist parties cannot be reduced to just one function. The parties were multifunctional organizations[27] and not just in charge of political rule or cadre selection.[28] They felt also responsible for the societies' integration and the dissemination of worldviews and collective identities. The principal aim of this volume is to make the multifunctional character of the CPs more visible in the research on communism and thereby give them a more prominent place in historiography.

The volume collects contributions that implement approaches of social and cultural history on the CPs. Their joint starting point is first an understanding of the CPs that emphasizes their status as independent organizations, with clear borders to state institutions and other mass organizations. Indeed, they never became an integral branch of the "mono-organizational state."[29] Although the merger of government and politburo came to be perceived as the archetypal feature of the Soviet model, even in the CPSU's case it was limited to the Second World War.[30] In its aftermath, the CPSU reestablished its central role and "advised" its "sister parties" in East Central Europe to persist in a similar fashion on certain borders between party and state. These "borders" became even more important as Khrushchev started to "revive" the party and use it as his power base from the Nineteenth Congress onwards.[31]

The decades of post-Stalinism were, consequently, not marked by the "mono-organizational institutional design" that dominates the current historiographical approaches.[32] In contrast, the "party states" were actually differentiated by organizational borders: borders most prominently between the state and the party, yet also "between the party's center (the 'inner party') and the 'outer party' of regional and local organizations."[33] The parties' role was always quintessential, and these boundaries were often blurred, but they constituted important references for the political and societal actors. If one aims to gain an understanding of state socialist political processes that does not stop at the underlying politburo decision, then these boundaries need to be considered.

Historians and political scientists have referred to the "mono-institutional organizational design" primarily when they dealt with the relationship between party and state. In contrast, when they have dealt with party-society relations they usually preferred a very different perspective. Starting from the works of contemporaries who interpreted Communist rule as a new form of class rule—most prominently Milovan Djilas with his *New Class* and Michael S. Voslensky with *Nomenklatura*—they categorically differentiated between the CPs and their societal environment, the parties as power organizations, and the subjugated societies. Again, this interpretation is not shared here. Instead, many of the contributions in this volume—and this is their second joint starting point—are based on an understanding of party-society relations that can be captured using the metaphor of the "metabolism." The CPs were not isolated "closed organizations" within the state socialist societies. They were integral parts of these societies, and it is only therefore that, for example, the privileges enjoyed by comrades had the potential to become societal conflicts (and cannot just be seen as elements of a contrast between the ruling "new class" and the subjugated people). The CPs were not closed, but reacted to the societal, cultural, and economic changes within their environment in the post-Stalinist decades. The tightening of their disciplinary regime and repression was one common reaction to societal and inner-party unrest. However, in the post-Stalinist decades they turned more frequently to "softer" methods of rule and to a greater amount of political flexibility.[34] Nevertheless, the limits of this change still needed to be evaluated and many of the contributions in this volume directly address this question.

Most of the articles deal with the CPSU and the East German SED, some of them with the Polish PZPR and the Czechoslovakian CPCS. Even though this might be a rather small sample of Soviet-style Communist ruling parties, it nevertheless already illustrates important organizational, political, and cultural differences.[35] To exemplify this, the identities of the CPSU and PZPR functionaries, along with their worldviews and political agendas, often referred to imperial or national ideas and traditions.[36] They also more often legitimized their rule in a way that Max Weber would have called "traditional": CPSU functionaries in particular were often part of career networks or members of political "clans" that gave support and requested loyalty.[37] In the SED or CPCS (after 1968), however, the situation was different: Here, the nation did not play an important role as a frame of reference. In its place, Marxism-Leninism seemed to have shaped the functionaries' public transcripts and their *habitus* much more strongly (though not necessarily their thinking).

These differences raise the question of whether the category "Soviet-style communist party" has any analytical value that might outweigh its shortfalls. However, another premise of this volume is based on the assumption that the parties *were* indeed connected by certain beliefs and practices—by the shared ideology, the joint orientation towards Moscow as the political and cultural center of the Eastern hemisphere, and the transnational interconnections (through student exchanges within party academies, for example). These connections are seen here as the predominant factors that shaped the collective mentalities as well as the political practices. Therefore, comparative perspectives, which have the potential to highlight the CPs' similarities as well as their differences, are of particular value. Three such perspectives structure this volume and serve as frames of reference to the particular contributions and are briefly explained in the next paragraph.

Parties and Societies

The first of these three perspectives is based on the obvious fact that all the CPs are to be considered as mass parties. Indeed, they all organized substantial amounts of the population for decades until the final crisis. Thus, at least nineteen million people belonged to the CPSU in the 1980s (6.5 percent of a total Soviet population of 290 million), 3.5 million to the PZPR 38 million (9.2 percent), 1.7 million to the CPCS (15.4 percent) and 2.3 to the SED 17 million (12.9 percent). A number of sociological questions therefore urge to be answered: what were the social implications of the integration of up to a fifth of the adult population into the party world as a sphere of meaning and organizational rituals? What consequences did this integration have for the dynamics of social stratification, the rebuilding of classes, and the social distribution of resources?[38]

Older historiography interpreted this quantitative dimension of the communist state parties first and foremost as a technique of securing power, as an outcome of the evolution of revolutionary cadre parties into "totalitarian parties of mass integration."[39] It showed only limited interest in the social consequences of that integration. However, even in the new social history on everyday life, ordinary party members were dubbed as an unstructured mass, not worthy of more detailed analysis. The starting point for this volume is the counter-hypothesis that party membership was the most important political—and thereby social—distinguishing divide in state socialist societies. This divide substantially contributed to the constitution of new structures of inequality.[40] All the CPs focused upon here developed into parties of upper state bureaucrats during the post-Stalinist decades. For instance, at least 40 percent of the East German SED was composed of such cadres, following their own internal (and secret) statistics. The CPs were frequently joined by younger and middle-aged males, for whom membership promised access to higher educational degrees and professional careers. Thus, these members had an above-average salary level and, accordingly, a relatively high standard of living. This reproduction of loyalty by reward obviously played an increasingly important role—not least for full-time functionaries within the party apparatus itself.

As was shown for the CPSU as well as the SED, the share of staff expenditures in the party budgets rose continually (and faster than the number of functionaries), while expenditure on ideological work (propaganda meetings, printing of brochures, etc.) decreased.[41] The post-Stalinist CPs, it could be argued, increasingly used the stimulation by material means to keep party functionaries both active and loyal. Lavish salaries and career opportunities for "young potentials" are not be underestimated—opportunities for consumption or vacations in attractive places proved to be more effective in keeping the parties together as mass organizations than the insistence on "criticism and self-criticism" (given that the latter, at least in the SED, was never dropped and kept its place in the organizational culture).

Nevertheless, it would be inadequate to conclude that the importance of material incentives proves that hundreds of thousands of party members were opportunists following rational decisions to maximize their advantage. The reasons for joining the CPs during the 1970s and 1980s were numerous. Career and an ambition for social advancement played a prominent role, but it should not be forgotten that the majority of young party members in this period had a party family background, with their parents and sometimes grandparents being members. This turned joining the party into a similar function to that of Protestant Confirmation or Catholic First Communion in some rural areas of Central Europe: at least in some milieus, it was an obvious step in coming of age.[42]

Apparatuses and Policies

The second perspective in this volume focuses on the concrete functions of the CPs and their apparatuses within their societies. Again, it is necessary to gain some distance from the self-image of the parties (and the images of their Western opponents), presenting them as not only wholly responsible for the repression of the secret police, but also for the empty shelves in the supermarkets. Beyond these images, some confined fields of action came into view, all of them primarily directed to the goal of maintaining power.

The first field of action was to legitimize the power of the CPs by the *production and distribution of ideology*. From the perspective of a history of society, this production remains somewhat enigmatic: on the one hand, it was obviously extremely important for the CPs to enforce their philosophy as compulsory in the public sphere. The CPs had their own departments for agitation and propaganda, party schools, etc., with thousands of employees. Substantial resources were spent on disseminating exclusive party information bulletins on sensitive issues,[43] teaching Marxism-Leninism and, of course, controlling media coverage.[44]

On the other hand, broader layers of the population and at least some party members were aware of the fictional character of ideology. "Trust by faith" in Marxism-Leninism in the strict sense played a role only for a minority of party members.[45] The majority did not measure the party by its charismatic ideas, but rather by its practical qualities: standards of living, future prospects, and material and immaterial achievements of the sociopolitical order. Therefore, the CPs did not practice their claim for conviction and inner education in real life. Instead, they limited themselves to installing their doctrinal system in all public situations as an obligatory authoritative discourse. Beyond the public sphere, in private or semi-public life (in the workplace, on the streets), it was secondary or even totally negligible whether one was convinced by it or just paid it lip service.[46]

The key question resulting from this contradiction is about the real status of "ideology" for the stability of socialist systems.[47] If the significance of ideology for the rank-and-file party members was low, what was the attitude of higher functionaries: do they have to be imagined as "true believers," convinced by the theory of stages of lawfully ascending formations of society? Or is it more appropriate that with de-Stalinization, the ideological "cement" also crumbled in the upper echelons? Do we therefore have to deal with a pragmatic power elite occupied with intrigues, turf battles, and practices of corruption, as suggested in interviews with former Polish party officials?[48] Was the production of ideology and enforcement of authoritative discourse therefore just a power technique, recognized by all participants as fictional? Or did it hint at something more substantial, such as the specific organizational culture of the CPs with their rituals of militancy and self-devotion? While the practical relevance of this organizational culture did decrease, it was obviously not possible to question it openly without paying the price of self-demolition, as shown in Gorbachev's perestroika and the beginnings of social democratization of the Polish PZPR.[49]

The second area of the CPs' activity was securing power through either the threat or the actual practice of *physical violence*. Indeed, this area did not lose its relevance for any of the parties focused on here even in the post-Stalinist era. Of course, mass terror as an instrument of policy faded after 1953. After the period of establishing the Communist system, party functionaries only acted as "professional revolutionaries" on rare occasions, agitating against farmers or stirring up "class hatred." However, even after 1953, it was part of the political practice of top party officials in Poznan or Magnitogorsk, Halle or Prague, to exchange information with their secret police heads about dissidents, nationalist or religious milieus, etc., or, as in East Germany, about people who wanted to leave the country. Only in a few cases did the secret police dare to observe, arrest, or psychologically "decompose" without the explicit permission of the respective party heads.

It was, however, part of the style of these post-Stalinist decades that despite individual cases of hardship, attempts at finding implicit solutions came to the fore. In fact, all Communist parties after 1953 sought a new mode of dictatorial rule. This mode can be characterized by the term "reliability of expectations," but it included not only the channeling and retraction of direct repression; it was also designed to achieve acceptance in other fields and for other party roles,[50] such as the caring "troubleshooter," which (in contrast to the "cold" state administration) took the concerns of ordinary people seriously and made bureaucrats take action.

With the revisionist current of social history and the history of everyday life in so-called new Communist studies, it has become more and more clear that the CPs did more than just instruct the secret police and indoctrinate the population. Considerable portions of their activities were devoted to a third field that can be summarized as "management of society." This field proved to be particularly important because it rapidly became clear to the party leadership that consent, loyalty, and willingness in the population depended first and foremost on issues of practical quality of life. Particularly at the district, county and local levels, countless examples can be found of party secretaries diverting investment funds for the benefit of their own territory, procuring workers for enterprises lacking a workforce, and, conversely, informal bargaining with local companies to support their plans for leisure attractions. The East German town of Brandenburg/Havel, for example, showed that in 1969 local party officials even managed to finance and build a whole public swimming pool that had never appeared in the planned state budget.[51]

It is remarkable that this unlawful political practice was by no means limited to the lower spheres of society—those levels for which the historiography of everyday life stated the importance of "Eigensinn" (stubbornness), colorful informal networks of mutual support, and a "grey" economy. CPSU and SED district party secretaries acted first and foremost as lobbyists for their territory, gaining symbolic capital by organizing its economic success.[52] Even the departments of the central committee (CC) apparatus developed to some extent into intermediary organizations: in addition to executing politburo resolutions, in particular those of the economic departments in the 1970s and 1980s, they cooperated in a somewhat flexible manner with their respective partner ministries for industrial branches, in some cases even including alliances against competing CC departments and "their" ministries.[53]

It is important to acknowledge that these "network improvisations"[54] cannot be interpreted as phenomena of demise. Networking and informal arrangements within the party and state bureaucracy had been gaining strength since the sixties. This was part of a homogenization of the functional elite, at least in East Central Europe, overcoming the former social and political conflicts between party and state cadres. To summarize, state socialism—apart from periods of war and the violent implementation of power—was reliant not only on an informal "secondary economy," but also on a "secondary policy" for its existence.

Internal Workings and Leadership Styles

A third perspective in this volume deals with the parties as political organizations that differentiated themselves from the outside world using the membership criterion and enforcing specific conditions and interpretations of reality for those members. At the same time, the parties were subject to change by the cohorts of members and functionaries, even though that change took place at a remarkably slower pace than its societal environment. From this perspective, different levels within the parties come into focus and show specific patterns of thought, speech, and action. These different levels can be defined as partial cultures within the party.

The party leaderships, for which only a few biographies of top functionaries are at hand despite a relatively strong interest in this level of party life,[55] are still as important as ever. One of the most striking research requirements is the very limited knowledge about concrete decision-making both within and outside the politburo meetings, which at least in the later decades often consisted only of rubber-stamping preformulated agendas and resolutions. The answers to questions of who, how, and when the power centers initiated political procedures, what defined political success, and the influence of informal relations is still quite unclear for East Central European CPs. The inner workings of the outwardly homogenous party apparatuses were more communicative and more dynamic and contained more areas of conflict than had been formerly recognized.

For instance, Leonid Brezhnev, of all people the ideal "apparatchik," maintained a quite cooperative leadership style and consulted experts with diverging opinions.[56] Moreover, the foreign policy-making process was shaped by persistent turf battles by a number of actors.[57] The seemingly monolithic CC apparatus of the SED was characterized, from the sixties onwards, by a substantial division between "technocrats" and "ideologues,"[58] and top officials in the PZPR openly followed their personal interests, be they political or material.[59]

The political style in the upper echelons of the parties was characterized by the particular style of individual party leaders. In contrast, grassroots party life in the thousands of party groups and cells was shaped much more by the experiences, attitudes, and expectations of "ordinary" comrades. One can observe a limited openness to external influences. The CPs responded to changes in societal norms, attitudes, and values—even if these responses were at odds with the respective party and organizational cultures of earlier decades of Stalinism or even the founding period of the parties.

An example of the conflict between organizational culture and the changing social framework can be seen in the attempts of the CPSU leadership in the Khrushchev era to strengthen the party's role as an agency for education and discipline.[60] During this period of the early sixties, "socialist morals" were at the center of inner-party discourses, and issues such as discipline at work, restrained consumption of alcohol, and marital fidelity were prominent at party meetings. However, at the same time, the number of party disciplinary sentences for exactly these kinds of misbehavior decreased to an all-time low: such values could still be propagated by the party, but were actually no longer enforced. The East German SED also did not rely on coercion or punishment until revisiting this option in the seventies and eighties.[61] Even this in some respects most Stalinist party in the Eastern bloc offered integration, and basic organizations functioned not only as instruments of discipline, but also as social environments enabling a variety of social exchanges that had little to do with Marxism-Leninism.

The time frame for this collection is limited by the basic transformation that took place after Stalin's death and gained more strength after 1956. For the Soviet Union, this decisive moment was the starting point for a renaissance of the Communist Party as the central institution of power, from which a rearrangement of institutions and societal policy in post-Stalinism was initiated and negotiated in conflicts. In the Communist dictatorships of East Central Europe, this transformation coincided with the establishment of a hegemonic position through the suppression of the bourgeois elites, the collectivization of agriculture and industry, as well as the creation of a resilient and loyal socialist service class. As mentioned above, in the medium-term, the paths of the individual parties separated—towards the Prague Spring, towards a state of conservative ultra-stability (as in the Soviet Union and GDR), or towards partial economic and social reforms (as in Poland and Hungary), but the basic patterns of the parties remained similar enough to be useful as common ground for questions about variations and cultural differences.

Rüdiger Bergien is Privatdozent at the Humboldt University Berlin and a postdoctoral research fellow at the Centre for Contemporary History in Potsdam. His publications include *Die bellizistische Republik. Wehrkonsens und "Wehrhaftmachung" in Deutschland 1918–1933* (2012); "Activating the 'Apparatchik': Brigade Deployment in the SED Central Committee and Performative Communist Party Rule," in *Journal of Contemporary History* 47, no. 4 (2012): 793–811; and *Im Generalstab der Partei. Organisationskultur und Herrschaftspraxis in der SED-Zentrale (1946–1989)* (2017).

Jens Gieseke is head of the research department "Communism and Society" at the Centre for Contemporary History in Potsdam, Germany. His publications include (coeditor) *Handbuch der kommunistischen Geheimdienste in Osteuropa* (2008), (editor) *Staatssicherheit und Gesellschaft* (2007), (coeditor) *Die Geschichte der SED* (2011), (author) *The History of the Stasi: East German Secret Police 1945–1990* (2014, published in seven languages), and (coeditor) *The Silent Majority in Communist and Post-Communist States* (2016).

Notes

1. Due to the inconsistent usage of abbreviations, we stick to the most common versions for the respective Communist parties, which in some cases is the English version, such as CPSU, but in some cases is the original version, such as SED (Sozialistische Einheitspartei Deutschlands) and PZPR (Polska Zjednoczona Partia Robotnicza).
2. Ilko-Sascha Kowalczuk, *Endspiel: die Revolution von 1989 in der DDR* [Endgame. The revolution of 1989 in the GDR] (Munich, 2009); Andrzej Paczkowski, *The Spring Will Be Ours: Poland and the Poles from Occupation to Freedom* (University Park, PA, 2003).
3. Leonard Schapiro, *The Communist Party of the Soviet Union* (New York, 1960); Hermann Weber, *Die Sozialistische Einheitspartei Deutschlands 1946–1971* [The Socialist Unity Party of Germany 1946–1971] (Hannover, 1971).
4. Sheila Fitzpatrick, "New Perspectives on Stalinism," *Russian Review* 45 (1986): 357–373.
5. See, e.g., Jörg Baberowski, *Der rote Terror. Die Geschichte des Stalinismus* [Red terror. The history of Stalinism] (Munich, 2003); id., *Scorched Earth: Stalin's Reign of Terror* (New Haven, 2015); Stephen Kotkin, *Magnetic Mountain: Stalinism as a Civilization* (Berkeley, 1995).
6. Oleg Khlevniuk, *Das Politbüro. Mechanismen der politischen Macht in der Sowjetunion der dreißiger Jahre. Aus dem Russ. von Ruth und Heinz Deutschland* [The politburo. Mechanisms of political power in the Soviet Union of the 1930s] (Hamburg, 1998).
7. Martin Malia, *Soviet Tragedy: A History of Socialism in Russia, 1917–1991* (New York, 1995); Paczkowski, *The Spring Will Be Ours*; Klaus Schroeder, *Der SED-Staat: Partei, Staat und Gesellschaft 1949–1990* [The SED state: Party, state, and society 1949–1990] (Munich, 1998); for an overview, Robert Service, *Comrades! A History of World Communism* (Cambridge, MA, 2007); and David Priestland, *The Red Flag: A History of Communism* (New York 2009).

8. Yoram Gorlitzki and Oleg Khlevniuk, *Cold Peace: Stalin and the Soviet Ruling Circle, 1945–53* (Oxford, 2004); Simon Sebag Montefiore, *Stalin: The Court of the Red Tsar* (London, 2004); Andreas Malycha and Peter Jochen Winters, *Die SED: Geschichte einer deutschen Partei* [The SED: History of a German party] (Munich, 2009); Robert Service, *Lenin: A Biography* (Cambridge, MA, 2000); id., *Stalin: A Biography* (London, 2004); William Taubman, *Khrushchev: The Man and His Era* (New York, 2003).
9. However, see for oral history approaches Lutz Niethammer, Alexander von Plato, and Dorothee Wierling, *Die volkseigene Erfahrung: eine Archäologie des Lebens in der Industrieprovinz der DDR. 30 biographische Eröffnungen* [The nationally-owned experience: An archeology of life in GDR's industrial province. 30 biographic revelations] (Berlin, 1991); Donald J. Raleigh, *Soviet Baby Boomers: An Oral History of Russia's Cold War Generation* (Oxford, 2012); Dorothee Wierling, *Geboren im Jahr Eins: der Jahrgang 1949 in der DDR. Versuch einer Kollektivbiographie* [Born in year one: The age-group 1949 in the GDR. Attempt at a collective biography] (Berlin, 2002).
10. But see the intensive debate on identity formation in Stalinism, starting with Jochen Hellbeck, *Revolution on My Mind: Writing a Diary under Stalin* (London, 2009); and Kotkin, *Magnetic Mountain*.
11. See, e.g., Piotr Gontarczyk, *Polska Partia Robotnicza. Droga do władzy (1941–1944)* [The Polish Workers Party. The road to power] (Warsaw, 2006); Gorlitzki and Khlevniuk, *Cold Peace*; Malycha, *Die SED*.
12. Approaches in Sigrid Meuschel, *Legitimation und Parteiherrschaft: zum Paradox von Stabilität und Revolution in der DDR 1945–1989* [Legitimacy and party rule: On the paradox of stability and revolution in the GDR 1945–1989] (Frankfurt a.M., 1992); Stephen Kotkin and Jan Tomasz Gross, *Uncivil Society: 1989 and the Implosion of the Communist Establishment* (New York, 2009).
13. For the Eigensinn concept see Thomas Lindenberger, "Die Diktatur der Grenzen. Zur Einleitung" [The dictatorship of borders. To the introduction], in *Herrschaftsstrukturen und Erfahrungsdimensionen der DDR-Geschichte* [Structures of rule and dimensions of experience in the history of the GDR] (Cologne, 1999), 13–44; Thomas Lindenberger, "Eigen-Sinn, Domination and No Resistance," *Docupedia-Zeitgeschichte*, 3 August 2015, http://dx.doi.org/10.14765/zzf.dok.2.646.v1; Alf Lüdtke, *The History of Everyday Life: Reconstructing Historical Experiences and Ways of Life* (Princeton, 1995); Sandrine Kott, *Communism Day-To-Day: State Enterprises in East German Society* (Ann Arbor: University of Michigan Press, 2014).
14. See, e.g., Donna Harsch, *Revenge of the Domestic: Women, the Family and Communism in the German Democratic Republic* (Princeton, 2007); Jan Palmowski, *Inventing a Socialist Nation: Heimat and the Politics of Everyday Life in the GDR, 1945–1990* (Cambridge, 2009); Andrew I. Port, *Conflict and Stability in the German Democratic Republic* (Cambridge, 2007); Alexei Yurchak, *Everything Was Forever, Until It Was No More: The Last Soviet Generation* (Princeton, 2006).
15. E.g., Sheila Fitzpatrick and Robert Gellately, *Accusatory Practices: Denunciation in Modern European History, 1789–1989* (Chicago, 1997); Catriona Kelly, *Comrade Pavlik: The Rise and Fall of a Soviet Boy Hero* (London, 2005); Jens Gieseke, ed., *Staatssicherheit und Gesellschaft. Studien zum Herrschaftsalltag in*

der DDR [State security and society. Studies about the everyday life of rule in the GDR] (Göttingen, 2007).
16. Cf. Ralph Jessen and Jens Gieseke, "Die SED in der staatssozialistischen Gesellschaft" [The SED in the state socialist society], in *Die Geschichte der SED. Eine Bestandsaufnahme* [The history of the SED. A review], ed. J. Gieseke and H. Wentker (Berlin, 2011), 16–60.
17. Milovan Djilas, *The New Class: An Analysis of the Communist System* (San Diego, 1957).
18. See, e.g., Andrew I. Port, "The Banalities of East German Historiography," in *Becoming East German: Socialist Structures and Sensibilities after Hitler*, ed. M. Fulbrook and A. I. Port (New York, 2013), 1–30, esp. 3.
19. Martin Sabrow, "Einleitung: Geschichtsdiskurs und Doktringesellschaft" [Introduction: Historical discourse and society of doctrines], in *Geschichte als Herrschaftsdiskurs. Der Umgang mit der Vergangenheit in der DDR* [History as discourse of power. Dealing with the past in the GDR], ed. M. Sabrow (Cologne, 2000), 9–35.
20. Yurchak, *Everything Was Forever*.
21. Palmowski, *Inventing a Socialist Nation*.
22. Martin Sabrow, "Sozialismus als Sinnwelt. Diktatorische Herrschaft in kulturhistorischer Perspektive" [Socialism as world of meaning. Dictatorial rule in perspective of cultural history], *Potsdamer Bulletin für Zeithistorische Studien* 40–41 (2007): 9–23.
23. For first reflections, see Rüdiger Bergien, "'Parteiarbeiter.' Die hauptamtlichen Funktionäre der SED" ["Party workers." The full-time staff of the SED], in *SED-Geschichte*, ed. Gieseke and Wentker, 164–186; id., "Activating the 'Apparatchik': Brigade Deployment in the SED Central Committee and Performative Communist Party Rule," *Journal of Contemporary History* 47, no. 4 (2012): 793–811; Michel Christian, "Ausschließen und disziplinieren. Kontrollpraxis in den kommunistischen Parteien der DDR und der Tschechoslowakei" [Expulsion and discipline. Control practices in the Communist parties of the GDR and Czechoslovakia], in *Die ostdeutsche Gesellschaft: eine transnationale Perspektive* [The East German society: A transnational perspective], ed. S. Kott and E. Droit (Berlin, 2006), 53–70.
24. Christoph Boyer, "'1989' und die Wege dorthin" [The paths to "1989"], *Vierteljahrshefte für Zeitgeschichte* 59, no. 1 (2011): 101–118.
25. Jörg Baberowski, "Criticism as Crisis, or Why the Soviet Union Still Collapsed," *Journal of Modern European History* 9 (2011): 148–165; Manfred Hildermeier, "'Well Said Is Half a Lie': Observations on Jörg Baberovski's 'Criticism as Crisis, or why the Soviet Union Still Collapsed,'" *Journal of Modern European History* 9, no. 3 (2011): 289–297.
26. However, first see approaches in Kotkin and Gross, *Uncivil Society*; furthermore, see the contributions in Martin Sabrow, ed., *1989 und die Rolle der Gewalt* [1989 and the role of violence] (Göttingen, 2012).
27. Eugenia Belova and Valery Lazarev, *Funding Loyalty: The Economics of the Communist Party* (New Haven, 2013), 13–14.
28. See Michael Voslensky, *Nomenklatura: Anatomy of the Soviet Ruling Class* (London, 1984).
29. Belova and Lazarev, *Funding Loyalty*, 7.

30. Gorlitzki and Khlevniuk, *Cold Peace*.
31. Yoram Gorlitzki, "Party Revivalism and the Death of Stalin," *Slavic Review* 54 (1995): 1–22; Alexander Titov, "The Central Committee Apparatus under Khrushchev," in *Khrushchev in the Kremlin: Policy and Government in the Soviet Union 1953–64*, ed. J. Smith and M. Ilic (London, 2011), 41–60.
32. This domination is noteworthy especially since this concept can be traced back to the idea of a "unity between party and people," which was developed and firmly supported by the CPs themselves.
33. Belova and Lazarev, *Funding Loyalty*, 5. For the differentiation between the "inner" and "outer" party as early as in George Orwell, *1984*, see Voslensky, *Nomenklatura*, 30.
34. Boyer, "1989."
35. For different types of CPs and their particular "path dependencies," see Christopher Boyer's contribution in this volume.
36. While Polish party leaders and functionaries understand themselves more and more as patriots and representatives of the Polish nation, in the CPSU the classic imperial self-understanding played a crucial role. The first secretary of the Soviet Republic, for example, always originated from the titular nation, while the second secretary was regularly a Russian from the Moscow party headquarters. Saulius Grybkauskas, "The Role of the Second Party Secretary in the 'Election' of the First: The Political Mechanism for the Appointment of the Head of Soviet Lithuania in 1974," *Kritika: Explorations in Russian and Eurasian History* 14 (2013): 343–366.; Marcin Zaremba, *Komunizm, legitymacja, nacjonalizm. Nacjonalistyczna legitymizacja władzy komunistycznej w Polsce* [Communism, legitimacy, nationalism. Nationalist legitimacy of Communist rule in Poland] (Warsaw, 2001).
37. Jan Pakulski, "Bureaucracy and the Soviet System," *Studies in Comparative Communism* 19, no. 2 (1986): 1–3; Yoram Gorlitzki, "Too Much Trust: Regional Party Leaders and Local Political Networks under Brezhnev," *Slavic Review* 69, no. 3 (2010): 676–700.
38. Cf. T. H. Rigby, *Communist Party Membership in the U.S.S.R. 1917–1967* (Princeton, 1968).
39. Wolfram Adolphi, "Kaderpartei. Skizze für ein HKWM-Stichwort" (Cadre party. Sketch of a reference for the historical-critical dictionary of Marxism), *Utopie kreativ* 193 (2006): 982–994, see 983.
40. This hypothesis of course refers to "new-class" theories by Trockij and Djilas, as well as Stephen Kotkin, who dubbed the socialist upper class as the "uncivil society," i.e., a caste of profiteers of the system, who let the system go to rack and ruin due to their immobility and personal interests in 1989–91. Kotkin, *Uncivil Society*.
41. Belova and Lazarev, *Funding Loyalty*.
42. In reference to the CPCS, see the contribution of Michael Christian in this volume.
43. See the contribution of Sabine Pannen in this volume.
44. Anke Fiedler, *Medienlenkung in der DDR* [Controlling the media in the GDR] (Cologne, 2014).
45. Concerning the topic of communism being a "political religion" and the interpretation of the party as holder of "charisma" in the sense of Max We-

ber's "Herrschaftsformenlehre," see Martin Sabrow, "Das Charisma des Kommunismus. Überlegungen zur Anwendung des Weberschen Herrschaftstypus auf die DDR" [Charisma of Communism. Thoughts about the application of Max Weber's typology of power], in *ZeitRäume. Potsdamer Almanach des Zentrums für Zeithistorische Forschung 2006*, ed. M. Sabrow (Berlin, 2007), 162–174.

46. See Palmowski, *Inventing a Socialist Nation*, with his juxtaposition of "public" and "hidden" or "private transcripts," as well as Yurchak, *Everything Was Forever*.
47. For the period of post-Stalinism, see Pavel Kolar, *Der Poststalinismus. Ideologie und Utopie einer Epoche* [The post-Stalinism. Ideology and utopia of an epoch] (Cologne, 2016).
48. See the contribution of Krzysztof Dąbek in this volume.
49. See the contributions of Jan C. Behrends and Frédéric Zalewski in this volume.
50. Jörg Baberowski, "Wege aus der Gewalt. Nikita Chruschtschow und die Entstalinisierung 1953–1964" [Ways out of violence. Nikita Khrushchev and the de-Stalinization 1953–1964], in *Gesellschaft—Gewalt—Vertrauen. Jan Philipp Reemtsma zum 60. Geburtstag (Society—violence—trust. For the 60th birthday of Jan Philipp Reemtsma)*, ed. Ulrich Bielefeld, Heinz Bude, and Bernd Greiner (Hamburg, 2012), 401–437.
51. See the contribution of Andrea Bahr in this volume.
52. See the contribution of Jay Rowell in this volume.
53. See the contribution of Rüdiger Bergien in this volume.
54. See Annette Schumann, ed., *Vernetzte Improvisationen. Gesellschaftliche Subsysteme in Ostmitteleuropa und in der DDR* [Cross-linked improvisations. Subsystems of societies in Eastern and Central Europe and in the GDR] (Cologne, 2008); Alena Ledeneva, *Russia's Economy of Favours: Blat, Networking, and Informal Exchange* (Cambridge, 1998).
55. See the contribution of Martin Sabrow in this volume.
56. See Donald J. Raleigh, "'Soviet Man of Peace.' Leonid Il'ich Brezhnev and His Diaries," *Kritika* 27, no. 4 (2016): 837–868; Susanne Schattenberg. "Trust, Care, and Familiarity in the Politburo: Brezhnev's Scenario of Power," *Kritika* 16, no. 4 (2015): 835–858.
57. See the contribution of Mark Kramer in this volume.
58. See the contribution of Rüdiger Bergien in this volume.
59. See the contribution of Krzyztof Dąbek in this volume.
60. See the contribution of Edward Cohn in this volume.
61. See the contribution of Sabine Pannen in this volume.

Bibliography

Adolphi, Wolfram. "Kaderpartei. Skizze für ein HKWM-Stichwort" [Cadre party. Sketch of a reference for the historical-critical dictionary of Marxism]. *Utopie kreativ* 193 (2006): 982–994.

Baberowski, Jörg. "Criticism as Crisis, or Why the Soviet Union Still Collapsed." *Journal of Modern European History* 9 (2011): 148–165.

———. "'Wege aus der Gewalt. Nikita Chruschtschow und die Entstalinisierung 1953–1964" [Ways out of violence. Nikita Khrushchev and the de-Stalinization 1953–1964]. In *Gesellschaft—Gewalt—Vertrauen. Jan Philipp Reemtsma zum 60. Geburtstag* [Society—violence—trust. For the 60th birthday of Jan Philipp Reemtsma], ed. Ulrich Bielefeld, Heinz Bude, and Bernd Greiner, 401–437. Hamburg: Hamburger Ed., 2012.

———. *Der rote Terror. Die Geschichte des Stalinismus* [Red terror. The history of Stalinism]. Munich: Deutsche Verlags-Anstalt, 2003.

———. *Scorched Earth: Stalin's Reign of Terror*. New Haven: Yale University Press 2015.

Belova, Eugenia, and Valery Lazarev. *Funding Loyalty: The Economics of the Communist Party*. New Haven: Yale University Press, 2012.

Bergien, Rüdiger. "Activating the 'Apparatchik': Brigade Deployment in the SED Central Committee and Performative Communist Party Rule." *Journal of Contemporary History* 47, no. 4 (2012): 793–811.

———. "'Parteiarbeiter.' Die hauptamtlichen Funktionäre der SED" ["Party workers." The full-time staff of the SED]. In *Die Geschichte der SED. Eine Bestandsaufnahme* [The history of the SED. Taking stock], ed. Jens Gieseke and Hermann Wentker, 164–186. Berlin: Metropol, 2011.

Boyer, Christoph. "'1989' und die Wege dorthin" [The paths to "1989"]. *Vierteljahrshefte für Zeitgeschichte* 59, no. 1 (2011): 101–118.

Christian, Michel. "Ausschließen und disziplinieren. Kontrollpraxis in den kommunistischen Parteien der DDR und der Tschechoslowakei" [Expulsion and discipline. Control practices in the Communist parties of the GDR and Czechoslovakia]. In *Die ostdeutsche Gesellschaft, eine transnationale Perspektive* [The East German society. A transnational perspective], ed. Emmanuel Droit and Sandrine Kott, 53–70. Berlin: Christoph Links Verlag, 2006.

Djilas, Milovan. *The New Class: An Analysis of the Communist System*. New York: Praeger, 1957.

Fiedler, Anke. *Medienlenkung in der DDR* [Controlling the media in the GDR]. Cologne: Böhlau, 2014.

Fitzpatrick, Sheila, and Robert Gellately, eds. *Accusatory Practices: Denunciation in Modern European History, 1789–1989*. Chicago: University of Chicago Press, 1997.

Fitzpatrick, Sheila. "New Perspectives on Stalinism." *Russian Review* 45 (1986): 357–373.

Gieseke, Jens, ed. *Staatssicherheit und Gesellschaft. Studien zum Herrschaftsalltag in der DDR* [State security and society. Studies about the everyday life of rule in the GDR]. Göttingen: Vandenhoeck & Ruprecht, 2007.

Gieseke, Jens, and Ralph Jessen. "Die SED in der staatssozialistischen Gesellschaft" [The SED in the state socialist society]. In *Die Geschichte der SED. Eine Bestandsaufnahme* [The history of the SED. Taking stock], ed. Jens Gieseke and Hermann Wentker, 16–60. Berlin: Metropol Verlag, 2011.

Gontarczyk, Piotr. *Polska Partia Robotnicza. Droga do władzy (1941–1944)* [The Polish Workers Party. The road to power (1941–1944)]. Warszawa: Fronda, 2006.

Gorlitzki, Yoram. "Party Revivalism and the Death of Stalin." *Slavic Review* 54, no. 1 (1995): 1–2.

———. "Too Much Trust: Regional Party Leaders and Local Political Networks under Brezhnev." *Slavic Review* 69, no. 3 (2010): 676–700.

Gorlitzki, Yoram, and Oleg Khlevniuk, *Cold Peace: Stalin and the Soviet Ruling Circle, 1945–53.* Oxford: Oxford University Press, 2004.

Grybkauskas, Saulius. "The Role of the Second Party Secretary in the 'Election' of the First: The Political Mechanism for the Appointment of the Head of Soviet Lithuania in 1974." *Kritika: Explorations in Russian and Eurasian History* 14 (2013): 343–366.

Harsch, Donna. *Revenge of the Domestic: Women, the Family and Communism in the German Democratic Republic.* Princeton: Princeton University Press, 2007.

Hellbeck, Jochen. *Revolution on My Mind: Writing a Diary under Stalin.* London: Harvard University Press, 2009.

Hildermeier, Manfred. "'Well Said Is Half a Lie': Observations on Jörg Baberowski's 'Criticism as Crisis, or Why the Soviet Union Still Collapsed.'" *Journal of Modern European History* 9, no. 3 (2011): 289–297.

Kelly, Catriona. *Comrade Pavlik: The Rise and Fall of a Soviet Boy Hero.* London: Granta, 2005.

Khlevniuk, Oleg. *Das Politbüro. Mechanismen der politischen Macht in der Sowjetunion der dreißiger Jahre* [The politburo. Mechanisms of political power in the Soviet Union of the 1930s]. Trans. from Russian by Ruth and Heinz Deutschland. Hamburg: Hamburger Ed., 1998.

Kolar, Pavel. *Der Poststalinismus. Ideologie und Utopie einer Epoche* [Post-Stalinism. Ideology and utopia of an epoch]. Cologne: Böhlau, 2016.

Kotkin, Stephen. *Magnetic Mountain: Stalinism as a Civilization.* Berkeley: University of California Press, 1997.

Kotkin, Stephen, and Jan Gross. *Uncivil Society: 1989 and the Implosion of the Communist Establishment.* New York: Modern Library, 2009.

Kott, Sandrine. *Communism Day-To-Day: State Enterprises in East German Society.* Ann Arbor: University of Michigan Press, 2014.

Kowalczuk, Ilko-Sascha. *Endspiel. Die Revolution von 1989 in der DDR* [Endgame. The revolution of 1989 in the GDR]. Munich: C. H. Beck, 2009.

Ledeneva, Alena. *Russia's Economy of Favours: Blat, Networking, and Informal Exchange.* Cambridge: Cambridge University Press, 1998.

Lindenberger, Thomas. "Die Diktatur der Grenzen. Zur Einleitung" [The dictatorship of borders. To the introduction]. In *Herrschaftsstrukturen und Erfahrungsdimensionen der DDR-Geschichte* [Structures of rule and dimensions of experience in the history of the GDR], ed. Thomas Lindenberger, 13–44. Cologne: Böhlau, 1999.

Lindenberger, Thomas. "Eigen-Sinn, Domination and No Resistance." *Docupedia-Zeitgeschichte*, 3 August 2015. http://dx.doi.org/10.14765/zzf.dok.2.646.v1.

Lüedtke, Alf. *The History of Everyday Life: Reconstructing Historical Experiences and Ways of Life.* Princeton: Princeton University Press, 1995.

Malia, Martin. *Soviet Tragedy: A History of Socialism in Russia, 1917–1991.* New York: Free Press 1995.

Malycha, Andreas, and Peter Jochen Winters. *Die SED: Geschichte einer deutschen Partei* [The SED: History of a German party]. Munich: C. H. Beck, 2009.
Meuschel, Sigrid. *Legitimation und Parteiherrschaft. Zum Paradox von Stabilität und Revolution in der DDR 1945–1989* [Legitimacy and party rule. On the paradox of stability and revolution in the GDR 1945–1989]. Frankfurt/M.: Suhrkamp, 1992.
Niethammer, Lutz, Alexander von Plato, and Dorothee Wierling. *Die volkseigene Erfahrung: eine Archäologie des Lebens in der Industrieprovinz der DDR. 30 biographische Eröffnungen* [The nationally-owned experience: An archeology of life in GDR's industrial province. 30 biographic revelations]. Berlin: Rohwohlt, 1991.
Paczkowski, Andrzej. *The Spring Will Be Ours: Poland and the Poles from Occupation to Freedom*. University Park: Pennsylvania State University Press, 2003.
Pakulski, Jan. "Bureaucracy and the Soviet System." *Studies in Comparative Communism* 19, no. 2 (1986): 1–3.
Palmowski, Jan. *Inventing a Socialist Nation: Heimat and the Politics of Everyday Life in the GDR, 1945–1990*. Cambridge: Cambridge University Press, 2009.
Port, Andrew I. *Conflict and Stability in the German Democratic Republic*. Cambridge: Cambridge University Press, 2007.
———. "The Banalities of East German Historiography." In *Becoming East German: Socialist Structures and Sensibilities after Hitler*, ed. Mary Fulbrook and Andrew I. Port, 1–30. New York: Berghahn Books, 2013.
Priestland, David. *The Red Flag: A History of Communism*. New York: Grove/Atlantic, 2009.
Raleigh, Donald J. *Soviet Baby Boomers: An Oral History of Russia's Cold War Generation*. Oxford: Oxford University Press, 2012.
———. "'Soviet Man of Peace.' Leonid Il'ich Brezhnev and His Diaries." *Kritika* 27, 4 (2016): 837–868.
Rigby, Thomas H. *Communist Party Membership in the U.S.S.R. 1917–1967*. Princeton: Princeton University Press, 1968.
Sabrow, Martin. "Einleitung: Geschichtsdiskurs und Doktringesellschaft" [Introduction: Historical discourse and society of doctrines]. In *Geschichte als Herrschaftsdiskurs. Der Umgang mit der Vergangenheit in der DDR* [History as discourse on power. Dealing with the past in the GDR], ed. M. Sabrow, 9–35. Cologne: Böhlau, 2000.
———. "Das Charisma des Kommunismus. Überlegungen zur Anwendung des Weberschen Herrschaftstypus auf die DDR" [The charisma of communism. Thoughts about the application of Max Weber's typology of power]. In *ZeitRäume. Potsdamer Almanach des Zentrums für Zeithistorische Forschung 2006*, ed. Martin Sabrow, 162–174. Berlin: Wallstein, 2007.
———. "Sozialismus als Sinnwelt. Diktatorische Herrschaft in kulturhistorischer Perspektive" [Socialism as world of meaning. Cultural perspectives on dictatorial rule]. *Potsdamer Bulletin für Zeithistorische Studien* 40–41 (2007): 9–23.
———, ed. *1989 und die Rolle der Gewalt* [1989 and the role of violence]. Göttingen: Wallstein Verlag, 2012.
Schattenberg, Susanne. "Trust, Care, and Familiarity in the Politburo: Brezhnev's Scenario of Power." *Kitika* 16, no. 4 (2015): 835–858.

Schroeder, Klaus. *Der SED-Staat* [The SED state]. Cologne: Böhlau, 2013.
Schumann, Annette, ed. *Vernetzte Improvisationen. Gesellschaftliche Subsysteme in Ostmitteleuropa und in der DDR* [Cross-linked improvisations. Subsystems of societies in Eastern and Central Europe and in the GDR]. Cologne: Böhlau, 2008.
Sebag Montefiore, Simon. *Stalin: The Court of the Red Tsar.* London: Orion, 2004.
Service, Robert. *Comrades! A History of World Communism.* Cambridge, MA: Harvard University Press, 2007.
———. *Lenin: A Biography.* Cambridge, MA: Harvard University Press, 2000.
———. *Stalin: A Biography.* London: Belknap Press, 2004.
Shapiro, Leonard. *The Communist Party of the Soviet Union.* London: Eyre and Spottiswoode, 1960.
Taubman, William. *Khrushchev: The Man and His Era.* New York: Free Press, 2003.
Titov, Alexander. "The Central Committee Apparatus under Khrushchev." In *Khrushchev in the Kremlin: Policy and Government in the Soviet Union 1953–64,* ed. Jeremy Smith and Melanie Ilic, 41–60. London: Routledge, 2011.
Voslensky, Michael. *Nomenklatura: Anatomy of the Soviet Ruling Class.* London: The Bodley Head, 1984.
Weber, Hermann. *Die Sozialistische Einheitspartei Deutschlands 1946–1971* [The Socialist Unity Party of Germany 1946–1971]. Hannover: Verlag für Literatur und Zeitgeschehen, 1971.
Wierling, Dorothee. *Geboren im Jahr Eins: der Jahrgang 1949 in der DDR. Versuch einer Kollektivbiographie* [Born in year one: The age-group 1949 in the GDR. Attempt at a collective biography]. Berlin: Christoph Links Verlag, 2002.
Yurchak, Alexei. *Everything Was Forever, Until It Was No More: The Last Soviet Generation.* Princeton: Princeton University Press, 2006.

 1

The Paradox of Party Discipline in the Khrushchev-Era Communist Party
Edward Cohn

In October 1961, the Twenty-Second Congress of the Soviet Communist Party enacted a historic change: as part of the party's new program, the congress announced a new "Moral Code of the Builder of Communism," the first formal ethical code in the movement's history.[1] In the early days of the Soviet Union, as David Hoffmann has noted, many Communists had actively resisted the idea of a written code of conduct, arguing that "whatever advanced the cause of the proletarian state was morally correct."[2] By the early 1960s, however, the attitude of the country's leadership had sharply changed. Nikita Khrushchev and other party leaders had begun devoting more attention to the private behavior of Communists and other citizens, emphasizing in particular the need for party members to speak out against all violations of "the norms of socialist life" that they witnessed around them. The new Moral Code was an important part of this shift. It elucidated twelve principles that should define the behavior of all "builders of Communism" (both party members and other citizen activists), including "intolerance of injustice, parasitism, dishonesty, careerism, [and] greed," and "mutual respect in the family, [and] care about the upbringing of children."[3] The new party charter, also enacted in 1961, added teeth to the code when it announced that the country's party cells should "see to it that each Communist observe in his own life and cultivate among workers the moral principles set forth in the CPSU program, the Moral Code of the Builder of Communism."[4] In the years that followed, state publishers released a growing number of pamphlets and books describing the principles of the code and detailing the responsibilities of Communists, beautifully illustrating the regime's new attitude to the behavior of party members.[5]

Although the enactment of the moral code suggested that party leaders were increasingly concerned with the behavior of Communists, the Twenty-Second Congress also endorsed changes that made it more difficult to punish Communists for committing misconduct. The new party charter, for instance, declared that a Communist could only be expelled from the party by a two-thirds vote of his or her primary party organization (PPO), rather than a simple majority.[6] Many of the congress's speakers denounced the crimes of the Stalin era and hailed "the triumph of the Leninist norms of party life" since 1953, which included a curtailment in the number of expelled Communists; party publications bragged that the number of expulsions between 1956 and 1961 had fallen to 40 percent of the total for the five years before Khrushchev's secret speech, and that the figure for 1960 was the lowest in twenty years.[7] Soviet leaders, in short, sent the country a powerful signal that expulsion from the party should be a punishment of last resort, representing a step back from the strict supervision of Communists' behavior.

The result of these changes was an apparent paradox: the percentage of Communists expelled from the party each year fell to an all-time low at the same time that discussions of citizens' behavior became more intense than they had been in decades. Khrushchev-era party officials seemed to care more than ever before about the behavior of Soviet citizens, while being less inclined to punish errant Communists than they had been since the revolution. This chapter seeks to explain the forces behind this apparent paradox. In particular, it argues that the Khrushchev-era party's efforts to define and enforce the regime's behavioral norms were driven by several competing—and often contradictory—forces, including the leadership's desire for a larger and more vibrant Communist Party, its interest in fighting public disorder by Soviet citizens, its efforts to move away from the coercive and repressive tactics of the Stalin years, and its desire both to eliminate improper behavior in party members' private lives and to avoid the embarrassment posed by the public discussion of Communists' misconduct. Ultimately, these forces helped ensure that the public discussion of Communists' behavior would increase at the very moment that the enforcement of the regime's behavioral norms slackened—a fact of life that would continue, largely unabated, until 1991.

The Decline of Expulsion in the Postwar Communist Party

On 27 October 1961, Frol Kozlov—then seen as Khrushchev's likeliest successor—introduced a series of revisions to the party charter in a speech to the Twenty-Second Congress. Near the end of his remarks, he announced that in order to prevent "the unfounded use of the utmost measure of party punishment," the new charter would allow expulsion from the party only by a two-thirds vote of the primary party organization, rather than a simple majority. He added that the very institution of expulsion was on the decline: "The intensification of the party's ideological life, the strengthening of party discipline, and the rise in consciousness of Communists have resulted in the fact that in recent years, the number of cases of expulsion from the CPSU has sharply decreased. We must continue to assume that exclusion from the party, as the highest measure of party punishment, should apply only to those who are unworthy of being in the party's ranks."[8] N. M. Shvernik, the chairman of the Committee of Party Control, had made similar remarks to the congress two days before. "More and more there is no need to resort to the extreme measure of punishment, which is expulsion from the party," he announced, ascribing this decline to "the restoration of Leninist norms of party life, the prevalence of the method of persuasion in educational work, the power of influence of the party collective, and the growth of consciousness of party members." Shvernik proudly announced that the expulsion rate had declined by 2.5 times since 1956.[9]

These comments represented the first half of the paradox described in this chapter: party leaders were not merely reporting on a decline in expulsions since Khrushchev's rise to power, but were also making expulsion more difficult and sending lower party organizations the unmistakable signal that they should continue to downplay "the utmost measure of party punishment."[10] These trends were driven by several important changes in Soviet politics. First, and most importantly, the rise of de-Stalinization had weakened the party discipline system and made expulsion from the Communist Party far more difficult, as Soviet leaders strove to repudiate "coercion" and to denounce the excesses associated with the Stalinist personality cult. Second, party leaders also felt that expulsion was incompatible with their goal of expanding and revitalizing the Communist Party as a force for change in Soviet life. In the years after 1953, the party grew dramatically in size, and its leaders emphasized the enthusiasm, ideological fervor, and political consciousness of the country's Communists. Expelling a large number of Communists would hinder the party's growth while belying its message of unity, strength, and enthusiasm—a message that was crucial to party leaders at a time when the divisive policies of de-Stalinization threatened to tear the party apart.

On one level, of course, the weakening of the party discipline system in the Khrushchev-era Communist Party was such a dramatic trend that Kozlov and Shvernik hardly needed to bring it to the congress's attention. In the decades before World War II, most expulsions had taken place in the context of a periodic party purge, which typically resulted in the expulsion of more than 10 percent of the USSR's Communists. (The party expelled 24.3 percent of its members in the 1921 purge, 11.8 percent in the 1929 purge, and 18.3 percent in 1933, for example.[11]) The party's Eighteenth Congress abolished the mass purge in 1939, replacing it with an expanded series of everyday investigations and hearings on the local level; in the late Stalin years, between 1945 and 1953, the party expelled an average of roughly a hundred thousand members each year, a high absolute total that never exceeded 3 percent of all Communists.[12] Once Stalin had died, moreover, party organizations began to curtail expulsion even further. The number of Communists expelled from the party plummeted by nearly 40 percent between 1953 and 1954 (dropping from 134,293 to 82,362), before dropping another 54 percent in 1955. By the early 1960s, the party was expelling roughly 30,000 Communists each year for misconduct and declaring that between ten thousand and forty thousand Communists had "mechanically left" the party when they failed to pay dues or attend meetings. In all, between 0.42 percent and 0.67 percent of the party lost its membership each year during the early 1960s, an increasingly tiny percentage,[13] and the expulsion rate for political offenses and anti-Soviet activity declined by an even greater proportion.[14]

The single most important trend leading to the decline of expulsion was the leadership's decision to repudiate the "cult of personality" and de-Stalinize the party.[15] It was no coincidence, after all, that Shvernik dated the decline in expulsion not to Stalin's 1953 death, but to the Twentieth Congress in February 1956, when Nikita Khrushchev had famously denounced the crimes of his predecessor. Khrushchev recited a litany of Stalinist crimes in that address, often highlighting the evils of the Great Terror and frequently mentioning the wrongful expulsion of innocent Communists. "A majority of the Central Committee members and candidates, elected by the Seventeenth Congress and subjected to arrests in 1937–38, were illegally expelled from the party, a gross violation of the party charter,"[16] he announced at one point. At another moment, he directly linked Stalin's egotism and more violent crimes with the mass expulsions that greatly curtailed the party's size: "Arbitrariness (*proizvol*) by one person encouraged and permitted arbitrariness in others. Mass arrests and the deportations of thousands and thousands of people, execution without trial and without normal investigation created insecurity in people, leading to fear and even desperation. This, of course, did not contribute toward the unity of the party ranks and of all strata of working people, but, on the contrary, brought about the annihilation and amputation from the party of workers who were loyal but inconvenient to Stalin."[17] Five years later, Shvernik explicitly linked the party's present-day efforts to change the process of expulsion to its efforts to combat the personality cult. "In accordance with the decisions of the Twentieth Congress, directed at the restoration of Leninist norms of party life and the liquidation of the consequences of the cult of personality," he announced, "serious insufficiencies and mistakes in the work of the Committee of Party Control and local party organs, that existed in the past, were eliminated." He singled out several "defects [in the investigative process] that were ingrained under the influence of the personality cult," including "excessive suspicion" toward party members, the expulsion of Communists in absentia, and the insufficient review of accusations.[18] The result, as noted above, was not merely a dramatic drop in all expulsions under Khrushchev, but the near elimination of cases involving dissent or anti-Soviet activity.

The declining expulsion rate was also linked to another major initiative of the Khrushchev years: the explosive growth of the Communist Party in the years after 1953 (see Figure 1.1). The party had begun growing in 1939, after the conclusion of the Great Purges, and expanded rapidly during World War II—a period when party membership jumped from 3,872,465 to 5,760,369.[19] This growth continued at a slower pace in the late 1940s and early 1950s, when the party membership increased to 6,897,224 (a 19.7 percent increase in eight years.) After 1953, Khrushchev and his allies endorsed the concept of a large party membership and even increased the party's size by 59.8 percent—a rate that vastly exceeded both the growth of the population as a whole under Khrushchev and the growth of the party in the late Stalin years.[20] By the end of

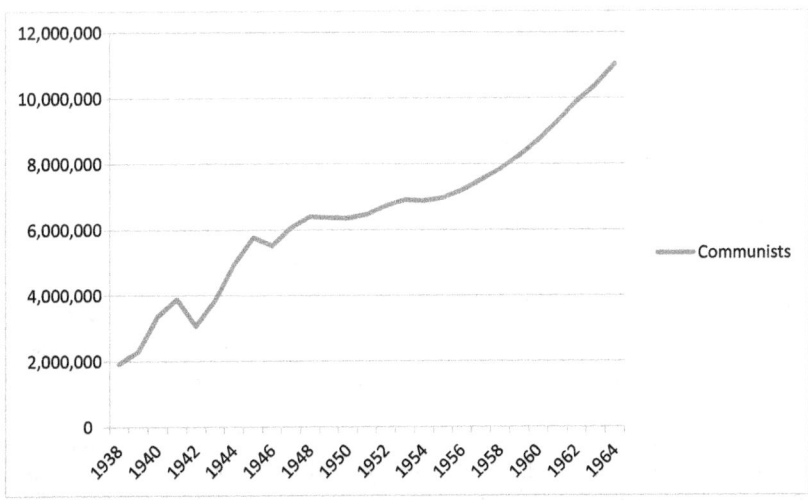

Figure 1.1. Communist Party Membership by Year, 1938–1964

1964, the Communist Party had 11,022,369 members, the highest total in the USSR's history both in absolute terms and as a percentage of the country's population (see Table 1.1).[21]

Table 1.1. Communist Party Membership, 1938–1964

Year	Full members	Candidate members	All Communists	Female Communists	% Women
1938	1,405,879	514,213	1,920,002	286,273	14.9%
1939	1,514,181	792,292	2,306,973	333,821	14.5%
1940	1,982,743	1,417,232	3,339,975	490,244	14.4%
1941	2,490,479	1,381,986	3,872,465	575,853	14.9%
1942	2,155,336	908,540	3,063,876	442,321	14.4%
1943	2,451,411	1,403,190	3.854,701	567,354	14.7%
1944	3,126,627	1,791,934	4,918,561	784,280	15.9%
1945	3,965,530	1,794,839	5,760,369	969,289	16.8%
1946	4,127, 689	1,383,173	5,510,862	1,033,115	18.7%
1947	4,774,886	1,277,015	6,051,901	1,102,424	18.2%
1948	5,181,199	1,209,082	6,390,281	1,143,187	17.9%
1949	5,334,811	1,017,761	6,352,572	1,141,086	18.0%
1950	5,510,787	829,396	6,340,183	1,160,938	18.3%
1951	5,658,577	804,398	6,462,975	1,206,203	18.7%
1952	5,853,200	854,339	6,707,539	1,276,560	19.0%
1953	6,067,027	830,197	6,897,224	1,335,336	19.4%
1954	6,402,284	462,579	6,864,863	1,346,971	19.6%
1955	6,610,238	346,867	6,957,105	1,364,713	19.6%
1956	6,767,644	405,877	7,173,521	1,414,456	19.7%
1957	7,001,114	493,459	7,494,573	1,477.678	19.7%
1958	7,296,559	546,637	7,843,196	1,533,078	19.5%
1959	7,622,356	616,775	8,239,131	1,605,804	19.5%
1960	8,017,249	691,418	8,708,667	1,692,164	19.4%
1961	8,472,396	803,430	9,275,826	1,809,688	19.5%
1962	9,051,934	839,134	9,891,068	1,942,080	19.6%
1963	9,581,149	806,047	10,387,196	2,050,371	19.7%
1964	10,182,916	839,453	11,022,369	2,195,004	19.9%

Source: The Russian State Archive of Contemporary History [Rossiiskii gosudarstvennyi arkhiv noveishei istorii] (f. 77, o. 1, d. 26, l. 21); "KPSS v tsifrakh 1961–1964 gody" [CPSU in figures 1961–1964], *Partiinaia zhizn'* [Party life], May 1965, 8–17.

A high rate of expulsion from the party would have been incompatible with the party's explosive Khrushchev-era growth, which was intended not only to expand the party, but also to cement its status as an activist force in society. Khrushchev sought not only to increase the ranks of the party, but to recruit thousands of new members from the working class and peasantry, rather than the bureaucracy and the administrative apparatus. In the secret speech and on many other occasions, Khrushchev had portrayed party members as one of the main victims of Stalin,[22] and now he sought make it larger, more activist, more proletarian, and less bureaucratic in nature. He accompanied the party's expansion with a series of reforms intended to shake up the party bureaucracy and to emphasize the voluntary mobilization of party members, including a campaign against "bureaucratism" launched in 1954, and a 1958 plan to reform the party apparatus on the basis of "the public principles" (*obshchestvennye nachala*), by which nonprofessional party activists would voluntarily take on administrative work that was normally conducted by salaried officials, forming new committees and councils to fight bureaucracy and mobilize activists to expand economic production.[23] Together, these campaigns were intended to further the Khrushchev-era regime's populist vision of a party that took its strength not from the bureaucracy, but from the working population.[24]

By the time of the Twenty-Second Congress, Khrushchev had begun to describe the Communist Party not just as a vanguard of the working class, but as a "party of the entire people." Party pamphlets emphasized that as Soviet society entered "the period of the construction of communism," the party had become a "ten-million-member army" with a growing role in politics; it had evolved from a party of the working class into a "vanguard of the Soviet people" whose social composition resembled that of the country at large.[25] The reality behind this rhetoric was more complex, however. Khrushchev was most successful in his goal of expanding the party's membership—a triumph that was widely heralded in party pamphlets and speeches.[26] But he was less successful in changing its social composition. Between 1953 and 1964, the percentage of women in the party edged up slightly, from 19.4 percent to 19.9 percent. (The fact that the party was still mostly male would shape its approach to family issues and the problem of drunkenness, under Khrushchev.) The percentage of Communists who came from the proletariat rose substantially, from 32.1 percent in 1953 to 37.3 percent in 1964, but less substantially than party rhetoric had promised. (Before 1941, after all, more than 60 percent of Communists had been workers, and the share of workers in the party lagged behind their share of the overall population.) The percentage of Communists who were peasants actually decreased in the Khrushchev era, dropping from 17.8 percent in 1953 to 16.5 percent in 1964. The percentage of white-collar workers, finally, dropped slightly—declining from 50.1 percent in 1953 to 46.2 percent in 1964.[27]

The party's Khrushchev-era membership policies helped shape the regime's vision of how Communists should behave in two main ways. First, these policies made it more difficult for party organizations to punish Communists who violated the party's behavioral code, both by discouraging expulsion as a repressive Stalinist tactic and by prioritizing the growth of the party over the purity of its ranks. Second, they emphasized the gulf between the rhetoric of the Khrushchev-era party leadership and the realities of Soviet political life. On the one hand, Khrushchev's vision of the party was unabashedly revolutionary: he sought to restore the Leninist ways of the past while returning the party to its proletarian roots. On the other hand, Khrushchev failed to change

Table 1.2. The Class Breakdown of Communists, 1945–1953

Year	Workers in the party	Peasants in the party	White-collar workers in the party (*Sluzhashchie*)
1946	1,865,126 (33.85%)	1,023,903 (18.58%)	2,621,833 (47.58%)
1947	2,041,317 (33.73%)	1,091,362 (18.03%)	2,919,222 (48.24%)
1948	2,125,910 (33.27%)	1,173,180 (18.36%)	3,091,191 (48.37%)
1949	2,101,527 (33.60%)	1,160,465 (18.27%)	3,090,580 (48.65%)
1950	2,084,714 (32.88%)	1,148,753 (18.12%)	3,106,716 (49.00%)
1951	2,107,453 (32.61%)	1,165,208 (18.03%)	3,190,314 (49.36%)
1952	2,162,059 (30.44%)	1,206,668 (16.99%)	3,338,812 (49.78%)
1953	2,213,667 (32.10%)	1,226,040 (17.78%)	3,457,517 (50.13%)
1961	35.0%	17.3%	47.7%
1964	37.3%	16.5%	46.2%

Source: The Russian State Archive of Contemporary History (f. 77, o. 1, d. 26, l. 21); "KPSS v tsifrakh 1961–1964 gody" [CPSU in figures 1961–1964], *Partiinaia zhizn'* [Party life], May 1965, 8–17.[28]

the party's fundamentally bureaucratic and conservative nature. As it entered the 1960s, in short, the regime combined new revolutionary rhetoric about the party's growth and vitality with a sense of bureaucratic maturity that had grown in the twenty years since the Great Terror. Khrushchev wanted to make the party a more vital and activist institution without limiting its growth or unleashing the repression of the past.

The Party's New Behavioral Code

At the same time that party organizations throughout the Soviet Union were beginning to expel fewer Communists, a second—seemingly contradictory—trend was reshaping the experiences of party members throughout the USSR: an effort to emphasize the many responsibilities of Communists and to make the behavioral code surrounding party membership more explicit and restrictive, especially when it came to everyday life. This effort was evident in a number of trends, including the promulgation of the Moral Code of the Builder of Communism, the party charter's redefinition of the "obligations and rights" of Communists, the publication of pamphlets emphasizing Communists' responsibility to fight violations of "the norms of socialist life," and a new country-wide emphasis on "intolerance" (*neterpimost'*) toward misconduct of all kinds. These efforts became apparent as early as 1953, but grew in intensity throughout the decade and reached their peak at the Twenty-Second Congress in 1961. In broad terms, they were driven by the same forces that resulted in a drop in expulsions—the leadership's desire to achieve social change without coercion from above and to make party members a more active and vital force in society. More often than not, however, the effect of the regime's policies was to direct the attention of the USSR's Communists toward poor behavior by other citizens, not to crack down on the misconduct of party members. Party leaders often resolved the Khrushchev-era paradox of party discipline by assuming that their members were paragons of good behavior and urging them to enforce the regime's behavioral code on the rest of the population.

Nikita Khrushchev helped set the tone for much of the decade to come even before Joseph Stalin's death, when he delivered an address proposing changes to the party charter at the Nineteenth Congress in 1952.[29] The previous version of the charter, enacted in 1939, had included only four duties of Communists in its section on the "obligations and rights" of party members: their need "to work tirelessly to raise their consciousness," "to strictly observe party discipline," "to be a model of compliance with labor and state discipline," and "to strengthen ties with the masses daily."[30] The charter's 1939 language was both terse and traditionally minded; it emphasized ideology, discipline, and workplace concerns, barely mentioning the need for "communist morality" or for good behavior in the home. Khrushchev's new charter expanded the number of duties from four to eleven and championed a populist vision of party membership. Most importantly, it included new language emphasizing the need for Communists to obey the party's will, to fight bureaucratic inertia, and to resist the temptations of political offices and administrative positions. Several provisions dealt with this theme, emphasizing the need for every Communist to be "an active fighter for the fulfillment of party decisions" and calling for the punishment of all wrongdoers, regardless of position—one of many signs that party leaders were worried about the party's bureaucratization and the growth of an administrative elite that was safe from criticism.[31]

The party's vision of its members' responsibilities entered a final stage with the 1961 party charter, which remained in effect until 1986. The new charter emphasized a broader vision of party activism that extended beyond the workplace to the family and the home. Most strikingly, it required Communists to play a larger role in everyday life, mandating that they "bring about the formation and upbringing of a person of communist society" and "struggle decisively against all manifestations of bourgeois ideology, against the remnants of a private-property psychology, religious prejudices, and other vestiges of the past; to comply with the principles of communist morality and put the public interests above the private."[32] None of these duties would have struck the party's Communists as a total surprise or a clear break with the past, but each one helped to emphasize a Communist's duties in his or her private life and to emphasize the "public duty" of party members. In particular, the charter emphasized that Communists needed to be activists for the transformation of society. It took it for granted that a Communist would not be personally involved in "vestiges of the past," such as religion, but reiterated that a party member must speak out against remnants of the past in society at large. Communists were expected not only to move beyond bureaucratic inertia, but to return to the citizen activism of the past.

During the same period, the regime launched both a series of press campaigns and a tough criminal crackdown on "vestiges of the past" that were corrupting the behavior of Soviet citizens. As Brian LaPierre and Miriam Dobson have noted, both the regime and the public at large were growing increasingly concerned about hooliganism and juvenile delinquency during the 1950s—a fear that seems to have spread both because some Soviet social problems were growing worse and because the post-Stalin regime was willing to discuss these problems more openly than before.[33] Beginning soon after Stalin's death in 1953, Soviet newspapers began to stigmatize offenders guilty of hooliganism, drunkenness, child abandonment, and "amoral behavior" that threatened the family.[34] The regime launched tough new campaigns to crack down on "petty hooliganism" and "parasitism" and launched more halfhearted attempts to rein in drunkenness,[35] while increasing the crime-fighting role of public institutions, such as the comrade's court and the volunteer crime-fighting squad known as the *druzhina*. As will be discussed below, many of these efforts sought to mobilize members of "the public" (*obshchestvennost'*) to speak out against "anti-social acts" like hooliganism and drunkenness, and all of them involved the public stigmatization of citizens whose actions violated "the norms of socialist communal life." The regime's new focus on reforming personal behavior was exemplified by several Khrushchev-era pamphlets titled *Everyday Life is Not a Private Matter*, which were firm in their denunciation of "vestiges of the past," like "drunkenness, foul language, disrespect to women, and disregard for the rules of socialist collective life."[36]

The centerpiece of the regime's efforts to redefine citizens' behavior came when the Twenty-Second Congress enacted the Moral Code of the Builder of Communism. This code was part of the new party program enacted at the congress, a document that consistently championed a more activist role for the party in society. When it introduced the party's vision of ideology, culture, and education, for example, the program was quick to attack attitudes and practices that threatened to corrupt society. "Even after the victory of the socialist order," the program declared, "vestiges of capitalism survive in the consciousness and behavior of people, which impedes the forward movement of society."[37] In particular, the program emphasized the theme of communist morality and attacked the regime's past use of coercion from above. "In the process of the transition to communism, the role of moral principles in the life of society increases even more, the scope of the moral factor increases, and the meaning of the administrative regulation of relations between people accordingly decreases," the program declared, suggesting both that citizens need to pay increased attention to the tenets of Communist morality and that those principles could be best enforced by methods other than administrative coercion.[38]

Instead, the party program championed another approach to Communists' behavior: the Moral Code of the Builder of Communism. In particular, it endorsed twelve tenets that (in the words of one pamphlet) "include[d] the most important moral principles that characterize the shape of the New Man":[39]

- devotion to the cause of Communism, love of the socialist Motherland and of the socialist countries.
- conscientious labor for the good of society: he who does not work, neither shall he eat.
- concern on the part of everyone for the preservation and growth of public property.
- a high sense of public duty; intolerance of actions harmful to the public interest.
- collectivism and comradely mutual assistance: one for all and all for one.
- humane relations and mutual respect between individuals: man is to man a friend, a comrade, and a brother.
- honesty and truthfulness, moral purity, unpretentiousness and modesty in social and private life.
- mutual respect in the family, concern for the upbringing of children.
- irreconcilability towards injustice, parasitism, dishonesty, careerism, and profiteering.
- friendship and brotherhood among all peoples of the USSR, intolerance of national and racial hatred.
- intolerance towards the enemies of communism, peace, and freedom of nations.
- fraternal solidarity with the working people of all countries, and with all peoples.[40]

These principles, the program proclaimed, were a rejection of "the class morality of the exploiter" and of the "perverted and egoistic views and morals of the old world"[41] and should guide the behavior of all "builders of Communism," whether they were party members or non-party activists. In fact, the new party charter announced that primary party organizations should "see to it that each Communist observe in his own life and cultivate among workers the moral principles set forth in the CPSU program, the Moral Code of the Builder of Communism."[42]

The new Moral Code was an unusual document: it was far more specific than any past statement of moral principles endorsed by the party leadership, while remaining far too abstract and vague to provide concrete ethical guidance to a "builder of communism." Many of the code's principles represented socialist principles that would have been unsurprising to a Marxist at any point in history, such as "conscientious labor for the good of society." Other principles (such as "honesty and truthfulness") were so vague that they were essentially useless. Still others represented a growing postwar interest in preserving the Soviet family, an approach that had been growing in prominence since the 1936 family law. A final group of provisions captured the tenor of the times, either in their specifics or in the general principles behind them. The Moral Code was enacted in the midst of a tough state campaign against "parasitism," for example—a theme that made the familiar quotation that "he who does not work, does not eat" especially timely. Three provisions, moreover, called for builders of communism to display "intolerance" (*neterpimost'*) toward misconduct, while two others endorsed "irreconcilability" (*neprimirimost'*) toward wrongdoing—a theme that was extremely prominent in the rhetoric of the Khrushchev years.[43] As Miriam Dobson has noted, the Moral Code's call for "intolerance" toward parasites and other wrongdoers was one of its most popular provisions.[44]

The Moral Code of the Builder of Communism, in short, helped create the paradox at the heart of this chapter, since the Twenty-Second Congress had endorsed a moral code championing the "intolerance" of misconduct at the same time that the party took measures to curtail expulsion from its ranks. Party leaders immediately sought to resolve this paradox by explaining *how* Communists should combat the vestiges of the past. To some degree, party leaders simply assumed that their members would be paragons of good behavior for their peers. One party pamphlet, published in 1962, perfectly encapsulated this approach to good behavior: it was titled *The Personal Example of a Communist* and provided the stories of five party members whose model behavior should inspire all citizens.[45] Another pamphlet proclaimed that "to serve as an example for others means to raise the high title of a Communist, to live in full accordance with the demands of the party charter," before describing a Mordovian collective farmer who was a "great worker" and a "model public-spirited person" (*primernyi obshchestvennik*). "Comrade Tomilin behaves as befits a Communist, not only in labor, but in his everyday life and his family," it concluded.[46]

Party sources were vaguer on what should be done with Communists who committed misconduct. One pamphlet, which focused on the lessons of the Moral Code, emphasized the heavy responsibilities of Communists while remaining essentially silent on the issue of expulsion:

> A Communist is responsible to his party organization for every misdeed. It is necessary that all interventions provided for by the party charter be applied to those who do not consider it necessary to follow the moral principles of our moral code. And we cannot gloss over, but must hold a discussion of, each case of the behavior of a party member in the collective, in production, or in everyday life. The more demandingly Communists relate to themselves, the better they will fulfill their roles as leaders and the more productive the work of party organizations in cultivating the new man will be.[47]

In fact, this passage's suggestion that Communists guilty of misconduct would be subjected to a "discussion" hinted at the regime's larger approach to wrongdoing and Communist morality. In a section on "the eradication of the vestiges of capitalism in the consciousness and behavior of people," the 1961 party program declared, "In the struggle with vestiges of the past and with manifestations of individualism and egoism, the public (*obshchestvennost'*), the influence of public opinion, and the development of criticism and self-criticism will play a large role. The comradely condemnation of anti-social behavior will gradually become the main means of eradicating bourgeois views, customs, and habits. The power of example in public and private life, and in the fulfillment of public duty, acquires great educational significance."[48] The regime's main weapons against "vestiges of the past," then, would be "comradely criticism," ideological propaganda, and "education" (*vospitanie*). The state would crack down on "superstition" and "religious belief" through atheist propaganda and scientific education. It would seek to transform the consciousness of the population through new measures at moral education. Most prominently, it would seek to stigmatize wrongdoers through "public opinion," often in the form of hearings held by comrades' courts, workplace collectives, and other "comradely" institutions representing "the public."[49]

In fact, the main lesson sent to Communists by the Moral Code of the Builder of Communism was not that party members should fear expulsion and tough punishment if they violated its principles, but that they should fight for its values among the broader population. "The person of the epoch of Communism is a fighter," one pamphlet proclaimed[50]; another announced that every party member should be a "fighter for a Communist everyday life."[51] The solution to social problems was for Communists and other citizens to "speak out" (*vystupat'*) about them, denouncing any violations of the norms of society that they witnessed. As one pamphlet declared, "Unfortunately, a significant number of citizens still shows unnecessary delicacy where they should give a strong slap on the wrists to various thieves, embezzlers, hooligans, and so on. It is not uncommon to observe cases where tens of people see the carousing of a drunken hooligan, but cowardly avoid him, not wanting to interfere, trying to stay out of trouble."[52] Communists, in short, were expected to take the lead in struggling with "vestiges of the past" and to fight wrongdoing via "comradely condemnation." This activity would sometimes take place on the individual level, when a Communist witnessed an infraction and immediately spoke out against it. Sometimes it would take place at the collective level. One pamphlet told the story of a Communist who had ignored his son, who ran into trouble, inspiring his colleagues to hold a collective meeting, where they told him, "We want to help you as Communists and friends."[53] (As a result, the man was inspired to take his childrearing more seriously and the son became a model student.) Other Communists were expected to join the *druzhina*, a comrades' court, or another organization representing "the public." The Moral Code of the Builder of Communism was intended to challenge not just amorality, but passivity and non-interference as well, at least when it came to infractions by non-Communists and everyday citizens.

This approach offered a number of advantages to the regime. First, encouraging expulsion would have risked acknowledging that many Communists were guilty of misconduct and thereby embarrassing the party at a time when Khrushchev was hailing the high political consciousness of its members; shifting the focus onto non-Communists with a poor education and a low level of political consciousness allowed the regime to sing the praises of "moral education" as a tool for social change. Second, party officials at the time of the Twenty-Second Congress were keen to emphasize that as the USSR approached communism, the state and its institutions would wither away.[54] This focus on non-state actors paved the way for newly reinvigorated "public" institutions, such as the comrades' court and the *druzhina*, which would rally everyday citizens in the fight against antisocial acts.[55] Finally, encouraging members of "the public" (*obshchestvennost'*) to speak out against vestiges of the past had a final advantage for Khrushchev: it enabled the regime to take a tough, hardline stance against misconduct without resorting to coercion from above. As one writer concluded, many citizens "try to explain their failure to intervene with violations of the public interest, by saying that only the organs of the state are obligated to struggle with anti-social acts."[56] In principle, the Moral Code of the Builder of Communism encouraged bottom-up citizen activism, not a coercive, top-down effort to crack down on misbehaving Communists and other citizens. To be sure, as Oleg Kharkhordin and Brian LaPierre have shown, public organizations like the *druzhina* could be violent and coercive, but their harsh approach could be more easily justified by their populist politics.[57]

In short, the regime's growing interest in the behavior of Communists and other citizens presented Nikita Khrushchev with a problem: how could he champion "intolerance" for misbehavior and "the vestiges of the past" without purging the party of wrongdoers? As Miriam Dobson has noted, many citizens responded to the Moral Code by calling for a purge of immoral and corrupt Communists,[58] but Khrushchev opted for another approach. He diverted the party's moralizing tendencies outward and emphasized the need for "moral education" to change the consciousness and behavior of Soviet citizens. The party's new moral code became a permanent part of Soviet life, but did not result in a new purge or the tougher punishment of Communists.

Conclusion: The Changing Nature of Party Membership in the Era of Late Socialism

The Communist Party's Twenty-Second Congress, then, highlighted many of the tensions and contradictions that defined Soviet life and ideology in the Khrushchev years. But it also helped to shape the experiences of Communists and other Soviet citizens for decades to come. Although several of the trends discussed in this chapter, including the regime's efforts at de-Stalinization and its focus on "intolerance" toward wrongdoing, were characteristic products of the Khrushchev years that lost some of their prominence under Leonid Brezhnev, the regime's rhetoric on Communist morality remained strong, the party's expulsion rate remained low, and the number of Communists continued to climb in the years following Khrushchev's ouster. As a result, Khrushchev's policies resulted in a subtle long-term change in how the ideal behavior of Communists was viewed and in a growing divide between the rhetoric of the regime and the realities of Soviet life.

To name one example, Khrushchev-era rhetoric on Communist morality helped to change the party's expectation of its members in subtle ways, even if it did not result in the expulsion of large numbers of offenders. The number of Communists expelled for "unworthy behavior in everyday life"—basically, for drunkenness or misconduct in the family—seems to have remained steady or grown slightly in the 1950s and 1960s, at the same time that the overall expulsion rate was dropping sharply; the expulsion rate for these offenses rose in the Brezhnev years, although at a slower rate than the growth of the party.[59] The definition of "unworthy behavior" also began to expand, encompassing cases of marital infidelity that earlier would have been ignored because they did not directly threaten the upbringing of children. Moreover, from the mid-1950s onward, workplace-based party organizations spent increasing amounts of time debating and judging the misconduct of their members, looking into intimate matters in excruciating detail and airing Communists' dirty laundry for all to see. Even when they did not expel Communists for drunkenness, child abandonment, and marital infidelity, these organizations spent increasing amounts of time debating members' private behavior and censuring them for their misdeeds.[60]

Just as importantly, the party's new emphasis on "the norms of socialist life" had more subtle effects on how it defined its members' behavior. With the growing importance of *obshchestvennost'*, many party sources began to emphasize that a Communist's responsibilities extended beyond merely following the party line and included work in other public organizations. "In the past there were cases when a Communist, who conscientiously fulfilled his party assignments, neglected his responsibilities as a deputy to the local soviet or as a member of a trade union," one pamphlet noted. "The new charter puts an end to any undervaluing of work in public organizations and stresses its growing importance during the transition to communism."[61] Scholars have noted the rising importance of activism in public organizations in the late Soviet years, for Communists and non-Communists alike.[62] Even when party organizations were not pushing their members to fight hooliganism in a comrades' court or to demonstrate their "intolerance" of public disorder in a *druzhina*, they often encouraged Communists to participate in other newly expanded organizations, such as a parents' council; some party officials even argued that membership of such a board should be considered a party assignment akin to running a "wall newspaper" or engaging in agitation.[63] This change, in turn, highlighted the regime's growing focus on parenting and the family within the party's behavioral code, which became more insistent that Communists be good parents as well as good workers. In 1964, the journal *Partiinaia zhizn'* even published a letter from a Communist asking whether he was worthy of serving as party cell secretary, given that his son was a weak student and had been expelled from the Pioneers.[64] The journal replied that to resign as PPO secretary would be "to leave active public work" and urged him not to do so, while reiterating that Communists must raise their children well and provide an example to others through their private behavior.

Ultimately, the biggest legacy of the Khrushchev-era policies discussed in this chapter was a growing divide between party rhetoric and party reality. Even when the passions of the Khrushchev years had faded, the party's call for its members to be moral paragons and citizen activists remained a permanent part of the political landscape, as the Communist Party continued to grow and the expulsion rate remained a shadow of what it had been under Stalinism. Khrushchev had promised to transform the political consciousness and the everyday behavior of the Soviet people, but his utopian rhetoric was never translated into success. The Moral Code of the Builder of Communism remained a prominent feature of Soviet life until the USSR's 1991 collapse, while the party continued to grow and the tough enforcement of the party's behavioral code for its members faded into the past.

Edward Cohn is an associate professor of history at Grinnell College. His publications include *The High Title of a Communist: Postwar Party Discipline and the Values of the Soviet Regime* (2015) and "Coercion, Re-education, and the Prophylactic Chat: Profilaktika and the KGB's Struggle with Political Unrest in Lithuania, 1953–64," in *The Russian Review* 76, no. 2 (2017): 272–293.

Notes

Earlier versions of parts of this chapter appear in Edward Cohn, *The High Title of a Communist: Postwar Party Discipline and the Values of the Soviet Regime* (DeKalb, IL: Northern Illinois University Press, 2015).
1. For the code's text, see *Materialy XII s"ezda KPSS* (Moscow, 1962), 410–11. See Deborah Field, *Private Life and Communist Morality in Khrushchev's Russia* (New York, 2007), esp. 9–11, and Richard T. De George, *Soviet Ethics and Morality* (Ann Arbor, 1969) for scholarly writings on communist morality.
2. David Hoffmann, *Stalinist Values: The Cultural Norms of Stalinist Modernity, 1917–1941* (Ithaca, 2003), 58–59.
3. *Materialy XII s"ezda*, 411.
4. "Ustav Kommunisticheskoi partii Sovetskogo Soiuza," *Pravda*, 3 November 1961, 2.
5. See, for example, B. Khanenko, *Kakie neset obiazannosti i kakie imeet prava chlen KPSS* [What are the responsibilities and what are the rights of a member of the CPSU] (Moscow, 1963); G. Ukhov, *Chego partiia trebuet ot kommunista* [What the party demands from a Communist] (Moscow, 1962); V. Markov, *Byt–ne chastnoe delo* (Moscow, 1964); V. Moskovskii, *Partiia vsego naroda: besedy o KPSS* (Moscow, 1962); and *Printsipy tvoei zhizni (besedy o moral'nom kodekse stroitelia kommunizma)* (Moscow, 1963).
6. *Materialy XII s"ezda*, 430–435.
7. "KPSS v tsifrakh (1956–1961 gg.)," *Partiinaia zhizn'*, 1962: 1 (January), 47.
8. F. R. Kozlov, "Ob izmeneniiakh v ustave Kommunisticheskoi partii Sovetskogo Soiuza," *Pravda*, 28 October 1961, 4.
9. N. M. Shvernik, "Okonchanie rechi tovarishcha N. M. Shvernika," *Pravda*, 26 October 1961, 4.
10. For an analysis of the role of expulsion and censure in the postwar Communist Party, see Edward Cohn, *The High Title of a Communist: Postwar Party Discipline and the Values of the Regime in the Postwar Soviet Union, 1945–1964* (DeKalb, 2015).
11. See Rossiiskii gosudarstvennyi arkhiv sotsial'no-politicheskoi istorii [The Russian State Archive of Social-Political History], f. 17, o. 7, d. 309, l. 138.

12. See Rossiiskii gosudarstvennyi arkhiv noveishei istorii [The Russian State Archive of Contemporary History, hereafter RGANI], f. 77, o. 1, d. 26, l. 25.
13. *Spravochnik "KPSS v tsifrakh" na 1 yanvarya 1962 g* (RGANI f. 77, o. 1, d. 26, l. 21) and "KPSS v tsifrakh 1961–1964 gody," in *Partiinaia zhizn'*, May 1965, 8–17.
14. See RGANI f. 77, o. 1, d. 5, ll. 77 and 166; d. 6, ll. 73 and 174; d. 7, ll. 68 and 164; d. 8, ll. 76 and 175; d. 9, ll. 20, 69; d. 10, ll. 5, 65, 131; d. 11, ll. 5, 63, 124; d. 12, ll. 5, 54, 158, 217. For more on repression and anti-Soviet activity under Khrushchev, see Robert Hornsby, *Political Reform and Repression in Khrushchev's Soviet Union* (New York, 2013) and Vladimir Kozlov, Sheila Fitzpatrick, and Sergei V. Mironenko, eds., *Sedition: Everyday Resistance in the Soviet Union under Khrushchev and Brezhnev* (New Haven, 2011).
15. For a recent monograph on this theme, see Polly Jones, *Myth, Memory, Trauma: Rethinking the Stalinist Past in the Soviet Union, 1953–1970* (New Haven, 2013).
16. Nikita Khrushchev, "O kul'te lichnosti i ego posledstviiakh," in *Doklad N. S. Khrushcheva o kul'te lichnosti na XX s"ezde: dokumenty*, 51–119 (Moscow, 2002), 74.
17. Ibid., 60.
18. Shvernik, "Okonchanie," 4.
19. Statistics in this paragraph come from *Spravochnik "KPSS v tsifrakh" na 1 yanvarya 1962 g* (RGANI f. 77, o. 1, d. 26, l. 21) and "KPSS v tsifrakh 1961–1964 gody," *Partiinaia zhizn'*, May 1965, 8–17.
20. See E. M. Andreev et al., *Naselenie sovetskogo soiuza, 1922—1991* (Moscow, 1993) for information on the population's growth rate under Khrushchev.
21. For a classic account of party membership policies, see T. H. Rigby, *Communist Party Membership in the U.S.S.R., 1917–1967* (Princeton, 1968).
22. See Cynthia Hooper, "What Can and Cannot Be Said: Between the Stalinist Past and New Soviet Future," *Slavonic and East European Review* 86 no. 2 (April 2008): 306–327.
23. See Barbara Ann Chotiner, *Khrushchev's Party Reform: Coalition Building and Institutional Innovation* (Westwood, CT, 1984) and Soo–Heon Park, "Party Reform and 'Volunteer Principle' under Khrushchev in Historical Perspective" (doctoral dissertation, Columbia University, 1993) for more on Khrushchev-era party reform.
24. See George Breslauer, *Khrushchev and Brezhnev as Leaders: Building Authority in Soviet Politics* (Boston, 1982), esp. 52–58, for a discussion of Khrushchev's populism.
25. Moskovskii, *Partiia vsego naroda: besedy o KPSS*, 4.
26. See, for example, S. Sutotskii, *10 millionov idushchikh vperedi (KPSS—partiia vsego naroda)* (Moscow, 1963).
27. See table 2.
28. RGANI f. 77, o. 1, d. 26, l. 21, and "KPSS v tsifrakh 1961–1964 gody," *Partiinaia zhizn'*, May 1965, 8–17.
29. Khrushchev's speech to the congress was published in *Pravda* (13 October 1952, page 1) and is discussed in Yoram Gorlizki, "Party Revivalism and the Death of Stalin," *Slavic Review* 54, no. 1 (Spring 1995): 1–22.

30. "Ustav Vsesoiuznoi Kommunisticheskoi partii (bol'shevikov)," *Pravda*, 27 March 1939, 1.
31. "Ustav Kommunisticheskoi partii Sovetskogo Soiuza," *Pravda*, 14 October 1952, 1. For more on the growth of a party elite that was safe from prosecution, see Cynthia V. Hooper, "A Darker 'Big Deal': Concealing Party Crimes in the Post-WWII Era," in *Late Stalinist Russia: Society Between Reconstruction and Reinvention*, ed. Juliane Fürst (New York, 2006), 142–163, and "Terror from Within: Participation and Coercion in Soviet Power, 1924–1964" (doctoral dissertation, Princeton University, 2003
32. "Ustav Kommunisticheskoi partii Sovetskogo Soiuza," *Pravda*, 3 November 1961, 1.
33. Brian LaPierre, *Hooligans in Khrushchev's Russia: Defining, Policing, and Producing Deviance during the Thaw* (Madison, 2012); Miriam Dobson, *Khrushchev's Cold Summer: Gulag Returnees, Crime, and the Fate of Reform after Stalin* (Ithaca, 2009).
34. For an overview of press coverage related to drunkenness in the early Khrushchev years, see Mark Field, "Alcoholism, Crime, and Delinquency in Soviet Society," *Social Problems* 3, no. 2 (October 1955): 100–109.
35. See LaPierre, *Hooligans in Khrushchev's Russia*, chapter 3, on petty hooliganism; Sheila Fitzpatrick, "Social Parasites: How Tramps, Idle Youth, and Busy Entrepreneurs Impeded the Soviet March to Communism," *Cahiers du monde russe* 47, no. 1–2 (January–June 2006), 377–408, on parasitism; and *Spravochnik partiinogo rabotnika*, vyp. 2 (Moscow, 1959), 404–408, for a December 1958 decree of the Central Committee and Council of Ministers calling for a stronger "struggle with drunkenness" and home-brewing.
36. The quotation comes from Markov, *Byt–ne chastnoe delo*, 57. For a pamphlet with the same title, see O. Kuprin, *Byt–ne chastnoe delo* (Moscow, 1959).
37. *Materialy XXII s"ezd*, 408.
38. *Materialy XXII s"ezd*, 410.
39. *Printsipy tvoei zhizni*, 127.
40. *Materialy XXII s"ezd*, 411.
41. *Materialy XXII s"ezd*, 410.
42. "Ustav Kommunisticheskoi partii Sovetskogo Soiuza," *Pravda*, 3 November 1961, 2.
43. See LaPierre, *Hooligans in Khrushchev's Russia*, 102, for a discussion of how the regime's response to the moral panic around hooliganism led to efforts to create "a society of all-encompassing intolerance toward every imaginable type of deviancy."
44. Dobson, *Khrushchev's Cold Summer*, 211.
45. S. Indurskii, *Lichnyi primer kommunista* (Moscow, 1962).
46. *Printsipy tvoei zhizni*, 128–129.
47. *Printsipy tvoei zhizni*, 130–31.
48. *Materialy XXII s"ezd*, 412.
49. See, for example, N. F. Kuznetsova, *Dela o prestupleniiakh, rasmatrivaemykh tovarishcheskimi sudami* (Moscow, 1962).
50. *Printsipy tvoei zhizni*, 11.
51. Markov, *Byt–ne chastnoe delo*, 45.
52. *Printsipy tvoei zhizni*, 50.

53. Kuprin, *Byt–ne chastnoe delo*, 50.
54. Alexander Titov, "The 1961 Party Programme and the Fate of Khrushchev's Reforms," in *Soviet State and Society under Nikita Khrushchev*, ed. Jeremy Smith and Melanie Ilic (London, 2009), 8–26.
55. Harold J. Berman and James W. Spindler, "Soviet Comrades' Courts," *Washington Law Review* 38 (1963): 842–910; Gorlizki, "Delegalization"; Darrell P. Hammer, "Law Enforcement, Social Control and the Withering of the State: Recent Soviet Experience," *Soviet Studies* 14, no. 4 (April 1963): 379–397.
56. *Printsipy tvoei zhizni*, 50–51.
57. See LaPierre and Oleg Kharkhordin, *The Collective and the Individual in Russia: A Study of Practices* (Berkeley, 1999).
58. Dobson, *Khrushchev's Cold Summer*, 210–211.
59. See, for example, Edward Cohn, *The High Title of a Communist*, chapter 5. For Brezhnev-era expulsion statistics, see RGANI f. 77, o. 1, d. 13, ll. 90, 102, 171.
60. See Cohn, *The High Title of a Communist*, chapter 5.
61. E. I. Bugaev and B. M. Leibzon, *Besedy ob ustave KPSS* (Moscow, 1962), 66.
62. See, for example, Vladimir Shlapentokh, *Public and Private Life of the Soviet People: Changing Values in Post-Stalin Russia* (New York, 1989), 115–122.
63. See, for example, Markov, *Byt–ne chastnoe delo*, 59–60, and N. Bogdanov, "Obshchenarodnoe, partiinoe delo," *Sem'ia i shkola* 12 (December 1962): 2.
64. "Dostoin li ia doveriia?," *Partiinaia zhizn'* 12 (June 1964): 44–45.

Bibliography

Andreev, E.M., Darskii, L.E., and Khar'kova, T.L.. *Naselenie sovetskogo soiuza, 1922–1991* [The population of the Soviet Union, 1922–1991]. Moscow: Nauka, 1993.

Berman, Harold J., and James W. Spindler. "Soviet Comrades' Courts." *Washington Law Review* 38 (1963): 842–910.

Breslauer, George W. *Gorbachev and Yeltsin as Leaders*. Cambridge: Cambridge University Press, 2002.

Bugaev, E. I., and B. M. Leibzon. *Besedy ob ustave KPSS* [Conversations about the charter of the CPSU]. Moscow: Gosudarstvennoe izdatel'stvo poiticheskoi literatury, 1962.

Bugaev, E., E. Bagramov, Z. Demysheva, S. Elizarenko, V. Kirsanov, A. Klimov, G. Krivoshchen, I. Mitin, N. Mora, F. Petrenko, P. Svechnikov, A. Svinarenko, V. Tolstov, and I. Shvets. *Printsipy tvoei zhizni (besedy o moral'nom kodekse stroitelia kommunizma)* (Principles of your life [Conversations about the moral code of the builder of Communism]). Moscow: Gosudarstvennaia izdatel'stvo politicheskoi literatury, 1963.

Chotiner, Barbara Ann. *Khrushchev's Party Reform: Coalition Building and Institutional Innovation*. Westport, CT: Greenwood Press, 1984.

Cohn, Edward. *The High Title of a Communist: Postwar Party Discipline and the Values of the Regime in the Postwar Soviet Union, 1945–1964*. DeKalb: Northern Illinois University Press, 2015.

CPSU. *Spravochnik partiinogo rabotnika, vyp. 2* [Handbook of a party worker]. Moscow: Izdatel'stvo politicheskoi literatury, 1959.
De George, Richard T. *Soviet Ethics and Morality*. Ann Arbor: University of Michigan Press, 1969.
Dobson, Miriam. *Khrushchev's Cold Summer: Gulag Returnees, Crime, and the Fate of Reform after Stalin*. Ithaca: Cornell University Press, 2009.
Field, Deborah. *Private Life and Communist Morality in Khrushchev's Russia*. New York: Peter Lang, 2007.
Field, Mark. "Alcoholism, Crime, and Delinquency in Soviet Society." *Social Problems* 3, no. 2 (October 1955): 100–109.
Fitzpatrick, Sheila. "Social parasites: How Tramps, Idle Youth, and Busy Entrepreneurs Impeded the Soviet March to Communism." *Cahiers du monde russe* 47, no. 1–2 (January–June 2006): 377–408.
Gorlitzki, Yoram. "Party Revivalism and the Death of Stalin." *Slavic Review* 54, no. 1 (1995): 1–22.
Hammer, Darrell P. "Law Enforcement, Social Control and the Withering of the State: Recent Soviet Experience." *Soviet Studies* 14, no. 4 (April 1963): 379–397.
Hoffmann, David. *Stalinist Values: The Cultural Norms of Stalinist Modernity, 1917–1941*. Ithaca: Cornell University Press, 2003.
Hooper, Cynthia V. "A Darker 'Big Deal': Concealing Party Crimes in the post–WWII Era." In *Late Stalinist Russia: Society between Reconstruction and Reinvention*, ed. Juliane Fürst, 142–163. New York: Routledge, 2006.
———. "What Can and Cannot Be Said: Between the Stalinist Past and New Soviet Future." *The Slavonic and East European Review* 86 no. 2 (April 2008): 306–327.
Hornsby, Robert. *Political Reform and Repression in Khrushchev's Soviet Union*. New York: Cambridge University Press, 2013.
Indurskii. S. *Lichnyi primer kommunista* [The personal example of a Communist]. Moscow: Moskovskii rabochii, 1962.
Jones, Polly. *Myth, Memory, Trauma: Rethinking the Stalinist Past in the Soviet Union, 1953–1970*. New Haven: Yale University Press, 2013.
Khanenko, B. *Kakie neset obiazannosti i kakie imeet prava chlen KPSS* [What are the responsibilities and what are the rights of a member of the CPSU]. Moscow: Gosudarstvennoe izdatel'stvo politicheskoi literatury, 1963.
Kharkhordin, Oleg. *The Collective and the Individual in Russia: A Study of Practices*. Berkeley: University of California Press, 1999.
Khrushchev, Nikita. "O kul'te lichnosti i ego posledstviiakh" [About the cult of personality and its consequences]. In *Doklad N.S. Khrushcheva o kul'te lichnosti na XX s"ezde: dokumenty* [The report of N. S. Khrushchev about the cult of personality to the Twentieth Congress: Documents], 51–119. Moscow: Rosspen, 2002.
Kozlov, Vladimir, Sheila Fitzpatrick, and Sergei V. Mironenko, eds. *Sedition: Everyday Resistance in the Soviet Union under Khrushchev and Brezhnev*. Trans. Olga Livshin. New Haven: Yale University Press, 2011.
Kuprin, O. *Byt–ne chastnoe delo* [Everyday life is not a private matter]. Moscow: Izdatel'stvo politicheskoi literatury, 1959.

Kuznetsova, N. F. *Dela o prestupleniiakh, rasmatrivaemykh tovarishcheskimi sudami* [Cases on crimes, considered by comrades' courts]. Moscow: Izdatel'stvo Moskovskogo universiteta, 1962.
LaPierre, Brian. *Hooligans in Khrushchev's Russia: Defining, Policing, and Producing Deviance during the Thaw*. Madison: Wisconsin University Press, 2012.
Markov, V. *Byt–ne chastnoe delo*. Moscow: Izdatel'stvo politicheskoi literatury, 1964.
Materialy XII s"ezda KPSS (Everyday life is not a private matter). Moscow: Gosudarstvennoe izdatel'stvo politicheskoi literatury, 1962.
Moskovskii, V. *Partiia vsego naroda: besedy o KPSS* [Party of the entire people: Conversations about the CPSU]. Moscow: Gospolitizdat, 1962.
Park, Soo–Heon. "Party Reform and 'Volunteer Principle' under Khrushchev in Historical Perspective." Doctoral dissertation, Columbia University, 1993.
Rigby, Thomas H. *Communist Party Membership in the U.S.S.R. 1917–1967*. Princeton: Princeton University Press, 1968.
Shlapentokh, Vladimir. *Public and Private Life of the Soviet People: Changing Values in Post-Stalin Russia*. New York: Oxford University Press, 1989.
Sutotskii, S. *10 millionov idushchikh vperedi (KPSS—partiia vsego naroda)* [10 million going forward (The CPSU—party of the entire people)]. Moscow: Izdatel'stvo politicheskoi literatury, 1963.
Titov, Alexander. "The 1961 Party Programme and the Fate of Khrushchev's Reforms." In *Soviet State and Society under Nikita Khrushchev*, ed. M. Ilic and J. Smith, 8–26 London: Routledge, 2009.
Ukhov, G. *Chego partiia trebuet ot kommunista* [What the party demands from a Communist]. Moscow: Moskovskii rabochii, 1962.

 2

"It Is Not Possible to Allow Past Mistakes to Come Again"
Recruitment Policy in the CPCS in the 1970s and 1980s
Michel Christian

"It is not possible to allow past mistakes to come again." This assertion was formulated in the introduction to the new recruitment directive issued by the Central Committee (CC) of the Communist Party of Czechoslovakia (CPCS) in September 1971.[1] It referred to the poor situation in the party after the CPCS experienced its deepest crisis, and the largest purge in its history: more than 28 percent of party members either left or were expelled from the party between January 1968 and December 1970.[2] What, according to the directive, were considered as "past mistakes," was the recruitment of members "according to quantitative rather than qualitative criteria" and "the admission of individuals who should not belong to the Party," which was regarded as the cause of the 1968 crisis. Another issue was the aging of party members. As the number of party recruits had been lower in the 1960s, and many young members had been expelled, older cohorts were not replaced, and the average age therefore rose.

However, the solution envisioned by the directive was by no means new. At a meeting in November 1970, CPCS Presidium members had already developed the following line of reasoning: "since the working class is the youngest and the largest class, there are real conditions to help lower the average age of the members by taking young workers into the party."[3] According to the directive, which was adopted in September 1971, workers and peasants should thus comprise a "large majority" of the new recruits, and new members were supposed to be younger than thirty-five years old. Party functionaries were invited to rely on mass organizations, such as the youth organization and the union, a channel that had been mentioned in the party statutes since 1962.[4] The only new directive consisted of particularly targeting the individuals whose parents were already members of the party. That directive indicated that party leaders had become aware of the long-term effects of the historical mass recruitment into the CPCS that might, from then on, provide the opportunity to recruit young people from families in which party membership had become an intergenerational phenomenon, thereby resulting in family tradition.

Whether the new recruitment policy indeed helped overcome "past mistakes" is the subject of this essay. Monitoring the evolution of party membership during the 1970s and 1980s will first help us assess whether the post-crisis recruitment directive constituted a break with the past. The reasons people joined the CPCS is the second question that needs to be addressed. Given the context in which the "post-crisis" recruitment policy was formulated, the reasons for which one would become a party member—especially in the case of "young workers"— were hard to fathom, knowing that the party had abandoned its reform course, ousted its most popular leaders, and accepted military occupation by the Soviet Union. This view is in accordance with existing literature. Many Czech historians, many of whom were in exile, saw the so-called "normalization era" as a second "age of darkness" for the Czech and Slovak nations. The members who joined the CPCS after 1970 are said to have been motivated either by fear or by material interest. More generally, the whole of Czechoslovakian society is considered to have fallen into moral disarray after 1970, with people acting on an individualistic basis, busying themselves with the building of their dachas, and putting up a façade of political conformity when so required by the regime. After the fall of the regime, that description in political and moral terms remained part of the historiography.[5]

However, this assumption is questionable. The description in itself, which often came from people who had been part of the reform movement, was originally meant to deny any legitimacy to the regime after 1970, showing that it rested only on an "abnormal social contract" in which everyday security and consumption came as a reward for political conformity.[6] New works that challenge such a description have only recently been published.[7] Contrary to that approach in moral terms, I resort to a historical and sociological perspective to assess the CPCS recruitment policy, measuring its successes and limits, while interpreting the motivations of the people who joined the Communist Party during that period by taking into account the social context of which they were part.

To that end, one central issue was to find reliable material that provided information about membership composition in terms of age, gender, education, and social background. At the beginning of the 1990s, an international group of sociologists, led by Ivan Szelényi and Donald J. Treiman, carried out an ambitious study of several East European countries called *Social Stratification in Eastern Europe after 1989: General Population Survey*.[8] Many sociologists in the study used some data collected in the 1990s to draw conclusions on the 1950s and 1960s, which is questionable since the majority of older people, and especially party members, who were alive in the 1950s and 1960s had died by the 1990s. However, this chapter is partly based on the study's more reliable data on party members in the 1970s and 1980s. Equally useful was the oral history project of the Oral History Center of the Institute for Contemporary History (*Ústav pro soudobé dějiny*), which published a set of interviews and analyses concerning workers and members of intellectual professions (intelligentsia).[9] Finally, some pre-1989 studies based on party material have focused on the composition of the CPCS.[10] Party material has often been dismissed as unreliable, notably because the CPCS was suspected of manipulating the data, especially when it came to "social class," in order to appear as a "proletarian" party. Yet I argue that in addition to post-1989 sociological studies and oral histories, it is indeed possible to use party material by combining material from the higher organs,[11] which provide figures about the party as a whole, with material from the lower organs in the districts (*okresy*), which provide a local but more precise picture of the recruitment process.[12]

A Successful Recruitment Policy? Stricter Recruitment Criteria after the 1968 to 1970 "Crisis"

Paradoxically, the criteria for joining the party became stricter at the very moment when the party leaders called for a mass recruitment policy. The process of joining the Communist Party became longer and more difficult, first because of the "candidate" status that was restored as early as 1971, after having been suppressed in 1966.[13] While they were still candidates, the members-to-be were supposed to become acquainted with party life before being admitted as full members. This probationary period was extended to two years, the longest of all Communist parties. In addition, the past activities of the new candidates, especially in the years between 1968 and 1970, were carefully scrutinized. In the membership applications that the local CPCS organs had to validate,[14] it was not uncommon to read comments about their conduct in 1968. Most of them certified that "there is no remark about him/her concerning the years 1968 to 1969." Some others had to justify their behavior (e.g., "What was happening was not clear to him").[15] In some rare cases, the routine checks led to an investigation resulting in an expulsion, for instance when it appeared that a candidate had not mentioned that he had supported Dubček.[16] Not every candidate received a comment about his/her attitude in 1968 to 1969. At the same time, a party functionary could systematically write "1968?" in the margins of all CVs when the candidate's attitude in 1968 was not mentioned.[17]

Such suspicion emanated not only from the top; it also came from the bottom of the party apparatus. In 1976, CPCS leaders around Husák decided to relent on the candidacy requirements and open party recruitment up to those who had been expelled or struck off[18] from the party in the years 1968 to 1971. In June 1976, a CC directive was issued to implement "a balanced approach to re-admit into the party those whose membership had been cancelled or who were expelled in the years 1968 to 1971."[19] Cautiously based on a report titled "CPSU Evaluation Practice in Matters of Readmission of Former Members into the Party,"[20] the directives allowed the readmission of every former member, provided he had not been an "active right-wing opportunist element."[21] However, the directive caused discontent in the lower party organs. A secret report, obtained by East German Communists through their embassy in Prague, described how the directive was received, telling them that "some comrades criticized the fact that this decision was taken without referring to the bottom party organs. Some local secretaries stated that in their district, they knew of "no such cases of people who could apply to be readmitted."[22] The top-down reintegration project had obviously underestimated the human consequences of the 1970 purge. In fact, the purge, which is usually viewed as a merely negative move, also had positive effects in forming a new core of loyal members and drawing a line between "us" and "them." Between 165,000 and 235,000 members, amounting to far more than a small "Stalinist core," contributed to the purge by participating in commissions to interview each member individually.[23] Many functionaries in the lower party organs were therefore reluctant to readmit people they had ousted from the party in 1970 in a very tense situation. As a result, twelve years later, hardly more than four thousand former members had been readmitted into the party following this procedure.[24] Former members had not constituted the expected recruitment reservoir.

A Steadily Growing Number of Party Members

Despite the political context of the 1970s and the strict recruitment criteria, the new recruitment policy succeeded in winning large numbers of people for the party soon after it was formulated, and for as long as the party remained in power. Between 1971 and 1988, an average of more than 60,000 people each year joined the party, with higher figures in the 1970s and lower figures in the 1980s (table 2.1).

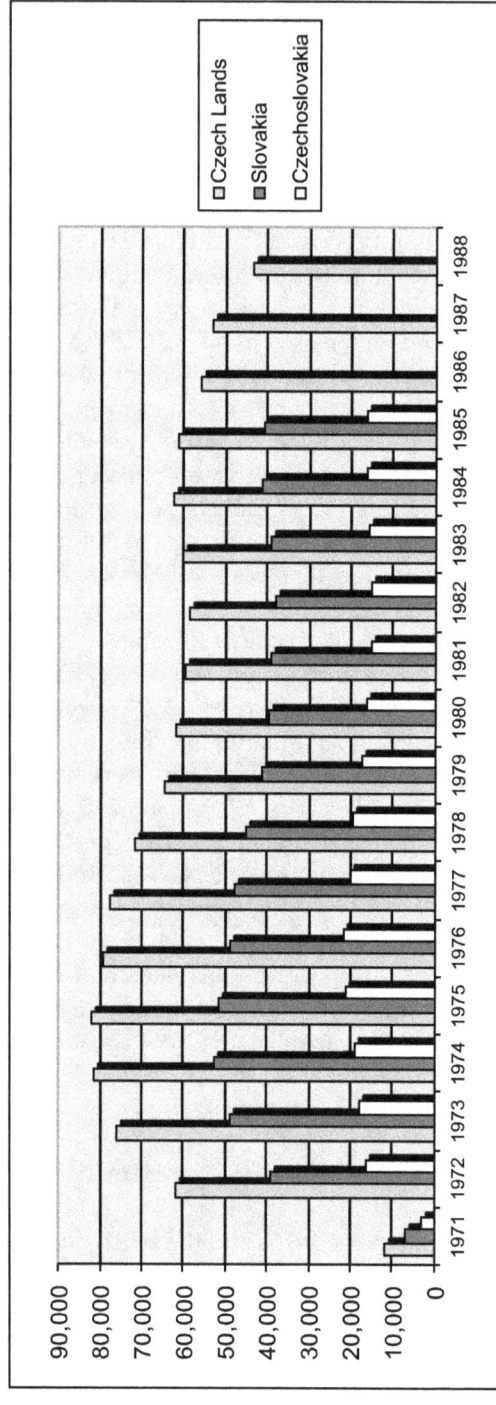

Figure 2.1. Number of Candidates to the CPCS between 1971 and 1988

Source: These figures were found in the booklets prepared for party congresses between 1971 and 1986. They were complemented by figures about the years 1986–1989 from Prague National Archives (PNA), Oddělení 1 (uncatalogued), Údaje o vývoji členské základny KSČ od 1.1.1971 do 1.1.1989 [Data on the development of the CPCS basis from 1.1.1971 to 1.1.1989].[25]

This large intake of new members ensured that party membership figures kept on growing until 1988, although the number of pre-1970 members declined progressively for demographic reasons (see table 2.2). Membership was thoroughly renewed as a result. In 1981, 43 percent of the members had joined the party after 1971. By 1988, this figure had risen to 59 percent. Most of the new members were young; between 1971 and 1976, 51 percent of party candidates were under twenty-five. To some extent, the recruitment policy took advantage of a favorable demographic trend because the so-called baby boomers, who were born in the 1950s, were reaching their twenties by the 1970s. Conversely, the lower figures of the 1980s seem to reflect a declining demographic trend. Probably as a result of this less favorable trend, the age at which candidates applied for membership increased slightly in the 1980s, when only 42 percent of party candidates were under twenty-five between 1981 and 1986.[26]

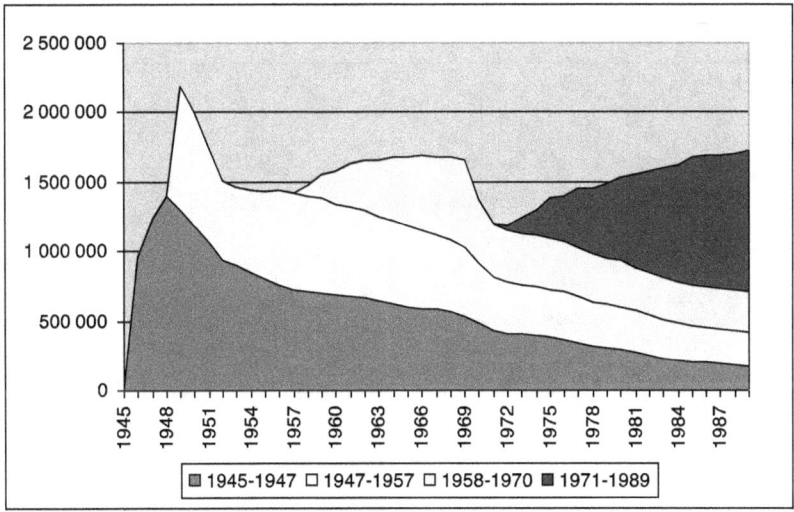

Figure 2.2. Membership Evolution between 1945 and 1988, according to the Year When Members Joined the Party

Source: This diagram was made on the basis on the data collected by Jiří Maňák.

However, on the whole, the rate of party membership among the population increased steadily during the entire period of time, from 11.6 percent in 1971 to 15.4 percent in 1988 (table 2.3). This means that the membership figures of the party reflected not only demographic trends, but also rose faster than the population. The rate of membership in the Czech lands rose from 10–15 percent to 14–17 percent between 1971 and

1986 (depending on the region). The trend was still stronger in Slovakia, where the rate of membership, though lower than in the Czech lands, jumped from 7–8 percent to 11–12 percent during the same period (table 2.4).[27] The proportion of Slovaks in the CPCS ranks increased from 21 percent in 1971 to 28 percent in 1986.[28] With this trend, the Slovaks, who made up only 13 percent of the CPCS members in 1953 and had originally been strongly underrepresented,[29] pursued their catching-up process in the long run.

Table 2.1. Average Rate of Party Membership in the Czechoslovakian Population (in Percentages)[30]

1971	1976	1981	1986	1989
11.6	12.9	14.2	15.1	15.4

Source: PNA, Oddělení 1 (uncatalogued), Údaje o vývoji členské základny KSČ od 1.1.1971 do 1.1.1989 [Data on the development of the CPCS rank and file from 1.1.1971 to 1.1.1989], 8.

Table 2.2. Evolution of the Rate of Party Membership in the Czech and in the Slovakian Regions between 1971 and 1986 (in Percentages)[31]

		1971	1986
Czech lands	Prague	12.6	16.5
	Central Bohemia	15.6	17.5
	South Bohemia	12.5	15.3
	West Bohemia	12.4	15.6
	North Bohemia	12.1	15.1
	East Bohemia	11.5	13.9
	South Moravia	11.5	15.0
	North Moravia	10.6	14.4
Slovakia	Bratislava	11.4	16.8
	West Slovakia	7.4	10.9
	Central Slovakia	8.5	12.1
	East Slovakia	8.9	12.2
	CPCS overall	11.6	15.1

Source: UV KSČ, Vývoj členský základny KSČ a složení nomenklaturních kádrů mezi XVI. a XVII. Sjezdem [Development of the party basis and composition of the nomenclature cadres between the 16th and 17th Congresses], 1986, 52.

A Majority of Workers and Peasants among the New Recruits

The recruitment policy succeeded in attracting large numbers of relatively young people within the party; moreover, the young people were indeed mainly workers. The official figures produced by the CC on the occasion of party congresses show that the share of workers among newly recruited candidates remained as high as 60 percent in the 1970s and 1980s, while candidates from the "intelligentsia" amounted to only approximately 20 percent of the overall candidate intake. Of course, one could easily argue that these figures are not reliable as they were produced by the party apparatus and primarily had a legitimization function. This was the case, for instance, in the East German SED (*Sozialistische Einheitspartei Deutschland,* or German Socialist Unity Party), where statistical categories were vague and aggregated people who came from different social backgrounds into the same category. For instance, the category of "workers" was made up of real industrial and agricultural workers and employees in services, but also foremen and people who had once been workers but who had later been trained to become functionaries or supervisors.[32]

That the recruitment of workers served to prove the working class identity of the party was of course also true in the CPCS. However, in that particular case, this is not contradictory to the fact that people recruited as workers really were workers. A confrontation with the data that was produced at the local level helps put official figures to the test. In order to be admitted to the party, individuals applied in the workplace where the party primary organizations were set up. They were elected as party members by other party members of the primary organization. However, before the vote, every application had to be validated by the local CPCS committee (*okresní výbor*), which examined each application individually and, at the same time, produced statistics based on a short CV kept in their archives. The statistics were used to supervise the implementation of the local recruitment plan, mainly based on age and social class quotas, and were also simultaneously transmitted to the upper levels, which produced general statistics. This allowed for a comparison of biographical information with statistical categories—to check, for instance, whether a worker on paper actually was a worker in real life. The comparison of the occupation of candidates within their CV and the social category under which they were registered shows that the statistics produced by the party apparatus did not widely differ from social reality. In particular, party functionaries did not use any tricks to boost the proportion of workers in the official statistics. People who had once worked as blue-collar workers and had then risen to white-collar positions were not, for example, registered as "workers," but as "administrative employees," as shown by the CV of Comrade J. (see epigraph below), who was once a worker in a book factory, then later became a payroll accountant—and as such, was registered as an "administrative employee." The practice in the CPCS consisted, therefore, of registering the real occupation of the candidates and members.

> J. D.
> 34 years old, born X. X. 1941
> CPCS candidate since 22.10.1974
> Worker, now an accountant in charge of the payroll
> Primary organization Sfinx in Žleby
> Address: Žleby
> Father employee on the Czechoslovakian railroads, now retired. Mother agricultural worker, then member of the agricultural cooperative, also retired. Both parents not party members. After having completed her training in a vocational school, Comrade J. was hired as a worker in a book factory in Golč. Jeníkově. From 1961 onwards she has worked in the national Company Sfinx in Žleby. She is a member of the Union. She is married, husband worker, member of the CPCS. Comrade J. joined the party out of ideological commitment and she wants to work actively. Opinions from her neighborhood about her are good. Nothing to note about her concerning the years 1968–1969. She has been informed about the party statutes and she has got a party mission as an assistant to the party group supervisor.[33]

The finding that the CPCS could recruit more than 60 percent of its candidates among workers over 20 years is surprisingly consistent with the results of some sociological studies conducted after 1989. The comparison of official party figures with sociological data shows that the "intelligentsia" category corresponds to that of "administrators and professionals," while "manual workers" were part of the "routine non-manual workers," and "agricultural workers" corresponds to the "workers" category in use in the party apparatus (tables 2.5 and 2.6.) Sociologists have often blamed internal party material for being heavily

Table 2.3. Party Members' Occupation When Joining the Party, according to Figures Based on the Social Stratification in Eastern Europe Survey (in Percentages)

Occupation	1971–81	1981–89
Manual and routine non-manual work	51	56
Agriculture	6	4
Administrators and professionals	24	29
Not working / missing	19	10

Source: Gary Marks, "Communist Party Membership in Five Former Soviet Bloc Countries." *Communist and Post-Communist Studies* 37 (2004): 241–263, esp. 257.

Table 2.4. Party Members' Occupation When Joining the Party, according to Figures Issued by the Central Committee of the CPCS (in Percentages).

Occupation	1971–81	1981–89
"Workers"	61	58
"Members of agricultural cooperatives"	8	6
"Intelligentsia"	19	22
"Students"	3	3
Others	9	11

Source: PNA, Oddělení 1 (uncatalogued), Údaje o vývoji členské základny KSČ od 1.1.1971 do 1.1.1989 [Data on the development of the CPCS rank and file from 1.1.1971 to 1.1.1989], 11.

biased, while sociological reconstruction was supposed to unveil the "real" Communist societies. Yet, a critical use of internal party material leads to conclusions similar to the findings of sociological studies, which means that the widespread distrust by sociologists of internal party material rests on an insufficient analysis of historical sources.

Influence of Social Class and Sector on Recruitment

The group called "party members" was in fact very heterogeneous because members held very different positions and worked in various fields of activity where membership did not mean the same thing. Although workers represented the majority among party candidates, the rate of party membership among workers in the country remained low. Conversely, engineers, technicians, teachers, and jurists, while making up a minority of the candidates, were professions with a high rate of membership of the party (table 2.7). This was confirmed by sociological studies produced after 1989, which showed that the higher the level of education one had, the higher the odds were of joining the party.[34] However, a CPCS specificity was that the odds of people with tertiary education (university degree) joining the CPCS at the end of the 1980s, while being 2.7 times higher than those of people with just a primary school education, were in fact the lowest among Communist parties in the Soviet bloc.[35] This was due to the rate of party membership among intellectuals, which was in fact quite heterogeneous. While the rate of party membership was very high among managers, it was lower among other nonmanagerial professions such as scientists, physicians, and cultural employees (table 2.7). Although these professionals were more frequently party members than the rest of the population, in fact

Table 2.5. Rate of Party Membership in the CPCS in Different Social Groups and Professions in 1981 (in Percentages)

Foremen and sector directors in factories	50.4
Clerks and state apparatus	34.5
Engineers and technicians in factories	24.7
Teachers, professors, school directors	29.0
Physicians	15.3
Scientists	10.8
Culture institutions	16.5
Factory workers	13.2
Population overall	14.2

Source: PNA, Oddělení 1, (uncatalogued), *Vývoj členský základny KSČ a složení nomenklaturních kádrů mezi XV. a XVI. sjezdem* [Evolution of the CPCS membership and composition of the cadre of the nomenclature between the 15th and the 16th Congresses], 1981, 18.

they had a lower rate of membership compared to other countries in the Eastern bloc, especially the Soviet Union[36] or Hungary.[37]

The recruitment dynamics also did not occur at the same pace everywhere, and depended very much on the sector of activity, as shown by table 2.8, based on statistics from the district of Mělník. Taking into account the sector of activity, two main factors appear to have influenced recruitment practices. First, recruitment depended on the extent to which a sector of activity was viewed as strategic, as that was a very

Table 2.6. Size and Proportion of Post-1968 Membership in Some Primary Party Organizations in the Mělník District in 1979

Primary party organizations	Size of the primary organization in 1979	Members since 1968 (in percentages)
District administration	114	18
Machine tool factory (TOS)	58	21
ČSAD (bus public transportation)	77	38
Public police	74	45
Electricity plant	211	53
Spolana chemical plant	683	54
State security	19	63

Source: Státní okresní (local archive, hereafter SOkA) Mělník OV KSČ, 326–306: Hlášení o složení členstva ZO KSČ k 31.12.1971 [Statement about the composition of the membership on 31.12.1971], and SOkA Mělník OV KSČ, 327–310: Hlášení o složení členstva ZO KSČ k 1.1.1979 [Statement about the composition of the membership on the 1.1.1979].

important activity in the state apparatus. Recruitment was also important in some plants, such as the Spolana chemical plant, because the latter's role was of strategic importance to the economy. The second factor is how big the work unit was. Recruitment appeared to be easier in bigger units, wherit was supported by important party and economic apparatuses. The large plants were explicitly mentioned as targets in the directive on recruitment that was issued by the CC in 1971.[38]

Underrepresentation and Discrimination towards Women

The recruitment policy of the CPCS also favored men over women. On the whole, women's share in the party ranks remained stable at around 28 percent. However, there was a sharp contrast between the situations in Slovakia and in the Czech lands; women were less numerous in the party ranks in Slovakia, and Slovakian women were less organized than their Czech counterparts (table 2.9). The contrast between Czech and Slovakian territories had existed since 1945 and was hardly modified in the 1970s and 1980s. Although the absolute number of women in the party did increase, the rate of CPCS membership among women increased less than the rate of membership among men. This again differed from the situation in other Communist parties, where the proportion of women in the party and/or the rate of membership among the female population actually grew during the same period. In the SED for instance, the proportion of women in the party rose from 28 percent to 36 percent between 1970 and 1989, and the rate of membership of East German women rose from 8 percent to 12 percent during the same period of time.[39]

There are several explanations for this. Since admission into the party occurred in the workplace, women were less likely to join the party because they stayed home more often than men; but even at work,

Table 2.7. Organization Rates among Women and among Men in Slovakia, in the Czech lands, and in Czechoslovakia Overall in 1981 (in Percentages)

	Men	Women	Men and women together
Slovakia	18.5	4.1	11.0
Czech lands	22.6	9.0	15.0
Czechoslovakia	21.3	7.5	14.0

Source: PNA, Oddělení 1 (uncatalogued), Rozbor výsledků soupisu členů a kandidátů KSČ k 1.1.1980 za ženy [Analysis of the results of the registration of CPCS candidates and members—women], 1980, 1–2.

they were less likely to be recruited than men. A sociological study conducted after 1989 showed that, in net effect, men were three times more likely than women to join the Communist Party before 1989, one of the highest rates among Communist parties in Eastern Europe.[40] This was in part due to the recruitment directives themselves, which did not consider recruiting women as a priority, placing the emphasis on recruiting women only in sectors where they were already numerous and that had "an important role in social life and the education of young people."[41] As a result, in the first years of the 1970s, the proportion of women among new candidates was even lower than their proportion in the party (23 percent). Their proportion among new candidates grew only gradually and reached 33 percent by the end of the 1980s. Thus the recruitment policy of the 1970s and 1980s hardly challenged female underrepresentation and discrimination in the CPCS.

Why Join the Party?

Many historians have already given an interpretation of the reasons people joined the party. However, most of them did so in moral terms, without being fully aware of the sociological specificities of CPCS recruitment compared to that of other Communist parties in the Eastern bloc. For instance, Karel Kaplan wrote that during the six years he spent working in a boiler room after he lost his functions in the CC apparatus, five of his colleagues joined the party. Among them, he wrote in his memoirs, three had been told they would get an apartment if they joined the party; one wanted above all to leave the factory and his condition as a worker. He then became a functionary in the youth organization before being recruited by the political police.[42] Based on such testimonies, the assumption that the majority of people who joined the CPCS after 1970 were hypocrites or careerists is still well established today. Similar to the rest of the population, new party members were supposed to have concluded that they were part of an "abnormal social contract" in which everyday security and consumption came as a reward for political conformity.[43]

Yet, Kieran Williams has shown that the CPCS regime recovered its stability even before any new economic policy in favor of consumption and housing was implemented.[44] Rather, even as early as 1970, the CPCS leaders around Husák were able to find a political strategy to discredit their opponents, use the people's weariness, and appear to many people as leaders coping with everyday life issues. From August 1968 onwards, Husák encouraged a depoliticization of party life, talking about the necessity of putting a stop to endless debates, to stop sending resolutions from the base to the CC, and restoring order to address specific issues. His discourse was somewhat effective, as it contributed to giving the members who stayed in the party a new sense of their role; they would be the responsible ones who chose to stay and cope with down-to-earth issues, and set aside ideological debates.[45] Likewise, the fact that such masses of members were recruited to the CPCS during the "normalization years" cannot be explained only by material rewards, but also by an element of acceptance that the CPCS managed to create among the people. Not only did their acceptance result from a political strategy, it was also favored by the social trends that the Czech and Slovak societies underwent during the "normalization years."

Joining the Party as a Social Rite

A first favorable condition to mass recruitment was that from the 1970s onwards, the first generation that was entirely socialized under a Communist regime became adults. Recruiting young people very much depended on demographic trends. By the beginning of the 1960s, there had already been an important recruitment drive in the party, at a time when the first generation that had been educated in the new socialist society started to work. The party leaders were fully aware of the demographic shift that occurred at the beginning of the 1970s. For instance, a summary report about the purges of the CPCS in 1970 projected that as many as "181,000 people between the ages of fifty-five and sixty" and "99,000 between the ages of fifty and fifty-four" would retire every year. At the same time, "259,000 young people between sixteen and twenty-five" should replace them. The report stated, "In that age group there is a large reservoir of new forces for the party," because only 49,416 members of the CPCS were under twenty-five, whereas they were more than two million in the national population at the time.[46]

Having been entirely socialized in the socialist system and not having experienced other social systems, young people were probably more likely to join the Communist Party, not as a political act but rather as a normal step, whatever they thought of party policies. The effect of recruiting young people under twenty-five implies that joining the party became a normal step in their personal life, like studying, starting work, becoming an army conscript, or getting married. This contributed to the depoliticization of one's personal decision to join the party, which became part of the socialization processes, and a social rite. This factor, although relevant, was nevertheless not specific to the CPCS.

Other countries experienced it with similar consequences on recruitment in the Communist Party.[47]

Joining the Party for Career Purposes

Joining the Communist Party often had positive consequences on one's career. Being a member was an asset in gaining a better position, and many positions implied party membership. One should keep in mind that a genuine shift took place within the party elite and Czechoslovakian State apparatuses after the purges of 1970. In 1975, as many as 60.3 percent of the 56,000 cadres who belonged to the central nomenclature had been appointed since 1971.[48] This trend also appeared at the shop-floor level in factories and plants with a high rate of membership in the CPCS among foremen and sector directors (around 50 percent; see table 10 below).

The effect, however, was not systematic. Although being a member of the CPCS could have an impact on one's career, it depended much on local conditions. For instance, in the medium-sized machine tool plant TOS, where party organization remained stable throughout the 1960s and 1970s, promotion to directing positions after 1970 were not made in favor of new CPCS members, but rather in favor of older members with long experience at the TOS factory. In contrast, in Spolana, a large chemical plant that underwent a process of modernization in the 1970s, party organization followed an uneven path from the 1960s to the 1970s. In Spolana, due to thorough purges and the expansion of the plant, promotion to directing positions was easier after 1970, including for new CPCS members who had just begun to work in the plant.

However, membership of the CPCS could make sense for motivations other than career reasons. As shown below, the CPCS did not attract a large proportion of intellectuals, who were already part of the elite of the country. A first explanation was that intellectuals were not keen to join the CPCS, especially after the purge of the party that followed the Prague Spring and struck them very hard. However, a second interpretation, which is not incompatible with the first, is that the recruitment policy did not target them as a priority, but rather tried to broaden the legitimacy of the party among lower classes, and especially among workers and peasants. One goal of such a policy might have been to rely on and support some forms of social resentment against intellectuals by targeting people with less or little cultural capital, who viewed themselves as "normal citizens," as opposed to intellectuals, whom they considered to be arrogant.

This sort of strategy had, for instance, already appeared during the party purge in 1970, when ad hoc commissions in charge of implementing the purge had shown much more understanding towards workers than intellectuals. In a report written about the task of the latter commissions, the emphasis was placed on the fact that "control organs often did not confirm the striking off of workers, rather they acted to overcome the causes of their passivity. But when it came to the striking off of rightist elements, they demanded a more radical treatment: expulsion."[49] This formulation implicitly lumps intellectuals and "rightists" together and distinguished them from the normal working people; it was not only a way of dividing of political opposition, but also expressed a genuine antipathy towards intellectuals. This was not new. The phenomenon took its roots in the "workerist" culture that had long prevailed in the CPCS and continued, to some extent, to exist in the 1970s.[50] It might have been one of the sources that enabled the CPCS to successfully implement its recruitment policy until the end of the regime.

The Decisive Role of the Family

Family was another factor that was very specific to the Czechoslovakian case. The CPCS had been a mass party since the very beginning of its history before 1938, and especially after 1945. After it came into power in 1948, it had the highest rate of party membership in the whole Eastern bloc, with more than 27 percent of the population in the party in the Czech lands, and 10 percent in Slovakia in 1950, and still 18 percent and 10 percent respectively at the end of the 1960s.[51] As a result, in the long run, more and more young people happened to have one or both parents who were in the CPCS.

Some sociological studies[52] showed that the proportion of party members was twice as high among people whose father had been a member of the CPCS at any time than among the rest of the population (table 2.10). This phenomenon can be observed in the Czech lands as well as in Slovakia, though the effect was stronger in the Czech lands because the rate of party membership had been very high from the end of the 1940s onwards. In addition, the proportion of party members at the end of the 1980s was similar among people whose father had ever been a party member at the end of the 1980s and among people whose father *or* mother were members at the time of their joining the party (table 2.11). This means that people had often joined the CPCS even though their fathers had either been expelled from the party, struck off, or had left of their own accord.

Table 2.8. People Whose Father Had Ever Been in the CPCS by the End of the 1980s (in Percentages)

	Cz. lands	Slovakia
Among the population overall	23	18
Among party members	45	35

Source: Eric Hanley, "A party of workers or a party of intellectuals? Recruitment into Eastern European communist parties 1945-1988." *Social Forces* 81/4 (2003) 1073-1105.

Table 2.9. People with a Mother or Father Still in the CPCS at the End of the 1980s (in Percentages)

Among the population overall	23
Among members who joined in the 70s	38
Among members who joined in the 80s	41

Source: Gary Marks, "Communist Party Membership in Five Former Soviet Bloc Countries." *Communist and Post-Communist Studies* 37 (2004): 249 and 252.

Another way to test the role played by family in joining the party consists of using biographical material produced by the party apparatus itself, such as the short biographies contained in the document the CPCS district secretariats had to validate in order to admit people as candidates or full members. A survey based on 131 candidate applications in Kutná Hora in spring 1975 shows that 53 percent of the applicants either had a father or a mother in the party, which is consistent with the results mentioned above, as Central Bohemia was a region with the highest rate of CPCS membership in Czechoslovakia.

Also available are the individual evaluation forms that were produced on the occasion of the party card exchanges. Such material moves the focus from the people who were about to join the party to those already in the party. This shows party membership to be an intergenerational phenomenon, as the document mentioned the membership of the member's parents as well as of his/her children. A survey based on the eighty-seven individual evaluations made within the CPCS primary organization at the TOS machine tool factory in 1979 shows, for instance, that forty-five of the eighty-seven CPCS members in the TOS factory had sixty-four children older than eighteen. Among them, eighteen (28 percent) were Communist Party members, a much higher percentage than the 17.5 percent average rate of party membership in Central Bohemia. However, the most interesting point is that all of these eighteen "communist children" had not only one parent in the CPCS, but also one or two grandparents (five cases), their mother *and* father (six cases), or both (five cases). This finding underlines two factors, namely family education and family tradition, which could only emerge as relevant factors in the long-term history of a socialist society.

Both are helpful in understanding what social processes favored the expansion of the CPCS in the 1970s.

In examining intergenerational social mobility among candidates of whom at least one parent was already a party member, it appears that party membership did not systematically result in social reproduction, or even personal or intergenerational social mobility. In fact, a variety of situations existed. For instance, the applications validated by the Kutná Hora district secretary in spring 1975 reveal the existence of three profiles of intergenerational mobility among candidates who had father or a mother in the party.[53] The first included young people from intellectual or state-employed families (among which were the mayor, police officers, and party functionaries), who joined the party while still in high school and who were already active in the socialist youth. In such cases, the applicants' parents had often experienced strong social advancement, and their children indeed took advantage of a social reproduction process of which party membership was a by-product. The second profile included people who experienced social advancement in comparison to their parents. They either took advantage of vocational training or were promoted during their career (for instance from worker to foreman, from glass worker to policeman). Party membership was obviously a condition in accessing some functions. It was not, however, uncommon for people to join the party long after they had assumed their new functions. In such cases, it must be noted that the applicants' parents were often already party members, which could mean that people with Communist parents might have been considered as reliable enough to be left undisturbed for a while, before they either joined the party of their own accord or were demanded to. A third profile included people from working-class families who were themselves workers and experienced no particular career advancement even though they had joined the party; sometimes, father and son happened to work in the same plant. In such cases, young people did not join the party for career reasons but primarily because, having been raised by Communist parents, joining the party was the normal thing to do, regardless of the social class they belonged to.

The Marginal Role of Mass Organizations

The family, where "primary socialization" took place, is thus a decisive factor in interpreting why people joined the CPCS. The survey on candidate applications in Kutná Hora, on the contrary, shows that membership of mass organizations such as the youth organization, the

Table 2.10. Membership of Mass Organizations among Candidates Recruited in Kutná Hora in 1975 (in Percentages)

Youth organizations	49
Union	73
Brigades of Socialist Work	27
Sports organizations	8
Czechoslovakian-Soviet Friendship	17
Red Cross	7
Civil Defense	10
Svazarm	3
Czechoslovakian Women's League	7

Source: Based on 131 candidate applications made between June 1974 and March 1975 and examined by the CPCS district secretariat of Kutná Hora between February and April 1975; see SOkA Kutná Hora, OV KSČ, 96, Zápis POV KSČ dne 19.2.1975, 19.3.1975 and 16.4.1975.

union, the society for friendship with the Soviet Union, the sports organization, etc., was far from general among party candidates (table 2.12). These organizations, where the so-called "secondary socialization" took place, did not really prepare potential candidates for the CPCS. On the contrary, one gains the impression that instead the CPCS prepared functionaries for the mass organizations, because many new candidates were sent to mass organizations in order to take on responsibilities, ensuring the "leading role of the party" there (table 2.13).[54]

A similar survey concerning applicants admitted as candidates to the SED in 1979 in the district of Nauen, near Berlin, revealed completely opposite results (table 2.14): a low proportion of candidates with either

Table 2.11. Participation of CPCS candidates in Kutná Hora in 1975 (n=131) as Functionaries in Mass Organizations and in the CPCS (in Percentages)

Mass organizations	Already in function	Intended to take a function as "party mission"
Youth organizations	11	24
Union	5	11
Popular militia	0	5
Other mass organizations	0	8
CPCS	0	11

Source: Candidate applications made between June 1974 and March 1975 and examined by the CPCS district secretariat of Kutná Hora between February and April 1975; see SOkA Kutná Hora, OV KSČ, 96, Zápis POV KSČ dne 19.2.1975, 19.3.1975 and 16.4.1975.

Table 2.12. Comparable Membership of Mass Organizations among Candidates Recruited in Kutná Hora in 1975 (n=131) to the CPCS and in Nauen in 1979 to the SED (n=134) (in Percentages)[55]

Mass organizations	CPCS candidates in Kutná Hora in 1975	SED candidates in Nauen in 1979
Youth organizations	49	77
Youth organizations (function)	11	22
Union	73	95
Sports organizations	8	28
Czechoslovak/German-Soviet Friendship	17	95
Svazarm/Gesellschaft für Sport und Technik (GST)	3	28
Czechoslovak/German Women's League	7	6
Either parent in the Communist Party	53	16

Sources: For the CPCS, candidate applications made between June 1974 and March 1975 and examined by the CPCS district secretariat of Kutná Hora between February and April 1975; see SOkA Kutná Hora, OV KSČ, 96, Zápis POV KSČ dne 19.2.1975, 19.3.1975 and 16.4.1975. For the SED, Brandenburgisches Landshauptarchiv, Rep 531 Nauen 1310–1315: Protokolle Sekretariat der Kreisleitung der SED Nauen, 2.2.1979–25.7.1979 [Minutes of the SED Committee of the Nauen district].

a parent in the party, on the one hand, and a very high proportion of candidates who were members of several mass organizations, on the other. Unlike in Czechoslovakia, "secondary socialization" seems to have been more influential than primary socialization in people joining the SED.

Conclusion

Party recruitment practices should not only be understood in terms of coercion and material interest. It is fair to say that both existed, as evidenced by many oral studies based on interviews with former party members,[56] but recruitment practices included a variety of arrangements rather than any "social contract." The variety of arrangements implied that being a member was viewed as something that was reasonably possible to deal with, especially if one's parents were already in the party, or for young people looking for some sort of social status. Personal motivation could be a variety of reasons, and does not have to be coherent; people joined the party for material reasons and at the same time for political reasons or because of family tradition. To account for such incoherent choices, Albert Hirschman has resorted to the notion of "secondary will," which comes together with primary will, although is not necessarily coherent with it, and is in a subordinate position. The notion is helpful in understanding how the CPCS could recruit at a high pace right up until the end, why it collapsed so suddenly, and perhaps also why it continued to remain in existence under the same name, even after 1989.

In addition, the Communist Party did not merely express the rule of the new bureaucratic class, or of the intelligentsia, while maintaining a "workerist" facade for propaganda purposes. The thesis of the so-called "status inconstancy"[57] has proved to be an exaggeration; it argued that the suppression of private property and the concentration of power in the Communist Party had produced a society in which inequalities were not crystalized, and economic, cultural, and political capital were not concentrated in the same social group. On the contrary, the theory of the "new class," first formulated by Milovan Djilas[58] and refined by Iván Szelényi,[59] argued that economic, cultural, and political capital was increasingly concentrated on party members. It seems reasonable to adopt a balanced position. On the one hand, it is true that party membership structured social inequalities, as shown by the high rate of CPCS membership in the State and economic apparatus. On the other hand, however, many people joined the party despite their lower social status—or they did not—despite their own strong cultural capital. It means that party membership was only one factor in structuring social inequalities. It also means that people who joined the party might have found some benefits in being members, not only in material terms, but also more in more general terms of social status, regardless of the career opportunities linked to party membership. From that standpoint, the recruitment policy of the 1970s and 1980s continued the trends of the previous decades. The CPCS never gave up the project of being a "people's party."

Michel Christian is a postdoctoral research fellow at the University of Geneva. His publications include *Camarades ou apparatchiks ? Les communistes en RDA et en Tchécoslovaquie?* (Paris, 2016); "How Transnational Were Eastern Bloc Communist Parties? The Case of Party Institutions of Higher Education," *Vingtième siècle. Revue d'histoire* 129 (2011): 1, 31–43; and (coeditor) *Planning in the Cold War: Competition, Cooperation, Circulations* (forthcoming 2018).

Notes

1. *Směrnice ÚV KSČ k soustavnému zkvalitňování členské základny strany* [Central Committee directives for the systematic improvement of the party base], 16.9.1971, in *Usnesení orgánů ÚV KSČ—Rukověť' pro členy kontrolních a revizních komisí* [Decisions of the CC of the CPCS. Handbook for members of the supervision and control commissions], 60–78.
2. Jiří Maňák, *Čistky v Komunistické straně Československa v letech 1969–1970* (Prague, 1997), 117.
3. Prague National Archives (hereafter PNA), 1261/0/5, 144–223-2, 45–52: *Návrh zásad dalšího růstu a formování strany* [Proposal of principles for the growth and the constitution of the party], 20.11.1970, 48.
4. Stanovy strany [Statutes of the party], 1962, chapters 67 to 69.
5. Lenka Kalinová, "Mythos und Realität des 'Arbeiterstaates' in der Tschechoslowakei" [Myths and reality of the "worker state" in Czechoslovakia], in *Arbeiter im Staatssozialismus: ideologischer Anspruch und soziale Wirklichkeit* [Workers in state socialism: Ideological ambitions and social reality], ed. Peter Hübner, Christoph Klessmann, and Klaus Tenfelde (Cologne, 2005), 87–108.
6. See, for example, Zdeněk Hejzlar, *Reformkommunismus. Zur Geschichte der Kommunistischen Partei der Tschechoslowakei* [Reform Communism. On the history of the Communist Party of Czechoslovakia] (Cologne, 1976), 375–383.
7. Due to the scarcity of works on the social history of socialist Czechoslovakia, most recent studies about the CPCS focus on discrete, well-rounded spheres that the researcher can grasp to study the influence of the CPCS in everyday life. See, for instance, Katka Volná et al., eds., *Prověřená fakulta. KSČ na Filozofická fakultě UK v letech 1969–1989* [Screened department. CPCS in the philosophy department of Charles University 1969–1989] (Prague, 2009).
8. For a presentation of that project, see https://www.library.ucla.edu/social-science-data-archive/sseehome, accessed 3 September 2017.
9. Miroslav Vaněk, ed., *Obyčejní lidé . . . ?! Pohled do života tzv. mlčící většiny. Životopisná vyprávění příslušníků dělnických profesí a inteligence* [Ordinary people?! A picture of the life of the so-called silent majority. An autobiographical account by workers and members of intellectual professions] (Prague, 2009).
10. Gordon Wightman, "Membership of the Communist Party of Czechoslovakia in the 1970s: Continuing Divergence from the Soviet Model," *Soviet Studies* 35, no. 2 (1983); 208–222.
11. Material from the higher organs used in this article are kept in the National Archives in Prague and were produced by the Central Committee's First Department in charge of party organization. It consisted mainly of booklets produced on the occasion of party congresses in 1971, 1976, 1981, and 1986, as well as in some uncatalogued statistical reports about the years 1986 to 1989.
12. The material from lower party organs used in this article was found in the two local archives (*Státní okresní*, hereafter SOkA) of Mělník and Kutná

Hora, two towns located in the former region (*kraj*) of Central Bohemia (*středočeský kraj*). Of particular interest for this article were statistical reports on local membership, evaluation forms, and candidate's application forms.
13. PNA 1261/0/5, 144–223–2, p.45–52: *Návrh zásad dalšího růstu a formování strany* [Proposal of principles for the growth and the constitution of the party], 20.11.1970, 52.
14. This observation was based on 131 candidate applications made between June 1974 and March 1975 and examined by the CPCS district secretariat of Kutná Hora between February and April 1975; see SOkA Kutná Hora, OV KSČ, 96, Zápis POV KSČ dne 19.2.1975, 19.3.1975 and 16.4.1975.
15. See for instance SOkA Kutná Hora, OV KSČ, 96, Zápis POV KSČ dne 19.2.1975, 100.
16. SOkA Kutná Hora, OV KSČ, 96, Zápis POV KSČ dne 5.3.1975, 102.
17. SOkA Kutná Hora, OV KSČ, 96, Zápis POV KSČ dne 16.4.1975.
18. Being "struck off" (*zrušení*) the party was a milder sanction than "expulsion" (*vyloučení*), which was reserved for overt "party enemies."
19. PNA, Předsednictvo UV KSČ 1976–79, 8/7/1: Návrh směrnice UV KSČ o diferencovanem přistupu při opětném přijeti do strany těch, kterym bylo v letech 1968–70 členstvi ve straně zrušeno, připadně byli ze strany vyloučeni [Proposal of a Central Committee directive about the balanced approach to readmit into the party those who had been struck off or expelled in the years 1968 to 1971], 11.6.1976.
20. PNA, Předsednictvo UV KSČ 1976–79, 6/5/1e: O praxi KSSS při posuzování otázek souvisejících s obnovou členství bývalých komunistů ve straně [On the practice of the PCUS in dealing with questions linked with readmission of former members in the party], 28.5.76, 14–22.
21. PNA, Předsednictvo UV KSČ 1976–79, 8/7/1, 11.6.1976, 7.
22. Stiftung Archiv der Partei und Massenorganisationen—Bundesarchiv (hereafter SAPMO BArch) DY 30 IV B2/20/150: Information über die erneute Aufnahme von ehemaligen Parteimitgliedern in die KSČ [Information report about the readmission of former party members in the CPCS], 18.5.1976, 4.
23. Maňák, Čistky, 45.
24. PNA, Oddělení 1 (uncatalogued), Přehled o počtu a sociálním složení přijatých kandidátů—bývalých členů KSČ od XV. sjezdu do 1.10.1989 [Summary table on the number and social composition of admitted candidates—former members of the CPCS between the 15th Congress and 1.10.1989].
25. These figures can be considered as reliable because the party apparatus was at that time efficient enough to register every individual joining or leaving the party. The probability that CPCS functionaries falsified the number of party candidates to match some unofficial goals is very low. In fact, party statistics registered positive as well as negative trends, as showed by many articles in the party press criticizing "negative trends" in some regions. For instance, see Wightman, "Membership of the Communist Party of Czechoslovakia in the 1970s," 210–211.
26. PNA, Oddělení 1 (uncatalogued), Vývoj členské základny [Development of the party basis?], 1976, 24; and PNA, Oddělení 1 (uncatalogued), Vývoj členský základny KSČ a složení nomenklaturních kádrů mezi XVI. a XVII.

Sjezdem [Development of the party basis and composition of the nomenclature cadres], 1986, 26.
27. UV KSČ, Vývoj členský základny KSČ a složení nomenklaturních kádrů mezi XVI. a XVII. Sjezdem (Development of the party basis and composition of the nomenclature cadres between the 16th and 17th Congresses), 1986, 52.
28. Ibid.
29. PNA 1261/2/1, 272–1596, p. 1–37: Složení strany 28.2.1953 [Composition of the party 28.2.1953], 5.
30. NA, Oddělení 1 (uncatalogued), Údaje o vývoji členské základny KSČ od 1.1.1971 do 1.1.1989 (Data on the development of the CPCS basis from 1.1.1971 to 1.1.1989), 8.
31. Č, Vývoj členský základny KSČ a složení nomenklaturních kádrů mezi XVI. a XVII. Sjezdem (Development of the Party basis and composition of the nomenclature cadres between the XVIth and the XVIIth congress), 1986, 52.
32. SAPMO BArch, DY 30 J IV 2 3A/1828, p. 28–46: Gutachten zur Einstufung der Mitglieder und Kandidaten der Partei in die Kategorien der sozialen Gliederungen [Study on the sorting of the party members and candidates in social categories], 20.11.1969.
33. SOkA Kutná Hora, OV KSČ Kutná Hora, 96, Zápis POV KSČ dne 19.2.75, 103.
34. Figures from Marks, "Communist Party Membership," 252.
35. This odds ratio was of 5 for Hungary, 4.2 for Bulgaria, and 3.7 for Russia. Ibid.
36. See Wightman, "Membership of the Communist Party of Czechoslovakia in the 1970s," 217.
37. Raymond Sin-Kwok, "The Social Composition of the Czechoslovak and Hungarian Communist Parties in the 1980s," *Social Forces* 75, no. 1 (1996): 61–89.
38. *Směrnice ÚV KSČ*, 68.
39. See SAPMO BArch DY 30 J/IV 2/3/1725, 7–25, *Analyse über die Mitgliederbewegung der SED seit dem VII. Parteitag und im Jahre 1970* [Analysis of the membership figures of the SED since the 7th congress and during 1970], 10.3.1971 and SAPMO BArch DY 30/J IV 2/3/4347, 5–29: Anlage Nr.1 zum Protokoll Nr4 vom 10.1.1989 [Attachment no.1 of the 4th record on 10.1.1989], 19.
40. Marks, *Communist Party Membership*, 255.
41. *Směrnice ÚV KSČ*, 67.
42. Karel Kaplan, *Dans les archives du Comité Central: trente ans de secrets du bloc soviétique*. (Paris, 1978), 325.
43. See, for example, Zdeněk Hejzlar, *Reformkommunismus*, 375–383.
44. Kieran Williams, *The Prague Spring and Its Aftermath: Czechoslovak Politics, 1968–1970* (Cambridge, 1997), 42–43.
45. Ibid., 40.
46. PNA 1261/0/5, 144–223–2, p. 45–52: *Návrh zásad dalšího růstu a formování strany* [Proposal of principles for the growth and the constitution of the party], 20.11.1970, 29.

47. The same can be observed for the East German SED; see Michel Christian, "Les politiques de recrutement des partis communistes en RDA et en Tchécoslovaquie" [Recruitment policies of the Communist parties in the GDR and in Czechoslovakia], *Transitions* 47, no. 2 (2007): 41.
48. DY 30 J IV 2/2J/7223: Information an das Politbüro zur Frage der Kaderpolitik der KSČ, 1976 [Information to the politburo on the question of cadre policy of the CPCS], no date (1975).
49. PNA 1261/0/5, 144–223–2, 139–148: *Poznatky a doporučení ústřední kontrolní a revizní komise KSČ vyplývající z průběhu výměny stranických legitimacyí* [Lessons and recommendations of the central audit and revision commission resulting from the implementation of the party cards exchange], 20.11.1970, 139.
50. Mark Wright, "Ideology and Power in the Czechoslovak Political System," in *Eastern Europe: Political Crisis and Legitimation*, ed. Paul G. Lewis, 111–136. (London, 1984), 131.
51. Maňák, *Proměny strany moci*, 22.
52. The studies of Eric Hanley and Gary Marks mentioned above were based on data collected at the beginning of the 1990s, and they provide an accurate picture of the situation at the end of the 1980s.
53. Based on 131 candidate applications made between June 1974 and March 1975 and examined by the CPCS district secretariat of Kutná Hora between February and April 1975; see SOkA Kutná Hora, OV KSČ, 96, Zápis POV KSČ dne 19.2.1975, 19.3.1975 and 16.4.1975.
54. Ibid.
55. The district (*Kreis*) of Nauen, in the economically mixed periphery of Berlin, had a profile very similar to the profile of the district (*okres*) of Kutná Hora.
56. Miroslav Vaněk, "Jsem dělník a kdo je víc? Sonda do života příslušníků dělnických profesí v socialistickém Československu," in Vaněk, *Obyčejní lidé . . . ?!*, 509–512.
57. Pavel Machonin, "Social Stratification in Contemporary Czechoslovakia," in *American Journal of Sociology* 75 (1970): 725–741.
58. Milovan Djilas, *The New Class: An Analysis of the Communist System* (New York, 1957).
59. György Konrád and Iván Szelényi, *The Intellectuals on the Road to Class Power* (New York, 1979).

Bibliography

Christian, Michel. "Les politiques de recrutement des partis communistes en RDA et en Tchécoslovaquie" [Recruitment policies of the Communist parties in the GDR and in Czechoslovakia]. *Transitions* 47 (2007): 2, 33–46.
Djilas, Milovan. *The New Class: An Analysis of the Communist System.* New York: Praeger, 1957.
Hanley, Eric. "A Party of Workers or a Party of Intellectuals? Recruitment into Eastern European Communist Parties (1945–1988)." *Social Forces* 81 (2003): 4, 1073–1105.

Hejzlar, Zdeněk. *Reformkommunismus. Zur Geschichte der Kommunistischen Partei der Tschechoslowakei* [Reform Communism. On the history of the Communist Party of Czechoslovakia]. Cologne: Europäische Verlagsanstalt, 1976.

Kalinová, Lenka. "Mythos und Realität des 'Arbeiterstaates' in der Tschechoslowakei" [Myths and reality of the "worker state" in Czechoslovakia]. In *Arbeiter im Staatssozialismus: ideologischer Anspruch und soziale Wirklichkeit* [Workers in state socialism: Ideological ambitions and social reality], ed. Peter Hübner, Christoph Klessmann, and Klaus Tenfelde, 87–108. Cologne: Böhlau, 2005.

Kaplan, Karel. *Dans les archives du Comité Central: trente ans de secrets du bloc soviétique* [In the archives of the Central Committee. Thirty years of secrets of the Soviet bloc]. Paris: Albin Michel, 1978.

Konrád, György, and Iván Szelényi. *The Intellectuals on the Road to Class Power.* New York: Harcourt Brace Jovanovich, 1979.

Machonin, Pavel. "Social Stratification in Contemporary Czechoslovakia." *American Journal of Sociology* 75 (1970): 725–741.

Maňák, Jiří. *Čistky v Komunistické straně Československa v letech 1969–1970* [The purges in the Communist party of Czechoslovakia in the years 1969–1970]. Prague: Ústav pro soudobé dějiny AV ČR, 1997.

Marks, Gary N. "Communist Party Membership in Five Former Soviet Bloc Countries, 1945–1989." *Communist and Post-Communist Studies* 37 (2004): 241–263.

Sin-Kwok Wong, Raymond. "The Social Composition of the Czechoslovak and Hungarian Communist Parties in the 1980s." *Social Forces* 75, no. 1 (1996): 61–90.

Vaněk, Miroslav, ed. *Obyčejní lidé . . . ?! Pohled do života tzv. mlčící většiny. Životopisná vyprávění příslušníků dělnických profesí a inteligence* [Ordinary people?! A picture of the life of the so-called silent majority. An autobiographical account by workers and members of intellectual professions]. Prague: Academia, 2009.

Volná, Katka, Jakub Jareš, Matěj Spurny, and Klára Pinerová, eds. *Prověřená fakulta. KSČ na Filozofická fakultě UK v letech 1969–1989* [Screened department. CPCS in the philosophy department of the Charles University 1969–1989]. Prague: Ústav pro soudobé dějiny AV ČR, 2009.

Wightman, Gordon. "Membership of the Communist Party of Czechoslovakia in the 1970s: Continuing Divergence from the Soviet Model." *Soviet Studies* 35, no. 2 (1983): 208–222.

Williams, Kieran. *The Prague Spring and Its Aftermath: Czechoslovak Politics, 1968–1970.* Cambridge: Cambridge University Press, 1997.

Wright, Mark. "Ideology and Power in the Czechoslovak Political System." In *Eastern Europe: Political Crisis and Legitimation*, ed. Paul G. Lewis, 111–136. London: Croom Helm, 1984.

 3

Behind Closed Doors
The Erosion of SED Party Life in the 1980s

Sabine Pannen

The images and events of fall 1989 were extremely powerful and are firmly anchored in the collective German memory. Political opponents as well as the silent majority of ordinary citizens of the GDR (German Democratic Republic) held the mass demonstrations that led to the end of the dictatorial system. In addition to the visible and full-throated protests, an inconspicuous loss of loyalty had taken place, which was why the revolution was peaceful and why party rule came to an end. Party members were no longer willing to perform their role as representatives of the state party. By 1989, the majority was unwilling to continue to support the maintenance of power of the SED (Socialist Unity Party). Some joined the demonstrations. Many more withdrew their party membership. While the protest marches grew in size, SED members returned their membership documents en masse, which eventually led to the collapse of the state party. This was not, however, an inevitable event, nor did anyone expect a silent decline of the powerful Unity Party. Even in the summer of 1989 a decline was unimaginable. According to the security police at that time, the opposition consisted of 150 groups and 2,400 activists.[1] In contrast, the state party had 2.3 million members who were organized into approximately 60,000 primary party organizations (PPOs). The reasons party members were no longer willing to advocate the political system, and why they eventually left the party in droves, are phenomena which deserve an explanation.

This loss of loyalty begs the question of what motivated rank-and-file party members to participate up until 1989, and what factors created cohesion and stability? The most obvious difference between comrades and nonmembers was the "party life." The mandatory meetings and the party "schooling" lessons created a particular joint experience. The state party also had a specific membership body. In order to preserve power, the state party was a cadre party that organized functional elites within their ranks. At the same time, the SED was driven by its own perception of being a worker's party and the apparatus made a great effort to recruit workers. As a result, the membership body was a meticulously designed group of people. Like a pyramid, it consisted of three different functional groups. At the top was the small group of decision-making functionaries. Below the top level were a large number of members who belonged to the functional elite, which was divided into different sectors: the power-preserving elite, which embraced full-time (party) functionaries, and the security sector of the military, police, and secret police. There was also an ideological elite covering the (party) press, (party) universities, and the educational sector, as well as the art scene. In addition to the administrative sector that contained the public authorities, there was also the management elite that contained experts such as engineers and economists. At the base of the pyramid, below the heterogeneous functional elite, were the rank-and-file members. Among them were industrial workers as well as students, pensioners, schoolchildren, housewives, and a small number of freelancers. This chapter follows a broader concept of party rank-and-file members. As well as the "ordinary" comrades, this study also considers the lower ranks of the functional elite to be the rank-and-file members because workers and their superiors, pupils and teachers, students and professors, shared their work, life, and the party environment on a day-to-day basis. Two different groups dominated the membership body. In the 1970s and 1980s, approximately 500,000 party members (22 percent) belonged to the power preserving elite, and between 650,000 and 750,000 party members (34 percent) were industrial workers.[2] In this essay, the rank-and-file members will be represented by party members from the steel mill in the town of Brandenburg an der Havel. In contrast to the district capital Potsdam, which had a large administrative sector, Brandenburg was the industrial heart of the area. The steel mill was not only an infrastructural lifeline; it also formed the identity of Brandenburg as a "steel city."[3] Large industrial companies were "key enterprises" because they represented the image of the GDR as a workers' state,[4] so the level of SED membership there was particularly high. In 1981, close to one-third of 7,489 employees at the steel mill held a membership document. The party organization was dominated by middle-aged and older men, and only 17 percent of members were women. What is also striking are the following statistics: almost three-quarters of party members were engaged in the production sector, whereas about a quarter of party members belonged to the category of "intelligentsia."[5] The social composition of the membership has to be interpreted as an expression of the efforts of the party to court steelworkers and to promote its identity as a workers' party.

On the one hand, steelworkers, ordinary clerks, and middle-management engineers and economists—who were mainly holders of membership documents—shared their environment and experiences with colleagues who were not affiliated with the party. On the other hand, they were involved in the party organization with its particular obligations and therefore had to advocate the official party-leadership interpretations of reality in everyday life. While their colleagues went home to their families, party members gathered every Monday after work in the meeting rooms of the steel mill and elsewhere across the GDR for their closed party sessions. What did they actually deal with behind closed doors, and what relevance did it have for members in particular, and the political system at large?

There are currently three accepted interpretations of party life. First, it is seen as a place of repression, sparked by the purging of party members between the end of the 1940s and the beginning of the 1950s.[6] Second, there is the narrative of mandatory, ritualized, and boring party meetings. Irene Böhme, a writer and former party member who fled to West Germany, recalled an anecdote describing the nature of party life in her 1982 publication on the mentality of the East German people. At one party gathering, an old comrade and experienced warrior of the good old days of 1920s Communist youth organizations, gave this advice to a young comrade: "Just take notes, then you won't fall asleep."[7] Recent studies, such as that by Alexei Yurchak about Komsomol, the Soviet youth organization, focus on the manifold self-interests of members. He found that they would only comply with meaningless party rituals in order to have the opportunity to follow their own particular interests.[8] This "performative shift" didn't lead to a delegitimization of the political system, but rather created an unquestionable implicitness for the people. How, then, should SED party life and the role of rank-and-file members be evaluated? Was membership just a formal relationship and the so-called "party life" just ballast that was dragged along for matters of legitimacy? Following this reasoning, the mass demonstrations of 1989 also unveiled an inoperable structure. Or did grassroots membership and party life have functions that made it lose its power in the run-up to the peaceful revolution? To what extent were the grassroots members at all a relevant historical factor in the events of 1989?

Despite the dominant retrospective narrative of boredom, I will argue that the reconstruction of those Monday meetings reveals two functions that were of crucial importance to cohesiveness beyond their well-known disciplinary power. First, the information produced by the Central Committee for the PPO held additional value. This exclusive background information, available to party members, provided a knowledge advantage that facilitated the mediation of the party positions through everyday life. This transfer of authority from the party's headquarters to its basic PPOs also aimed to enhance community spirit. In addition, the bottom-up communication was also meaningful. Officially declared as "advice, suggestions, and critique," the seemingly nonpolitical issues of everyday life demonstrated the management capacity of the party. This allowed rank-and-file members to use the party's power to improve living conditions in their communities. However, these factors of integration and stabilization lost their power through an accumulation of problems in the 1980s.

Integration before Exclusion: Conditions of Post-Stalinist Party Life

Party trials and penalties were distinctive instruments of Soviet-style communist parties. The expulsion of 750 thousand members between 1948 and 1951, for reasons of power-implementation by the leadership, are notorious.[9] Although disciplinary instruments were always present, they became less dominant after the purges. As Michel Christian has argued, elements of participation were increasingly preferred.[10] A paradigm shift in the context of the revival of the party under Khrushchev took place in 1954.[11] Expulsions as a punishment were replaced by the idea of the so-called "education" of members, and in 1963 "educational instruments" were introduced. In addition to a "warning," the new party penalties of "criticism" and "deprecation" could also be inflicted on members. The hostile expulsion was no longer the tool of first resort.[12] In line with the changing disciplinary practice, a low number of party proceedings were established. In the 1970s and 1980s, the central party control commission statistics showed an average number of about 19,000 proceedings per year. Remarkably, in 1988, this number rose to 22,998.[13] Compared to the growing level of membership, which grew to more than two million in the 1970s, those numbers are in fact very low. Even the number of deaths within the party, at 30,000 per year, was higher than the number of party trials.[14] The internal statistics of the central party control commission also indicate that the "need" for repression declined in favor of integration tools. Therefore, the commission dealt not only with their supposed enemies but also with minor misdemeanors. They predominantly got involved when rank-and-file members disobeyed the law or annoyed their community by not following rules and ignoring obligations. In Brandenburg, (as well as elsewhere), drunk driving or the consumption of alcohol in the workplace was one of the main topics the local control commissions had to deal with as a force of law and order among party members.[15]

In addition to this change in disciplinary practice, which followed the premise of integration before exclusion, the SED leadership expanded integrative instruments of party life. In 1957, the Central Committee started releasing an information bulletin for the PPOs,[16] which contained facts not found in the central party newspaper, *Neues Deutschland*. This information bulletin by the party headquarters provided party members exclusively with prior and additional information on events and changes, as well as the party positions and arguments covering a wide range of current domestic and foreign policy. At the beginning, this information service was only available to the party secretaries of the most important companies. In 1968, this service was expanded, and from then on, every party secretary was provided with the internal bulletin sent by the headquarters in Berlin.[17] This expansion was not just a reaction to the growth of party membership. The development of this channel of information aimed to integrate the rank and file in order to facilitate political agitation. This expansion indicates that the role of rank-and-file members as facilitators of ideology should have been strengthened. Information available only to party members not only led to a distinction between them and people who did not have a party document, but also strengthened the bond between the center and the periphery as the transfer of knowledge equaled a transfer of authority. In addition to ideological legitimacy, societal steering also became more important. Party meetings had always been a forum where problems about the workplace, the neighborhood, and the community could be addressed, but from the 1960s, issues of everyday life were given a more prominent role in party communications. In 1963, internal petitions by party members were introduced and the party apparatus also paid great attention to problems reported by the party secretaries from PPOs.[18] This kind of seemingly nonpolitical critique was appreciated and sent by the party secretary in his monthly report to the local apparatus under the terms of so-called "advice, suggestions, and critique." In an ideal scenario, the district party committee responded quickly and informed the PPO about their plan of action to resolve these problems. This flow of information was of great importance to the party apparatuses at all levels. It was a source of popular opinion as well as an opportunity to compensate shortcomings and to solve problems before they created serious conflicts. The perspective of the leadership was that party members should not only be facilitators of ideology. Membership, therefore, not only had an individual dimension in enhancing career opportunities, for example, which was inseparable from the party document; members also had to perform the role of being a social agent in everyday life. How did the rank-and-file members deal with these offers, and were these instruments important to them?

Social Practice in Party Life

In 1977, the GDR was hit by the coffee crisis, when prices on the world market rose.[19] The costs of importing coffee caused a drop in imports. The Kosta coffee brand that had been sold at a reduced rate was replaced by Kaffee-Mix, which consisted partly of roasted coffee, but with many added replacements. In the early summer of 1977, while the majority of citizens were still unaware of what was about to happen, party members received an information bulletin from the Central Committee about the upcoming changes.[20] The information provided more in-depth background reasons than were later reported by the media, and gave insights into the practical consequences concerning the changes to the product line. Factory canteens and those in the administration sector had to reduce their consumption of coffee, cocoa, and tropical fruit. Beyond giving information about these changes to everyday life, the information explained what had caused them. Price rises on the capitalist world market were mentioned as well as capitalist countries such as West Germany, France, and the United States; the price hikes forced the introduction of savings through a large supply of "coffee mix" brands.

The handling of the Central Committee's information bulletin required that particular rules were followed. They were addressed personally to the party secretaries of PPOs and were sent through the post only. Party apparatuses at all levels received post through the party's courier service. Large companies and institutions, such as Humboldt University in Berlin, had a party apparatus equal to the local SED secretariats, and therefore also received documents through this courier service. Members who did not hold an office hardly ever saw the confidential papers sent by the party headquarters. In fact, they had to request to see them and were allowed only to read them; copying even a single section was prohibited. These clandestine rules were based on the organizational principles of a Leninist Soviet-type party. This exclusive knowledge benefited party secretaries as they were more involved in advocating party positions than ordinary members, and were thus in need of that authority. In addition to this aura of mystery, the information bulletin sent by the party headquarters also had a practical value.

First, it informed party secretaries earlier, and provided more insights than the information given in press reports. This knowledge advantage provided party secretaries with authority in the political opinion battle in everyday life. Second, it also offered a relevant pattern of orientation. The official interpretation of reality had to be plausible in order to gain acceptance in party policy. This applied not only to party members as facilitators of ideology, but also for people who had no SED affiliation.

Letters sent by party secretaries to the department of agitation of the Central Committee indicated that the Central Committee information bulletin was important to party members and provided orientation. They asked for additional copies or requested it to be sent again later, as they sometimes received an empty or very light envelope. In 1979, the party secretary of an engineering school, for example, wrote to the party's headquarters, "Still send me the designated information as it is always a great help, as well as a source of good information."[21] A year later, the secretary of the party organization of the city council of Borna in Saxony wrote to the Central Committee as he had received only one instead of eleven copies: "Our party organization has appreciated the information from our leadership for a long time, and is taking advantage of it. . . . The heads of our party organization use it in our party meetings. . . . We hope to receive this information, arguments, and explanations of resolutions as previously. There are plenty of other opportunities to save paper."[22]

These mistakes in distribution indicate that the information bulletin produced by the Central Committee was of real additional benefit for party secretaries of PPOs as they were particularly involved in facilitating the party position and in need of additional information and arguments. But what significance did it have for rank-and-file members without a voluntary function? They hardly ever saw this paper sent by the headquarters in Berlin. The opinion that the bulletin had no meaning at all seems to be exaggerated as well as the idea that it caused a stir in the party meeting room. One needs instead to differentiate. The bulletin offered a wide range of topics concerning foreign and domestic affairs, which were not of interest to all rank and files. They were only relevant if the topic raised was linked to their specific living or working space. The prior information about the coffee reductions in the face of the coffee crisis provided those party members who had a lower income, and no access to West German coffee brands, the chance to stock up on coffee.

The public sphere of socialist societies was characterized by the information monopoly of the party, which established a hierarchical access system. At the same time a vivid grapevine existed. Dictatorial rule created a strong need for information by the party apparatus as well as by the people.[23] In this context, the information bulletin privileged rank-and-file members. In addition to practical information, the arguments and the party standpoint were not only helpful for party secretaries in performing their role, but also for professions that were strongly associated with facilitating the party position, such as teachers, or employees of the administration sector. Of course, the information bulletin was not the only tool to provide rank-and-file members with knowledge. Among other party information channels there were also the monthly instruction meetings for party secretaries, organized by the district party committee, where local issues were discussed and networking took place.[24] Eventually, they all refer to the role of rank-and-file members as facilitators of ideology. Their profession as well as their position in the party depended on their performance being full of verve.

The coffee crisis not only illustrates the relevance of the top-down communication in general, and the information bulletin in particular; it also shows that the "bottom-up" information channel was important. An opinion report of 19 September 1977 by the Ministry of State Security stated that the political work at the grassroots level would be difficult as there were indications that party members were backing down and giving up.[25] In fact, they had more information available, but the absence of press reports concerning these issues created widespread frustration, and party members, particularly party secretaries and middle management, could do nothing against it. From their perspective, a prompt press release and reports explaining these actions would have prevented these emotional reactions. An earlier *Stasi* report on this issue stated an "open and sincere attitude towards citizens"[26] would have always been met with understanding. They felt that the responsibility of propagating the policy and the response to questions should be passed on to the local party level. At the same time, they were dissatisfied with the reverse communication and doubted that the "view and opinions" of the grassroots level were being taken seriously. Party secretaries informed the party district committee about the emotional reactions and the need for public information, as well as information on actions to improve the coffee supply through their monthly reports. In the absence of a response by the apparatus, the secret police noted that they thought the central organs were apparently oblivious to the problems and issues that average people had to deal with. This led to decisions being made that were almost inexplicable.[27] Four days after the *Stasi* recorded these frustrations among the rank and file, the party organ *Neues Deutschland* published a short article to take the heat out of the situation.[28]

The coffee crisis was just a short episode in the long history of supply shortages, but it demonstrates that the party apparatus's offer of finding solutions was taken for granted by the rank and files. The records of PPOs at the steel mill in Brandenburg also show that a number of different problems in everyday life were reported to the district party committee, and they illustrate that the apparatus took action. In September 1985, for example, the rank-and-file members at the steel mill were provided with feedback on reported supply problems concerning two city districts. Party secretaries were able to announce that the city council, together with the department of economy of the district party committee, was working on a solution.[29]

While workplace affairs and problems concerning the work environment could be resolved in situ, issues regarding the supply of goods and services or local infrastructure were not only reported but also resolved by the district party committee. Not only the party and *Stasi* records indicate that this problem-solving channel was relevant for the rank and files. A former party member and ambulance driver at the steel mill in Brandenburg explains in an interview that he apparently always addressed workplace problems at party gatherings and he achieved a positive outcome: "You also had the feeling that you were somehow able to make a difference. Later this changed, but at least up until the mid-1980s. You really had the feeling, yes, if I go there and say something at the party meeting or at a party school event, something would change. It would improve. Yes, and to some extent, it actually did get better, at first, at least."[30]

This narrative indicates that the articulation of everyday life issues at party meetings gave political participation a practical value because it led to improvements in conditions for neighbors and colleagues. To be able "to make the difference," as the ambulance driver pointed out, could be a motivation to perform the role of a "social agent" and gave political participation a social meaning. How and when this integration function lost its power, as indicated by the ambulance driver at the Brandenburg steel mill, will be discussed in the last section.

Supply Crisis as a Factor of Erosion

During the 1980s, the integration functions of party life were challenged and lost their power. A major factor was the supply crisis that developed at the end of the 1970s and the beginning of the 1980s. Indeed, economic problems and supply shortages were, like the issue of limited travel opportunities, in particular to West Germany and West

Berlin, topics that people in the GDR always discussed.[31] But under the rule of Erich Honecker, these areas of conflict became more vibrant. The claim that the socialist system was more efficient and fairer than the capitalist system remained, but the strategy changed.[32] Honecker's policy of socialist consumerism, which combined extensive social welfare and consumer interests, created manifold follow-up problems. While in foreign affairs a policy of détente towards West Germany took place, the party leadership was facing major domestic problems: the economy started to lurch, the level of debt and the financial dependence on the West grew, and this decreased the scope for political action. In 1974, the party leadership legalized the West German currency—the "deutsche mark"—in order to generate revenue in the face of rising numbers of visitors from the West. At the same time they expanded "Intershops," where Western products were sold to East Germans if they paid in West German currency. This development was not the only one that led to a large presence of the West in everyday life. In the 1970s and 1980s, almost every East German was able to watch West German television, so the West German way of life was considered a template.[33] The perception of supply shortages became more explosive in the face of the well-known West German living standards.

Party and security police records show that rank-and-file members did not deal with particular issues and topics; in fact, they shared the issues on supply of goods and services and absent travel opportunities to the West, yet their membership required them to perform the roles of mediators of ideology and social agents. At the beginning of the 1980s, it became increasingly difficult to meet these requirements. The export of clothing and fabrics increased, while the import of fruit and vegetables decreased. This caused shortages in day-to-day life, and the supply of goods became consistently worse during the 1980s than it had been in the 1970s.[34] The economic slump was taboo to the party leadership, and it was ignored in the media. Both issues created widespread frustrations within society in general, as well as among the rank-and-file members. In April 1980, an anonymous complaint addressed to Erich Honecker, signed by "comrades with good intentions," provides an insight into the low morale. The letter stated,

> As a comrade, I can't look at the outrageous conditions that we have to deal with in our state any longer. I am talking about the supply of indispensable goods. Again today, I saw a long queue of people who wanted to buy soap, standing in front of a shop. There are even difficulties with the supply of mustard. We have shortages like this in every field. People are grumbling, and they are right. How is it possible that thirty-five years after the war, we still have conditions like this? There is no understand-

ing for this among the people. It really is time now for orderly conditions. This was possible previously. We can't get any information about the reasons for this situation from anywhere.[35]

This complaint from alleged party members not only illustrates the impact of the economic decline in everyday life; it also shows that for those who experienced the scarcities of the postwar period, massive supply shortages were unacceptable such a long time after the Second World War. The West German living standard is not mentioned here, but it was nevertheless a relevant comparative figure for most people. Additionally, the demand for information on this downward development grew but was not met. These frustrations had an additional dimension for party members. The security police stated that party members found themselves on the defensive and did not hold convincing arguments.[36] They neither received special information from the party headquarters—such as an information bulletin on this issue—nor did they obtain information on sustainable actions taken by the district party committee on the issues that had been reported. A full-time party secretary from the steel mill in Brandenburg explains, in retrospect, that the supply of information by the party apparatus in the 1980s did not decline in quantity, but in quality. He recalls what consequences this situation held for him in his everyday life: "You can say what you want. If there were no panties for women, then there were none. If you said the delivery is due tomorrow and you could find the necessary items the day after tomorrow, you could say: Listen, stop moaning and grumbling. Tomorrow it will be fine again. And so on. But we only got information that didn't help convince people. You weren't able to say: 'See, I was right!'"[37] Without being able to provide practical solutions, the party secretary experienced a loss of authority. The economic downturn increased in the first half of the 1980s and was not only experienced at the consumer level, but also in the workplace. In 1986, the ministry for state security (*Stasi*) reports claimed that the people perceived the supply crisis as a permanent problem, and the GDR was referred to as a "society of scarcity."[38] This perception of a supply crisis was boosted by the relaxation of travel restrictions to the West. In 1987 and 1988, more than one million East German citizens visited their relatives in West Germany, and this also included party members.[39] Generally, it was only members of the armed forces who were prohibited from traveling to the West, as well as so-called "secret carriers," such as the upper and middle management of companies who faced particular restrictions. A membership document was common within those groups. Due to the *Stasi* reports, the relaxation of travel restrictions created an increasing need to travel to the West, including among party members. It even led to a loss of acceptance of existing travel restrictions.[40] It also had another boomerang effect insofar as the stories of the returnees—who were able to compare living circumstances with their own eyes—increased the perception of a supply crisis. In summer 1987, the mainstream was dominated by doubts concerning the economic situation, and information on the reasons for this development were now vehemently expected.[41] It became increasingly difficult for party members to perform their role as facilitators of ideology. Not only did they share the opinions of their colleagues and neighbors who were not party members, but they were also not given any additional information on the reasons for the economic downward trend.

In this tense atmosphere, another integration tool lost power, and more and more problems were articulated at party meetings. The monthly reports by party secretaries to the local apparatus became longer and longer, and became lists of deficits.[42] This also applied to the party organizations in the steel mill in Brandenburg. In 1985, party members were still provided with information about the actions taken to improve the situation, but information about these initiatives stopped in 1987. The local party leadership seemed unable to cope with the accumulation of problems. Party secretaries at the steel mill reported to the local apparatus that many members were now of the opinion that "it's not worth the effort of articulating these issues at party meetings as the leadership no longer supplies sufficient answers."[43] Since the local apparatus failed to provide answers to pressing questions and problems, political participation became increasingly meaningless. Rank-and-file members were unable to perform their role as social agents, and faith in the management skills of the party leadership declined.

This alarming situation was exacerbated in September 1988. The introduction of the new Wartburg 1.3 car caused a scandal and created an outrage about the leadership, particularly amongst party members.[44] The announcement that this car would go into series production in October 1988 had already caused outbursts of anger. Initially, the price created a furor. The vehicle was supposed to be sold for a price of 30,200 ostmarks (the East German currency). In the context of an average income of about 1,300 ostmarks per month, this was a prohibitive price.[45] Therefore, this vehicle became not only a symbol of the price explosion of consumer goods, but also an allegory for the increasing social divide both within society and within the membership. A *Stasi* report stated that the following argument was very common: "It doesn't help a worker if a bread roll costs five pennies, but a Wartburg car is a prohibitive expense. There is more expected from life than cheap bread rolls."[46] As well as the high price of technical equipment, the design also created resentment. Aside from the VW engine, the car showed no further developments. Members of the sports club in Grünau in Berlin were of opinion that the Wartburg, despite its improvements, "is like an old granny with a pacemaker."⁴⁷ They were referring to the VW engine and the outdated design. Two lines of discussion thereby met: the inflationary price development of consumer goods, and, compared to West Germany, the miserable domestic economy with its pathetic lack of strength.

The perception held by party members did not differ from those with no party affiliation. This time, the Central Committee released an information bulletin on the issue, but it increased the frustrations even further. In sixteen pages, the information bulletin justified the high price of the vehicle. The innovations of the new vehicle were listed, and it was argued that not only the development costs needed to be covered, but a profit should also be achieved in order to finance social welfare.⁴⁸ This interpretation ignored growing perceptions of an economic crisis and the loss of acceptance of the party's policy. Hence, the widespread opinion among party members was that the authors of this information did not have a clue about the situation at the grassroots level, and, as if that were not enough, instead of providing party members with orientation in order to empower them to perform their role as facilitators of ideology, the information bulletin caused further critical discussions about the pricing policy and the efficiency of the economy. It reinforced the discontent at the grassroots of the party. Not only did comrades doubt the content of the information and reject it as implausible, but even in party meetings they expressed opinions that were in conflict with the official party standpoint.⁴⁹ Criticism and discontent with the party's policy was addressed not only in the private sphere, among friends or colleagues, but also expanded to the level of party publicity. Two months later, in November 1988, the *Stasi* recorded that members rejected (party) functions and sporadically left the party.⁵⁰

In the fall of 1988, an alarming scenario had already taken place at the party's grassroots level. On the one hand, the pressure on party members increased, which made it almost impossible to facilitate the party's interpretation of reality, while on the other hand, they were also no longer willing to advocate a policy that they rejected. Not only did the party apparatus lose its power to solve reported problems in the growing economic slump; the leadership also ignored the rising perception of crisis, and could therefore no longer benefit from its social and ideological instruments of integration. This situation also had an impact on the aforementioned party secretary. He recalls this situation: "Actually, me myself, I was not convinced either. And I also lost the inner, inner, let's call it, the urge to convince people, as I myself was not convinced by the arguments. If you've lost the spark, you can't light a fire. You know?"[51]

Summary

This exploration has shown that previous perceptions of party life as a place of repression and boredom were insufficient in describing the function of the mandatory meetings and the role of the rank-and-file members within the political system. After the purges and in the context of the revival of the party under Khrushchev in the USSR, an integration strategy was instigated in East Germany. Expulsions as a method of first choice were replaced by the idea of "educating" members. Along with the changes in disciplinary practice, the leadership expanded integration instruments in the 1960s. An information bulletin by the Central Committee was sent to all party secretaries of PPOs to provide the rank and files with more information, the party standpoint, and their arguments. In addition to ideological mediation, the party apparatus paid more attention to societal steering, namely problems reported by the party secretaries in their monthly reports. The local apparatus tried to solve the reported issues on the supply of goods and problems with infrastructure before they created serious conflicts. Performing the role of facilitators of ideology and social agents could be meaningful to rank-and-file members. They benefited from the information surplus and the possibility of receiving support from the party apparatus. The latter gave political participation a social meaning, and rank-and-file members, as well as party secretaries, performed as agents for their fellow colleagues or neighbors. Indeed, repression was still an important factor of cohesion, but it was put in the background while ideological and social facilitation dominated the social practice of party life.

In the face of the economic decline in the 1980s, a gradual erosion of the two integration factors took place. Shortages in the supply of goods and services made it increasingly difficult for rank-and-file members to perform their roles as facilitators of ideology and social agents. In 1986 and 1987, the perception of a crisis increased and the need for information grew, but for the party leadership, the downward economic trend and the supply problems were taboo topics and party members were not provided with reasons for this downward development. Monthly reports by party secretaries became lists of deficits. In 1987, the PPOs of the steel mill in Brandenburg no longer received any response to the problems they reported, and their political participation became meaningless. In 1988, the frustrations reached an elevated level when rank-and-file members started to articulate their discontent with the policy of the leadership at party meetings. The integration tools lost their power when the apparatus proved unable to solve problems, and the leadership continued to be reluctant to address the growing perception of a crisis. Ideological and social steering lost its grip so that only repression provided a precarious stability. This last pillar of cohesion eventually lost its power in 1989.

The supply crisis was an explosive issue among workers and their superiors at (industrial) companies, but only highlights one area of conflict in the 1980s. West German products, currency, and travel opportunities were also increasingly important reasons for friction. In addition, "glasnost and perestroika" had a great impact on the growing perception of crisis among rank-and-file members and the function of party life. Indeed, the conflicts varied in significance for different groups in the membership, and they also ultimately contributed to the loss of integration. Eventually, the rank-and-file members who had served for the stability and functionality of the political system halted their loyalty and assent.

Sabine Pannen is a research fellow at the Centre for Contemporary History in Potsdam. Her publications include "Abwarten, austreten oder protestieren? Der innere Zerfall der SED-Parteibasis in Brandenburg an der Havel," in *Agonie und Aufbruch. Das Ende der SED-Herrschaft und die Friedliche Revolution in Brandenburg*, edited by Jutta Braun and Peter Ulrich Weiß (2014); and *Loyalitätsverlust, Der innere Zerfall der SED-Parteibasis 1979–1989* (forthcoming 2018).

Notes

1. Martin Sabrow, "Der Konkurs der Konsensdiktatur. Überlegungen zum inneren Zerfall der DDR aus kulturgeschichtlicher Perspektive" [The failure of consensus dictatorship. Considerations about internal decay of the GDR from a cultural perspective], in *Weg in den Untergang, Der innere Zerfall der DDR* [Road to collapse. The internal decay of the GDR], ed. Konrad H. Jarausch and Martin Sabrow (Göttingen, 1999), 88.
2. Dietrich Staritz and Siegfried Suckut, "Alte Heimat oder neue Linke? Das SED-Erbe und die PDS-Erben?" [Old home or new left? The legacy of the SED and the PDS as heir?], *Deutschland Archiv* 24 (1991): 1040; Florian Peters, "Arbeitermythos und Staatspartei, Zusammensetzung und Rekrutierung von Mitgliedschaft und Funktionärskörper (1961–1989)" [Worker myth

and state party, social composition and recruitment of party members and functionaries], unpublished manuscript, 33–34.
3. Brandenburg was not a preplanned steel city like Magnitogorsk in the Soviet Union. In contrast to other industrial cities in the GDR, such as the "oil city" of Schwedt, it had an industrial and steel tradition. See Stephen Kotkin, *Magnetic Mountain: Stalinism as a Civilization* (Berkeley, 1995); Philipp Springer, *Verbaute Träume, Herrschaft, Stadtentwicklung und Lebensrealität in der sozialistischen Industriestadt Schwedt* [Obstructed dreams. Power, urban development and people's lives in the socialist industrial city of Schwedt] (Berlin, 2006). Also see Andrea Bahr, who analyzes the rule of the district party committee of Brandenburg in this volume.
4. Jens Gieseke, "Social Inequality in State Socialism—An Outline," *Zeithistorische Forschungen* [Studies in Contemporary History] Online edition 10, no. 2 (2013), Accessed 21 August 2017 from http://www.zeithistorische-forschungen.de/2-2013/id=4493#en; and Christoph Kleßmann, "Arbeiter im 'Arbeiterstaat' DDR: Deutsche Tradition, sowjetisches Modell, westdeutsches Magnetfeld (1945 bis 1971) (Workers in the 'Worker State' GDR: German Tradition, Soviet Model, West German Magnetic Field), (Bonn, 2007) 9–40.
5. The records of the party organization of the steel mill in Brandenburg are kept by the main archive of the federal land of Brandenburg, the Brandenburgisches Landeshauptarchiv (hereafter BLHA). "Zusammensetzung der Mitglieder und Kandidaten nach ausgewählten GO, Jahresbericht 1981 Stand November 1981" [Composition of members and candidates of selected PPO, annual report November 1981] in BLHA, Rep. 531 Brbg., Nr. 1843. In 1981 the district party committee of Brandenburg counted 2,136 SED members at the steel mill. In November the number increased to 2,285. According to internal statistics of the district party committee of Brandenburg an der Havel, 1,543 workers within a total volume of 5,538 workers held a membership document; see "Organisationsgrad und Parteischulbesuch ausgewählter Betriebe und Einrichtungen 1981" [Membership and party school attendance of selected companies and institutions], in BLHA, Rep. 531 Brbg., Nr. 1843.
6. Bernd Florath, "Der Untergang der SED" [The downfall of the SED], in *Das Revolutionsjahr 1989. Die demokratische Revolution in Osteuropa als transnationale Zäsur* [The revolutionary year of 1989. The democratic revolution in Eastern Europe as transnational turning point], ed. Bernd Florath (Göttingen, 2011), 63–104; Thomas Klein, *"Für die Einheit und Reinheit der Partei." Die innerparteilichen Kontrollorgane der SED in der Ära Ulbricht* ["For the unity and purity of the party." The control organs of the SED in the Ulbricht era] (Cologne, 2002); Thomas Klein, Wilfriede Otto, and Peter Grieder, *Visionen, Repression und Opposition in der SED* [Visions, repression and opposition in the SED] (Frankfurt, 1996); Wilfriede Otto, "Zu Normen und Ritualen im SED-Alltag," [About norms and rituals of party life], in *Die DDR—Erinnerungen an einen untergegangenen Staat* [The GDR—Memories of a defunct state], ed. Heiner Timmermann (Berlin, 1999), 295–306.
7. Irene Böhme, *Die da drüben. Sieben Kapitel DDR* [Those over there. Seven chapters GDR] (Berlin, 1982), 48.

8. Alexei Yurchak, *Everything Was Forever, Until It Was No More: The Last Soviet Generation* (Princeton, 2005).
9. Michel Christian, "Ausschließen und disziplinieren. Kontrollpraxis in den kommunistischen Parteien der DDR und der Tschechoslowakei" [Expulsion and discipline. Control practices in the Communist parties of the GDR and Czechoslovakia], in *Die ostdeutsche Gesellschaft, eine transnationale Perspektive* [The East German society, a transnational perspective], ed. Emmanuel Droit and Sandrine Kott (Berlin, 2006), 53–70.
10. Ibid., 59. This phenomenon was also pointed out for the CPSU by Edward Cohn in "Sex and the Married Communist: Family Troubles, Marital Infidelity, and Party Discipline in the Postwar USSR, 1945–64," *The Russian Review* 68 (July 2009): 429–450. See also: Idem, *The High Title of a Communist: Postwar Party Discipline and the Values of the Soviet Regime* (Illinois, 2015).
11. Entwurf für neue Richtlinien für Parteiverfahren [Draft for new guidelines for party proceedings], 23.11.1954, in SAPMO-BArch, DY 30/IV 2/4/8, Bildung und Tätigkeit der ZPKK. The records of the Central Committee of the Socialist Unity Party of Germany are kept by the Foundation Archives of Parties and Mass Organizations of the GDR in the federal archives Stiftung Archiv der Parteien und Massenorganisationen der DDR im Bundesarchiv (hereafter SAPMO-BArch). See also: Yoram Gorlitzki, "Party Revivalism and the Death of Stalin," in *Slavic Review* 54, no. 1 (1995): 1–22; Thomas Bohn, Rayk Einax, and Michel Abeßer, eds., *De-Stalinisation Reconsidered: Persistence and Change in the Soviet Union* (Frankfurt, 2014); Stephan Merl, "Entstalinisierung, Reformen und Wettlauf der Systeme 1953–1964" [De-Stalinization, reforms and the race of political systems], in *Handbuch der Geschichte Russlands, Vom Ende des Zweiten Weltkriegs bis zum Zusammenbruch der Sowjetunion, Bd. 5/1: 1945–1991* [Handbook of Russian history, from the Second World War until the decline of the Soviet Union], ed. Stefan Plaggenborg (Stuttgart, 2002), 175–318.
12. Protokoll des VI. Parteitages der Sozialistischen Einheitspartei Deutschlands [Minutes of the 6th Party Congress of the Socialist Unity Party of Germany] 15–21 Januar 1963, Bd. IV, Berlin 1963, 415.
13. See Statistische Analysen der Zentralen Parteikontrollkommission [Statistical analyses of the central party control commission], SAPMO-BArch, DY 30/11075.
14. See Analysen der Mitgliederbewegung der SED des Sektors Mitgliederbewegung in der Abteilung Parteiorgane des ZK [Analyses of SED membership development by the CC department of party organs], SAPMO-BArch, DY 30/ J IV 2/2 J/ 7064.
15. Edward Cohn analyzes the changing disciplinary practice of the CPSU and the role of CPSU members in the Khrushchev era in this volume.
16. Sitzung des Sekretariats des ZK der SED [Session of the SED CC secretariat], 2.05.1957, in SAPMO-BArch, DY 30/J IV 2/3/559 57.
17. Sitzung des Sekretariats des ZK der SED [Session of the SED CC secretariat], 17.01.1968, in SAPMO-BArch, DY 30/ J IV 2/3A 1533.
18. Statut der Sozialistischen Einheitspartei Deutschlands [SED statute], 9. Aufl. Berlin 1968, 28.

19. Mark Allinson, "1977: The GDR's Most Normal Year?," in *Power and Society in the GDR 1961–1979: The "Normalization of Rule,"* ed. Mary Fulbrook (New York, 2009), 256–259; Anne Dietrich, "Kaffee in der DDR—'Ein Politikum ersten Ranges'" [Coffee in the GDR—'A first-rate political issue'], in *Kaffeewelten. Historische Perspektiven auf eine globale Ware im 20. Jahrundert* [Coffee worlds. Historical perspectives of a global product in the 20th century], ed. Christiane Berth, Dorothee Wierling, and Volker Wünderich (Göttingen, 2015), 225–248; Monika Sigmund, *Genuss als Politikum: Kaffeekonsum in beiden deutschen Staaten* [Pleasure as a political issue: Coffee consumption in both German states] (Berlin, 2015); Stefan Wolle, *Die heile Welt der Diktatur: Alltag und Herrschaft in der DDR 1971 bis 1989* [The ideal world of dictatorship: Everyday life and power in the GDR 1971 to 1989] (Bonn, 1999), 199–201; Volker Wünderich, "Die 'Kaffeekrise' von 1977, Genussmittel und Verbraucherprotest in der DDR [The "Coffee Crisis" 1977, luxury food and consumer protest in the GDR]," *Historische Anthropologie* 11 (2003): 240–261.
20. Information bulletin, "Zur Versorgung mit Kaffee- und Kakaoerzeugnissen" [On the supply of coffee and cocoa products], 1977/6, Nr.152, in BStU, MfS, SED-KL 3944, 149–150.
21. Letter of a party secretary of the engineering school Feinwerktechnik Glashütte Sachsen, 27 September 1979, in SAPMO-BArch, DY 30/9231.
22. Letter from the Borna city council party secretary, 28 August 1980, in SAPMO-BArch, DY 30/9231.
23. Arpád Szakolczai and Agnes Horváth, "Information Management in Bolshevik-Type Party States: A Version of the Information Society," *East European Politics and Societies* 5, No. 2 (Spring 1991) 268–305, here 292–293.
24. Andrea Bahr, *Parteiherrschaft vor Ort, Die SED-Kreisleitung Brandenburg 1961–1989*, [Party rule in local practice. The SED's local party apparatus in Brandenburg/Havel 1961–1989] (Berlin, 2016), 66–89.
25. ZAIG, "Tendenzen auf Hinweise der Unzufriedenheit in der Reaktion der Bevölkerung der DDR" [Trends of indications of discontent in the reactions of the people of the GDR], 19 September 1977, in *Die DDR im Blick der Stasi 1977. Die geheimen Berichte an die SED-Führung* [The GDR in the light of the Stasi 1977. The secret reports to the party leadership], ed. Henrick Bispinck (Göttingen, 2012), 231.
26. ZAIG, "Weitere Hinweise über Reaktionen der Bevölkerung zu den Maßnahmen des Ministerrates der DDR zur Versorgung mit Kaffee und Kakaoerzeugnissen" [Further information aboutf the reactions of people related to the measures of the ministerial council of the GDR concerning the supply of coffee and cocoa products], 1 September 1977, in *Die DDR im Blick der Stasi 1977*, 228.
27. ZAIG, "Tendenzen auf Hinweise der Unzufriedenheit in der Reaktion der Bevölkerung der DDR" [Trends of indications of discontent in the reaction of the people of the GDR], 19 September 1977, in *Die DDR im Blick der Stasi 1977*, 231.
28. "Weltmarktpreise und Kaffeeversorgung," *Neues Deutschland*, 23 September 1977, vol. 32, 2.

29. Informationsbericht für den Zeitraum 21.8. bis 20.9.1985 der ZBPL über Probleme, die in Mitgliederversammlungen angesprochen wurden [Report by the party leadership at the steel mill for the period 21 August until 20 September 1985 concerning problems raised in party meetings], BLHA, Rep. 532 Nr. 6137.
30. Interview between the author and a former ambulance driver at the steel mill in Brandenburg on 4 August 2010.
31. Jens Gieseke "'Seit Langem angestaute Unzufriedenheit breitester Bevölkerungskreise'—Das Volk in den Stimmungsberichten des Staatssicherheitsdienstes ["Long-term pent-up dissatisfaction of the widest sections of the population"—The people in state security popular opinion reports], in *Revolution und Vereinigung: Als Deutschland die Realität die Phantasie überholte* [Revolution and unification: When reality overtook fantasy in Germany], ed. Klaus-Dietmar Henke (Munich, 2009), 139–140; see also Jens Gieseke, "Bevölkerungsstimmungen in der geschlossenen Gesellschaft. MfS-Berichte an die DDR-Führung in den 1960er- und 1970er-Jahren" [Popular opinion in the closed society. MFS reports to the GDR leadership in the 1960s and 1970s], *Zeithistorische Forschungen* [Studies in contemporary history] Online edition 5, no. 2 (2008): 236–257. Accessed 21 August 2017 from http://www.zeithistorische-forschungen.de/2-2008/id=4491.
32. Jens Gieseke, "Die Einheit von Wirtschafts-, Sozial- und Sicherheitspolitik, Militarisierung und Überwachung als Probleme einer DDR-Sozialgeschichte der Ära Honecker [The unity of economic, social and security policy, militarization and surveillance as problems for a social history of the Honecker era]," *Zeitschrift für Geschichtswissenschaft* 51, no. 11 (2003): 996–1021.
33. Michael Meyen, *Denver Clan und Neues Deutschland. Mediennutzung in der DDR* [The Denver clan and Neues Deutschland. Media use in the GDR] (Berlin, 2003), 38.
34. Matthias Judt, "Bananen, gute Apfelsinen, Erdnüsse u.a. sind doch keine kapitalistischen Privilegien" [Bananas, good oranges, peanuts etc. are no capitalistic privileges], in *Alltäglicher Mangel am Ende der 1980er Jahre in der DDR* [Everyday shortage at the end of the 1980s in the GDR], DA online. Accessed 21 August 2017 from http://www.bpb.de/geschichte/zeitgeschichte/deutschlandarchiv/163470/bananen-gute-apfelsinen-erdnuesse-u-a-sind-doch-keine-kapitalistischen-privilegien?p=all, 12.07.2013; see also Jonathan R. Zatlin, *The Currency of Socialism, Money and Political Culture in East Germany* (Cambridge, 2007), 110.
35. Anonymous letter by "Comrades with good intentions," 1 April 1980, in BStU, MfS, HA XX 13426, 78.
36. ZAIG, "Hinweise zur Reaktion der Bevölkerung" [Information on reactions among the people] 5. September 1980, in BStU, MfS, ZAIG 4165, 2–3.
37. Interview by the author with a former full-time party secretary at the steel mill in Brandenburg on 12 November 2010.
38. ZAIG, "Hinweise über Reaktionen der Bevölkerung der DDR zu Problemen des Handels und der Versorgung" [Information about reactions among the people of the GDR concerning problems with trade and with supply of goods], 17 November 1986, in BStU, MfS, ZAIG 4165, 53–60, here 60.
39. Hans Hermann Hertle, *Chronik des Mauerfalls—Die dramatischen Ereignisse*

um den 9. November 1989 [Chronicle of the fall of the Berlin wall—The dramatic events around 9 November 1989] (Berlin, 1996), 45–50.
40. ZAIG, "Weitere Hinweise zu Reaktionen der Bevölkerung auf den offiziellen Besuch des Generalsekretärs des ZK der SED und Vorsitzenden des Staatsrates der DDR, Genossen Honecker, in der BRD, 2. Zusammenfassung" [Further information about reactions among people on the official visit of the general secretary, Comrade Honecker, in the FRG, 2nd summary] 16 September 1987, in BStU, MfS, ZAIG 4229, 25.
41. ZAIG, "Hinweise über Reaktionen der Bevölkerung zu Problemen des Handels und der Versorgung" [Information about reactions among the people about problems with trade and supply of goods], 14 April 1987, in BStU, MfS, ZAIG 4165, 62.
42. Monatsberichte der Grundorganisationen des SWB 1987 [Monthly report of a PPO in the steel mill in Brandenburg an der Havel] in BLHA, Rep. 532, Nr. 6234. See also Sönke Friedreich, *Autos bauen im Sozialismus: Arbeit und Organisationskultur in der Zwickauer Automobilindustrie nach 1945* [Car-making in socialism: Labor and organizational culture of the car industry in Zwickau after 1945] (Leipzig, 2008), 365–366.
43. APO-Berichtsprotokoll des SWB. Meinungen zu Versorgungsfragen 15 December 1987 [Monthly report of a PPO in the steel mill. Opinions on supply issues] in BLHA, Rep. 532, Nr. 6234.
44. Martin Sabrow, "Die Wiedergeburt des klassischen Skandals. Öffentliche Empörung in der späten DDR" [The rebirth of the classic scandal. Popular outrage in the late GDR] in *Skandal und Diktatur: Formen öffentlicher Empörung im NS-Staat und in der DDR* [Scandal and dictatorship: Types of popular outrage in the Nazi state and the GDR], ed. Martin Sabrow (Göttingen, 2004), 231–265.
45. Wolle, *Die heile Welt der Diktatur*, 191.
46. ZAIG, "Hinweise auf Reaktionen der Bevölkerung auf die in den Massenmedien der DDR erfolgten Veröffentlichungen zum Personenkraftwagen 'Wartburg 1.3'" [Information on reactions among people about the mass media–published information on the new vehicle "Wartburg 1.3"], 26 September 1988, in BStU, MfS, ZAIG 4241, 4.
47. Reaktionen der Bevölkerung [Reactions of the people], 20 September 1988, in BStU, MfS, BV Berlin, Abt. XX 3720, 103; see also Zatlin, *The Currency of Socialism*, 225–227.
48. Information bulletin, "Zum neuen Wartburg" [On the new Wartburg], 1988/11, Nr. 252, in BStU, MfS, HA VI Nr. 15338, 395–410.
49. ZAIG, "Weitere Hinweise zur Reaktion der Bevölkerung im Zusammenhang mit dem PKW 'Wartburg 1.3'" [Further information on reactions among people in the context of the new vehicle "Wartburg 1.3"], 27 October 1988, in BStU, MfS, ZAIG 4241, 8–11.
50. ZAIG, "Hinweise über einige beachtenswerte Entwicklungstendenzen in der Reaktion der Bevölkerung auf innenpolitisch Fragen" [Information about some remarkable trends in the reactions of people concerning domestic issues], 24 November 1988, in BStU, MfS, ZAIG 4158, 110.
51. Interview by the author with a former full-time party secretary of the steel mill in Brandenburg on 12 November 2010.

Bibliography

Allinson, Mark. "1977: The GDR's Most Normal Year?" In *Power and Society in the GDR 1961–1979: The "Normalization of Rule,"* ed. Mary Fulbrook, 256–259. New York: Berghahn Books, 2009.
Bahr, Andrea. *Parteiherrschaft vor Ort. Die SED-Kreisleitung Brandenburg 1961–1989* [Party rule in local practice. The SED's local party apparatus in Brandenburg/Havel 1961–1989]. Berlin: Christoph Links Verlag, 2016.
Bispinck, Henrik, ed. *Die DDR im Blick der Stasi 1977. Die geheimen Berichte an die SED-Führung* [The GDR in the light of the Stasi 1977. The secret reports to the party leadership]. Göttingen: Vandenhoeck & Ruprecht, 2012.
Böhme, Irene. *Die da drüben. Sieben Kapitel DDR.* [Those over there. Seven chapters GDR]. Berlin: Rotbuch-Verlag, 1982.
Bohn, Thomas M., Rayk Einax, and Michel Abeßer, eds. *De-Stalinisation Reconsidered: Persistence and Change in the Soviet Union.* Frankfurt/M.: Campus Verlag, 2014.
Christian, Michel. "Ausschließen und disziplinieren. Kontrollpraxis in den kommunistischen Parteien der DDR und der Tschechoslowakei" [Expulsion and discipline. Control practices in the communist parties of the GDR and Czechoslovakia]. In *Die ostdeutsche Gesellschaft, eine transnationale Perspektive* [The East German society, a transnational perspective], ed. Emmanuel Droit and Sandrine Kott, 53–70. Berlin: Christoph Links Verlag, 2006.
Cohn, Edward. *The High Title of a Communist: Postwar Party Discipline and the Values of the Regime in the Postwar Soviet Union, 1945–1964.* DeKalb: Northern Illinois University Press, 2015.
———. "Sex and the Married Communist: Family Troubles, Marital Infidelity, and Party Discipline in the Postwar USSR, 1945–64." *The Russian Review* 68 (July 2009): 429–450.
Dietrich, Anne. "Kaffee in der DDR—'Ein Politikum ersten Ranges'" [Coffee in the GDR—"A first-rate political issue"]. In *Kaffeewelten. Historische Perspektiven auf eine globale Ware im 20. Jahrundert* [Coffee worlds. Historical perspectives on a global product in the 20th century], ed. Christiane Berth, Dorothee Wierling, and Volker Wünderich, 225–248. Göttingen: Vandenhoeck & Ruprecht, 2015.
Florath, Bernd. "Der Untergang der SED" [The downfall of the SED]. In *Das Revolutionsjahr 1989. Die demokratische Revolution in Osteuropa als transnationale Zäsur* [The revolutionary year of 1989. The democratic revolution in Eastern Europe as transnational turning point], ed. Bernd Florath, 63–104. Göttingen: Vandenhoeck & Ruprecht, 2011.
Friedreich, Sönke. *Autos bauen im Sozialismus: Arbeit und Organisationskultur in der Zwickauer Automobilindustrie nach 1945* [Car making in socialism: Labor and organizational culture of the car industry in Zwickau after 1945]. Leipzig: Leipziger Universitätsverlag, 2008.
Gieseke, Jens. "Bevölkerungsstimmungen in der geschlossenen Gesellschaft. MfS-Berichte an die DDR-Führung in den 1960er- und 1970er-Jahren" [Popular opinion in the closed society. MFS reports to the GDR leadership in the 1960s and 1970s], *Zeithistorische Forschungen* [Studies in Contemporary His-

tory] Online edition 5, no. 2 (2008): 236–257. Accessed 21 August 2017 from http://www.zeithistorische-forschungen.de/2-2008/id=4491.

———. "Die Einheit von Wirtschafts-, Sozial- und Sicherheitspolitik, Militarisierung und Überwachung als Probleme einer DDR-Sozialgeschichte der Ära Honecker" [The unity of economic, social and security policy, militarization and surveillance as problems for a social history of the Honecker era]. *Zeitschrift für Geschichtswissenschaft* 51, no. 11 (2003): 996–1021.

———. "'Seit Langem angestaute Unzufriedenheit breitester Bevölkerungskreise'—Das Volk in den Stimmungsberichten des Staatssicherheitsdienstes" ["Long-term pent-up dissatisfaction of the widest sections of the population"—The people in state security popular opinion reports] In *Revolution und Vereinigung: Als Deutschland die Realität die Phantasie überholte* [Revolution and unification: When reality overtook fantasy in Germany], ed. Klaus-Dietmar Henke, 130–148. Munich: Deutscher Taschenbuch Verlag, 2009.

———. "Social Inequality in State Socialism—An Outline." *Zeithistorische Forschungen* 10, no. 2 (2013): 171–198. Accessed 21 August 2017 from http://www.zeithistorische-forschungen.de/2-2013/id=4493#en.

Gorlitzki, Yoram. "Party Revivalism and the Death of Stalin." *Slavic Review* 54, no. 1 (1995): 1–22.

Hertle, Hans Hermann. *Chronik des Mauerfalls—Die dramatischen Ereignisse um den 9. November 1989* [Chronicle of the fall of the Berlin wall—The dramatic events around 9 November 1989]. Berlin: Christoph Links Verlag, 1996.

Judt, Matthias. "Bananen, gute Apfelsinen, Erdnüsse u.a. sind doch keine kapitalistischen Privilegien" [Bananas, good oranges, peanuts etc. are no capitalistic privileges], *Alltäglicher Mangel am Ende der 1980er Jahre in der DDR* (DA online). Accessed 21 August 2017 from http://www.bpb.de/geschichte/zeitgeschichte/deutschlandarchiv/163470/bananen-gute-apfelsinen-erdnu esse-u-a-sind-doch-keine-kapitalistischen-privilegien?p=all, 12.07.2013.

Klein, Thomas. *"Für die Einheit und Reinheit der Partei." Die innerparteilichen Kontrollorgane der SED in der Ära Ulbricht* ["For the unity and purity of the party." The control organs of the SED in the Ulbricht era]. Cologne: Böhlau Verlag, 2002.

Klein, Thomas, Wilfriede Otto, and Peter Grieder. *Visionen, Repression und Opposition in der SED* [Visions, repression and opposition in the SED]. Frankfurt (Oder): Frankfurter/Oder-Editionen, 1996.

Kleßmann, Christoph. *Arbeiter im "Arbeiterstaat" DDR: Deutsche Tradition, sowjetisches Modell, westdeutsches Magnetfeld (1945 bis 1971)* [Workers in the "worker state" GDR: German tradition, Soviet model, West German magnetic field]. Bonn: Verlag J. H. W. Dietz Nachf, 2007.

Kotkin, Stephen. *Magnetic Mountain: Stalinism as a Civilization*. Berkeley: University of California Press, 1997.

Merl, Stephan. "Entstalinisierung, Reformen und Wettlauf der Systeme 1953–1964" [De-Stalinization, reforms and the race of political systems]. In *Handbuch der Geschichte Russlands, Vom Ende des Zweiten Weltkriegs bis zum Zusammenbruch der Sowjetunion, Bd. 5/1: 1945–1991* [Handbook of Russian history, from the Second World War until the decline of the Soviet Union], ed. Stefan Plaggenborg, 175–318. Stuttgart: Hiersemann Verlag, 2002.

Meyen, Michael. *Denver Clan und Neues Deutschland. Mediennutzung in der DDR* [The Denver clan and Neues Deutschland. Media use in the GDR]. Berlin: Christoph Links Verlag, 2003.
Otto, Wilfriede. "Zu Normen und Ritualen im SED-Alltag." [On norms and rituals of party life]. In *Die DDR—Erinnerungen an einen untergegangenen Staat* [The GDR—Memories of a defunct state], ed. Heiner Timmermann, 295–306. Berlin: Verlag Duncker & Humboldt, 1999.
Peters, Florian. "Arbeitermythos und Staatspartei. Zusammensetzung und Rekrutierung von Mitgliedschaft und Funktionärskörper (1961–1989)" [Worker myth and state party. Social composition and recruitment of party members and functionaries]. Unpublished manuscript, 1–37.
Sabrow, Martin. "Der Konkurs der Konsensdiktatur. Überlegungen zum inneren Zerfall der DDR aus kulturgeschichtlicher Perspektive" [The failure of consensus dictatorship. Considerations about the internal decay of the GDR from a cultural perspective]. In *Weg in den Untergang. Der innere Zerfall der DDR* [Roads to collapse. The internal decay of the GDR], ed. K. H. Jarausch and M. Sabrow, 83–116. Göttingen: Vandenhoeck & Ruprecht, 1999.
———. "Die Wiedergeburt des klassischen Skandals. Öffentliche Empörung in der späten DDR." [The rebirth of the classic scandal. Popular outrage in the late GDR]. In *Skandal und Diktatur: Formen öffentlicher Empörung im NS-Staat und in der DDR* [Scandal and dictatorship: Types of popular outrage in the Nazi state and the GDR], ed. Martin Sabrow, 231–265. Göttingen: Wallstein Verlag, 2004.
Sigmund, Monika. *Genuss als Politikum: Kaffeekonsum in beiden deutschen Staaten* [Pleasure as a political issue: Coffee consumption in both German states]. Berlin: de Gruyter Oldenbourg, 2015.
Springer, Philipp. *Verbaute Träume. Herrschaft, Stadtentwicklung und Lebensrealität in der sozialistischen Industriestadt Schwedt* [Obstructed dreams. Power, urban development and people's lives in the socialist industrial city of Schwedt]. Berlin: Christoph Links Verlag, 2006.
Staritz, Dietrich, and Siegfried Suckut. "Alte Heimat oder neue Linke? Das SED-Erbe und die PDS-Erben?" [Old home or new left? The legacy of the SED and the PDS as heir?] *Deutschland Archiv* 24 (1991): 1038–1049.
Szakolczai, Arpád, and Agnes Horváth. "Information Management in Bolshevik-Type Party States: A Version of the Information Society." *East European Politics and Societies* 5, No. 2 (Spring 1991): 268–305.
Wolle, Stefan. *Die heile Welt der Diktatur. Alltag und Herrschaft in der DDR 1971–1989* (The cozy world of dictatorship. Everyday life and political power in the GDR from 1971 to 1989). Bonn: Christoph Links Verlag, 1998.
Wünderich, Volker. "Die 'Kaffeekrise' von 1977, Genussmittel und Verbraucherprotest in der DDR" [The "Coffee Crisis" 1977, luxury food and consumer protest in the GDR]. *Historische Anthropologie* 11 (2003): 240–261.
Yurchak, Alexei. *Everything Was Forever, Until It Was No More: The Last Soviet Generation*. Princeton: Princeton University Press, 2006.
Zatlin, Jonathan R. *The Currency of Socialism, Money and Political Culture in East Germany*. Cambridge: Cambridge University Press, 2007.

 4

The Successive Dissolution of the "Uncivil Society"
Tracking SED Members in Opinion Polls and Secret Police Reports, 1969–1989

Jens Gieseke

Being Bolshevik or Hiding Behind a Mask?

Microhistorical studies from different periods of Communist Party history draw controversial images of what party members thought about their roles both within the party, and within society itself. Two interpretations are influential here. Studies that go back to the implementation and development phase of the Communist regime often focus on the comrades' responsiveness regarding their claims of "revolutionary" enthusiasm and mobilization as expected by the organization. The idea of being a "Bolshevik" or a "Communist" was an extraordinary challenge to the subjects themselves, which occupied them intensively. Becoming a party cadre, and to actually become one from the inside, represented sophisticated identity work.[1]

From the contrary "cool" perspective of functionalist sociology, membership of the Communist state party appears to have been simply a necessity, an external offer made by the system whereby adaptable parts of the population accepted the ability to participate in the power structure, or just the opportunity to secure or advance their personal position in exchange. This perspective tends to play a role in the later stages of party history when becoming a party member no longer represented a commitment to embattled social situations but was more an act of conformism. However, it may also apply to the construction phase, where it is often associated with narratives of opportunism and corruption through privileges. Such a perception can particularly be found in cases of countries in which Communist movements were only weakly anchored culturally, and in which the establishment of the Communist regime showed strong signs of imperial domination in a religious or social "foreign" environment such as the Central Asian periphery of the Soviet Union or Catholic Poland. Moreover, the importance of this perspective increases for the late stages of Communist rule due to the necessities of modern complex industrial societies.[2]

Both perspectives can claim evidence, and ultimately it is necessary to investigate the interaction between them in terms of historical change and for different groups and milieus within the party membership.

The Communist labor movement had been strong in East Germany previously, and appeared to be particularly legitimized by the struggle against fascism. At the same time, however, the Communists in the German Democratic Republic (GDR) acted under conditions of external occupation and in a society in which the previous Nazi dictatorship could rely on a substantial mass base. The following analysis focuses on the second half of GDR history, which was characterized by stability and the omnipresence of party rule on the one hand, and by severe economic, social, and cultural pressure in the competition between the systems of East and West Germany, as well as the looming crisis on the other.

The following analysis aims to track East German Socialist Unity Party of Germany (Sozialistische Einheitspartei Deutschlands, or SED) members' self-image. It begins with some considerations of its political and social composition and then follows two contemporary series of sources about the mindsets of party members, among others. The first series is a proxy survey program by the West German opinion research institute Infratest, which in the years 1969 to 1973 aimed to get a more detailed image of the SED membership by interviewing West German visitors to East Germany who met party members. The second series are reports on the "reactions of the population" to current political events and general moods by the East German Ministry of State Security (Ministerum für Staatssicherheit, or *Stasi*). Both sources contain a number of hints on the questions of how homogeneous or heterogeneous the SED membership was, how—in the sense of the regime—functional or dysfunctional party members were at this stage of "mature" and "late socialism," and how they positioned themselves within the dynamics of the decay of the state socialist system. A starting point is the concept of "uncivil society"—that is, the assumption that party members formed a block of sociopolitical stakeholders in late socialist societies and tried to secure their privileged position in face of a possible system change, therefore acting as key players in the transition to postcommunist restructuring.[3] It is obvious that membership of the party played a significant role among the forces of "uncivil society," but how party members, or subgroups of them, acted within (or beyond) this block deserves a more detailed exploration.

The Two Bodies of Membership

Despite the careful formulation and manipulation of data about the social composition of the party, it is clear from a social-statistical perspective that the SED was primarily a party of higher state officials. Reassembled internal party data shows a level of at least 40 percent of such cadres among the 2.3 million members (in 1989).[4] If we could choose our own samples on the basis of individual members' data, not of aggregated statistics, this share would even be higher. As the composition of the membership was subject to detailed decisions on the SED's recruitment policy, the degree of organization in various areas of society can be read as a sociopolitical ranking of value preferences: at the top we find the security forces and ideological elites at the core of "uncivil society,"[5] with several hundred thousand members. In these sectors, SED members constituted a majority among all employees. In the secret police, and of course in the party apparatus itself, practically all employees were party members. Tiered by rank and sector, this also applied to the large number of leading cadres in the economy and civil state apparatus in all sectors (justice, health, culture, etc.)[6]

Most members entered the party as young or middle-aged men, for whom party membership opened or secured access to higher levels of education and professional careers. Following this ranking, party members enjoyed above-average salary levels, privileged access to scarce goods and services, and an appropriate standard of living. As can be seen, material reward played an increasingly important role in the production of loyalty—not least among full-time employees of the party themselves. As Rüdiger Bergien has ascertained, SED finances show that the share of staff expenditures on the total budget rose continuously (and more quickly than the growth of staff), while expenditure for ideological work, such as events, printing of material, etc., decreased. These continuous increases were also fueled by competition with salaries in other areas of state and economic management.[7]

However, the SED membership had a dual character; in many ways, it was also a "constructed" body that due to recruitment and advertising policies should have represented the "working class" mass base in terms of statistics and public representation. From 1971 onwards, the total number of members and annual growth rates were no longer subject to the interplay of rapid expansion and purges, as they had been in the 1940s and 1950s, in order to broaden the power base, but rather followed the rhythm of party conventions and the associated recruitment campaigns, which were strictly choreographed to document the constantly "growing" leading role in the membership. These total numbers, as well as the proportion of "workers and employees" of between 70 and 80 percent, are almost the only information that had been publically presented. However, even the strictly internal proportion of "real" production workers had practically been fixed since the mid-sixties to a standard rate of about 37 percent, although it is not clear whether this just followed the role model of the Communist Party of the Soviet Union (CPSU), which reported a similar value.[8] Yet in 1986, the figure followed this standard with a rate of 37.8 percent.

This kind of membership policy was not limited to fiction and statistical manipulation (through, among other things, the attribution of functionaries, students, and pensioners to the percentage of "workers") but deployed its own reality in "party life." Party officials at all levels made great efforts to meet the requirements in that respect, especially in companies with workforces that corresponded to the ideal image of the "proletariat."

The results of this policy can, for example, be tracked in a 1981 statistical report by the SED district leadership of Brandenburg an der Havel. According to this report, the twenty-five largest party organizations in factories, etc., in the district had 5,700 SED members. This was approximately half of the total number of SED members in Brandenburg an der Havel. The SED share of employees was 18.7 percent on average, which approximately concurred with the average in the East German adult population. But the degree of organization was very unevenly distributed; peak values could be found among the bureaucracies in the city council and the county administration with 55 and 52 percent rates of SED membership respectively. The report did not include the *Stasi* or the People's Police district offices, with presumably significantly higher numbers, and several other places that were not captured in the local statistics of the county party organization. However, Brandenburg an der Havel was not an administrative center, and therefore industrial enterprises played an important role there, especially the steel plant in Brandenburg, with an SED membership rate of 29 percent among its workforce. Among the nearly three-quarters of employees at the steelworks who were categorized as workers, the rate of SED membership was approximately the same level, at 27.9 percent. The steel plant, as well as the other above-average businesses (the local railway switch factory at 24.7 percent; VEB road transport at 22.3 percent), represented the ideal type of labor aristocracy with large numbers of skilled male German workers, preferably in large heavy-industrial factories, and was therefore particularly suitable for the "construction" of the desired membership structure. The SED membership rate in businesses where mainly women, unskilled laborers, and in some cases foreigners worked were considerably lower as they did not correspond to the ideal image of the industrial proletariat—for example, the local clothing factory, which had an 8.1 percent SED membership rate, and the retail trade organization Konsum at 8.8 percent.[9]

In other words, in addition to the state employees, who formed the core group of the SED membership, this milieu of "workers" represented a secondary, yet still important, clientele, in which, however, women, migrants, and unskilled workers from small businesses were underrepresented. The cherished "production workers" enjoyed certain moderate privileges among the party membership and in SED policy as a whole, such as relatively high wages, access to new housing, etc., for example. They did not really expect sanctions to be taken against them for debts in their membership dues, nor against inactivity. They also felt themselves under far less pressure to execute and represent the course of the party in their working brigades. In fact, rather, they performed a balancing function by displaying to their colleagues their knowledge of exclusive information attained from the internal party information system. They were also able to communicate practical problems within their own working unit to the party or factory operatives responsible, usually with a certain chance of success.[10]

Overall, in terms of membership policies, the SED was a body with two functions. It existed as an agglomeration of the state party and insofar can be dubbed as the "uncivil society" of the GDR. At the same time, it was a large body with an artfully elaborated legitimizing membership policy. This constructed, dual-function party meant that the SED obviously incorporated many members who met the related requirements with differing degrees of enthusiasm and with different attitudes, and who met the biographical and statistical criteria in different manners.

Infratest Polls on Party Members

How homogeneous or heterogeneous were the SED members in terms of their political attitudes, value orientations, and attitude profiles? One way to approach this question is the analysis of secret West German opinion polls conducted by the Infratest institute using the proxy method. Infratest interviewed West German visitors to the GDR about attitudes and opinions of one of their East German interlocutors (the so-called "person X") in a large-scale program of annual surveys from 1968 to 1989. This method was, in a sense, a continuation of refugee interviews developed in the Harvard project on the Soviet social system and adopted by Infratest for the GDR in the 1950s. The Harvard project was regarded as an opportunity to take an "alternative view" of the societies of the Soviet sphere, and to prove the very existence of such a thing as "society as a communicative space" under the Communist regime. The refugee interviews indeed brought a wealth of new findings. They showed that "public opinion" was relatively autonomous and at some points a surprisingly positive picture of some aspects of life in the Eastern Bloc was held, even among the refugees.[11]

It goes without saying that such surveys cannot be incorporated at face value in our present reconstruction of popular opinion and society. Nevertheless, they offer a number of questions and findings that can be pursued in compliance with the very specific positions of both the pollsters and their clients in Western governments respectively.

When Infratest, the West German polling institute, started conducting surveys on the East German population in the late 1960s, SED members were of particular interest. First, their attitudes and opinions were important for the question of stability or instability of the Communist regime in general. The federal government felt that it was an important area of interest in which to learn more about SED members. This included the question of how many "true believers" the SED could muster, whether party members could actually be regarded as instruments that could be controlled and as homogeneous social actors for the SED leadership, or whether they were an opportunistic mass, potentially disloyal to the totalitarian regime. The SED members among the "persons X" were therefore analyzed separately in survey waves from 1969, 1970, and again in 1973.

Moreover, the percentage share of SED membership was a kind of acid test for the "proxy" interview method through West German visitors to the GDR, which Infratest used because they were unable to contact respondents across the border. Infratest was concerned that no SED members could be reached for the sample due to their seclusion from contacts in the West. Therefore, one of the surprising results of the first surveys was that SED members were not only present, but even overrepresented among the so-called "persons X" on whom the Western interviewees reported. While in 1969 the rate of party membership within the general adult population of East Germany was around 16 percent (1.9 million members), the share in the sample was 23 percent. In the next wave of 1970, the party members had a more or less expected share of 18 percent. In the last wave of 1973, the share was—for reasons that could not be clarified here—remarkably low at 8.6 percent.

Nevertheless, Infratest assumed that party members who had access to classified information (such as army and police officers, for whom it was strictly prohibited to have contact to the West) were underrepresented or absent altogether. Moreover, the sample group of only one hundred party members was too small and heterogenous to deliver representative data.

In particular, the survey design brought with it an inherent distortion concerning the issue of party loyalty versus Western orientation: "They [people x] will definitely be rather open-minded comrades, because they are willing to maintain contact with visitors from the West. A strictly dogmatically-thinking SED member will be less likely to maintain personal relations with West Germany."[12]

As a comparison with official party statistics shows, the Infratest sample was indeed not representative in some respects. The gender distribution was more or less correct with a rate of around 70 percent male members, but the cohort between thirty and fifty years of age was overrepresented, and the group aged over sixty was underrepresented. These distortions exaggerated the character of the SED as a party of state employees (who typically were social climbers in the middle-age group range), a characterization that can nonetheless be confirmed by the (then secret) official party data (see tables 4.1 and 4.2). According to Infratest, 58 percent (1970) and 64 percent (1973) of SED members among the "persons X" were white-collar employees, while the percentage share of workers was determined as only 14 and 11 percent respectively. The relationship between the two groups was significantly more balanced among the non-SED members of "persons X" (in 1970, 21 percent workers compared to 27 percent white-collar employees; and in 1973, 30 percent compared to 17 per cent). These numbers corresponded with an above-average educational profile among SED members with more than 20 percent of them being college graduates.

The strong differences in the "workers" as well as the "white-collar" subgroups are a result of different categorization. The official SED statistics were generous in the way they counted members as workers, including, for example, people with office jobs such as "skilled worker for writing technology." The Western categories (which Infratest did not explain in detail) were different. Additionally, it is possible that East German workers hid their (possibly dutiful) party affiliation to Western visitors or the visitors simply did not pay attention to this question. The latter assumption corresponds with several validity tests made by Infratest that revealed that "apolitical" people with a low level of education (among both visitors and the GDR population) confined themselves largely to personal subjects, and therefore could generally provide only limited information about political issues.

Table 4.1. Demographic Structure of SED Members from Internal SED Statistics and the Infratest Sample (in Percentages)

	SED members: Party statistics		SED members: Infratest statistics	
	1970	1973	1970	1973
Total/Sample	1,909,859	1,950,784	84	107
Male	71.3	70.4	66	76
Female	28.7	29.6	34	24
Age				
Under 31 (Party statistics) / 30 (Infratest)	19.5	17.8	15	24
31 to 40 years / 30 to 39	25.5	25.4	19	29
41 to 50 years / 40 to 49	21.8	22.5	30	25
51 to 60 years / 50 to 59	12.7	13.9	25	14
Over 60 / 59 years	20.5	20.4	11	9
Secondary education (8 years)	–	–	26	34
Secondary education (10 years)	–	–	15	13
Higher education (without high school diploma)	–	–	5	9
Higher education (with high school diploma)	–	–	11	4
Vocational college	–	–	16	19
University degree	–	–	29	22

Sources: Infratest GDR program 1970, questions 25, 77, and 81; 1973, questions 19 and 85; Party Statistics: Analyse über die Entwicklung der Mitgliederbewegung der SED seit dem VII. Parteitag und im Jahre 1970, 10.3.1971 [Analysis of the development of party membership of the SED after the 7th party conference and in 1970, 10.3.1971]; Stiftung Archiv der Parteien und Massenorganisationen im Bundesarchiv (hereafter SAPMO BA) [Foundation Archive of the Parties and Mass Organizations in the Federal Archive], I IV 2/3/1725, Bl. 7–15; im Jahr 1974 (in 1974), 8.1.1975; SAPMO BA, I IV 2/3/2253, Bl.; 39f.

The Infratest surveys provide us with two reference groups for the analysis of the political attitudes among SED members (see table 4.3). The first is the contrasting group of non-SED members, the second is a compilation of all those "persons X" who were evaluated by the respondents to be full or at least partial "supporters" of the GDR system. The latter group was of course identical to the party members to some degree, but not completely: a number of "persons X" supported the SED system but were not party members, and, on the other hand, party

Table 4.2. Social Composition of SED Members (in Percentages)

Occupation (according to respective categorizations)	Party statistics		Infratest	
	1970	1973	1970	1973
White-collar employees / civil servants	13.2	12.4	–	–
Full-time functionaries	8.8	8.7	–	–
Intelligentsia	17.1	18.6	–	–
Total white-collar employees, functionaries, intelligentsia	39.1	39.9	64	58
Workers	36.9	36.8	14	11
Collective farmers/artisans	5.9	5.2	9	14
Self-employed/private craftsmen/tradesmen	0.6	0.5	1	3
Apprentices	–	–	0	2
Pensioners	14.1	14.0	1	7
Housewives	2.0	1.9	4	0
Students	1.5	2.0	8	5

Sources: See sources for table 4.1.

members did not always present themselves to their West German visitors as "supporters" of the Communist system.

On a scale of one to five—from unconditional support, gradual combinations of criticism and acceptance, up to total refusal—SED members presented a mixed profile (see table 4.3); while approximately 20 percent were evaluated as being "totally convinced of the justness of the regime," 30 to 40 percent had a positive attitude combined with some criticism. Another 30 percent—according to the impressions of the West German respondents—were not convinced of, but only *outwardly* accommodated to, the system. Moreover, in the 1973 wave, Infratest detected a share of 14 percent who had expressed strong criticism.

The attitudes of the SED members as shown above differ remarkably from the nonmembers in the East German population, who were mainly to be found in the group of "externally aligned." However, only 50 to 60 percent of SED members were attributed an attitude of general approval towards the regime. In addition, Infratest identified a significant proportion of SED members who were perceived by West Germans as merely externally aligned. Surprisingly, the number of people who were classified as full, or at least critical, "followers" of the GDR system was even larger among the general population than the number

Table 4.3. "Which of these political attitudes apply to person X?" (in percentages)

	Supporters of the GDR system		SED-members		Nonmembers	
	1970	1973	1970	1973	1970	1973
Absolute number of respondents	151	288	84	107	380	1141
Totally convinced by the regime	28	23	22	21	1	4
Generally positive towards the regime, but sometimes critical about some issues	72	77	43	30	12	17
Not convinced, but externally aligned	0	0	31	31	59	39
Rejects regime, strong criticism on government and political conditions	0	0	3	14	15	19
Indifferent towards the regime, not interested in politics	0	0	0	2	10	12
Don't know	0	0	1	2	3	10

Source: Infratest GDR program 1970, question 63; 1973, question 69.

of SED members. The pattern confirmed the western view of "Out-and-Outers" (*Hundertfünfzigprozentiger*) and opportunistic followers (*Mitläufer*) to a certain degree, while there was an extremely large middle group. This group did not obviously conform to the Western cliché of fanatical Communists, but—at least in talks with West Germans—combined loyalty with some criticism.

This pattern of a "mixed" composition of SED members who had a high political commitment and those whose membership was perceived as an instrumental adaptation is not entirely surprising. However, the detailed characterization of these attitudes in questions about the political setting is revealing. In the first exploration in 1969 Infratest stated, "According to our surveys, membership of the SED does not however necessarily lead to an image of absolute political integrity in the sense of driving SED policies. Despite their party badge, remarkably many SED members do not feel very well in their everyday lives, they complain about political pressure and a general feeling of insecurity."[13] In questions of political pressure, the values of SED members were relatively close to those of nonmembers. Among the latter, the feeling of pressure was relatively limited, at least insofar as West German analysts—with their image of totalitarian, all-encompassing repression—anticipated. One can speculate that SED members felt significantly less able to escape from party orders or internal discipline than nonmembers.

This general finding corresponded to the results that 41 percent of party members who complained about spending "too much time" on political events and meetings, compared to the rate of only around 20 percent among (the more convinced) "supporters" and (in that respect less burdened) nonmembers (see table 4.4).

Table 4.4. "Did X complain about spending too much time on political and societal events or did X express the view that the expenditure of time is acceptable?" (in percentages)

	Supporters	SED members	Nonmembers
Total (respondents only)	82	60	186
Too much time	20	41	23
Does not matter	78	58	82

Source: Infratest GDR program 1970, question 46.

Beyond the waste of time, between 30 and 43 percent of party members complained about political pressure (see table 4.5), obviously bearing in mind party orders or internal disciplinary issues, like "criticism and self-criticism." This share was only slightly lower than that of nonmembers. Even among "supporters" a certain percentage expressed concerns about such pressure.

Table 4.5. "Did X complain about political pressure, or did you have the impression that X did not feel under pressure?" (in percentages)

	Supporters		SED members			Nonmembers		
	1970	1973	1969	1970	1973	1969	1970	1973
Total	134	234	224	76	93	719	323	798
Complained about pressure	13	13	35	30	43	45	34	43
No complaints	87	87	65	70	57	55	65	57

Source: Infratest GDR program 1969, p. 16; 1970, question 50; 1973, question 67.

This pattern of a "mixed" composition of SED membership can be specified in two respects. First, the affiliation to the party can be seen as ambivalent even in the cases of a generally positive attitude towards the political system. The question regarding why "persons X" decided to join the SED or one of the mass organizations (see table 4.6) led Infratest to find that the rate was distributed relatively evenly among SED members who stated an "inner conviction" (33 percent), the incentives of "advantages" (28 percent), and the aim of preventing trouble (39 percent). Remarkably, even in the "supporter" group the rate of "instrumental" reasons was almost as high as "idealistic" reasons. Assumably, these people did not join the organization because of, but despite or independently from their regime-friendly political attitude.[14]

Table 4.6. "Did X occasionally mention the reasons why he/she joined mass organizations or the Party (SED, Free German Youth, trade union, Society for Sports and Technology, etc.)? Which ones?" (in percentages)

1970	Supporters	SED members	Nonmembers
Total	122	68	98
Inner conviction	51	33	17
Advantages	26	28	36
Prevention of trouble	23	39	17

Source: Infratest GDR program 1970, question 45.

Finally, Infratest respondents attributed to 33 percent of members the opinion that being a party member was the most important factor in professional success, while this rate was only 14 percent within the "supporter" group (see table 4.7).

Table 4.7. "Please tell me what X mentioned as the most important factors in professional success in the GDR" (in percentages, multiple answers possible)

	Supporters	SED members	Nonmembers
Total	143	–	–
Party membership	15	33	41
Intelligence, good expert knowledge	47	34	24
Job performance	24	20	15
Membership of mass organizations (Free German Youth, trade union, etc.)	8	13	16
Social background	7	7	8
Good connections	4	5	6

Source: Infratest GDR program 1970, question 41.

Beyond issues of organizational behavior, the Infratest data delivered a major modification of the true-believer/opportunist pattern by showing a differentiated variety of judgments on the qualities of the East German and West German systems in comparison (see table 4.8). Confirming the aforementioned images, a broad majority of 95 percent of party members (and even 71 percent of nonmembers) attributed "strong participation in political life" as a feature of the Communist system—obviously bearing in mind the high degree of ritualized participation in meetings, demonstrations, etc.

The other issues show, to some degree at least, similar trends for members and nonmembers. The education and health systems and the promotion of science and technology were seen as strong features of the GDR, while the supply of consumer goods, personal freedom, economic power, and even a fair distribution of income were attributed to the West German system.

The "hot" topics of social performance within the system, such as pensions, income equality, or future opportunities found that SED members were, on the whole, rather on the side of the general population than the ideologically loyal "followers," who seemed to identify with the interpretations of the party leadership.

Interestingly, the biggest differences between "supporters" and SED members were to be found to be more or less evenly distributed. For example, a slight majority of party members attributed the "prospect of better future living conditions" to West Germany (49 to 42 percent), while among "supporters," preferences were on the East German side (20 to 58 percent).

Without being able to discuss all the dimensions of the data here, these results show a high readiness and ability to show differentiated judgments in several practical fields of political and social competition between the two systems. Once again, party members can be found in an intermediate position between the reference groups of loyal supporters and nonmembers.

For a number of strongly contested features of the system, the results show a relatively even distribution within the SED membership. Additionally, general attitudes were not at all diametrically opposed to the nonmember population, but distributed in at least similar patterns.

In other words, Infratest could conclude that there were relatively diverse attitudes among SED members and that the proportion of combative, ideology-driven Communists was relatively low, not only within society generally, but also within the party itself. The duties of party life were primarily seen as a burden. These findings also had implications

Table 4.8. "Please tell me for each of these features if it is more a feature of the GDR system or the Federal Republic system" (selected features, 1973; in percentages)

Key: dark grey = GDR positive; light grey = approximately the same; white = FRG positive; n.d. = no difference

	Supporters			SED members			Nonmembers		
Total no. of responses[1]	288			107			1141		
	GDR	n.d.	FRG	GDR	n.d.	FRG	GDR	n.d.	FRG
Strong participation in political life	82	16	2	95	3	2	71	18	11
Appropriate provisions for health	75	16	9	72	16	12	50	26	23
Promotion of science and technology	81	16	2	71	18	11	60	20	20
Equal opportunities in education	81	12	7	67	20	13	56	21	23
Readiness to help each other	60	37	2	67	29	4	46	45	8
Appropriate prices	49	18	30	43	10	47	27	15	57
Chances for better living conditions in the future	58	20	20	42	9	49	25	21	53

Feature								
Proper working conditions	53	21	25	42	11	47	24	24	51
Economic security for citizens	53	19	24	40	20	40	23	21	55
Equal rights for all	50	19	27	38	19	43	16	19	62
Just income distribution	49	15	33	35	7	58	18	12	69
Wages appropriate to performance	38	16	43	26	7	67	12	12	75
Good pension schemes	30	12	57	24	8	68	11	11	78
Efficient economy	34	13	48	22	15	62	11	14	74
Protection against environmental damage	9	29	61	17	28	56	6	39	54
Personal freedom	21	26	52	15	19	67	4	7	88
Supply with consumer goods	4	13	80	7	7	86	2	4	93

[1.] Reduced totals for specific features.
Source: Infratest GDR program 1973, question 23.

for the design of future research; Infratest decided to no longer record party members separately in its regular program, but to differentiate primarily between the groupings of different attitudes, as they were expected to be more relevant in terms of system stability.

As already explained at the beginning, all these categorizations and findings are to be read as reflections of Western images about the role of party members and will at best provide us with rough indications on the internal conditions within the SED from a very specific perspective. Nevertheless these indications invite the possibility of being followed more closely in other sources, particularly insofar as they did not meet the outcomes anticipated by the pollsters.

Party Comrades in the View of the Stasi

In addition to the secret Western opinion polls, a second information channel is available that was designed to capture popular opinion on a macro level—that is, secret police reports made for the East German leadership. As in the case of the poll surveys, they require consideration of a number of preconditions in terms of issues and findings. They were designed for the purposes of system stabilization, which meant that on the one hand they pointed to the "hostile" potential of hazards to the consolidation of power, and at the same time had to indicate fields of political action where corrections might stabilize the existing order. These purposes shaped the way in which the officers in charge constructed their societal categories and communication about attitudes, moods, etc.[15] The intelligence officers involved did not do this from a position of neutral objectivity, but had (and usually *wanted*) to comply with the relevant principles of societal perception as defined by the party leadership. If they ignored or openly challenged the general patterns of legitimatizing Communist rule in their reports, they risked the possibility of finding themselves targets of party criticism. As an outcome of this particular mode of representation, the reports were shaped in a typical pattern. First, they regularly stated that the majority of the population and especially the "working class" agreed fully with the party line, while, second, they reported a more or less large number of specific statements as critical and defined minority groups as holding a "hostile" attitude.[16]

These intelligence reports (contrary to popular belief) do not usually depict what East Germans thought in private, but what they articulated in semipublic situations (at work, in the bar, in a shopping queue), where *Stasi* informers could pick it up, and are of interest insofar as they show what was (barely) regarded as permitted to be said in public at a given time.[17]

It goes without saying that party members were not a top priority in that respect, but were nonetheless important because of their role as buttresses of the system in everyday life and defenders of party rule in case of emergency. Thus their attitudes played a role in the reports when the *Stasi* collected reactions to current events that were important to party members (for example, speeches by Communist leaders) or if they registered signals that set this function in question.

SED members in general, or specific party cadre groups, were only mentioned in a handful of reports from the beginning in the late 1950s until the end of the 1970s (see table 4.9). However, these numbers rose visibly from 1980 onwards and exploded after 1985. In this last period, practically every single report directly mentioned the attitudes of party members.

Table 4.9. Number of Stasi Reports Mentioning Party Members or Specific Groups of Party Cadres, 1960–87

Year	1960–64	65–69	70–74	75–79	80–84	85–87
Total SED membership mentioned	6	4	7	3	15	39

Source: Personal calculations based on the corpus of reports on "reactions of the population."

In the reports up to 1980, SED members were considered relevant to the *Stasi* in two respects. First, they were frequently the only group within the East German population who showed an active interest in party congresses and Central Committee plenary sessions of the SED and CPSU, on which the *Stasi* had to report. Second, their main concern was to obtain a clear and "correct" official interpretation of events and resolutions in order to represent the party line in societal life. This interest also applied to political crises such as the Sino-Soviet Split or the Prague Spring.

Similar to the Infratest surveys, the *Stasi* reports did not show any differentiation in the 1960s and early 1970s. They presented the SED membership as a homogenous community of propagators of ideology—a community of suffering, however, in an environment of people who obtained their political views, and even the most basic information on events first and foremost from Western media. For instance, one report on the dismissal of Khrushchev in 1964 said,

> Several reports show that SED members . . . speak indignantly and are dissatisfied about the present announcements. They have repeatedly commented that, due to insufficient information, the enemy would impose his arguments on the party. Larger parts of the population would take up the propaganda line of the NATO broadcasters due to their interest in details. . . . (Some party members have even expressed the view that they were forced to listen to Western stations so as not to be caught off guard against such "arguments" and therefore be ill-prepared to confront with them in the workplace.) . . . In a number of cases a certain resignation can be observed among party members, which in their view was due to the fact that they had previously praised comrade Khrushchev as a model in discussions and lectures, but would probably now have to change their minds.[18]

In addition to this general desire for a clear political line, the *Stasi* reports showed party members as being particularly skeptical towards the party leadership's détente policy and its intensifying contact with the West. Comments stressed the risks of any further opening up of East German society to Western influence. The *Stasi* officers noted not least their own reservations in such reports. For instance, one report on the West German parliamentary elections in November 1972 reads as follows: "A number of arguments by progressive citizens of the GDR contain concerns about—as they see it—the current reluctance of the SED in the political-ideological dispute with the SPD [Social Democratic Party]. . . . The currently tolerated 'political lull' bears the risk that politically interested, but ideologically unsteady GDR citizens would be drawn to the path of 'democratic socialism.'"[19]

This perception of SED members as a relatively homogenous, potentially "left radical" counterpart of the party leadership was dissolved in the following years and gave room to a new kind of categorization in terms of concrete professional groups and more diversified role interpretations. The first and most important group was the economic cadres, at all levels, in the late 1970s. They were mostly shown as judging from the angle of their everyday struggle within the plan economy, distancing themselves from the desire for ideological clarity. According to one of the first such reports in 1978, these cadres circulated, and in some cases printed, several hundred copies of political jokes and humorous texts, "in which the economic policy of the SED and the economic development of the GDR were vilified and denigrated with irony and alleged satire. . . . The circulators and clients of these reproductions of the . . . texts were . . . mostly senior and middle-level executives from the state and economic administration, combines, enterprises and institutions, as well as other members of the scientific-technological intelligentsia—among them a considerable number of SED members."[20]

Even meetings of local mayors and trainings for the directors of local editorial offices of party newspapers were used to disseminate such texts—resulting in them being published by Western news magazines such as *Der Spiegel* or the *Der Stern*. During the debt crisis in 1982, this humorous distancing, which presumably was not a totally new phenomenon, turned into a wave of "resignation, pessimism and bafflement amongst executive cadres," according to the *Stasi* view. In the same period, the Ministerum für Staatssicherheit (MfS, or *Stasi*) came to a generalization of such moods for the societal base of the SED: "Party members and other progressive forces, among them members of the bloc parties, express their concerns that it is becoming more difficult to find convincing arguments related to questions of the economic and supply situation in talks at the workplace, with neighbors, or during leisure activities. Thereby the population has the impression that the party and state leadership is not informed about the real situation."[21] From as early as 1981—that is, before the emergence of Gorbachev and even Andropov—a classic "legitimatization" of articulating criticism in the Soviet Union was to make positive reference to the (perceived or real) greater openness.[22]

This change in perspective from the image of a homogenous, loyal body of party members to a plurality of attitudes and a critical distance to ideology as a source of orientation could not be directly correlated with the Infratest results. The data does, however, at least suggest that the *Stasi* started to focus on the party members who had primarily joined due to their professional obligations, or who related their loyalty to the practical advantages and achievements of the socialist system.

The Disintegration of the Ideological Elite: Journalists for More Openness in Media Politics

Among the party cadres, journalists from the SED newspapers and state electronic media were a second group who had begun to visibly distance themselves from the party line. Traditionally, the main task of these cadres was to communicate the partisan SED view of events within the country and around the world, and thereby strengthen the legitimacy of party rule. They were therefore a crucial professional group in the fields of "window dressing" and creating "the euphoria of success," as the population now frequently aired criticisms. In 1985/86, due to the *Stasi* reports, these groups began to redefine their own professional self-awareness by invoking Gorbachev's glasnost beyond the rules of being "collective organizers" and instruments of mass agitation. To quote one statement from January 1986,

> Particularly progressive citizens, including numerous journalists, students and parts of the journalism faculty section at the Karl Marx University in Leipzig, as well as employees from several departments of the Ministry of Foreign Affairs have made very critical comments on media policy. In particular they stressed the low level of information in news programs made by GDR television, mainly *Aktuelle Kamera* [the main news program]. Due to strictly confidential evidence, journalists from the capital (who work at the *Berliner Zeitung* [the local SED newspaper], *Neues Deutschland* [the central SED organ] the *Berliner Verlag* and for GDR radio and television) have expressed the opinion that the mass-media would distance themselves from the working people with such coverage, because the latter would not find their problems represented there.[23]

It goes without saying that such criticism was not made visible in the pages of newspapers or TV programs, but was voiced in a "hidden" (but conflict-laden) manner within editorial offices. The *Stasi* recognized similar attempts in at least some parts of the social sciences and even law faculties (which had traditionally been a stronghold of ideological conformity).[24] Although these activities took place more or less behind closed doors, these reports documented the departure of these scholars from roles as communicators of party rule. Furthermore, these were party members who could be mainly identified as representatives of the loyal-critical subgroup in the Infratest surveys. One can summarize the *Stasi* reports as identifying a reform intelligentsia who articulated their views under the roof of the ruling party. The importance of these "reformers" was also strengthened by the fact that its main aim was not to establish elaborate alternative theories (like the earlier Marxist dissidents), but to depict and analyze the virulent realities of social life. The *Stasi* thereby recorded that two key party groups present in society only reluctantly continued to follow their commitments to the rules of SED organizational culture such as party discipline and active representation of the party in society.

The "Progressive Forces" and the Fate of the SED

Hence, the question of crosscurrents within the membership has to be raised. The *Stasi* had indeed already mentioned such currents in nearly all of its situation reports from 1985 onwards under the striking, albeit blurred, term of "progressive forces." These forces were characterized, on the one hand, as advocates of a sharp dissociation from Soviet reform policy and from the West. On the other hand, however, the secret police could not help but state that there were pronounced signs of helplessness and bafflement within this milieu.

These "progressive forces" were mostly located in the field of ideological education, such as civics teachers, the full-time party apparatus itself, and the power-securing elites.[25] Party secretaries, for example, avoided dealing with the reform policy of the Soviet leadership in their propaganda work by confining themselves to the elucidation of Soviet foreign policy or Erich Honecker's welcoming address at the CPSU conferences. This denial annoyed SED members from both the academy of arts and the FDJ youth organization.[26]

The strongest bastions of such party-conservative positions were not unsurprisingly located within the armed forces (i.e., army, police, state security — though the latter was not openly mentioned). They showed themselves to be aghast at the revelations of the Soviet "discussion of errors," which would shake the "international reputation of the USSR" and would lead to an "increase in activities of hostile-negative forces."[27]

The most decisive event for this faction of SED members was the adoption of the joint paper between the West German Social Democrats and the SED on the "battle of ideologies and joint security" in 1987, in which the SED leadership accepted the goal of not stereotyping the enemy. As the *Stasi* reported, statements concerning this agreement included — "besides general support" — a "very differentiated variety of remarkable opinions . . . [and] notable positions, including doubts and skepticism about the sincerity and trustworthiness of the SPD as a partner to this agreement, reservations and ambiguities regarding certain statements in the document, and the resulting fears, questions and expectations."[28]

Older SED members, and functionaries in particular, implied their intentions to infiltrate the SPD and recalled their "bitter experience" of the labor movement with the Social Democrats.

> Demands for a reduction in images of the enemy laid down in the document provoked debates and questions that came mainly from officers of the armed forces, teachers, but also from employees of state institutions. Several expressions of opinion showed the stance that imperialism and all the forces that sustain this societal system should still be seen as the class enemy, even if they dismissed war as a solution of contradictions and tried to avoid war by all means. . . .
>
> A substantial number of members and SED candidates, including employees of state and economic administrations, scientists, teachers and other progressive forces, expressed their lack of understanding for the document's statements on the readiness for reform and the right of both societal systems to exist. These remarks were followed by apprehension about a "liberalization" with more "pluralism" in the GDR.[29]

As the *Stasi* stated with great concern, this progressive differentiation of party membership escalated in the following two years and culminated in a statement in September 1989 that the attitudes of SED members "hardly differ from non-party members."[30]

Some Conclusions

So what do these two very different sources tell us about the SED membership? The incomplete treatment and the specificities of surveys and secret police reports suggest the use of caution, but they—at least somewhat—invite educated guesses as to their meaning as well. During the most stable phase of GDR history in the 1960s and the first half of the 1970s, they provided the image of SED members as a functional base in society, which was nevertheless only partially identical to the minority of GDR citizens who actively identified with the system in terms of its ideological program. The Infratest data corresponds to the image of a hybrid composition in the sense of the "two bodies" of the party— that is, the logic of party affiliation, which was primarily based on two features: the functionality as a state party and a symbolic substructure of "worker" members outside of this sphere. Significant numbers of members (approximately half to two-thirds, according to Infratest, but these are rough estimates at best) did not differ in their pragmatic, but in fact rather pro-Western, attitude to the rest of the population. Hence, the disciplinary integration into the machinery of conformity in "party life" was more important to party members than issues of political belief. This resulted in the seemingly paradoxical yet characteristic result for the period of late socialism, that more party members than non-members felt themselves under political pressure, as they claimed to their West German friends and relatives. This concurs with *Stasi* reports from the early decades that show the public role of SED members as ideological guards, which means that externally they performed according to the rules of party discipline. Other roles, such as advocates of particular interests, were not articulated in *Stasi* reports at this stage.

Such findings also raise questions on the dynamics from the mid-1970s onwards. During this period, Infratest recognized that the number of loyal supporters of the SED regime was in decline, while the *Stasi* reports show a slow differentiation of attitudes, followed by the final landslide among party members concerning their support of the SED regime.

This dynamic comprises three interwoven levels that cannot be clearly separated. First, the inner attitudes of party members may have actually changed. Causes may have been generational or other structural shifts within the membership, or the worsening performance of SED policy. Second, the change could have taken place on the level of a "more public" articulation of previously existing attitudes. In this case, the change would indicate an erosion in terms of the pressure to conform to the organizational culture of the party. Third, it is conceivable that the actual change was carried out at the level of the rapporteurs themselves, as they dared (or felt obliged) to mention more critical statements made by formerly loyal supporters of the regime.

My assumption is that all three dimensions played a role in the process; as the Infratest surveys and much other evidence shows, and not least as theories of organizational sociology suggest, an institution of such scope and relevance as the SED could not be homogenous. The profiles of the various subgroups, however, were subject to social dynamics, such as positive incentives like upward mobility and sociopsychological guidance by the authoritarian-paternalistic societal frame, which decreased, while the "social costs" of representing the party in society increased. Thus, while the "hybrid" character of mass membership may have strengthened the SED's integrative power for decades, centrifugal forces finally overstretched the capacities of the militarized internal constitution and organizational culture.

The party as a uniform power bloc had been significantly more eroded before the existential crisis than was outwardly visible. The authoritarian party still kept up its pressure on members to publicly follow their roles as executors of party orders, informants on deviant behavior, etc., within a closed society. These roles visibly dissolved only with a considerable delay—a process that then accelerated rapidly during the last two years of GDR history, culminating in the sudden disintegration of autumn 1989. The party as a whole was certainly not the "uncivil society" of the GDR, but proved to be a relatively heterogeneous unit in regard to the attitudes of its members. This may be one reason for the only moderate success as a political force after the revolution compared to other postcommunist countries.

Finally, it can be considered to be an echo of the tension between sympathy for the GDR system and the repulsive party culture of the SED that its postcommunist successor, the Party of Democratic Socialism (PDS), was able to draw significant numbers of voters (of up to a quarter of votes), but had to deal with a small (and continually shrinking) member corpus of old functionaries and the remains of the "progressive forces." But that is another story.

Jens Gieseke is head of the research department "Communism and Society" at the Centre for Contemporary History in Potsdam, Germany.

His publications include (coeditor) *Handbuch der kommunistischen Geheimdienste in Osteuropa* (2008), (editor) *Staatssicherheit und Gesellschaft* (2007), (coeditor) *Die Geschichte der SED* (2011), (author) *The History of the Stasi: East German Secret Police 1945–1990* (2014, published in seven languages), and (coeditor) *The Silent Majority in Communist and Post-Communist States* (2016).

Notes

1. Sheila Fitzpatrick, *Tear off the Masks! Identity and Imposture in Twentieth-Century Russia* (Princeton, NJ, 2005); Jochen Hellbeck, *Revolution on My Mind: Writing a Diary under Stalin* (Cambridge, 2006); Stephan Kotkin, *Magnetic Mountain: Stalinism as a Civilization* (Berkeley, 1997).
2. M. Rainer Lepsius, "Die Institutionenordnung als Rahmenbedingung der Sozialgeschichte der DDR" [Institutional order as a general condition of the social history of the GDR], in *Sozialgeschichte der DDR* [Social history of the GDR], ed. H. Kaelble, J. Kocka, and H. Zwahr (Stuttgart, 1994), 17–30; Gary N. Marks, "Communist Party Membership in Five Former Soviet Bloc Countries, 1945–1989," *Communist and Post-Communist Studies* 37 (2004): 241–263; Sigrid Meuschel, *Legitimation und Parteiherrschaft. Zum Paradox von Stabilität und Revolution in der DDR 1945–1989* [Legitimacy and party rule. On the paradox of stability and revolution in the GDR 1945–1989] (Frankfurt/M., 1992); Raymond Sin-Kwok Wong, "The Social Composition of the Czechoslovak and Hungarian Communist Parties in the 1980s," *Social Forces* 75, no. 1 (1996): 61–90.
3. Stephan Kotkin and Jan Gross, *Uncivil Society: 1989 and the Implosion of the Communist Establishment* (New York, 2009).
4. For detailed data see the documentation of party statistics in: Florian Peters, *Arbeitermythos und Staatspartei. Zusammensetzung und Rekrutierung von Mitgliedschaft und Funktionärskörper (1961–1989)*, (forthcoming).
5. Ibid.
6. Compare Jens Gieseke, "Social Inequality in State Socialism: An Outline," *Zeithistorische Forschungen* 10 (2013): 2. Accessed 4 September 2017, http://www.zeithistorische-forschungen.de/2-2013/id=4493#en; Jens Gieseke and Ralf Jessen, "Die SED in der staatssozialistischen Gesellschaft" [The SED in the state socialist society] in *Die Geschichte der SED. Eine Bestandsaufnahme* [The history of the SED. Taking stock], ed. Jens Gieseke and Hermann Wentker (Berlin, 2011); Heike Solga, *Auf dem Wege in eine klassenlosen Gesellschaft? Klassenlagen und Mobilität zwischen Generationen in der DDR* [On the way to a classless society? Class positions and mobility between generations in the GDR] (Berlin, 1995).
7. Rüdiger Bergien, *Im "Generalstab der Partei": Organisationskultur und Herrschaftspraxis in der SED-Zentrale (1946–1989)* [In the "general staff of the party": Organizational culture and practice of rule in the center of the SED (1946–1989)] (Berlin, 2017); for the CPSU see Eugenia Belova and Valery

Lazarev, *Funding Loyalty: The Economics of the Communist Party* (New Haven, 2012).
8. Thomas H. Rigby, *Communist Party Membership in the U.S.S.R. 1917–1967* (Princeton, 1968), 325.
9. All data from the table "Degree of Organization and Party School Visits" in "SED District Organization, Brandenburg an der Havel, 7.1.1981," Brandenburgisches Landeshauptarchiv [Brandenburg State Archive] Rep. 531, Brbg. Nr. 1843. I thank Sabine Pannen for this document.
10. See the chapter by Sabine Pannen in this volume.
11. Alex Inkeles and Raymond Bauer, *The Soviet Citizen: Daily Life in a Totalitarian Society* (Cambridge, MA,1959); for an appraisal as a historical source, see Sheila Fitzpatrick, "Popular Opinion under Communist Regimes," in *Oxford Handbook of the History of Communism* (Oxford, 2014), 371–386; idem, "Popular Opinion in Russia under Pre-War Stalinism," in *Popular Opinion in Totalitarian Regimes*, ed. Paul Corner (Oxford, 2009), 17–32; Jens Gieseke, "Opinion Polling Behind and Across the Iron Curtain: How West and East German Pollsters Shaped Knowledge Regimes on Communist Societies," *History of the Human Sciences* 29, no. 4–5 (2016): 77–98.
12. Infratest GDR program 1969, 17.
13. Infratest GDR program 1969, 15.
14. For the sake of precision it has to be mentioned here that the reasons may have differed for the respective organizations, such as the Society for Sports and Technology, for example.
15. For a theoretical assessment of secret police reports as a historical source, see P. Holquist, "'Information is the Alpha and the Omega of our Work': Bolshevik Surveillance in its Pan-European Context," *Journal of Modern History* 69 no. 3 (1997): 415–450.
16. Martin Dimitrov, ed., *Why Communism Did Not Collapse: Understanding Authoritarian Regime Resilience in Asia and Europe* (Cambridge, 2013). Fitzpatrick, *Popular Opinion*; P. Holquist, *Information*.
17. For a general account on *Stasi* reports, see Jens Gieseke, "Annäherungen und Fragen an die 'Meldungen aus der Republik'" [Approaches and questions to the "reports from the republic"), in *Staatssicherheit und Gesellschaft. Studien zum Herrschaftsalltag in der DDR* [State security and society. Studies on everyday rule in the GDR), ed. Jens Gieseke (Göttingen, 2007), 79–98; idem, "Bevölkerungsstimmungen in der geschlossenen Gesellschaft. MfS-Berichte an die DDR-Führung in den 60er und 70er Jahren" [Public opinion in the closed society. MfS reports to the GDR leadership in the 1960s and 1970s), *Zeithistorische Forschungen* 5, no. 2 (2008): 236–257. Accessed 4 September 2017, http://www.zeithistorische-forschungen.de/16126041-Gieseke-2-2008.
18. Ministerum für Staatssicherheit (hereafter MfS), "Information Nr. 933/64, 3. Inf. über Reaktion zur Ablösung Chruschtschows" [Information about reactions to the replacement of Khrushchev], 22.10.64, BStU (Federal Commissioner for the Stasi Records), MfS, ZAIG 957, 21.
19. MfS, "Information Nr. 1100/72, "Reaktion der Bevölkerung der DDR zur Politik Brandt/Scheel-Regierung im Zusammenhang mit dem Ergebnis der Bundestagswahl vom 19.11.1972" [GDR people's reactions to the policies

of the Brandt/Scheel government in West Germany to the West German elections from 19.11.1972], BStU, ZA, ZAIG 2095, 14 (quotation marks in the original document).
20. MfS, "Information über Vervielfältigung und Verbreitung die gesellschaftlichen Verhältnisse in der DDR diskriminierender Texte" [Information on copying and publishing of texts that discriminate against the social conditions in the GDR], 21.12.1978, BStU, ZA, ZAIG 4131, 4; see "DDR: Leere Regale vor Weihnachten" [Empty shelves before Christmas], *Der Spiegel* 51/1978, 18 December 1978.
21. MfS, "Hinweise über weitere aktuelle Gesichtspunkte der Reaktion der Bevölkerung der DDR im Zusammenhang mit Problemen der Volkswirtschaft und der Versorgung" [Comments about further current aspects of the people's reactions to problems of the GDR national economy and provisions], 6.9.1982, BStU, ZA, ZAIG 4165, 26f.
22. MfS, "Erste Hinweise über Reaktionen der Bevölkerung der DDR zu den veröffentlichten Materialien der 13. Tagung des ZK der SED" [First indications on the people's reaction to information from the 13th meeting of the SED Central Committee], 17.12.1980, BStU, ZA ZAIG 4154, 2–7; MfS, "Weitere Hinweise zur Reaktion der Bevölkerung der DDR zum XXVI. Parteitag der KPdSU" [Further information about the people's reactions to the 26th CPSU conference], 9.3.1981, BStU, ZA, ZAIG 4155, 11–16.
23. MfS, "Hinweise über beachtenswerte Reaktionen zur Medienpolitik der DDR" [Information about relevant reactions to the GDR media policy], 13.1.1986, BStU, ZA ZAIG 4202, 2, 4.
24. MfS, "Beachtenswerte Hinweise über Reaktionen der Bevölkerung der DDR auf die Entscheidung der sowjetischen Führung, dem Ersuchen Sacharows auf Rückkehr nach Moskau stattzugeben" [Notable points on the people's reactions on the Soviet leadership's decision to allow Sacharov to move back to Moscow], 13.1.1987, BStU, ZA, ZAIG 4215, 2–6; MfS, "Erste Hinweise über Reaktionen der Bevölkerung auf das Plenum des ZK der KPdSU" [First indications on the people's reactions to the plenum of the CPSU Central Committee], 3.2.1987, BStU, ZA, ZAIG 4217, 2–15.
25. MfS, "Hinweise auf beachtenswerte Reaktionen der Bevölkerung der DDR im Zusammenhang mit der Vorbereitung des XI. Parteitages der SED" [Indications on the notable people's reactions to the preparations of the 11th SED Party Conference], 11.10.1985, BStU, ZA, ZAIG 4199, 8f.
26. MfS, "Weitere Hinweise über beachtenswerte Reaktionen der Bevölkerung der DDR in Vorbereitung auf den XI. Parteitag der SED" [Further indications on the relevant people's reactions to the preparations of the 11th SED Party Conference], 14.4.1986, BStU, ZA, ZAIG 4199, 19.
27. MfS, "Erste Hinweise über Reaktionen der Bevölkerung auf das Plenum des ZK der KPdSU" [First indications on the people's reactions to the CPSU Central Committee plenum], 3.2.1987, BStU, ZA, ZAIG 4217, 5.
28. Ibid.
29. MfS, "Hinweise über beachtenswerte Aspekte aus der Reaktion der Bevölkerung auf das von der SED und der SPD gemeinsam erarbeitete Dokument 'Der Streit der Ideologien und die gemeinsame Sicherheit'" [Indications on relevant aspects of the people's reactions to the SED and SPD joint docu-

ment "The dispute of ideologies and joint security"], 24.9.1987, BStU, ZA, ZAIG 4230, 3 and 6.
30. MfS, "Hinweise auf beachtenswerte Reaktionen von Mitgliedern und Funktionären der SED zu einigen Aspekten der Lage in der DDR und zum innerparteilichen Leben" [Indications to relevant reactions of members and functionaries of the SED on aspects of the situation of GDR and party life], 11.9.1989, printed in Arnim Mitter and Stefan Wolle, eds., *Ich liebe Euch doch alle. Befehle und Lageberichte des Ministeriums für Staatssicherheit Januar bis November 1989* [I love you all! Orders and reports of the ministry for state security from January to December 1989] (Berlin, 1990), 148–150.

Bibliography

Belova, Eugenia, and Valery Lazarev. *Funding Loyalty: The Economics of the Communist Party.* New Haven: Yale University Press, 2012.

Bergien, Rüdiger. *Im "Generalstab der Partei." Organisationskultur und Herrschaftspraxis in der SED-Zentrale (1946–1989)* [In the "general staff of the party." Organizational culture and practice of rule in the center of the SED]. Berlin: Christoph Links Verlag, 2017.

Dimitrov, Martin, ed., *Why Communism Did Not Collapse: Understanding Authoritarian Regime Resilience in Asia and Europe.* Cambridge: Cambridge University Press, 2013.

Fitzpatrick, Sheila. "Popular Opinion in Russia under Pre-War Stalinism." In *Popular Opinion in Totalitarian Regimes,* ed. Paul Corner, 17–32. Oxford: Oxford University Press, 2009.

———. "Popular Opinion under Communist Regimes." In *Oxford Handbook of the History of Communism,* ed. Stephen A. Smith, 371–386. Oxford: Oxford University Press, 2014.

———. *Tear Off the Masks! Identity and Imposture in Twentieth-Century Russia.* Princeton: Princeton University Press, 2005.

Gieseke, Jens. "Annäherungen und Fragen an die 'Meldungen aus der Republik'" [Approaches and questions to the "reports from the republic"]. In *Staatssicherheit und Gesellschaft. Studien zum Herrschaftsalltag in der DDR* [State security and society. Studies on everyday rule in the GDR], ed. J. Gieseke, 79–98. Göttingen: Vandenhoeck & Ruprecht, 2007.

———. "Bevölkerungsstimmungen in der geschlossenen Gesellschaft. MfS-Berichte an die DDR-Führung in den 1960er- und 1970er-Jahren" [Popular opinion in the closed society. MFS reports to the GDR leadership in the 1960s and 1970s]. *Zeithistorische Forschungen* (Studies in contemporary history), Online edition 5, no. 2 (2008): 236–237, http://www.zeithistorische-forschungen.de/2-2008/id=4491. Accessed 4 September 2017.

———. "Opinion Polling Behind and Across the Iron Curtain: How West and East German Pollsters Shaped Knowledge Regimes in Communist Societies." *History of the Human Sciences* 29, no. 4–5 (October/December 2016): 77–98.

———. "Social Inequality in State Socialism: An Outline." *Zeithistorische Forschungen* 10, no. 2 (2013): 171–198, http://www.zeithistorische-forschungen .de/2-2013/id=4493#en. Accessed 4 September 2017.

Gieseke, Jens, and Ralph Jessen. "Die SED in der staatssozialistischen Gesellschaft" [The SED in the state socialist society]. In *Die Geschichte der SED. Eine Bestandsaufnahme* [The history of the SED. Taking stock], ed. Jens Gieseke and Hermann Wentker, 16–60. Berlin: Metropol Verlag, 2011.

Hellbeck, Jochen. *Revolution on My Mind: Writing a Diary under Stalin.* London: Harvard University Press, 2009.

Holquist, Peter. "'Information is the Alpha and the Omega of our Work': Bolshevik Surveillance in its Pan-European Context." *Journal of Modern History* 69, no. 3 (1997): 415–450.

Inkeles, Alex, and Raymond Bauer. *The Soviet Citizen: Daily Life in a Totalitarian Society.* Cambridge, MA: Harvard University Press, 1959.

Kotkin, Stephen. *Magnetic Mountain: Stalinism as a Civilization.* Berkeley: University of California Press, 1997.

Kotkin, Stephen, and Jan Gross. *Uncivil Society: 1989 and the Implosion of the Communist Establishment.* New York: Modern Library, 2009.

"Leere Regale vor Weihnachten" [Empty shelves before Christmas]. *Der Spiegel* 51/1978, 18 December 1978. Accessed 4 September 2017, http://www.spiegel .de/spiegel/print/d-40605950.html.

Lepsius, M. Rainer. "Die Institutionenordnung als Rahmenbedingung der Sozialgeschichte der DDR" [The institutional order as a general condition of the social history of the GDR]. In *Sozialgeschichte der DDR* [Social history of the GDR], ed. H. Kaelble, J. Kocka, and H. Zwahr, 17–30. Stuttgart: Klett-Cotta, 1994.

Marks, Gary N. "Communist Party Membership in Five Former Soviet Bloc Countries, 1945–1989." *Communist and Post-Communist Studies* 37 (2004): 241–263.

Meuschel, Sigrid. *Legitimation und Parteiherrschaft. Zum Paradox von Stabilität und Revolution in der DDR 1945–1989* [Legitimacy and party rule. On the paradox of stability and revolution in the GDR 1945–1989]. Frankfurt/M.: Suhrkamp, 1992.

Mitter, Armin, and Stefan Wolle, eds. *Ich liebe Euch doch alle. Befehle und Lageberichte des Ministeriums für Staatssicherheit Januar bis November 1989* [I love you all! Orders and reports of the ministry for state security from January to December of 1989]. Berlin: BasisDruck, 1990.

Peters, Florian, *Arbeitermythos und Staatspartei. Zusammensetzung und Rekrutierung von Mitgliedschaft und Funktionärskörper (1961–1989)*, (forthcoming).

Rigby, Thomas H. *Communist Party Membership in the U.S.S.R. 1917–1967.* Princeton: Princeton University Press, 1968.

Sin-Kwok Wong, Raymond. "The Social Composition of the Czechoslovak and Hungarian Communist Parties in the 1980s." *Social Forces* 75, no. 1 (1996): 61–90.

Solga, Heike. *Auf dem Wege in eine klassenlose Gesellschaft? Klassenlagen und Mobilität zwischen Generationen in der DDR* [On the way to a classless society? Class positions and mobility between generations in the GDR]. Berlin: Akademie Verlag, 1995.

 5

On the Way to Party Pluralism?
The PZPR and the Reform of the Socialist Party System in 1988–1989

Frédéric Zalewski

This essay deals with the political reforms carried out by the Polish communist party—the Polish United Worker's Party (*Polska Zjednoczona Partia Robotnicza*, or PZPR)—from 1986 to 1989, with a special emphasis on the years 1988 to 1989. Its main thesis is that the instigators of the reforms wanted first to radically reform the political order of state socialism and reshape its legitimacy through the rejection of the Stalinist state model. The reforms were also the starting point of when the party agreed to start official talks with the democratic forces of *Solidarność* (solidarity). It could be described as the Polish version of perestroika, and the Polish word *Przedubowa*, whose meaning is very close (i.e., reconstruction or restructure), was sometimes used as an equivalent in some political and ideological texts of this period. This set of policies is very well known to specialists of history or political science, but more so by its output (the roundtable talks with *Solidarność* and the "democratic transition" that began in June 1989), and its inputs (the collapse of the regime in 1980 and the failure of the earliest reforms from 1986 to 1988). This essay proposes a study of these reforms, and focuses on the analysis of the political rationality of the whole plan of the political opening up of the communist regime, in which the question of pluralism was an important but delicate concern.

The first approximation of our topic is that these political reforms tried to establish a new ideological beginning for the communist regime and had to produce a new base of legitimacy for the party. In that sense, political actors, who were the main organizers of this new policy, must be regarded as involved in a process that had to succeed despite the high level of uncertainty. This position is of course an analytical position, and not a political assessment on the quality of this political program. Indeed, we cannot assume a teleological point of view in which the whole process is analyzed according to one issue—that is, the final collapse of state socialism—which seems obvious today, but which was highly improbable for all actors, including the opposition leaders, such as Bronislaw Geremek or Adam Michnik, for example. The literature seems reluctant to attribute all the implications of this remark, in my opinion, because of the influence of the totalitarian approach of state socialism. In a way, it is not "politically correct" to suggest that these reforms had the potential to radically reform the regime, and that history could have an issue other than the collapse of communism. Moreover, the main historical evidence of this aspect of political reforms was an intense ideological production in various arenas of the party—such as conferences and meetings of the Central Committee sections, for example—or in the party's publications, such as the theoretical monthly journal *Nowe Drogi*. Yet, this ideological production is tacitly regarded as a manifestation of an "Orwellian Newspeak," as a mass manipulation that turned into empty words when the ideology of communism was lost. Consequently, most authors, especially Polish historians, focus on the strategic choices of the party leaders, referring mainly to General Jaruzelski and his close political entourage, such as General Kiszczak. Methodologically, it implies basing the analytical work on the huge amount of material in party archives of this period and establishing the individual political preferences of the actors during this process.[1] This essay does not intend to deny that this approach was a very important and necessary step in understanding the issue of the party strategy in the years 1988 to 1989. However, this process must be seen as a sort of "daily monitoring" of all the reforms in which General Jaruzelski made all the strategic decisions, but which does not describe the political and ideological framework of this Polish version of perestroika.[2] This topic is more often viewed as a second-order concern, and this leads to misunderstandings. For example, the Polish historian Paweł Kowal, in his significant study of the years of 1986–89, remarks on an ideological conference in May 1989: "On the basis of a rational political practice, it is really difficult to explain why such attention was accorded to these less important issues than the electoral struggle."[3] However, a few lines later, he quotes one of the party leaders, the prime minister Mieczysław Rakowski, who later said of this conference, "The local first secretaries did good work. The delegate's speeches were critical toward the (party) direction, but there was no demagogy."[4] In other words, this device (after Foucault)[5] had to produce some mobilization in the party apparatus and to standardize the political analysis of the new political course at the lower levels of the party. The proximity of the elections could, on the contrary, be regarded as an important indicator of the relevance of this work to the actors. To be clear, my aim is not to suggest that the ideological texts produced then were the source of the reforms, but to underline that ideology was an important issue for the party leaders. Moreover, there is no doubt that this ideological framework was highly speculative and incomplete—as one of the party leaders, Marian Orzechowski, said, the main goal was to establish a "minimum ideological order" as a background to further political transformations.[6]

Nevertheless, it is important to study the different aspects of political transformation that took place in Poland from 1988 to 1989. The first set of hypotheses are, among other ideas, that perestroika and its local variations were a political move to restore the party leadership in society through the democratization of State socialism and the examination of the Leninist principles of state rule. Despite the global collapse of communism provoked by the different national crises and their alignments,[7] the reformers started the process of designing a new regime.[8] The institutional and political setup of this policy tended to create some possibilities for formalization and the expression of social interests because those who conceived of these reforms identified this evolution as a condition for the economic transformation, which was also the initial concern not only of Mikhail Gorbachev, but also of Polish party leaders. The Polish Round Table Agreement talks of February to April 1989 between the party and the opposition in Poland were a desperate move to save the regime in the face of social unrest, as well as an attempt toward a deeper transformation of the concept of state rule by the party. In brief, the main theoretical direction here is to consider not the political regimes and their classification, but the political order and its transformations.[9] This way of questioning this political process allows new directions to emerge in understanding the latest period of communism in Poland. One of these is the question of an emerging pluralism. In previous research I showed that the official peasants' party, the United People's Party (*Zjednoczone Stronnictwo Ludowe*, or ZSL), took advantage of this context to question its ability to be a representative political party in a future "democratic socialism."[10] This chapter aims to expand this topic and study the political setup of the formalization of interests and emerging pluralism.

This approach must be compared and cross-analyzed with a set of questions about the various trends of de-Stalinization. Despite the fact that this notion is more a political tool than a scientific concept, it can be used to understand how it was defined by political actors, for what purposes, and what content they gave to this idea—often in competition with other actors who wanted to impose their own definition. The context of political reforms in Poland in 1989–1989 was characterized by the emergence of a political norm defining the previous stage of state communism as Stalinist or influenced by relics of Stalinism. In this way, the party drew the outlines of a new interpretation of the communist regime in Poland, which had democratic trends, according to this interpretation, between 1944 and 1948, but only became a Stalinist dictatorship after 1949. If the "people's democracy" of the 1944 to 1948 period could become a new reference for the regime and the party, it implies, however, a deep redefinition of the process of mobilization and the distribution of resources in the party rank and file. In January 1989, the resolutions of the Tenth Plenum of the Central Committee gave special attention to this matter and started a stage of political and administrative work in the party in order to organize a new congress.[11] This process was of course inconclusive, but the analysis of its concrete forms shows that the party leadership was under pressure because of the frustrations and various expectations of party members, who started to be de facto its only real constituency. Furthermore, this process shows that the 1988–89 party crisis was a new occurrence of the communist organization's inability to move beyond the Stalinist model, in a long history of de-Stalinization that started in 1956.[12] Moreover, this period is characterized by a specific tension for party members between loyalty to the party identity and rejection of its centralization.

This essay explores these topics by describing the political implications of the political reforms of 1988 to 1989 in terms of pluralism in two complementary directions: first, the process of new "institutional design" on the scale of the global political order of state socialism in Poland; and second, the question of de-Stalinization within the party apparatus and rank and file, especially in June and July 1989—that is, after the electoral disaster of the coalition between the party and its allies. Analysis will be based on the answers of the grassroots party members to a questionnaire published by the daily newspaper *Trybuna Ludu* in July 1989. The results of my previous research will be used for a comparison with the ZSL, which was involved in the same process of transformation as the Communist Party and had undertaken research with its members in a detailed questionnaire a few weeks earlier. This essay should be seen as a work in progress; it presents the first results of research started in 2012 and is therefore partially inconclusive, and its empirical bases are still narrow.

Did the Polish Reforms Include Party Pluralism?

Between 1986 and 1988, the PZPR attempted to introduce some pluralistic rules in the official political sphere. For example, in 1986 a consultative council (*Rada Konsultacyjna*) was created with fifty-six so-called independent members. This group of news institutions was *supposed* to be "legitimacy catchers," as Georges Mink[13] so rightly said. Indeed, this first version of pluralism had very little in common with democratic pluralism.[14] It was a limited pluralism whereby the highly centralized rules of state socialism remained intact.[15] In short, the party leaders wanted to employ a kind of institutional diversification, without any supportive mobilization for pluralism in "civil society."

This new politics must also be related to the evolution of the PZPR itself from 1980. Of course, it's difficult to stress all the transformations this organization underwent in a few words, mostly because on the one hand it was deeply devitalized after the "Polish revolution" in 1980 and after the coup under General Jaruzelski in December 1981, while on the other hand it remained one of the most important mass organizations of the regime, and still had to fulfill the political and ideological functions of leading state socialism. The main effect of the 1980 crisis was the drastic fall in numbers of members (see table 5.1).[16] As Andrzej Friszke noticed, the percentage of industrial workers fell from 46 to 42 percent between 1980 to 1981; workers made up two-thirds of the members who resigned from membership of their own volition. Moreover, the PZPR membership was no longer attractive to the younger generation; 47.6 percent of people who resigned their membership between 1980 and 1981 had joined the party between 1972 and 1979.[17] Between 1988 and 1989, the ability of the party to recruit younger members was viewed as a crucial issue, but, as observed by Georges Mink, it was already a priority in 1982, just after the introduction of the martial law, because one-third of all members were already in retirement in 1980.[18] Furthermore, the PZPR conducted a classical—in terms of Soviet political norms—process of "normalization" through purges, particularly among its own bureaucracy. The long-term process of bureaucratization of the party reached its highest level during the leadership of Edward Gierek in the 1970s, and this evolution was then stigmatized in official rhetoric as passivity and opportunism from the rank-and-file members.

Table 5.1. Total Number of Party Members (in Thousands)

Year	1970	1980	1984	1985	1986	1987
Members	2,320	3,091.9	2,117.3	2,115.4	2,129	2,149.3
Applicants	189.2	291.6	57.9	104.5	1,335	156.8

Source: Georges Mink, *La Force ou la raison. Histoire sociale et politique de la Pologne (1980–1989)* [Force or reason. Political and social history of Poland (1980–1989)] (Paris, 1989), 163.

Of course, such a process of purges reveals that the PZPR faced a deep crisis in their party model, which remained the Stalinist version of the Leninist vanguard party, despite the fact that the function of political representation of the working class was de facto transferred to *Solidarność*, the independent trade union. Moreover, Soviet rule prevented all tentative transformation and did not allow any deviation from the previous Stalinist model. In a very interesting remark, the Polish sociologist Jadwiga Staniszkis noted that the preparatory work for the Ninth Congress, which took place in July 1981, excluded three possible new orientations for the PZPR because each of them were viewed as "a step backwards in the direction of socialism." The first was a kind of socialist catch-all party, with social integration functions, and with a withdrawal of its ideological leadership. The second was the exact opposite—that is, a return to the Leninist model of the vanguard party. The third option was the rediscovery of the socialist traditions of the PZPR through promoting the legacy of the PPS (*Polska Partia Socjalistyczna* / Polish Socialist Party), which was absorbed into the PPR (*Polska Partia Robotnicza* / Polish Workers Party) in 1948.[19] Interestingly, all three directions were rejected again after 1986. It could be suggested that this document proved that the PZPR leadership was aware of the tensions between liberalization trends and a possible conservative backlash, especially after the emergence of new transversal links. For example, some "horizontal structures" (*Struktury poziome*) emerged in 1980–81, which wanted to claim more democracy inside the party and ideological references to the West European social democratic parties.

Debates about the party model were frozen from 1982 to 1986 as a consequence of martial law; the main development during this period was mainly concerned with the PZPR leadership. The collegial form of leadership in the politburo did not disappear, but it took on new forms. The first secretary, General Jaruzelski, progressively eliminated all of his opponents, such as the prominent leader of the conservative wing, Stefan Olszowski, and transferred power to the close circle of his entourage, in less or more formal arenas, without any specific support from the lower levels of the party organization. In fact in the 1980s, all of the PZPR leadership moved toward a more personalized politics and political style. Leaders such as Mieczysław Rakowski, for instance, were not only public figures, but also had their own political views on the future of the regime. Following the interpretation of Ken Jowitt, one could suspect a charisma transfer from the PZPR to its various leaders,[20] and many authors have underlined that one of the central pieces of the political reforms in 1989 was to give General Jaruzelski the responsibility of securing the PZPR position by becoming president. Moreover, the regime developed its use of opinion polls from the early 1980s, and these showed the increasing popularity of General Jaruzelski at the end of the decade.[21]

The failure of the institutional diversification strategy became obvious when the 1987 referendum on reforms failed and when new strikes among young workers took place in 1988. The party leaders then made the decision to negotiate with *Solidarność*, and the Tenth Plenum of the Central Committee (December 1989 to January 1990) formalized this strategy. This decision opened the way to the roundtable talks and consequently to the 1989 general elections, but it was also an ideological step toward a broader definition of pluralism. Indeed, the resolutions from the plenum accepted pluralism as an important direction for the future of the regime. However, the actual meaning of this "pluralism" was still vague. The resolutions said, "The PZPR recognizes the need for a pluralism of interests and aspirations, and the enlargement of a coalition in state government by giving a role to the opposition."[22]

The gradual introduction of the concept of pluralism in official politics was both a pragmatic adjustment to the change of an uncertain political situation as well as a label for various institutional or political experiments, which were not always consistent or fully conceptualized. As a label, it was a convenient concept for negotiations with opposition and for the legalization of *Solidarność*, which the plenum resolutions presented as trade union pluralism. As a broader frameworking process it was vague, but provided context for the new motto of "socialist parliamentary democracy" that the PZPR presented as a perspective for the regime. In this way, this concept or label could therefore be analyzed as an arrangement—that is, a temporary solution that prevented disorder and informed the various protagonists about the meaning and direction of action.[23]

The reference to pluralism was therefore not an ideological jump to the pluralistic understanding of democracy according to the liberal ideology of a democratic regime. The word pluralism was applied to "social life," to a "representation of interests," and aimed to show that the party intended to plan a less centralized political order, with a renewed set of organizations that could go deeper into society than the prior institutional novelties of the 1986–1988 period. In other words, this pluralism was disconnected from the question of the party system, which did not itself change in the short term. The plenum resolutions stated that the governing coalition must be grounded in the PZPR, the "allied parties," meaning the ZSL and the Democratic Party (*Stronnictwo Demokratyczny*). In January 1989, the party reformers were still very careful about political parties and did not want to radically change the model established in 1949 whereby, based on ideas in Leninist theory, the "allied parties" were de facto "transmission belts" to mobilize the constituencies that the party gave them—that is, the peasantry (ZSL) and the intellectuals and independent workers (SD).

Furthermore, this new policy must also be considered by the limitations caused by its strategy. As many authors have already pointed out, the ZSL and the SD saw all this political opening as an opportunity to claim more weight in the state government, but also (and maybe mainly) as a threat that the center of the regime's political partnership would go in the direction of a PZPR/*Solidarność* partnership and power-sharing.[24] In this context, the Tenth Plenum's resolutions reflected the concern of the party leadership in securing the "old" coalition with the PZPR as the main player.

However, these growing references to pluralism were an emerging norm for political actors.[25] As the case of the ZSL shows, actors developed more adaptive strategies because they anticipated new constraints and roles for themselves in the future political order. If in the years between 1981 and 1984 this party was mainly engaged in a process of formalization of its own "invented traditions,"[26] 1988 was a moment of connecting this process with a broader challenge about its constituency, its representative functions in the political system, and what it had to offer politically. As the ZSL only had restricted political functions and was limited in its implementation to a single status group, this political reflection gradually moved far away from its "transmission belt" function assigned by the existing model of the party system. At the end of 1988, *Wieś Współczesna*, the ZSL theoretical monthly journal, published a series of articles in answer to the question "Does the peasants' political movement need a revival?," for example. Last but not least, the ZSL tended to adopt the word *partia* (party), which was explicitly linked with the political functions of the pluralistic parties in these theoretical essays, instead of the Slavic equivalent *stronnictwo*.[27] The ZSL strategy was obviously congruent with the main objectives of the PZPR and aligned itself with them to a certain extent, but the point is that this internal work was quite effective and early compared to the same process within the PZPR. As an additional argument, it could be said that the ZSL then had a competitive interaction with various "independent" peasant organizations that the PZPR did not have. In other words, pluralism gradually became a salient issue for the main actors, challenging the subordinated party system of Polish state socialism.

In brief, the Polish reforms included some formal references to a limited pluralism, a starting point from which to look for a new basis of legitimacy for state socialism. This pluralism was still under-theorized when the political and parliamentary crisis of July to August 1989 took place, when *Solidarność* refused to support a government led by the PZPR. Furthermore the framing of the situation was changing and the various interpretations by the political actors in regard to this concept reflected this uncertainty. Nevertheless, the situation forced the various ideologists of the official political sphere to formalize the representative functions of political parties, and many texts referred explicitly to categorizations as "aggregation of interest" or "political representation" — that is, to a liberal set of ideas. Party pluralism as a normative reference was a kind of by-product of those reforms, to some extent.

Political Reforms as an Institutional Device

It is quite difficult to analyze the political reforms of 1986 to 1989 through only their political content. Instead, I propose the hypothesis that their meaning is to a large extent connected to the set of institutional forms and discourses they constitute. Indeed, this institutional device shows that political and administrative practices, despite the declarative intentions of the party officials, were still appropriate to the Stalinist state model and politics.

As many authors have already pointed out, many actors were embodied in the political framing of the reforms. General Jaruzelski had his own advisers, such as Wiesław Górnicki; some of the party's authorities created informal groups of experts or developed their personal view of the political trends of state socialism (such as the prime minister, Mieczysław Rakowski, who stated that socialism as a state and international system was in a deep crisis).[28] Moreover, the "classical" places for ideological work, such as ideological journals, newspapers, etc., have also been occupied by many authors who started to publish various essays and analyses on reforms. In 1987, the official Central Committee monthly journal *Nowe Drogi* started to publish political evaluations of the situation and the reforms, for example.[29] These various activities were initially only partially connected to each other, but their "weak ties" gave a global meaning to the reforms.[30] From 1988, the party leaders tried to make the political content of the reforms more homogenous, and one way in which to do this was to encapsulate these ideological activities in a united body of fewer, or more formal, institutions.

The starting point of this process was the Sixth Plenum of the Central Committee in November 1987. Still under the careful label of "socialist revival" (*socjalistyczna odnowa*), the plenum planned a new ideological conference: the Third Theoretical Ideological National Conference

(*Ogólnopolska Konferencja Teoretyczno-Ideologiczna—OKTI*), whose goal was, in accordance with the plenum's decisions, to question the "core issues of the socialist revival."[31] The ideological process then became more centralized and the party began to create some institutional arenas and political literature around the conference preparation. A special group (*zespół*) was created in order to prepare the conference, in coordination with the permanent Central Committee's Ideological Commission, which prepared the substantive issues of the process. On 8 June 1988, these commissions organized an internal working meeting about "socialist pluralism and national agreement." This meeting then contributed to the formalization of the concept of "socialist pluralism," in an exposé by Janusz Reykowski.[32] During this mobilization process, the party's (and more specifically Central Committee's) official publications (mainly *Nowe Drogi*), as part of the "propaganda apparatus" published large extracts of the exposés and also, as before, individual contributions. The Third OKTI took place in January 1989, after the Tenth Plenum, and was the basis of the gradual diffusion of the new ideological trend in the party's organization and administration. A few months later, in May 1989, the National Delegates Conference was organized, for example. Last but not least, these ideological activities were gradually connected to more organizational work—as the delegates' conference shows. The Central Committee's officials attempted to identify and co-opt young and dynamic middle managers, such as Zygmunt Czarzasty, for example, who saw his career boosted by its integration into the political organization of the reforms.[33] Zygmunt Czarzasty, who was born in 1942, was a Central Committee administrative manager, who became the regional first secretary in Słupsk in 1986, where his mobilization work was positively evaluated. His regional section was then chosen for the National Delegates Conference. He was later co-opted as a member of the Central Committee, where he was in charge of a section of the internal reforms in 1989 (see "Creating a Constituency" below).

This institutional device should be seen as supportive of the formalization of political reforms and especially for the emerging political discussions and "under construction" problematic. As an example, we can refer to a text about democratic centralism by Józef Oleksy, published in April 1989 in *Nowe Drogi*, in which the author—beyond his political preferences—gave a new definition to this central concept of the Stalinist political practices. According to him, the party should build a "new party of a new type" with more democratic discussions, while keeping its unity in action.[34] The tensions between the reformist conceptions and the "old" Stalinist habits and practices—here, the production of ideological texts whose purposes were to reassert the political value of the founding texts of State socialism—can then be seen more clearly in the analysis of this aspect of the 1986 to 1989 transformations.[35]

The PZPR Member Survey: Creating a Constituency?

The question of pluralism within the party gradually became an important matter in the party's activities because the political trends of reform challenged the internal relations and distribution of power that came from the institutionalization of the Leninist "party of a new type" model. The PZPR leadership suddenly realized that the party's transformation implied creating "internal opinion" that had not previously been necessary. A part of the internal reform was indeed dedicated to the formalization of such a "constituency" in the party. But in this matter, too, the party leadership proceeded very carefully and, in fact, wanted to test some general ideas about the future.

In July 1989, the PZPR asked its members in which directions the party should go. For the first time, the respondents were free to express their opinions, but the process was strictly controlled by the party's authorities. On 6 July 1989, the "Commission for the party's organization" (*Komisja Pracy Partyjnej*) had a meeting during which it was decided to send a questionnaire to the base organization, but this survey was placed in a strictly supervised political process: the survey was indeed presented as an application of the process decided during the Tenth Plenum in January 1989 and the delegate's conference in May 1989. Furthermore, the framing of the questions seems to have been a by-product of the opinions transmitted in June by the voivodeship (administrative area) committees to the commission. The formal starting point of the consultation was the new party's official statutes, but the basis of the process was indeed political. A communiqué from the commission was published separately from the report, and its official statements indicated the way in which this survey is embodied in a broader process of organized mobilization of the base organization:

> The search for a new party model is going in the direction of answers to the following questions: what should its constituency be, what interest should it pursue? How should it define the membership's criteria? In what locations could the party efficiently reach its goals? Consequently, can the democratic centralism model offer each party member real weight in the party's activities? How is the party supposed to function in the context of parliamentary democracy? The new form of the party must emerge from a broad discussion among party rank-and-file mem-

bers. The Commission of Party Work for the Central Committee asked the members to take part in this discussion. The Commission also asked the voivodeship committees to do organizational work in their territories to support the creation of various political clubs.[36]

The discussion during the meeting of the Commission, under the direction of Zygmunt Czarzasty, showed that the strategic goal of this consultation was with the base organization. Its members stressed that the internal reforms would be impossible if they were disconnected from the grassroots trends. Waldemar Świrgon, for example, said that "the program which is being discussed everywhere can only arise on the basis of a broad social movement and not in cabinets, drinking Coca-Cola and eating canapés."[37] The Commission hoped, as Czesław Borowski said, to define two or three main projects and build a broad coalition for the next general elections, which should take place four years later.[38] This level of reform was then under the pressure of recent political events, but tried in the same way to adapt the organizational work already done within the party and mobilize the rank-and-file members in various ways.

The questionnaire was published on 9 July 1989 in the party's official daily paper, *Trybuna Ludu,* in very similar terms to the Commission's report a few days previously.[39] Moreover, the Commission created a working group of thirteen members who were in charge of organizing the survey. People were invited to write to the party or to call by phone, and a special phone service was created to collect the various opinions, daily from 9 A.M. to 3 P.M. The working group wrote a daily report to the party's authorities in which each phone call was presented. Opinions were usually nominative and the reports very carefully noted some points, such as the age, place of residence, professional activity, education, and, last but not least, the duration of party membership. Typical presenters of opinions were identified as follows: "Jacek B., 31 years old, PZPR member since 1980, lawyer from Łódź"; "Czeslaw M., Warsaw, 82 years old, communist and working class activist since 1924"; or "Worker, PZPR member." The survey was immediately presented as a success among members. The official Commission statements, sent to the Central Committee members on 7 July 1989, underlined that this initiative was regarded as "very interesting by the party's members from the first day" and that this "dialogue about the future of the party was considered very useful, by giving—in the context of the absence of a similar (process) at the local level—direct possibilities to make suggestions and propositions." However, the daily reports show a more moderate mobilization. On 10 July 1989, the phone service collected the opinions of eleven people, and on 11 July, of nine, for example. On

16 August, the daily report stated that "200 people have called since the phone service was established on 7 July, and 80 percent were party members. The Commission also received 84 written responses, in which the majority, i.e. 60, reflected individual positions, others were statements or discussions of various party's organizations."[40] In addition to this well-organized consultation, the Commission also undertook face-to-face consultations. On 10 July, Leszek Miller, for example, met some members who had sent individual responses.[41]

The final product of this survey was an eight-page document prepared by the Commission to the Fifteenth Plenum of the Central Committee, dated 9 September 1989. This document presented a summary of the opinions expressed by party members, but located them in formulations and categorizations that fitted with the previous ideological work done at the centralized level. Concerning the democratic centralism, the document appealed for a reform of this way of functioning: "The form of the internal democracy requires a change toward a new formula of democratic centralism ... with guarantees of expressing their own opinions for those who will be in the minority after a vote. A minimum of democratic centralism must be kept for governing the party and for discipline in the realization of resolutions."[42] In fact, the party leadership had to ideologically ground its strategic considerations because it was worried about the centripetal tendencies that appeared during those transformations and because of the defeat during the elections.[43] The "constituency of the future party" (*baza społeczna partii*) should be, according the work of the Commission, not only the working class, but all of society, in a "socialist" and "national" perspective. The party should not "make distinctions between workers, peasants and intellectuals."[44] The Eleventh Congress must, according to the document, "prepare a new formula of program and organization that allows the PZPR to become a party representing the Polish left and the working people." The party should end its prior activities by changing its name and in this way "make a clear separation with Stalinism." But the conclusion also stressed that "there is a strong tendency to give the party a working-class orientation," with links to the trade unions.[45]

The number of responses was surprisingly small for an organization with more than two million members, which in addition purported to be a mass mobilization party. Interestingly, this point was not noted in the final report. The Commission members were probably fully aware of this problem, but also focused on other issues. Indeed, the content of the responses was evidently interpreted as an additional sign that the party could no longer manage itself through the "old" democratic centralism. The survey was seen by many respondents as an opportunity to voice their opinions,[46] and they were very critical about the bureaucratization of the party. Some respondents expressed anger and frustration toward the party's apparatchiks very directly, pointing out that they should be given "real jobs" or, less radically, asking for staff cuts at different levels of the party organization. These criticisms were combined with complaints about the rupture between the PZPR and the working class, which was supposed to be its "natural" constituency. For example, a worker called the phone service and said, "The working class base must separate and create a new party. Workers feel unrecognized in the party because of the weight of bureaucrats and intellectuals."[47] In similar terms, many respondents underlined the ideological vacuum in the party's daily activities. In addition, if the moral authority of the party still held a political value for most respondents, the concrete bodies of direction (such as local and voivodeship committees, for example, but even the Central Committee) were mistrusted, and the flow of authority turned in favor of party leaders, mainly General Jaruzelski, and more occasionally Leszek Miller. It can then, by the way, be suggested that this evolution could seriously worry a political leadership that had tried to break away from the Stalinist legacy and consequently therefore also with the cult of personality. However, many respondents demonstrated more reformist opinions and proposed a social democratic turn, by reference to the Western European experiences or the Polish Pre-Soviet Socialist Party (the PPS). Nevertheless, the opinions expressed by respondents were not always politically or ideologically consistent: one respondent asked for more democratization in the party, but proclaimed "maximum discussion before decisions, maximum discipline in its realization" as a political norm for the party.[48]

Moreover, because of the very specific questions asked by the Commission, the respondents only pointed out the reforms as part of a more global process a few times, despite the frequency of their references to democratic centralism as a norm to challenge the party. One respondent appealed for example to an "examination of the Stalinist stage of the party."[49] In a similar way, only a few respondents noticed that the PZPR was late in its transformations in comparison with the "allied parties" of the official coalition: a typewritten letter collected by the Commission complained, for example, that the ZSL had organized a survey about its future and that the party "just published some vague appeals in its press."[50] This was true, as the ZSL had already published a similar but more specific survey in its press in June.[51]

If the survey created a new de facto "internal opinion" by PZPR members, the political processing of collected opinions shows a very careful democratic opening of the party, which prevented the possibility for party members to actively contribute to the key decisions of the party's transformation. The survey was rather an additional tool with which to frame reform after the ideological process that had been led by the top of the party since 1988. This was also an opportunity to test this plan. In this way, the party leaders could check that this coalescent new base could support the new political course and legitimate it. This was also the creation of a new "public sphere" in the party and was an opportunity to secure the reform plans. But it was also a tool for mobilization. If some general orientations were already available, the party was uncertain about the participation of the base in a context of apathy (especially after the electoral defeat), which the members of the Commission had underlined many times. That is why the survey was presented as part of a "package" in which there was also the creation of several political alternative ways of activation from the top of the party, such as political clubs or less formal internal party meetings.

Conclusion

Despite a gradual and careful introduction of pluralistic rules, the whole process of reform was rather elitist and was controlled by party leaders. Until June 1989, this pluralism was a convenient label to a certain extent—a kind of "umbrella" for incremental changes—and was not a full conversion to party pluralism. Concerning the party and its internal democratization, the process of opening up was incremental. It started with the medium-level apparatus during the delegate's conference in May 1989, which was a prior stage to framing the reforms, and then in July of the same year it involved ordinary members. In fact, the PZPR leadership tried to enlarge the base of support for its reforms rather than switch to a more member-inclusive party model. In other words, the survey, and maybe all the political experiments of this period, can be analyzed as a Weberian process in which the holders of power tried to strengthen their legitimacy through a top-down process of the circulation of the political norms of domination.[52]

The author would like to thank Rüdiger Bergien, Jens Gieseke and Stephanie Karmann. The author would also like to thank Professors Padraic Kenney and Bernard Pudal for their remarks on previous versions of this text. Of course, as the expression goes, the author assumes full responsibility for the content of this article.

Frédéric Zalewski is an associate professor in political science at the Université Paris Nanterre and a member of the CNRS unit Institut des Sciences Sociales du Politique (ISP CNRS). His publications include *Paysannerie et politique en Pologne* (2006), *Introduction à l'Europe post-communiste* (2009), (coeditor) *L'Europe contestée : espaces et enjeux des positonnements contre l'Union européenne* (2008), and *Révolutions conservatrices en Europe centrale et orientale*, a special issue of the *Revue d'Etudes Comparatives Est-Ouest* (vol. 47, no. 4, 2016).

Notes

1. This orientation is close to the games of transition analysis in political science, by focusing on strategic choices of the soft-liners. See Adam Przeworski, *Democracy and the Market: Political and Economic Reforms in Eastern Europe and Latin America* (Cambridge, 1991).
2. We refer here explicitly to the frame theory in political science. See Doug MacAdam, "Tactical Innovation and the Pace of Insurgency," *American Sociological Review* 48 (1983): 735–754; D. Snow et al., "Frame Alignment Processes, Micromobilization, and Movement Participation," *American Sociological Review* 51 (1986): 735–754.
3. Paweł Kowal, *Koniec systemu władzy* [The end of the power system] (Warsaw, 2012), 468.
4. Ibid.
5. Michel Foucault, *Dits et Ecrits II 1976–1988* [Writings II 1976–1988] (Paris, 2001), 299.
6. *Trybuna Ludu*, 31 January 1989.
7. Ken Jowitt, *New World Disorder: The Leninist Extinction* (Berkeley, 1991); Jacques Lévesque, *1989, la fin d'un empire. L'URSS et la libération de l'Europe de l'Est* [1989, the end of an empire. The USSR and the liberation of Eastern Europe] (Paris, 1995).
8. Michel Dobry, *Sociologie des crises politique* [The political crisis of sociology] (Paris, 1992).
9. Bernard Lacroix, "Ordre politique et ordre social" in "Traité de science politique" [Political order and social order in: Political science handbook], ed. M. Grawitz and J. Leca (Paris, 1985), 469–565.
10. Frédéric Zalewski, *Paysannerie et politique en Pologne. Trajectoire du parti paysan polonais du communisme à l'après-communisme 1945–2005* [Peasantry and politics in Poland. The path of the Polish peasant party from communism to postcommunism] (Paris, Michel, 2006); idem, "L'improbable autonomisation d'un "parti satellite". Réflexions sur les rapports de pouvoir entre le ZSL et le PZPR dans la Pologne communiste (1949–1989)" [The unlikely empowerment of a "satellite party." Reflections on the power relations between the ZSL and the PZPR in communist Poland (1949–1989)], *Revue d'Histoire moderne et contemporaine* 49, no. 2 (2002).
11. *Trybuna Ludu*, 19 January 1989.

12. Bernard Pudal, *Un monde défait. Les communistes français de 1956 à nos jours* [A defeated world. The French communists from 1956 to today] (Bellecombes-en-Bauge, 2009).
13. Georges Mink, *La force ou la raison. Histoire sociale et politique de la Pologne (1980–1989)* [Force or reason. Social and political history of Poland (1980–1989)] (Paris, 1989), 178.
14. Including free and regular elections, turnover in office and competitive party system; see Arend Lijphart, *Democracy in Plural Societies: A Comparative Exploration* (New Haven, 1977); S. M. Lipset, *Political Man* (New York, 1960).
15. Andrzej-Leon Sowa, *Historia polityczna Polski* [Political history of Poland] (Warsaw, 2011).
16. Mink, *La Force ou la raison* [Force or reason], 163.
17. Andrzej Friszke, "Próba portretu zbiorowego aparatu partyjnego" [Tentative collective portrait of the party apparatus], in *PZPR Jako machina władzy* [The PZPR as a power machine], ed. D. Stola and K. Persak (Warsaw 2012), 63.
18. Mink, *La Force ou la raison* [Force or reason], 90, 141.
19. Jadwiga Staniszkis, *Pologne. La révolution autolimitée* [Poland. The self-limited revolution] (Paris, 1982), 101.
20. Ken Jowitt, *The New World Disorder.*
21. Stanislaw Gebethner, "Geneza i tło polityczno-ustrojowe wyborów przydenckich 1990 r" [Genesis and background of the 1990 presidential elections], in *Dlaczego tak głosowano. Wybory prezydenckie'90* [Why this vote. The 1990 presidential elections], ed. Stanisław Gebethner and Krzysztof Jasiewicz (Warsaw,1993), 37.
22. *Trybuna Ludu* 16, no. 13783 (19 January 1989).
23. Luc Boltanski and Laurent Thévenot, *De la justification. Les économies de la grandeur* [On justification. Economies of worth] (Paris: Gallimard, 1991).
24. Georges Mink, *La force ou la raison* [Force or reason] (Paris, 1989),199; Tadeusz Kisielewski, *Zapiski historyczno-polityczne z lat 1981–1991* [Political and historical notes from the years 1981–1991] (Częstochowa, 1994).
25. Michel Dobry, "Les causalités de l'improbable et du probable: Notes à propos des manifestations de 1989 en Europe centrale et orientale" [The causalities of the improbable and the probable: Notes about the 1989 demonstrations in Central and Eastern Europe], *Cultures & Conflicts* (spring 1995): 322.
26. Eric Hobsbawm and Terence Ranger, *The Invention of Tradition* (Cambridge, 1983).
27. Frédéric Zalewski, "L'improbable autonomisation d'un "parti satellite." Réflexions sur les rapports de pouvoir entre le ZSL et le PZPR dans la Pologne communiste (1949–1989)" [The unlikely empowerment of a "satellite party." Reflections on the power relations between the ZSL and the PZPR in communist Poland (1949–1989)], *Revue d'Histoire moderne et contemporaine* 49, no. 2 (2002): 78–101.
28. Andrzej-Leon Sowa, *Historia polityczna Polski* [Political history of Poland] (Warsaw 2011), 596ff.
29. Georges Mink, *La force ou la raison* [Force or reason] (Paris, 1989), 198ff.

30. Mark Granovetter, "The Strength of Weak Ties," *American Journal of Sociology* 78, no. 6 (1973): 1360–1380.
31. Andrzej Czyż, "Kontynuacja i wzbogacenie socjalistycznej odnowy" [Continuation and enrichment of the socialist renewal], *Nowe Drogi* 4, no. 467 (1988): 13.
32. Reykowski Janusz, "Pluralizm socjalistyczny" [Socialist pluralism], *Nowe Drogi* 6 (1989).
33. Antoni Dudek, *Reglamentowana rewolucja. Rozkład dyktatury komunistycznej w Polsce 1988–1990* [The adjusted revolution. The collapse of the communist dictatorship in Poland], (Warsaw, 2004), 203.
34. Józef Oleksy, "Od centralizmu biurokratycznego do centralizmu demokratycznego" [From bureaucratic centralization to democratic centralization] *Nowe Drogi* 4, no. 469 (1989): 14–25.
35. Bernard Pudal, *Un monde défait*.
36. Komunikat z posiedzenia Komisji Pracy Partyjnej [Communication from the meeting of the commission for the party work], KC PZPR, Archiwum Akt Nowych (hereafter AAN), PZPR KC IV/1.
37. Komisja Pracy Partyjnej [Commission for the party work], 6.07.89, p. 16, KC PZPR, AAN, PZPR KC IV/1.
38. Ibid., 30.
39. "Komisja KC czeka na listy i telefony" [The CC commission is waiting for calls], *Trybuna Ludu*, 9 July 1989.
40. Informacja Nr II/134/89, Warszawa, dnia 16 sierpnia 1989 r [Information NrII/134/89, Warsaw, 16 August 1989], AAN, PZPR KC, IV/3.
41. Informacja Nr II/117/89, Warszawa, dnia 17 lipca 1989 r [Information Nr II/117/89, Warsaw, 17 July 1989], AAN, PZPR KC, IV/3.
42. Komisja Pracy Partyjnej [Commission for the party work], 6.07.89, KC PZPR, AAN, PZPR KC IV/1.
43. Ibid.
44. Ibid.
45. Dyskusja nad modelem partii—Oczekiwania związane z XI Zjazdem PZPR [Discussions on the party model—Expectations related to the 11th Party Congress], KC PZPR, AAN, PZPR KC IV/1.
46. Albert Hirschman, *Exit, Voice, and Loyalty: Responses to Decline in Firms, Organizations, and States* (Cambridge, 1970).
47. Informacja Nr II/108/89, Warszawa, dnia 10 lipca 1989 r [Information Nr II/108/89, Warsaw, 10 July 1989], 1, AAN, PZPR KC, IV/3.
48. Informacja Nr II/117/89, Warszawa, dnia 17 lipca 1989 r [Information NrII/117/89, Warsaw, 17 July 1989], 3, AAN, PZPR KC, IV/3.
49. Informacja Nr II/113/89, Warszawa, dnia 13 lipca 1989 r [Information Nr II/113/89, Warsaw, 13 July 1989], 5, AAN, PZPR KC, IV/3.
50. KC PZPR, AAN, PZPR KC IV/1.
51. *Dziennik Ludowy* [The peasant daily] 145, no. 9892 (22 June 1989).
52. Michel Dobry, "Valeurs, croyances et transactions collusives. Notes pour une réorientation de l'analyse de la légitimation des systèmes démocratiques [Values, beliefs and collusive transactions. Notes for the redirecting of analysis of legitimacy of democratic systems], in À la recherche de la

démocratie. Mélanges offerts à Guy Hermet [In search of democracy. Papers in tribute to Guy Hermet], ed. Javier Santiso (Paris, 2002).

Bibliography

Archiwum Akt Nowych [New Documents Archive] (AAN). Warsaw. Polska Zjednoczona Partia Robotnicza, Komitet Centralny [Polish United Workers Party, Central Committee]. Records IV1, IV3.

Benford, Robert D., and David A. Snow. "Frame Alignment Processes, Micromobilization, and Movement Participation." *American Sociological Review* 51, no. 4 (1986): 464–481.

Boltanski, Luc, and Laurent Thévenot. *De la Justification. Les économies de la Grandeur* [On justification. Economies of worth]. Paris: Gallimard, 1991.

Czyż, Andrzej. "Kontynuacja i wzbogacenie socjalistycznej odnowy" [Continuation and enrichment of the socialist renewal]. *Nowe Drogi* 4, no. 467 (1988): 11–21.

Dobry, Michel, "Valeurs, croyances et transactions collusives. Notes pour une réorientation de l'analyse de la légitimation des systèmes démocratiques" [Values, beliefs and collusive transactions. Notes for the redirecting of analysis of legitimacy of democratic systems]. In À la recherche de la démocratie. Mélanges offerts à Guy Hermet [In search of democracy. Papers in tribute to Guy Hermet], ed. Javier Santiso. Paris: Karthala, 2002

Dobry, Michel. "Les causalités de l'improbable et du probable: Notes à propos des manifestations de 1989 en Europe centrale et orientale" [The causalities of the improbable and the probable: Notes about the 1989 demonstrations in Central and Eastern Europe]. *Cultures & Conflicts*, spring 1995.

———. *Sociologie des crises politiques* [The political crisis of sociology]. Paris: Presses de la Fondation Nationale des Sciences Politiques, 1992.

Dudek, Antoni. *Reglamentowana rewolucja. Rozkład dyktatury komunistycznej w Polsce 1988–1990* [The adjusted revolution. The collapse of the communist dictatorship in Poland]. Warsaw: Arcana, 2004.

Foucault, Michel. *Dits et Ecrits II 1976–1988* [Writings II 1976–1988]. Paris: Gallimard, 2001.

Friszke Andrzej. "Próba portretu zbiorowego aparatu partyjnego" [Sketch of a collective portrait of the party apparatus]. In *PZPR jako machina władzy* [The PZPR as a power machine], ed. Dariusz Stola and Krzysztof Persak, 55–74. Warsaw: ISP PAN, 2012.

Gebethner, Stanisław, and Krzysztof Jasiewicz, eds. *Dlaczego tak głosowano Wybory prezydenckie '90* [Why this vote? The 1990 presidential elections]. Varsovie: ISP-INP, 1993.

Granowetter, Mark, "The Strength of Weak Ties." *American Journal of Sociology* 78, no. 6 (1973): 1360–1380.

Hirschman, Albert O. *Exit, Voice, and Loyalty: Responses to Decline in Firms, Organizations, and States*. Cambridge, MA: Harvard University Press, 1970.

Hobsbawm, Eric, and Terence Ranger. *The Invention of Tradition*. Cambridge: Cambridge University Press, 1983.

Jowitt, Ken. *New World Disorder: The Leninist Extinction.* Berkeley: University of California Press, 1991.
Kisielewski, Tadeusz. *Zapiski historyczno-polityczne z lat 1981–1991* [Political and historical notes from the years 1981–1991]. Czestochowa: WSP, 1994.
Kowal, Pawel. *Koniec systemu władzy* [The end of the power system]. Warsaw: ISP PAN/IPN/Trio, 2012.
Lacroix, Bernard. "Ordre politique et ordre social" [Political order and social order]. In *Traité de science politique* [Political science handbook], ed. Madeleine Grawitz and Jean Leca, 469–565. Paris: Presses Universitaires de France, 1985.
Levesque, Jacques. *1989, la fin d'un empire. L'URSS et la libération de l'Europe de l'Est* [1989, the end of an empire. The USSR and the liberation of Eastern Europe]. Paris: PFNSP, 1995.
Lijphart, Arend. *Democracy in Plural Societies: A Comparative Exploration.* New Haven, CT: Yale University Press, 1977.
Lipset, Seymour-Martin. *Political Man: The Social Basis of Politics.* New York: Anchor Books, 1960.
MacAdam, Doug. "Tactical Innovation and the Pace of Insurgency." *American Sociological Review* 48 (1983): 735–754.
Mink, Georges. *La force ou la raison. Histoire sociale et politique de la Pologne (1980–1989)* [The force or the reason. Political and social history of Poland (1980–1989)]. Paris: La Découverte, 1989.
Oleksy, Józef. "Od centralizmu biurokratycznego do centralizmu demokratycznego" [From bureaucratic centralization to democratic centralization]. *Nowe Drogi* 4, no. 469 (1989): 14–25.
Przeworski, Adam. *Democracy and the Market: Political and Economic Reforms in Eastern Europe and Latin America.* Cambridge: Cambridge University Press, 1991.
Pudal, Bernard. *Un monde défait. Les communistes français de 1956 à nos jours* [A defeated world. The French communists from 1956 to today]. Bellecombes-en-Bauge: Le Croquant, 2009.
Reykowski, Janusz. "Pluralizm socjalistyczny" [Socialist pluralism]. *Nowe Drogi* 6 (1989).
Snow, David A., R. Burke Rochford Jr., Steven K. Worden, and Robert D. Benford. "Frame Alignment Processes, Micromobilization, and Movement Participation." *American Sociological Review* 51 (1986): 735–754.
Sowa, Andrzej-Leon. *Historia polityczna Polski 1944–1991* [Political history of Poland, 1944–1991]. Warsaw: Wydawnictwo Literackie, 2011.
Staniszkis, Jadwiga. *Pologne. La révolution autolimitée* [Poland. Self-limited revolution]. Paris: PUF, 1982.
Zalewski, Frédéric. *Paysannerie et politique en Pologne. Trajectoire du parti paysan polonais du communisme à l'après-communisme 1945–2005* [Peasantry and politics in Poland. The path of the Polish peasant party from communism to postcommunism]. Paris, Michel Houdiard, 2006.

 6

Communist Party Apparatuses as Steering Organizations
Paths of Development in East Central Europe
Christoph Boyer

The following essay presents a comparative view of party apparatuses as steering organizations in East Central European (ECE)[1] state socialism between 1945 and 1989. The basic premise is that we should drop the simplified concept of the apparatus as a smoothly operating machine, steering and administering society under the primacy of politics, in perfect accordance with political inputs. Instead, we should focus on the "disorderly phenomena": on internal fractions and the conflicts of interest inside allegedly homogeneous and hierarchical administrative bodies; on the ample space for maneuvering that results from the fact the functionaries are not smoothly-rotating little wheels, but players with egotistical interests. They may form networks or clans behind and below the formal institutional arrangements. Last but not least, the diffuse borderlines between the apparatus and its environment should be taken into account. It would be would be a gross oversimplification to talk about the bipolarity of "society" and "party" or about a top-down relationship between both. Instead, we should look for more complex forms of interaction, such as negotiations, for example; and we should watch out for consensus (even if it was, to a considerable extent, manipulated and urged from above).[2] One is almost tempted to call these structures "polycratic" if this would not insinuate a homology between state socialism and National Socialism—which should not be flatly denied, but rather discussed intensively.

On the other side, the essence of state socialism undoubtedly *is* one-party rule[3] in combination with a centrally planned and administered economy, both in the service of the great transformation that intends to shift the working class to the center of society. In other words, state socialism functioned, to a large extent, as a monocratic hierarchy.

On the whole, this implies that we have to think about ways and methods of reconciling these contradictory findings and conflicting interpretations. First, we have to assign both elements (i.e., "hierarchy" on the one side, and the "disorderly dimension" on the other) an appropriate place in a more comprehensive tableau. Second, we have to add the dynamic dimension. The question is, in other words, whether, and above all *why*, the distribution of weight between the two elements shifts—and whether the single shifts add up to a continuous long-term drift—to a path of development that follows a plausible logic. The next question is whether this intrinsic logic will be able to yield adequate and sufficient explanations per se—or if we need additional—that is, external—determinants.

As one can easily see, these questions add up to a highly ambitious research program, but the essay can of course only present a very rough and superficial sketch. Nevertheless, it is crucial that we keep a more comprehensive system of coordinates at the back of our minds; otherwise the danger is that we will get stuck in a heap of unconnected details. The principal perspective of the following considerations is "macro" and "systemic"—mainly from the economic aspect. The focus is on the party apparatus and primarily on the economic bureaucracy, leaving the administrative bodies of the state to a large extent aside. At first glance, the functions and dysfunctions of the state look principally similar to those of the party[4]—but this reasonable-looking hypothesis with regard to a comparison of the "two pillars" and the relationship between them cannot be tested here without running the danger of overloading the text.

The starting point of the following analysis is the party apparatus in the context of the "classical model,"[5] as it was installed in ECE after 1945, in the period of "building socialism."[6] The model was defined by the primacy of politics; the power monopoly (unlimited by law, and if necessary, backed by terror) of the Marxist-Leninist Party over economy, society, and culture, exerted by the apparatus. Party rule was backed by the ideological monopoly—and vice versa. The party steered a megaproject of socioeconomic transformation that expropriated and liquidated (not only in a metaphorical, but also in a physical sense) the small bourgeoisie, landowners, and industrial entrepreneurs, thereby pushing the industrial working class and the proletarian peasants into a central position in society. The second element of the model consisted of the predominance of collective property, which tended to imply the elimination of the market and private entrepreneurs. This constituted the basis of (at least in theory, and as a regulative idea) comprehensive central administrative economic planning and regulation, which preferably relied on moral and emotional stimulation through nonmarket incentives, and particularly on the mobilization of "enthusiasm" by means of campaigns. The extortion of achievement through physical force replaced economic cost-benefit calculations and economic incentives. The third element was a policy of forced extensive industrial growth, with a marked preference for the primary industries, energy, and the production of investment goods. The imitation of the Soviet model of the 1920s and 1930s implied big push heavy industrialization from the beginning in the agrarian or agrarian-industrial ECE countries (Poland, Hungary, and Slovakia). It meant a restructuring of the existing industrial base, and its reorientation from light, and consumer goods industries toward heavy industry in older industrial regions such as East Germany and Bohemia/Moravia.

The planning bureaucracy entrusted with the implementation of this policy, at least at first glance, looked very much like an ideal type of Weberian bureaucracy operating on the basis of explicit policy programs enacted by the political steering center (i.e., the party leadership), and preferably implemented top-down. *Sachlichkeit* (neutrality/objectivity), *Herrschaft des Fachwissens* (preponderance of expertise), and *Regelgebundenheit der bürokratischen Verwaltungstätigkeit* (the principle of rule-bound bureaucratic administration)[7] exerted by a monocratic, hierarchically organized staff of professional, personally detached but politically loyal functionaries were of essential importance.[8] Here, the appropriate metaphor is, in fact, "apparatus." It expresses the pronouncedly technocratic optimism of the earlier postwar years regarding "scientific methods" of steering and regulation: a sort of mechanical engineering, as it were. The basic premise was an *ex ante* identity of the common interests of society and the party. The primacy of politics was obvious; it was in perfect accordance with a rather strong and, initially at least, unbroken belief in the "dialectic unity" of technical, economic, and administrative expert logic on the one side, and the politically correct Marxist-Leninist position (embodying the interests of the working class) on the other.

Quite a number of irritations and malfunctions arose almost at once from the fact that the apparatus *intended* to and was *supposed* to act and function as a machine—and exactly this turned out to be impossible. One can make this rather long story very short: it is practically conventional wisdom that bureaucracies that overload themselves with regulatory ambitions significantly reduce their steering capacities. They produce mismanagement and disorientation, a lack of efficiency and productivity, frictions and waste. To a certain extent, they enable the cadres to pursue "egotistical interests." The mere size of the apparatus diminishes its ability to learn. The result was a combination of rigidity and chaos—the details of the story can be found in the chapters on the pathologies of "redtapeism" in sociological textbooks.

Socialist party apparatuses apparently generated such dysfunctions a fortiori, simply because they showed many more regulatory ambitions than other bureaucracies.[9] Massive overregulation and overcentralization generated a severe principal agent (i.e., control) problem: the command economy was permanently thwarted and foiled by "soft plans" and soft budget constraints. Plan discipline on a command-and-obey basis periodically decayed; it was not possible to effectively and permanently reinforce it given the absence of market incentives and sanctions. This holds true even if one takes into consideration that ways and methods of planning and administration were not ready-made and at hand in the disorderly early postwar times. Quite a number of tools and procedures had to be developed on the spot through trial and error, under conditions of material austerity and extreme time pressure.[10]

It should be stressed at this point that some of these ostensible imperfections may ultimately have turned turn out to be advantages; precisely because the apparatus did not have an iron grip on everything and everybody, it left, at least to a certain extent, options open for self-regulation, for *Eigen-Sinn* (self-will), etc. Speaking in a more technical-sociological manner, these "deficits" enabled "loose coupling"—that is, a more flexible method of steering and regulating. Moreover, stressing the manifest and manifold dysfunctions of the apparatus certainly does not imply that state socialism should be seen as a failure from the very beginning—as a story of inevitable decay. As a relatively simple and highly effective instrument to organize the initial steps of large-scale, big push heavy industrialization, mobilizing and exploiting the industrial work force en masse, centrally planned and administered economies undoubtedly had their merits. The apparatus was, in other words, relatively successful in this respect (if we neglect for the time being the social and moral costs). This holds true at least with regard to the agrarian or semi-industrialized countries of the region, such as Hungary and Poland (and the Slovak parts of Czechoslovakia). However, it should immediately be added that the policy of forced extensive industrial growth with its marked preference for investment goods industries (at the same time grossly neglecting standard of living problems) almost inevitably created massive social tensions. Against this background, the density and intensity of violent eruptions against the apparatus and its functionaries in times of terrorist high-Stalinism were only initially astonishing.[11] The uprising in the German Democratic Republic (GDR), the turbulence in Czechoslovakia in 1953, the riots in Poland, and the 1956 revolution in Hungary were only the tips of the iceberg.

The first attempts at repairing the malfunctions of the apparatus—still *within* the limits of the classical system—came rather soon. They formed systematic and plausible patterns. First, the installation and subsequent refinement of a system of controls may be observed. They came through commissions, in reports, or through legal action against corruption, etc. Second, there were various campaigns aimed at improving plan fulfillment, for example. This entailed, third, a certain overall reorganization of the planning and steering mechanism in order to make it more efficient—this was already sometimes with the assistance of cybernetics and early computers. This meddling and tampering with the apparatus had already started in the late fifties, still in the period of building socialism. Examples illustrating this included the Rozsypal reforms in Czechoslovakia or Friedrich Behrens's and Arne Benary's initiative[12] in the GDR. In addition to the above, there were also a number of devices used in order to improve communication with society: petitioning[13] played a prominent role in this respect. Here, the secret service also had its systematic place. Beyond the intrusion into the private lives of people, the *Stasi* (East German secret police) and its equivalents in other countries, such as the Czechoslovak *státní bezpečnost* (state security), were commissioned to deliver the information necessary for "scientific steering." They were also meant to function as early warning systems in a society that had neither the market nor free discussion to work successfully as information-producing agencies. Other problem-solving devices were the much-discussed networks. They existed in a semiofficial sphere, in niches and grey zones, but in general they were tacitly tolerated, as they were, for example, apt to mobilize scarce resources that the official planning mechanism was unable to procure in sufficient quantities.[14]

Still another field of activity was cadre policy. Its systematic flaw, however, was that it tended to attribute the malfunctions of the apparatus to the individuals who ran it. Consequently, cadre training primarily invested in the education of the "socialist personality." But a policy of moral appeals missed the point insofar as it ignored the structural deficits that (mainly) deformed people. Nevertheless, the constant efforts to improve the professional qualities of the personnel (pushing political loyalty to the background, but never really replacing it) seem to have been fairly successful in the long run, at least to a certain extent.[15]

It is important to stress that all these "first-stage activities" evidently remained within the systemic limits of the command system. The intention was to improve the existing structures by perfecting and tightening the mechanisms of control; trying to expel the devil with the help of Satan, as it were. Following the paths of state socialist development further, one arrives at the stage of socialist reforms.

Socialist reforms represent a more subtle, creative, and ambitious response to the deficits of the classic system and its apparatus. These reforms were enacted from approximately the early sixties onwards, after the end of the period of building socialism. This was the case in Hungary (1968), and Ulbricht's New Economic System and the Prague Spring also fit into this context. Socialist reforms basically aimed to decentralize the system and make it more flexible. There were three principal strategies. First, private ownership of the means of production was legalized again, at least to a certain extent. Second, market elements were inserted into and combined with planning—again to a certain extent. Third, socialist reforms were intended to mobilize the individual, to release the "personal material interests" and the creative potential of society through numerous forms and methods of participation, on the shop floor and beyond, at least to a certain extent. To a certain degree, socialist reforms allowed and even supported social differentiation. Last, but not least, as a reaction to the dramatic destabilization of 1953/56, the reforms began to improve the working and living conditions of "the people," in a rather broad sense of the concept, in the vast field of social and consumer policy.

Generally speaking, socialist reforms were intended as modernization programs. There are quite a few variations to the theme. Some of them were more technocratic, the center paradoxically trying to decentralize the apparatus from above, as in the case of the GDR. In other cases, such as in Czechoslovakia, reform initiatives originated outside the apparatus, or they came from below, subsequently transcending the economy and soon expanding into the field of politics and culture. Be that as it may, reform activities should by all means be taken as an indicator that the party apparatus possessed intrinsic capacities to stabilize itself through change, maybe even significantly diminishing the operating range of the apparatus, at least for a certain time.

However, it is essential to also promptly state that the success of all reform movements was structurally limited by the power interests of the cadres, who may have been temporarily weakened in their capacity to act and react, but whose power was in principle unbroken. Even if reforms reduced the level of bureaucratic regulation, they were, at the same time, characterized by a certain tendency to "refill the regulatory gap." Administrative interventions tended, as ever, to transgress the limits beyond which the new autonomy was in danger of being overthrown again. These encroachments may have been based on legal procedures. In quite a number of cases, there were ambiguous and permanently changing micro-regulations, which possibly even conflicted with formal law. Correspondingly, on the level of organization, the competences of private and bureaucratic actors were not clearly defined. Corrupt relationships and the individual opportunism in relation to the bureaucrats seem to have been more important than market performance. Socialist reform economies were, in short, an environment that favored the evolution of "political entrepreneurs," of adventurers, or even mafiosi. "Politics" outplayed efficiency and Weberian *Sachlichkeit*. Seen against this background, it is not surprising that the tension between the modernization of "administrative socialism" and the power interests of the party ultimately turned out to be unresolvable. In other words, the central dilemma of socialist reform was in practically all cases[16] solved in favor of the logic of power and the material interests of the bureaucrats connected with it.

At the end of the 1960s, all ECE state socialist regimes had a more or less long record of reforms, relapses, and new attempts at reform. However, for two principal causes, this potentially infinite story then reached a new stage of development.[17] Whereas the deficits of the apparatus had primarily been of an intrinsic or systemic nature thus far—and the limitations of its capacity to act had been caused intrinsically—from the early seventies onwards, external restrictions came to the forefront.

First, ECE state socialism was confronted with a new technical and economic challenge: the transition to the third industrial revolution—that is, from a classical industrial society to a post-Fordist society, perhaps a postmodern "electronic and service economy," with the concomitant transition from extensive to intensive patterns of economic growth. It is important to note that this transformation was a challenge for industrial societies in general; in the special case of state socialism, far-reaching structural change was hampered, or at least slowed, by the barriers inherent in the central administrative planning system. Despite a certain opening up to global economic relations, ECE state socialist regimes remained, on the whole, for both economic and political reasons, entrenched behind "anti-imperialist walls." The consequence was that they only benefitted to a very limited extent from the synergies arising from global technological cooperation. As a plausible reaction to this problem, the socialist economies started to compensate their intrinsic weakness through imports of advanced Western technology and know-how. This strategy of "intensification," however, was unsuccessful within the given institutional framework; consequently, the modernization gap with the West became visibly deeper during the 1970s and 1980s. It is essential to make clear that this increasingly obvious lagging behind the West was not an *absolute* deficit of ECE state socialism, but a *relative* shortcoming compared to "the West." The consequence was, in any case, a drastic deterioration of the terms of trade of the socialist economies on the world market. As technology imports could no longer be sufficiently financed by export earnings, ECE countries were trapped, at least in the longer run, in massive foreign debts.[18]

The second bundle of restrictions arose from *within* socialist societies. However, from the point of view of the apparatus, it must have looked like an external limitation as well. In order to generate the loyalty that reforms had not been able to produce, at around the beginning of the 1970s, most ECE state socialist countries greatly intensified their social and consumer policy. This was not just a minor policy shift, but a fundamental change in paradigm. Any remains of utopian vision were discarded. Due to the costly social and consumer policy programs that implied an obvious over-stretching of economic resources, the import of consumer goods became a second major source of massive external borrowing in Poland, Hungary, and the GDR.[19] The turn to mass consumption looked like an ingenious problem-solver at the beginning, but the new policy was not really able to stop the erosion of mass loyalty in the longer run. Evidently, the relatively modest material achievements of late state socialism were not able to compete with Western affluence; the increasing osmosis between East and West (and above all the rising influence of Western media) meant that Western standards were increasingly accepted by the people as the quasi-natural standards.

If we take a closer look at the possible policy options and strategy choices made by the ECE state socialist countries in the 1970s and 1980s, they appear considerably and systematically restricted. In other words, the party apparatuses found themselves in an increasingly defensive position.

There are two main variations to this theme. First, East German *Realsozialismus*[20] and Czechoslovak *normalizace*[21] both followed the end of reform periods—that is, after the termination of Ulbricht's economic experiments and the Prague Spring respectively. In both regimes, the massive expansion of social and consumer policy, as the shibboleth of a renewed "socialism for the masses," was closely linked with the return to a planned economy of the classical type, under the strict control of the party apparatus whose undisputed rule had been restored after the liquidation of reforms. This trade-off between the power interests of the party and the material concerns of the people—the FDGB (Freier Deutscher Gewerkschaftsbund / Free German Confederation of Trade Unions) and the ROH (Revoluční odborové hnutí / Revolutionary Trade Union Movement) acting as their rather potent quasi-lobbies—became the "brand label" of *Realsozialismus* and *normalizace*. The raison d'être of the new paradigm was primarily political. It (re)stabilized the system. But the technical support of the party apparatus and its cadres,[22] in whose interests this paradigm stood in evident accordance, seems to have been an indispensable factor.

In the long run, the reestablishment of political and economic orthodoxy, combined with an innovative achievement (i.e., the expansion of social and consumer policy), turned out to be a highly immobile arrangement. The Parties had accepted a deadly serious obligation to concern themselves with the overall material wellbeing of the people, and this new social contract created strong and practically irreversible path dependencies. The covenant was noisily propagated; it was explicit, and it was utterly rigid. It produced expectations and demands that could not be slimmed down by a new austerity, except perhaps at the price of mass upheaval, which was the (well-documented) obsession of the elites. "Caring for the people" now became the foremost task of the apparatus on the lower levels of the socialist *Lebenswelt*, in towns and villages, and in the socialist enterprise.[23] However, this extensive and intensive piecemeal engineering for the wellbeing of the working people should be interpreted as an unmistakable sign of the inherent weakness of the party and its permanent (and ultimately unsuccessful) attempt at gaining mass loyalty.

Under these premises, a thorough transformation of the economy (and above all a reduction in the standard of living, which structurally overstrained resources) turned out to be impossible. It was no longer even attempted.[24] As the self-imposed captivity of the cadres implied a narrow limitation of their mental and conceptual horizons, the structural problems of *Realsozialismus* and *normalizace*, its economic and standard of living policies were postponed, suppressed, ignored, or at least kept behind the façade; social and economic frictions and deficiencies, en masse, were not able to break the iron clamp of the stabilization paradigm. Having fallen into a state of rigidity and sclerosis, the apparatuses imploded within a few months between spring and autumn 1989.[25] At the time, the breakdown was more or less a surprise, but looking at it in retrospect, it becomes evident that it had not come out of the blue. The loyalty of society (and in the end, even of the high and highest-ranking cadres) seems to have withered and waned, but regardless of the increasing social differentiation of late socialist society, this process evolved tacitly and subcutaneously—under cover, as it were—if one disregards the small groups of dissidents at the periphery of society.

Gierek's Poland[26] and late Kádár's Hungary[27] chose a substantial expansion of social policy and consumption as their primary raison d'être, as well as a new principal source of legitimacy. A basically similar socioeconomic macro-constellation drove both party regimes into foreign indebtedness, but the path of development of both countries differed from the trajectory of the East German and Czechoslovak implosion of their regimes in important respects. Whereas *Realsozialismus* and *normalizace* had established a narrow link between material pacification and restoration, reerecting a stable-looking bureaucratic structure, Hungary and Poland, faced with the debt crisis, initiated new rounds of economic reform, and even attempted austerity measures. But, contrary to plans and intentions, these last efforts at modernizing the economic mechanism and slimming down the social and consumption budgets in order to escape the debt trap resulted in the erosion of party rule as well as a significant loss of mass loyalty. In both countries, the lengthy decay and protracted decomposition of the apparatus were evident well before the *exitus*.

Poland was the first subvariation to the erosion theme. The disintegration process had already started there in the early 1970s in the context of Gierek's grand design of "economic modernization plus consumption for the people," when steeply rising imports stimulated an anarchic release of local and regional economic interest groups both inside as well as outside the party. As these lobbies bitterly competed and rivaled each other for imported resources, the center of the party increasingly lost its grip on the economy and society. A second factor of disintegration consisted of the attempts of the party to combat the external trade imbalance by reducing consumption and raising prices. This policy provoked the notoriously harsh antagonism between "them" and "us" that soon paved the road toward the rise of *Solidarność*. Martial law and the Jaruzelski government were a sort of last resort solution; they were implemented at a time when Polish society had already considerably expanded its room for maneuver. The initial disputes about standard of living problems had widened into fundamental conflicts about political and moral issues. In the 1980s, the countervailing power of society showed marked contours; the apparatus seems to have lost much of its steering capacities, maybe even its basic qualities as an administrative organization. The "Polish erosion" was by no means a carefully planned and orderly retreat from power, but an uncontrolled plunge into chaos and anarchy.

In Hungary, late Kádárism provided the second subvariation to the erosion theme. Since the revolution of 1956, there had been a tacit consensus within Hungary that another pretext for a Soviet intervention should be avoided at all costs. The antagonism between the party and the people developed against this background, albeit along generally softer lines in Hungary. In the 1980s particularly, the Kádár regime tried out a combination of gradual reform as well as austerity. However, at this time, the Hungarian party also tolerated, and even actively supported, the concomitant rise of a private agrarian and small-business sector (which led to the rise of a new social layer of small businessmen in town and country), both parallel to and behind the official economy. Life with austerity was intended to become easier this way, and the new *enrichissez-vous* was intended as a diversion strategy. The result might be called a "soft erosion" of the party apparatus and its planned economy. In contrast to the Polish harsh confrontation scenario, the border between the Hungarian party and "her" society became more and more diffuse as functionaries started to become businessmen using their economic and social capital to build up their starting positions for the new age to come.

Summary and Outlook

The empirical findings presented in these four case studies demonstrate that one and the same basic problem constellation developed in different directions between 1970 and 1989. A more detailed and thorough explanation of these divergences—which ought to refer back to the (very) long path dependencies, rooted in different economic and social structures, as well as political cultures—cannot be given in any more detail in the context of this essay.[28]

As regards the qualities of the apparatus as a steering organization, the case studies show a rather similar long-term developmental logic, which followed chronology, at least approximately. The classical system was at its starting point everywhere, and was then followed by a turn to imminent repairs. The next step was socialist reform, which in all cases ended in a more or less clearly visible (Poland, Hungary) or more or less concealed (GDR, ČSSR) impasse. It is important to note here that talking about a developmental logic implies strong path dependencies, but by no means an outright "necessity." A sufficient explanation of the long-term drift has to take external contingent factors into respect. State socialism was not doomed to perish because of *absolute* deficits, but it turned out to be *relatively* deficient—that is, compared with the Western world. To understand this basic fact, a global framework of interpretation is essential. At first glance, the revolutionary momentum which set an end to the rule of the apparatus seemed to come primarily from below and from within—but a second glance reveals the extremely important role of exogenous determinants.

The ECE example seems to prove that reforming a party apparatus with resounding results is impossible because socialist reforms are structurally at variance with the material as well as the power interests of the cadres. This almost looks like an "iron law." However, in taking a comparative perspective of a global system of coordinates, and particularly when looking at the Chinese scenario since 1978, one must realize that there is no such iron law; the Chinese case demonstrates the principal possibility of a partial and incremental transformation of the centrally planned economy. It proves that over time, socioeconomic reforms are in fact able to transcend the socialist economic system. In addition, this reform path is tolerated, even supported, by the party functionaries. The cadres have not lost their importance in the new environment; the Chinese political ancien régime has remained intact until today. It seems as if this transition (which looks amazing, at least to European eyes) is partly based on sociocultural patterns not congruent with "Western values." But this explanation seems a bit too easy and comfortable. The clue might be sought in the circumstance that, in the course of the Chinese transition, old (communist) and new (capitalist) elites have fused into a new corruptive coalition of interests. Elaborating this hypothesis would, however, lead to a new, long, and quite complicated story.[29]

Christoph Boyer is professor of contemporary European history at the Paris Lodron University of Salzburg. His publications include (coeditor) *European Economic Elites Between a New Spirit of Capitalism and the Erosion of State Socialism* (2009), and "Big '1989,' Small '1989': A Comparative View on Eastern Central Europe and China on Their Way into Globalization," in *1989 in a Global Perspective*, ed. Ulf Engel, Frank Hadler, and Matthias Middell (Leipzig, 2015), 177–204.

Notes

1. "ECE" means, in a pragmatic sense (i.e., ignoring a bulk of heavily value-laden and therefore almost endless and sterile semantic debates), the megaregion between Germany in the west and Russia/the Soviet Union in the east, between the Baltic Sea in the north and the Balkans in the south. More strictly speaking, the sample of ECE state socialisms on which this paper is based comprises the GDR, Czechoslovakia, Hungary, and Poland—four countries of a roughly similar geographic, demographic, and economic "format," on a medium level of socioeconomic modernization, which seems to be typical for ECE within a European frame of reference (cf. Iván T. Bérend, *Decades of Crisis: Central and Eastern Europe before World War II* (Berkeley, 1998); idem, *History Derailed: Central and Eastern Europe in the Long Nineteenth Century* (Berkeley, 2003). The commonalities between

these four countries are relatively strong, at least in comparison to "early socialisms" (Soviet Union), "big socialisms" (Soviet Union, China), or "third world socialisms" (e.g., Cuba or Vietnam). Looking at the longer lines of development, one has to state that legal traditions and mentalities are in principle "Western type"—i.e., the political culture is, despite many internal differences, characterized by a basic contrast to the autocratic and despotic traditions of Orthodox and Osman Europe. It is important to note that a certain internal modernization bias existed between the GDR and Czechoslovakia (at least in Bohemia and Moravia), with their relatively old industrial traditions on the one side, and agrarian or semi-industrial Poland and Hungary on the other (these two countries did not undergo industrialization before the postwar era). The history of ECE state socialism was situated between the end of WWII and 1989. Sovietization limited the maneuvering options everywhere (but in different subperiods this holds true with different intensity). Basically, the Soviet system was imposed from without—but at different times and in different countries the Soviet influence was amalgamated with autochthonous traditions in different specific mixtures.
2. At this point, the intermediate strata of socialist societies should also be introduced—e.g., the lower party or trade union functionaries who found themselves sandwiched in a position between orders from above and demands from below, functioning as a sort of buffer or filter in both directions. Split, partial, or diffuse loyalties of social groups and strata were quite a common affair; affinity to the system seems to have been a gradual phenomenon.
3. ECE state socialisms were, strictly speaking, not one-party states, but in a wider sense of the concept: the central role of the Communists was (more or less) camouflaged by the legal existence of other political groupings. But pluralism was limited again by the obligatory membership of all political forces in the "National Front"—where the leading role of the Communists was undisputed.
4. It would, for example, be misleading to assume that the party apparatus was in general the protagonist of "the political," whereas the administration of the state was the advocate of "objective," "neutral," "technocratic" issues. It seems more plausible that both orientations were to be found in both "compartments" of the apparatus.
5. János Kornái, *Das sozialistische System. Die politische Ökonomie des Kommunismus* (Baden-Baden, 1995), 35–428.
6. As the essay presents a comparative analysis on a higher level of generalization and as facts are presented in a strongly condensed form, literature is cited in an aggregated and very strict selection. On the classical system and the logic of its development, especially on socialist reforms in all four countries, cf. Manfred Alexander, *Kleine Geschichte Polens* (Stuttgart, 2008); Anne Applebaum, *The Iron Curtain: The Crushing of Eastern Europe, 1944–1956* (New York, 2012); Jaromír Balcar and Jaroslav Kučera, *Von der Rüstkammer des Reiches zum Maschinenwerk des Sozialismus. Wirtschaftslenkung in Böhmen und Mähren 1938 bis 1953* (Göttingen, 2013); Iván T. Bérend, *Central and Eastern Europe 1944–1993: Detour from the Periphery to the Periphery*

(Cambridge, 1996); idem, *Decades of Crisis: Central and Eastern Europe before World War II* (Berkeley, 1998); idem, *From the Soviet Bloc to the European Union* (Cambridge, 2009); idem, *History Derailed: Central and Eastern Europe in the Long Nineteenth Century* (Berkeley, 2003); László Borhi, *Hungary in the Cold War 1945–1956* (Budapest, 2004); Wlodzimierz Borodziej, *Geschichte Polens im 20. Jahrhundert* (Munich, 2010); Christoph Boyer, "Gesellschaften ohne Krise? Der Staatssozialismus," in *Krisen verstehen. Historische und kulturwissenschaftliche Annäherungen*, ed. Thomas Mergel (Frankfurt/M., 2012), 165–175; idem, ed., *Sozialistische Wirtschaftsreformen. Tschechoslowakei und DDR im Vergleich* (Frankfurt/M., 2006); idem, ed., "Zur Physiognomie sozialistischer Wirtschaftsreformen" (Frankfurt/M., 2007); idem and Friederike Sattler, "In Lieu of an Introduction: Big Structures, Large Processes and Huge Comparisons—A Frame of Interpretation," in *European Economic Elites Between a New Spirit of Capitalism and the Erosion of State Socialism*, ed. Christoph Boyer and Friederike Sattler (Berlin, 2009), 19–70; Christiane Brenner and Peter Heumos, eds., *Sozialgeschichtliche Kommunismusforschung. Tschechoslowakei, Polen, Ungarn und DDR 1948–1968* (Munich, 2005); Norman Davis, *Im Herzen Europas. Geschichte Polens* (Munich, 2000); Dierk Hoffmann, *Aufbau und Krise der Planwirtschaft. Die Arbeitskräftelenkung in der SBZ/DDR 1945 bis 1963* (Munich, 2002); idem, *Nachkriegszeit. Deutschland 1945–1949* (Darmstadt, 2011); idem, *Von Ulbricht zu Honecker: Die DDR 1945–1989* (Berlin, 2013); Dagmara Jajesniak-Quast, *Stahlgiganten in der sozialistischen Transformation. Nowa Huta in Krakau, EKO in Eisenhüttenstadt und Kunčice in Ostrava* (Wiesbaden, 2010); Wladyslaw W. Jermakowicz and Jane Tompson Follis, *Reform Cycles in Eastern Europe 1944–1987: A Comparative Analysis from a Sample of Czechoslovakia, Poland, and the Soviet Union* (Berlin, 1988); Gábor Révész, *Perestroika in Eastern Europe: Hungary's Economic Transformation 1945–1988* (Boulder, 1990); Dieter Segert, *Die Grenzen Osteuropas. 1918, 1945, 1989. Drei Versuche, im Westen anzukommen* (Frankfurt/M., 2002); André Steiner, *Die DDR-Wirtschaftsreform der Sechziger Jahre: Konflikt zwischen Effizienz- und Machtkalkül* (Berlin, 1999); Tibor Valuch, "Changes in the Structure and Lifestyle of the Hungarian Society in the Second Half of the XXth Century," in *Social History of Hungary from the Reform Era to the End of the Twentieth Century*, ed. Gábor Gyáni, György Kövér, and Tibor Valuch (New York, 2004), 509–671.

7. These are central concepts of Max Weber's theory of bureaucracy, cf. Max Weber, *Wirtschaft und Gesellschaft* (Tübingen, 1980), 571–579. In this context, *Regelgebundenheit* does not imply rule of law (and the pertaining judicial controls) in a "Western" sense; the term simply designates the ensemble of orderly, calculable, stable, and consistent administrative procedures that prevent a decline into chaos and anarchy.

8. This point is made against Bala Bálint, *Kaderverwaltung* (Stuttgart, 1972), who states a categorical difference between "administration by cadres" and "Weberian bureaucracy." Cf. Christoph Boyer, *"Die Kader entscheiden alles . . . ." Kaderentwicklung und Kaderpolitik in der zentralen Staatsverwaltung der SBZ und der frühen DDR (1945–1952)* ["The cadres decide everything . . . ." Cadre development and cadre policies in the central state administration of the SOZ and the early GDR (1945–1952)] (Dresden, 1996).

9. Such as (to give just one of many possible examples) "Western" regulatory bodies in the context of a Keynesian style economic policy.
10. Cf. Christoph Boyer, "Bürohelden? Zu Verwaltungsstil und Habitus der zentrale Planbürokratie in der formativen Phase der SBZ/DDR," in Peter Hübner, ed., *Eliten im Sozialismus. Beiträge zur Sozialgeschichte der DDR* (Cologne, 1999), 255–271; idem, "Stabilisierung durch Wandel. Institutionenevolution im Staatssozialismus," in *Das Europa der Diktaturen: Steuerung—Wirtschaft—Recht*, ed. Gerd Bender, Rainer Maria Kiesow, and Dieter Simon (Baden-Baden, 2002), 119–139.
11. Cf., e.g., Peter Heumos, "Aspekte des sozialen Milieus der Industriearbeiterschaft in der Tschechoslowakei vom Ende des Zweiten Weltkrieges bis zur Reformbewegung der sechziger Jahre," *Bohemia* 42, no. 2 (2001): 323–362.
12. Cf. their brochure "Zur ökonomischen Theorie und ökonomischen Politik in der Übergangsperiode" (Berlin, 1956).
13. The *Eingabewesen* in the GDR; functional equivalents existed in other state socialist countries.
14. From the vast literature, cf. Annette Schumann, ed., *Vernetzte Improvisationen. Gesellschaftliche Subsysteme in Ostmitteleuropa und in der DDR* [Crosslinked improvisations. Subsystems of societies in Eastern and Central Europe and in the GDR] (Cologne, 2008).
15. From the vast literature, cf., for example, the special issue "Kaderarbeit" [Cadre work], *Bohemia* 53, no. 2 (2013); Christoph Boyer, "Wirtschaftsfunktionäre. Das Personal der wirtschaftslenkenden Apparate in der formativen Phase der SBZ/DDR (1945–1961)" [Economical functionaries. The staff of the economic steering apparatus in the formative phase of the SOZ/GDR (1945–1961)], in *Vom Funktionieren der Funktionäre. Politische Interessenvertretung und gesellschaftlicher Integration in Deutschland nach 1933* [On the functioning of the functionaries. Political representation of interests and social integration in Germany after 1933], ed. Till Kössler and Helke Stadtland (Essen, 2004), 109–125.
16. This holds true for ECE state socialist regimes; for complex reasons (which cannot be discussed here), China is a different case (cf. the outlook of this essay).
17. Cf., again in an absolutely strict selection, on the European and the global frame of reference, Barry Eichengreen, *The European Economy since 1945: Coordinated Capitalism and Beyond* (Princeton, 2006); Ronald Findlay and Kevin H. O'Rourke, *Power and Plenty: Trade, War, and the World Economy in the Second Millennium* (Princeton, 2007); Jeffry A. Frieden, *Global Capitalism: Its Fall and Rise in the Twentieth Century* (New York, 2006); Eric Hobsbawm, *The Age of Extremes, 1914–1991* (London, 1995); Tony Judt, *Postwar: A History of Europe since 1945* (London, 2005); Hartmut Kaelble, *Sozialgeschichte Europas 1945 bis zur Gegenwart* (Munich, 2007).

On the two new challenges and their consequences, cf. Timothy Garton Ash, *Time for a Revolution?* (Colchester, 2009); Christoph Boyer, "'1989' und die Wege dorthin" [The paths to "1989"], *Vierteljahrshefte für Zeitgeschichte* 1 (2011): 1–18; idem, "Asymmetrische Verflechtung: Ein Beitrag zur Erklärung des Systemzusammenbruchs in Ostmitteleuropa," *Jahrbuch für Wirtschaftsgeschichte* (2014): 197–232; idem, "Lange Entwicklungslinien europäischer Sozialpolitik im 20. Jahrhundert. Eine Annäherung," *Archiv für Sozialgeschichte* (2009): 25–62; idem, "Lernresistenz und Kommunikationsverweigerung: Die Politbüros von SED und Kommunistischer Partei der Tschechoslowakei als retardierende Elemente im '1989er-Prozess,'" *Zeitschrift für Ostmitteleuropa-Forschung* 4 (2010): 472–488; Michael Brie, "Staatssozialistische Länder Europas im Vergleich. Alternative Herrschaftsstrategien und divergente Typen" in *Einheit als Privileg. Vergleichende Perspektiven auf die Transformation Ostdeutschlands,* ed. Helmut Wiesenthal (Frankfurt/M., 1996), 39–104; György Dalos, *1989 — Der Vorhang geht auf. Das Ende der Diktaturen in Osteuropa* (Munich, 2009); Peter Hübner and Jürgen Danyel, "Soziale Argumente im politischen Machtkampf: Prag, Warschau, Berlin 1968–1971," *Zeitschrift für Geschichtswissenschaft* (2002): 804–832; Tomasz Inglot, *Welfare States in East Central Europe, 1919–2004* (Cambridge, 2008); BélaTomka, *Welfare in East and West: Hungarian Social Security in an International Comparison, 1918–1990* (Berlin, 2004).

18. Peter Heumos, "Aspekte des sozialen Milieus."
19. Only Czechoslovakia was, for contingent causes, an exception in this respect. After the 1968 invasion, the Soviet Union propped up the normalization regime with subsidies, at least for a certain time, in order to make it more bearable for the people.
20. Cf. the detailed introduction and the single contributions in Christoph Boyer, Klaus-Dietmar Henke, and Peter Skyba, eds., *Deutsche Demokratische Republik 1971–1990: Bewegung in der Sozialpolitik, Erstarrung und Niedergang* (Baden-Baden, 2008); Klaus-Dietmar Henke, ed., *Revolution und Vereinigung 1989/90* (Munich, 2009); Peter Hübner and Christa Hübner, *Sozialismus als soziale Frage. Sozialpolitik in der DDR und Polen 1968–1976* (Cologne, 2008); Matthias Judt, *Der Bereich Kommerzielle Koordinierung. Das DDR-Wirtschaftsimperium des Alexander Schalck-Golodkowski — Mythos und Realität* (Berlin, 2013); Christoph Kleßmann, *Arbeiter im "Arbeiterstaat" DDR. Deutsche Traditionen, sowjetisches Magnetfeld (1945 bis 1991)* (Bonn, 2007); Ilko-Sascha Kowalczuk, *Endspiel. Die Revolution von 1989 in der DDR* (Munich 2009); Charles M. Maier, *Das Verschwinden der DDR und der Untergang des Kommunismus* (Frankfurt/M., 1999); Gerhard A. Ritter, *Wir sind das Volk! Wir sind ein Volk! Geschichte der deutschen Einigung* (Munich, 2009); Andreas Rödder, *Deutschland einig Vaterland. Die Geschichte der Wiedervereinigung* (Munich, 2009); Jörg Roesler, *Geschichte der DDR* (Cologne, 2012); Klaus Schröder, *Der SED-Staat* (Cologne, 2013); Peter Skyba, "Die Sozialpolitik der Ära Honecker aus institutionentheoretischer Perspektive," in *Repression und Wohlstandsversprechen. Zur Restabilisierung von Parteiherrschaft in der DDR und der ČSSR,* ed. Christoph Boyer and Peter Skyba (Dresden, 1999), 49–62; André Steiner, ed., *Überholen ohne einzuholen: die DDR-Wirtschaft als Fußnote der deutschen Geschichte?* (Berlin, 2006); idem, *Von Plan zu Plan. Eine Wirtschaftsgeschichte der DDR* (Munich, 2004); Stefan Wolle, *Die heile Welt der Diktatur. Alltag und Herrschaft in der DDR 1971–1989* (Bonn, 1998).
21. Franz-Lothar Altmann, *Wirtschaftsentwicklung und Strukturpolitik in der Tschechoslowakei nach 1968* (Munich, 1987); Beata Blehova, *Der Fall des Kommunismus in der Tschechoslowakei* (Vienna, 2006); Mikuláš Teich, Dušan

Kováč, and Martin D. Brown, eds., *Slovakia in History* (Cambridge, 2011); Christoph Boyer, "Normalisierung," *Bohemia* (2006/7): 348–360; idem, "'Sorge um den Menschen.' Tschechoslowakische Sozial- und Konsumpolitik im Übergang von der Reform zur 'Normalisierung,'" in *Sozialismus als soziale Frage*, ed. Peter Hübner and Christa Hübner (Cologne, 2008), 471–514; Jiří Kosta, *Die tschechische/tschechoslowakische Wirtschaft im mehrfachen Wandel*, (Muenster, 2005); Vladimir Kusin, *From Dubček to Charter: A Study of "Normalization" in Czechoslovakia 1968–1978* (Edinburgh, 1978); Martin Myant, *The Czechoslovak Economy 1948–1988: The Battle for Economic Reform* (Cambridge, 1989); Niklas Perzi, Beata Blehova, and Peter Bachmaier, eds., *Die Samtene Revolution. Vorgeschichte, Verlauf, Akteure* (Frankfurt/M., 2009); J. N. Stevens, *Czechoslovakia at the Crossroads: The Economic Dilemmas of Communism in Postwar Czechoslovakia* (New York, 1985), 226–259; Zdislav Šulc, *Stručné dějiny ekonomických reforem v Československu (České republice) 1945–1995* [A short history of economic reforms in Czechoslovakia (The Czech Republic) 1945–1995] (Brno, 1998); Alice Teichova, *Wirtschaftsgeschichte der Tschechoslowakei, 1918–1980* (Vienna, 1988); Otakar Turek, *Podíl ekonomiky na pádu komunismu v Československu* [The economic factor and the fall of Communism in Czechoslovakia] (Prague, 1995).
22. Assisted by an expert culture that seems to have gained importance in late socialism.
23. As an instructive report on late socialist social policy in everyday life, cf. Landolf Scherzer, *Der Erste. Eine Reportage aus der DDR* (Rudolstadt, 1988).
24. There was a last and rather feeble attempt at economic flexibility in Czechoslovakia in the late 1980s—but more or less as an academic initiative, without much practical relevance.
25. In order to explain this final breakdown, an additional bundle of "individual" events leading to the open revolt in autumn 1989 ought to be introduced, but this lies beyond the horizons of this essay.
26. Jane L. Curry, "The Solidarity Crisis, 1980–1981: The Near Death of Communism," in *Poland's Permanent Revolution*, 167–209; Andreas Hoessli, *Planlose Planwirtschaft. Krisenzyklus und Reformmodelle in Polen* (Hamburg, 1989); Hübner and Hübner, *Sozialismus als soziale Frage*; Lukas Imhof, "Polen und das Phänomen Solidarnosc," in *Transformation und historisches Erbe in den Staaten des europäischen Ostens*, ed. Carsten Goehrke and Seraina Gilly (Bern, 2000), 529–597; Wladyslaw W. Jermakowicz, *Das wirtschaftliche Lenkungssystem Polens. Indikatoren und Determinanten seiner Entwicklung 1944–1984* (Marburg, 1985); Zbigniew Kamecki, "Poland's Foreign Indebtedness," in *Economic Reform in Poland: The Aftermath of Martial Law*, ed. David M. Kemme (Greenwich, CT, 1991), 141–157; Bartolomiej Kaminski, *The Collapse of State Socialism: The Case of Poland* (Princeton, 1991); David M. Kemme, "Obstacles to Reform," in *Economic Reform in Poland: the Aftermath of Martial Law 1981–1988*, ed. idem (Greenwich, CT, 1991), 1–13; Sarah Meiklejohn, "1976: Anatomy of an Avoidable Crisis" in *Poland's Permanent Revolution: People vs. Elites, 1956 to the Present*, ed. Jane L. Curry and Luba Faifer (Washington, DC, 1996), 109–165; August Pradetto, *Bürokratische Anarchie. Der Niedergang des polnischen "Realsozialismus"* (Vienna, 1992); Ben Slay, *The Polish Economy: Crisis, Reform and Transformation* (Princeton, 1994);

Krystyna Szymkiewicz, "From Decentralization to Liberalization of Foreign Trade: The Experience of Poland," in *The Soviet Union and Eastern Europe in the Global Economy*, ed. Marie Lavigne (Cambridge, 1992), 190–204; Johannes von Thadden, *Krisen in Polen: 1956, 1970 und 1980. Eine vergleichende Analyse ihrer Ursachen und Folgen mit Hilfe der ökonomischen Theorie der Politik* (Frankfurt/M., 1986); Klaus Ziemer, *Polens Weg in die Krise: eine politische Soziologie der "Ära Gierek"* (Frankfurt/M., 1987).

27. Iván T. Bérend, "Economic Growth and Structural Changes in the Economy and Society: The State Socialist Attempt Fails," in *Evolution of the Hungarian Economy 1848–1998*, vol. 1, *One-and-Half Centuries of Semi-Successful Modernization 1848–1989*, ed. Iván T. Bérend and Tomás Csató, (New York, 2001), 362–384; idem, *The Hungarian Economic Reforms 1953–1988* (Cambridge, 1990); idem, "Post-Stalinist Reforms: Towards a Hungarian Model of State Socialism," in *Evolution of the Hungarian Economy 1848–1989*, vol. 1, 293–322; Tomás Csató, "Transport, Trade and the Services," in *Evolution of the Hungarian Economy 1848–1998*, vol. 1, 350–361; L. Izsák, *A Political History of Hungary 1944–1990* (Budapest, 2002); János Kornai, *Evolution of the Hungarian Economy 1848–1998*, vol. 2, *Paying the Bill for Goulash Communism* (New York, 2000); idem, *Unterwegs. Essays zur wirtschaftlichen Umgestaltung in Ungarn* (Marburg, 1996), 285–362; idem, "The Hungarian Reform Process: Visions, Hopes, and Reality," *The Journal of Economic Literature* 24 (1986): 1687–1737; Gábor Révész, *Perestroika in Eastern Europe: Hungary's Economic Transformation 1945–1988* (Boulder, 1990); Ignác Romsics, *Hungary in the Twentieth Century* (Budapest, 1999); Sándor Szakács, "From 'Goulash Communism' to Breakdown," in *The Ideas of the Hungarian Revolution, Suppressed and Victorious 1956–1999*, ed. Lee W. Congdon and Bela K. Király (New York, 2002), 194–230.

28. A (rather sketchy) outline of an explanation is presented in Christoph Boyer, "Sozialgeschichte der Arbeiterschaft und staatssozialistische Entwicklungspfade: konzeptionelle Überlegungen und eine Erklärungsskizze," in *Arbeiter im Staatssozialismus—Ideologischer Anspruch und soziale Wirklichkeit*, ed. Peter Hübner, Christoph Kleßmann, and Klaus Tenfelde (Cologne, 2005), 71–86.

29. For first hints, cf. Christoph Boyer, "Big '1989,' Small '1989': A Comparative View on Eastern Central Europe and China on their Way into Globalization," in *1989 in a Global Perspective*, ed. U. Engel, F. Hadler, and M. Middell (Leipzig, 2015), 177–204; Barry Naughton, *Growing Out of the Plan: Chinese Economic Reforms 1978–1993* (New York, 1996); idem, *The Chinese Economy: Transitions and Growth* (Cambridge, 2007); Peter Nolan, *Transforming China: Globalization, Transition and Development* (London, 2005).

Bibliography

Alexander, Manfred. *Kleine Geschichte Polens* [A short history of Poland]. Stuttgart: Reclam, 2008.

Altmann, Franz-Lothar. *Wirtschaftsentwicklung und Strukturpolitik in der Tschechoslowakei nach 1968* [Economic development and structural policy in Czechoslovakia after 1968]. Munich: Olzog, 1987.
Applebaum, Anne. *The Iron Curtain: The Crushing of Eastern Europe, 1944–1956*. New York: Doubleday, 2012.
Balcar, Jaromír, and Kučera Jaroslav. *Von der Rüstkammer des Reiches zum Maschinenwerk des Sozialismus. Wirtschaftslenkung in Böhmen und Mähren 1938 bis 1953* [From the armory of the Reich to the machine work of socialism. Economic governance in Bohemia and Moravia 1938–1953]. Göttingen: Vandenhoeck & Ruprecht, 2013.
Balla, Bálint. *Kaderverwaltung* [Administration by cadres]. Stuttgart: Enke, 1972.
Bérend, IvánT. *Central and Eastern Europe 1944–1993: Detour from the Periphery to the Periphery*. Cambridge: Cambridge University Press, 1996.
———. *Decades of Crisis: Central and Eastern Europe before World War II*. Berkeley: University of California Press, 1998.
———. "Economic Growth and Structural Changes in the Economy and Society: The State Socialist Attempt Fails." In *Evolution of the Hungarian Economy 1848–1998*. Vol. 1, *One-and-Half Centuries of Semi-Successful Modernization 1848–1989*, ed. Iván T. Bérend and Tomás Csató, 362–384. New York: Columbia University Press, 2001.
———. *From the Soviet Bloc to the European Union*. Cambridge: Cambridge University Press, 2009.
———. *History Derailed: Central and Eastern Europe in the Long Nineteenth Century*. Berkeley: University of California Press, 2003.
———. *The Hungarian Economic Reforms 1953–1988*. Cambridge: Cambridge University Press, 1990.
———. "Post-Stalinist Reforms: Towards a Hungarian Model of State Socialism." In *Evolution of the Hungarian Economy 1848–1989*. Vol. I, *One-and-Half Centuries of Semi-Successful Modernization 1848–1989*, ed. Iván T Bérend and Tomás Csató, 293–322. New York: Columbia University Press, 2001.
Blehova, Beata. *Der Fall des Kommunismus in der Tschechoslowakei* [The fall of communism in Czechoslovakia]. Vienna: Lit, 2006.
Borhi, László. *Hungary in the Cold War 1945–1956*. Budapest: CEU Press, 2004.
Boyer, Christoph. "'1989' und die Wege dorthin" [The paths to "1989"]. *Vierteljahrshefte für Zeitgeschichte* 59, no. 1 (2011): 101–118.
———. "Asymmetrische Verflechtung: Ein Beitrag zur Erklärung des Systemzusammenbruchs in Ostmitteleuropa" [Asymmetric interdependence: A contribution to the explanation of the system collapse in Eastern Central Europe]. *Jahrbuch für Wirtschaftsgeschichte* 55, no. 1 (2014): 197–232.
———. "Big '1989,' small '1989': A Comparative View on Eastern Central Europe and China on Their Way into Globalization." In *1989 in a Global Perspective*, ed. Ulf Engel, Frank Hadler, and Matthias Middell, 177–204. Leipzig: Leipziger Universitäts-Verlag, 2015.
———. "Bürohelden? Zu Verwaltungsstil und Habitus der zentrale Planbürokratie in der formativen Phase der SBZ/DDR" [Office heros? On the administrative style and the habitus of the central planning bureaucracy in the formative phase of the SOZ/GDR]. In *Eliten im Sozialismus. Beiträge zur Sozi-*

algeschichte der DDR [Elites in socialism. Contributions to the social history of the GDR], ed. Peter Hübner, 255–271. Cologne: Böhlau, 1999.

———. "*Die Kader entscheiden alles . . . .*" *Kaderentwicklung und Kaderpolitik in der zentralen Staatsverwaltung der SBZ und der frühen DDR (1945–1952)* ["The cadres decide everything . . . ." Cadre development and cadre policies in the central state administration of the SOZ and the early GDR (1945–1952)]. Dresden: Hannah-Arendt-Institut für Totalitarismusforschung, 1996.

———. "Gesellschaften ohne Krise? Der Staatssozialismus" [Societies without crisis? The case of state socialism]. In *Krisen verstehen. Historische und kulturwissenschaftliche Annäherungen* [Understanding crises. Historical and cultural approaches], ed. Thomas Mergel, 165–175. Frankfurt/M.: Campus, 2012.

———. "Lange Entwicklungslinien europäischer Sozialpolitik im 20. Jahrhundert. Eine Annäherung" [Long lines of development of European social policy in the 20th century. An approach]. *Archiv für Sozialgeschichte* (2009): 25–62.

———. "Lernresistenz und Kommunikationsverweigerung: Die Politbüros von SED und Kommunistischer Partei der Tschechoslowakei als retardierende Elemente im '1989er-Prozess'" [Learning resistance and refusal to communicate: The politburo of the SED and the Communist Party of Czechoslovakia as retarding elements in "the 1989 process"]. *Zeitschrift für Ostmitteleuropa-Forschung* 4 (2010): 472–488.

———. "Normalisierung" [Normalization]. *Bohemia* (2006/7): 348–360.

———. "'Sorge um den Menschen.' Tschechoslowakische Sozial- und Konsumpolitik im Übergang von der Reform zur 'Normalisierung'" ["Concern for the people." Czechoslovak social and consumer policy in the transition from reform to "normalization"]. In *Sozialismus als soziale Frage. Sozialpolitik in der DDR und Polen 1968–1976* [Socialism as a social issue. Social policy in East Germany and Poland 1968–1976], ed. Peter Hübner and Christa Hübner, 471–514. Cologne: Böhlau, 2008.

———. "Sozialgeschichte der Arbeiterschaft und staatssozialistische Entwicklungspfade: konzeptionelle Überlegungen und eine Erklärungsskizze" [The social history of the working class and state socialist development paths: Conceptual considerations and a sketch of an explanation]. In *Arbeiter im Staatssozialismus — Ideologischer Anspruch und soziale Wirklichkeit* [Workers in state socialism — ideological claim and social reality], ed. Peter Hübner, Christoph Kleßmann, and Klaus Tenfelde, 71–86. Cologne: Böhlau, 2005.

———. "Stabilisierung durch Wandel. Institutionenevolution im Staatssozialismus" [Stabilization through change. The evolution of institutions in state socialism]. In *Das Europa der Diktatur: Steuerung — Wirtschaft — Recht* [The Europe of dictatorship: Regulation — economy — law], ed. Gerd Bender, Rainer Maria Kiesow, and Dieter Simon, 119–139. Baden-Baden: Nomos, 2002.

———. "Wirtschaftsfunktionäre. Das Personal der wirtschaftslenkenden Apparate in der formativen Phase der SBZ/DDR (1945–1961)." [Economic functionaries. The staff of the economic steering apparatus in the formative phase of the SOZ/GDR (1945–1961)]. In *Vom Funktionieren der Funktionäre. Politische Interessenvertretung und gesellschaftlicher Integration in Deutschland nach 1933* [On the functioning of the functionaries. Political representation of

interests and social integration in Germany after 1933], ed. Till Kössler and Helke Stadtland, 109–125. Essen: Klartext, 2004.
———, ed. *Sozialistische Wirtschaftsreformen. Tschechoslowakei und DDR im Vergleich* [Socialist economic reforms. Czechoslovakia and East Germany compared]. Frankfurt/M.: Klostermann, 2006.
———, ed. *Zur Physiognomie sozialistischer Wirtschaftsreformen* [On the physiognomy of socialist economic reforms]. Frankfurt/M.: Klostermann, 2007.
Boyer, Christoph, and Friederike Sattler. "In Lieu of an Introduction: Big Structures, Large Processes and Huge Comparisons—A Frame of Interpretation." In *European Economic Elites between a New Spirit of Capitalism and the Erosion of State Socialism*, ed. Christoph Boyer and Friederike Sattler, 19–70. Berlin: Duncker & Humblot, 2009.
Boyer, Christoph, Klaus-Dietmar Henke, and Peter Skyba, eds. *Deutsche Demokratische Republik 1971–1990: Bewegung in der Sozialpolitik, Erstarrung und Niedergang* [The German Democratic Republic 1971–1990: Movement in social policy, sclerosis and decline]. Baden-Baden: Nomos, 2008.
Boyer, Christoph, and Peter Skyba, eds. *Repression und Wohlstandsversprechen. Zur Stabilisierung von Parteiherrschaft in der DDR und ČSSR* [Repression and promise of prosperity. On stabilization of party rule in the GDR and the ČSSR]. Dresden: Hannah-Arendt-Institut für Totalitarismusforschung, 1999.
Brenner, Christian, and Peter Heumos, eds. *Sozialgeschichtliche Kommunismusforschung. Tschechoslowakei, Polen, Ungarn und DDR 1948–1968* [Studies in the social history of communism. Czechoslovakia, Poland, Hungary and East Germany 1948–1968], Munich: Oldenbourg, 2005.
Brie, Michael. "Staatssozialistische Länder Europas im Vergleich. Alternative Herrschaftsstrategien und divergente Typen" [State socialist countries in Europe compared. Alternative strategies of governance and divergent types]. In *Einheit als Privileg. Vergleichende Perspektiven auf die Transformation Ostdeutschlands* [Unity as a privilege. Comparative perspectives on the transformation of East Germany], ed. Helmut Wiesenthal, 39–104. Frankfurt/M.: Campus, 1996.
Csató, Tomás. "Transport, Trade and the Services." In *Evolution of the Hungarian Economy 1848–1998. Vol. I, One-and-Half Centuries of Semi-Successful Modernization 1848–1989*, ed. Iván T. Bérend and Tomás Csató, 350–361. Boulder: Social Science Monographs, 2000.
Curry, Jane L. "The Solidarity Crisis, 1980–1981: The Near Death of Communism." In *Poland's Permanent Revolution*, ed. Jane L. Curry and Luba Faifer, 167–209. Washington, DC: American University Press, 1996.
Dalos, György. *1989—Der Vorhang geht auf. Das Ende der Diktaturen in Osteuropa* [1989—The curtain opens. The end of dictatorship in Eastern Europe]. Munich: C. H. Beck, 2009.
Davies, Norman. *Im Herzen Europas. Geschichte Polens* [In the heart of Europe. A history of Poland]. Munich: C. H. Beck, 2000.
Eichengreen, Barry. *The European Economy since 1945: Coordinated Capitalism and Beyond*. Princeton: Princeton University Press, 2006.
Findlay, Ronald, and Kevin H. O'Rourke. *Power and Plenty: Trade, War, and the World Economy in the Second Millennium*. Princeton: Princeton University Press, 2007.

Frieden, Jeffry A. *Global Capitalism: Its Fall and Rise in the Twentieth Century*. New York: Norton, 2006.
Garton Ash, Timothy. *Time for a Revolution?* Colchester: Routledge, 2009.
Henke, Klaus-Dietmar, ed. *Revolution und Vereinigung 1989/90* [Revolution and reunification 1989/90]. Munich: Deutscher Taschenbuch-Verlag, 2009.
Heumos, Peter. "Aspekte des sozialen Milieus der Industriearbeiterschaft in der Tschechoslowakei vom Ende des Zweiten Weltkrieges bis zur Reformbewegung der sechziger Jahre" [Aspects of the social milieu of the industrial working class in Czechoslovakia from the end of World War II until the reform movement of the sixties]. *Bohemia* 42, no. 2 (2001): 323–362.
Hobsbawm, Eric. *The Age of Extremes, 1914–1991*. London: Joseph, 1995.
Hoessli, Andreas. *Planlose Planwirtschaft. Krisenzyklus und Reformmodelle in Polen* [Chaos in the planned economy. The crisis cycle and reform models in Poland]. Hamburg: Junius, 1989.
Hoffmann, Dierk. *Aufbau und Krise der Planwirtschaft. Die Arbeitskräftelenkung in der SBZ/DDR 1945 bis 1963* [Building and crisis of the planned economy. The steering of the labor force in the SOZ/GDR 1945–1963]. Munich: Oldenbourg, 2002.
———. *Nachkriegszeit. Deutschland 1945—1949* [The postwar era. Germany 1945–1949]. Darmstadt: Wissenschaftliche Buchgesellschaft, 2011.
———. *Von Ulbricht zu Honecker: Die DDR 1945–1989* [From Ulbricht to Honekker: The GDR 1945–1989]. Berlin: be.bra-Verlag, 2013.
Hübner, Peter, and Jürgen Danyel. "Soziale Argumente im politischen Machtkampf: Prag, Warschau, Berlin 1968–1971" [Social arguments in the struggle for political power: Prague, Warsaw, Berlin 1968–1971]. *Zeitschrift für Geschichtswissenschaft* (2002): 804–832.
Imhof, Lukas. "Polen und das Phänomen Solidarnosc" [Poland and the solidarnosc phenomenon]. In *Transformation und historisches Erbe in den Staaten des europäischen Ostens* [Transformation and historical heritage in the countries of the European east], ed. Carsten Goehrke and Seraina Gilly, 529–597. Bern: Lang, 2000.
Inglot, Tomasz. *Welfare States in East Central Europe, 1919–2004*. Cambridge: Cambridge University Press, 2008.
Izsák, L. *A Political History of Hungary 1944–1990*. Budapest: Eötvös University Press, 2002.
Jajesniak–Quast, Dagmara. *Stahlgiganten in der sozialistischen Transformation. Nowa Huta in Krakau, EKO in Eisenhüttenstadt und Kunčice in Ostrava* [Steel giants in the socialist transformation. Nowa Huta in Krakow, EKO in Eisenhüttenstadt and Kunčice in Ostrava]. Wiesbaden: Harrassowitz, 2010.
Jermakowicz, Wladyslaw W. *Das wirtschaftliche Lenkungssystem Polens. Indikatoren und Determinanten seiner Entwicklung 1944–1984* [The economic steering system in Poland. Indicators and determinants of its development from 1944 to 1984]. Marburg: Herder-Institut, 1985.
Jermakowicz, Wladyslaw W., and Jane Tompson Follis. *Reform Cycles in Eastern Europe 1944–1987: A Comparative Analysis from a Sample of Czechoslovakia, Poland, and the Soviet Union*. Berlin: Duncker & Humblot, 1988.
Judt, Matthias. *Der Bereich Kommerzielle Koordinierung. Das DDR-Wirtschaftsimperium des Alexander Schalck-Golodkowski—Mythos und Realität* [The

commercial coordination sector. The GDR economic empire of Alexander Schalck-Golodkowski—Myth and reality]. Berlin: Links, 2013.
Judt, Tony. *Postwar: A History of Europe since 1945*. London: Penguin, 2005.
Kaelble, Hartmut. *Sozialgeschichte Europas 1945 bis zur Gegenwart* [Social history of Europe 1945 until today]. Munich: C. H. Beck, 2007.
Kamecki, Zbigniew. "Poland's Foreigns Indebtedness." In *Economic Reform in Poland: The Aftermath of Martial Law*, ed. David M. Kemme, 141–157. Greenwich, CT: Jai Press, 1991.
Kaminski, Bartolomiej. *The Collapse of State Socialism: The Case of Poland*. Princeton, NJ: Princeton University Press, 1991.
Kemme, David M. "Obstacles to Reform." In *Economic Reform in Poland: The Aftermath of Martial Law 1981–1988*, ed. David M. Kemme, 1–13. Greenwich, CT: Jai Press, 1991.
Kleßmann, Christoph. *Arbeiter im "Arbeiterstaat" DDR: Deutsche Tradition, sowjetisches Modell, westdeutsches Magnetfeld (1945 bis 1971)* [Workers in the "worker state" GDR: German tradition, Soviet model, West German magnetic field (1945 to 1971)]. Bonn: Verlag J. H. W. Dietz Nachf., 2007.
Kornai, János. *Evolution of the Hungarian Economy 1848–1998*. Vol. 2, *Paying the Bill for Goulash Communism*. New York: Columbia University Press, 2000.
———. The Hungarian Reform Process: Visions, Hopes, and Reality. *The Journal of Economic Literature* 24 (1986): 1687–1737.
———. *Unterwegs. Essays zur wirtschaftlichen Umgestaltung in Ungarn* [On the road. Essays on the economic transformation in Hungary]. Marburg: Metropolis, 1996.
Kosta, Jiří. *Die tschechische/tschechoslowakische Wirtschaft im mehrfachen Wandel* [The Czech/Czechoslovak economy in the process of continuous change]. Münster: Lit, 2005.
Kowalczuk, Ilko-Sascha. *Endspiel. Die Revolution von 1989 in der DDR* [Endgame. The revolution of 1989 in the GDR]. Munich: C. H. Beck, 2009.
Kusin, Vladimir. *From Dubček to Charter 77: A Study of "Normalisation" in Czechoslovakia 1968–1978*. Edinburgh: Q Press, 1978.
Maier, Charles M. *Das Verschwinden der DDR und der Untergang des Kommunismus* [The disappearance of the GDR and the fall of communism]. Frankfurt/M.: Fischer, 1999.
Meiklejohn, Sarah. "1976: Anatomy of an Avoidable Crisis." In *Poland's Permanent Revolution: People vs. Elites, 1956 to the Present*, ed. Jane L. Curry and Luba Faifer, 109–165. Washington: American University Press, 1996.
Myant, Martin. *The Czechoslovak Economy 1948–1988: The Battle for Economic Reform*. Cambridge: Cambridge University Press, 1989.
Naughton, Barry. *The Chinese Economy: Transitions and Growth*. Cambridge, MA: MIT Press, 2007.
———. *Growing out of the Plan: Chinese Economic Reforms 1978–1993*. New York: Cambridge University Press, 1996.
Nolan, Peter. *Transforming China: Globalization, Transition and Development*. London: Anthem Press, 2005.
Perzi, Niklas, Beata Blehova, and Peter Bachmaier, eds. *Die Samtene Revolution. Vorgeschichte, Verlauf, Akteure* [The velvet revolution. Prehistory, events, actors]. Frankfurt/M.: Lang, 2009.

Pradetto, August. *Bürokratische Anarchie. Der Niedergang des polnischen "Realsozialismus"* [Bureaucratic anarchy. The decline of Polish "real socialism"]. Vienna: Böhlau, 1992.
Révész, Gábor. *Perestroika in Eastern Europe: Hungary's Economic Transformation 1945–1988*. Boulder: Westview Press, 1990.
Ritter, Gerhard A. *Wir sind das Volk! Wir sind ein Volk! Geschichte der deutschen Einigung* [We are the people! We are one people! The history of German reunification]. Munich: C. H. Beck, 2009.
Rödder, Andreas. *Deutschland einig Vaterland. Die Geschichte der Wiedervereinigung* [Germany united fatherland. The history of the reunification]. Munich: C. H. Beck, 2009.
Roesler, Jörg. *Geschichte der DDR* [History of the GDR]. Cologne: Papyrossa, 2012.
Romsics, Ignác. *Hungary in the Twentieth Century*. Budapest: Osiris, 1999.
Sándor Szakács, "From 'Goulash Communism' to Breakdown." In *The Ideas of the Hungarian Revolution, Suppressed and Victorious 1956–1999*, ed. Lee W. Congdon and Bela K. Király, 194–230. New York: Social Science Monograph, 2002.
Scherzer, Landolf. *Der Erste. Eine Reportage aus der DDR* [The boss. A report from the GDR]. Cologne: Kiepenheuer & Witsch, 1988.
Schroeder, Klaus. *Der SED-Staat* [The SED state]. Cologne: Böhlau, 2013.
Segert, Dieter. *Die Grenzen Osteuropas. 1918, 1945, 1989. Drei Versuche, im Westen anzukommen* [The borders of Eastern Europe. 1918, 1945, 1989. Three attempts at arriving in the West]. Frankfurt/M.: Campus, 2002.
Skyba, Peter. "Die Sozialpolitik der Ära Honecker aus institutionentheoretischer Perspektive" [The social policy of the Honecker era from the perspective of institution theory]. In *Repression und Wohlstandsversprechen. Zur Restabilisierung von Parteiherrschaft in der DDR und der ČSSR* [Repression and the promise of prosperity. On the restabilization of party rule in East Germany and Czechoslovakia], ed. Christoph Boyer and Peter Skyba, 49–62. Dresden: Hannah-Arendt-Institut für Totalitarismusforschung, 1999.
Slay, Ben. *The Polish Economy: Crisis, Reform and Transformation*. Princeton, NJ: Princeton University Press, 1994.
Steiner, André, ed., *Überholen ohne einzuholen: die DDR-Wirtschaft als Fußnote der deutschen Geschichte?* [Overtaking without catching up: The East German economy as a footnote in German history?]. Berlin: Links, 2006.
Steiner, André. *Die DDR-Wirtschaftsreform der sechziger Jahre: Konflikt zwischen Effizienz- und Machtkalkül* [Economic reform in the GDR in the sixties: The conflict between efficiency and power considerations]. Berlin: Akademie-Verlag, 1999.
———. *Von Plan zu Plan. Eine Wirtschaftsgeschichte der DDR* [From one plan to the next. An economic history of the GDR]. Munich: Deutsche Verlags-Anstalt, 2004.
Stevens, John Z. *Czechoslovakia at the Crossroads: The Economic Dilemmas of Communism in Postwar Czechoslovakia*. New York: Columbia University Press, 1985.
Šulc, Zdislav. *Stručné dějiny ekonomických reforem v Československu (České republice) 1945–1995* [A short history of economic reforms in Czechoslovakia (The Czech Republic) 1945–1995]. Brno: Nakladatelství Doplněk, 1998.

Szymkiewicz, Krystyna. "From Decentralization to Liberalization of Foreign Trade: The Experience of Poland." In *The Soviet Union and Eastern Europe in the Global Economy*, ed. Marie Lavigne, 190–204. Cambridge: Cambridge University Press, 1992.

Teich, Mikuláš, Dušan Kováč, and Martin D. Brown, eds. *Slovakia in History*. Cambridge: Cambridge University Press, 2011.

Teichova, Alice. *Wirtschaftsgeschichte der Tschechoslowakei, 1918–1980* [An economic history of Czechoslovakia, 1918–1980]. Vienna: Böhlau, 1988.

Thadden, Johannes von. *Krisen in Polen: 1956, 1970 und 1980. Eine vergleichende Analyse ihrer Ursachen und Folgen mit Hilfe der ökonomischen Theorie der Politik* [Crises in Poland: 1956, 1970 and 1980. A comparative analysis of their causes and consequences with the help of the economic theory of politics]. Frankfurt/M.: Lang, 1986.

Tomka, Béla. *Welfare in East and West: Hungarian Social Security in an International Comparison, 1918–1990*. Berlin: Akadamie-Verlag, 2004.

Turek, Otakar. *Podíl ekonomiky na pádu komunismu v Československu* [The economic factor and the fall of communism in Czechoslovakia]. Prague: Ústav pro Soudobé Dějiny AV ČR, 1995.

Valuch, Tibor. "Changes in the Structure and Lifestyle of the Hungarian Society in the Second Half of the XXth Century." In *Social History of Hungary from the Reform Era to the End of the Twentieth Century*, ed. Gábor Gyáni, György Kövér, and Tibor Valuch, 509–671. New York: Social Science Monographs, 2004.

Weber, Max. *Wirtschaft und Gesellschaft* [Economy and society]. Tübingen: Mohr, 1980.

Wolle, Stefan. *Die heile Welt der Diktatur. Alltag und Herrschaft in der DDR 1971–1989* [The cozy world of dictatorship. Everyday life and political power in the GDR from 1971 to 1989]. Bonn: Christoph Links Verlag, 1998.

Ziemer, Klaus. *Polens Weg in die Krise: eine politische Soziologie der "Ära Gierek"* [Poland's way into the crisis: A political sociology of the "Gierek era"]. Frankfurt/M.: Athenäum, 1987.

7

THE CENTRAL COMMITTEE DEPARTMENT OF PARTY ORGANS UNDER KHRUSHCHEV

Alexander Titov

The Department of Party Organs (hereafter DPO) was one of the key units in the Central Committee apparatus of the Communist Party of the Soviet Union (CPSU)—the principal political, administrative, and ideological center in the Soviet system of governance.[1] This chapter[2] looks at the structure, personnel, and main functions of the department, focusing on the Khrushchev period from 1953 to 1964. It also examines reasons for the eventual dismantlement of the system formed under Khrushchev, and the impact this had on the long-term reforms of the Communist Party.

Khrushchev has been seen by historians as the champion of party supremacy in the Soviet Union.[3] At the end of Stalin's era there were three centers of power in the Soviet Union—the Soviet government, the security services, and the Communist Party apparatus. The two former centers of power—the state ministries and the security services—held predominance over the party machine. Lavrentii Beria's rapid removal from power by other Presidium members in June 1953 attested to their fears about the excessive influence of the security services, while also reducing the latter's significance.[4] The rivalry between the state and the party structures proved to be more enduring.

The post-Stalin struggle for power is best understood within the context of a Khrushchev-led successful shift in the balance of power away from the state institution in favor of the party apparatus. A critical component of this shift of power was the reform of the state and party apparatuses that took place in the decade following the death of Stalin in 1953. In this context, Khrushchev's term in power can be divided into three periods.

The first period, between 1953 and 1957, was marked by attempts to find solutions to the over-centralization and bureaucratization of both the state and party apparatuses. An important factor during this period was the ongoing political struggle for power among the Presidium members, which spilled over into institutional rivalries between the party and the state, represented respectively by Khrushchev and his colleagues in the Presidium who held ministerial posts.[5] That period ended in May 1957 with the *sovnarkhoz* (regional economic council) reform, which led to the abolition of some twenty-five ministries and replaced them with *sovnarkhozy*, and the defeat of the "anti-party group" at the June plenum of the Central Committee of the same year, following a failed attempt by the majority of the Presidium members to remove Khrushchev from the post of the first secretary of the CPSU.

The second period, between 1957 and 1962, saw the peak of Khrushchev's power, with little institutional reform in either the state or the party apparatuses, as the system of government built in the previous period was given a chance to show its worth. Finally, the third period, between 1962 and the removal of Khrushchev from office in October 1964, saw a new bout of reorganizations of the party and the state apparatuses, prompted by economic and political pressure on Khrushchev. The ultimate failure to invigorate the economy led to the end of Khrushchev's political influence and a scaling back of his reforms under the new post-Khrushchev collective leadership. The latter declared stability as the cornerstone of its policies, which defined Soviet politics for the next two decades. This broad periodization into three phases can be also applied to the analysis of reforms of the Central Committee apparatus.[6] Within this broader framework, the DPO was also subject to a series of reorganizations that exemplified its role and importance in the new system of government in the Soviet Union.

Structure of the Department of Party Organs

Since its inception, the Central Committee apparatus, the support office of the Communist Party's main decision-making bodies, had two unique functions in the Soviet system: responsibility for propaganda and agitation, and personnel policy. Although various other functions were added to the Central Committee apparatus remit over time—including, for example, responsibility for economic and international affairs—the ideological and personnel spheres always remained the prerogative of the Central Committee apparatus at least until Gorbachev's reforms of the Communist Party in the late 1980s.

The DPO was the key unit in personnel management, where its responsibilities included the running of the *nomenklatura* system of top-level appointments across the Soviet system, and the supervision of the entire structure of the Communist Party, including the interaction between the central party leadership and the regional elites in the Soviet Union. In the first post-Stalin decade, the DPO consolidated its place within the central party structures, while at the same time undergoing significant structural changes. Overall, there were two distinct changes to the way the DPO operated under Khrushchev. First, there was a greater emphasis on the regional organization of the department, which culminated in a division of the single DPO into two different departments, one for the Union Republics and one for the Russian Soviet Federated Socialist Republic (RSFSR). Second, the department and its successors were subject to larger staff cuts than the rest of the Central Committee apparatus.

One of the most distinct features of the Khrushchev period was the trend toward decentralization and campaigns against excessive bureaucracy.[7] Although the main brunt of reforms was aimed at state institutions, the Central Committee apparatus was also subject to restructuring and staff cuts, resulting in the loss of around 14 percent of its staff between 1953 and 1957.[8] The DPO was affected by this trend to a greater degree than other departments. If in April 1953 it had 298 staff members, by 1957 it had lost 22 percent of its staff, down to a total of 232 employees in the two departments that replaced the former DPO (132 for the Union Republics department, and 100 for the RSFSR department).[9]

Given the nature of its work in the supervision of local party organizations, the DPO always had a strong regional focus, reflected in its structure of ten regional sectors covering the main areas of the USSR and six functional sectors.[10] The trend toward regionalization meant that it was one of the earliest departments to be split on a territorial principle in May 1954, preceded only by the Department of Agriculture, which was split into the departments for the RSFSR and the Union Republics in January 1954. The two areas of special concern for Khrushchev, agriculture and the local party machine, were therefore exposed to new organizational methods from the earliest period.

The principle of territorial specialization in the Central Committee apparatus was fully implemented in 1956, when the Bureau for the RSFSR was established to serve as a substitute for a RSFSR Central Committee secretariat. This gave Khrushchev the opportunity to place his allies in key positions in the new structure, including Viktor Churaev as the head of the DPO, and Vladimir Mylarshchikov as the head of the Department of Agriculture.[11]

After the big reform of 1956, the size of the DPO remained almost unchanged in subsequent years. For example, the RSFSR department had one hundred employees in 1956, of which eighty-five were career party members with executive responsibilities and fifteen technical staff (assigned to the department's secretariat, the unit responsible for secretarial support of the executive staff). In June 1962, there were eighty-four staff members spread across ten regional and two functional sectors, as well as the head of department, two deputies, and four inspectors.[12] This structure, based on the division of responsibilities between the Union Republics and the RSFSR, remained unchanged until 1962, at which point organization of the party organs, including its Central Committee apparatus, was changed based on a new principle of bifurcation between industrial and agricultural branches.

Department Personnel

The composition of personnel in the DPO during this period had three distinct characteristics. First, there was a high proportion of staff that had work experience in local party organs. Second, there was a high representation of people from Ukraine. Finally, there was a high turnover in personnel, particularly in the top echelons.

The hierarchy in the DPO consisted of the department head, the first deputy, the assistant to the head of the department, deputies, the head of the department's secretariat, heads of sectors, inspectors, and, finally, instructors, who were at the bottom of the hierarchy list. Collectively, they were known as executive employees (*otvetstvennye rabotniki*) at the Central Committee apparatus, or employees with executive powers to make policy decisions at a level appropriate to their posts. In 1957, the Department of Union Republics had, in addition to its head and the first deputy, two further deputies, nine heads of sectors, four inspectors, and forty-seven instructors. The RSFSR department had a similar number of deputies, eight heads of sectors, eight inspectors, and sixty-five instructors.[13]

The post of head of the DPO was a key position in the CPSU power hierarchy. According to Anastas Mikoyan, one of the longest serving members of the Presidium, the head of department was almost equal in status to a Central Committee secretary.[14] A general cadre policy in the Central Committee apparatus was to appoint people with experience in the field they supervised. For example, personnel in a department dealing with heavy industry usually had staff with a background in that industry. Sergei Baskakov (1898–1991), who was in charge of the Department of Industry and Transport for the RSFSR from 1956 to 1962, began his career as an engineer at an armament factory in Perm (renamed Molotov from 1940 to 1957) then switching to a party career at the same factory and continuing it in the local *obkom* (oblast party committee), before being promoted to a Central Committee post in Moscow. Similarly, propaganda departments were often staffed by people who had previously worked in publishing or education.[15] In the same way, there was a large representation of former regional party committee secretaries in the departments that supervised *obkoms*. For example, Evgenii Gromov (1909–1981) was the head of the DPO in the transitional period between 1953 and 1957. Gromov made his career in the Moscow party organization during the 1940s, and was promoted to one of the deputy heads in the new DPO in 1948, eventually succeeding Averkii Aristov as head of the department in April 1953.[16]

A biographical study of the heads and the first deputies indicates the high degree of turnover, and relatively consistent background, of these incumbents. Khrushchev kept Gromov in his post until March 1957, when he was appointed the Soviet ambassador to Hungary, which was a form of honorary retirement for someone who had been at the center of Soviet politics for many years. After Gromov's removal, the post of department head remained vacant for almost a year. Alexander Shelepin (1918–1994), a rising star under Khrushchev from a Komsomol (All-Union Leninist Young Communist League, or VLKSM—the Communist party youth wing) background, headed the department from April to December 1958, at which point he was appointed as the chairman of the KGB instead of Ivan Serov, who had held that post since the creation of the KGB in 1954.

Vladimir Semichastnyi (1924–2001), Shelepin's close associate from their Komsomol days, was briefly put in charge of the department between March and December 1959, but he was demoted to the post of the second party secretary of Azerbaijan. The next head of the Union DPO was Viktor Churaev (1904–1982), who had previously held the corresponding post in the RSFSR DPO. Churaev was a former associate of Khrushchev from Ukraine, who rose through the ranks in the Kharkov *obkom* before being brought to Moscow in 1951. The appointment of Churaev and some of his successors supports historian Nikolai Mitrokhin's argument about Ukrainian cadres constituting one of the two principal pools from which Khrushchev drew his support and whom he actively promoted in the 1950s and early 1960s.[17]

Churaev was replaced in 1961, a year of substantial personnel changes, by Vitalii Titov (1907–1980), another appointee from Kharkov. In November 1962, Titov also became Central Committee secretary responsible for party and organizational matters, combining the two most powerful posts in the Central Committee. After Khrushchev's fall, Titov was replaced by Ivan Kapitonov (1915–2002), a former Moscow party boss demoted by Khrushchev in 1959 to head the Ivanovo region. Kapitonov retained his tenure as the head of the department from 1964 to 1983. This illustrates a greater degree of stability among the top Central Committee personnel under Brezhnev compared with the Khrushchev period.

Similarly, most of the deputies had regional party experience. Petr Pigalev (1911–1975) had a background in the Central Committee apparatus but also spent several years as the second secretary of the Molotov (as Perm was known from 1940 to 1957) *obkom*, before returning to the Central Committee and making his way up from inspector (1951–1954) to head of sector (1954–1957), to deputy head (1957–1961), and finally to first deputy head of department (1961–1966). Georgii Eniutin (1903–1969) was another of Khrushchev's associates from Ukraine (he was the first secretary of the Zaporozhie *obkom* from 1947 to 1951) serving as a deputy head of department from 1952 to 1954. Nikolai Petrovichev (1898–1991) came to the RSFSR DPO in 1961 from the Moscow *obkom*, another key circle for Khrushchev's patronage, and rose through its ranks from head of sector to deputy head of the department, retiring only in 1983 as the first deputy of the Department of Organizational and Party Work, the successor to the DPO. Iosif Shikin (1906–1973), the deputy head in 1954–1961, was an exception, having made his career in the army's political department in the 1940s before making his way to the Central Committee apparatus as an inspector in 1950.

The RSFSR DPO's first head was the aforementioned Viktor Churaev, the first secretary of the Kharkov *obkom* from 1949–1953. Churaev, before his promotion to head of the DPO for the RSFSR, had served as a deputy head of the former DPO, and in this sense he was the logical choice to head the RSFSR department when it was carved out of the DPO. He was replaced by Mikhail Efremov (1911–2000) in 1959, who until then had been Kuibyshev *obkom*'s first secretary. He was, however, demoted to head of the Cheliabinsk and then the Gorky *obkoms*, before returning to Moscow in 1965 as deputy chairman of the *Sovmin* (the Council of Ministers, the Soviet government), following the removal of Khrushchev from power a year earlier. In 1961, Efremov was succeeded by Mikhail Polekhin, a long-time deputy head of the department, and before that a secretary of the Primorsk regional party organization, who remained in charge of the RSFSR department until its abolition in 1965.

The fact that all heads of the party organs departments had experience at the *obkom* level indicates the close link between them and the people they supervised. The only exceptions to this rule were Shelepin and Semichastnyi, who came from Komsomol structures, but this does not undermine the general principle of appointments because the DPO also supervised the Komsomol.

Lower-level personnel at the DPO had a similar background of work experience at the local party level before being promoted to the Central Committee. After a period of work at the center, they were often shifted back to the region in a higher capacity. For example, Mikhail Ponomarev (1918–2001) made typical career progress rising through the ranks in the Molotov (Perm) *obkom* to become its second secretary from 1954 to 1955, before being assigned to head a sector at the RSFSR DPO between 1955 and 1959. His move to Moscow was perhaps helped by Pigalev, the former second secretary from the Molotov *obkom*, who was an inspector at the RSFSR DPO at the time of Ponomarev's appointment there. After four years in the Central Committee, Ponomarev was appointed first secretary of the Kalmyk *obkom* (1959–1961), and then, after a brief stint as an inspector in the Central Committee apparatus, was appointed as head of the Vladimir *obkom*, where he served as the first secretary until 1983.

What emerges, then, is a pattern of frequent rotations between local and central posts in the DPO. For many of its staff, work experience at the DPO served as an important step in their party career. This supports historian Nikolay Mitrokhin's thesis that the Central Committee apparatus served as a form of top management school in the Soviet system—an M.B.A.[18] for top Communist bureaucrats.[19]

The heads of the departments of party organs changed very frequently during Khrushchev's era compared to other departments in the Central Committee apparatus. Between 1953 and 1964, the DPO and its successor, the Union Republics DPO, had five different heads. Similarly, the RSFSR DPO had three different heads in that period. In contrast, other departments were more stable: the general department was headed by Vladimir Malin throughout, the culture department by Dmitrii Polikarpov; the two international departments were headed throughout by Boris Ponomarev and Iurii Andropov, and the RSFSR Department of Industry and Transport was headed by Sergei Baskakov. Only departments of agriculture for the RSFSR and the Union Republics, another problematic area for Khrushchev, had a similar rate of changes in its management with three and four different heads in that period respectively.

Khrushchev, as a leader, relied on frequent personnel rotations in the Central Committee apparatus to spur greater efficiency and achieve results in the key areas of concern. However, there is little evidence that this approach yielded the necessary results over the long term as, for example, the agricultural performance declined in the second half of Khrushchev's period, and there was an open revolt by the party *nomenklatura* against Khrushchev in the autumn 1964.

Functions

The two DPOs were a key element in the CPSU power hierarchy. This was on account of their three most important functions: the selection of cadres, supervision of local party organizations, and reporting to the Central Committee secretariat on the state of affairs in the regions. The supervision of the local party organizations can be subdivided into planned inspections by the department's staff, inspections in response to complaints from below, and finally, intervention in local disputes as the final arbiter of conflicts among regional elites.

Reporting to the Central Committee secretariat involved both submitting initial reports on the state of local affairs, and drafting the secretariat's decisions, based on those initial reports, into official decrees. Once the official decisions were formally approved by the secretariat or the Presidium, the DPO was charged with ensuring their implementation by the *obkoms*.

Supervision of local party organizations was carried out through inspections, meetings with regional party leaders both in Moscow and in local centers, as well as informal interventions—for example, by telephone. The two departments for party organs had the greatest number of inspections of all Central Committee departments. For example, in 1955 there were 545 trips to the regions (300 in the RSFSR and 245 in the Union Republics) that lasted between three and forty days. These constituted almost a third of all regional assignments by the Central Committee apparatus. They were often undertaken in cooperation with other departments, such as propaganda and agitation, agriculture, or one of the industrial departments, depending on the specialization of the region in question, so, for example, the Department of Agriculture was involved if the assignment was to an agricultural region. In contrast, the Central Committee department with the next largest number of regional inspections was the Department of Propaganda and Agitation, but it only received half as many inspection trips, at 233 per year.[20] Planned inspections of the regions were an important method of the supervision of *obkoms*.

A report by the DPO to the Central Committee secretariat, based on an inspection of the Smolensk oblast in 1959 is characteristic of the department's work of this period. A group of three representatives of the Central Committee apparatus—two from the DPO for RSFSR, and one from the Department of Agriculture for RSFSR—carried out an inspection of the Smolensk oblast in December 1959.[21]

One of the reasons for the inspection was the extremely poor agricultural results in the region. The report made a damning assessment of the region's economic performance and party work there. For example, meat procurements fell from 51,000 tons in 1957 to 40,800 tons in 1958, while for eleven months of 1959 this was down to only 38,900 tons. Milk production remained static. For the region to meet its procurement obligations, 212,000 pigs and 123,000 tons of grain had to be purchased from other regions. To purchase additional cattle and grain, 216 million rubles were spent, while only 142,000 rubles were received from the sale of cattle. The reported noted that in 1958 the oblast did not meet its target for the production of meat and milk. On 1 December 1959 only 49 percent of procurements for meat were fulfilled, and 72 percent for milk. As an illustration of the failing of the kolkhoz (collective farm) system, the annual procurement plan could only be achieved with the inclusion of agricultural output from private plots. The economy of the Smolensk oblast still struggled to reach pre–World War II levels of agricultural production, despite more than half a decade of intensive efforts to revive Soviet agriculture after Stalin's death in 1953. For example, its grain production was half of the 1940 level. For every ruble of salary, the *sovkhozy* (Soviet farm) returned 88 kopecks of production, so they were not viable economically.[22]

The report also criticized the unsatisfactory state of personnel work, which was particularly evident in the high turnover among kolkhoz chairmen. Many kolkhoz chairmen were expelled from the party; some were even prosecuted by the security organs. The DPO report claimed that the first secretary ruled in a dictatorial manner through his permanent representatives (*postoyannye upolnomochennye*), preferring to rely on punishment rather than helping to improve management in the failing kolkhozy. For example, 82 percent of kolkhoz chairmen were issued official party reprimands. Poor material conditions meant that few specialists sent to work in the oblast remained there, with 1,756 out of 2,000 having left the region over the previous three years.

Despite this damning report, including accusations of deliberate data inflation to meet official targets, there was little of immediate consequence for Pavel Doronin (1909–1976), the Smolensk oblast first secretary. Doronin was summoned to the DPO for an official talk, and was seen by Khrushchev on 29 December 1959 after the Central Committee plenum on agriculture. The reason for a mild reprimand to Doronin is to be found in the political context of the time.

The plenum passed a resolution "On the further development of agricultural production," which marked a high point in Khrushchev's campaign to dramatically increase meat production in the USSR. The Riazan oblast's apparent achievement of tripling meat production in 1959 (subsequently discovered to be based on deceit) was presented in official propaganda as an example for other meat-producing regions to follow. Only when the failure of meat production became impossible to ignore did Khrushchev authorize inspections by the Central Committee, which uncovered massive cheating, led to the Riazan oblast first secretary Aleksei Larionov's suicide, and dealt a severe blow to Khrushchev's prestige.[23]

At the time of the Smolensk inspection report in December 1959, the irregularities discovered in the Smolensk oblast were not given the full attention they deserved in order to avoid a distraction from the countrywide campaign. However, the poor performance and other failures uncovered by the inspection were not completely forgotten. At the next major reshuffle in 1961, Doronin was dismissed from his post and went into retirement at the relatively young age of fifty-two.

Inspections such as the one at Smolensk were a permanent feature of the Central Committee work and aimed to ensure the accountability of the regional elites, as well as access to accurate information about regional politics for the central authorities in Moscow. There is enough evidence to conclude that the relevant authorities at the Central Committee had a reasonably accurate account of conditions in the regions at their disposal. However, the possible implications and the response by the Central Committee were dependent on the political circumstances of the time, particularly on the type of policies and goals set by the top Soviet leadership. In practice, this meant that the response of the central authorities to similar types of misdemeanors by local elites could vary considerably.

Responses to "signals" from the regions in the form of letters of complaint to the Central Committee or other central party organs were another important mechanism for ensuring that the local party elites were aware that the Central Committee in Moscow could intervene at any moment. As a rule, if concrete facts were mentioned in a complaint, some form of enquiry had to be carried out. This could be anything from a written inquiry, to which the *obkom* in question had to formally respond, to an inspection by the department's staffers. For example, a letter to *Pravda* from the workers in Miass (a town in the Cheliabinsk oblast) highlighted terrible road conditions, a lack of transport, and the indifference of the local authorities to these problems. The letter was forwarded to Central Committee, and the DPO sent a request to the local *obkom* to investigate the complaint. The *obkom* responded by listing measures taken to alleviate the situation, including changes to bus schedules and a *subbotnik* (a voluntary unpaid work party on days off) to mend the roads. The department's instructor in charge of overseeing the Cheliabinsk oblast deemed these efforts as sufficient and closed the case.[24]

However, the large number of complaints meant that the majority of them did not receive a full investigation, and the Miass case points to a rather superficial attempt to solve an acute local transportation problem. Nevertheless, the threat of a random inspection ensured that local party elites could not completely ignore local problems because they knew that there was always a possibility that the central authority, through the Central Committee's DPO, could intervene, with potentially negative consequences for local bosses.

Another function of the DPO was the selection and appointment of cadres. On 1 January 1954, the DPO had 2,235 primary (i.e., directly appointed) *nomenklatura* (*osnovnaia nomenklatura*) officeholders and 4,539 secondary (supervised, but not directly appointed) officeholders (*uchetno-kontrol'naia nomenklatura*). Of the primary *nomenklatura*, 1,628 were leading party cadres; the rest were state, trade union, and Komsomol posts. Of the secondary *nomenklatura*, 4,065 were party appointments.[25] After the division of the department into the Union Republics and the RSFRS, the sector of the single party ticket (*sektor edinogo partiinogo bileta*) and the sector of records of the leading cadres (*sektor ucheta vedushchikh kadrov*) remained in the Union department, which managed *nomenklatura* records for all Central Committee departments, and made it the key element in the party appointments system.

The *nomenklatura* of the RSRSR DPO in 1956 included six first secretaries of regional party committees, known as *kraikoms* (*kraevye komitety partii*), sixty-seven first secretaries of *obkoms*, six secretaries of *obkoms* within the Primorsky *krai*, and second secretaries of Moscow and Leningrad *obkoms* (the first party secretaries of these two cities were appointed by the Presidium), second secretaries of *kraikoms* and *obkoms*, and all heads of departments of *obkoms* and *kraikoms* (578 positions). In addition, the RSFSR department supervised appointments to all Soviet organs, including the chair of the Presidium of the RSFSR Supreme Soviet, the chair of the RSFSR Council of Ministers (*Sovmin*), as well as top trade union and Komsomol appointments.[26] These appointees reported to the head of the department that had appointed them, making that head their de facto immediate superior. Since Khrushchev did not often meet *obkom* first secretaries one-on-one, the two heads of the party department were, in essence, his viceroys over the *obkom* secretaries.[27]

The department also reported to the Central Committee secretariat on the state of affairs in the regions. For example, between May and December 1963, the RSFSR DPO submitted thirty-one reports to the secretariat, ranging from a report on shortcomings in the selection of personnel by economic agencies, to the restructuring of Moscow's creative union branches (*tvorcheskie soiuzy*). It also prepared decrees on decisions made by the secretariat on all aspects of party work. In 1963, there were 110 decrees, reports, and other official documents prepared by the department.[28] The department was also responsible for the supervision of the implementation of the leadership's decision in the regions. The DPO thereby collected information from the regions, reported to the secretariat on its findings, drafted the decisions made by the latter, and supervised their implementation back in the regions concerned. This gave the leadership of the department (i.e., the head, his deputies, and heads of sectors) an enormous degree of power over the regional policies in the Soviet Union.

The departments of party organs performed another crucial function as the final arbiter in local disputes. This function was particularly important during the Khrushchev period, when there was a high turnover among *obkom* secretaries, creating conditions for conflicts with incumbent elites. For example, from 1958 to 1959 there was a conflict in the Kalmyk *obkom* between Nikolai Zhezlov, a newly appointed first secretary, and representatives of the local hierarchy.[29] The conflict was exacerbated by the recent return to their homeland from exile of the Kalmyks, who had been deported to Central Asia at the end of World War II. It was alleged that Zhezlov, a native of the neighboring Stavropol oblast, promoted only his friends (who were ethnic Russians) to positions of power, while the Kalmyks were relegated to secondary posts in their own titular republic. This dispute was taken to Churaev, the head of the RSFSR DPO. It was alleged that Zhezlov was informed about the Kalmyk opposition visits to the Central Committee and knew the contents of their conversations with Churaev and Ekaterina Furtseva, the Central Committee secretary and a member of the Presidium, from Orlov, who was the Central Committee instructor in charge of supervising the Kalmyk region. Eventually, Zhezlov was dismissed as first secretary in February 1959, and demoted to the post of the head of the meat and dairy industries in his native Stavropol *sovnarkhoz*.[30] Moscow decided to calm things down by appointing a familiar figure from the center, someone whom it could trust. Zhezlov's replacement was Mikhail Ponomarev, who until then had been the head of a sector in the RSFSR DPO.[31]

The departments of party organs, therefore, played a central role in the relationship between the center and local elites. Its broad sway of functions, from the selection of cadres to inspection of the regions and the supervision of the implementation of the central authorities' decisions, meant that local party elites viewed it as the most important central agency that they had to deal with.

Bifurcation of Party Organs

There is a prevalent view among historians, which is also supported by contemporary accounts, that Khrushchev's downfall was caused to a substantial degree by the excessive reorganizations of the state and party institutions, which unsettled the governing *nomenklatura* and undermined Khrushchev's authority.[32] In the last years of his rule, Khrushchev attempted a radical reform of the party apparatus against the background of mounting economic problems. This was in contrast to Khrushchev's first period in power, when he channeled his attention toward the fight against state bureaucracy and excessive centralization. Although from 1953 to 1957 the party elites were his core group of support, in the final years, Khrushchev turned them against him, and this ultimately cost him his job. The reform that caused the greatest amount of frustration among the Communist Party *nomenklatura* was the split of the Communist Party into agricultural and industrial branches.

The reforms of 1962–1964 were forced on Khrushchev by the deepening crisis in the economy, above all in agriculture. The rise of state-controlled food prices, which was introduced on 1 June 1962, resonated negatively around the country. This was damaging to Khrushchev personally because it came just several months after the adoption of the Third Party Program in October 1961, which had promised great abundance for the Soviet people.[33] The popular reaction was deeply negative: "I have three children. Together with my husband, we earn 120 rubles between us. With this state of affairs our children won't see any meat or butter," said one woman.[34] "The resolutions of the Twenty-Second Party Congress and the Party Program promised a continuous rise in workers' material conditions, while in practice the prices for meat and milk are rising, and living standards are falling," claimed a miner from the Tula oblast.[35] "We are advancing towards communism, while the material conditions are worsening," said workers from a Gorky city factory.[36]

Khrushchev's solution to the mounting problems in the field of agriculture was to strengthen the party's role in running the economy. Several reforms were attempted over the course of 1962. For example, at the Central Committee's March plenum on agriculture, it was decided to strengthen the party's control over agriculture by creating committees for agriculture headed by the first secretaries of lower party organizations.[37] Finally, in a more radical move, the whole party apparatus was split into agricultural and industrial branches at the Central Committee's November plenum in 1962.

Khrushchev's rationale behind the reform was to strengthen the party's economic role at the expense of its other duties, such as political work and propaganda. He argued that "the unification of communists according to their place in economic activity gives party organizations the ability to concentrate their main attention on economic questions, subjecting all other forms of work—organizational, ideological, culture and educational—to solving the principal task."[38] The principal task of the party organization became economic management, while other areas of party activity were now deemed of secondary importance. As a result, many party apparatchiks who did not have a background in economics were made responsible for results in a sphere in which they were not trained. Khrushchev's core constituency was turning against him.

The bifurcation of party organs led to confusion and resentment in the Central Committee apparatus and *obkoms*. This reorganization also caused particular frustration in the work of the departments of party organs as these departments had to reorganize themselves and simultaneously supervise similar reorganizations at lower levels. In December 1962, the RSFSR DPO was split into the Department of RSRSR Party Organs for Agriculture (headed by Mikhail Polekhin, previously the head of the RSFSR DPO) and the Department of RSFSR Party Organs for Industry (headed by Nikolai Voronovskii, the former deputy head of the old RSFSR DPO). These new departments had structures similar to that of the abolished department, with five regional and two functional sectors. The personnel also came from the abolished department.[39] Overall, this reform, while not changing the compositional substance of the Central Committee apparatus, did create uncertainty and confusion among staff, not least by complicating the chain of command in the party hierarchy.

In contrast to the RSFSR department, the Union Republics DPO was not split into industrial and agricultural units, and instead was renamed the Department of Party Organs. However, its structure was changed to reflect the new principle of party organization. They were two subdepartments now: for the management of industry and agriculture of the Union Republics, and the subdepartment of central organizations and organizational regulatory matters.[40]

Khrushchev's attempt at charging the party organs with responsibilities for economic performance at a time of a deepening economic crisis drew hostility from party bosses who did not want to "carry the can" for Khrushchev's own mistakes. For example, the first secretary of the Smolensk *obkom*, Nikolai Kalmyk (1913–2000), told a local party meeting that "everyone should understand that no other organs but *oblispolkom* [the local Soviet executive organ, distinct from the local party organization] can conduct direct management of the multitude of agricultural production, the work of production departments, and all other agricultural organs, enterprises and institutions."[41] Kalmyk, the first secretary, was severely reprimanded by the RSFSR DPO for agriculture for attempting to shift responsibility away from himself and his party organization for the poor performance of the region.[42] However, the mood among party secretaries remained strongly hostile to the new system of party organization.

One of the biggest problems caused by the reorganization was the ensuing rivalry between agricultural and industrial *obkoms*, which flared up almost immediately after their creation. For example, in December 1962 the Ukrainian first secretary Petro Shelest had already had to settle disputes between Aleksandr Liashko and Trofim Poplevkin, the secretaries of the industrial and the agricultural *obkoms* in the Donetsk oblast, barely a month after the introduction of the bifurcation principle at the Central Committee November plenum.[43] The two secretaries protected the interests of their respective clients in industry and agriculture.

At the same time, economic performance did not improve. After the 1962 reform, the Central Committee departments responsible for party work assumed greater responsibility for propping up a struggling economy, while at the same time continued to be undermined by the frequent reorganizations and personnel changes that were characteristic of the Khrushchev era.

The bifurcation of the CPSU proved to be one of the most calamitous reforms made by Khrushchev, and it was not a coincidence that it was also the first major policy revision by the new leadership. Barely a month after Khrushchev's ouster, the departments of party organs for agriculture and industry were again merged into a single RSFSR department in December 1964.[44] After the Twenty-Third Party Congress, in May 1966, a major reform of the Central Committee apparatus drew a line under Khrushchev's reforms and introduced a structure of the Central Committee apparatus that remained largely unchanged until perestroika in the second half of the 1980s. The RSFSR DPO was absorbed into the Department of Organizational and Party Work, as the old DPO for Union Republics was then known (see figure 7.1 for an overview of organizational changes). It was continuously headed by Ivan Kapitanov from 1964 to 1983, who was concurrently the Central Committee secretary in charge of cadres. This newly expanded department was a more formidable organ than its predecessors under Khrushchev. However, its functions and the principles of its work remained the same, as it continued its role as the main intermediary between the top leadership and the local party elites.

Conclusion

The DPO played a key role in the Soviet power hierarchy, serving as the main conduit between the top leadership in the center and regional party bosses. Despite the broad reforms within the state and party apparatus, the DPO retained its importance for most of the Khrushchev's period. There were, however, several distinct features of the DPO in this period. First, relating to its structure, there was a greater emphasis on regional specialization represented by the establishment of two departments of party organs in 1954. Second, concerning personnel, there was a substantial staff turnover, exemplified by the frequent changes in top management. In addition, there was a high representation of regional elites in the departments, particularly from Ukraine. Finally, the last bout of reforms unleashed in 1962 undermined stability and the normal functioning of the party organs, including the Central Commit-

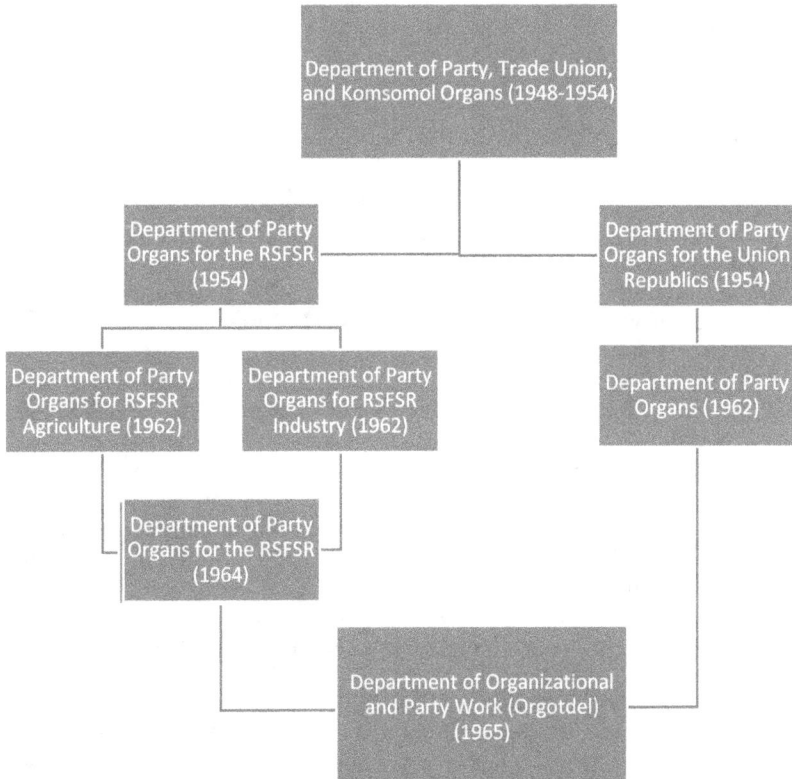

Figure 7.1. Organizational Chart of the Party Organ Departments of the CPSU, 1954–1964

tee departments responsible for their oversight. After Khrushchev's removal from power, a period of stability ensued, with the reinstatement of a single department that was responsible for the supervision of the local party machines. This drew a line under Khrushchev's erratic state and party reforms, and ushered in Brezhnev's period of stability, better known as "stagnation."

Alexander Titov is lecturer in modern European history at Queen's University Belfast. His publications on post-Stalin political history include "The Central Committee Apparatus under Khrushchev" in *Khrushchev in the Kremlin: Policy and Government in the Soviet Union, 1953–1964* (2011), and "The 1961 Party Programme and the Fate of Khrushchev's Reforms" in *Soviet State and Society under Nikita Khrushchev* (2009). Dr. Titov has also published extensively on Russian foreign policy, including "Which Way Out of Ukraine—Versailles, Yalta or Vienna?" in *History and Policy* (2014). He is currently working on a new biography of Nikita Khrushchev.

Notes

1. For a recent overview of the role of the Central Committee apparatus in the Soviet system, see Nikolay Mitrokhin, "The CPSU Central Committee Apparatus, 1970–85: Personnel and Role in the Soviet Political System," *Russian History* 41 (2014): 307–328, especially 312–317. For a classical analysis, see Jerry F. Hough and Merle Fainsod, *How the Soviet Union is Governed* (Cambridge, MA, 1979).
2. An earlier version of the chapter was presented at a workshop in Manchester in September 2008. Special thanks to Yoram Gorlizki and Nikolay Mitorkhin for their valuable comments on that earlier draft.
3. Rudolf Pikhoia, *Sovetskii Soiuz: Istoriia vlasti, 1945–1991* [Soviet Union: A history of power, 1945–1991] (Moscow, 1998), 110. For analysis of changes in power configuration in the late Stalin period, see Yoram Gorlizki and Oleg Khlevniuk, *Cold Peace: Stalin and the Soviet Ruling Circle 1945–1953* (Oxford, 2004).
4. Beria's vast Ministry of Internal Affairs was split into several institutions, one being the much-reduced Ministry of the Internal Affairs; and the status of the political police (the Committee for State Security, or better known by its Russian abbreviation as the KGB) in particular was lowered to that of a committee under the direct control of the Council of Ministers, rather than a separate ministry as it had been previously.
5. Analysis of this power struggle and its impact on institutional reorganizations is given in Y. Gorlizki, "Anti-Ministerialism and the USSR Ministry of

Justice, 1953–56: A Study in Organisational Decline," *Europe-Asia Studies* 48, no. 8 (1996): 1279–1318; V. P. Naumov, "Bor'ba Khrushcheva za edinolichnuiu vlast'" [Khrushchev's struggle for one-man rule], *Novaia i Noveishaia Istoriia* 2 (1996); E. Zubkova, "Malenkov i Khrushchev: Lichnyi faktor v politike poslestalinskogo rukovodstva" [Malenkov and Khrushchev: The personal factor in post-Stalinist leadership policies], *Otechestvennaia istoriia* 4 (1995).

6. For a detailed analysis of the reforms of the Central Committee apparatus under Khrushchev, see Alexander Titov, "The Central Committee Apparatus under Khrushchev," in *Khrushchev in the Kremlin: Policy and Governance in the Soviet Union, 1953–1964*, ed. Jeremy Smith and Melanie Ilic (London, 2011), 41–54.
7. Gorlizki, "Anti-Ministerialism and the USSR Ministry of Justice, 1953–56."
8. See Alexander Titov, "The Central Committee Apparatus under Khrushchev," 47–52.
9. Yoram Gorlizki, "Party Revivalism and the Death of Stalin," *Slavic Review* 54, no. 1 (1995): 20; Rossiiskii gosudarstvennyi arkhiv noveishei istorii [Russian state archive of contemporary history], hereafter RGANI, f. 5, op. 31, d. 70, ll. 82–83.
10. In April 1954, the department's ten regional sectors were the Trans-Caucasian Republics; the Baltic Republics and Belorussian SSR; Central Asian Republics and Kazakhstan; Ukraine and Moldova; Central regions; Black Earth Belt; Caucasus and Crimea regions; Northern, North-Western regions, and Karelo-Finnish SSR; Urals regions; and Far Eastern regions. Six functional sectors dealt with organizational and regulation matters: party information, single party card, trade union organs, Komsomol organs, training and retraining of party and Soviet personnel, and the department's secretariat.
11. For more details see Alexander Titov, "Partiia protiv gosudarstva: reform apparata TsK KPSS pri Nikite Khrushcheve" [Party versus state: The reform of the CC apparatus of the CPSU by Nikita Khrushchev], *Neprikosnovennyi zapas* 83, no. 3(2012): 155–166; and idem, "The Central Committee Apparatus under Khrushchev," 46–52;
12. RGANI, f. 13, op. 2, d. 426, l. 154. The sectors were the Sector of Central Districts, the Sector of the Black Earth Belt and Volga Region Districts, the Sector of North Caucuses Region, the Sector of the Urals and Western Siberia Districts, the Sector of Eastern Siberia and the Far East Districts, the Sector of Organizational and Regulatory Matters and Party Information, the Sector of Training and Retraining of Party and Soviet Employees, and the department's secretariat.
13. RGANI, f. 5, op. 31, d. 70, l. 82–83. The Department of Union Republics also had nine executive and fifty-seven technical staff in two sectors responsible for the record keeping of *nomenklatura* appointments.
14. A. Mikoyan, *Tak bylo: Razmyshleniia o minuvshem* [So it was: Reflections on the past] (Moscow, 1999), 602.
15. For analysis of the propaganda departments, see N. Mitrokhin, "Back-Office Mikhaila Suslova: Otdel propagandy TsK KPSS v kontse 1960-kh—

1985 godakh" [Mikhail Suslov's back office: The propaganda department of the CPSU Central Committee from the end of the 1960s to 1985], *Cahiers du Monde Russe* 54, no. 3–4 (2014): 409–440.

16. For biographic information, I rely on Iu.V. Goriachev, ed., *Tsentral'nyi Komitet KPSS, VKP(b), RKP(b), RSDRP(b): 1917–1991: istoriko-biograficheskiĭ spravochnik* [The Central Committee of the CPSU, VCP(b), RCP(b), RSDRP(b), 1917–1991: historical-biographical handbook] (Moscow, 2005); the excellent web resource www.knowbysight.info; A. A. Fursenko, ed., *Prezidium TsK KPSS 1954–1964: chernovye protokol'nye zapisi zasedanii, stenogrammy, postanovleniia* [The Presidium of the CPSU CC 1954–1964: Draft protocol notes, stenographs, resolutions], 3 vols (Moscow, 2003–2008); Iu. V. Goriachev, ed., "Posetiteli kremlevskogo kabineta N. S. Khrushcheva" [Visitors of the Kremlin office of N. S. Khrushchev], *Istochnik* 4 (2003): 76–112; David Wells and John Miller, eds., *A Directory of Heads and Deputy Heads of CPSU Central Committee Departments 1952–1991* (Manchester, 1993).

17. J. Smith and M. Ilic, eds., "The Rise of Political Clans in the Era of Nikita Khrushchev," in *Khrushchev in the Kremlin: Policy and Government in the Soviet Union 1953–64* (London, 2011), 26–40.

18. Master of Business Administration degree.

19. N. Mitrokhin, "Apparat TsK KPSS v 1953–1985 godakh kak primer 'zakrytogo' obshchestva" [The CPSU CC apparatus of 1953–1985 as example of the "closed" society], *NLO*, no. 100 (2009), accessed 17 June 2016, http://magazines.russ.ru/nlo/2009/100/mi44.html. Other works that mention the role of the Central Committee apparatus as an important career step for regional party elites, and specifically for second secretaries of the union republics, are Saulius Grybkauskas, "Imperializing the Soviet Federation? The Institution of the Second Secretary in the Soviet Republics," *Ab Imperio* 3 (2014): 267–292; and John H. Miller, "Cadres Policy in Nationality Areas," *Soviet Studies* 29, no. 1 (1977): 3–36.

20. RGANI, f. 5, op. 31, d. 51, ll. 6–7.

21. They were carried out by Milov, a Central Committee inspector in the RSFSR Department of Party Organs; Gromova, an instructor in the same department; and Novikov, an instructor from the RSFSR Department of Agriculture.

22. RGASPI, f. 556, op. 14, d. 134, ll. 103–110.

23. For a detailed account of the Riazan affair, see O. Khlevniuk, "Economy of Illusions," in *Khrushchev in the Kremlin: Policy and Governance in the Soviet Union, 1953–1964*, ed. J. Smith and M. Ilic (London, 2011), 171–186; and Yoram Gorlizki, "Scandal in Riazan: Networks of Trust and the Social Dynamics of Deception," *Kritika: Explorations in Russian and Eurasian History* 14, no. 2 (2013): 243–278.

24. RGASPI, f. 556, op. 14, d. 142, ll. 81–84.

25. RGANI, f. 5, op. 29, d. 33, l. 14–16.

26. RGANI, f. 13, op. 1, d. 445, l. 2.

27. For a general overview of the frequency of Khrushchev's personal appointments including *obkom* secretaries, see Murin, ed., "Posetiteli," 51–55.

28. RGANI, f. 5, op. 31, d. 214, ll. 119–141.

29. This included *obkom* secretary Dzhimbinov; the chairman of the Republic's Supreme Soviet, Ivanov; the chairman of the Republican Trade Union, Mantsynov; Republican minister of culture, Nadbitov; and writer, Indzhiev.
30. RGASPI, f. 556, op. 14, d. 139, ll. 11–12. Zhezlov resumed his party career after Khrushchev's removal from power in 1964, and later even replaced Mikhail Gorbachev as the second secretary of the Stavropol *kraikom* in 1970–1976, after Gorbachev was appointed the first secretary there.
31. See section on department personnel above.
32. Rudol'f Pikhoia, *Sovetskii Soiuz* (Moscow, 1999), 240. For a contemporary view, see A. Artizov and V. Naumov, eds., *Nikita Khrushchev, 1964* (Moscow, 2007), 193–196. For more details on the 1962 party reform, see John A. Armstrong, "Party Bifurcation and Elite Interests," *Soviet Studies* 17, no. 4 (April 1966): 417–430; and Barbara Ann Chotiner, *Khrushchev's Party Reform: Coalition Building and Institutional Innovation* (Westport, CT: Greenwood Press, 1984).
33. On the Third Party Program, see Alexander Titov, "The 1961 Party Programme and the Fate of Khrushchev's reforms," in *Soviet State and Society under Nikita Khrushchev*, ed. M. Ilic and J. Smith (London, 2009), 8–26.
34. RGASPI, f. 556, op. 14, d. 203, l. 12.
35. RGASPI, f. 556, op. 14, d. 203, l. 24.
36. RGASPI, f. 556, op. 14, d. 203, l. 36.
37. *KPSS v rezolutsiiakh i resheniiakh s'ezdov, koferentsii i plenumov TsK* [The CPSU in the resolutions and decisions of the party congresses, conferences and CC plenary meetings] (Moscow, 1986), vol. 10, 225.
38. Khrushchev's report to the November plenum, 1962. RGANI, f. 2, op. 1, d. 596, l. 33.
39. The new department increased in size and now had eighty-one responsible workers and seventeen technical personnel including the head of the department, two deputies, six inspectors, ten heads of regional sectors and two functional ones, and fifty-seven instructors. The new structure consisted of the sector of Central and North-Western districts; the Centre, the Black Earth and North Caucasus districts; the Urals and Western Siberia districts; East-Siberian and Far Eastern districts; Organizational and Regulatory Matters and Information; and Training and Retraining of Party and Soviet Employees. RGASPI, f. 556, op. 14, d. 249, l. 4, 17.
40. The first subdepartment had four regional sectors: Ukraine and Moldavia; the Kazakhstan and Central Asian republics; the Belorussia and Baltic republics; the Trans-Caucasian republics. The second one had four sectors on a functional basis: Organizational and Regulatory Matters and Information; Training and Retraining of Party and Soviet Cadres; Trade Union and Komsomol Organs; and the Single Party Card.
41. Khrushchev's report to the November plenum, 1962. RGANI, f. 2, op. 1, d. 596, l. 33.
42. RGASPI, f. 556, op. 14, d. 239, l. 14–15.
43. Petro Shelest, *Da ne sudimy budete* [Yes, you will not be judged] (Moscow, 1995), 162.
44. RGANI, f. 13, op. 2, d. 751, l. 47.

Bibliography

Archival Sources

RGASPI—Rossiiskii gosudarstvennyi arkhiv sotsial'no-politicheskoi istorii [Russian state archive of social and political history].
RGANI—Rossiiskii gosudarstvennyi arkhiv noveishei istorii [Russian state archive of contemporary history].

Primary Sources

Fursenko, A. A., ed. *Prezidium TsK KPSS 1954–1964: Chernovye protokol'nye zapisi zasedanii, stenogrammy, postanovleniia* [The Presidium of the Central Committee of the CPSU 1954–1964: Draft protocol notes, stenographs, resolution], 3 vols. Moscow: ROSSPEN, 2003, 2004, 2008.
KPSS v rezolutsiiakh i resheniiakh s'ezdov, koferentsii i plenumov TsK [The CPSU in resolutions and decisions of congresses, conferences and plenums of the Central Committee]. Moscow: Politizdat, 1986.
Murin, Iurii, ed. "Poseteliteli kremlevskogo kabineta N. S. Khrushcheva." *Istochnik* 4, no. 64 (2003): 51–112; and 5, no. 65 (2003): 76–112.

Secondary Sources

Armstrong, John A. "Party Bifurcation and Elite Interests." *Soviet Studies* 17, no. 4 (April 1966): 417–430.
Artizov, A., and V. Naumov, eds. *Nikita Khrushchev, 1964*. Moscow: Materik, 2007.
Chotiner, Barbara Ann. *Khrushchev's Party Reform: Coalition Building and Institutional Innovation*. Westport, CT: Greenwood Press, 1984.
Goriachev, Iu. V., ed. *Tsentral'nyi Komitet KPSS, VKP(b), RKP(b), RSDRP(b): 1917–1991: istoriko-biograficheskiĭ spravochnik* [The Central Committee of the CPSU, ACP(b), RCP(b), RSDLP(b): 1917–1991: Historical-biographical guide]. Moscow: Parad, 2005.
Gorlizki, Yoram. "Anti-ministerialism and the USSR Ministry of Justice, 1953–56: A Study in Organisational Decline." *Europe-Asia Studies* 48, no. 8 (1996): 1279–1318.
———. "Party Revivalism and the Death of Stalin." *Slavic Review* 54, no. 1 (1995): 1–22.
———. "Scandal in Riazan: Networks of Trust and the Social Dynamics of Deception." *Kritika: Explorations in Russian and Eurasian History* 14, no. 2 (2013): 243–278.
Gorlizki, Yoram, and Oleg Khlevniuk. *Cold Peace: Stalin and the Soviet Ruling Circle 1945–1953*. New York: Oxford University Press, 2004.
Grybkauskas, Saulius. "Imperializing the Soviet Federation? The Institution of the Second Secretary in the Soviet Republics." *Ab Imperio* 3 (2014): 267–292.
———. "The Role of the Second Party Secretary in the 'Election' of the First: The Political Mechanism for the Appointment of the Head of Soviet Lithuania in 1974." *Kritika: Explorations in Russian and Eurasian History* 14, no. 2 (2013): 343–366.

Hough, Jerry F., and Merle Fainsod. *How the Soviet Union is Governed.* Cambridge, MA: Harvard University Press, 1979.
Khlevniuk, Oleg. "Economy of Illusions." In *Khrushchev in the Kremlin: Policy and Governance in the Soviet Union, 1953–1964,* ed. J. Smith and M. Ilic, 171–186. London: Routledge, 2011.
Kibita, Nataliya. *Soviet Economic Management under Khrushchev: The Sovnarkhoz Reform.* London: Routledge, 2013.
Mikoyan, Anastas. *Tak bylo: Razmyshleniia o minuvshem* [This is how it was: Reflections about the past]. Moscow: Vagrius, 1999.
Miller, J. H. "Cadres Policy in Nationality Areas." *Soviet Studies* 29, no. 1 (1977): 3–36.
Mitrokhin, Nikolay. "Apparat TsK KPSS v 1953–1985 godakh kak primer "zakrytogo" obshchestva." NLO, no. 100 (2009). Accessed 17 June 2016, http://magazines.russ.ru/nlo/2009/100/mi44.html.
———. "Back-Office Mikhaila Suslova: Otdel propagandy TsK KPSS v kontse 1960-kh—1985 godakh" [Mikhail Suslov's back office: The propaganda department of the CPSU Central Committee from the end of the 1960s to 1985]. *Cahiers du Monde Russe* 54, no. 3–4 (2014): 409–440.
———. "The CPSU Central Committee Apparatus, 1970–85: Personnel and Role in the Soviet Political System." *Russian History* 41 (2014): 307–328.
———. "The Rise of Political Clans in the Era of Nikita Khrushchev." In *Khrushchev in the Kremlin: Policy and Government in the Soviet Union 1953–64,* ed. J. Smith and M. Ilic, 26–40. London: Routledge, 2011.
Naumov, V. P. "Bor'ba Khrushcheva za edinolichnuiu vlast'" [Khrushchev's struggle for one-man rule]. *Novaia i Noveishaia Istoriia* 2 (1996): 10–31.
Pikhoia, Rudolf. *Sovetskii Soiuz: Istoriia vlasti, 1945–1991* [The Soviet Union: A history of power]. Moscow: RAGS, 1998.
Shelest, Petro. *Da ne sudimy budete* [Yes, you will not be judged]. Moscow: Kvintisentsia, 1995.
Sushkov, A. *Prezidium TsK KPSS v 1957–1964 gg.: Lichnosti i vlast'* [Presidium of the Central Committee of the CPSU in 1957–1964: Personalities and power]. Ekaterinburg: UrO RAN, 2009.
Titov, Alexander. "The 1961 Party Programme and the Fate of Khrushchev's Reforms." In *Soviet State and Society under Nikita Khrushchev,* ed. M. Ilic and J. Smith, 8–26. London: Routledge, 2009.
———. "The Central Committee Apparatus under Khrushchev." In *Khrushchev in the Kremlin. Policy and Government in the Soviet Union 1953–64,* ed. Jeremy Smith and Melanie Ilic, 41–60. London: Routledge, 2011.
———. "Partiia protiv gosudarstva: reforma apparata TsK KPSS pri Nikite Khrushcheve" [Party versus state: The reform of the CPSU Central Committee under Nikita Khrushchev]. *Neprikosnovennyi zapas* 83, no. 3 (2012): 155–166.
Wells, D., and J. Miller, eds. *A Directory of Heads and Deputy Heads of CPSU Central Committee Departments 1952–1991.* Manchester: Lorton House, 1993.
Zubkova, Elena. "Malenkov i Khrushchev: Lichnyi faktor v politike poslestalinskogo rukovodstva" [Malenkov and Khrushchev: The personal factor in the policies of the post-Stalin leadership]. *Otechestvennaia istoriia* 4 (1995): 103–115.

 8

TRUE BELIEVERS BECOMING FUNDED EXPERTS?
Personnel Profile and Political Power in the
SED Central Committee's Sectoral Apparatus, 1946–89

Rüdiger Bergien

In early December 1989, some state security units were still performing their tasks as if nothing had happened. The Berlin Wall had fallen, citizens of the German Democratic Republic (GDR) were traveling to the West for shopping tours and family reunions, and although thousands of comrades of the Socialist Unity Party (SED) were returning their party documents every week, *Stasi* officers were still gathering information, writing analyses, and tapping telephone lines. The fact that they were now trying to protect a GDR that was no longer a party dictatorship did not make much of a difference regarding their methods.[1]

One "operative file" the *Stasi* was still working on used the code name "Händler" (trader). It had been pursued by the *Stasi* II/6 department since early 1986.[2] A telephone call between a certain "Karl" and his father regarding this case was taped on the morning of 2 December 1989. The written summary of this call reads as follows: "Karl simply wanted to get in touch with his father once again. The father is pleased. The father had just read in the newspaper that there is a conference tomorrow.[3] Karl agrees. We will gradually close down the whole thing. . . . On 1 January he will again start at the Charité.[4] His father thinks that he is right in doing so. Karl explains that he wants nothing to do with this gang of swindlers any more. It is a disgrace how they did all these things. One wouldn't have believed this before. The father thinks that jealousy and envy also play an important role. Karl agrees by pointing out that they performed truly grave misdeeds."[5]

In this phone call, Karl uses a narrative of justification that was very widespread in the SED in November and December 1989. Hundreds of thousands of SED comrades (and former comrades) were complaining bitterly about the "gang of swindlers"—the old SED party leadership—which had not only ruined the GDR, but had also performed "grave misdeeds." Allegedly they had lived in luxury and grown rich at the expense of the people.⁶ Karl, however, was not just a rank-and-file SED comrade. His full name was Professor Dr. Karl Seidel, a member of the SED Central Committee (CC). He had been head of the CC's health policy department since 1981 and was therefore one of a group of around forty top SED functionaries, some of whom were, informally, higher-ranking than the GDR's ministers and state secretaries. Seidel was at least the most influential man in GDR health policy, and he had presented himself as a loyal and convinced comrade throughout his career. Yet now, in early December 1989, he was the first CC department head to leave the sinking boat. In the call with his father, he seems less regretful about the collapse of his party and the downfall of communism than satisfied that he had managed to get a new job at the Charité so promptly.

One could handle this taped phone call as an anecdote and just note with a shake of the head that a leading SED functionary needed no more than a couple of weeks to sharply distance himself from a party leadership that he had loyally supported for decades. However, one could also take his case seriously. One could ask, for example, what Seidel's phone call tells us about the mentality, beliefs, and motives of the CC department heads in the late 1980s, or, to be more precise, about the mentalities of the heads of the CC sectoral departments.⁷ As these departments were in charge of political fields reaching from the GDR's basic industry to agriculture and health policy, and as most of its heads routinely had to be crisis managers, one could also ask why Seidel and his comrades had been loyal to the now so-called "gang of swindlers" for such a long time. Opportunism and cowardice are frequently used explanations for the socialist elites' failure to secure their political world. However, at least in view of Karl Seidel, these explanations are not fully convincing, as Seidel was an internationally renowned medical scientist who had led a clinic at the Berlin Charité until he entered the central party apparatus. He had had professional alternatives, and he was not known for his cowardice. Had he and his comrades simply not had the power to change anything? Did Marxist-Leninist education hinder them in thinking beyond the latest politburo decisions? Or did they, as a caste of the dictatorships' sated beneficiaries, voluntarily give up their party, as well as socialism, partly due to conflicting personal interests, and partly due to bureaucratic inertia?⁸

Even though these questions are too extensive to be fully addressed in this chapter, it aims at least to set a bold question mark behind the still widespread perception of Communist Party functionaries as inflexible "ideological watchdogs" whose political efficacy went only as far as putting through the latest politburo decisions.⁹ It argues first that the perception of CC apparatus staff as true believers and a homogeneous red avant-garde was not even true in the first postwar years, and departed even further from this image as the apparatus was largely augmented in the early 1950s and professionalized from the late 1950s onwards. Using the CC health policy department's example, this chapter points out, second, that the sectoral department heads could hold significant power if a certain configuration of power was given, and that it was this power, rather than ideology, that can be considered one of the most important motives for the GDR's expert functionaries and state officials to start working for the CC apparatus. Third, it asks what additional motivations might have worked as incentives for the sectoral department heads in keeping to the politburo's line and, furthermore, holding together the whole apparatus as a highly differentiated organization.

The Central Committee Apparatus's Career and Personnel Profile: Survivors and Specialists

At first glance, the SED central apparatus of the early postwar years was what the party leadership wanted it to be: a stronghold of "old communists" and antifascists and probably Germany's (in the view of its members' party experience) most communist organization. Ninety biographies of a total of 240 political employees who had been employed in the SED party headquarters in the summer of 1946 onwards are used as the empirical basis of this chapter.[10] Nearly half of these ninety employees had been more or less active in the antifascist resistance until 1945. Thirty-two employees had indeed been imprisoned in concentration camps, most of them for many years, and some of them, like Arthur Wyschka, who headed the SED central secretariat's[11] local policy department between 1946 and 1949, nearly the whole of the period of existence of the Third Reich.[12] However, many of the other fifty-eight employees had also faced extreme experiences prior to 1945. The "Moscow émigrés" among them had seen the deportations of friends and family members during the "great terror" in the Soviet Union, whereas those who had emigrated to Western countries usually had to go through life with great difficulty, such as Hugo Gräf, born in 1892, and between 1946 and 1948 the head of the central SED health policy department. Gräf was imprisoned—taken into "protective custody" (*Schutzhaft*)—for two years beginning in 1933, until he emigrated to Czechoslovakia and then, shortly before Czechoslovakia's occupation by Nazi Germany in 1938, to Great Britain. He spent all of the war years there working under poor conditions in his profession as a metal worker.

However, neither these common experiences of deprivation and terror nor Marxist-Leninist convictions made the SED central apparatus's first employees a homogenous group. Their biographies and social profiles were quite heterogeneous and ranged from young communist activists, such as the twenty-four-year-old Wolfgang Leonhard (who fled to the West in spring 1949, where he wrote his famous reckoning with the Stalinist system[13]), to Alfred Oelßner, who, born in 1879, could even look back on a functionary career in the social democracy of the *Kaiserreich* (German Empire). There were (at least a few) descendants of the Jewish bourgeoisie, such as Leo Zuckermann, who had earned his Ph.D. in law studies at the Berlin Humboldt University prior to 1933 and had spent the Nazi years in Mexico. In addition, there were also genuine "party soldiers," such as Richard Stahlmann, who, in his position as a *Comintern* instructor, had already participated in the Chinese Canton Uprising in 1934 and served as a partisan commander in the Spanish Civil War.

Some, or even the majority, of the SED first-generation apparatchiks might have been attracted by the prospect of finally building socialism in Germany, while others were driven by more profane motives for membership,[14] such as social security or material benefits. Anton Plenikowsky, for example, who was head of the party's central regional policy department between 1946 and 1950, secured himself a villa in the Berlin area of Bohnsdorf as soon as he had returned from his Swedish exile in 1946.[15] Nevertheless, with the Stalinist "cleansings" that started in fall 1948 and also concerned the central SED apparatus, a certain homogenization of its employees' biographical and political profiles took place. As "aberrations" such as "social democracy" were persecuted, a "correct" political habitus and use of the expected phrases became a matter of political survival. However, from 1950 onward under the apparatus's homogenized surface, a massive personal transformation took place that led it even further away from its avant-garde self-perception.

As the central SED apparatus's role in the political system increased in October 1949 (with the foundation of the GDR), the number of the central apparatus's political employees doubled from 320 to more than 600 between the summer of 1950 and late 1953.[16] As the turnover of staff was extremely high, several hundred new employees were engaged for the CC apparatus, most of them, on average, much younger than the first cohort's members. They brought different experiences, values, and expectations into the apparatus, which could only partially have been homogenized through the party high school courses.

One of these new, very young CC employees was Günter Mittag, the later infamous CC secretary for economics. He entered the apparatus in 1952 and was promptly promoted to the position of head of the railway and transportation department in 1953 at the age of just twenty-six. Mittag had no professional experience in this realm, yet at least he was young enough not to have been seriously involved into the National Socialist system, in contrast to Rudolf Weber, who served as a sector head in the CC social policy department and was responsible for health policies from 1953 onwards. Weber, who grew up in a family of medical practitioners, had entered the *Sturmabteilung* (SA) in 1933 and the NSDAP (Nazi Party) in 1940.[17] However, after he had fallen into Soviet captivity as a military physician in Stalingrad, he became one of the founders of the Soviet-steered "National Committee for a Free Germany," which enabled him not only to join the SED, but also to rise up in the party apparatus. Others had to be more discreet about their past. Walter Borning for example, who was promoted to the position of head of the CC security department in 1960, did not mention his NSDAP membership in the curriculum vitae he had to provide to the party.[18]

Weber and Borning's pasts are not mentioned here to suggest that even the SED CC apparatus had a "brown past."[19] However, together with Mittag they represented a new generation of functionaries who replaced the old communists (and old social democrats) of the late 1940s. In view of its personnel profile, the central party apparatus virtually grew into the postfascist GDR society, as its new employees, to a certain extent, shared this society's collective societal experiences and burdens. However, in view of the central party apparatus's main task during these years—to enforce the politburo's decision to "build socialism"— the apparatus "societalization" proved to be disadvantageous. Department heads such as Mittag or Borning could not refer to an antifascist biography to legitimize their claims to political power. Worse still, they could also not refer to their level of education, nor to their professional experience.

In 1953, only 15 percent of the CC employees had a university or technical college degree. By 1959 this share had risen to just 25 percent, despite huge efforts made by the CC cadre specialists. The CC secretariat was convinced that this insufficient formal education was one of the main reasons for its apparatus's alleged bad political performance. Therefore, from the late 1950s onwards, another extensive change in the personnel profile took place. The 1950s apparatus of young men (and fewer women) who lacked either education or professional experience (or both) developed into an apparatus of highly qualified professionals, in the sectoral departments at least. While the importance of the ideology departments decreased against the background of Ulbricht's 1960s reformist and technocratic agenda (at least until Erich Honecker raised their status again from the early 1970s onwards),[20] the power of the sector departments grew, as will be shown in the next section.

The sectoral departments' professionalization can be personified by Karl Seidel, whose call with his father in early December 1989 was cited at the beginning of this chapter. Seidel, born in Nuremberg in 1930, grew up in a family of medical practitioners and studied medicine in Leipzig in the 1950s. He became a medical consultant in psychiatry, qualified in Dresden as a university lecturer (with a thesis about suicide prevention), became an assistant medical director at the Dresden academy psychiatric clinic, and supervised the renowned Berlin Charité psychiatric clinic between 1975 and 1979. Seidel enjoyed a good reputation both in the GDR and internationally. He led negotiations with the West German Siemens electronic group on the delivery of Siemens's computerized tomography to GDR hospitals and frequently visited specialist conferences in Western countries.[21]

The fact that a renowned scientist like Seidel accepted an offer to take up a position in the CC health policy department in 1979 is only surprising if one maintains the apparatus's image as a stronghold of ideology and bureaucratic inertia. Due to the professionalization of the CC sectoral departments, the career profiles of its employees became increasingly similar to the CVs of GDR ministerial officials. Changes between state and party apparatuses grew ever more frequent, resulting in an interconnection between ministries and CC departments based on personal relations.[22] However, as the influence of the 1970s and 1980s CC department heads was based less on political exclusivity, this party–state interconnection was a premise for their political influence.

Political Power: The Rise of the Health Policy Department

In the late 1940s and 1950s, the CC apparatus had only a modest influence on health policies.[23] In meetings in the early 1950s between a responsible CC employee, comrade Holze, and state officials, only matters of lesser importance were discussed, such as the question of whether GDR health institutions should be allowed to accept Red Cross donations ("Yes, if they are given without conditions") or whether the Dresden-based Deutsches Hygiene Museum should be permitted to export its famous glass anatomic models.[24] Also, in the following years, the CC employees responsible were rather busy discussing drafts for a GDR professional medical association or inventing medals and awards for medical practitioners of outstanding merit (in order to keep them from leaving the GDR to go to the West).[25] The setting of the course of GDR health policy was in the hands of the health ministry, or rather of the politburo itself, but not in the party apparatus.

One of the first important actors in this field was Max Zetkin, the son of the communist icon Clara Zetkin. Max had worked for more than fifteen years as a chief physician in Soviet hospitals before returning to Germany in 1946 to take up the post of deputy director of the health policy administration. It is very telling that he had no scruples in telling the then central secretariat secretary Helmut Lehmann that he, Zetkin, and his staff were "so burdened with work" that they had "difficulties finding the time for closer cooperation" with the party apparatus.[26] Similarly, Zetkin's de facto successor, the SED state secretary Jenny Matern,[27] was not at all confined to the role of being the party's representative in the CDU-led health ministry.[28] Indeed, she exercised her function with confidence, and, on at least one occasion, she stood firmly against grave accusations from the party central[29] and obviously went as far as serving the medical profession's interests by ordering the destruction of a "central file" (*Zentralkartei*) that had contained all GDR medical practitioners' names, as well as their affiliation to National Socialist organizations up to 1945.[30]

Things changed in the late 1950s. From the politburo's perspective, the GDR health system had developed into a problem area as more and more GDR medical practitioners fled to the West. By 1959, at least seventy-five hundred medical practitioners and nearly fifteen hundred dentists had left GDR territory, half of these from 1954 onwards, which amounted to half of the medical personnel who had been located in Soviet-occupied Germany in 1946.[31] The party leadership reacted to this situation as it frequently did to growing problems: it established a CC department to increase the party's influence on the particular political field. In this case, the CC health policy sector was dissolved from the CC social policy department and made into an independent department. Its new head was Werner Hering, a just thirty-year-old law graduate with a doctorate, and a representative of the new generation of professionalized CC functionaries.

Hering proved to be a good choice insofar as he combined loyalty to the party line with a great deal of flexibility toward the special needs and interests of the status-conscious medical profession. In cooperation with the health ministry, he brought a series of proposals to the politburo's table—something that had been "more or less taboo up to this point"[32] and can best be described as "lobbying." The long-announced professional medical association was finally to be founded; doctors should again be allowed to use the traditional titles that had been banned in 1945 (such as *Sanitätsrat* and *Medizinalrat*), and they should even be allowed to settle down in private practices again. However, Hering also bolstered the party apparatus's influence on the health ministry as he inundated health minister Max Sefrin with "suggestions" in the following years. These suggestions included issues regarding the problems with the GDR drug supply after the building of the Berlin Wall, as well urging that heart surgeons would only be permitted to operate in the new heart surgery centers,[33] as well as judicial problems of the removal of deceased's organs.[34]

From the mid-1960s onwards, Hering tightened his party line and argued for the disposal of the private medical practices whose establishment he just had promoted in 1959 in view of the exodus of physicians (who were then contained by the building of the wall). Hering proved himself to be a talented political tactician here as he regularly confronted Kurt Hager, the responsible CC secretary and politburo member, with (alleged) complaints from local SED branches about these "excesses"— the private treatments—"which are inconsistent with socialism."[35] In the late 1940s and 1950s, the responsible CC's functionaries had rather been observers of health policy processes, but from the 1960s onwards, the professionalized health policy department became a political actor.

In the early 1970s, Hering even won a major success. After years of lobbying, in 1973, he, together with health minister Ludwig Mecklinger, achieved the so-called joint resolution (*gemeinsamer Beschluss*) about who gained approval from the politburo and the council of ministers.[36] This "joint resolution" led to a desperately needed increase in the state budget for the health system. The provision of medical care increased, as well as specialist fields such as orthopedics and surgery. Sickness allowances were augmented, and the construction of hospital buildings and nurses dormitories began. However, as the starting point was catastrophic, the measures were anything but sufficient. In 1976, an extensive *Stasi* report about the situation in the health system made it drastically clear that many old hospital buildings were still rotting, that the wages of nursing staff were miserable—that is, the same as housekeeping staff—and that clinic doctors who "deserted the republic" confronted the health system with very severe personnel shortages.[37]

The GDR health system's lasting precarious conditions illustrate that room for political maneuvering was quite limited even for a power-conscious CC department head like Werner Hering. Even Hering's relative successes depended on a specific figuration of power[38] within the GDR party and state leadership. Hering had an advantage over some of his department head colleagues in that he was the favorite of politburo member Kurt Hager, and in that his aim to get more money for the health system was favored by Erich Honecker's change of course toward socialist consumerism, which included an expansion of social services. However, this power configuration was not to last. Hering experienced this himself when he and Mecklinger prepared to introduce a bill into the CC secretariat in summer 1981 that should have finally brought about wage increases for the underpaid GDR nursing staff. However, the power configuration that had guaranteed Hering's influence had changed due to the rise of Günter Mittag, who, in view of the GDR's debt and economic crisis, demanded a strict spending freeze. Furthermore, it also changed as Erich Honecker had just learned from Leonid Brezhnev that the Soviet Union intended to decrease their crude oil exports to the GDR, which must lead to an intensification of the debt and economic crisis.[39] In addition, a few weeks before Hering and Mecklinger brought their bill to the CC secretariat's table, there had been protests in several GDR hospitals against underpayment and disastrous working conditions. In view of the Solidarity movement in Poland, the SED leadership was alarmed.

Against this background, Werner Hering and minister Ludwig Mecklinger entered the CC secretariat's conference room on Wednesday, 26 August 1981, to justify their bill. They triggered one of the few occasions when Erich Honecker had a public outburst of rage.[40] He shouted at Hering that "two-thirds of the doctors were unreliable citizens, who he would gladly get shot of." Moreover, the CC health policy department had not once started a campaign to improve medical personnel's political consciousness since its establishment. It had always asked for more money, but these times, Honecker shouted, were now over. "The cash-cow has been milked dry!" (*Die Geldkuh ist leergemolken!*) The doctors had to learn to obey. And, verbatim, "If anyone rebels, I will send them to the coalfields!" (*Wer aufmuckt, den schicke ich in die Braunkohle!*) When the meeting was over, Hering was de facto dismissed.

In view of the question of the role of the CC sectoral department heads in the GDR political system, the health department's further fate is quite telling. Its "execution" in August 1981 could be interpreted as an indication that the party leadership expected its CC departments to keep to their role as ideological watchdogs, but not to make their own policy. Indeed, Karl Seidel, who succeeded Hering in office, was strictly ordered to limit his department's work purely to political-ideological tasks.[41] However, as doctors continued to flee to the West and even basic health services were endangered, the party could not just stand by trying to raise medical staff's political consciousness. Consequently, in the course of the 1980s, Karl Seidel acted not as an ideologue, but as an expert politician and crisis manager, a role to which he was predestined through his scientific and medical career. In 1987, health minister Ludwig Mecklinger confided to his *Stasi* contact officer, that "things have gone as bad again as they were in the days of comrade Hering." In his opinion, Mecklinger continued, "there were too many doctors in the health policy department and too few party workers."[42] His reservations about the experts in the CC department who did not care about "party work" but acted as a kind of "super government" to his ministry, as Mecklinger had complained about as early as the mid-1970s, was proven true. Seidel replaced Mecklinger with Klaus Thiemann, a medical scientist and deputy minister at the university and technical college ministry in 1989. In Seidel's (and the politburo's) opinion, the seventy-year-old Mecklinger was no longer capable in his position in times of crisis.

The CC health department's example should have illustrated that sectoral department heads like Hering and Seidel *could* have significant room to maneuver. It was this room that attracted many already high-ranking state officials to move into the party apparatus. Karl Seidel resigned his post as Charité clinic director in favor of a position in the CC health policy department, as he believed the party headquarters to be the only place in the GDR where one could change the circumstances that he and his medical colleagues had to suffer from.[43] Similarly, in 1975, Gregor Schirmer, deputy minister for the university and technical college system, moved to the officially lower-ranking position of CC science department's deputy head. In an interview he explained that in his position as deputy minister he had "to suffer more criticism from below or from next-door than as a deputy CC department head. My authority . . . as a CC deputy department head was higher . . . . There I was beyond any criticism, so to speak. I was sacrosanct, because everything I said was to be equated with the party line."[44] However, the number of CC employees who could claim to yield political power, to make a difference in his or her political field, was rather small. Most of their working days passed with the preparation of extensive analyses of agricultural working conditions or the prospects of GDR's tin deposits, which did not change anything, and with many meetings in which countless "small" matters were discussed, but rarely resolved. Many, if not most, employees and even sector and department heads had reason to become depressed about the ineffectiveness of their organization. Although the apparatus was seen as the center of power, its employees were in many cases as helpless as any other state institution in view of the GDR's structural problems. So why did they remain in their positions? What motivated them?

Integrating Factors: Money and Medals

To start with, it seems easier to point out the factor that did *not* have the effect of integrating the apparatus—that is, ideology. In fact, ideology had always played a key role in the CC apparatus employees' self-perception. In an interview, a former CC employee, who was thirty-five in 1989 (and the daughter of a famous antifascist), assured me, "We were all believers."[45] On the other hand, there is no indication that CC employees (with the possible exception of a few older comrades) were in any way more trusting, more dogmatic, or more ideologically centered than other GDR citizens who were loyal to the regime. Most CC employees did not read the classic works of Marxism-Leninism before they were forced to do so at party high school. The CC library's lending list shows (at least for the 1950s) that CC employees borrowed fiction in great numbers, that they loved the satirical magazine *Eulenspiegel* as well as sports magazines and generally Western newspapers, but that theoretical works or Soviet magazines remained unread on the library shelves.[46] In addition, not even the minutes of bugging by the GDR state security (as well as West German intelligence) of CC employees' phone calls and informal talks in private contexts contain any direct references to ideology. Of course, the employees could have internalized certain basic beliefs to a degree that these were no longer explicitly mentioned. However, as long as they did not use the authoritative discourse in their talks, this discourse and its ideological premises could not have served as a matter of integration of the CC apparatus.

An integrating factor was certainly that CC employees shared a consciousness that they constituted a political elite. *Stasi* reports and interviews indicate that many of them were proud that they had risen to the party headquarters and behaved with great self-confidence. Their public appearances, a GDR state official complained in 1974, would often be like that of "demi-gods who were climbing down to earth," while the local party functionaries would even "treat them as gods."[47] In summer 1972, a CC employee caused public anger in a Berlin pub when, during an argument with another customer, he pulled out his CC identity card to prove that he—as opposed to his adversary—had a highly responsible position and was doing most important work (and earned 2500 ostmarks a month, with full justification).[48] And in 1986, on the occasion of his sixtieth birthday, a CC security department sector head told his comrades that when he was employed by the SED CC in the 1950s, he had been asked where his career might finally lead. He claimed that he had answered, "What else could come now? You can't get higher than the CC!"[49]

Combined with the possibility of wielding power, an elitist self-perception might also have bent "technocrats" like Seidel to the apparatus. Belonging made it easier for them to ignore some of the dogmatic or even Stalinist features that they might have sneered at from their previous positions as clinic directors or deputy ministers, such as the quasi-military discipline within the "big house" and, not least, Erich Honecker's autocratic leadership style, which was especially visible through his habit of addressing his CC department heads as the "party's general staff" (which is very telling in regard to Honecker's hierarchical thinking).[50] However, there were further integrating factors that also attracted rank-and-file CC employees, not just the small group of department heads—that is to say, monetary incentives and privileges.[51]

Of course, these fields need to be dealt with carefully as there is some danger of repeating the opposition's fall 1989 accusations. However, there can be no doubt that CC employees were always well paid. When Walter Borning, who was later to become security department head, entered the apparatus in 1952 as a rank-and-file political employee, he earned 1,000 ostmarks per month,[52] whereas the GDR gross average wage was just 225 ostmarks. This stands in sharp contrasts to the contemporaries' claim that party functionaries were kept quite short in the Ulbricht era but compensated for their underpayment with idealism and strong beliefs.[53] In the 1970s and 1980s, confronted with a general growth of income in the GDR, the CC salary commission frequently argued that the party needed to raise their full-time employees' salaries to be able to compete with the salaries offered by ministries and combines.[54] CC employees did indeed enjoy large pay increases. The average income of a CC department head rose from 2,500 ostmarks in 1965 to 4,300 ostmarks in 1984. A rank-and-file political employee received at least 2,200 ostmarks in 1984, compared to 1,300 ostmarks in 1965. Compared to other members of the GDR functional elites, these pay increases were not disproportionate.[55] However, they prove the contemporary claims that money did not count in the party apparatus to be false. In the words of Horst Wambutt, the former basic industries department head, "Our employees were able to calculate. It wasn't like that, after all. Nobody worked in the apparatus just because of his convictions, even if he was the most loyal comrade."[56]

However, the contemporary claims do contain a core of truth. In an economy of short supply, money plays a less important role than in a market economy. Therefore, the importance of symbolic capital and privileges was correspondingly great. The general secretary was aware of that. It characterizes Erich Honecker's leadership style that he awarded his highest-ranking functionaries—the CC department heads—with privileges to an extent that suggests similarities to Leonid Brezhnev's patronage policy.[57]

In the late Ulbricht years, there were only four CC department heads who were simultaneously elected members of the CC, a position that included not only reputation but also monthly expense allowances of 300 to 500 ostmarks. In the late 1980s, there were twenty CC department heads that were elected CC members, as Honecker had initiated their election to strengthen their loyalty. Another measure the general secretary frequently used to intensify the bonds between him and his "general staff" was the award of high decorations. Even though hundreds of different kinds of decorations and medals were very generously awarded to comrades and noncomrades alike at any important and less important occasions,[58] there were indeed some very prestigious decorations. The "hero of the working class" title or the "Karl Marx medal"—the latter was worth 20,000 ostmarks in prize money—were generally rarely awarded, yet nearly all CC department heads of Honecker's inner circle received these awards. Gisela Glende, who led the office of the politburo (and was therewith de facto Erich Honecker's office manager), was awarded the Karl Marx medal twice.

That the "material interests" of the department heads were so skillfully satisfied by Honecker was at least an important reason for them to serve the party and can be further illustrated by their proneness to their abuse of authority and unjustified enrichment. Wolfgang Herger, the last CC security department head, admitted in an interview that this tendency was indeed a problem in the CC apparatus and called it "corruption by habituation." Herger explained that comrades from the CC machine construction department received Lada cars for their private use. Their reasoning was that if their colleagues got cars "through their connections to the machine construction industry," they "therefore also feel justified in trying to get one."[59] Günter Glende, the CC infrastructure department head, also offered Herger a "Neckermann house," as a certain type of West German prefabricated house was nicknamed. Herger would have refused this offer, but some of his department head comrades had not. They accepted a "Neckermann house" or a color TV set from Glende, and were therefore obliged to him from then on—part of an informal network for the exchange of political and material favors.

One of the department heads that did not resist the temptation to abuse his position was Karl Seidel, the health policy department head. The reason that Seidel's phone calls were taped by the *Stasi* even in early December 1989 was corruption of a singular extent. From the mid-1980s onwards, Seidel had abused his diplomatic passport to undertake shopping trips to West Berlin. There he visited not only the *Kaufhaus des Westens,* the famous West Berlin department store, but also computer stores. He bought personal computers, together with peripheral devices, smuggled them to East Berlin (protected again by his diplomatic passport) and resold them at great profit—Western personal computers were overpriced in the GDR in secondhand goods businesses. By October 1987, he had already sold computers totaling a value of nearly 277,000 ostmarks; by fall 1989, he had made a profit of 130,000 ostmarks.[60] He used his profits not least to furnish his country house with antiques and buy a VW estate car in West Berlin. His GDR-produced "Wartburg" did not have enough power output to carry his two German shepherds, he confided to a friend, as the *Stasi* learned through its bugging campaign.[61]

It may be tempting to condemn Seidel and, with him, all of the CC department head comrades as corrupt hypocrites. However, from an analytical perspective, things were definitely more complex, at least if one keeps in mind that these political elites' opportunities to express their elitist status were severely limited within the context of a regime that was forced to present itself as highly egalitarian. Even if Seidel's activities seem plainly illegal and corrupt from a Western perspective, they also need to be seen as attempts to compensate for the restrictions that the Marxist-Leninist ideology imposed on Seidel and his comrades, who, due to their positions, were regularly confronted with Western elitist styles when they attended international conferences, trade fairs in the Federal Republic of Germany (FRG), etc.

Conclusion

All in all, in view of their motivation, political practice, and even in view of their materialist interests, the CC sectoral department heads prove to be rather a "normal" state socialist elite than an isolated, ideology-filled caste of "party workers" or "professional revolutionaries." Bearing in mind their dispositions, it is anything but surprising that they started looking for new jobs when their party dissolved rapidly from October 1989 onwards instead of preparing for a last stand. At least some of the sectoral department heads were indeed able to find new, although lower-ranking, jobs in a post-socialist GDR and in a united Germany. A telling example is Horst Wambutt, who, after he had led the CC machine construction and basic industry departments for more than two decades, found a position in a West German machine construction business and stayed there even beyond his retirement age in 1997.[62]

However, Karl Seidel's attempt to restart his Charité career failed. He was arrested on 15 December 1989, by order of the GDR public prosecutor's office and charged with corruption and abuse of authority, and a fine was imposed upon him in 1992. It is questionable whether he would have been able to continue his academic career in a united Germany that was rigidly disbanding GDR scientific institutions. However, if Seidel's transfer to the Charité had worked and he had become a professor again, he might have been the sole CC department to rise to such a high position again after the socialist GDR's downfall. It is quite telling that it was his material interests that hindered this possibility, and not his ideological beliefs.

Rüdiger Bergien is a lecturer (Privatdozent) at the Humboldt University Berlin and a postdoctoral research fellow at the Centre for Contemporary History in Potsdam. His publications include *Die bellizistische Republik. Wehrkonsens und "Wehrhaftmachung" in Deutschland 1918–1933* (2012); "Activating the 'Apparatchik': Brigade Deployment in the SED Central Committee and Performative Communist Party Rule," in *Journal of Contemporary History* 47, no. 4 (2012): 793–811; and *Im Generalstab der Partei. Organisationskultur und Herrschaftspraxis in der SED-Zentrale (1946–1989)* (2017).

Notes

1. From late November 1989, the *Ministerium für Staatssicherheit* (Ministry for State Security) was renamed the *Amt für Nationale Sicherheit* (Office for National Security). The aim of its command was to transform at least parts of the former *Stasi* into an interior secret service that might resemble the West German Verfassungsschutz (Federal Office for the Protection of the Constitution). On the Stasi's last months, see Walter Süß, *Staatssicherheit am Ende: warum es den Mächtigen nicht gelang, 1989 eine Revolution zu verhindern* [The end of state security: Why the rulers failed to prevent a revolution in 1989] (Berlin, 1999); Jens Gieseke, *Die hauptamtlichen Mitarbeiter der Staatssicherheit. Personalstruktur und Lebenswelt 1950–1989/90* [The full-time employees of the secret police. Staff structure and milieu 1950–1989/90] (Berlin, 2000).
2. For this case, see also Rüdiger Bergien, *Im "Generalstab der Partei." Organisationskultur und Herrschaftspraxis in der SED-Zentrale 1946–89* ["General staff of the party." Organizational culture and practice of rule in the center of the SED] (Berlin, 2017), 448–449.
3. This conference was the twelfth (extraordinary) meeting of the SED Central Committee that ended with the politburo's resignation and the Central Committee's self-dissolution.

4. The Charité is the name of the internationally recognized Berlin Humboldt University hospital.
5. Information A 7776/86/133/89, Bd. 63142, 2.12.1989, BStU, MfS, HA II/6, Nr. 2041, 261–262.
6. Hans-Hermann Hertle and Gerd-Rüdiger Stephan (eds.), *Das Ende der SED. Die letzten Tage des Zentralkomitees* [The end of SED. The last days of the Central Committee] (Berlin, 1997).
7. By dividing the nearly forty CC departments, working groups, and commissions into several groups, I follow an approach similar to Nikolay Mitrokhin, who makes a distinction between the CPSU CC apparatus "ideological" groups (Propaganda, Culture, and Science and Education), the "international" (International Information, and Tied with Socialist Countries), the "sectoral" (more than a dozen departments answering to various economic sectors), and the "functional" groups who were responsible for the work of the party apparatus as a whole. Nikolay Mitrokhin, "CPSU Central Committee Apparatus, 1970–85: Personnel and Role in the Soviet Political System," *Russian History* 41, no. 3 (2014): 307–328, here 311.
8. Stephen Kotkin and Jan Tomasz Gross, *Uncivil Society: 1989 and the Implosion of the Communist Establishment* (New York, 2009).
9. For such a perception see the—generally extremely inspiring—work of Robert Darnton, *Censors at Work* (New York, 2014), 183–4. Darnton, however, used the "ideological watchdog" phrase not for the SED CC apparatus in total, but just in view of the (indeed watchdog-like) employees of the CC culture department.
10. For more details, see Rüdiger Bergien, *Generalstab der Partei*.
11. The SED Central Committee was introduced not earlier than 1950 in the course of a general "sovietization" of the party's structures. Until then the central party apparatus was called apparatus of the central secretariat (*Apparat des Zentralsekretariats*) or apparatus of the party executive (*Apparat des Parteivorstands*).
12. Wyschka was imprisoned for the first time in May 1933 and then spent nearly all the coming years until 1945 in concentration camps in Esterwegen, Lichtenburg, Buchenwald, and Sachsenhausen.
13. Wolfgang Leonhard, *Child of the Revolution*, transl. C. M. Woodhouse (Chicago, 1958).
14. For the concepts of "motives for membership" (*Mitgliedschaftsmotive*), see Stefan Kühl, *Organisationen. Eine sehr kurze Einführung* [Organizations. A very short introduction] (Wiesbaden, 2011), 30–33.
15. Michael F. Scholz, *Skandinavische Erfahrungen erwünscht? Nachexil und Remigration; die ehemaligen KPD-Emigranten in Skandinavien und ihr weiteres Schicksal in der SBZ/DDR* [Scandinavian experience desired? Post-exile and remigration; the former German Communist Party immigrants in Scandinavia and their further fate in the Soviet Occupied Zone/GDR] (Stuttgart, 2000), 66.
16. Heike Amos, *Politik und Organisation der SED-Zentrale 1949–1963. Struktur und Arbeitsweise von Politbüro, Sekretariat, Zentralkomitee und ZK-Apparat* [Policy and organization of the SED central control office. The structure

and operation of the politburo, secretariat, Central Committee and Central Committee apparatus] (Münster, 2003), 183.
17. However, Weber entered these organizations probably in view of his career as a hospital physician rather than because of his ideological convictions.
18. However, his joining of the Nazi Party in 1939 and having grown up in quite a nationalistic family obviously had some long-term effects on his basic beliefs. In 1970 during a military maneuver, he insulted a group of NVA (National People's Army) officers as "weak bastards" (*lahme Säcke*) who should take example of how "we did things thirty years ago" (*wie wir das vor 30 Jahren gemacht haben*). *Anlage Nr. 14 zum Protokoll der Politbürositzung vom 29.2.1972, Veränderung der Funktion des Abteilungsleiters für Sicherheitsfragen des ZK der SED*... [Enclosure Nr. 14 to the politburo report meeting of 29.2.1972. Reform of function of the head for security of the SED Central Committee], Stiftung Archiv der Parteien und Massenorganisationen im Bundesarchiv [Foundation Archive of the Parties and Mass Organizations in the Federal Archive], hereafter SAPMO-BArch, DY 30/J IV 2/2/1381, 135–6. See also comments under endnote 5.
19. At no point in time had more than around 10 percent of all political CC employees been former NSDAP or SA/SS members prior to 1945. At least two-thirds of this group had entered the Nazi organizations as very young men in the last years of the war. For more detail, see Rüdiger Bergien, "Das Schweigen der Kader. Ehemalige Nationalsozialisten im zentralen SED-Parteiapparat—eine Erkundung" [The silence of the cadre. Former National Socialists in the SED party apparatus—An investigation], in *Kontinuitäten und Diskontinuitäten. Der Nationalsozialismus in der Geschichte des 20. Jahrhunderts* [Continuities and discontinuities. National Socialism in the history of the 20th century], ed. Birthe Kundrus and Sybille Steinbacher (Göttingen, 2013), 134–53.
20. See especially Monika Kaiser, *Machtwechsel von Ulbricht zu Honecker: Funktionsmechanismen der SED-Diktatur in Konfliktsituationen 1962 bis 1972* [Change of government from Ulbricht to Honecker. How the SED-dictatorship worked in situations of conflicts] (Berlin, 1997).
21. For Seidel's CV, see Sonja Süß, *Politisch missbraucht? Psychiatrie und Staatssicherheit in der DDR* [Politically abused? Psychiatry and state security in the GDR] (Berlin, 1998) (= Analysen und Dokumente [Analyses and documents], vol. 14), 182.
22. This interconnection is illustrated by the fact that ten of the twenty-nine SED ministers who were in office in 1980 had served for a longer period in a leading position at the party headquarters. See Bergien, *Im "Generalstab der Partei"*; for similar findings for the Soviet Union, see Mitrokhin, *CPSU Central Committee Apparatus*, 315.
23. See Anna-Sabine Ernst, *"Die beste Prophylaxe ist der Sozialismus." Ärzte und medizinische Hochschullehrer in der SBZ/DDR 1945–1961* ["The best prophylaxis is socialism." Physicians and medical professors in the SBZ/GDR 1945–1961] (Münster, 1997), 40–43.
24. Professor Zetkin, Aktennotiz, betr.: Besprechung mit Gen. Holze vom ZK am 29.3.51. 30.03.1951 [Professor Zetkin, memorandum, concerning: meet-

ing with comrade Holze from the ZK on 29.3.52, 30.03.1951], Bundesarchiv Berlin [BArch Berlin], DQ 1/20167, unnumbered.
25. Anne-Sabine Ernst, *"Die beste Prophylaxe ist der Sozialismus,"* 138.
26. Maxim Zetkin to Helmut Lehmann, 9.1.1948, BArch Berlin, DQ 1/20167, unnumbered.
27. It was common practice that the ministries not led by SED ministers were given a strong SED state secretary in order to secure the party's control over the particular political field. Jenny Matern was one such "strong" state secretary—not least due to her marriage to Hermann Matern—in the first postwar years, alongside Wilhelm Pieck and Walter Ulbricht, the most famous German communist.
28. As Ernst suggests in *"Die beste Prophylaxe ist der Sozialismus,"* 142–143.
29. Matern remained unimpressed when Otto Schön, a CC department head close to Ulbricht, tried to initiate a Stalinist-style newspaper campaign against the health ministry's alleged insufficient cadre policy in 1953. She replied tersely to Schön that his accusations were not true, and she did not experience any consequences for her actions. Jenny Matern to Otto Schön, 12.5.1953, BArch Berlin, DQ 1/3156, 308.
30. Ernst, *"Die beste Prophylaxe ist der Sozialismus,"* 187.
31. Ibid., 54.
32. Ibid., 52–53.
33. Werner Hering to Max Sefrin, 29.7.1964, BArch Berlin, DQ 1/5263, unnumbered.
34. Werner Hering to Max Sefrin, 24.1.1963, BArch Berlin, DQ 1/5263, unnumbered.
35. Werner Hering to Kurt Hager. See Information to the Secretary of the Central Committee concerning the gradual disposal of private treatment in medical institutions in the GDR, 11.9.1967, SAPMO-BArch, DY 30/IV A 2/19, 33, unnumbered.
36. Jürgen Wasem, Doris Mill, and Jürgen Wilhelm, "Gesundheitswesen und Sicherung bei Krankheit und im Pflegefall" [Healthcare and security in case of illness and nursing care], in *Geschichte der Sozialpolitik in Deutschland seit 1945*, vol. 10, *Deutsche Demokratische Republik 1971–1989* [History of social policy in Germany since 1945, vol. 10, German Democratic Republic 1971–1989], ed. Christoph Boyer, Klaus-Dietmar Henke, and Peter Skyba (Baden-Baden, 2008), 372.
37. See Siegfried Suckut, "Seismographische Aufzeichnungen. Der Blick des MfS auf Staat und Gesellschaft in der DDR am Beispiel der Berichte an die SED-Führung 1976. Beispiel der Berichte an die SED-Führung 1976" [Seismic recordings. The secret police's view of state and society in the GDR through the example of reports to the SED leaders 1976], in *Staatssicherheit und Gesellschaft*, ed. Jens Gieseke (Göttingen, 2007), 116–118. See also Wasem, Mill, and Wilhelm, *Gesundheitswesen*, 385.
38. The sociological concept "configuration of power" is elaborated in Wolfgang Sofsky and Rainer Paris, *Figurationen sozialer Macht. Autorität—Stellvertretung—Koalition* [Figurations of social power. Authority—deputy—coalition] (Opladen, 1991).

39. The GDR economy depended on the profits generated by the refinement of crude oil and its reexport to Western countries.
40. We are informed about the meeting's course by two independent sources: first, by an account given by health minister Mecklinger, who attended the meeting, to his state security contact officer a few days later (HA XX/1: Vermerk über ein Gespräch mit dem Minister für Gesundheitswesen, Genossen Mecklinger, 31.8.1981, BStU, MfS, HA XX, Nr. 527, Teil 1, 139–40); second, in the memoirs of Hering's closest staff member, Erich Fischer, *Geständnisse und Bekenntnisse* [Admissions and confessions] (Schkeuditz, 2002), 150–153.
41. MfS, HA XX/1: Vermerk. 11.9.1981, BStU, MfS, HA XX, Nr. 41, 1–3, here 1.
42. "Seiner Meinung (seien) in der (ZK-)Abteilung Gesundheitspolitik zu viele Ärzte und zu wenig Parteiarbeiter." [In his opinion there were too many doctors and not enough party workers in the (CC) health policy department.] MfS, HA XX/1: Vermerk, 20.1.1987, BStU, MfS, HA XX, Nr. 527, Teil 1, 3.
43. Süß, *Politisch missbraucht?* 182.
44. Interview with Gregor Schirmer, 5 February 2010, 7, author's transcript and audio file.
45. Interview with Renate Michalik-Erxleben, 18 January 2016, 31, author's transcript and audio file.
46. Fritz Gäbler: Bericht über die Überprüfung des technischen Apparats beim Büro des Politbüros [Report on the audit of the technical apparatus at the office of the politburo], 12.2.1957, SAPMO-BArch, DY 30/IV 3/58, unnumbered.
47. This quotation by an official of the GDR state travel agency was documented by an unofficial *Stasi* collaborator: Report IM "Renn." 16.7.1974, BStU, MfS, AIM 15396, 89, Bd 7, 41–44, here number 44.
48. Bruno Beater: 1. Stellvertreter des Ministers für Staatssicherheit, an Bruno Wansierski, ZK-Abteilung Sicherheitsfragen, ref.: Äußerungen des Mitarbeiters des ZK der SED, Genossen Walter Rädel [Bruno Beater: First deputy to the minister of state security, to Bruno Wansierski, Central Committee department of security, concerning: Statements from Walter Rädel, member of staff of the SED Central Committee], 6.9.1972, BStU, MfS, SdM, Nr. 1092, 27; Peter Raab: Information, 6.7.1972, BStU, MfS, SdM, Nr. 1092, 28–31.
49. Diary entry by Dieter Mechel, who was a political employee in the CC security department between 1986 and 1989, dated 9.9.1986. I am very grateful to Dieter Mechtel for providing me with his contemporary notes.
50. It is to be left open whether Honecker consciously cited his hero Stalin when using that phrase.
51. Much inspiration to the following explanations were provided by Eugenia Belova and Valery Lazarev, *Funding Loyalty: The Economics of the Communist Party* (New Haven, CT, 2012).
52. Cadre file Walter Borning, SAPMO-BArch, DY 30/IV 2/11/v. 2998, 83.
53. Fischer, *Geständnisse und Bekenntnisse* [Admissions and confessions], 123.
54. Vorlage für das Sekretariat des ZK betr. Gehaltsregulativ für den Parteiapparat der SED, [Presentation for the secretary of ZK, concerning the payment regulation for the party-apparatus of the SED], 17.10.1980, SAPMO-BArch, DY 30/J IV 2/3A/3549, 143–65.

55. Due to many salary bonuses, high-ranking *Stasi* officers were even better paid. See J. Gieseke, "Zwischen Privilegienkultur und Egalitarismus. Zu den Einkommensstrukturen des Ministeriums für Staatssicherheit" [Between a culture of privilege and egalitarianism. On the structure of income of the ministry for state security], *Deutschland Archiv* 43, no. 3 (2010): 442–453.
56. "Unsere Mitarbeiter konnten ja rechnen. So war das ja nicht. Nur aus Überzeugung hat keiner im Apparat gearbeitet, und wenn er noch so ein treuer Genosse war." Interview with Horst Wambutt, 5 June 2013, 5–6, author's transcript and audio file.
57. John P. Willerton, "Patronage Networks and Coalition Building in the Brezhnev Era," *Soviet Studies* 39, no. 2 (1987): 175–204.
58. Stefan Hornbostel, "Ehre oder Blechsegen? Das Auszeichnungswesen der DDR" [Honor or just a piece of metal? Honors in the GDR], in *SFB 580-|Mitteilungen* [SFB 580-Messages] 3 (2002): 33–39.
59. Interview with Wolfgang Herger, 29 April 2014, 33, author's transcript and audio file.
60. Information, August 1989, BStU, MfS, HA II/6, Nr. 1059, 4.
61. Gesprächsprotokoll mit dem DDR-Bürger . . . . [Communication protocol with GDR citizens], 26.10.1989, BStU, MfS, HA II/6, Nr. 1059, 13.
62. Interview with Horst Wambutt, 7 November 2012, 58, author's transcript and audio file.

Bibliography

Amos, Heike. *Politik und Organisation der SED-Zentrale 1949–1963. Struktur und Arbeitsweise von Politbüro, Sekretariat, Zentralkomitee und ZK-Apparat* [Politics and organization of the SED central control office. The structure and operation of the politburo, secretariat, Central Committee and Central Committee apparatus]. Münster: LIT Verlag, 2003.

Belova, Eugenia, and Valery Lazarev. *Funding Loyalty: The Economics of the Communist Party*. New Haven: Yale University Press, 2012.

Bergien, Rüdiger. "Das Schweigen der Kader. Ehemalige Nationalsozialisten im zentralen SED-Parteiapparat—eine Erkundung" [The silence of the cadre. Former national socialists in the central party apparatus—An investigation], in *Kontinuitäten und Diskontinuitäten. Der Nationalsozialismus in der Geschichte des 20. Jahrhunderts* [Continuities and discontinuities. National Socialism in the history of the 20th century], ed. B. Kundrus and S. Steinbacher, 134–153. Göttingen: Wallstein Verlag, 2013.

———. *Im "Generalstab der Partei." Organisationskultur und Herrschaftspraxis in der SED-Zentrale (1946–1989)* [In the "general staff of the party." Organizational culture and practice of rule in the center of the SED]. Berlin: Christoph Links Verlag, 2017.

Darnton, Robert. *Censors at Work*. New York: W. W. Norton & Company, 2014.

Epstein, Catherine. *The Last Revolutionaries: German Communists and their Century*. Cambridge, MA: Harvard University Press, 2003.

Ernst, Anna-Sabine. *"Die beste Prophylaxe ist der Sozialismus."* Ärzte und medizinische Hochschullehrer in der SBZ/DDR 1945–1961 ["The best prophylaxis is socialism." Physicians and medical professors in the Soviet Occupation Zone/GDR 1945–1961]. Münster: Waxmann Verlag, 1997.

Fischer, Erich. *Geständnisse und Bekenntnisse* [Admissions and confessions]. Schkeuditz: Schkeuditzer Buchverlag, 2002.

Gieseke, Jens. *Die hauptamtlichen Mitarbeiter der Staatssicherheit. Personalstruktur und Lebenswelt 1950–1989/90* [The full-time employees of the state security. Staff structure and milieu]. Berlin: Christoph Links Verlag, 2000.

———. "Zwischen Privilegienkultur und Egalitarismus. Zu den Einkommensstrukturen des Ministeriums für Staatssicherheit" [Between a culture of privilege and egalitarianism. On the structure of income of the Ministry for State Security]. *Deutschland Archiv* 43, no. 3 (2010): 442–53.

Hertle, Hans-Hermann, and Gerd-Rüdiger Stephan, eds. *Das Ende der SED. Die letzten Tage des Zentralkomitees* [The end of the SED. The last days of the Central Committee]. Berlin: Christoph Links Verlag, 1997.

Hornbostel, Stefan. "Ehre oder Blechsegen? Das Auszeichnungswesen der DDR" [Honor or just a piece of metal? Honors in the GDR]. *SFB 580-Mitteilungen* 3 (2002): 33–39.

Kaiser, Monika. *Machtwechsel von Ulbricht zu Honecker: Funktionsmechanismen der SED-Diktatur in Konfliktsituationen 1962 bis 1972* [Change of government from Ulbricht to Honecker. How the SED dictatorship worked in situations of conflicts]. Berlin: Akademie Verlag, 1997.

Kotkin, Stephen, and Jan Gross. *Uncivil Society: 1989 and the Implosion of the Communist Establishment.* New York: Modern Library, 2009.

Kühl, Stefan. *Organisationen. Eine sehr kurze Einführung* [Organizations. A very short introduction]. Wiesbaden: VS Verlag für Sozialwissenschaften, 2011.

Leonhard, Wolfgang, *Child of the Revolution.* Transl. C. M. Woodhouse. Chicago: H. Regnery Co, 1958.

Mitrokhin, Nikolay. "The CPSU Central Committee Apparatus, 1970–85: Personnel and Role in the Soviet Political System." *Russian History* 41 (2014): 307–328.

Port, Andrew I. *Conflict and Stability in the German Democratic Republic.* Cambridge: Cambridge University Press, 2007.

Scholz, Michael F. *Skandinavische Erfahrungen erwünscht? Nachexil und Remigration; die ehemaligen KPD-Emigranten in Skandinavien und ihr weiteres Schicksal in der SBZ/DDR* [Scandinavian experience desired? Post-exile and remigration; the former German Communist Party immigrants in Scandinavia and their further fate in the Soviet Occupation Zone/GDR]. Stuttgart: Franz Steiner Verlag, 2000.

Sofsky, Wolfgang, and Rainer Paris. *Figurationen sozialer Macht. Autorität—Stellvertretung—Koalition* [Figurations of social power. Authority—substitution—coalition]. Opladen: Suhrkamp Verlag, 1991.

Suckut, Siegfried. "Seismographische Aufzeichnungen. Der Blick des MfS auf Staat und Gesellschaft in der DDR am Beispiel der Berichte an die SED-Führung 1976" [Seismic recordings. The state security's view of state and society in the GDR through the example of reports to the SED leaders 1976]. In

Staatssicherheit und Gesellschaft [State security and society], ed. Jens. Gieseke, 99–128. Göttingen: Vandenhoeck & Ruprecht, 2007.

Süß, Sonja. *Politisch missbraucht? Psychiatrie und Staatssicherheit in der DDR* [Politically abused? Psychiatry and state security in the GDR]. Berlin: Christoph Links Verlag, 1998.

Süß, Walter. *Staatssicherheit am Ende. Warum es den Mächtigen nicht gelang, 1989 eine Revolution zu verhindern* [The end of state security. Why the rulers failed to prevent a revolution in 1989]. Berlin: Christoph Links Verlag, 1999.

Wasem, Jürgen, Doris Mill, and Jürgen Wilhelm. "Gesundheitswesen und Sicherung bei Krankheit und im Pflegefall" [Healthcare and security in case of illness and nursing care]. In *Geschichte der Sozialpolitik in Deutschland seit 1945. Vol. 10, Deutsche Demokratische Republik 1971–1989* [History of social policy in Germany from 1945. Vol. 10: German Democratic Republic 1971–1989], ed. C. Boyer and K-D. Henke, 363–415. Baden-Baden: Nomos Verlag, 2008.

 9

Paternalism in Local Practice
The Logic of Repression, Ideological Hegemony,
and the Everyday Management of Society
in an SED Local Secretariat

Andrea Bahr

The Reichstein villa, a magnificent and stately building in the center of the town of Brandenburg an der Havel,[1] was once the residence of a successful family of entrepreneurs. The Reichstein brothers established a factory in the 1870s that produced prams, and later bicycles and cars, under the brand name Brennabor. After World War II, the Soviet Union dismantled the production facilities, but the Reichstein villa remained a significant place in Brandenburg. For the Socialist Unity Party (SED), this manor house seemed precisely the proper place to establish their local representation. The building symbolized and demonstrated the SED's claim to power in the form of architecture. From here, the local party apparatus guided the affairs of the town and the rural district of Brandenburg. Around fifty-five political employees were concerned with implementing and maintaining party rule.[2] The local SED secretariat, which consisted of the leading functionaries of the party apparatus, the State organs, and the so-called mass organizations, was the decision-making body.[3]

The local party apparatus and its functionaries not only had to control the processes inside the SED organization, but also had to manage both the economy and societal life in the territory in line with the ideological imperatives of the central SED leadership. After all, the SED strove for nothing less than the total transformation of society and every individual in terms of Marxist-Leninist ideology. One of the SED's central aims was to create the "new man," the "socialist personality."[4] Thus, the local party officials acted as "managers of society" and demanded complete and utter competence in the social space of both the town and the rural district. There, at the interface between people's everyday lives and the SED's sphere of power, the regime and its politics could be experienced directly by citizens. Local party officials had to act in all societal fields and could not just remain on the level of claims and proposals. They had to make decisions regarding everyday life in the territory, and implement them. Furthermore, they also had to enforce the decisions and guidelines of the party leadership. The local party officials did all this face-to-face with state and economic actors, as well as the population. Therefore, the local party apparatuses were of great importance for the stability and function of the SED regime.

Although local party officials were crucial in maintaining party rule, very little is known about their practices and the logic that was relevant to their decisions. Therefore, in this chapter, I focus on the social practices of local party functionaries in the period between the building of the Berlin Wall in 1961 and the collapse of the SED regime in 1989.[5]

Starting Points: Local Functionaries' Self-Perception and Other Narratives

In examining local party functionaries, a variety of narratives and images exist that have shaped them in terms of both public and scholarly perception. First of all, one dominant and typical narrative can be found among local party officials themselves insofar as they tried then, and still try, to justify their experience and behavior in hindsight by recounting the difficult "sandwich" position that characterized their rule. In addition to ideological pressure from "above"—from the regional party apparatus and the party leadership—they were also under pressure from the local population. On the one hand, they were forced to implement the SED's unrealistic and dogmatic principals, and, on the other, they had to face the requirements of "real life" in their territory and secure the economic and social functions there as well. Local party functionaries have often portrayed themselves as officials who wanted the best, but were unfortunately under constant and negative pressure from "above" and "below."[6] This self-perception, however, remains nonspecific in respect of the local practice of their rule. Very similar narrative patterns are typical for all other functionaries in the SED apparatus, and at all levels of the hierarchy.[7]

This image of the caring party functionary also dominates the narrative of the famous report "Der Erste."[8] In the mid-1980s, the journalist Landolf Scherzer portrayed the day-to-day work of the first secretary of the town of Bad Salzungen. Furthermore, Scherzer emphasized the first secretary's universal responsibility. As his book was published in 1988, it requires a critical understanding of the period. He was not allowed to observe when it came to any security concerns. In addition, we must bear in mind that it took Scherzer several years to get permission from the party leadership for to undertake his report. Thus, it can be assumed that the journalist met the limits of what he felt he was allowed to do in order to get his text published. Besides its limitations, Scherzer's book provides rare insights into the local party apparatus.

Patterns of Behavior

Even though these self-perceptions and contemporary narratives are problematic, they are able to provide a starting point for a praxeological analysis of the local party functionaries' social practice. From a praxeological point of view, every individual's practice is determined by two aspects: the social structures in which the individual acts on the one side, and his or her own frame of reference on the other.[9] The latter includes the actor's norms, values, and interpretive models. To reconstruct and explain the local party officials' practice, it is first necessary to consider the SED's organizational culture.[10] It involved hierarchical structures of authority, and narrow horizons of thoughts and perceptions.[11] Second, we must take into account the society of the GDR (German Democratic Republic) and its structures. In this chapter, I will follow concepts that describe socialist society as a modern industrial society and question the idea of an "immobilized society."[12] The SED did indeed try to enforce its claim to power in all fields of society. Nevertheless, social autonomy, *Eigensinn* (obstinacy), and other guiding principles, such as economic efficiency, remained, albeit in a restricted way.[13]

One aspect that becomes palpable in these self-perceptions is the tensions resulting from the local party officials' "sandwich" position. These tensions also become visible in a praxeological analysis of the day-to-day work of a local party secretariat. Three functional patterns of behavior coexisted in the local party officials' repertoire of action. The first of these patterns was repression, which was either applied or threatened in order to secure power. The second pattern is found in the constant production and reproduction of the legitimation of rule through ideological interpretation. These persuasive practices were part of the "educational dictatorship" in which the authoritative discourse[14] had to be maintained by convincing or persuading ordinary East Germans to conform. However, the individual's actual beliefs also played a minor role. Of greater importance, however, was the dominance of the authoritative discourse in public. Finally, the third pattern is the pacification of social life through palpable benefits and economic efficiency. In addition to ideological persuasion and repression, social pacification was one of the key tasks of a territorial party secretariat, which the local officials had to perform with "socialist creativity" and the ability to negotiate informal agreements and trade-offs.

Each of these three patterns of behavior was of substantial importance to the performance of local party rule. At the same time, however, these patterns conflicted and competed with each other. This gives the impression that local party officials worked under constant pressure and paid for successes in one area with setbacks or defeats in another. This pressure meant that the local party functionaries demanded a reward for their efforts. This reward was either monetary or in the form of other material privileges.[15] There were undoubtedly cases of corruption and personal enrichment gained by using one's position inside the party or state apparatus at a local level. Some functionaries used their "good relations" with managers of local companies to obtain, for example, construction materials for their dachas. Even though there is evidence of corruption, a scholarly analysis remains to be done.[16] However, it can be assumed that personal enrichment on a local level had a different dimension to that on a central level because local party officials' power position in relation to big companies with large resources was limited. These big companies dealt directly with functionaries of the party leadership, or at least at the district level.[17] In addition to material rewards, local functionaries were also remunerated through a strong feeling of power and the satisfaction that they successfully ruled their territory even under adverse conditions.

Previous research has already shown the juxtaposition and opposition of the three patterns of behavior in society as a whole.[18] However, these conflicting practices especially affected the local practice of party rule in the towns and rural districts. I will argue that in this social space, the requirements of a modern industrial society created pragmatic solutions and triggered a process of deideologization both much more intensively, and sooner, than in the central party apparatus.

I will illustrate my point using some examples from Brandenburg. Furthermore, these examples can be used to show how the patterns changed over time. The local SED secretariat of Brandenburg controlled a territory that, though not representative in a technical sense, is in many respects typical of the GDR. The town of Brandenburg and the rural district had more than 130 thousand inhabitants in the 1980s. The urban area was characterized by its heavy industry. The local steel mill, which at times was the biggest steel producer in the GDR, especially dominated the picture of Brandenburg. Other important factories were the VEB Getriebewerk (a transmissions factory) and the VEB Reichsbahnausbesserungswerk (National Railway Repair Works). There were also some medium-sized factories, as well as the usual service and supply companies. In the rural district of Brandenburg, however, agrarian structures predominated.[19]

Repressive and Persuasive Practices after the Construction of the Berlin Wall

After the construction of the Berlin Wall in 1961, which stopped the flow of refugees to the West, the SED faced a new situation. The closed border offered the chance to again take drastic actions. At the same time, the party had to redefine its relationship to the population and to map out a new strategy in respect of sociopolitical issues. The weeks and months directly after the construction of the Berlin Wall were marked by repression and hardship against presumed enemies of the regime.[20] In the first days after 13 August 1961, around a hundred people were accused of being "provocateurs" in the district of Potsdam alone. They were sentenced to prison or hard manual labor measures.[21]

Moreover, the local party officials' persuasive practices of agitation became more aggressive and intense. These practices ranged from banners and flags to face-to-face communication, and were based on the ideological concept of the educability of man. It was one of the SED's basic ideological imperatives that every individual could be transformed into the "new man" with a "socialist personality" by internalizing the SED's convictions. The party therefore tried hard to enforce their norms and values. Following the party's perspective, socialist convictions were unquestionable and universally valid because they were based on scientific and a kind of over-empirical knowledge. If the individual complied with the party's values and norms, his or her own life would change for the better. The "right consciousness" in turn would generate loyalty and commitment to the regime.[22] These convictions were part of SED organizational culture and thus a matter of fact for the local party functionaries. Political agitation and propaganda therefore formed a central part of their day-to-day practice.

In practice, the promotion of ideological justifications for specific actions such as the construction of the Berlin Wall had a dual nature. On the one hand, the ideological justifications were necessary—at least from the propagandists' perspective—to legitimate such unpopular actions. For example, the construction of the Berlin Wall was presented as a necessary evil on the way to socialism. The SED narrative described the Berlin Wall as an "antifascist rampart" against the "imperialists" in the West. On the other hand, the SED could not force East Germans to believe in the party's worldview. Instead, the SED's interpretations had to compete against others that were either spread by Western media or were based on the individual's personal experiences and assumptions. Therefore, the aim of convincing every individual turned into an aim of enforcing the authoritative discourse. People had to stick to this set of statements in public or fear sanctions.

Nevertheless, the alleged or actual persuasive power of ideological convictions was not the only incentive the SED had to offer to East Germans. It is likely that even as early as the 1950s, other incentives were central to loyalty or passive acceptance, such as the chance of upward social mobility.

The Pacification of the Population: Incentives for Integration

As early as the end of October 1961, only two months after the construction of the Berlin Wall, local party officials in Brandenburg took into account considerations that went beyond the persuasive power of their own ideological framework. In fall 1961, the first local party secretary suggested, at a meeting of the local party secretariat, "The fact is that we can't take a step forward with the agitation among the population if we don't address the issues of supplies, repairs, housing arrangements, etc."[23] From his point of view, it was necessary to meet the population's basic material needs in order to convince the people of Brandenburg of the SED's values and norms. By the end of the 1960s, this strategy of pacification was established in local party officials' practice. From 1971 onwards, after Erich Honecker's accession to power, retaining social peace became more and more dominant, and not only in the reasoning of local party officials. Honecker's concept of "unity of economic and social policy" offered a wide array of social policy measures and material incentives to satisfy the population's material demands. These measures performed an integration function for the regime. They were expected to generate loyal behavior or at least passive acceptance.

Local party functionaries pursued this strategy of pacification as early as October 1961 because of their relative proximity to the social reality experienced by the population. Unlike the party functionaries of the Central Committee and the politburo—who resided in Wandlitz near Berlin, in isolation from ordinary citizens—their local counterparts lived in ordinary housing areas in towns or rural districts. Only the local party apparatus building was equipped with security measures.

Following his considerations in October 1961 regarding material incentives, the first party secretary of Brandenburg distanced himself from the perceptions held at a higher party level. Some functionaries on the regional level apparently preferred tougher measures. This becomes obvious in regard to the campaign against consumers of Western media. Western radio programs in particular provided the population in the GDR with alternative interpretations regarding the building of the Berlin Wall. In order to enforce their sole privilege of interpreting society, the SED tried to ban the consumption of Western media and thus diffuse alternative interpretations. The party launched campaigns such as Aktion Ochsenkopf. As a result of this campaign, members of the FDJ (Free German Youth), the socialist youth movement in the GDR, dismantled radio and television receivers or aligned them to GDR programs.[24] At the end of August 1961, the first secretary of the SED in the district of Potsdam made it abundantly clear that he expected hard measures to be taken against consumers of Western media: "You have to tell people that the time of Western media consumption is over. And if they don't change the direction of their receiving aerials, then you have to remove it. You have to get those people arrested and sentence them to a labor camp. There, they can watch from the camp home."[25] In contrast, the first party secretary of Brandenburg proposed a more moderate line of action: "You cannot imprison all these people, but you have to end discussions. You have to investigate where people organize collective consumption of Western media and unmask them in public. . . . you have to consider how to repel these people without antagonizing the masses."[26] He was equally concerned about the SED's sole privilege of interpreting the situation, but he tried to find a modus vivendi that he considered feasible. In his statement he proposed how this modus vivendi could be designed. He wanted to enforce and secure the SED's hegemony in public by banning open discussion about information from Western media. Therefore, people who watched or listened to Western programs but did not exchange information and views with their neighbors or colleagues could hope to remain undisturbed.

The strategy of pacification, which the first party secretary of Brandenburg considered as early as October 1961, corresponds with the fact that many local party officials developed a decidedly paternalistic conception of rule. The term "welfare" is central here, which includes two simultaneous meanings. On the one hand, a caring aspect, but on the other, a patronizing and punitive one.[27] The latter is mainly excluded from the power elite's narrative. However, from the 1960s onwards, these efforts toward integration dominated the local party officials' day-to-day work. In addition, officials underlined this aspect of their rule in their public staging. Repression, in contrast, became more subtle and less apparent in public.

One example—the construction of a new outdoor swimming pool in Brandenburg at the end of the 1960s—can be used to illustrate the importance and impact of such incentives for integration. The construction was supposed to be a project that would orchestrate community-building in Brandenburg, as well as participation in that community. Everyone—from workers, to housewives, to whole factories—should become involved in the construction and thereby experience fellowship, solidarity, and participation.

Thus, the SED local secretariat provided an opportunity to identify with Brandenburg beyond the official propaganda and beyond any political reasoning. It is likely that many people in the town felt directly addressed by the apolitical character of this incentive toward integration; they wished to improve their immediate surroundings. Most did not link their financial support or free labor to the regime as a whole. Their input was probably independent of political considerations and was more likely to be defined by their identification with Brandenburg. A woman from Brandenburg mentioned her attachment to and pride in the town as reasons for her donation of 1,000 ostmarks. She wrote, "I was born in Brandenburg, and I'm interested in my town's development. In particular, I am pleased with the construction of the outdoor swimming pool. I myself cannot use it, but the world belongs to the youth. I have decided to donate 1,000 ostmarks."[28]

Nevertheless, by strengthening this local identity, the local SED secretariat also produced commitment, which in the end supported the regime.[29] Local party functionaries camouflaged the dictatorial nature of the regime in everyday life; instead, they promoted solidarity, fellowship, and welfare. On the occasion of the official opening of the swimming pool, the first secretary of the SED in Brandenburg, Gerhard Pannhausen, did not miss the opportunity to cut the ribbon. He was together with the secretary of economy of the regional party secretariat in the front row, while the formal head of the town, the mayor, took a back seat. Pannhausen took the opportunity to promote his and the SED's caring role.

In the end, the new outdoor swimming pool became a success for local officials, but it was only made possible by violating SED norms. As there were no central funds available, the local party secretariat had to depend on local factories and their resources, and were thereby able to circumvent the grand party plan. The consequences of this violation were limited and manageable. They could be accepted in favor of satisfying the population. A former local secretary stated, in hindsight: "Yes, definitely, we ... did good things for our population. But the higher authorities registered that with mixed feelings and always with a wagging finger: What you are doing here is not in accordance with our financial discipline."[30] In his experience, however, the response was never more than remonstrations. He never experienced dismissals or other punishments of party functionaries in respect to such projects.

Ideological Imperatives and Economic Efficiency in Conflict

This strategy of pacification meant that the local SED secretariat had to depend on local factories and their contributions. This was not only the case for construction projects such as the swimming pool. Rather, the personal and material resources of the companies were also essential to daily life and included less prestigious tasks such as improving the infrastructure or living conditions. It was economic performance that formed the basis of satisfying the population's daily needs. Economic efficiency therefore became a guiding principle for local party officials in addition to ideological imperatives; this was particularly the case from the 1970s onwards and clearly in the 1980s, when the GDR's economic crisis deepened. What is most striking is the fact that sometimes economic efficiency even outweighed ideological imperatives regarding decisions made by local party functionaries.

This can be clearly seen at the beginning of the 1970s in the VEB Kohlehandel in Brandenburg, which supplied the territory with coal. As work at the plant was physically demanding and of low social prestige, the employees were mainly workers who had a critical attitude toward the regime, or who belonged to marginalized social groups and therefore could not find any other type of employment. Among them were, for example, former members of fascist organizations and people who had tried to flee the GDR. From the local party secretariat's point of view, the social composition of the workforce was highly problematic. Therefore, the local SED secretariat instructed the local office of the *Stasi* (secret police) to analyze "particular occurrences" in the company and to keep the situation under surveillance.[31] At the beginning of 1972, the second party secretary of Brandenburg, along with the secretary of economy, visited the VEB Kohlehandel to get an idea of what was going on. They talked to the company's party functionaries. However, the two secretaries could not achieve positive changes, which the local SED secretariat had to realize by the end of the year.[32]

In the light of these issues, the way in which the local secretariat handled a conflict between the party secretary of the company on the one side, and staff and the company leadership on the other, is very surprising. Given the problematic social composition of the workforce, the party secretary of the company tried hard to implement the party's worldview. Some workers described him as "dogmatic" and "authoritarian." The workers complained about his behavior and even described a "climate of fear" that existed in the company from their point of view. They turned to the SED local secretariat for help and thus took seriously the SED's claim of regulating society.[33]

However, the local party apparatus did not react according to the SED's ideological imperatives. Instead of backing the party secretary of the company in his "fight" against "hostile and negative forces" and for the SED's sole privilege of interpreting society, the local SED secretariat dismissed its representative. In doing so, the apparatus opted in favor of the workforce and its demands. Why, one must ask, was the local party secretariat not pleased with the performance of the party secretary at the VEB Kohlehandel? He had at least tried hard to secure the SED's power of interpretation.

In this case, supplying the population with coal was paramount for the SED local party secretariat. Cold homes in fall and winter would have provoked trouble and discontent. That is why the local SED officials did not adhere to their ideological imperatives at all costs, and did not try hard to enforce the SED's interpretations against "hostile and negative forces." Their main goal was rather to integrate and motivate the whole workforce in order to ensure the supply of coal. It was economic efficiency instead of ideological imperatives that guided the local party functionaries' decisions. From the local SED apparatus's point of view, even workers who had physically or verbally violated the limits laid down by the SED regime in the past, for instance by trying to flee the country, had to be integrated.

Of course, the enforcement of this authoritative discourse and the repression of individuals and societal groups who had acted critically toward or against the regime continued. Nevertheless, the 1960s saw a transformation in the local party functionaries' repressive practices. The following modus vivendi was developed: the SED spied on its enemies or presumed enemies, kept an eye on their plans, and cracked down on collective or public actions. Local party officials, however, tried to stay in the background in respect to hard repression. While on the one side they highlighted the "welfare" and caring nature of their rule, they tried to cover up repression and especially their involvement in tough measures against disobedience. Local party functionaries limited themselves to social pressure and social control. They left harsh repression to the *Stasi*.

Negotiations between Local Party Functionaries and the Population

Similar to the workers in the VEB Kohlehandel, who called on the SED local party secretariat to settle their work conflict, from the mid-1960s onwards more and more citizens demanded that the SED local party apparatus not only regulate social relations, but also supply them with necessary day-to-day supplies. Thus, parts of the population took the SED's claims seriously.

This became particularly visible in the run-up to major events that were of great importance for the SED's staging of power in order to legitimate and secure party rule. Elections were one of these major events that undoubtedly fulfilled an important function for the SED in respect of legitimation.[34] What is more, elections were crucial points of self-assurance for the local party functionaries up until the local elections in May 1989. Until then, the SED regime's social order and power relations were actively reproduced and confirmed during elections by the majority of the populace. People submitted to the SED's claim to power and rules by voting for the National Front's single list of candidates.

Some individuals and groups, however, used the elections to raise their own demands, and some even made their vote dependent on them being fulfilled. Generally, these demands were about the provision of housing, better supplies of daily necessities, or improved public transport, and the local party apparatus could not ignore or repress these demands because party officials themselves gave priority to these aspects. At the same time, they were in charge of securing a high election turnout and approval for the regime. Local party officials were therefore obligated to negotiate with these individuals and groups.

Ultimately, however, this type of communication could be ended through repression, but if these individuals and groups played the SED's game, they could expect that their demands would be taken seriously and fulfilled if possible. Under no circumstances was the political sphere — that is, the power structures and the authoritative discourse — allowed to be questioned by citizens. Furthermore, the social status of citizens and their previous behavior toward the regime was also relevant. If one could demonstrate that she or he had contributed to the success of the GDR in the past, for example by working hard in an important branch of production, then she or he could hope for the fulfillment of her or his demands. Those who were renowned for their critical attitude toward the regime or who tried repeatedly to get their demands met by blackmailing local officials could expect repressive measures to be taken against them, resulting in disadvantages related to professional advancement or educational opportunities.

This can be clearly seen in the run-up to the elections in 1967. A group of employees from the *Werk für Gleisbaumechanik* (factory for railway track construction), an important subsidiary of the *Deutsche Reichsbahn* (German Reich Railway), complained about the public transport between their workplace and their housing areas. They voiced this complaint in an election meeting in front of the SED's local secretary for economy, Günter Schilling. Two years previously, he had demanded that in the run-up to elections the apparatus should particularly focus its attention on general supplies to the population. Schilling and certainly other local party officials were aware of the fact that a good supply situation influenced the decisions that citizens made during elections. In 1965, with local elections only a few weeks away, the secretary of economy pointed out in front of his colleagues in the local party apparatus that the supply of daily goods and services was crucial to the outcome of the election because the apparatus could influence "daily and hourly the mood of the population through our good or bad performance"[35] in these fields.

In light of this conviction, it is no surprise that Schilling immediately tried to meet the demands of the workforce at the *Werk für Gleisbaumechanik*. He instructed the mayor to take the necessary steps because the state organs were in charge of public transportation. The party official had promised the workers an answer "in the next few days," because he wanted to find a solution to the problem before Election Day. In order to increase pressure to get things done as quickly as possible, the secretary underlined the "progressiveness" of the labor collective within the company in correspondence with the mayor.[36] The workers had proven their loyalty to the regime through good economic results and a progressive cultural life in their brigade. The latter had been documented in the local press. Therefore, they were able to build on the care they received from local party functionaries. It is probable that the workers knew how to put their demands forward in order to get things done. They had to stress their "progressiveness" and, furthermore, they voiced their demands to the secretary of economy. Thus, they accelerated the negotiation of their problems by appealing to the SED's own claims, and by addressing a higher rank in the hierarchy of power, although the local SED secretariat and its functionaries had no formal right to give orders to the state organs, but in practice the latter was subordinated to the party.[37]

Most local party functionaries perceived themselves as lobbyists for the population who pushed state officials to develop "a style of work, which is realistic and close to the people . . . which has open ears, open hearts and the willingness to find solutions to the demands of the population."[38] The first secretary of the SED in the district of Potsdam demanded this style of work in 1978. He emphasized the SED's caring role. Then as well as now, a lot of regional and local party officials saw themselves as actors who did a great deal for the population. In return, state officials were blamed for "bureaucratic" and "heartless" behavior toward citizens.[39]

Schilling, the secretary for economy in Brandenburg, also played this role by advocating workers' demands toward the mayor and by claiming a quick solution. He was successful because the mayor reacted immediately and informed the responsible department in the state administration, which quickly organized that the tramways run every twenty minutes during rush hour.[40] The demands of workers from the *Werk für Gleisbaumechanik* were fulfilled. Schilling and the local party apparatus thereby proved in the run-up to the elections that they kept their promises to supply people with daily goods and services. It is probable that this influenced the workers' election decision in favor of the single list of the *National Front.*

From the mid-1970s onwards, elections in Brandenburg showed that citizens linked their vote to the fulfillment of basic needs. This could be clearly seen in respect to the living conditions in the old center of Brandenburg. The local SED secretariat noted this with concern. Shortly after the *Volkskammer* (East German Parliament) elections in 1976, the first party secretary of Brandenburg declared, in front of party functionaries from the district of Potsdam, that living conditions in the housing areas of the old center were one of the biggest and most urgent problems, and that this became particularly clear in the run-up to the elections.[41] The local SED secretariat admitted the limits of their own opportunities regarding reconstruction, and it asked the district SED secretariat for help.

Nevertheless, three years later, in 1979, when local elections were held, the living conditions in the old center had worsened and the effects on election turnout could not be ignored. These housing areas were a "red flag" in the elections, and although only 38 percent of eligible voters lived there, local officials realized that 60 per cent of nonvoters came from this area. The first party secretary advanced a variety of reasons for this development. Besides an adverse political persuasive praxis, he made the poor living conditions responsible for the election outcome. He noticed that "the election outcome of 1979 in the housing areas of the old center . . . was obviously an answer to our policy of modernization and reconstruction in our town."[42]

One decade later, in the mid-1980s, the conviction that material incentives were crucial to the party apparatus's performance, especially in the run-up to elections, was well established:

> "In order to guarantee a strong political effect of direct communication with voters, we pay attention to such aspects that can influence the voter's snap decisions. These aspects are the range of goods and supplies in shops and factories, as well as responding to petitions, hints, and suggestions . . . . Until now citizens have not remarked that they will not participate in the election if certain demands are not met. We expect, however, that further talks with citizens will lead to the manifestations of such phenomena. In that case, we will check the necessity of these demands, but we refuse to be blackmailed. Justified demands are to be discussed and decided upon before Election Day."[43]

Also mentioned in this statement was the phenomenon that individuals linked their vote directly to the fulfillment of their demands, and thus blackmailed local party functionaries. It was clear that the majority of East Germans and most of the people of Brandenburg knew what consequences nonattendance on Election Day could bring.[44] As a result, most of them did not try to blackmail local officials.[45] Nevertheless, this phenomenon occurred, and the reaction of local party officials shows their willingness to meet the population's demands in order to ensure a high election turnout.

The above serves to show that the negotiation of material concessions in preelection periods was a central part of the local party apparatus' strategy of pacification. These negotiations ensured—alongside propaganda and repression—that the majority of East Germans submitted to the SED's claim to power on Election Day.

Conclusion

The examples from Brandenburg show that local party officials adopted not only persuasive and repressive practices in order to secure power from the 1960s onwards, but also offered material incentives to ensure integration. In order to secure power in the social space of a town or a rural district, the local party secretariat had to accept other ways of functioning in addition to their own ideological imperatives, such as economic efficiency. Pragmatic solutions accompanied the local party functionaries' persuasive and repressive practices. Local party secretariats and their officials therefore substantially contributed to the stability of the SED regime. They aimed to establish and retain social peace, and to react immediately to demands and dissatisfaction in the territory. Thus, they made a crucial contribution to maintaining the often-propagated consensus between the population and the regime.[46] Nevertheless, local party officials could only achieve short-term successes. They repeatedly had to find solutions to the systemic problems and deficits of the socialist regime. A reform of the system as a whole, and change to its functional principles, was neither possible nor sought after by officials. The pragmatic solutions were designed to stabilize and secure the regime, although some of them violated the organizational culture of the SED.

In the 1980s, however, developments increasingly undermined the local party officials' strategy of pacification. Economic difficulties were not the only issues that contributed to this. The articulation of critical voices, especially in church-related milieus, also grew over time. Of course, Brandenburg was not comparable to Jena or other centers of opposition, yet, some oppositional groups were still formed there, such as environmental groups, as well as support groups for individuals who refused to do military service or those who tried to leave the country by applying for an exit permit, for example. This collective and public articulation of alternative interpretations, as well as the population's increased requirements and demands, which arose from the strategy of pacification, asked too much of local party officials. They clung to this strategy, nevertheless. On 18 October 1989, after the big demonstrations in Leipzig, the first secretary of Brandenburg still wrote, "In the current situation, we concentrate especially on such questions that contribute to the wellbeing of our citizens. Therefore, we pay particular attention to the supply of daily goods and services, the health services, and public transport, because they are important trend indicators for us. Furthermore, these aspects are standards of our own performance, which aims to make changes."[47]

Even though the first party secretary was confident about changes, more and more local officials lost their self-assurance. The local party apparatus suffered its first serious setback during the local elections in May 1989. Up to this point, all past elections had demonstrated the power of the regime and the subjugation of the majority of the population to the SED's rules. In 1989, however, the opposition revealed the regime's election fraud, which demonstrated the potential for protest and the breadth of dissatisfaction among the population.

During 1989, it became apparent that the SED and its functionaries could not counter these attacks on its rule. Instead, they repeated the old patterns—namely, agitation was intensified. However, by the 1980s, these persuasive practices were no longer accompanied by attractive material incentives. It became obvious even to SED functionaries that their ideological imperatives had increasingly lost their persuasive and integrative power.

This direct attack on their power made it clear to local party officials that the consensus between the SED regime and East German citizens, which they had propagated for so long, and which supported their local rule, was without a real base in society. As a result, many local officials could not endow their rule and actions with meaning, and they lost their orientation. This was exacerbated by the lack of interpretations, guidance, and declarations from above. Many local party functionaries were paralyzed and some gave up, declining to fight for their power.

The public role of local party officials suddenly changed. In the past, they had often presented themselves as "town fathers" and most of the citizens of Brandenburg had accepted that as their role. On 12 November 1989, three days after the wall came down, however, eight thousand people demonstrated against the SED regime and for free elections in the town. The first party secretary, who tried to address the demonstrators, was booed by the masses. He was forced to leave the speaker's platform before the rage of the demonstrators turned into physical violence aimed at his person. The local party apparatus disintegrated in the following months. More and more members left the party, and on 1 December 1989, the SED's claim to power, the so-called "leading role of the party," was eliminated from the constitution of the GDR. Thus, the party apparatus lost the justification for its existence.

Andrea Bahr is postdoctoral research fellow with the Federal Commissioner for the Records of the State Security Service of the former GDR. Her publications include *Parteiherrschaft vor Ort. Die SED-Kreisleitung Brandenburg 1961–1989* (2016); and (coauthor) *Die Staatssicherheit und die Grünen* (2016).

Notes

1. In the following, the town and the rural district will hereafter be called Brandenburg. The town and the rural district are located near Potsdam and Berlin and cover an area of approximately 1,050 sq km.
2. The apparatus was divided into four departments: party organs, agitation and propaganda, economy, and agriculture. Some employees were directly assigned to the first secretary, i.e., the person responsible for security matters.
3. Members of the secretariat from 1967 to 1989: first secretary, second secretary, secretaries for agitation and propaganda, economy and agriculture, mayor, chairmen of the local council, of the local planning commission, of

the local agricultural council (only until 1975), chairman of the local FDGB, first secretary of the FDJ, and chairman of the local party control commission (from 1975 onwards). See, e.g., "Wahlordnung für die Wahlen der leitenden Parteiorgane, für die Wahlen der Delegierten zu den Delegiertenkonferenzen, Parteikonferenzen und zu den Parteitagen (Beschluss des Zentralkomitees der SED vom 17.9.1966)" [Election order for the elections of the leading party organs, for the elections of the delegates to delegation conferences, party conventions and the congresses (Decision of the Central Committee of the SED of 17 September 1996)], in *Dokumente der Sozialistischen Einheitspartei Deutschlands. Beschlüsse und Erklärungen des Zentralkomitees sowie seines Politbüros und seines Sekretariats.* Band XI [Documents of the Socialist Unity Party of Germany. Resolutions and declaration of the Central Committee as well as its politburo and its secretariat. Vol. 11]. Berlin (East): Dietz Verlag Berlin, 1969), 179–180; Heinrich Best and Heinz Mestrup, eds., *Die Ersten und Zweiten Sekretäre der SED. Machtstrukturen und Herrschaftspraxis in den thüringischen Bezirken der DDR* [The first and second secretaries of the SED. Structures of power and practice of rule in the Thuringian Districts of the GDR] (Weimar, 2003), 70–173.
4. Peter Fritzsche and Jochen Hellbeck, "The New Man in Stalinist Russia and Nazi Germany," in *Beyond Totalitarianism: Stalinism and Nazism Compared*, ed. Sheila Fitzpatrick and Michael Geyer (Cambridge, 2009), 302–341.
5. For the period prior to 1961, see Andrew Port, *Conflict and Stability in the German Democratic Republic* (Cambridge, 2007).
6. A typical example for this narrative of the "sandwich" position and the caring role can be found in the self-perception of Heinz Vietze, former first secretary of the town of Oranienburg and later Potsdam. This can be clearly seen in an interview published in Brigitte Zimmermann and Hans-Dieter Schütt, *Noch Fragen, Genossen!* [Any more questions, comrades!] (Berlin, 1994), 200–219.
7. See, e.g., H. Modrow, ed., *Das Große Haus von außen. Erfahrungen im Umgang mit der Machtzentrale in der DDR* [The big house from the outside. Experiences with the center of power in the GDR] (Berlin, 1996).
8. Landolf Scherzer, *Der Erste* [The boss] (Berlin, 1997). A similar image can be found in the short text, Gerhard Holtz-Baumert, "Der Erste von O." [The boss of O.], *Neue Deutsche Literatur. Monatszeitschrift für Literatur und Kritik* 2 (1986): 13–20.
9. Pierre Bourdieu, Outline of a Theory of Practice (Cambridge, 1977); Thomas Lindenberger, "SED-Herrschaft als soziale Praxis—Herrschaft und 'Eigen-Sinn': Problemstellung und Begriffe" [SED-rule as social practice—Rule and 'Eigen-Sinn': Problems and concepts], in *Staatssicherheit und Gesellschaft. Studien zum Herrschaftsalltag in der DDR* [State security and society. Studies on the day-to-day rule], ed. Jens Gieseke (Göttingen, 2007), 23–47; Sven Reichardt, "Praxeologische Geschichtswissenschaft. Eine Diskussionsanregung" [Praxeological history. Ideas for discussion], in *Sozial Geschichte. Zeitschrift für historische Analyse des 20. und 21. Jahrhunderts* 22, no. 3 (2007): 43–65; Reinhard Sieder, "Sozialgeschichte auf dem Weg zu einer historischen Kulturwissenschaft?" [Social history on the way to a historical cultural science?], *Geschichte und Gesellschaft* 20 (1994): 445–468.

10. Edgar Schein, "Coming to a New Awareness of Organizational Culture," *Sloan Management Review* (winter 1984): 3.
11. Martin Sabrow, "Sozialismus als Sinnwelt. Diktatorische Herrschaft in kulturhistorischer Perspektive" [Socialism as world of meaning. Cultural perspectives on dictatorial rule], *Potsdamer Bulletin für Zeithistorische Studien* 40–41 (2007): 9–23.
12. Sigrid Meuschel, "Überlegungen zu einer Herrschafts- und Gesellschaftsgeschichte der DDR" [Reflections on the GDR's history of rule and society], *Geschichte und Gesellschaft* 19 (1993): 5–14.
13. Ralph Jessen, "Die Gesellschaft im Staatssozialismus. Probleme einer Sozialgeschichte der DDR" [Society in state socialism. Problems of a social history of the GDR], *Geschichte und Gesellschaft* 21 (1995): 96–110; Detlef Pollack, "Die konstitutive Widersprüchlichkeit der DDR-Gesellschaft. Oder: War die DDR homogen? Eine Fortsetzung der Diskussion zwischen Sigrid Meuschel und Ralph Jessen" [The constituent contradictory nature of the GDR Society. Or: Was the GDR homogenous? Continuing the discussion between Sigrid Meuschel and Ralph Jessen], *Geschichte und Gesellschaft* 24 (1998): 110–131; Detlef Pollack, "Wie modern war die DDR" [How modern was the GDR?], in *Koordinaten deutscher Geschichte in der Epoche des Ost-West-Konflikts* [Coordinates of German history in the epoch of the East-West conflict], ed. Hans Günter Hockarts (Munich 2004), 175–205.
14. Martin Sabrow, "Einleitung: Geschichtsdiskurs und Doktringesellschaft" [Introduction: Historical discourse and society of doctrines], in *Geschichte als Herrschaftsdiskurs. Der Umgang mit der Vergangenheit in der DDR* [History as a discourse on power. Dealing with the past in the GDR], ed. Martin Sabrow (Cologne, 2000); Alexei Yurchak, *Everything Was Forever, Until It Was No More: The Last Soviet Generation* (Princeton, 2006).
15. In the mid-1980s, the wage of an ordinary political employee in the local party apparatus was approximately 1,600 ostmarks, while the average gross wage in the GDR was approximately 1,100 ostmarks. There is relatively little difference if we bear in mind that a function inside the party apparatus entailed greater responsibilities and an extreme pressure to conform. Of course, the higher ranks—secretaries and heads of departments—earned more. A first secretary earned 3,000 ostmarks a month in the mid-1980s. See Protokoll Nr. 3 der Sitzung des Sekretariats des ZK (9 January 1985) [Minutes Nr. 3 on the meeting of the secretariat of the ZK (9 January 1985)], Stiftung Archiv der Partei und Massenorganisationen—Bundesarchiv (SAPMO-BArch) [Foundation Archives of the Party and Mass Organizations of the GDR in the Federal Archives], DY 30/ J IV 2/3 A 4191, n.p.
16. André Steiner, "Bolsche Vita in der DDR? Überlegungen zur Korruption im Staatssozialismus" [Bolsche Vita in the GDR? Reflections on corruption in state socialism], in *Geld—Geschenke—Politik. Korruption im neuzeitlichen Europa* [Money—gifts—politics. Corruption in early modern Europe], *Beihefte der Historischen Zeitschrift*, vol. 48, ed. Jens Ivo Engels, Andreas Fahrmeir, Alexander Nützenadel (Munich, 2009), 252. Some cases of corruption on a local level are documented in *Strafjustiz und DDR-Unrecht*, Bd. 3, *Amtsmissbrauch und Korruption* [Criminal justice and injustice in the GDR, vol. 3, Abuse of office and corruption], Klaus Marxen and Gerhard Werle (Berlin,

2002). In Brandenburg, the SED/PDS (Socialist Unity Party/Party of Democratic Socialism) installed a "Commission for the Examination of the Abuse of Office and Corruption" in December 1989. Apparently, only two cases of corruption were detected. See Märkischen Volksstimme (local party newspaper) Edition Brandenburg, 22.12.1989, 8.
17. Such extreme cases of personal enrichment as Rüdiger Bergien has analyzed regarding the Central Committee apparatus seem unlikely on the local level. See Rüdiger Bergien, *"Im Generalstab der Partei." Organisationskultur und Herrschaftspraxis in der SED-Zentrale (1946–1989)* [In the general staff of the party. Organizational culture and practice of rule in the center of the SED] (Berlin, 2017).
18. Christoph Boyer and Peter Skyba, eds., *Repression und Wohlstandsversprechen. Zur Stabilisierung von Parteiherrschaft in der DDR und CSSR* [Repression and promise of prosperity. On stabilization of party rule in the GDR and the USSR] (Dresden, 1999); Frank Ettrich, "Neotraditionalistischer Staatssozialismus. Zur Diskussion eines Forschungskonzeptes" [Neotraditional state socialism. Discussing a research concept], *Prokla* 86 (1992): 98–114; Konrad H. Jarausch, "Fürsorgediktatur" [Welfare dictatorship], Docupedia-Zeitgeschichte, 11 February 2010, accessed 27 September 2013, http://docupedia.de/zg/F.C3.BCrsorgediktatur?oldid=84610; Sigrid Meuschel, *Legitimation und Parteiherrschaft. Zum Paradox von Stabilität und Revolution in der DDR 1945–1989* [Legitimation and party rule. About the paradox of stability and revolution in the GDR 1945–1989] (Frankfurt/M., 1992).
19. Gerd Heinrich, Klaus Heß, Winfried Schich, and Wolfgang Schößler, eds., *Stahl und Brennabor. Die Stadt Brandenburg im 19. und 20. Jahrhundert* [Steel and Brennabor. The city of Brandenburg in the 19th and 20th century] (Potsdam, 1998).
20. On repression after the building of the wall and the role of the judiciary, or rather its instrumentalization by the SED, see Falco Werkentin, *Politische Strafjustiz in der Ära Ulbricht. Vom bekennenden Terror zur verdeckten Repression* [Political criminal justice in the Ulbricht era. From open terror to hidden repression] (Berlin, 1997), 225–259.
21. Protokoll über die Beratung des Büros der SED-Bezirksleitung Potsdam mit den Blockparteien und den Massenorganisationen am 18.8.1961 [Minutes on the consultation of the office of the SED district apparatus Potsdam with the block parties and the mass organizations on 18 August 1961], Brandenburgisches Landeshauptarchiv (hereafter BLHA) [Central State Archive of Brandenburg], Rep. 530 Nr. 247, 187f.
22. Peter Fritzsche and Jochen Hellbeck, "The New Man in Stalinist Russia and Nazi Germany," in *Beyond Totalitarianism: Stalinism and Nazism Compared*, ed. Sheila Fitzpatrick and Michael Geyer (Cambridge, 2009), 302–341.
23. Protokoll der Sitzung des Büros der SED-Kreisleitung Brandenburg (Stadt) am 31. Oktober und 1. November 1961 [Minutes of the meeting of the office of the SED local apparatus Brandenburg (city) on 31 October and 1 November 1961], BLHA, Rep. 531 Brandenburg Nr. 147, n.p. All quotations of non-Englisch sources have been translated by the author.
24. Franziska Kuschel, "'Keine NATO-Sender mehr dulden.' Westmedien in der DDR der Sechzigerjahre" ["Don't tolerate NATO-stations anymore."

Western media in the GDR in the sixties], *Deutschlandarchiv* 2 (2012), accessed 20 April 2012, http://www.bpb.de/geschichte/zeitgeschichte/deuts chlandarchiv/74942/keine-nato-sender.
25. Protokoll der Sitzung des Büros der SED-Bezirksleitung Potsdam am 25. August 1961 [Minutes of the meeting of the office of the SED district apparatus Potsdam on 25 August 1961], BLHA, Rep. 530 Nr. 248, 65.
26. Protokoll der Sitzung des Büros der SED-Kreisleitung Brandenburg (Stadt) am 15. August 1961 (16.8.1961) [Minutes of the meeting of the office of the SED local apparatus Brandenburg (city) on 15 August 1961 (16 August 1961)], BLHA, Rep. 531 Brandenburg Nr. 144, n.p.
27. Konrad H. Jarausch, "Fürsorgediktatur" [Welfare dictatorship], *Docupedia-Zeitgeschichte*, 11 Feburary 2010, accessed 27 September 2013, http://docu pedia.de/zg/F.C3.BCrsorgediktatur?oldid=84610.
28. Information des Organisationsstabes "Schwimmbad" über den Stand der Aktion per 31.1.1968 [Information on the "Swimming Pool" organizational chart on the status of the action as of 31 January 1968], BLHA, Rep. 531 Brandenburg Nr. 1336, n.p.
29. Adelheid von Saldern, ed., *Inszenierter Stolz. Stadtpräsentationen in drei deutschen Gesellschaften (1935–1975)* [Staged pride. Representations of cities in three German societies (1935–1975)] (Stuttgart, 2005), 11–27 and 409–459.
30. Interview with a former second party secretary of Brandenburg on 5 April 2011 undertaken by the author.
31. Bericht der Arbeitsgruppe der SED-Kreisleitung Brandenburg zur Untersuchung der Vorkommnisse im VEB Kohlenhandel (13.3.1973) [Report of the working group of the SED local apparatus Brandenburg to investigate the incidents in the VEB Coal Supply (13 March 1973)], BLHA, Rep. 531 Brandenburg Nr. 1568, n.p.
32. Aktennotiz eines Mitarbeiters der SED-Kreisleitung Brandenburg über die Aussprache mit einem Mitglied der Parteileitung des VEB Kohlehandel Brandenburg (12.12.1972) [Brief note of an employee of the SED local apparatus Brandenburg about the discussion with a member of the party leadership of the VEB Coal Supply Brandenburg (12 December 1972)], BLHA, Rep. 531 Brandenburg Nr. 1552, n.p.
33. Bericht des Direktors der Bezirksdirektion VEB Kohlehandel Potsdam an den Sekretär für Wirtschaftspolitik der SED-Kreisleitung Brandenburg— Vorkommnisse im VEB Kohlehandel Brandenburg (12.12.1972) [Report of the director of the district directorate-general VEB Coal Supply Potsdam to the secretary for economic policy of the SED Brandenburg—Events in the VEB Coal Supply Brandenburg (12 December 1972)], BLHA, Rep. 531 Brandenburg Nr. 1552, n.p.
34. See especially Ralph Jessen and Hedwig Richter "Non-Competitive Elections in 20th Century Dictatorships: Some Questions and General Considerations," as well as Stephan Merl's article "Elections in the Soviet Union, 1937–1989: A View into a Paternalistic World from Below," both in *Voting for Hitler and Stalin: Elections under 20th Century Dictatorship*, ed. Ralph Jessen and Hedwig Richter (Frankfurt/M., 2011), 9–36, 103–125, 276–308. See also Hans Michael Kloth, *Vom "Zettelfalten" zum freien Wählen. Die Demokratisierung der DDR 1989/90 und die "Wahlfrage"* [From "Zettelfalten" to free

elections. The democratization of the GDR and the "Wahlfrage"] (Berlin, 2000).
35. Diskussionsbeitrag des Sekretärs für Wirtschaftspolitik der SED-Kreisleitung Brandenburg bei der Sitzung der gewählten Kreisleitung am 29.9.1965 (ohne Datum) [Discussion report of the secretary for economic policy of the SED local apparatus Brandenburg at the meeting of the elected board of the SED Brandenburg on 29 September 1965 (no date)], BLHA, Rep. 531 Brandenburg, Nr. 982, n.p.
36. Schreiben des Sekretärs für Wirtschaftspolitik der SED-Kreisleitung Brandenburg an den Oberbürgermeister der Stadt zu in Wahlversammlung geäußerten Mängeln (13.6.1967) [Letter from the secretary for economic policy of the SED local apparatus Brandenburg to the mayor of the city regarding deficiencies expressed in the election meeting (13 June 1967)], Stadtarchiv Brandenburg [Municipal Archives of Brandenburg], 2.0.2 (Rat der Stadt—Bereich Oberbürgermeister) Nr. 97, 151–153.
37. Christoph Bernhardt, "Zwischen Herrschaft und Selbstbehauptung—Ambivalenzen sozialistischer Stadtpolitik und Urbanität" [Between domination and autonomy—Ambivalences of socialist urban policy and urbanity], in *Sozialistische Städte zwischen Herrschaft und Selbstbehauptung. Kommunalpolitik, Stadtplanung und Alltag in der DDR* [Socialist cities between domination and autonomy. Local government, urban planning and everyday life in the GDR], ed. Christoph Bernhardt and Heinz Reif (Stuttgart, 2009), 301–303.
38. Prüfungsbericht Nr. 1.8/78 der Bezirksrevisionskommission Potsdam—Thematische Prüfung zur Arbeit mit den Eingaben, Hinweisen, Vorschlägen und Kritiken sowie mit der Bevölkerungspost in den SED-Grundorganisationen der Räte der Kreise und in den SED-Grundorganisationen von ausgewählten Städten bzw. Gemeinden sowie der Lokalredaktion der *Märkischen Volksstimme* (10.8.1978) [Report No. 1.8/78 of the district audit commission Potsdam—Thematic review of the work with the input, tips, suggestions, and criticisms as well as with the people's letters in the basic SED organizations of the councils of the counties and in the basic SED organizations of selected cities and municipalities as well as the local editor of the *Märkischen Volksstimme* (10 August 1978)], BLHA, Rep. 530 Nr. 6596, n.p.
39. Hinweise der SED-Kreisleitung Brandenburg für die Erhöhung der Qualität der monatlichen Einschätzung über die Ergebnisse der Mitgliederversammlungen und der politischen Massenarbeit (18.04.1975) [Suggestions provided by the SED local apparatus Brandenburg for increasing the quality of the monthly assessment of the results of the general meetings and the political labor (18 April 1974)], BLHA, Rep. 531 Brandenburg Nr. 1537.
40. Schreiben des Oberbürgermeisters der Stadt Brandenburg an den Sekretär für Wirtschaftspolitik der SED-Kreisleitung Brandenburg (30.8.1967), n.p. [Letter from the mayor of the city of Brandenburg to the secretary for economic policy of the SED local apparatus Brandenburg (30 August 1967)], Stadtarchiv Brandenburg, 2.0.2 (Rat der Stadt—Bereich Oberbürgermeister) Nr. 97, 202.
41. Aktennotiz der Abteilung Parteiorgane der SED-Bezirksleitung Potsdam zur Problemdiskussion im Sekretariat der SED-Kreisleitung Brandenburg

am 8.11.1976 (11.11.1976) [Brief note of the department of party organs of the SED district apparatus Potsdam on the discussion of problems in the secretariat of the SED local apparatus Brandenburg on 8 November 1976 (11 November 1974)], BLHA, Rep. 530 Nr. 4877, n.p.
42. Cf. the following Bericht des 1. Sekretärs der SED-Kreisleitung Brandenburg an den 1. Sekretär der SED-Bezirksleitung Potsdam (23.5.1979) [Report by the first secretary of the SED local apparatus Brandenburg to the first secretary of the SED district apparatus Potsdam (23 May 1979)], BLHA, Rep. 531 Brandenburg Nr. 1805, n.p.
43. Monatsbericht des 1. Sekretärs der SED-Kreisleitung Brandenburg an den 1. Sekretär der SED-Bezirksleitung Potsdam (18.4.1984) [Monthly report of the first secretary of the SED local apparatus Brandenburg to the first secretary of the SED district apparatus Potsdam (18 April 1984)], BLHA, Rep. 531 Brandenburg Nr. 2091, n.p.
44. These consequences could range from social and political pressure to outright disadvantages regarding career development. See Kloth, Vom "Zettelfalten" zum freien Wählen.
45. In the run-up to the elections of 1986, only 220 people in Brandenburg considered not voting. Approximately half of them gave reasons that suggest they tried to blackmail local officials. Problems of housing and supply, as well as problems on the shop floor, were dominant. See Bericht der SED-Kreisleitung Brandenburg zur Vorbereitung auf die Wahlen 1986 [Report of the SED local apparatus Brandenburg in preparation for the 1986 elections], BLHA, Rep. 531 Brandenburg Nr. 2112, n.p.
46. Martin Sabrow, "Der Konkurs der Konsensdiktatur. Überlegungen zum inneren Zerfall der DDR aus kulturgeschichtlicher Perspektive" [The failure of consensus dictatorship. Considerations about the internal decay of the GDR from a cultural perspective], in Weg in den Untergang. Der innere Zerfall der DDR [Roads to collapse. The internal decay of the GDR], ed. Konrad H. Jarausch and Martin Sabrow (Göttingen, 1999), 83–116.
47. Monatsbericht des 1. Sekretärs der SED-Kreisleitung Brandenburg an den 1. Sekretär der SED-Bezirksleitung Potsdam (18.10.1989) [Monthly report of the first secretary of the SED local apparatus Brandenburg to the first secretary of the SED district apparatus Potsdam (18 October 1989)], BLHA, Rep. 531 Brandenburg Nr. 2126, n.p.

Bibliography

Bergien, Rüdiger. Im "Generalstab der Partei." Organisationskultur und Herrschaftspraxis in der SED-Zentrale (1946–1989) [In the "general staff of the party." Organizational culture and practice of rule in the center of the SED]. Berlin: Christoph Links Verlag, 2017.

Bernhardt, Christoph. "Zwischen Herrschaft und Selbstbehauptung—Ambivalenzen sozialistischer Stadtpolitik und Urbanität" [Between domination and autonomy—Ambivalences of socialist urban policy and urbanity]. In Sozialistische Städte zwischen Herrschaft und Selbstbehauptung. Kommunalpoli-

tik, Stadtplanung und Alltag in der DDR [Socialist cities between domination and autonomy. Local government, urban planning and everyday life in the GDR], ed. C. Bernhardt and Heinz Reif, 301–303. Stuttgart: Steiner, 2009.

Best, Heinrich, and Heinz Mestrup, eds. *Die Ersten und Zweiten Sekretäre der SED. Machtstrukturen und Herrschaftspraxis in den thüringischen Bezirken der DDR* [The first and second secretaries of the SED. Structures of power and practice of rule in the Thuringian Districts of the GDR]. Weimar: Hain Verlag, 2003.

Bourdieu, Pierre. Outline of a Theory of Practice. Cambridge: Cambridge University Press, 1977. Previously published as *Entwurf einer Theorie der Praxis. Auf der ethnologischen Grundlage der kabylischen Gesellschaft*. Frankfurt/M.: Suhrkamp Verlag, 1976.

Boyer, Christoph, and Peter Skyba, eds. *Repression und Wohlstandsversprechen. Zur Stabilisierung von Parteiherrschaft in der DDR und CSSR* [Repression and promise of prosperity. On stabilization of party rule in the GDR and the USSR]. Dresden: Hannah-Arendt-Institut für Totalitarismusforschung, 1999.

Ettrich, Frank. "Neotraditionalistischer Staatssozialismus. Zur Diskussion eines Forschungskonzeptes" [Neo-traditional state socialism. Discussing a research concept]. *Prokla* 86, no. 1 (1992): 98–114.

Fritzsche, Peter, and Jochen Hellbeck. "The New Man in Stalinist Russia and Nazi Germany." In *Beyond Totalitarianism: Stalinism and Nazism Compared*, ed. S. Fitzpatrick and M. Geyer, 302–341. Cambridge: Cambridge University Press, 2009.

Heinrich, Gerd, Klaus Hess, Winfried Schich, and Wolfgang Schössler. *Stahl und Brennabor. Die Stadt Brandenburg im 19. und 20. Jahrhundert* [Steel and Brennabor. The city of Brandenburg in the 19th and 20th century]. Potsdam: Verlag für Berlin-Brandenburg, 1998.

Holtz-Baumert, Gerhard. "Der Erste von 'O'" [The boss of "O"]. *Neue Deutsche Literatur. Monatszeitschrift für Literatur und Kritik* 2 (1986): 13–20.

Jarausch, Konrad H. "Fürsorgediktatur" [Welfare dictatorship]. Docupedia-Zeitgeschichte, 11 February 2010. Accessed 27 September 2013, http://docupedia.de/zg/F.C3.BCrsorgediktatur?oldid=84610.

Jessen, Ralph. "Die Gesellschaft im Staatssozialismus. Probleme einer Sozialgeschichte der DDR" [Society in state socialism. Problems of a social history of the GDR]. *Geschichte und Gesellschaft* 21, no. 1 (1995): 96–110.

Jessen, Ralph, and Hedwig Richter. "Non-Competitive Elections in 20th Century Dictatorships: Some Questions and General Considerations." In *Voting for Hitler and Stalin: Elections under 20th Century Dictatorship*, ed. R. Jessen and H. Richter, 9–36. Frankfurt/M.: Campus Verlag, 2011.

Kloth, Hans Michael. *Vom "Zettelfalten" zum freien Wählen. Die Demokratisierung der DDR 1989/90 und die "Wahlfrage"* [From "Zettelfalten" to free elections. The democratization of the GDR and the "Wahlfrage"]. Berlin: Christoph Links-Verlag, 2000.

Kuschel, Franziska. "'Keine NATO-Sender mehr dulden.' Westmedien in der DDR der Sechzigerjahre" ["Don't tolerate NATO stations anymore." Western media in the GDR in the sixties]. *Deutschlandarchiv* 45, no. 2 (2012). Accessed 20 April 2017, http://www.bpb.de/geschichte/zeitgeschichte/deutschlandarchiv/74942/keine-nato-sender.

Lindenberger, Thomas. "SED-Herrschaft als soziale Praxis—Herrschaft und 'Eigen-Sinn': Problemstellung und Begriffe" [SED-rule as social practice—Rule and 'Eigen-Sinn': Problems and concepts]. In *Staatssicherheit und Gesellschaft. Studien zum Herrschaftsalltag in der DDR* [State security and society. Studies on the day-to-day rule], ed. J. Gieseke, 23–47. Göttingen: Vandenhoeck & Ruprecht, 2007.

Marxen, Klaus, and Gerhard Werle, eds. *Strafjustiz und DDR-Unrecht*. Bd. 3, *Amtsmissbrauch und Korruption* [Criminal justice and injustice in the GDR. Vol. 3, Abuse of office and corruption]. Berlin: de Gruyter, 2002.

Merl, Stephan. "Elections in the Soviet Union, 1937–1989: A View into a Paternalistic World from Below." In *Voting for Hitler and Stalin: Elections under 20th Century Dictatorship*, ed. R. Jessen and H. Richter, 276–308. Frankfurt/M.: Campus Verlag, 2011.

Meuschel, Sigrid. *Legitimation und Parteiherrschaft. Zum Paradox von Stabilität und Revolution in der DDR 1945–1989* [Legitimacy and party rule. On the paradox of stability and revolution in the GDR 1945–1989]. Frankfurt/M.: Suhrkamp, 1992.

Pollack, Detlef. "Die konstitutive Widersprüchlichkeit der DDR-Gesellschaft. Oder: War die DDR homogen? Eine Fortsetzung der Diskussion zwischen Sigrid Meuschel und Ralph Jessen" [The constituent contradictoriness of the GDR society. Or: Was the GDR homogenous? Continuing the discussion between Sigrid Meuschel and Ralph Jessen]. *Geschichte und Gesellschaft* 24, no. 1 (1998): 110–131.

———. "Wie modern war die DDR" [How modern was the GDR?]. In *Koordinaten deutscher Geschichte in der Epoche des Ost-West-Konflikts* [Coordinates of German history in the epoch of the East-West conflict], ed. H. G. Hockerts, 175–205. Munich: Oldenbourg, 2004.

Port, Andrew I. *Conflict and Stability in the German Democratic Republic*. Cambridge: Cambridge University Press, 2007.

Reichardt, Sven. "Praxeologische Geschichtswissenschaft. Eine Diskussionsanregung" [Praxeological history. Ideas for discussion]. *Sozial Geschichte. Zeitschrift für historische Analyse des 20. und 21. Jahrhunderts* 22, no. 3 (2007): 43–65.

Richter, Hedwig. "Mass Obedience: Practices and Functions of Elections in the German Democratic Republic." In *Voting for Hitler and Stalin: Elections under 20th Century Dictatorship*, ed. R. Jessen and H. Richter, 103–125. Frankfurt/M.: Campus Verlag, 2011.

Sabrow, Martin. "Der Konkurs der Konsensdiktatur. Überlegungen zum inneren Zerfall der DDR aus kulturgeschichtlicher Perspektive" [The failure of consensus dictatorship. Considerations about the internal decay of the GDR from a cultural perspective]. In *Weg in den Untergang. Der innere Zerfall der DDR* [Roads to collapse. The internal decay of the GDR], ed. K. H. Jarausch and M. Sabrow, 83–116. Göttingen: Vandenhoeck & Ruprecht, 1999.

———. "Einleitung: Geschichtsdiskurs und Doktringesellschaft" [Introduction. Historical discourse and society of doctrines]. In *Geschichte als Herrschaftsdiskurs. Der Umgang mit der Vergangenheit in der DDR* [History as discourse on power. Dealing with the past in the GDR], ed. M. Sabrow, 9–35. Cologne: Böhlau, 2000.

———. "Sozialismus als Sinnwelt. Diktatorische Herrschaft in kulturhistorischer Perspektive" [Socialism as world of meaning. Cultural perspectives on dictatorial rule]. *Potsdamer Bulletin für Zeithistorische Studien* 40–41 (2007): 9–23.

Saldern, Adelheid von, ed. *Inszenierter Stolz. Stadtpräsentationen in drei deutschen Gesellschaften (1935–1975)* [Staged pride. Representations of cities in three German societies (1935–1975)]. Stuttgart: Steiner, 2005.

Schein, Edgar. "Coming to a New Awareness of Organizational Culture." *Sloan Management Review* 25, no. 2 (1984): 3–16.

Scherzer, Landolf. *Der Erste. Eine Reportage aus der DDR* [The boss. A report from the GDR]. Cologne: Kiepenheuer & Witsch, 1988.

Sieder, Reinhard. "Sozialgeschichte auf dem Weg zu einer historischen Kulturwissenschaft?" [Social history on the way to a historical cultural science?]. *Geschichte und Gesellschaft* 20, no. 3 (1994): 445–468.

Steiner, André. "Bolsche Vita in der DDR? Überlegungen zur Korruption im Staatssozialismus" [Bolsche Vita in the GDR? Reflections on corruption in state socialism]. In *Geld—Geschenke—Politik. Korruption im neuzeitlichen Europa* [Money—gifts—politics. Corruption in early modern Europe], *Beihefte der Historischen Zeitschrift*, vol. 48, ed. Jens Ivo Engels, Andreas Fahrmeir, Alexander Nützenadel, 249–274. Munich: Oldenbourg, 2009.

Werkentin, Falco. *Politische Strafjustiz in der Ära Ulbricht. Vom bekennenden Terror zur verdeckten Repression* [Political criminal justice in the Ulbricht era. From open terror to hidden repression]. Berlin: Christoph Links Verlag, 1997.

Yurchak, Alexei. *Everything Was Forever, Until It Was No More: The Last Soviet Generation*. Princeton: Princeton University Press, 2006.

Zimmermann, Brigitte, and Hans-Dieter Schütt. *Noch Fragen, Genossen!* [Any more questions, comrades!]. Berlin: Verlag Neues Leben, 1994.

10

THE SED *BEZIRK* SECRETARIES AS BROKERS OF TERRITORIAL INTERESTS IN THE GDR

Jay Rowell

The extremely productive historiography of the German Democratic Republic (GDR) state and party apparatus has paid scarce attention to the local and district (*Bezirk*) levels.[1] With a few notable exceptions, historical research has focused on the centers of power—the central party apparatus and the *Stasi* in particular.[2] This focalization was in large part based on the idea that the GDR represented a perfectly centralized political system capable of enforcing strict discipline on subnational state and SED (Socialist Unity Part of Germany / *Sozialistische Einheitspartei Deutschlands*) organs, as "all important decisions, but also the most insignificant ones, were taken by the General Secretary of the SED."[3] Local and district officials were seen to simply relay central decisions, and their discipline was assumed to be based on a series of mechanisms that placed local actors in a web of constraints: the nomenclature system,[4] the internalization of the culture and ideology of the SED, the stringent hierarchical control over subaltern organizations of party and state, and, last but not least, a diffuse cultural hypothesis in which the GDR was seen as being influenced by a Prussian relationship to authority. As the GDR was reputed to be the most centralized country of the Communist bloc, there simply seemed to be little to be learned about the workings of the political system by looking at the lower echelons. This perspective was paradoxically reinforced by the extremely rich historiography in social history of the GDR, in which the variety of tactics deployed by social groups in the face of rigid political directives was a central theme of research, but left party and state actors as a reified and monolithic entity that remained largely outside of the scope of enquiry.

In this chapter, I propose to connect some of the insights of social history to take a closer look at the *Bezirk* and local levels of the state and party bureaucracies. The central research question will be that of the emergence of what can be termed territorial interests, and the way in which these territorial interests were articulated and expressed. A first clue to the possibility of the development of territorially defined interests, and, by extension, an indication of the possible limits to a purely "top down" practice of power, appears in the variety of terms used by the public to designate the *Bezirk* first secretary of the SED: the *Bezirks Fürst*, which can be translated as the "district prince," or more simply *der Erste*, or "number 1."[5] These expressions imply an autonomy of action and a form of sovereignty over a territory that lies somewhere between a feudal sovereign and an appointed governor or French-style prefect, whose role it is to represent central authority in provinces and oversee the application of central directives. Like nominated governors or prefects, the *Bezirk* first secretaries were named and could be revoked by central authorities. However, unlike the former two functions, in which central authorities generally organized a rotation of personnel to limit the risks of "going native," the GDR first secretaries often remained in place for several decades and built their political reputations on their stewardship of their territory.

In the daily exercise of their functions, territorial representatives of the SED or nominally elected representatives of *Bezirk* or local (*Kreis*) executives performed many of the same tasks as elected officials in liberal democracies when serving their electorate. They attended banquets, commemorations, and inaugurations of buildings and monuments; they personally handed out awards and medals; they visited construction sites, factories, universities, and hospitals, where they gave speeches and conversed with workers, engineers, doctors, etc.; they held visiting hours for members of the public and received numerous letters asking for help in solving administrative problems. This ritualized and partially mediatized production of proximity with the public indicates that their role was not just limited to that of a "transmission belt" between central authorities and the population. In their often long terms in office as territorial "boss," the first secretaries developed patronage relationships and established long-term working relationships with local industry and state administrations, which, as I will seek to demonstrate, progressively transformed the role of the first secretary of the *Bezirk*, at least in part, to that of a representative of territorial interests in Berlin.

Understanding the mechanisms leading to the definition of this role of the "Bezirk prince" requires the study of both horizontal networks within the political territories and the vertical linkages—both personal and structural/institutional—with central authorities. In the first section of the chapter, I will focus on the transformations in territorial SED and state bureaucracies that progressively changed a tense and adversarial relationship between local political elites to a more cooperative relationship by the early 1960s. This created the necessary conditions for the emergence of shared interests among territorial bureaucracies.[6] In the second section, I will more closely examine the territorial inscription of careers of the first secretaries and discuss patterns of legitimation of holders of this function. Finally in the last section, I will show how territorial state and SED representatives organized a pragmatic division of labor that was geared toward maximizing the flow of centrally allocated resources to the *Bezirk*.

The Progressive Pacification of the Relationship between Territorial Elites

Between 1945 and 1989, one can schematically identify two separate institutional configurations of territorial institutions. In the phase of the conquest and consolidation of the dominant role of the SED from 1945 to the early 1960s, interactions between territorial SED organs and state bureaucracies were rife with conflict and marked by overlapping competencies. However, from the late 1950s on, these relationships gradually become more pacified and were increasingly marked by a division of labor. Better access to centrally allocated resources was both a consequence and a cause of improved cooperation between territorial actors.

Between 1945 and 1952, the Soviet zone of occupation in the GDR preserved the inherited institutional architecture of *Kreis* (county) and *Länder* (regions). In their relationship to these administrations, the SED concentrated on the political cleansing of former members of the Nazi party and the occupation of key positions by Party members and industrial workers, a transformation justified by the affirmation of a "socialist" administrative model where the sociological composition of the administration should reflect the "dominant role of the working class." The territorial reforms of 1952 brought an end to the *Länder* and replaced them with fourteen, then fifteen, *Bezirke*. This reform destabilized the political-administrative space, bringing with it a high degree of uncertainty, battles over competencies, high turnover, and increased tensions between cadres working in industry, territorial administrations, and the SED. However, beginning in the late 1950s, interactions moved in a more cooperative direction. Several factors explain this gradual shift. First, SED leaders in Berlin became aware of the counterproductive effects of uncontrolled interventions of local party officials in the economy and began to codify the division of labor. Second, the sociological composition of local SED leaders changed as the SED strove to promote officials with more "technical" skills. This led to a circulation of personnel between industry, administrations, and the party apparatus, thus reinforcing personal relationships and trust. The SED officially maintained its preeminent role, but the reaffirmation of this role gradually became ritualized, and the intrusive and often counterproductive incursions of members of the SED apparatus into economic or administrative affairs became rarer.

The "Democratization" of the Local State (1952–1960)

The ill-prepared and wide-sweeping administrative and economic reforms of 1952 not only destabilized precarious administrative routines by creating overlapping competencies in industry and state administrations, it also profoundly reorganized (and destabilized) SED organizations as the party organization mirrored the territorial state organization. Between 1952 and 1954, there was a phenomenal turnover in the rank and file working in the local SED apparatus, as 60 percent of full-time party workers were replaced.[7] In the city of Leipzig, party statistics show that in 1953, only 18 of the 283 permanent party workers had been working in the apparatus for more than three years.[8] This extraordinary fluctuation is not only linked to the campaigns to cleanse party membership of the early 1950s that particularly targeted former Social Democrats. It is also related to the fact that many party workers in the early 1950s had little schooling or experience in bureaucratic work, and had difficulties in using the correct party terminology, especially as party doctrines often shifted.[9]

Sociologically, the higher ranks of the local state administrations and the members of the local SED apparatus could hardly be more different if one compares the statistics dating from August 1952 on the 263 most senior officials in the Leipzig municipal administration with their counterparts in the SED bureaucracy, whose role was to oversee the work of state bureaucracies. On the side of the SED, 259 out of 283 were registered as "being from working-class families," and only twenty-three had more than the standard eighth grade education.[10] On the side of the state administrations, there is no information on diplomas; however, only 26 percent were registered as being from a working-class background, with 56 percent coming from a family of employees or civil servants.[11] If these high-ranking members of the city administration were in their vast majority members of the SED (86 percent), their cadre files, established by their counterparts in the SED bureaucracy, are a testimony to the intensity of the social tensions between representatives of the two organizations. The evaluators had almost without exception a working-class background and much less educational capital. This sociological asymmetry transpires in the categories of judgment of the administrative elites. For example, in 1960, there was a local SED campaign to remove several department heads from office.[12] The director of the administration in charge of construction, an architect by profession, was said to "possess all the necessary professional qualities, but does not participate regularly in the meetings of the party cell. He is very critical and his opinions and attitudes are often counterproductive, thereby producing a negative political influence on the entire department."[13] Another architect in the same department was seen to be "responsible for the absence of criticism and self-criticism in his service. H. is ideologically unreliable and an opportunist."[14] The engineer and technical director of the district building Kombinat VEB Bau-Union (State Enterprise Builder's Union), was removed from his functions by the SED for having "lied to the party and for keeping to himself"; the report also claimed that "E. is arrogant and displays opportunistic tendencies."[15] At the heart of these power struggles for ascendancy is the social condescendence felt by party members or the open reluctance of state employees to "confide" or to consider party meetings and campaigns as important as their professional tasks. Critical remarks, aloof body language or facial expressions, or other forms of verbal or nonverbal resistance to the authority of party workers were seen as visible signs of an inauthentic relationship to the Party and were immediately translated into disqualifying political categories: "opportunism," "ideological weakness," "careerism," or "ambivalence."

The Rebalancing the Local Institutional Space

Several transformations gradually contributed to the reduction of frictions between the SED apparatus and the local state, so by the end of the 1950s, tensions began to structurally subside. The extraordinarily high turnover in the SED apparatus of the early 1950s slowed so much that, by 1961, more than two-thirds of permanent party workers in the Leipzig *Bezirk* SED organization had been in place for more than three years.[16] In parallel, the shambles of the early 1950s, created in part by the constant intervention of party officials in the running of the local administrations and *Kombinate*, set into motion a learning process leading to a relative division of labor.

After the insurrectional strikes of June 1953, the multiplication of rival state and party administrations responsible for "controlling" companies came to be seen as a political problem and led to attempts to codify the relationships between economic actors, the state, and the SED. For example, a central directive defining the mandate of SED cells within administrations defined nine functions, which were essentially limited to the domains of "agitation and propaganda," the organization of political education, and the selection of candidates for Party schools. The evaluation of personnel in leading positions remained a direct and important power, but the directive was keen to avoid giving any powers in directly intervening in daily management.[17] The observable interventions of SED officials into administrative activities gradually declined and the numbers of state cadres removed from office after falling into disfavor with party officials became increasingly rare after the early 1960s.

However, the codification of relationships was not the only factor at play. First, there was a perceptible learning process by state and economic cadres in their dealings with SED officials through the progressive incorporation of the rules of interaction, which can be summarized as recognizing the leading role of the SED in verbal and nonverbal communication to avoid trouble and gain autonomy. Second, there was a sociological convergence in profiles of state and party functionaries that reduced tensions between the two types of personnel.

Administrative cadres, most of whom were SED members, progressively mastered the expected rhetoric and standardized ideological statements that provided tangible signs of submission to the collective intelligence of the party of the working classes. This made it harder to stigmatize top cadres of bourgeois social origins with university educations for "opportunism" or "arrogance." They progressively learned the expected rhetoric and body language, which visibly demonstrated their symbolic recognition of SED supremacy in a tactic of blame avoidance. This sense of tact, diplomacy, and ease, to use Goffman's terminology,[18] was the price to pay for increased professional autonomy. Relationships between representatives of the two organizations became increasingly ritualized and had fewer practical consequences, as party workers were symbolically confirmed in their dominant role, and state and economic functionaries could get on with their jobs. To give one example, in November 1969, the SED organization of the city of Leipzig demanded "explanations and concrete measures" when learning that the level of productivity was only 54 percent of plan targets in housing construction.[19] Party criticism failed to take into account the actual causes that were linked to the diversion of cement deliveries from housing to a high-priority power station. But in reality, SED actions had more to do with reasserting its authority and proving to central party organs that it was active than with finding a solution or even sanctioning those responsible. The SED demanded a "better organization of construction sites and a more scientific and less bureaucratic way of working."[20] The state cadres promised action, taking the form of meetings where SED resolutions and Walter Ulbricht's article in *Neues Deutschland* would be studied, and as well as political meetings on each construction site. The proposed action could not have any effect on the causes of the problems of productivity, and none of the actors involved would probably have believed that they would, but the local SED officials demonstrated to their hierarchy that they were active and obtained signs of submission from local cadres. State cadres in turn would lose a few hours in meetings and discussions, but the proposed plan of action left them free to address the economic and technical questions that were the origin of SED intervention.

The second factor that explains the pacification of interactions in the local political spaces is a sociological convergence. Technical training and skills became essential criteria for cadre politics in the central instances of the SED in the second half of the 1950s. At the *Bezirk* and *Kreis* level, the effort to prepare party workers for the "scientific and technical revolution" became tangible after 1960. The numbers of party workers with a degree in higher education rose from 5 percent in 1958 to 15 percent three years later in the SED organization of the city of Leipzig;[21] by 1963, 36 percent of the 479 party workers of the *Bezirk* SED organization and full-time SED secretaries in companies had a higher education degree, with a further 20 percent enrolled in continuing education.[22] This rapid rise of the educational capital came through training programs or the hiring of personnel with a university degree, often with prior experience in state administration or industry. The porosity between the different local structures created the conditions for a more cooperative relationship in a context where all local organizations were evaluated by their respective hierarchies on a single central criterion: fulfilling plan targets. In other words, as good economic results were primordial in establishing the reputations of actors in all institutions, there was the progressive recognition of the existence of common interests and interdependence.

The Territory as a Resource for *Bezirk* "Princes"

A subnational territory and its population can only exist politically if public institutions and their representatives impose the territory as a natural entity with specific characteristics and interests. This supposes that political and administrative elites have an interest in articulating regional or local identities and that the institutional configuration provides incentives. Actors will defend and formulate territorial interests if and when they perceive a positive relationship between the economic performance of "their" territory and the accumulation of political capital and career advancement

The Political Trajectories of the First Secretaries of the Bezirk

In the late 1940s, the construction of a central state and the strengthening of the central party apparatus necessitated the co-option of the personnel in the territorial apparatus of the party and the *Länder* (*Bezirk* after 1952) executives. Between 1947 and 1949, leading figures of the SED moved to Berlin, thereby creating a vacuum in the party apparatus of the *Länder,* filled predominantly by young party cadre. In 1955, five of the fifteen *Bezirk* first secretaries of the SED were under the age of 35, and only three were older than 50.

The classic criteria used to study GDR elites point to a high level of homogeneity among the fifteen first secretaries in the early 1950s. All were male and members of the KPD (German Communist Party, *Kommunistische Partei Deutschlands*) at the moment of the creation of the SED in 1946 (ten entering before 1933, three in 1945, and Alois Pisnik, first secretary of Magdeburg District from 1955 to 1979, an Austrian, joined the Austrian Socialist Party in 1928. According to their official biographies, all were of working-class origin, none had a university degree, but all had completed at least a one-year course in an SED or a CPSU (Communist Party of the Soviet Union) party school.

However, if one looks at the career trajectories in their territorial dimension, one can distinguish between three paths: (1) a first ascending career pattern in which future first secretaries held a succession of increasingly important positions in *Kreis*, state, or SED organs; (2) a second trajectory in which first secretaries previously held positions in *Land* governments or party organizations and then moved to *Bezirk* positions within the borders of the former *Land*; (3) a third trajectory where a first secretary is sent to a *Bezirk* where he had not worked before.

Six of the fourteen first secretaries in place in 1955 worked their way up through local positions in the same territory: Walter Buchheim (Karl-Marx-Stadt 1952–1959), Paul Fröhlich (Leipzig 1952–1970), Gerhard Grüneberg (Frankfurt/Oder 1952–1958), Alfred Neumann (Berlin 1953–1957), Bernhard Quandt (Schwerin 1952–1974), and Albert Stief (Cottbus 1953–1969). They generally began their careers in 1945 at the municipal level or as a functionary in the SED youth organization *Frei Deutsche Jugend* (FDJ; Free German Youth) and worked their way up to a position of first secretary in increasingly important *Kreis* party organizations. This is, for example, the case of Paul Fröhlich, first secretary of the Leipzig *Bezirk* between 1952 and 1970. A miner by trade, Fröhlich joined the KPD in 1930. After the war, he was successively SED secretary for propaganda and culture in the Dresden Party organization, first secretary of the SED in *Kreis* Bautzen, then first secretary of the important SED organization of Leipzig between 1950 and 1952, before being named first *Bezirk* secretary in 1952.

Six first secretaries in office in 1955 had previously held positions in the executives or SED organizations of the *Länder*: Otto Funke (Suhl 1952–1968), Karl Mewis (Rostock 1952–1964), Helmut Müller (Gera 1952–1955), Alois Pisnik (Magdeburg 1952–1979), Hans Riesner (Dresden 1952–1957), and Max Steffen (Neubrandenburg 1953–1960). For example, Karl Mewis, former SED first secretary of the *Land* Mecklenburg became first secretary of the Rostock *Bezirk,* and the five others in this group were either members of the SED bureau (Müller, Pisnik, and Funke) or ministers for education of their *Land* (Steffen and Riesner).

Finally, in the last configuration, three first secretaries "discover" their territory when taking office. In this case, the career moves were horizontal, from one *Bezirk* to another: Franz Bruk (Halle 1954–1958), Eduard Götzl (Potsdam 1955–1957), and Hans Kiefert (Erfurt 1953–1957). For example, Hans Kiefert built up his SED career in Berlin before a stint of four years as first secretary of Erfurt, then resumed his career in Berlin.

In all cases, the first secretaries of the mid-1950s were second-tier SED elites. At the times of their designation, only two were members of the central committee of the SED, even if most would be co-opted into this central organ in subsequent years. If none of the first secretaries were in exile in Moscow between 1933 and 1945, ten, or all those who entered the KPD before 1933, spent at least two years in a Nazi concentration camp, which demonstrates the importance of antifascist resistance in personal biographies in a state whose principal claim to legitimacy was antifascism. This biographical attribute was also essential in the designation of mayors in important cities or at the head of the *Bezirk* council (ten of fifteen in 1955). These biographies provide important clues to the more or less implicit definition of the role that was expected of these territorial representatives. Before 1945, they proved their loyalty to the party and they owed their rapid promotion to their party loyalty. As incontestable antifascists with working-class backgrounds, these cadres represented the noblest attributes of German communism: resistance to Nazism and the claim to democratic representativity, in that people of humble origins could become mayor, president of a *Bezirk* council, or "boss" of the Party organization.

Patronage as a Means to Cultivate Ties to the "Masses"

Beyond their working-class and antifascist pedigree, an important role of the first secretaries consisted in visibly demonstrating that they were in constant contact with the "masses." In doing so, they regularly used the problems that the public drew to their attention as a means to reassert their authority over state administrations. The Leipzig municipal archives contain countless interventions of first secretaries (*Kreis* or *Bezirk*) concerning a wide span of relatively mundane problems that were transformed into political issues by first secretaries, such as the empty shop shelves, public transportation, or housing. For example, in a letter to the mayor of Leipzig, the first secretary Paul Fröhlich raised the following issues: "During my recent visit to Portitz [a Leipzig suburb], a large number of inhabitants brought the transportation problem to my attention. Indeed, three changes of the tramway are necessary to get to the city center. In addition, residents complained about the presence of an industrial pigsty, which pollutes the air and attracts swarms of flies. Thank you for taking care of these problems and informing me of the solutions you propose."[23] Local inhabitants had expressed their objections to the construction of an industrial pigsty and the difficulties in urban mobility to city officials on numerous occasions, but lacked the resources to weigh in on the organization of public transportation or to curb the SED's plans to increase meat production during the final push of agricultural collectivization at the end of the 1950s. In this case, the intervention of Fröhlich resulted in an increase of the frequency of trams to Portitz as a way to shorten travel times, a measure which the SED took full credit for.

The first secretaries of the 1950s harnessed popular dissatisfaction by turning it against state administrations accused of being "bureaucratic," "distant," or "cold hearted." In doing so, they institutionalized the circumvention of bureaucratic rules, allowing them, to use Pierre Bourdieu's terminology, to "obtain symbolic profits from the administrative rigidity of dominated institutions."[24] By representing the "problems of the masses" and intervening on behalf of ordinary citizens, or by publishing articles in the press criticizing "bureaucratism," "the sloppy work of local administrations," or the "distance between the public administrations and the masses," local party leaders sought symbolic legitimacy with the public and ascendancy over other local actors. These resources were part of a local zero-sum game characteristic of the 1940s and 1950s. First secretaries used public demands as a way to assert authority by imposing a reallocation of state resources, and taking credit for themselves when individual citizens or local clients benefitted. However, as this reallocation of funds and investments was only possible by reallocating resources, the interventions of the first secretaries to satisfy one clientele came at the expense of another (less vocal or influential) and weakened the overall efficiency of the system. Local administrations were left with the task of explaining to individuals, groups, or institutions why their resources were reduced, or their needs not met.

Transformations of the Role of the First Secretaries

As a result of the pacification of the relationships between SED and state organizations at the local and *Bezirk* level, and the increasingly important role of *Bezirk* "bosses" in the central institutions, the attentions of first secretaries were gradually less centered on asserting their authority locally than on securing more resources and investments for their territory at the national level. In other words, the zero-sum game at the local level became a zero-sum game at the national level, with *Bezirk* secretaries in competition to secure the prosperity of their territory.

We can recall that, in 1955, only two of fourteen district first secretaries were part of the central committee and none were members of the politburo. By 1958, eleven first secretaries who were in office in 1955 had been co-opted into the central committee and four were candidates for the politburo or full members. Their arrival occurred in 1958 with the exclusion of the "Schirdewan-Wollweber faction" from the politburo. The *Bezirk* leaders had shown their loyalty to Walter Ulbricht; Alfred Neumann (Berlin 1953–1957) became a full member of the politburo, and Karl Mewis (Rostock 1952–1967), Hans Kiefert (Erfurt 1953–1957, Berlin 1957–1959), and Paul Fröhlich (Leipzig 1952–1970) became candidates. This rapid rise suggests that they were able to convert the resources of their position in the provinces to increase their authority within the central institutions of the SED to such an extent that they were considered to be valuable allies in the internal struggles of the politburo and "natural" candidates for the highest positions.

From the late 1950s on, a more or less long tenure in an "important" *Bezirk* (Berlin, Dresden, Halle, Leipzig) became one of the principal paths to access the politburo, alongside career trajectories in the mass organizations (particularly in the FDJ) and responsibilities in central party organs.[25] Typical careers of cadres who became *Bezirk* first secretaries in the 1960s and entered the politburo in the 1960s and 1970s went from the central committee administration to *Bezirk* boss and then to the politburo, as if the capacity to perform well as *Bezirk* first secretary was an ultimate test for rising party cadres. For example, Horst Sindermann was director of the Bureau for Agitation and Propaganda of the central committee (1954–1963), first secretary of Halle (1963–1971), candidate for the politburo in 1963, and full member in 1967. In this area, as in others, the 1970s and 1980s were marked by little turnover and consequently a progressive aging of the entire political elite. In 1989, only four of the fifteen *Bezirk* first secretaries had been in place for less than ten years, and six had been in place for more than two decades.

The increasing longevity in the same territory provided the structural preconditions for multiple forms of identification between the first secretary and the territory. At the same time, these first secretaries held strong positions in Berlin, which compensated for the very weak personal networks and formal relationships between *Bezirk* executives and state ministries.[26] In contrast to the 1940s and 1950s, in later years first secretaries interceded actively in central planning to ensure the economic success of their territory, which would provide tangible signs of their own skills and help their chances of rising to—or staying in— the most central places of power.

First secretaries progressively became brokers relaying the interests of *Bezirk* industries and administrations, ensuring that the territory got its share of investments and consumer goods. The reach of the first secretary depended in large part on his political capital, but also on more informal relationships and on a web of exchanges of services and goods, which created an informal economy of credits and debts, part of which took the following form: high-level SED officials or ministers often contacted *Bezirk* first secretaries for their support in solving a personal problem or intervening on a "sensitive" issue, very often concerning housing allocation for a family member, friend, or an important personality. *Bezirk* bosses addressed their problem to local executives and relied on their efficiency to find adequate solutions. By rendering this service, first secretaries could later hope to obtain favors in more official central negotiations, and local executives could hope to enlist the first secretary's support in negotiations in Berlin.

The archives of the housing department of the Leipzig *Bezirk* council contain a large number of such cases dating from the 1970s.[27] A first example is a letter dated 18 November 1976, sent by the minister for the glass and ceramics industry, asking for the first secretary Horst Schumann to help find a modern two-room apartment for his daughter, who was to begin her studies at the University of Leipzig.[28] Schumann forwarded the letter to the administrative services with a brief word: "The comrade minister asks for our support in this case. Please inform me by the end of the month about the solution you have found, and I will personally inform the comrade minister."[29] In another letter to the president of the *Bezirk* council, the first secretary of the Leipzig city SED organization mentions a phone call from Kurt Hager, an influential member of the politburo. Hager hoped to find a large apartment (at least five rooms and 150 square meters) for a renowned university professor: "At the request of comrade Kurt Hager, I have to ensure that the comrade Professor M. will get good working conditions. Besides the fact that I gave my personal word to comrade Hager and to the comrade professor, if we don't keep our promise, it would corroborate the impression that Prof. M. has of the incompetence of the state organs and the disinterest that we [the SED] have for ensuring that he finds the conditions he needs for his work. For us, it is the perfect opportunity to establish a better relationship with this important comrade."[30] In this type of circuit of exchange, a minister, member of the politburo, another *Bezirk* first secretary, or member of the central committee uses a personal relationship to solve a problem for a family member, friend, or for someone influential. The local administrations set aside a "special reserve" of empty flats and houses to solve precisely this type of unplanned—if frequent—problem. This cemented collaborative relationships in the local institutional space and gave leverage to first secretaries in future negotiations with central elites. When these transactions are interpreted not as isolated forms of corruption or rule-breaking, but in a larger framework of transactions, one can appreciate the degree of interdependence, in a configuration comparable to court society, as analyzed by Norbert Elias.[31]

Accessing the Political Center

What is striking in reading documents exchanged between central and *Bezirk* administrations is less the inflexibility of "top-down" central planning than the capacity of local actors to renegotiate the allocation of resources: to obtain decreases in plan targets or to obtain supplementary resources. These negotiations often involved relatively limited investments or deliveries of goods in short supply. For example, a few thousand tons of cement or steel, or the reduction of production targets by 1 or 2 percent, for a *Kombinat* or industrial sector were important, in that they could permit achieving 100 percent of plan targets and thereby avoid any negative consequences. At the same time, supplementary resources allowed local actors to build up "reserves" to compensate the eventuality of future supply problems, or for use in more discretionary ways.

The Institutional Expressions of Territorial Interests

Negotiations between representatives of *Bezirk* councils and central ministries brought together cadres with similar sociological characteristics but very different career trajectories.[32] From the early 1960s on, *Bezirk* directors for economic planning were mainly young SED members with diplomas in economics, as were their homologues of the *Staatsplankommission* (SPK; State Plan Commission). Directors of *Bezirk* construction administrations were also economists, as were most of their counterparts in the Ministry of Construction. However, for ministerial elites, career paths rarely began in territorial administrations, as was the case for only five of thirty-seven ministerial elites in the years 1960–1980 for whom I was able to find biographical information.[33] Ministerial elites were primarily co-opted out of positions in industry, thereby explaining in part the very formal relationships between ministerial elites and *Bezirk* councils. Indeed, in written interactions, the formal *Sie* is preferred to the more familiar *du* form of address, contrary to the norms of communication characterizing exchanges between *Bezirk* administrations and Party functionaries, or between ministerial personnel and the bureaus of the central committee.

In the complex process of plan negotiations, the struggle to find an agreed-upon objective between central ambitions and territorial objections often ended in a compromise, as expressed in a speech by the vice director of the SPK before *Bezirk* presidents in 1959: "Each time we meet, we spend hours discussing and we almost invariably arrive at a 50 percent to 50 percent solution. I think everybody here understands what I mean. . . . If the central plan for Construction foresees a 9 percent gain in productivity with an increase of 6 percent in investment, the *Bezirk* plan proposes a 7 percent productivity gain with a 7 percent increase in investment. Invariably, the final result is an increase in productivity of 8 percent with the same investments, or an increase of 9 percent with a considerable increase in investments. This is our common problem."[34] This logic of negotiation based on fixing a median point contributed to weakening the imperative nature of central plan directives, and local decision-makers shifted resources from one sector to another according to the differential in the importance in plan targets between economic sectors. In a partially successful attempt to obtain more construction capacity, the director of the Leipzig *Bezirk* Plan Commission indicated to central authorities that "the imperatives of building new housing has led us to reduce productive capacity for repairs and reconstruction of housing. The continual disruption and delays in delivering cement and steel has also delayed the construction of schools, day care centers and shops in the new neighborhoods, much to the discontent of the masses."[35]

Continually confronted with delays or reductions in the supply of raw materials, semi-finished goods for industries, or consumer products, territorial administrations had three options: reallocate disposable resources from one sector to another, protest against unilateral decisions or broken promises of central authorities, or ask the first secretary to intervene. In some more critical situations, first secretaries politicized the issue and managed to secure "exceptional contingents" by mobilizing the figure of "the masses" who would be "disappointed," "upset," or "wouldn't understand the policies of the SED." Sometimes things went so far that the specter of another 17 June 1953 was mobilized by *Bezirk* representatives. For example, on 8 June 1961, Willi Stoph, Walter Ulbricht's right-hand man, spoke before the *Bezirk* council presidents in a meeting in Berlin: "It has become next to impossible for us in Berlin to know what is really happening in the *Bezirk*. We get reports that say that most everything is fine, then suddenly we get a phone call and hear that the situation is urgent. How can we solve the problems of delivering butter and meat when we get a phone call with an ultimatum? 'Give me something immediately, I've got nothing in store, the shops are empty. If I don't get something fast, the situation could spin out of control.'"[36] Despite the thousands of reports sent to Berlin, *Bezirk* representatives were able to master the sources of uncertainty as they were reputed to intimately "know" what was happening on the ground, so they regularly instrumentalized the public "mood": "growing dissatisfaction of citizens who have been waiting two years for the construction of the grocery store"[37] or "the disappointment and anger of families to whom we promised the delivery of a new apartment this year."[38]

The Pivotal Position of the Prince of the Bezirk

The multipositioning of Bezirk first secretaries in central and territorial institutions, as well as their capacity to accumulate political capital and credit, was based in part on their capacity to exert a discretionary control over local material and symbolic resources. If officially the first secretary had a mandate from the party to control the execution of SED resolutions, his reputation was also inextricably linked to the economic performance of his *Bezirk*. As territorial administrations had only formal access to central institutions where plan negotiations were structured by the 50 percent logic described above, only the *Bezirk* first secretary had power to influence key investment decisions in a more structural and long-term basis by engaging the credit and personal contacts with ministers and members of the politburo.

The capability to intervene successfully depended on his reputation and weight in central places of power, his capacity to articulate territorial (and/or personal) interests with the interests of party leaders, and his position relative to other territorial representatives in competition. I will try to illustrate this role through the successes, then failures, of the first secretary of the Leipzig *Bezirk*, Horst Schumann, who was in position from 1970 to early 1989.

In the 1970s, Schumann was asked by the president of the council of Leipzig to intervene in Berlin on numerous occasions to try to divert more central investments to Leipzig. For decades, the local state apparatus had been making the recurring argument that the *Bezirk* contributed more to national wealth than it got back in investments. For example, in 1974, Schumann presented the catastrophic housing situation and the chronic underinvestment, both in absolute and relative terms, to Gerhard Schürer, director of the SPK,[39] and managed to obtain an "outside of plan" factory to produce the concrete wall elements necessary to accelerate housing construction in the *Bezirk*. In 1975, he followed up on another report by the *Bezirk* council president underscoring the fact that the *Bezirk* had still not attained the national average of per capita housing construction and that the accumulated effects of underinvestment in housing and infrastructure required the transfer of 3,600 construction workers to the *Bezirk*.[40] Throughout the 1970s, Schumann was very active in Berlin and multiplied meetings with ministers, members of the politburo, and the director of the SPK. His role was undoubtedly important in the increase in the proportion of investments flowing to the Leipzig *Bezirk* in the 1970s. However, an open conflict with the politburo in the early 1980s destroyed much of the political capital that Schumann had accumulated through his activism. In an interview, a former secretary of state in the Ministry of Construction presented the conflict in the following terms:

> In the high spheres of power, it was decided that Leipzig-Grünau [a housing project for 100,000 inhabitants] needed two churches. Berlin had to impose that by force. Two churches had to be constructed, no discussion . . . except that everyone in town remembered what Schumann had said: "As long as we haven't built a cinema, I won't allow the construction of two churches." From a local standpoint, that's perfectly OK, but from a political and economic viewpoint, a part of an overall strategy, it was more important to bring a loyal church closer to the state . . . that was good for the stability of the regime, and the churches were financed by the West, in convertible currency, at a time when foreign debt was becoming a critical problem.[41]

Schumann's mistake was to engage his political credit in a situation where realpolitik dictated the outcome. As territorial representative of the SED, Schumann failed in his role as guardian of centrally defined party policies, thereby weakening his standing in the most central party circles. At the same time, he lost face locally, both among SED members and local inhabitants, as he was unable to defend a position he had made public. This episode seemed to mark the decline of the capacity of Schumann to intervene effectively. However, it is perhaps not only his tactical mistake that explains this, but also his political and social trajectory, which limited his social capital in Berlin as well as his implantation in Leipzig. As the son of a celebrated communist resistant executed by the Nazis during the last months of the war, Schumann accomplished much of his career in the Free German Youth, first in Leipzig (1945–1953), then as secretary of the central council of the FDJ between 1959 and 1969, with a three-year stint at the Bureau for Agitation of the central committee and three years at the party school in Moscow. Schumann returned to Leipzig in 1969 as second *Bezirk* secretary and would become number one following the untimely death of Paul Fröhlich in 1970. If Schumann's career in the FDJ brought him close to Honecker and opened doors, his career did not provide him with some essential resources, as he neither disposed of a solid local foothold after a fifteen-year absence from Leipzig, nor did his previous functions place him in close contact with economic sectors or decision-makers.

Conclusion

Each time central authorities had difficulties in providing agreed-upon supplies or investments, territorial officials were asked to "mobilize all local resources" to fill the gaps. In other words, improvisation and give-and-take at the local level were not an act of resistance to the rigidity of central planning, hidden from central authorities, but an integral part of the stability of the plan economy itself. This routinization of improvisation not only followed an economic rational, but was also linked to the accumulation of political capital and the pursuit of careers. Deprived of electoral legitimacy, local political elites remained attentive to their legitimacy with the public and went to great lengths to visibly demonstrate not only that they listened to grievances, but also that they could act, in a sort of patronage relationship where resources were distributed in exchange for political loyalty. Instrumentalizing public concerns gave first secretaries public legitimacy and, at the same time, provided endless ammunition to assert primacy over "cold-hearted" bureaucracies "cut off from the masses." The conflictual relationships between local SED and state personnel gradually became more cooperative, and the circulations and conversions of goods, symbols, and legitimacy was based on a shared interest in providing the first secretary with political and relational capital in order to make him more efficient as a broker of territorial interests in Berlin. The first secretaries did not just oversee the economic improvisation in their territories. By calling in personal favors or past loyalty, by heading a *Bezirk* that was always close to fulfilling its plan targets by 100 percent, and by mastering the sources of political uncertainty through strategically interpreting the "moods" of the masses, they ultimately contributed in large part to the improvisation of economic planning in Berlin.

Jay Rowell is a CNRS research professor at the Society, Actors, and Government in Europe Research Center at the University of Strasbourg. His publications include *Le totalitarisme au concret: Le logement en RDA 1945–1989* (Paris, 2006), and «L'Eigensinn bureaucratique en RDA: Distanciation au rôle et autonomie des pratiques administratives," in *Sociétés contemporaines* 99–100 (2015).

Notes

1. Helga Welsh, "Die kommunistischen Eliten als Gegenstand der Forschung" [Communist elites as subject of research], in *Gesellschaft ohne Eliten? Führungsgruppen in der DDR* [Society without elites? Leadership groups in the GDR], ed. Arnd Bauerkämper, Jürgen Danyel, Peter Hübner, and Sabine Ross (Berlin, 1997), 148–149.
2. Jens Gieseke, *Die hauptamtlichen Mitarbeiter der Staatssicherheit: Personalstruktur und Lebenswelt 1950—1989/90* [The full-time employees of the state security. Staff structure and milieu 1950–1989/90] (Berlin, 2000); Thomas Lindenberger, *Volkspolizei. Herrschaftspraxis und öffentliche Ordnung im SED-Staat, 1952–1968* [The people's police. Practices of domination and public order in the SED state, 1952–1968] (Vienna, 2003); Heinrich Best and Heinz Mestrup, eds., *Die Ersten und Zweiten Sekretäre der SED. Machtstrukturen und Herrschaftspraxis in den thüringischen Bezirken der DDR* [The first and second secretaries of the SED. Structures of power and practice of rule in the Thuringian districts of the GDR] (Weimar, 2003); Mario Niemann, *Die Sekretäre der SED-Bezirksleitungen 1952–1989* [The SED district secretaries, 1952–1989] (Paderborn, 2007).
3. Ralph Jessen, "Diktatorische Herrschaft als kommunikative Praxis. Überlegungen zum Zusammenhang von 'Bürokratie' und Sprachnormierung in der DDR-Geschichte" [Dictatorial rule as communicative practice. Reflections on the context of "bureaucracy" and discursive norms in GDR history], in *Akten. Eingaben. Schaufenster. Die DDR und ihre Texte* [Archives,

Petitions and Shopwindows: The GDR and its Texts], eds. Alf Lüdtke and Peter Becker (Berlin, 1997), 72.
4. This system of organizing and controlling employment was first used within communist party organizations before being progressively extended to all important economic and bureaucratic functions at all levels: Christoph Boyer, *"Die Kader entscheiden Alles." Kaderentwicklung und Kaderpolitik in der zentralen Staatsverwaltung der SBZ und der frühen DDR (1945–1952)* ["The cadres decide everything." Cadre development and cadre policies in the central state administration of the SOZ and the early GDR (1945–1952)] (Dresden, 1996).
5. Landolf Scherzer, *Der Erste. Eine Reportage aus der DDR* [The boss. A report from the GDR] (Cologne, 1997).
6. The empirical basis of the chapter is largely based on the example of the *Bezirk* and city of Leipzig studied through central, *Bezirk*, and municipal archives of the SED and the state.
7. Hermann Weber, *DDR: Grundriß der Geschichte 1945–1990* [GDR: A historical outline 1945–1990] (Hannover, 1991), 98.
8. Report dated December 1953, SED city of Leipzig, Staatsarchiv Leipzig (hereafter STAL), SED IV 5/01/416.
9. In December 1953, 217 out of 283 permanent party workers were employed as industrial workers before entering employment for the SED. SED city of Leipzig, STAL, SED IV 5/01/416.
10. Cadre statistics of the SED city of Leipzig December 1953, SED ville de Leipzig, STAL, SED IV 5/01/416.
11. Report dated 1 August 1952, Bureau of Organization and Instruction of the city of Leipzig, Leipzig municipal archives (hereafter MA Leipzig), STVuR (1) 1507.
12. Christian Kurzweg and Oliver Werner, "SED und Staatsapparat im Bezirk: Der Konflikt um den Rat des Bezirkes Leipzig 1958/1959" [The SED and the apparatus of state in districts: The conflict about the district council of Leipzig 1958/1959], in *Länder, Gaue und Bezirke* [Regions, gaue and districts], ed. Michael Richter, Thomas Schaarschmidt, and Mike Schmeitzner (Dresden, 2007), 255–276.
13. SED city of Leipzig, STAL, SED IV/01/358
14. Ibid.
15. Ibid.
16. Ibid.
17. Directive on the objectives of SED organizations in municipal councils. MA Leipzig, STVuR (1) 3545. In the same line, SED organizations of the *Kreis* were asked in 1956 to write a report to the central committee answering the following questions: "How does the party influence the work of state organizations without substituting themselves for the latter? Are there examples where comrades of the party apparatus intimidate comrades from the state apparatus, thereby creating phenomena of insecurity and lack of initiative which are harmful to the efficiency of our institutions?" Circular dated 2 November 1956, MA Leipzig, STVuR (1) 3545.
18. Erving Goffman, *Interaction Ritual: Essays on Face-to-Face Behavior* (New York, 1982).

19. Letter to the Chief Architect of Leipzig and the director of the Construction Department of the city of Leipzig dated 21 November 1969, SED city of Leipzig, STAL, SED IVB-5/01/145.
20. Ibid.
21. SED city of Leipzig, STAL, SED IV 5/01/416.
22. Analysis of the professional training of permanent SED workers, Cadre bureau, SED *Bezirk* Leipzig, STAL, SED IV A-2/6/230.
23. Letter dated 19 December 1959 in the SED archives of the city of Leipzig, STAL, SED IV/01/358.
24. Pierre Bourdieu, "Droit et passe-droit. Le champ des pouvoirs territoriaux et la mise en œuvre des règlements" [Right and unjust privilege. The field of territorial authorities and the implementation of regulations], *Actes de la recherche en sciences sociales* 81–82 (March 1992): 91.
25. In 1989, eight of the twenty-one members of the politburo had been a *Bezirk* first secretary for more than five years, four of whom were still in office; see Helga Welsh, "Zwischen Macht und Ohnmacht. Zur Rolle der 1. Bezirkssekretäre der SED" [Between power and powerlessness: About the role of the first secretaries of the districts in the GDR], in *Sozialistische Eliten: Horizontale und vertikale Differenzierugsmuster in der DDR* [Socialist elites: Horizontal and vertical differentiation in the GDR], ed. Stefan Hornbostel (Opladen, 1999), 105–123.
26. Of the fifteen presidents of *Bezirk* councils in position in 1955, only two had previously held positions in another *Land* or *Bezirk* or in the central SED organization. In 1975, there had been little change in this pattern where careers began and ended in the same territory.
27. Leipzig *Bezirk* council, STAL, 24784.
28. Most students from out of town lived four to a room in dorms.
29. Letter from Karl Grünheid to Horst Schumann dated 16 November 1976. Leipzig *Bezirk* Council, STAL, 24784.
30. Letter from Roland Wötzel, Leipzig city SED first secretary to the president of the *Bezirk* council, 27 July 1982, Leipzig *Bezirk* council, STAL, 25557.
31. Norbert Elias, *The Court Society* (Oxford, 1983).
32. This paragraph is based on the construction sector.
33. Ministry of Construction, Berlin Federal Archives (hereafter BarchB), DH 1 19918–19921, 26103 ; and Council of Ministers, BarchB DC 20 8137.
34. Minutes of a meeting at the State Plan Commission (SPK), nondated, but probably early 1959, BarchB DC 20 7046.
35. Letter from Roland Wötzel to Gerhard Müller of the SPK dated 31 March 1975, Council of the *Bezirk* Leipzig, STAL, 24597.
36. BarchB, DC 20 7147.
37. Report from the *Bezirk* council Leipzig to the Ministry dated 12 May 1976, Council *Bezirk* Leipzig, STAL, 24597.
38. Letter to the Ministry of Construction following the announcement that Leipzig construction companies were ordered to build 767 apartment units in Berlin, 28 October 1984, Council *Bezirk* Leipzig, STAL, 25457.
39. Notes concerning a meeting with Gerhard Schürer in Berlin dated 10 January 1974, SED *Bezirk* Leipzig, STAL, SED IV C-2/6/04/552.

40. Note from Schumann to the president of the Leipzig Bezirk council relating a private meeting with the director of the SPK during preparations for the 1976–1980 five-year plan, 6 June 1975, Leipzig *Bezirk* council, STAL, 24597.
41. Interview, 26 May 1998 in Leipzig.

Bibliography

Best, Heinrich, and Heinz Mestrup, eds. *Die Ersten und Zweiten Sekretäre der SED. Machtstrukturen und Herrschaftspraxis in den thüringischen Bezirken der DDR* [The first and second secretaries of the SED. Structures of power and practice of rule in the Thuringian districts of the GDR]. Weimar: Hain Verlag, 2003.

Bourdieu, Pierre. "Droit et passe-droit. Le champ des pouvoirs territoriaux et la mise en œuvre des règlements" [Right and unjust privilege. The field of territorial authorities and the implementation of regulations], *Actes de la recherche en sciences sociales* 81–82 (March 1992): 86–96.

Boyer, Christoph. *"Die Kader entscheiden alles . . . ." Kaderentwicklung und Kaderpolitik in der zentralen Staatsverwaltung der SBZ und der frühen DDR (1945–1952)* ["The cadres decide everything . . . ." Cadre development and cadre policies in the central state administration of the SOZ and the early GDR (1945–1952)]. Dresden: Hannah-Arendt-Institut für Totalitarismusforschung, 1996.

Elias, Norbert. *The Court Society.* Oxford: Basil Blackwell, 1983 (1969).

Gieseke, Jens. *Die hauptamtlichen Mitarbeiter der Staatssicherheit. Personalstruktur und Lebenswelt 1950–1989/90* [The full-time employees of the state security. Staff structure and milieu 1950–1989/90]. Berlin: Christoph Links Verlag, 2000.

Goffman, Erving. *Interaction Ritual: Essays on Face-to-Face Behavior.* New York: Pantheon Books, 1982.

Jessen, Ralph. "Diktatorische Herrschaft als kommunikative Praxis. Überlegungen zum Zusammenhang von 'Bürokratie' und Sprachnormierung in der DDR-Geschichte" [Dictatorial rule as communicative practice. Reflections on the context of "bureaucracy" and discursive norms in GDR history], in *Akten. Eingaben. Schaufenster. Die DDR und ihre Texte* [Archives, Petitions and Shopwindows: The GDR and its Texts], ed. Alf Lüdtke and Peter Becker, 57–75. Berlin: Akademie Verlag, 1997.

Kurzweg, Christian, and Oliver Werner. "SED und Staatsapparat im Bezirk: Der Konflikt um den Rat des Bezirkes Leipzig 1958/1959" [The SED and the apparatus of state in districts: The conflict around the district council of Leipzig 1958/1959], in *Länder, Gaue und Bezirke* [Regions, gaue and districts], ed. Michael Richter, Thomas Schaarschmidt, and Mike Schmeitzner, 255–276. Dresden: Mitteldeutscher Verlag, 2007.

Lindenberger, Thomas. *Volkspolizei. Herrschaftspraxis und öffentliche Ordnung im SED-Staat, 1952–1968* [The people's police. Practices of domination and public order in the SED state, 1952–1968]. Vienna: Böhlau, 2003.

Niemann, Mario. *Die Sekretäre der SED-Bezirksleitungen 1952–1989* [The SED district secretaries, 1952–1989]. Paderborn: Ferdinand Schöningh Verlag, 2007.

Scherzer, Landolf. *Der Erste. Eine Reportage aus der DDR* [The boss. A report from the GDR]. Cologne: Kiepenheuer & Witsch, 1988.

Weber, Hermann. Die DDR 1945–1990. Grundriss der Geschichte [The GDR: A historical outline 1945–1990]. Hannover: Fackelträger, 1991.

Welsh, Helga. "Die kommunistischen Eliten als Gegenstand der Forschung" [Communist elites as subject of research], in *Gesellschaft ohne Eliten? Führungsgruppen in der DDR* [Society without elites? Leadership groups in the GDR], ed. Arnd Bauerkämper, Jürgen Danyel, Peter Hübner, and Sabine Ross. Berlin: Metropol-Verlag, 1997.

———. "Zwischen Macht und Ohnmacht: Zur Rolle der 1. Bezirkssekretäre der SED" [Between power and powerlessness: About the role of the first secretaries of the districts in the GDR], in *Sozialistische Eliten: Horizontale und vertikale Differenzierugsmuster in der DDR* [Socialist elites: Horizontal and vertical differentiation in the GDR], ed. Stefan Hornbostel, 105–123. Opladen: Leske und Budrich, 1999.

11

THE IDEA OF SOCIAL UNITY AND ITS INFLUENCE ON THE MECHANISMS OF A TOTALITARIAN REGIME IN THE YEARS 1956–1980

Krzysztof Dąbek

This chapter emerged out of my research on the authorities of the People's Republic of Poland (PRL).[1] The main idea of this research is to explain the social mechanisms of these authorities in the period of liberalization and the reduction of the ideological offensive (1956–1980). It also aims to show the mentality of the Polish United Workers' Party (*Polska Zjednoczona Partia Robotnicza*, or PZPR) authorities and the reality of the authorities through specific examples of their activities. The latter aim requires referring to empirical material. I obtained this material by recording interviews with former members of the authorities.

All the interviews were recorded by the author. I talked with thirty-two former members of the apparatus of the PZPR. The interviews lasted between two and three hours, and I talked with some interviewees on more than one occasion. The interviewees were PZPR apparatus employees and represented all departments and all levels of the hierarchy. I spoke with seven former secretaries of the Central Committee of the PZPR (one of them was the first secretary), as well as with former secretaries of provinces and districts. During their careers, many of them also worked in public administration or other important governmental institutions (there were among them a prime minister, a deputy prime minister, and five ministers). The interviews were not standardized and consisted of free conversations concerning the interviewees' activity in the authorities of the PRL. All interviewees were assured anonymity in advance of the interviews, and are identified in this chapter only by a number.

The interviews were recorded in 1999 to 2001. It was a perfect time for interviews because the left wing, which descended from the PZPR, was strong and popular, which made my interviewees feel confident and willing to talk about their experiences in government. In my work, I assumed that after the collapse of the old system it would be easier for them to talk about their experiences. They were outside the former organization and no longer active, so it could be satisfying for them to speak about old times when they had been very important and influential. As they wanted to be understood by modern, ordinary people, they used terms from the capitalist society, such as "groups of interests," "lobbies," etc. As a consequence, they revealed the mechanisms of life in the former apparatus that could not be exposed in any other way because the public documents of the party rarely gave information about such a phenomenon as a conflict in the authorities of the People's Republic of Poland.

I analyzed the totalitarian authorities, referring interviewees' statements to numerous sociological, historical, and political studies on totalitarianism. Among them, I should emphasize Andrzej Walicki's analysis of Marxist ideology—*Marksizm i skok do królestwa wolności* (Marxism and the leap to the kingdom of freedom),[2] from which I derived his main idea that the totalitarian regime rose from a Marxist utopia and its main principle of "social unity"—a society without any conflict.[3] According to Walicki, a distinctive feature of a totalitarian regime is the high intensity of ideological propaganda, and, therefore, in his opinion, resignation from the ideological crusade that took place after October 1956 meant a process of detotalitarization of the regime. Thus, according to Walicki, the PRL in the Gomułka period was a post-totalitarian, authoritarian state.

Hanna Świda-Ziemba disagrees with this conclusion.[4] According to Świda-Ziemba, although the authorities, after the upheaval that took place in October 1956, reduced terror and indoctrination, the Polish party and state system still maintained many features of a totalitarian system.

In this chapter, I have assumed Andrzej Walicki's ideas on the close relationship between communist totalitarianism with Marxist ideology and the essential idea of the unity of socialist society. However, analyzing the speech of the former officers of the party apparatus, I came to the same conclusion as Hanna Świda-Ziemba: although the breakthrough of October 1956 brought a restriction of terror and ideological indoctrination, the system of government retained many totalitarian features.

First, after October 1956, the idea of unity was still in force, though it was limited to the public sphere of life. There was still censorship, and the authorities controlled all public life and made every effort to maintain an appearance that they and Polish society were united and respected principles of the ideology. Since the reality of the Polish Peoples' Republic was far different from this project, there were constant attempts to disguise it through careful control of the public sphere of social life and the adoption of public ritual activities, which Świda-Ziemba identified as theater (*teatrum*): the world of rituals included sham elections, demonstrations-of-support assemblies, mass community work, 1 May parades, the display of appropriate slogans; it was an unrealistic world of "verbal reality" created by propaganda and expressed in a special language that came to be called "newspeak."[5] This world of rituals existed even though everyone knew election results were fixed, for example, and members of parliament were appointed to posts by the party authorities according to the *nomenklatura*. Nevertheless, my interviewees emphasized that the authorities were particular about the elections. During such "elections," the main concern of functionaries focused on preventing any objections that could shatter the picture of "unity." Therefore, it was hard work to organize such elections:

> In 1965 there were the next elections, so I took part. I had two regions to penetrate—Kędzierzyn and Racibórz. I went to Kędzierzyn and Racibórz several times and there I conducted different conversations with various people. I did not reveal that I was looking for a candidate to become a member of parliament. I wanted to figure out who deserved to be elected on the grounds of his general competence, and bonds with the community in which he acted. And first of all, I talked with secretaries, and members of the executive in the committee.... When I had prepared the list, I came back to the authorities of the *Voivodship* (regional) committee and there were more consultations. There were such meetings in Kędzierzyn, within the company.... Somebody proposed a candidate at the meeting, because they were known, and the proposal was accepted. And this is how they became an official candidate. It involved a lot of work. ... I was scared that if he was proposed at the meeting that there could be objections—well, there weren't any. (Interviewee no. 11)

A similar situation took place when there were significant shifts in the composition at the headquarters. Then there was a strange, irrational ritual. Piotr Osęka mentioned such elements of this ritual:[6] the principle was that the first secretary who was leaving had to accept his own dismissal. Another principle was that if he wanted to go of his own free will, some members of the politburo would try to persuade him not to. I would add one more: that after an upheaval took place, the composition of the politburo could not be instantly completely changed: "From Gomułka's headquarters, Loga-Sowiński, Jędrychowski, Kociołek, and Moczar still remained until March. The others were dismissed immediately. Those who stayed had already ... lost. They were aware that the dismissals were staggered in time so as not to dismiss the whole office. Because if these four had gone away, it would have meant it was changed 100 percent. So, a formula was created so that five members of the bureau went away, but others remained. It was known in advance that after a few months the rest of Gomułka's staff at the headquarters would be dismissed" (Interviewee no. 29). The ritual appears to be irrational, but if we take into consideration the principle of maintaining unity, or rather keeping up the appearance of unity, as the main principle of behavior in the regime, then the rituals, especially the principle of a slow exchange of members at the headquarters, seems quite reasonable. It enabled hiding and softening the quarrels about personnel matters and keeping up the appearance of unity.

However, after October 1956, the obligation of maintaining "unity" was limited to the public sphere, and people who were active in this sphere. The authorities could not, without the use of terror, force ordinary people (who did not occupy any important positions) to hold ideologically correct attitudes. An ordinary nonparty member or even an ordinary party member could enjoy freedom of speech and safely participate in religious rituals in their private life. The situation of members of the apparatus was different. They were obliged to present ideologically correct attitudes, so, for example, they could not go to church: "The majority of party members believed in God. I will tell you, the requirements were such that party employees could not go to church, for sure. Nor could members of the executive. But members of the district committees were affected by this to a lesser extent. To a lesser extent for sure. In fact, sometimes there were situations in which communal party conferences were held mostly on Sundays, after mass" (Interviewee no. 3). A higher position in the hierarchy meant the necessity to conform to the formal principles that defined the ideologically correct attitude, and also a greater involvement in—to use Erving Goffman's term[7]—the secondary adjustments of the apparatus,[8] namely being a member of one of the party groups and having an influential patron:

> If you held an unimportant post, then you just belonged to one or another secretary of the communal committee's faction. But generally these choices were not important. Then, one was calmly promoted, sometimes one was transferred to the economic apparatus, and back . . . . One's whole life passed quietly as in the case of a professional officer in a garrison. But, if one came into a higher position . . . such as a secretary, no, I think that a head of a department in a provincial committee, then it was a post at which one had to align themself. . . . And of course, a secretary of a provincial committee had to be someone's client. (Interviewee no. 12)

The obligation to present ideological unity could not exclude the divisions inside the apparatus, but it made them informal. The informal groups and their rivalry were camouflaged: "They camouflaged [factions], but it was inevitable. Because it was the apparatus, so there was the issue of being more important and the issue of promotions. . . . And it was natural that what you might call coteries had to be created. They were groups of people that worked together in close cooperation. They did not always trust each other, but they always worked together in close cooperation in order to prevent domination by some other groups" (Interviewee no. 6).

It was paradoxical then that functionaries had to present a unity of opinions, because they were members of informal cliques and they competed against each other. Functionaries were at risk of being excluded from the apparatus if they stood out with their opinions and behavior, or strayed from the party line. That is why the party groups had to avoid distinguishing themselves with a peculiar program. I spoke with only one functionary who openly declared that he was connected to a faction that had a different program. It was a group of orthodox communists whose leader was Kazimierz Mijal. This group was not influential, and it was later dismantled (at the end of the 1950s). I spoke with a few functionaries who were considered to be connected with Franciszek Szlachcic; this group was known to be a nationalist one. However, none of them admitted to this connection.

It is not easy to define either the program or the composition of the party groups, although functionaries knew it, because they were united by common interests and friendships (which were changeable). The party groups were formed on the basis of the functionaries' social background. Interviewees usually mentioned groups of people who came from the same regions, or groups based on a common interest such as hunting. They also emphasized that there was still a division between functionaries who came from PPR (Polska Partia Robotnicza, or Polish Workers' Party) and those from PPS (Polska Partia Socjalistyczna, or Polish Socialist Party), but the most important factor was their membership in youth organizations: "First of all, the cliques lasted and intrigues among the cliques were enormous, for example between the ZMW [Związek Młodzieży Wiejskiej—Polish rural youth association] 'Wici'[9] and the ZSP [Związek Studentów Polskich—Polish students' association]. On the one hand, there was Barcikowski and Tejchma, and on the other, Olszowski. And they fought each other. Babiuch didn't belong to either, because he had never studied at university, and he had not been active anywhere beyond the ZMP [Związek Młodzieży Polskiej—Union of Polish youth].[10] No, Babiuch was active in the ZWM"[11] (Interviewee no. 10). The idea of "unity" did not eliminate the divisions of the apparatus, but it made them clandestine and impossible to distinguish through a particular program. It also created peculiar methods of behavior in the apparatus, which could be hidden behind a closed door.

Thus social life was split into two spheres—the public sphere, in which ordinary citizens and outside observers presented an official image of a unified society, and an unofficial sphere, which hid the decision-making processes and any accompanying conflicts. Of course, this official public unity could only exist because the mechanisms behind the authorities' decisions were hidden and carefully prepared, and finished "creations" of the authorities' work were presented in the public forum.

Political rivalry within the apparatus could not be made public, so it could therefore not be democratic; it had to be hidden, so it took on secret forms. Functionaries could not speak freely and express their opinions in public. The PZPR conferences had to present "unity," in spite of the fact that they revealed a lot of information to the functionaries who knew and understood their symbolic language: "The floor was given according to territory and trade: a builder from Warsaw, a farmer from Mysiadło, in this way! . . . there were only small differences that showed the authorities what was going on. And it was enough, because everyone was vigilant about it. And it showed whether the plenary session was successful or not. And, if it was rebellious . . . somebody from outside would not catch that it was rebellious, but it was known—we knew. So, on the one hand it was directed, but on the other hand, it provided real information. It was a phenomenon of communication techniques" (Interviewee no. 12).

This chapter does not enable me to present the special character of communication within the PZPR, but it can be said that such an oblique way of conveying information was common: "Then, Gierek behaved a little, so to speak, strangely toward me, in the presence of some of the first secretaries of provincial committees. It was in Poznan at the central inauguration. He decided that I could not sit in the Presidium. It was a signal, evidently. . . . Someone went to the Presidium, it doesn't matter. . . . But I lost the ability to act effectively with the first secretaries of provincial committees because such a thing spread all around the country immediately. But Gierek was such a man. And when I went back to Warsaw, I started to pack up my things at the Central Committee" (Interviewee no. 19). The aforementioned signal was clear. It meant that the post would be lost, but there were also signs that were more difficult to recognize. Functionaries had to formulate a specific type of ability to observe the "messages" from the higher levels of authority and to properly "position" themselves toward changes therein: "The trick was to maneuver within all these compositional changes. Gomułka, Gierek, it is not known who. Holy shit! In order not to get into trouble, one had to observe watchfully; three-quarters of my energy was spent on observation, like a weathercock. What was going on at the top. How to connect with someone. And in difficult situations, to hide. The best thing was to fall ill, or to go to Bulgaria on holiday" (Interviewee no. 8). A lot of orders from high-ranking officials were expressed in this way, especially, if they were targeted against rivals. For example, the expectations of an official could be suggested by a symbolic gesture: "This is a good example. There is an order: write about youth participation in pilgrimages to Częstochowa and a wink—you should show that they do participate. . . Then Szydlak wanted to show that there was a strong clerical influence in Szlachcic's sector" (Interviewee no. 12). Through acting informally, an official could remove an employee who was not his direct subordinate and could thereby avoid conflicts with other officials: "In conversation with the first secretary of the provincial committee: 'You should think about removing the director of the department and send him to a different post; a good boy, but he is unfit in my opinion. Do you agree?' 'Yes.' And it was done this way" (Interviewee no. 12).

This resulted in a dispersal of responsibility. In the case of many activities and decisions, it is difficult to find out who was responsible. It is difficult to say whether the secretary suggested some activities informally, or if the subordinates showed their own initiative, and the secretary just turned a blind eye to these activities: "The police didn't do it for pleasure. The order was given by a minister or it came from the Central Committee. Did Gierek give the order himself? I would not tell you, I am not sure. If he had banned it, then they wouldn't have done it. I could not say that he ordered it. I could say he turned a blind eye" (Interviewee no. 28).

This way of working made the formal division of competences unimportant. Decisions were made as a result of informal influences. Thus, in such an organization, the rivalry was based on denunciation, manipulation of information, and intrigue. According to one of my interviewees, "It could be said that no holds were barred, especially such as dragging somebody through the mud. I am sorry, but it is the best expression—to drag somebody through the mud in front of the first secretary and 'big brother' [the USSR]" (Interviewee no. 12). This kind of action was not taken by individuals, but by informal groups—cliques that aimed to gain power: "The old communists were going to Gierek telling him that I was an old revisionist. The truth is that the Warsaw committee, Kania, influenced Gierek to dismiss me from the Central Committee. And so I was transferred to the central statistical office (GUS), and I was transferred and I was really satisfied" (Interviewee no. 17).

Everything could be a matter of denunciation, but there were three main popular issues used in a political fight: first, everything connected with the church and religion; second, everything connected with the activities of the opposition; and third, simple business scandals. These affairs were used as instruments in the political game, so it did not matter if the accusations were true or false. The members of an informal group put the blame on their opponents, for example, for being in favor with the church, or being involved in an economic scandal, but at the same time, they turned a blind eye to similar offenses if they came from their political allies. For example, according to the ideology, a party employee could not participate in religious rituals. Nevertheless, many of my interviewees emphasized that they defended people who participated in religious rituals: "Then, anonymous letters were written. I knew such a case concerning religious beliefs. The father of a secretary of a district committee died. There was a funeral with a priest. He attended the funeral. And they wanted to remove him from the party. The commission of party control came to investigate . . . I remember what I said: 'I would remove him from the party if he had not gone to his father's funeral'" (Interviewee no. 7).

However, functionaries very often hid their participation in religious rituals. On the one hand, a functionary lived in a normal society, and there were different norms from those proclaimed by the official ideology, and on the other hand, he had to hide his own religiousness if he wanted to keep his position in the party, and because of that many functionaries led a double life: "Leading a double life was very common in this case. They hid that their children had been baptized. The children were taken away, they got baptized, took communion somewhere else, to hide it. Because people lived in such a society. And one should respect its opinion, but there were different requirements from the party authorities" (Interviewee no. 28).

Functionaries took a similar attitude if they encountered the activities of the opposition. For a functionary it meant a lot of problems: "If one had [responsibility for] higher education and the school system at the same time, then it took more time to deal with a politically incorrect poster made by a group of students than with the collapse of a program to transport children to school. Several people worked on the program to transport children to school for half an hour, but dozens of people dealt with this poster for several days, because it was demanded by a superior authority. . . . There were such isolated cases, which, because of political perception, drew away from systemic issues, and the party became the ideological police" (Interviewee no. 12).

According to the interviewees, a functionary had to struggle against opposition, because if they did not they could be attacked by their rivals. They could accuse him of dawdling in preventing counter-activity:

> Karkoszka didn't want people to think that he had a mess in his area, because the Central Committee, people from the politburo, put pressure on him.... The person who was in charge of higher education was afraid of being bitten to death by his rivals, who proved him to be weak, and he could not prevent political counteractivities. Now, some professor wrote a text... and of course his colleague found this text. He showed that it was antisocialist and he sent information about this to every level of the apparatus, to everyone he could, and then the Professor Janion[12] affair burst out, because she wrote or said something, somewhere. So, it could be possible not to care about it [what Janion had said, and what would happen if the authorities found out about it] completely, but then one took a risk and they would say that he had a mess in his area, and that he was inefficient. (Interviewee no. 12)

The hidden competitiveness within the apparatus was also a factor that preserved the ideological principles of the system. Although officials did not believe in the ideology, they had to struggle against the opposition to support socialism. If an official did not, he would be dismissed. So, despite the fact that most of the activists did not believe in the ideology, they had to behave as if they did. However, because they did not really believe in the ideology, their fighting with the opposition and the church was in fact just a matter of keeping up the appearance that they did, though it did mean that sometimes officials did have to oppress the opposition or the church:

> Somebody in the institute of meteorology and hydrology got involved in the opposition and I even demanded myself that the first secretary of this institute dismiss him. But when there were no colleagues around, I told him that in my opinion it would be enough if we didn't hear about this person for a while. Or there were academics that were involved in DiP [a debating society][13] or *Latające Uniwersytet* [an underground education movement][14] or they signed a letter (to the authorities). And now what could we do? Fire him? Well, it could be a problem to fire him, but he could be transferred from one position to another, from one room to another, to make him invisible to the authorities. Interviewee no. 12)

The same could be said about their attitude toward corruption—that is, taking advantage of one's position for private purposes, simple bribery, etc. Certainly, they condemned corruption, but a post in the apparatus provided many unofficial privileges. Most of the interviewees did not like talking about it, but some of them were more sincere, like a former minister who said, "I could do everything unofficially. I could phone every factory which produced something I liked and ask if could buy something from them. And then I paid normally, or I paid with a discount" (Interviewee no. 12). According to my interviewees, it was no big deal, but in the situation where there was a permanent lack of supply of day-to-day products, it was important that a functionary had a lot of colleagues, and that they could help him. However, such relationships could involve a functionary in corruption: "Once I was forced to ask my colleague from a provincial committee for a favor. There were no tourist gas canisters anywhere. I called my colleague and I said: 'Listen to me. Phone one of your sports shops so that they will keep a gas canister for me, because I can't get one anywhere.' 'Okay, old fellow, Roger, I'll deal with it.' After two days he phoned and said, 'Come and get it.' I went and I asked: 'How much do I owe you?' He answered, 'Don't talk rubbish!' I said, 'Don't you talk rubbish!' Of course, I paid" (Interviewee no. 19). However, even if a functionary handled his day-to-day affairs in the usual way, he had to hide it. And he had to fix such things through his trusted friends: "However, frankly speaking, at least in Maków, I did not encounter such a situation where someone would bring me ham [a very marketable product in PRL] To be honest, if I wanted to buy something, I would rather go to Warsaw. There I had such relations that I called Warsaw and I preferred buying something in Warsaw than keeping up appearances there. And I can tell you, I queued, really!" (Interviewee no. 3).

Thus, in the period of stabilization, the strategy of members of the apparatus first consisted of keeping numerous offenses secret. It led to a phenomenon that Adam Podgórecki named a "dirty community" — that is, team loyalty resulting from knowledge about reciprocal offenses and the possibility of blackmail.[15] The principle of the party's unity led to splitting party life into two spheres: official and unofficial. Unofficially, in private relationships, functionaries could speak more openly than at official party meetings: "In private, one could speak very openly. And I'll tell you more, the difference between what the active members said in public and what they said in private was increasing. It meant that they were very critical, but in public it wasn't manifested because they were subordinate to the headquarters. So to speak, criticism stopped at the doors of private flats" (Interviewee no. 16). A functionary could talk openly only with some trusted colleagues:

> There were people that I trusted and I could speak candidly with them, and there were people that I had limited trust in. But it concerned everyone. The lack of mutual trust was one of the features, especially because there was a courtly atmosphere in the Central Committee. I remember one of the conferences of the interparliamentary union. It was in the 1970s. I went to one of the deputy foreign ministers. I won't tell you his name. And I said that I would like to talk a little bit because MSZ [the Ministry of Foreign Affairs] coordinated foreign policy, or maybe I said, controlled foreign policy. He said, "Comrade, foreign policy is controlled

by the Central Committee of the PZPR." So, he was kidding me! I knew who controlled this state, but the Ministry of Foreign Affairs directly conducted foreign policy. But I am sure he was afraid because I was a Central Committee employee and he thought I wanted to egg him on to say that he controlled the policy. Then I laughed. I said, "All right, all right, I know what the leading role of the party is," but I wanted to talk about specific matters. (Interviewee no. 19).

Every functionary had some friends that he or she trusted. Friendships were very important for functionaries; of course, they enabled the satisfaction of social needs, but above all they were necessary if you wanted to be promoted: "Rakowski called me to talk to him. Rakowski was the deputy prime minister and he was responsible for the superstructure, as it was called. He wanted me to go to Tejchma as an undersecretary to deal with the association of writers and the union of authors, because I had good contacts. And Rakowski applied to Jaruzelski, who was the prime minister, to make me an undersecretary at Tejchma's. So to speak, we—Rakowski, Tejchma, and me—drank a half liter of vodka at my home. And we waited for the confirmation of the prime minister" (Interviewee no. 10).

In the system in which there was an obligation to present ideological unity, a promotion could not be based on universal criteria of qualifications because it could lead to open competition and conflicts. The mechanism in a socialist society had to be hidden, and it was based on informal connections. Acquaintances and contacts that would be important for future careers had already been made at the level of youth organizations. Sometimes, the career of a young functionary started when he was noticed by an influential member of the authorities: *"He was at a meeting of the rural youth association, he listened to my speech and the speeches of activists of the rural youth association . . . and as I said, he liked my pragmatic attitude at that time . . . I caught his eye, and simply I was one of the candidates for the members of the Central Committee before some convention of the party, and I was elected, and next I became the director of the department of agriculture of the Central Committee" (Interviewee no. 28).* A lot of functionaries who made a career in the authorities had such a mentor. Later they promoted colleagues from youth organizations: "I myself took three or four people with me from the rural youth association [ZMW]. You could say 'my people'; that's what it is called now. There was always such an element that if you knew someone, you appreciated him, then you took him" (Interviewee no. 28).

Then, as the Polish sociologist Jacek Tarkowski explains, "the patron-client relationships" were defined by a relatively constant exchange of goods and favors between two individuals who held different positions in the social structure.[16] Tarkowski notes that relations of this kind were very often fostered within the state and party hierarchy, but he also stresses that the deal between the patron and the client was informal. According to my interviewees, their attitude to this principal very often became one of a very informal character. Certainly, such friendly relationships could be of different kinds—they could be less or more durable, less or more formal, and there was a greater or smaller age gap between functionaries: "The relation to Motyka was like between father and son. We were treated by him in that way. It was different in the case of Klasa, it was more like a friendship, but it also involved some much more intensive informal contacts than in the case of Lucjan Motyka" (Interviewee no. 14). For its participants, a relationship brought mutual benefits, which were different for the patron and his protégé, his client. The patron gained a loyal subordinate. According to the interviewees, it was very important: "One always needed to rely on somebody. If you inherited a set of old office workers, you didn't know which of them would be loyal. For example, Karkoszka inherited one lady secretary who was clearly more loyal to Kępa and Łukaszewicz than to him . . . . So, I suppose that I was taken to cover her, that I was a counterbalance to her" (Interviewee no. 12).

What was also important was that the loyalty of a client came not only from gratitude, but also from dependency: "Yes, it meant my subordinates, they had to like me instantly. Anyway, I played old tricks— immediately I promoted two people. They had to support me for this promotion, especially because it was not to somebody's liking" (Interviewee no. 12). A client's position depended on the influence of his patron. Sometimes, in case of an influential activist's demotion, there were mass demotions of his people or people who were considered to be his: "Well, as there was a cleaning after Szlachcic in the CC [Central Committee] and in the provincial committees—it was even said that it was a hunt for Franciscans because he was Franciszek (Francis) Szlachcic—then I saw how deeply it went. Even second-rate office workers from the provincial committees were dismissed because they were in his faction. Anyway, it was a bit of a nationalist-type faction, so they stood out, and they were easy to recognize" (Interviewee no. 12).

In addition, this mechanism of promotion let patrons strengthen friendships with other officials through the appointment of their protégés: "Because I came to him [Szlachcic] as if it was on his initiative on a proposal from Klasa. Because he [Szlachcic] asked Klasa: 'Do you have someone like that for a deputy?' And he answered: 'I have, but what can I give you?' he said, 'He has just started working for me.' But then they made a deal. So, as a result of this agreement, I came. As I said, I saw him for the first time when he offered me a post. But I have to say that he was absolutely fair to me afterwards." (Interviewee no. 2)

On the other hand, a loyal client was also first in line for promotion. What is more, he could gain easy access to the patron, and sometimes he could also decide who else should be permitted access to him; thus he could shape his patron's opinions and decisions. He also gained access to other members of authorities and information, and he could build his political background: "They tried to act in a normal way, but they took every opportunity to gain support. Of course, they also came to me, and then I went to the first [secretary]. Sometimes I organized a meeting for them with the first [secretary] or a meeting with someone from the Central Committee" (Interviewee no. 12). However, first of all, the client gained an influential mentor, who defended him: "So, for example my deal with Karkoszka, it was known that if there was someone who would want to kick me, and there were many such people, then I had a powerful mentor behind the bush, who showed his head and yelled not to touch me" (Interviewee no. 12).

Patrons defended their clients not only because they sympathized with them, but also because it was very important for the apparatus's employees not to allow others to fire their close associates. If the statement of my interviewee is to be believed, it sometimes led to unexpected consequences: "There were orders from the Central Committee via the Warsaw committee that Onyszkiewicz . . . had to be fired from University. Rybicki[17] could run the matter in such a way, play tricks, [so] that nobody was dismissed. Why? . . . If someone accepted that his close associates were dismissed, he would be dismissed soon, too" (Interviewee no. 12).

The statements made by interviewees show that cooperation between the PZPR first secretaries and a provincial governor very often became "patron-client relationships." Thanks to his power, the first secretary of a province committee could be a patron and defend an employee of the local administration. Such protection was needed especially if the local authorities carried out unplanned investments:

> The overpass was built by us in secret, I did it with Pękala.[18] We did it quietly, off the government, . . . against the prime minister's decision. I can tell you more because it is interesting. I went on holiday, and Pękala finished this overpass and there was an opening ceremony. Jaroszewicz called me. "Comrade, it is anarchy, there was a ban, you mock it, and you aren't cutting the ribbon." The minister came. He didn't tick off the minister who cut the ribbon. However, he knew where the power was, who did it. I said, "Comrade prime minister, there is the overpass so that one can drive to Kraków faster. So, there is little to worry about." Here, the prime minister wanted to dismiss Drapich[19] immediately. I had to phone Babiuch and ask him not to dismiss Drapich. (Interviewee no. 10)

In the configuration, every official had his own relationships in order to get someone's support. Therefore, it was very difficult to replace someone in an important post, and that is why the apparatus tended to increase in size. When an official wanted to promote their protégé, but he could not fire the protégés of other dignitaries, they could find a solution to the problem by creating a new post (of course, it had its costs.) Therefore, a real exchange of members of authorities could only be possible during violent periods of political and economic crises.

Another field of my research was my interviewees' activity in the economy. This was a very important sphere of officials' activity after October 1956, when there was a reduction in ideological offensives and terror, and when the authorities felt that they had lost their ideological legitimization. It therefore became very important for them to satisfy the needs of ordinary people and the interests of their own members. Although it was costly, it allowed them to buy peace throughout society as well as support from party activists.

According to the ideology, socialist society was to be completely rational and work smoothly like a supercomputer. The ideological project was based on the assumption that the center could control all of the economy and play the role of the great redistributor, one that distributes goods with consideration to the good of society as a whole. This could be possible because according to the doctrine in socialism, thanks to social (public) ownership over the means of production, citizens had noncontradictory interests; a given citizen had the same interests as other citizens, and they were also the same as the interests of the whole country. Of course, the reality was totally different. Party members were not unanimous, and the interest of society as a whole was not easy to recognize. First, there was no free market and therefore no market parameters to estimate the efficiency of economic activities. Second, functionaries occupied different positions in the authorities, and even if we presupposed their good intentions, they had a different standpoint on the good of society.

Certainly, there was the central plan, and the central authorities controlled the realization of that plan. However, according to my interviewees, the secretary of the local or branch organization had some room to maneuver in his activity. The role of the party secretary was not exactly defined, and therefore it depended on his personal will about what he would be interested in first. One of the province secretaries was interested in the development of a road system: "He had a passion, or he paid particular attention to traffic and roads. And really, he did a lot for the roads in the province and Kraków city" (Interviewee no. 27). Another functionary was interested in supporting makers of culture in society: "The artists and scholars had a terrible view of the provincial committee as people who were against culture, ignoramuses, etc. So, I tried to improve the image of the party in these spheres. But it couldn't be repaired artificially; it was necessary to make concessions, it was necessary not to support party members as rectors, it was necessary to allow the 'Teatr Stary' [theater] to show plays that Warsaw didn't like. Here, I had my good friend, Kraśko, who was responsible for culture in the Central Committee" (Interviewee no. 10). A functionary could become interested in every matter in the area of his work. One of my interviewees noticed that it was a weakness:

> There were satirical situations sometimes. Such a subject was . . . we exported a lot of vodka then . . . . But they complained about . . . the bottle, that it didn't unscrew. One could cut themselves while unscrewing it because it was necessary to use a knife. . . . So, I took this single case. I spoke with the minister. I told him about this matter. He said it was not so simple, but I researched the matter. So, in time I received a few-page report, about why this screw cap was as it was and why it couldn't be changed. But I said, "Listen, I won't accept this explanation. Think about it. Buy metal sheeting if it is the problem." In some time screw caps appeared, I looked at them—they were excellent. . . . We did not import metal sheet, but the whole screw caps. So, we had problems with such details. And generally, I have to say that the central authorities took care of too many details. It was a sore point in this structure of authorities. (Interviewee no. 16)

The idea of "social unity" did not eliminate the competition for goods in a socialist society; beneath the official unity of the party, there was hidden competition for limited goods. The competition for goods connected with the competition for power; a member of the authorities who gained the most goods could also show their power. Certainly, the first secretary of the PZPR had the main impact on the distribution of goods. He decided on the location of the major investments: "Well, over at *Huta Katowice* [ironworks], there was a lot of controversy. But, of course, Gierek looked after what was going on with the modernization of Silesia because his origins and his political power came from there" (Interviewee no. 29). He also satisfied the needs of people from his party base: "But, of course, when one carried out big investments, then one also had cash, then one had car coupons, flats, high salaries, bonuses, and so on" (Interviewee no. 10).

Low-ranking functionaries were less influential, but according to my interviewees, a regional secretaries of the party could manage to do a lot for their region if they only made an effort: "Sir, if a secretary of the party was enterprising, meaning he had connections, acquaintances, colleagues, friends—he was in good relationship with the headquarters—then he could gain extra resources for investment in the province. Because there were always reserves" (Interviewee no. 24).

The superior authorities settled struggles between the lower-level employees. Therefore, the conflicts transferred to the top of the party and state organization: "I remember when this 'Tin Box' [a factory] was built. There was a company in Kraków called Opakometr; they produced food cans. They built a factory in Brzesko. So of course I visited Cyrankiewicz; I took a chairman of the national council of the district with me. We secured his support and the 'Tin Box' was built. There was a kind of war. We went to Cyrankiewicz further on a suggestion by Motyka. We met a professor from AGH there who had come from the Bochnia district. We could not convince him in any way about our concept. The prime minister decided in the end" (Interviewee no. 1). In the centrally planned system, a given plant, industry, or region was only one element, which was not an independent entity, and its economic success did not depend on its activity:

> There was an incentive system for saving coal and coke, and the bonuses were quite significant. . . . So, people indeed made an effort to save coal and coke . . . . Especially workers at Huta Lenina (Lenin Ironworks) . . . saved a really significant quantity of coal and coke. So, they deserved a significant bonus. . . . And suddenly, it turned out that they wouldn't get it, because the whole metal industry had not saved energy resources, so there was no money. I said, "But, for the steel works of that ironworks it doesn't matter, because there were regulations." I went to the minister, he was a man from Kraków, so I had no problem to schedule an appointment—but he said, "I can't manage to do it—I mean, there is no money; the metal industry did not make a profit." I said, "But this ironworks did it and people are waiting for money." . . . I went to the Central Committee . . . . Anyway, the problem was not solved, the people were outraged, but it was a calm period, so they accepted it." (Interviewee no. 27)

In this system, the rational strategy for an economic organization and its employees did not consist of increasing efficiency, but in trying to make the superiors provide the desired goods and services, as well as social protection. Informal meetings with high-ranking officials were often used as an opportunity to influence the redistribution of wealth and goods. As the statements of the interviewees showed, all the spheres of entertaining officials were important:

> One needed to have colleagues in the budget committee. Connections. One had to invite W. here to show him, to invite him for dinner. The same, the minister of the chemical industry came from here—the former director of industrial works in Oświęcim. He liked Kraków. So if we wanted any investment . . . we asked O.—the minister of chemistry. We entertained him. He drank and ate here for two or three days and

the problem was solved. We didn't manage it in a democratic way. We managed it through connections. It was like that everywhere. So, if I went to Warsaw, I didn't go to department directors of the Central Committee, never. But I only went to the secretary of the Central Committee or to the minister, to corrupt them a little bit. I invited them to Kraków, I gave them some souvenirs from Kraków, and it was done. Or the head of the office of the council of ministers, he was a person, if you were good to him, you could do anything and you could hide it from the prime minister. He was a very important person from the PPS. (Interviewee no. 10)

Decisions on the development of the whole region or a state-owned enterprise were very often made during hunting trips: "There were whole provinces in which hunting was the base of activity of the provincial committee of the party. The main important deals were done there" (Interviewee no. 7). Local-level officials of the apparatus tried to gain important goods for their regions by offering decision-makers unofficial profits. My interviewees emphasized that it was usually a gift: "It was done in various ways, various official meetings, unofficial meetings, a glass of cognac, sometimes a large glass of cognac. Sometimes an allotment could be taken into account. Various things came into consideration if you wanted to get something for a district" (Interviewee no. 20). One of my interviewees, who was a minister, gave me this anecdote: "I remember when I became a minister, then after the sitting, I was surrounded by the first secretaries of the provincial committees, and they were asking what I liked doing. Maybe I liked hunting, because there was a good area for hunting in their province. Maybe I liked fishing. . . . So, I cracked a joke that I liked girls. They answered, 'Ok, it is possible.' So, there were informal influences and such corruption" (Interviewee no. 12).

These methods turned out to be very effective in gaining goods from the center of power. They led to the chaotic process of the outflow of goods from the center to the local and industry lobbies. The authorities very often had to change their economic plans as soon as they were confirmed. Thus, in fact, the result of the planned economy was in contradiction to its ideological assumptions; the socialist economy was not rational, and the obligatory "unity" of the party led only to the situation in which the process of distribution of goods was beyond any social control. Therefore, the authorities could only gain a short-term stabilization, which was limited by the weakness of the socialist economy.

Although it was always possible to create a new post, the quantity of goods in the socialist economy was limited. Competition within the socialist authorities did not lead to an increase in the pool of goods; it concerned only the distribution of goods, so it could only change the location of goods. Thus, the end of communism was caused by economic factors. All my interviewees agreed with this conclusion. They complained about the problems of the socialist economy. For example, one of my interlocutors, a former minister of economy, talked about one of the state-owned factories that had caused him a lot of problems: "There was a matter of building a cotton wool factory in the province of Bialystok in order to build a part of industry in undeveloped areas, and it was successful. . . . The efficiency was lower there than in Łódź, and there was a problem with personnel. For example, I remember girl workers who came from villages, and as they came to work there, they went away again quickly. They didn't want to work there. But when a regiment of tanks was stationed there, then the personnel [issue] was immediately stabilized. Such things took place sometimes" (Interviewee no. 17). This example above shows that in the period of the reduction of ideological offensive and terror, the authorities could not force ordinary people to increase efficiency. On the contrary, there was a process in the opposite direction. The center of power, which controlled all the distribution of goods, was under pressure from different interest groups.

I would like to finish by mentioning the development of the mentalities of functionaries. Generally speaking, the political competition in the apparatus impelled members of the apparatus to be more—to use David Riesman's term—"other-directed."[20] Thus, it could be concluded that the attitude of members of the apparatus changed. In the years 1956–1970, in the Gomułka period, most of the authorities' party members were "inner-directed"—they believed in communism, and it was in terms of their own inner gyroscope. That is why they very often did not care about the opinions of their companions, especially the opinions of less influential companions. In addition, according to my interviewees, they were sometimes rude toward their subordinates:

> [The] first time I met Gomułka in 1957, when I was the secretary of economy in Bydgoszcz . . . there was a big strike at the rail rolling stock repair workshops in Bydgoszcz. . . . Gomułka invited the delegation from the factory, and me, to come. We went there—twenty workers and me. Gomułka said that he would like to talk with me first. I went to him, but he was looking through a pile of papers. He asked, "So you are this son of a bitch from Bydgoszcz?" and he slammed [down] the pile of papers. I was a young boy, I didn't know what to do—to pick up the papers or to listen to him. But his personal secretary came and picked up the papers. He gave me a hard time for this strike, but he calmed down at last. And he said, "Now, tell me how it was," and I told him that I had discussed this issue with the minister on this matter three weeks ago, and that he had categorically refused to meet the demands of workers. Then,

he called the minister and the situation was repeated. So we went to these workers, he made a speech to them, he spoke for two hours; he liked to address people." (Interviewee no. 21)

Their successors in the Gierek period, in the years 1970–1980, were more polite and more sensitive to the party groups' needs. Although this also led to negative consequences: "Well, unfortunately, he [Gierek] wanted to be generous, and gave things to everybody. The last interlocutor was right, according to him. He gave things very easily and made promises. Then, there was a problem with realization, not everything was possible. But if it was carried out, it would be with harm to the economic equilibrium. Therefore, we over-invested at that time" (Interviewee no. 17).

Conclusion

To sum up, after October 1956, due to the reduction of terror and indoctrination, the authorities did not have the means to force ordinary people to adopt ideologically correct attitudes in their private lives. However, the situation for members of the apparatus was different; in public, the functionaries had to present a tight community of views and opinions. All divisions and rivalry in the authorities had to be hidden inside the informal sphere of party life. The authorities also maintained their centralized, hierarchical organization. In such an organization, a single institution, state-owned factory, or territorial organization lost their autonomy. The main decisions were made beyond them, by the higher-level authorities. It meant that decisions were very often made by informal centers of power. In addition, the competition for power and limited goods was also transmitted into the informal part of life, and the decisions were made by informal institutions in which people satisfied their needs. It meant that these processes progressed without any formal social control—without formal procedures. It led to the dispersal of responsibility and to the chaotic process of the outflow of goods from the center to local and industrial lobbies. In this situation, informal, cultural norms and patterns of action were very important. However, they were shaped by an ideological project, and they preferred to make secondary adjustments to the political system. These adjustments enabled communication, the exertion of influence, and struggles for positions and material goods, while keeping up the appearance of unity. Thus, the idea of "social unity" enforced artificial methods of behavior in all spheres of the activity of the authorities.

Krzysztof Dąbek is a freelance researcher and member of the Committee for the Defense of Democracy (KOD). His publications include *PZPR retrospektywny portret własny* (Warsaw, 2006), and "Debata nad totalitaryzmem. Sporu ciąg dalszy," *Przegląd Polityczny* 89 (2008): 136–142; he is also the author of various entries in the *Encyclopedia of Solidarity*, vol. 2 (2013).

Notes

1. Krzysztof Dąbek, *PZPR retrospektywny portret własny* [The PZPR in a retrospective self-portrait], with a preface by Marcin Kula, in the series W Krainie PRL: Ludzie, Sprawy, Problemy (Warsaw, 2006).
2. Andrzej Walicki, *Marksizm i skok do królestwa wolności. Dzieje komunistycznej utopii* [Marxism and the leap to the kingdom of freedom: The rise and fall of the communist utopia] (Warsaw, 1996).
3. A similar opinion was expressed by Ralf Dahrendorf, who claimed that totalitarianism was based on Marxism's attempt to eliminate class conflicts; cf. Ralf Dahrendorf, *Nowoczesny konflikt społeczny* [The modern social conflict] (Warsaw, 1993), 127.
4. Hanna Świda-Ziemba, *Człowiek wewnętrznie zniewolony: Mechanizmy i konsekwencje minio formacji—analiza psychologiczna* [Inherently enslaved men. Psycho-sociological problems of the past formation] (Warsaw, 1997).
5. Hanna Świda-Ziemba, *Młodzież PRL. Portret pokoleń w kontekście historii* [The youth of PRL. Portrait of a generation in historical context] (Kraków, 2010), 57; idem, "System totalitarny—kontrowersje intelektualistów polskich" [Totalitarian systems—The controversy between the Polish intellectualists], *Przegląd Polityczny* [Political review] 84: 83–97. The term "newspeak" was introduced by George Orwell in his book *Nineteen Eighty-Four*.
6. Piotr Osęka, "Nie wybierać na żywioł—model zmiany na stanowisku I sekretarza KC PZPR" [Keeping it under control: The model of change in the post of first secretary of the Polish United Workers Party], in *PRL—trwanie i zmiana* [PRL—Persistence and change], ed. Stola Dariusz and Marcin Zaremba (Warsaw, 2003).
7. Erving Goffman, "Charakterystyka instytucji totalnych" [The characteristics of total institutions], in *Współczesne teorie socjologiczne* [Modern sociological theories], vol. 1, ed. A. Jasińska-Kania, et al., (Warsaw, 2006), 316–335.
8. Hanna Świda-Ziemba, *Człowiek wewnętrznie zniewolony*, 66–80.
9. The youth movement in the countryside had many currents during the one hundred years of its history. The Rural Youth Association of the Republic of Poland's *Wici* was one of them. It was established in 1944. In 1948 it was included into the Union or Association of Polish Youth (ZMP), but after the disintegration of the ZMP it was reactivated as ZMW (Związek Młodzieży Wiejskiej—Polish Rural Youth Association).
10. The Związek Młodzieży Polskiej [Union of Polish Youth] was a Polish

youth organization that existed from 1948 to 1956. It was subordinated to the Polish Workers' Party (and later to the Polish United Workers' Party) and acted as a tool of political indoctrination.
11. The Związek Walki Młodych [Association of Fighting Youth] was a Polish communist youth organization founded in 1943. It was subordinated to the Polish Workers' Party. In 1948 it was included in the ZMP.
12. Maria Janion, born in 1926, was a Polish historian and professor of liberal arts. Her independent opinions increased authority among students and scholars, as well as the political opposition's involvement, and were a great problem to the government in the 1970s.
13. Doświadczenie i Przyszłość [Experience and future] was a debating society and an independent social research center founded by Stefan Bratkowski. The club integrated the Polish intelligentsia cooperating with the opposition. Its activity included the writing of reports on the situation in Polish society.
14. Latający Uniwersytet [Flying university] was the name of an underground educational institution that originated in the nineteenth century. The tradition of the Flying University was revived by Polish dissidents; from autumn 1977 they organized lectures in private homes.
15. Adam Podgórecki, *Społeczeństwo Polskie* [The Polish society] (Rzeszów, 1995), 92–94.
16. Jacek Tarkowski, *Socjologia świata polityki. Patroni i Klienci* [Sociology of the political world. Patrons and clients] (Warsaw,1994), vols. 1 & 2.
17. Zygmunt Rybicki was the rector of Warsaw University (1968–1980). He is known as the person responsible for persecutions after March 1968.
18. Jerzy Pękala was president of Kraków (1969–1978).
19. Wit Drapich was provincial governor of Kraków (1973–1975).
20. I refer to the terms "inner-directed" and "other-directed" used by David Riesman, Nathan Glazer and Reuel Denney in the book: *The Lonely Crowd: A Study of the Changing American Character,* to show the evolution of American character. In my opinion, these terms may be used in a different cultural context, to present an analogous attitude change.

Bibliography

Dąbek, Krzysztof. "Debata nad totalitaryzmem. Sporu ciąg dalszy" [Debate on totalitarianism. The continuation of the dispute]. *Przegląd Polityczny* [Political review] 89 (2008): 136–142.

———. *PZPR retrospektywny portret własny* [The PZPR in a retrospective self-portrait]. With a preface by Marcin Kula. Series W Krainie PRL: Ludzie, Sprawy, Problemy. Warsaw: Wydawnictwo Trio, 2006.

Dahrendorf, Ralf. *Nowoczesny konflikt społeczny* [The modern social conflict]. Warsaw: Czytelnik, 1993.

Goffman, Erving. "Charakterystyka instytucji totalnych" [The characteristics of total institutions]. In *Współczesne teorie socjologiczne* [Modern sociological theories], vol. 1, ed. Aleksandra Jasińska-Kania, Lech M. Nijakowski,

Jerzy Szacki, Marek Ziółkowski, 316–335. Warsaw: Wydawnictwo Naukowe Scholar, 2006.

Narojek, Winicjusz. *Jednostka wobec systemu. Trwanie i Zmiany* [The individual in the face of the system. The anthropology of persistence and change]. Warsaw: IFiS PAN, 1996.

Orwell, George. *Nineteen Eighty-Four*. London: Secker & Warburg, 1949.

Osęka, Piotr. "Nie wybierać na żywioł—model zmiany na stanowisku I sekretarz a KC PZPR" [Keeping it under control: The model of change in the post of first secretary of the Polish United Workers Party]. In *PRL—trwanie i zmiana* [PRL—Persistence and change], ed. Stola Dariusz and Marcin Zaremba, 19–37. Warsaw: Wydawnictwo Wyższej Szkoły Przedsiębiorczości i Zarządzania im. Leona Koźmińskiego, 2003.

Podgórecki, Adam. *Społeczeństwo Polskie* [The Polish society]. Rzeszów: Wydawnictwo Wyższej Szkoły Pedagogicznej, 1995.

Riesman, David, and Nathan Glazer. *The Lonely Crowd: A Study of the Changing American Character*. London: Yale University Press, 2001.

Świda-Ziemba, Hanna. *Człowiek wewnętrznie zniewolony: Mechanizmy i konsekwencje minio formacji—analiza psychologiczna* [Inherently enslaved men. Psycho-sociological problems of the past formation]. Warsaw: ISNS UW, 1997.

———. *Młodzież PRL. Portret pokoleń w kontekście historii* [The youth of PRL. Portrait of a generation in historical context]. Kraków: Wydawnictwo Ludowe, 2010.

———. "System totalitarny—kontrowersje intelektualistów polskich" [Totalitarian systems—The controversy between the Polish intellectualists]. *Przegląd Polityczny* [Political review] 84: 83–97.

Tarkowski, Jacek. *Patroni i Klienci. Socjologia świata polityki* [Patrons and clients. Sociology of the world of politics], vols. 1, 2. Warsaw: ISP PAN, 1994.

Walicki, Andrzej. *Marksizm i skok do królestwa wolności. Dzieje komunistycznej utopii* [Marxism and the leap to the kingdom of Freedom: The rise and fall of the communist utopia]. Warsaw: PWN, 1996.

12

FOREIGN POLICYMAKING AND PARTY-STATE RELATIONS IN THE SOVIET UNION DURING THE BREZHNEV ERA

Mark Kramer

This essay examines the foreign policymaking process in the USSR during the eighteen years that Leonid Brezhnev served as the highest leader of the Communist Party of the Soviet Union (CPSU), from October 1964 to November 1982. (The top post in the CPSU was known as the First Secretary from October 1952 until March–April 1966 but was otherwise known as the General Secretary.) Foreign policy in the USSR, as in other countries, was shaped not only by external pressures and events but also by domestic bureaucratic procedures, the interactions of policymakers, and high-level political maneuvering and infighting. The first section of the essay discusses the chief decision-making bodies and their role in foreign policymaking. The second section considers how high-level political maneuvering and rivalries affected foreign policy, and vice versa. The third section provides an overview of the state and party bureaucracies responsible for various aspects of foreign policy, including military affairs, intra-bloc relations, and foreign economic policy. The concluding section explores what this analysis of foreign policymaking tells us about the relationship between the CPSU and the Soviet state during the Brezhnev era.

The declassification of immense quantities of Soviet archival materials over the past twenty-five years, combined with the publication of a large number of important memoirs by former Soviet officials and diplomats, has provided enormously rich evidence for this essay. Until Soviet archival materials became available, scholars who tried to analyze Soviet foreign policymaking during the Brezhnev era had to rely predominantly on official Soviet newspapers and periodicals, along with a good deal of speculation and reading between the lines.[1] Often the work these scholars produced was perspicacious, but the dearth of reliable information at their disposal was a formidable barrier that led to many glaring inaccuracies and gaps.

The release of invaluable archival collections in Moscow since the early 1990s, particularly over the past few years (despite the increasingly dismal political situation in Russia under Vladimir Putin), has drastically changed the situation, enabling scholars to make use of vastly greater quantities of evidence than in the past—evidence that Soviet leaders had never intended to release. Although excellent studies of Soviet foreign policy under Joseph Stalin, Nikita Khrushchev, and Mikhail Gorbachev have appeared over the past twenty years, very little has been published about Brezhnev's foreign policy. The few items on this topic that have come out do not give any real sense of the dynamics of foreign policymaking during the Brezhnev era—the interactions among key decision-makers and the wide range of party and state organizations that dealt with foreign policy and military affairs on a day-to-day basis and during crises.[2] The analysis here is intended to fill in this lacuna by drawing on newly available primary sources (archival documents and memoirs) that reveal how Soviet foreign policy was made during the Brezhnev era.

Decision-Making Structures

Throughout the Brezhnev period, all major decisions concerning Soviet foreign policy were adopted in secret at the highest political level, primarily by the CPSU Politburo, the CPSU Secretariat, and the USSR Defense Council, each of which had its own coterie of advisers and support personnel. Numerous other individuals and organizations had input into foreign policy decision-making, but the decisions themselves were hashed out at the very top. The centralization of decision-making was especially pronounced during crises.

According to CPSU documents, the Brezhnev-era Politburo set up working groups and commissions in "certain priority areas" consisting of a few Politburo members with relevant spheres of responsibility, a few officials from outside the Politburo, and a few support staff.[3] Several of these bodies dealt with foreign policy and military affairs. One such commission was responsible for questions pertaining to military issues and the defense industry; another was responsible for overseeing nuclear arms control talks with the United States; and others supervised relations with the People's Republic of China (PRC) and policy toward the Middle East and the Arab-Israeli conflict.[4] In addition, a Politburo working group oversaw East-West trade; another working group focused on international human rights concerns (with the aim of countering international criticism of abuses in the USSR); and additional bodies were set up on an ad hoc basis to deal with international crises (East-West confrontations, armed clashes with the PRC, Arab-Israeli conflicts, political instability in Eastern Europe, etc.) or other exigent issues as needed.

The composition of these Politburo subgroups was often remarkably stable over lengthy periods, in line with Brezhnev's tendency to rely on the same people year after year ("stability of cadres"). For example, the membership of the "Commission to Supervise Soviet-American Negotiations" on strategic arms control, which was formed by a CPSU Politburo resolution in late November 1969, underwent almost no changes during the Brezhnev era.[5] Four key officials—Dmitrii Ustinov, Yurii Andropov, Andrei Gromyko, and Leonid Smirnov—were members of the commission throughout this time. Defense Minister Andrei Grechko was a member from November 1969 until his death in April 1976 (when he was succeeded as defense minister by Ustinov, who already wielded prodigious influence on military issues), and Mstislav Keldysh, the head of the Soviet missile and space program, served on the commission from November 1969 until his death in June 1978. Only one other official, Yakov Ryabov, served on the commission during the Brezhnev era, and his tenure was very brief. Ryabov, who had become the CPSU Secretary overseeing the weapons industry in 1976 after Ustinov replaced Grechko as defense minister, served on the commission from 1977 until 1979, when he fell out with Ustinov and was abruptly removed as CPSU Secretary and appointed first deputy head of the USSR State Planning Committee, a humiliating demotion.[6]

The Politburo commissions and working groups that dealt with foreign policy and military issues met regularly and received summaries of pertinent intelligence traffic (and sometimes raw data), briefings, and analytical reports from the First Main Directorate (foreign intelligence) of the State Security Committee (KGB) and the Main Intelligence Directorate (GRU) of the Soviet General Staff. In 1969, for example, as armed hostilities erupted between the Soviet Union and China, the GRU provided daily situation reports and other highly classified materials regarding Chinese intentions, goals, and troop deployments to the CPSU Politburo commission on China.[7] In 1980 and 1981, the KGB and GRU provided analogous materials about the crisis in Poland to the CPSU Politburo commission on Poland headed by a senior Politburo member, Mikhail Suslov.[8] Occasionally, the KGB and GRU coordinated their reports for Politburo commissions, but most of the time they sent information separately, especially during the many years that Yurii Andropov headed the KGB (1967–1982) and also served on the CPSU Politburo, initially as a candidate member and from 1973 as a full member.

The commissions had authority to take a wide range of actions on their own but would also frequently offer proposals and recommendations to the full Politburo and prepare drafts of resolutions and other documents pertaining to their spheres of responsibility.[9] Their recommendations and drafts were almost invariably adopted by the Politburo.

The available transcripts and notes of CPSU Politburo meetings from the Brezhnev era show that Brezhnev, as the party's General Secretary, closely guided the discussions of national security issues during his first decade in power.[10] All of the Politburo's commissions and working groups reported directly to him, allowing him to determine how issues were presented to the full Politburo. Moreover, as General Secretary, he was able to set the agenda for sessions of the CPSU Politburo and Secretariat and to make nominations at Politburo meetings for top foreign policy and military posts.[11] Brezhnev used these agenda-setting and nomination powers to good effect in shaping the Politburo's consideration of security issues.

In addition to heading the CPSU Politburo and Secretariat, Brezhnev chaired the USSR Defense Council, a highly secretive state body. The very existence of the Defense Council was not publicly disclosed until 1976, when two fleeting references to it appeared in the Soviet press.[12] In 1977, a brief (and misleading) mention of the Defense Council was included in Article 121 of the new Soviet constitution, which supposedly empowered the Presidium of the USSR Supreme Soviet to "form the USSR Defense Council and confirm its composition." A few other elusive references to the Defense Council subsequently appeared in the Soviet Union in the early 1980s, but no concrete information about the body's composition and areas of responsibility was available from official Soviet sources until 1989, when two members of the Defense Council, Lev Zaikov and Mikhail Gorbachev (both of whom were also on the CPSU Politburo), commented publicly about the body's primary tasks and functions.[13] These revelations were useful but were not sufficient to dispel the aura of mystery long enshrouding the Defense Council.

Not until after the collapse of the Soviet Union did greater information about the USSR Defense Council emerge. The full records of the Defense Council are still sealed, but a good deal of information about it can be found in other declassified documents (including notes from some Defense Council meetings) and memoirs. The Defense Council was created in February 1955 by the CPSU Presidium (the name then used for the Politburo) as a high-level "standing organ" that would "examine issues concerning the defense of the country and the Armed Forces," including military strategy, weapons production, military mobilization, and the use of force abroad.[14] At that same February 1955 meeting, the CPSU Presidium formed a Supreme Military Council (later renamed the Military Council) as an advisory body to the Defense Council, which itself was to consist of the highest-ranking officials responsible for security issues.[15]

The membership of the Defense Council varied only slightly during the Brezhnev era. When the body was first established in February 1955, it consisted of seven members, six of whom were members of the CPSU Presidium. In subsequent years, the number of members increased somewhat (mostly by bringing in a few more military commanders who were not on the CPSU Presidium), but it never numbered more than thirteen. In effect, the Defense Council, despite formally being a state body, functioned as little more than a subgroup of the Politburo. Both before and during the Brezhnev era, the CPSU General Secretary invariably served as head of the Defense Council, regardless of the state position he held. Nikita Khrushchev, as the CPSU First Secretary (the name then used for the top official in the party), was designated the head of the Defense Council in 1955, even though he held no senior state posts until March 1958. Brezhnev served as head of the Defense Council from 1964 on, even though he did not attain the highest state office—the chairmanship of the Presidium of the USSR Supreme Soviet—until 1977.[16]

The members of the Defense Council, in addition to the CPSU General Secretary, included the prime minister, the defense minister, the foreign minister, a few of the highest military-industrial officials, the chairman of the KGB, the director of Gosplan, the head of the military's Main Political Directorate, the chief of the Soviet General Staff, and (starting in late 1989), a deputy head who was also a senior member of the CPSU Politburo and Secretariat. In the late 1980s, when an official effort was under way to disparage the entire Brezhnev period as an "era of stagnation," Soviet Foreign Minister Eduard Shevardnadze publicly claimed that in the 1970s and early 1980s the Defense Council "often worked only spasmodically and was merely formal."[17] This characterization seems highly questionable. By all indications, Brezhnev played an active role until the late 1970s as chair of the Defense Council and established close working relations with high-ranking military officers as well as with his long-time ally Dmitrii Ustinov, who oversaw the defense industry during Brezhnev's first twelve years and then served as Soviet defense minister during the final phase of the Brezhnev period. These personal interactions allowed Brezhnev to use the Defense Council as a power base as well as a national security policymaking body.

High-Level Rivalries

The declassified transcripts of CPSU Politburo meetings indicate that Ustinov was more hawkish than Brezhnev on most issues, but the two men were in agreement about the need to allocate large quantities of resources to Soviet military industries and to the Soviet armed forces, helping to consolidate what Viktor Grishin in his memoirs described as the "historic achievement of putting the USSR at least on an equal footing with the world's strongest powers."[18] A consensus about this basic point—Brezhnev's legacy—existed.

Nevertheless, detailed notes from Soviet leaders' internal discussions reveal occasional sharp disagreements about the magnitude of resources that should be committed to Soviet military programs and activities. In at least two cases, these disagreements became the pretext for (and may have partly inspired) efforts to remove Brezhnev from office. Because high-level Soviet politics was characterized by frequent infighting and jockeying for power (declassified documents eliminate any lingering doubt about the Machiavellian nature of Soviet leadership politics), scholars who try in retrospect to analyze a political clash within the Soviet Politburo will usually find it hard to ascertain the precise weight of substantive disagreements versus less principled political attempts to gain an edge over rivals and amass greater power. What is interesting, however, is that during both of the major efforts to oust Brezhnev from the top party post, the challengers to the General Secretary felt the need to invoke national security issues.

The first move against Brezhnev occurred in June 1967, when he came under a forceful challenge behind the scenes from the head of the Moscow municipal Communist Party committee, Nikolai Egorychev, who condemned Brezhnev for not having provided a larger defense around Moscow against a U.S. nuclear missile and bomber attack. Egorychev unexpectedly laid down the gauntlet at a CPSU Central Committee plenum held on the eve of preliminary talks the Soviet Union was planning to initiate with the United States to see whether the two sides should hold formal negotiations to achieve a treaty limiting (or even banning) antimissile defense deployments, including those around Moscow.[19] Egorychev had privately written a cordial note to Brezhnev a few days before the plenum asking for the opportunity to speak there, though without giving any hint of what he wanted to discuss.[20] Brezhnev readily agreed, not realizing what was to come. Because the plenum was being convened to review Soviet policy vis-à-vis the Arab-Israeli war that had been fought earlier in the month (a brief war that ended with a decisive Israeli victory over the Soviet-backed

Arab armies), Brezhnev must have assumed that Egorychev wanted to address that issue or perhaps to speak about preparations in Moscow for the upcoming celebrations in November 1967 to mark the fiftieth anniversary of the Bolsheviks' ascendance to power.

After Brezhnev's initial lengthy report to the plenum about the Arab-Israeli conflict and subsequent discussion of the report, Egorychev was given the floor.[21] Rather than addressing the topic under discussion, he unexpectedly offered a blistering critique of what he claimed was the inadequate defense of Moscow against nuclear attack, a critique that was unmistakably targeted against Brezhnev.[22] Regardless of how much Egorychev actually cared about the substance of the issue —he acknowledged during the heated debate in the wake of his remarks that he had never bothered to attend a Moscow Oblast Military Council meeting dealing with air defense or other matters pertaining to protection of the capital—he clearly saw national security affairs as the main issue he should use in trying to displace Brezhnev. With this surprise move, Egorychev briefly seemed to gain an important political advantage at the plenum, catching Brezhnev and his CPSU Politburo allies wholly off guard. But after a break in the proceedings, Brezhnev returned and launched a furious counterattack, backed up by other Politburo members and senior military commanders, all of whom offered high praise of Brezhnev's commitment to the Soviet armed forces.[23] Having regained his footing, Brezhnev swiftly put an end to Egorychev's challenge, removing him from his party posts and appointing him deputy minister of tractor and agricultural machine-building. A few years later, Brezhnev struck a further blow against Egorychev, banishing him to Denmark to serve as Soviet ambassador.[24] Egorychev remained in the political wilderness in Copenhagen for nearly fifteen years.

The other major challenge to Brezhnev came in the mid-1970s from another full member of the CPSU Politburo, Alexander Shelepin, who was twelve years younger than Brezhnev and had been elevated to the Politburo in November 1964 as a reward for supporting the ouster of Khrushchev. According to Evgenii Primakov (who himself later became a CPSU Politburo member and head of Soviet foreign intelligence), Brezhnev "was continually wary of [Shelepin] upon receiving reports that Shelepin enjoyed considerable support, especially among younger *Komsomol* officials, who might accuse the General Secretary of lacking resolve" in responding to dangers abroad.[25] Primakov claims that the USSR's threat of military intervention in the October 1973 Arab-Israeli War was spurred in part by "Brezhnev's concern that [a failure to take a strong stand] would be exploited by his opponents in the leadership," particularly Shelepin.[26] The threat to send Soviet troops to the Middle East proved sufficient to forestall a direct challenge to Brezhnev at the time, but it did not eliminate Brezhnev's misgivings about Shelepin, who by all accounts was extraordinarily ambitious and aspired to gain the party's highest post.

Even if Shelepin was ready to make a bid for power earlier, he waited until after Brezhnev was weakened by a stroke in November 1974 at the start of a summit meeting in Vladivostok with U.S. President Gerald Ford.[27] Like Egorychev earlier, Shelepin seized on national security policy as a key issue to exploit against Brezhnev, focusing especially on the Soviet leader's effort to improve relations with the United States and pursue strategic arms control agreements. In late 1974 and early 1975, Shelepin voiced harsh criticism of the United States, implying that Soviet efforts to achieve détente had failed and left the country in greater danger. Prior to this time, Shelepin had always carefully endorsed Brezhnev's détente policies when speaking at CPSU Central Committee plenums,[28] but in late 1974 and early 1975 he warned about the importance of defending the USSR against "imperialist encroachments," warnings clearly intended to discredit Brezhnev's showcase foreign policy achievement, détente with the West.

In light of Shelepin's earlier strong endorsements of the push for détente and nuclear arms control, his shift in criticizing ties with the United States was undoubtedly driven less by the merits of the issue than by a simple bid for power, which suddenly seemed more feasible after Brezhnev was sidelined for prolonged periods by the stroke. Whatever the motive, Shelepin's comments posed an unmistakable challenge to Brezhnev. The struggle between the two men came to a head in April 1975, after a Soviet trade union delegation led by Shelepin traveled to Great Britain and encountered mass protests against Soviet human rights abuses. The demonstrators, whom Shelepin denounced as "Zionists," "paid agents," "anti-Soviet hooligans," and "enemies of the British working class," forced an early end to the delegation's visit, causing intense political embarrassment for the Soviet Union. The incident afforded Brezhnev a suitable pretext to get rid of Shelepin.[29] At a CPSU Central Committee plenum on 16 April 1975, Brezhnev presided over the removal of Shelepin from the Politburo and other senior posts and coupled that step with a lengthy report to the CPSU Central Committee strongly defending the Soviet Union's national security record, including the détente with the United States and nuclear arms control accords.[30]

Brezhnev's report stressed that the Soviet Union's "policy of peace" had not prevented the Soviet government from "intensifying its cooperation with all the socialist countries" or from "fulfilling its internationalist duty" to promote "national liberation struggles" and "revolution" in (what was then termed) the Third World, notably in Vietnam.[31] Brezhnev boasted that "our deep involvement in the struggle" in Vietnam had produced a "magnificent victory" for the Vietnamese Communists and had decisively resolved this "test of forces of the two social systems" in favor of the Soviet Union and the whole socialist bloc. The Soviet Union's "tireless work" in support of "class struggle," he argued, was fully consistent with "efforts to reduce the risk of nuclear war," and he emphasized that only an "enemy of peace" would claim otherwise. By conspicuously linking Shelepin's ouster with an elaborate justification of Soviet foreign policy, Brezhnev attained two goals simultaneously: he consolidated his own political power and eliminated a potentially dangerous rival, and he signaled his determination to rebuff hard-line attacks on his détente policies.

In this latter respect, Brezhnev's move against Shelepin reinforced the message conveyed by a change of high-level personnel a few years earlier, when Brezhnev suddenly demoted the long-time leader of the Ukrainian Communist Party (UkrCP), Petro Shelest, who was also a full member of the CPSU Politburo. The relationship between Brezhnev and Shelest had begun deteriorating in the mid-1960s—shortly after Brezhnev became CPSU General Secretary—but initially the tensions stemmed solely from concerns over Shelest's aspirations to build a power base in Ukraine. In October 1965, at Brezhnev's behest, the CPSU Presidium rebuked Shelest for having sent a note to the Presidium in early August 1965 proposing that the Ukrainian government be allowed to establish its own foreign economic ties.[32]

Even though foreign policy was generally not the main point of dispute in the deepening rift between Brezhnev and Shelest in later years, the UkrCP leader in late 1971 and early 1972 did begin expressing skepticism about the steady warming of the Soviet Union's relations with "imperialist aggressors."[33] His emphasis on the need for "strict vigilance" against the United States raised doubts about proposed arms control agreements that would restrict the deployment of antimissile defenses and set limits on the number of nuclear forces—precisely the type of agreement Brezhnev was getting ready to sign with President Richard Nixon. As a landmark summit meeting in Moscow between Brezhnev and Nixon approached in the spring of 1972, Brezhnev moved to sideline Shelest. A few days before Nixon arrived in Moscow for the summit meeting, Shelest was abruptly forced to step down as UkrCP first Secretary, a post he had held since July 1963. That same day, in a keynote speech at a crucial plenum of the CPSU Central Committee, Brezhnev presented a sweeping and impassioned defense of Soviet foreign policy.[34]

The Soviet leader repeatedly stressed that "the [strategic arms control] agreements will not in any way hinder our pursuit of the [weapons] programs we have long intended for the further strengthening of the defense of our country." He assured the Central Committee that "we [on the Politburo] understand that neither these [strategic arms control] documents nor any other will change the aggressive reactionary nature of American imperialism," and he noted with pride that the Soviet Union had been "giving comprehensive support," including armaments and economic aid, to the "progressive forces of the entire world," especially "the Vietnamese patriots in their liberation struggle against imperialism."[35] A key hard-line ally of Brezhnev, Soviet Defense Minister Marshal Andrei Grechko reinforced this point by outlining for the Central Committee the magnitude of Soviet contributions to North Vietnam's military victory:

> Our policy is profoundly internationalist. . . . An example of this is our unflagging, enormous assistance to the heroic people of Vietnam. We are helping the Democratic Republic of Vietnam with all types of weapons and combat equipment needed to wage war. In recent years alone, we have transferred to [North] Vietnam 70 divisions of air defense missile launchers and thousands of missiles, more than 500 aircraft and helicopters, roughly 900 tanks, more than 6,500 grenade launchers and howitzers, roughly 350,000 firearms, some 20 million artillery shells, and a good deal more. In addition, our country is sending a huge quantity of other material supplies needed to equip the armed forces and people of [North] Vietnam. . . . All of this is being provided by our people without complaint to the Vietnamese people in order to assist them in their heroic struggle. Without such assistance, without our weaponry, and without the support of our party, the Vietnamese people could not have gained the upper hand in the prolonged, intense struggle against imperialism and could not have withstood the onslaught of the U.S. military machine. It is only because of our support that they were able both to defend themselves and to achieve success in destroying the American occupiers."[36]

The following year, when Brezhnev delivered a final blow to Shelest in removing him from the CPSU Politburo, the Soviet leader again coupled this action with a report to the CPSU Central Committee justifying Soviet détente with the United States.[37] He declared "with complete certainty that, thanks to the work carried out by the Politburo and the entire Central Committee and by the USSR Supreme Soviet and the Soviet government, the international standing of the USSR and the international situation overall over the past two years [i.e., during the push for détente] have greatly improved." But he took care to add that the Soviet Union's "remarkably successful effort" to "reduce the risk of nuclear war" had not diminished Soviet "vigilance against imperialist intrigues" in the slightest. Throughout the détente years, he declared, the Soviet Union had continually "bolstered the economic and military might of the countries" of the Warsaw Pact and had been instrumental in the victory of the Vietnamese Communists: "The Soviet Union has given [North] Vietnam state-of-the-art weaponry and has provided broad economic assistance. Thousands of our military and civilian specialists have helped the Vietnamese friends in building up their country's defense capacity." Brezhnev noted that at the very time Nixon was coming to Moscow in May 1972, "we undertook additional military assistance to our Vietnamese friends." These steps to "champion the cause of world socialism," Brezhnev argued, had "cleared the way for an improvement of the situation in Europe and for a dialogue with the United States of America *on an equal basis*" (emphasis in original)[38] The implication was that the Soviet Union's long-cherished goal of becoming a coequal superpower on par with the United States—a goal dating back to Stalin's time—had finally been achieved.

These pronouncements undermined the basis for any hard-line complaints about the Soviet Union's opening to the West, adumbrating the position Brezhnev took when confronting Shelepin two years later. Thus, on repeated occasions from the late 1960s through the mid-1970s—from the ouster of Egorychev in June 1967 through the demotion and dismissal of Shelest in 1972–1973 and the removal of Shelepin in April 1975—Brezhnev demonstrated a credible willingness to move decisively against anyone who he believed was double-crossing him. In the process, he sent a warning to all other potential rivals that they would be punished if they attempted to exploit foreign policy in the intra-CPSU leadership struggle.

That warning proved effective. No further direct challenges to Brezhnev's leadership emerged on the question of foreign policy. Indeed, by the late 1970s, even as Brezhnev's health took a turn for the worse and his vigor diminished, his political position remained surprisingly robust. According to Viktor Grishin, the core figures of the CPSU Politburo had an informal conversation in the fall of 1978 to discuss whether, in light of Brezhnev's growing infirmities, they should persuade him to accept honorable retirement, an option he had actually brought up himself on a few occasions.[39] Mikhail Suslov, the most powerful figure on the Politburo and Secretariat after Brezhnev, told the others it was better to keep Brezhnev in place to preserve stability in the country, especially because they had not decided who should ultimately replace him. (Suslov himself was clearly not a successor, being five years older than the aging Brezhnev.) In effect, Suslov was saying that he had not yet decided who the best person was to replace Brezhnev, and until he did he would not endorse any proposal to ask Brezhnev about retiring. Rather than presenting the matter as a political prerogative, however, Suslov justified his reluctance on grounds of national security, arguing that it was crucial to preserve stability amid escalating tensions with the United States.

Foreign Policy Bureaucracies

Although major decisions about Soviet foreign policy rested with the highest organs of the Communist Party and Soviet government (the CPSU Politburo, the CPSU Secretariat, and the USSR Defense Council), numerous ministries and agencies performed crucial advisory and support functions. These functions often enabled them to wield immense influence on the shaping as well as the implementation of policy.

Chief among the agencies involved were the Soviet Defense Ministry and the Soviet General Staff. Unlike in the United States, where the Department of Defense was (and is) under firm civilian control, the Soviet Defense Ministry was staffed and controlled by professional military officers.[40] The Soviet General Staff oversaw all aspects of Soviet military planning, including preparations for nuclear war. The General Staff was the leading architect of military policy throughout the Soviet era, but at no time was it more influential than during the eighteen years under Brezhnev. The Defense Ministry and General Staff not only played dominant roles in the USSR's own military affairs but also carried out important tasks pertaining to military cooperation with the other Warsaw Pact member-states, with Communist countries in the "Third World" (Cuba, Vietnam, North Korea, etc.), and with other developing states. They also controlled the Soviet Union's arms control negotiating posture throughout the Brezhnev era.[41]

The Defense Ministry and General Staff offered guidance to the vast complex of Soviet military industries (a complex known by its Russian acronym, VPK) for the production of new weapons, but the VPK and its sprawling network of military factories often had their own ideas about the best types of new armaments. Occasionally, the VPK's preferences were at odds with those of the Soviet Defense Ministry and General Staff.[42] Whereas the Defense Ministry and General Staff were eager to pursue technological breakthroughs and qualitatively new weapons and support equipment, the VPK tended to prefer more incremental change. At times the result was a mismatch of weapons with key missions. The bureaucratic clout of the VPK rose to new heights during the Brezhnev era, in part because of the ascendance of Dmitrii Ustinov, the official who had been involved in defense production since 1941 and had overseen the entire weapons complex for many years. The appointment of Ustinov as defense minister in 1977 mitigated the potential for friction between the VPK and the Defense Ministry but did not fully eliminate it.

The Soviet Ministry of Foreign Affairs (MID) was in charge of most aspects of Soviet foreign policy, including political relations with the United States and other Western countries. Andrei Gromyko, who had become foreign minister in 1957, remained in that post for the entire Brezhnev period. The elevation of Gromyko to candidate membership on the CPSU Politburo in 1971 and full membership in 1973 at the height of détente reinforced his overarching authority on foreign policy.[43] Under his leadership, MID attained a bureaucratic status greater than at any time since the days of Vyacheslav Molotov in the 1940s and 1950s. MID was able to extend its influence into areas that in the past had been mostly outside its purview, such as relations with other Warsaw Pact countries. During the prolonged negotiations to set up the Conference on Security and Cooperation in Europe (CSCE) in 1973–1975, for example, MID played a lead role in coordinating the Soviet bloc's negotiating strategy, a complex and often delicate task.[44] Although CPSU officials also played an important part in coordinating Warsaw Pact positions vis-à-vis CSCE, MID's influence was crucial throughout, helped in part by Gromyko's personal stature.

The central apparatus of the CPSU included roughly twenty-five departments (the precise number fluctuated over time) that dealt with domestic and international affairs.[45] Most of the departments handled internal matters, but several played a direct role in national security policy. Among these were the International Department, the Department for Ties with Communist and Workers' Parties of Socialist Countries, the Cadres Abroad Department, the Administrative Organs Department, and the Defense Industry Department. The CPSU Propaganda Department also had important functions relevant to national security policy, and the CPSU General Department dealt with national security issues at least indirectly through its coordination of materials for policymakers. The departments were nominally accountable to the CPSU Central Committee but reported directly to one of the members of the CPSU Secretariat. The departments operated with considerable autonomy, and their input was often crucial in shaping the CPSU Secretariat's and CPSU Politburo's decisions. Because the departments' jurisdiction partly overlapped with the functions of government ministries and agencies, "turf" battles at times were intense.

The CPSU International Department (ID) was headed throughout the Brezhnev period by Boris Ponomarev, who was also a CPSU Secretary and (from May 1972) a candidate member of the CPSU Politburo.[46] Ponomarev's political clout—and the ID's bureaucratic standing—were bolstered by his long-standing close ties to Mikhail Suslov, dating back to their years in the Communist International (*Comintern*) under Stalin. Suslov for many years had been a leading figure in the highest party organs, and his authority in the CPSU during the Brezhnev era was second only to that of the General Secretary himself. The International Department handled relations with Communist parties in non-Communist countries, including large parties such as the Italian and French. Under Ponomarev's leadership, the ID became a champion of Soviet intervention in the Third World in the 1970s. The department worked with the KGB to aid Communist parties operating underground and to provide weaponry, financial support, and political assistance to radical leftwing "national liberation" movements and terrorist groups. One of Ponomarev's deputies, Rostislav Ulyanovskii, was especially active in promoting these efforts. The ID also was responsible for an aggressive program of "active measures," working again in conjunction with the KGB.[47] The department's active measures included elaborate propaganda and disinformation efforts to discredit Western governments and undermine U.S. influence throughout the world.

The CPSU Department for Ties with Communist and Workers' Parties of Socialist Countries, which was headed during almost all of the Brezhnev period by Konstantin Rusakov and Konstantin Katushev, handled relations with other Communist countries (the Warsaw Pact member-states, the PRC, Mongolia, North Korea, Cuba, Vietnam, Laos, and Cambodia).[48] The department was the main source of briefing memoranda and analytical reports for the highest organs of the CPSU, and its guidelines and recommendations were often adopted intact by the CPSU Politburo. The role of the department was especially important during periods of tension in Soviet–East European relations (in 1968, 1970, 1976, and 1980–1981) and during the armed clashes along the Sino-Soviet border in 1969.[49] The long-time first deputy head of the department, Oleg Rakhmanin, who was an expert on China and a harsh critic of Mao Zedong's regime, wielded far-reaching influence on Soviet policy toward China throughout the Brezhnev era.[50] Among other things, he was a key aide for the CPSU Politburo commission on China from the very start. Another senior official in the department, Georgii

Shakhnazarov, was an influential adviser to the highest party leaders on Soviet policy toward Eastern Europe. He served as staff director for the CPSU Politburo commission that was set up under Mikhail Suslov in August 1980 to deal with the crisis in Poland.

The CPSU Cadres Abroad Department was responsible, in conjunction with the KGB, for verifying the steadfastness and views of all party members who were chosen to serve in diplomatic and foreign trade postings except in Warsaw Pact countries (which were handled by the CPSU Department for Ties with Workers' and Communist Parties of Socialist Countries). In 1973 the department was merged with the CPSU Commission for Foreign Travel, and the unified body was renamed the CPSU Department for Work with Cadres Abroad and for Foreign Travel.[51] Aside from vetting personnel assigned overseas, the department got involved in numerous substantive issues relating to diplomatic representation and embassy staffing as well as the oversight of Soviet citizens traveling to countries outside the Communist bloc.

The CPSU Administrative Organs Department was broadly responsible for overseeing the KGB and the Soviet armed forces. The department's chief focus was on the many aspects of internal security, but it also wielded a good deal of influence on defense policy and oversaw the nuclear weapons complex, which was run by the Ministry of Medium Machine-Building. The relationship between the department and the institutions under its aegis (the KGB, the Ministry of Internal Affairs, the Ministry of Defense, the Ministry of Medium Machine-Building, etc.) was not antagonistic, but at times the department had to recommend that the CPSU Politburo tighten discipline within the armed forces or at the various ministries and agencies. Although occasional breaches of discipline within the Soviet armed forces were hardly surprising (similar infractions occur from time to time in most large militaries), the disciplinary problems that arose periodically at Soviet nuclear weapons laboratories and at Soviet ballistic missile factories were more surprising—some caused by alcohol, some by disaffection, and some by personal conflicts. The Administrative Organs Department at times had to conduct lengthy investigations into the nature of these problems.[52]

The CPSU Defense Industry Department, headed by Ivan Serbin from 1958 until his death in February 1981, worked closely with the Ministry of Defense and the VPK, but the triangular relationship was not always free of tension.[53] Although Serbin (a mechanical engineer by training who was known among his subordinates as "Ivan the Terrible") was only a candidate member of the CPSU Central Committee, his many years as head of the department gave him a great deal of bureaucratic leverage.[54] Moreover, the Defense Industry Department's long-time overseer on the CPSU Secretariat, Dmitrii Ustinov, was able to cut through bureaucratic obstacles. The department's relative standing vis-à-vis the Ministry of Defense declined somewhat after Ustinov was appointed to head the ministry in 1977, but the department continued to work not only on coordination of military production but on a broad range of other issues, including strategic arms control, military policy in outer space, and contingency planning for war.

The CPSU Propaganda and Agitation Department (usually referred to as just the Propaganda Department) was responsible for several activities pertaining to national security policy.[55] In conjunction with the KGB, the department coordinated the Soviet Union's massive effort to negate the impact of Western shortwave radio broadcasts. Numerous ministries and agencies were involved in this effort—ranging from the comprehensive jamming undertaken by the Ministry of Communications to the counterprogramming devised by the State Committee on Radio and Television Broadcasting—and they all came under the broad supervision of the Propaganda and Agitation Department. Other sections of the department oversaw the Soviet mass media's presentations of foreign policy and military affairs. The depictions in Soviet newspapers and broadcasts reached both domestic and foreign audiences and were regarded by Soviet leaders as a crucial element of Soviet foreign relations. In addition, the Propaganda Department played a key role in Czechoslovakia in the late summer and fall of 1968 after Soviet troops had occupied the country. The department's first deputy head, Aleksandr Yakovlev, supervised the reinstatement of censorship in the Czechoslovak media and the preparation of broadcasts for all major outlets.[56] The following year, the department closely supervised all media coverage of the hostilities with China.

By the time subsequent major crises broke out—the Soviet war in Afghanistan that began in December 1979 and the prolonged crisis in Poland in 1980–1981—a separate CPSU Department of Foreign Policy Propaganda had been set up. Established in February 1978, the department (which was renamed the Department of International Information in 1982) was headed by Leonid Zamyatin, a seasoned diplomat and propaganda official, throughout its eight-year existence. The new department took over most of the Propaganda and Agitation Department's erstwhile responsibilities for overseeing the foreign bureaus of Soviet mass media organs (TASS, Novosti, etc.) and for coordinating Soviet press coverage of foreign policy and national security affairs. The division of responsibilities between the two departments was sometimes ambiguous, and archival records make clear that jurisdictional disputes were hard to avoid.[57] Nonetheless, the creation of the

CPSU Department of Foreign Policy Propaganda underscored how crucial the role of propaganda still was in Soviet foreign policy during the Brezhnev era. From the earliest days of the Bolshevik regime, Soviet leaders had relied heavily on propaganda to shape people's outlooks both inside and outside the Soviet Union.[58] The establishment of the new CPSU Department of Foreign Policy Propaganda was a clear sign of continuity with institutions and practices of the past.

Conclusions

Throughout the Brezhnev era, the CPSU dominated the party-state relationship in the Soviet Union, as reflected by Brezhnev's performance of the functions of a head of state long before he became the actual head of state. His position as CPSU General Secretary was sufficient for him to serve as the country's highest leader in all respects. That said, one important thing to note is that the party-state relationship in foreign policymaking was by no means antagonistic. Key policymakers in the government—such as Gromyko, Ustinov, and Andropov—also became full members of the CPSU Politburo under Brezhnev. On the most crucial issues, a symbiotic relationship often existed between the Soviet government and the CPSU.

Nevertheless, at lower levels of the policymaking process, the relationship between party and state organs (or between some state agencies) was not always harmonious. The Ministry of Foreign Affairs and the CPSU International Department, as well as some of the other CPSU departments that had a role in foreign policymaking, would at times engage in turf battles or would even work at cross purposes. Much the same was true of the leading intelligence services, the KGB and GRU. Often their relationship was cooperative and mutually supportive, but at times the two agencies would compete for resources and influence, especially on high-profile assignments. The sorts of bureaucratic conflicts that have been a notable feature of policymaking in Western countries were also present in the Soviet Union. The closed nature of the Soviet system usually kept these conflicts from flaring into the open, but behind the scenes the maneuvering could be intense. When Brezhnev and other CPSU Politburo members exerted tight control over the policymaking process, they could offset the impact of bureaucratic conflicts, but as the Politburo members aged and especially as Brezhnev's health declined in the late 1970s and early 1980s, officials at lower levels had greater leeway to try to shape the agenda, parameters, and outcomes of policy deliberations.

The lack of institutionalized procedures for leadership succession in the Soviet Union inevitably had an effect on foreign policymaking from time to time. Brezhnev had witnessed firsthand the numerous challenges and political conflicts that arose during Khrushchev's time as CPSU leader, including the climactic confrontation in mid-October 1964 that resulted in Khrushchev's downfall and Brezhnev's ascendance. Brezhnev was therefore mindful of the possibility of facing a similar fate himself. The political challenges to Brezhnev's rule that did take place—in 1967 and in the first half of the 1970s—were all framed in terms of foreign policy and national security. In retrospect, it seems strange that his rivals chose to confront him on these issues. Foreign affairs and defense policy were Brezhnev's strongest suit, and the emergence of the Soviet Union as a coequal superpower with the United States during his tenure was his proudest achievement. On economic and social issues he was not as sure-footed or successful, but when disagreements arose during Brezhnev's early tenure over economic issues, as in 1965 with Alexei N. Kosygin (who wanted to undertake much bolder reforms), they did not precipitate challenges to Brezhnev's leadership and were resolved in Brezhnev's favor without changes of high-level personnel.

By the time Brezhnev was potentially more vulnerable to removal in the late 1970s and early 1980s because of his declining physical vigor, he had carried out many personnel changes (elevating key loyalists, such as Konstantin Chernenko and Dmitrii Ustinov; displacing potential challengers, such as Nikolai Podgornyi; and sidelining those with whom he had fallen out, such as Kosygin and Andrei Kirilenko) and had enacted institutional safeguards that enabled him to maintain his positions without significant disruption. Even when he himself broached the issue of stepping down late in his life, his colleagues on the Politburo urged him to stay, not least because they wanted to postpone deciding who would succeed him. After Suslov died in early 1982 and Andropov emerged as the clear successor, one might have expected that Brezhnev would be eased out, but he remained in office for another ten months until his death in November 1982—a reflection of the institutional inertia that had set in during his final years.

Brezhnev's longevity in office, second only to Stalin, put an imprint on Soviet foreign policymaking that endured during the brief tenures of his two immediate successors, Andropov and Chernenko, both of whom died in office less than a year and a half after becoming General Secretary. When Gorbachev came to power in March 1985, the nature of foreign policymaking in both the CPSU and the Soviet government still embodied Brezhnev's legacy. That is precisely why Gorbachev realized that if he wanted to enact major changes in Soviet foreign policy, he would have to restructure the foreign policymaking bureaucracies and procedures. Not only did he replace both Andrei Gromyko and Boris Ponomarev soon after taking office, but he also embarked on far-reaching changes in the party and state organizations that dealt with foreign policy and national security.[59] Moreover, Gorbachev and his new foreign minister, Eduard Shevardnadze, fostered the rise of "new political thinking in foreign policy" that broke with the precepts of the Brezhnev era. Within just a few years, the foreign policymaking process in the Soviet Union had been thoroughly overhauled, facilitating Gorbachev's bold new initiatives in foreign policy.

Gorbachev's restructuring of the foreign policymaking apparatus and the momentous changes that ensued amounted to a rejection of Brezhnev's legacy. The first fifteen years of the Brezhnev period had witnessed major achievements in Soviet national security policy, elevating the USSR to global superpower status. The commitment of vast resources for a military buildup, the consolidation of the Warsaw Pact, and a series of Soviet advances in the Third World after some initial setbacks were all hallmarks of Brezhnev's initial decade and a half in power. These gains, impressive though they were in bolstering Soviet power, began to come undone during Brezhnev's final years, and the slowdown of the Soviet economy reinforced the perception among some high-ranking officials that significant changes were needed. After the interregnum with Andropov and Chernenko, Gorbachev came to power and concluded early on that his prospects for revitalizing the Soviet Union at home would be greatly improved if he could undertake dramatic changes in foreign policy that would markedly ease East-West relations, fostering a stable climate in which he could proceed with wide-ranging domestic reforms. To go down this route, he dismantled Brezhnev's foreign policymaking apparatus and established one with his own imprint.

Mark Kramer is the director of cold war studies at Harvard University and a senior fellow of Harvard's Davis Center for Russian and Eurasian Studies. Among his recent books are *Imposing, Maintaining, and Tearing Open the Iron Curtain: The Cold War and East-Central Europe, 1945–1989* (2013); *Reassessing History from Two Continents* (2013); and *Spies: Espionage and International Politics during the Cold War*. He is the editor and lead author of three forthcoming volumes on *The Fate of Communist Regimes, 1989–1995*.

Notes

1. See, for example, Richard D. Anderson, *Public Politics in an Authoritarian State: Making Foreign Policy during the Brezhnev Years* (Ithaca, NY, 1993); Curtis Keeble, ed., *The Soviet State: The Domestic Roots of Soviet Foreign Policy* (Boulder, CO, 1987); Harry Gelman, *The Brezhnev Politburo and the Decline of Détente* (Ithaca, NY, 1984); Karen Dawisha, *The Kremlin and the Prague Spring* (Berkeley, 1984); Seweryn Bialer, ed., *The Domestic Context of Soviet Foreign Policy* (Boulder, CO, 1981); Jiří Valenta, *Soviet Intervention in Czechoslovakia, 1968: Anatomy of a Decision* (Baltimore, 1979); and Vernon V. Aspaturian, ed., *Process and Power in Soviet Foreign Policy* (Boston, 1971), esp. 555–698. Of these, Dawisha's book is the best. Valenta's study came out in a revised edition in 1991 that incorporates some newly released Czechoslovak archival materials, but his discussion of Soviet decision-making remains flawed, in part because of the unhelpful analytical framework he chose. See also the top-secret forty-page report produced in June 1976 by the U.S. Central Intelligence Agency, Directorate of Intelligence, Office of Political Research, *The Soviet Foreign Policy Apparatus*, PR-76 10037C, now declassified and available in the CIA's online Electronic Reading Room (https://www.cia.gov/library/readingroom/home).

2. For example, Fred Wehling, in his brief analysis of Soviet decision-making during the Middle East conflicts in 1967, 1970, and 1973, *Irresolute Princes: Kremlin Decision Making in Middle East Crises, 1967–1973* (New York, 1997), presents a new (though not fully convincing) theoretical perspective on crisis decision-making but offers nothing new empirically about actual policymaking in Moscow. Vladislav Zubok's illuminating survey of Soviet foreign policy, *A Failed Empire: The Soviet Union in the Cold War from Stalin to Gorbachev* (Chapel Hill, 2007), provides a trenchant discussion of the Brezhnev period but does not probe into foreign policymaking in any detail. Thomas Crump's brief account of Brezhnev's domestic and foreign policies, *Brezhnev and the Decline of the Soviet Union* (New York: Routledge, 2014), provides only cursory discussion of foreign policymaking. William J. Tompson's brief overview of the Brezhnev era, *The Soviet Union under Brezhnev* (New York: Routledge, 2003), includes a cogent discussion of foreign policy but says almost nothing about foreign policymaking. An essay by Svetlana Savranskaya and William Taubman, "Soviet Foreign Policy, 1962–1975," in *The Cambridge History of the Cold War*, vol. 2, *Crises and Détente*, ed. Melvyn P. Leffler and Odd Arne Westad (New York, 2010), 134–157, provides no coverage of foreign policymaking. In my own work on Soviet policy toward Eastern Europe during the Brezhnev period, I have discussed foreign policymaking in detail, but only with regard to that specific issue. See, for example, Mark Kramer, "The Kremlin, the Prague Spring, and the Brezhnev Doctrine," in *Promises of 1968: Crisis, Illusion, and Utopia*, ed. Vladimir Tismaneanu (Budapest, 2010), 276–362; idem, "The Soviet Union, the Warsaw Pact, and the Polish Crisis of 1980–1981," in *The Solidarity Movement and Perspectives on the Last Decade of the Cold War*, ed. Lee Trepanier, Spasimir Domaradzki, and Jaclyn Stanke (Krakow, 2010), 27–67;

and idem, *Soviet Deliberations during the Polish Crisis, 1980–1981*, CWIHP Special Working Paper No. 1 (Washington, DC, April 1999).

3. S. A. Mesyats, *Istoriya vysshikh organov KPSS* [History of the CPSU's Highest Organs] (Moscow, 2000), 27. All translations of non-English sources are my own.

4. "Koordinatsiya v SSSR voprosov kontrolya nad vooruzheniyami do 1985 goda" [Coordination of Arms Control Issues in the USSR before 1985], no date. Excerpts from classified Soviet Politburo documents, compiled by Vitalii Kataev, in Hoover Institution Archives (Stanford University), Vitalii Leonidovich Kataev Papers, Box 15, Disk 2, File PAB-GRUP, 1–5.

5. The remainder of this paragraph is based on the CPSU Politburo decrees excerpted in "Koordinatsiya v SSSR voprosov kontrolya nad vooruzheniyami" and on the declassified CPSU Politburo records in Rossiiskii Gosudarstvennyi Arkhiv Noveishei Istorii (Russian State Archive of Recent History, RGANI), Fond (F.) 3, esp. Opisi (Op.) 18 and 72. Many other CPSU Politburo commission materials are stored in the collections of documents amassed in the files of Brezhnev, Mikhail Suslov, Konstantin Chernenko, and Yurii Andropov, stored in RGANI, Ff. 80, 81, 84, and 82 respectively.

6. In a memoir published in 2000, Ryabov provided a fascinating first-hand account of his appointment as CPSU Secretary and his subsequent work in that post, including the genesis and nature of his conflict with Ustinov. See L. P. Ryabov, *Moi XX vek: Zapiski byvshego sekretarya TsK KPSS* [My 20th century: Notes *of a Former* CPSU CC Secretary] (Moscow, 2000), 188–217. A somewhat compressed version was published as a two-part feature "Yakov Ryabov o Borise El'tsine i Dmitrii Ustinove" [Yakov Ryabov on Boris Yeltsin and Dmitrii Ustinov] in two successive issues of *Rossiiskii kto est' kto: Zhurnal biografii* [Russian Who's Who: Journal of Biography], no. 4 (July–August 1999): 9–13, and no. 5 (September–October 1999), 30–34, esp. part 2. For further biographical information about Ryabov, see V. I. Ivkin, ed., *Gosudarstvennaya vlast' SSSR: Vysshie organy vlasti i upravleniya i ikh rukovoditeli, 1923–1991 — Istoriko-biograficheskii spravochnik* [State Power of the USSR: The Highest Organs of Power and Control and Their Leaders] (Moscow, 1999), 201–202.

7. The GRU's daily reports in 1969, each titled "Brief Report about the Situation" (*Kratkaya spravka ob obstanovke*) along with the report number and date, were declassified in August 2015 and are available in RGANI, F. 5, Op. 61, Dd. 11, 12, 13, 14, 15, 16.

8. Many of these materials are now available in RGANI, F. 82, Op. 1, Dd. 691, 692, 693; in RGANI, F. 5, Op. 77, Dd. 771, 782, 785, 785, 790; and in RGANI, F. 84 Op. 1, Dd. 872, 873, 874, 878, 889.

9. "Koordinatsiya v SSSR voprosov kontrolya nad vooruzheniyami," 1–2; and Mesyats, *Istoriya vysshikh organov KPSS*, 27–29. Analysis of archival materials from some of the commissions, cited below, reinforces this point.

10. Some declassified transcripts are stored in Fond 89 at RGANI, and excerpts from a few others were published in *Istochnik* (which ceased publication in 2004) and *Istoricheskii arkhiv* after 1992. Others have not yet been declassified and are still stored in the Presidential Archive of the Russian Federation

(APRF), which is inaccessible. The declassified protocols and supporting documents from CPSU Politburo meetings, which are extremely illuminating, are accessible in RGANI, F. 3, Op. 72., and I have gone through many thousands of pages of them.

11. On the importance of the General Secretary's agenda-setting powers, see Matthew A. Evangelista, "Norms, Heresthetics, and the End of the Cold War," *Journal of Cold War Studies* 3, no. 1 (Winter 2001): 5–35.

12. For citations of the brief public references to the Defense Council in the USSR from 1976 through the early 1980s, see Håkan Karlsson, "The Defense Council of the USSR," *Cooperation and Conflict* 23, no. 1 (1988): 69–83.

13. Zaikov's observations are in "Na Sovete oborony" [At the Defense Council], *Pravda* (Moscow), 27 November 1989, 2. Gorbachev's remarks, which came during the Supreme Soviet's scrutiny of the nomination of Dmitrii Yazov as defense minister, were transcribed in "Leglo li stat' ministrom: Spetsial'nye korrespondenty peredayut iz Kramlya" [Is It Easy to Become a Minister? Special Correspondents Report from the Kremlin], *Izvestiya* (Moscow), 5 July 1989, 2. Further comments about the Defense Council were made in 1989 by other officials, though in much less detail. See, for example, the speech by Army-General Aleksei Lizichev, the chief of the Soviet Army's Main Political Directorate, in "S"ezd narodnykh deputatov: Stenograficheskii otchet" [The *Congress of People's Deputies: Stenographic Account*], *Izvestiya* (Moscow), 8 June 1989, 5.

14. "Postanovlenie Prezidiuma TsK KPSS 7 fevralya 1955 goda: 'O sozdanii Soveta Oborony Soyuza SSR'" (Resolution of the CPSU CC Presidium of 7 February 1955: 'On the Creation of the Defense Council of the Soviet Union], CPSU Presidium Resolution No. P 106/III (Strictly Secret), 7 February 1955, in RGANI, F. 3, Op. 10, D. 126, List (L.) 2. For discussion of the matter in the CPSU Presidium, see "Protokol No. 99: Zasedanie Prezidiuma TsK KPSS 20 dekabrya 1954" [Protocol No. 99: Session of the CPSU CC Presidium on 20 December 1954], Handwritten Notes from CPSU Presidium Session (Strictly Secret), 20 December 1954, in RGANI, F. 3, Op. 8, D. 388, Ll. 19–22; and "Protokol No 106: Zasedanie Prezidiuma TsK KPSS 7 fevralya 1955 g" [Protocol no. 106: Session of the CPSU CC Presidium on 7 February 1955], Handwritten Notes from CPSU Presidium Session (Strictly Secret), 7 February 1955, in RGANI, F. 3, Op. 8, D. 388, Ll. 33–34.

15. "Postanovlenie Prezidiuma TsK KPSS 7 fevralya 1955 goda: 'Voprosy voennogo soveshchaniya'" [Resolution of the CPSU CC Presidium of 7 February 1955: "Issues of a military conference"], Presidium Resolution No. P 106/III (Strictly Secret), 7 February 1955, in RGANI, F. 3, Op. 10, D. 126, L. 3.

16. The year that Brezhnev became head of the Defense Council was first publicly revealed in a posthumous biographical sketch in Marshal N. V. Ogarkov, ed., *Voennyi entsiklopedicheskii slovar'* [Military Encyclopedic Dictionary] (Moscow, 1983), 100.

17. Comments transcribed in "Masshtab otvetsvennosti: Beseda chlena Politbyuro TsK KPSS, ministra inostrannykh del SSSR E. A. Shevardnadze so spetsial'nym korrespondentom 'Izvestiya'" [Scale of Responsibility: Conversation of the CPSU CC Politburo Member and USSR Minister of Foreign Affairs E. A. Shevardnadze with the Special Correspondent of "Izvestiya"],

Izvestiya (Moscow), 22 March 1989, 5, and in "Novyi impul's" [New Impulse], *Pravda* (Moscow), 29 March 1989, 4.
18. Viktor Grishin, *Ot Khrushcheva do Gorbacheva: Politicheskie portrety pyati gensekov i A. N. Kosygina* [From Khrushchev to Gorbachev: Political Portraits of Five General Secretaries and of A. N. Kosygin] (Moscow, 1996), 57.
19. "Plenum Tsentral'nogo Komiteta KPSS XXIII sozyva: Plenum TsK KPSS 20–21 iyunya 1967g.—'O politike Sovetskogo Soyuza v svrazi s agressiei Izrailya na Blizhnem Vostoke'" [Plenum of the CPSU Central Committee XXIII convocation: CPSU CC: Plenum 20–21 June 1967—"On the Soviet Union's Policy concerning Israel's Aggression in the Middle East"], Transcripts and supporting materials (Strictly Secret), 20–21 June 1967, in RGANI, F. 2, Op. 3, Dd. 57–77.
20. Egorychev's brief typewritten note to Brezhnev, dated 16 June 1967, with Brezhnev's approval marked in handwriting, is stored in RGANI, F. 80, Op. 1, D. 443, L. 116.
21. For Brezhnev's speech, see "Iyunskii Plenum TsK KPSS (20–21.VI.1967 g.): Stenogramma pervogo zasedaniya 20 iyunya 1967 g., utrennego" [June Plenum of the CPSU CC [20–21. VI. 1967]: Stenogram of the First Session, 20 June 1967, Morning], Marked-up verbatim transcript (Strictly Secret), 20 June 1967, in RGANI, F. 2, Op. 3, D. 65, Ll. 5–85.
22. "Iyunskii Plenum TsK KPSS (20–21.VI.1967 g.): Stenogramma vtorogo zasedaniya 20 iyunya 1967 g., vechernego" [(June Plenum of the CPSU CC [20–21. VI. 1967]: Stenogram of the Second Session, 20 June 1967, Evening], Marked-up verbatim transcript (Strictly Secret), 20 June 1967, in RGANI, F. 2, Op. 3, D. 66, Ll. 1–62.
23. "Plenum Tsentral'nogo Komiteta KPSS (20–21 iyunya 1967g.): Stenogramma tret'ego zasedaniya 21 iyunya 1967 g., utrennego" [(June Plenum of the CPSU CC [20–21. VI. 1967): Stenogram of the Third Session, 21 June 1967, Morning], Marked-up verbatim transcript (Strictly Secret), 21 June 1967, n RGANI, F. 2, Op. 3, D. 67, Ll. 1–156.
24. For Egorychev's perspective on the events, looking back thirty-five years later, see "'Versiyu o zagovore pridumali v TsK'" ["Allegations of a Conspiracy Were Concocted in the CC"], *Kommersant'-vlast'* (Moscow) 25 (2 July 2002): 50. He died in February 2005, a few months before his eighty-fifth birthday.
25. Evgenii Primakov, *Konfidentsial'no: Blizhnii vostok na stsene i za kulisami (Vtoraya polovina XX–nachalo XXI veka)* [Confidentially: The Middle East on Stage and behind the Curtains (Second Half of the 20th—Beginning of 21st Centuries)], revised and expanded edition, (Moscow, 2012), 164.
26. Ibid.
27. Brezhnev's stroke was not officially acknowledged at the time, though rumors of it were reported in the Western press and in dispatches from Western diplomats and Western intelligence reports. However, no solid information emerged until many years later, when Brezhnev's physician, Evgenii Chazov, discussed the matter in his memoirs. See E. I. Chazov, *Zdorov'e i vlast': Vospominaniya "kremlevskogo vracha"* [Health and Power: Memoirs of the "Kremlin Doctor"] (Moscow, 1992), 113–114. Chazov provided additional detailed information about Brezhnev's ailments in a subsequent,

more revealing book, *Khorovod smertei: Brezhnev, Andropov, Chernenko* [Procession of Deaths: Brezhnev, Andropov, Chernenko] (Moscow, 2014), 97–108, 128–130, 138, 141–144.

28. See, for example, Shelepin's remarks prepared for the April 1973 CPSU Central Committee plenum, "Vnutrennyaya opis': Aprel's kii Plenum TsK KPSS (26–27.IV.1973 g)" [Internal List of Contents: April Plenum of the CPSU CC [26–27 IV 1973)], Marked-up texts of plenum remarks (Secret), 26–27 April 1973, in RGANI, F. 2, Op. 3, D. 301, Ll. 36–47.

29. Shelepin's visit, hosted by the British Trades Union Council (TUC) in early April, had been sharply criticized from the moment it was announced in mid-March. See Laurie Johnston, "Shelepin Ends British Visit after Protests," *Times* (London), 3 April 1975, 33.

30. "Plenum Tsentral'nogo Komiteta KPSS, 16 aprelya 1975g.: Stenogramma zasedaniya 16 aprelya 1975 g., utrennego" [Plenum of the CPSU Central Committee, 16 April 1975: Stenogram of the Session on 16 April 1975: Morning], Marked-up verbatim transcript of CPSU Central Committee plenum (Strictly Secret), 16 April 1975, in RGANI, F. 2, Op. 3, D. 354, Ll. 1–87.

31. All quotations in this paragraph are from "Plenum Tsentral'nogo Komiteta KPSS, 16 aprelya 1975g.: Stenogramma zasedaniya 16 aprelya 1975 g., utrennego."

32. See "Postanovlenie Prezidiuma TsK KPSS 21 oktyabrya 1965 'O zapiske Pervogo sekretarya TsK KP Ukrainy t. Shelesta P. E. ot 2 avgusta 1965 g.'" [On the Note of the Ukrainian CP CC First SSecretary Cde. P. E. Shelest from 2 August 1965], CPSU Presidium resolution (Top Secret), 21 October 1965, in Rossiiskii Gosudarstvennyi Sotsial'no-Politicheskoi Istorii (Russian State Archive of Social-Political History, RGASPI), F. 84, Op. 3, D. 116, L. 28. For Anastas Mikoyan's notes from the CPSU Presidium discussion that preceded adoption of the resolution, see "Diktovka A. I. Mikoyana A. I. 21.IX.-65 g. po voprosu pis'ma Shelesta" [(Dictated Notes of A. I. Mikoyan, 21 IX 1965 on the Question of Shelest's Letter], 21 September 1965, in RGASPI, F. 84, Op. 3, Dl. 116, ll. 24–27.

33. See the three sets of handwritten diaries and typescripts covering 1971 and 1972 in "Tetradi P. E. Shelesta," in RGASPI, F. 666, Op. 1, which include excerpts from Shelest's speeches at the CPSU Politburo meetings he attended.

34. "XXIV sozyv: Maiskii Plenum TsK KPSS (19 may 1972 g.) — Zasedanie vtoroe (19 maya 1972 g.), vechernee" [(XXIV Convocation: May Plenum of the CPSU CC (19 May 1972) — Second Session (19 May 1972), Evening]. Marked-up verbatim transcript of CPSU Central Committee plenum (Strictly Secret), in RGANI, F. 2, Op. 3, D. 270, Ll. 1–147.

35. Ibid., Ll. 49, 51.

36. Ibid., Ll. 125–126.

37. "XXIV sozyv: Aprel'skii Plenum TsK KPSS (26–27. IV. 1973 g.) — Zasedanie pervoe (26 aprelya 1973 g.), utrennee" [(XXIV Convocation: April Plenum of the CPSU CC (26–27 IV 1973) — First Session (26 April 1973), Morning], Marked-up verbatim transcript of Brezhnev's report to the CPSU Central Committee plenum (Strictly Secret), in RGANI, F. 2, Op. 3, D. 297, Ll. 1–91. All quotations here are from this document.

38. Ibid.
39. Grishin, *Ot Stalina do Gorbacheva*, 78–79.
40. William Odom, *The Collapse of the Soviet Military* (New Haven, 1998), 117.
41. "Koordinatsiya v SSSR voprosov kontrolya nad vooruzheniyami do 1985 goda" (see note 9 supra), 1–5.
42. For a first-rate discussion of this phenomenon, see Peter Almquist, *Red Forge: Soviet Military Industry since 1965* (Cambridge, MA, 1992). See also I. V. Bystrova, *Sovetskii voenno-promyshlennyi kompleks: Problemy stanovleniya i razvitiya (1930–1980-e gody)* [The Soviet Military-Industrial Complex: Problems of Establishment and Development] (Moscow, 2006); and U.S. Central Intelligence Agency, *The Soviet Weapons Industry: An Overview*, DI 86-10016, September 1986.
43. No scholarly book-length study of Gromyko's nearly thirty-year tenure as Soviet foreign minister has yet appeared, and the only biography of him that has been published, by Svyatoslav Rybas, *Gromyko: Voina, mir i diplomatiya* [Gromyko: War, Peace, and Diplomacy] (Moscow, 2011), is uneven and sparsely sourced. Unfortunately, many of the vast collections of Gromyko's files stored at the MID archive (*Arkhiv vneshnei politiki Rossiiskoi Federatsii*) are still off-limits to researchers, though some important documents were released for a landmark compendium of declassified materials pertaining to U.S.–Soviet relations and détente (1969–1976), published jointly by the Russian Ministry of Foreign Affairs (in Russian) and the U.S. Department of State (in English) in 2007. See Russian Ministry of Foreign Affairs, *Sovetsko-amerikanskie otnosheniya: Gody razryadki, 1969–1976* [Soviet-American Relations: Years of Détente, 1969–1976], vol. 1, bk. 1, *Yanvar'–mai 1972* [January–May 1972] (Moscow: MID RF, 2007); Russian Ministry of Foreign Affairs, *Sovetsko-amerikanskie otnosheniya: Gody razryadki, 1969–1976* [Soviet-American Relations: Years of Détente 1969–1976), vol. 1, bk. 2, *1969–mai 1972* [1969–May 1972] (Moscow: MID RF, 2006); and U.S. Department of State, *Soviet-American Relations: The Détente Years, 1969–1972* (Washington, DC, 2007), as well as the five volumes in the State Department's *Foreign Relations of the United States* document series covering U.S. policy toward the Soviet Union and U.S.–Soviet relations during the Nixon and Ford administrations. Moreover, some revealing comments by Gromyko can be found in selected excerpts of declassified CPSU Politburo transcripts stored in Fond 2, Fond 3, and Fond 89 at RGANI (including those pertaining to events such as the invasion of Afghanistan in December 1979 and the prolonged crisis in Poland in 1980–1981) and in his declassified remarks to CPSU Central Committee plenums throughout the Brezhnev period. Gromyko's two-volume memoir, *Pamyatnoe* [Memoir] (Moscow, 1988), published a year before his death, is bland and uninformative. His son, Anatolii, who himself was a diplomat and MID adviser, published three collections of his own and other former Soviet officials' reminiscences about Gromyko, some of which are interesting. See, in particular, Anatolii Gromyko, *Andrei Gromyko—Polet ego strely: Vospominaniya i razmyshleniya syna* [Andrei Gromyko—The Flight of His Arrow: A Son's Recollections and Reflections] (Moscow, 2009). Other useful observations about Gromyko can be found in the memoirs of those who worked under or alongside him for many years,

including Anatoly Dobrynin, Georgii Kornienko, Anatolii Adamishin, and Andrei Aleksandrov-Agentov.

44. The MID's role in this process can now be studied in depth, thanks to the voluminous Politburo files, Foreign Ministry records, and CPSU department files recently transferred from the Russian Presidential Archive to RGANI, where they have been available since 2010. See the files (*dela*) in "Soveshchanie po bezopasnosti i sotrudnichestvu v Evrope: Postanovleniya Politbyuro TsK KPSS s prilozheniyami i materialami, 1969–1975 gg." [(Conference on Security and Cooperation in Europe: Resolutions of the CPSU CC Politburo with Appendices and Materials, 1969–1975], in RGANI, F. 3, Op. 73; and "Soveshchanie po bezopasnosti i sotrudnichestvu v Evrope: Zapisi besed sotrudnikov sovetskikh posol'stv s gosudarstvennymi i obshchestvennymi deyatelyami i sotrudnikami posol'stv zarubezhnykh stran, 1969–1976 gg." [Conference on Security and Cooperation in Europe: Notes from Conversations of Soviet Embassy Employees with State and Public Officials and Diplomats from Embassies of Foreign Countries, 1969–1976], in RGANI, F. 5, Op. 61, 62, 63, 64, 66, 67, 68, 69.

45. For listings of the CPSU Central Committee departments and the years they existed, see "Otdely, komissii, instituty RKP(b)—VKP(b)—KPSS" [Departments, Commissions, and Institutes of the RKP(b)—VKP(b)—CPSU], in *Spravochnik po istorii Kommunisticheskoi partii i Sovetskogo Soyuza, 1898–1991 gg.* [Handbook on the History of the Communist Party and of the Soviet Union] (Moscow, 2005), 57–71. The immense collections of files of all of these departments for the Brezhnev era, numbering tens of millions of pages, are now accessible again in Fond 5 at RGANI after being off-limits for 22.5 years.

46. See Mark Kramer, "The Role of the CPSU International Department in Soviet Foreign Relations and National Security Policy," *Soviet Studies* 42, no. 3 (July 1990): 429–446; and idem, "The CPSU International Department: Comments and Observations," in *The International Department of the CPSU Central Committee: Its Functions and Role in Soviet Foreign Policymaking* (Cambridge, MA, 1995), 99–127. The full formal name of the department was "International Department for Ties with Communist Parties in Capitalist Countries," but only the abridged name was ever used in either oral or written references.

47. See the sources adduced in the previous footnote as well as U.S. Department of State, *Soviet Active Measures: Forgery, Disinformation, Political Operations*, Special Report No. 88, October 1981, as well as many subsequent reports on the topic published by the Department of State and the U.S. Information Agency; Dennis Kux, "Soviet Active Measures: Overview and Assessment," *Parameters* 15, no.4 (fall 1985): 19–28; Christopher Andrew and Vasili Mitrokhin, *The Sword and the Shield: The Mitrokhin Archive and the Secret History of the KGB* (New York, 1999); and Christopher Andrew and Vasili Mitrokhin, *The World Was Going Our Way: The KGB and the Battle for the Third World* (New York, 2005).

48. An immense collection of files for this department, numbering millions of pages of documents, are stored in Fond 5 at RGANI. From mid-1992 through April 1993, they were fully accessible, and I used many of them.

From April 1993 until August 2015, all of the files, including the ones I saw earlier, were sealed. On the reasons for this setback, see Mark Kramer, "Archival Research in Moscow: Progress and Pitfalls," *Cold War International History Project Bulletin* 3, no. 1 (fall 1993): 18–39. Fortunately, however, the files through the mid-1970s were finally reopened in August 2015 and are now again accessible. The files from the mid-1970s through the mid-1980s, many of which I saw long ago, are in the process of being re-declassified.

49. See, for example, Kramer, "The Kremlin, the Prague Spring, and the Brezhnev Doctrine," 276–362; idem, "The Soviet Union, the Warsaw Pact, and the Polish Crisis of 1980–1981," 27–67; and idem, *Soviet Deliberations during the Polish Crisis, 1980–1981*.

50. For Rakhmanin's retrospective first-hand account of these years, see O. V. Rakhmanin, *K istorii otnoshenii Rossii-SSSR s Kitaem v XX veke: Obzor i analiz osnovnykh sobytii* [*On the History of Relations between Russia/the USSR and China in the 20th Century: A Survey and Analysis of Basic Events*], 3rd ed. (Moscow, 2002).

51. "Postanovlenie Politbyuro TsK KPSS 15 marta 1973 g.: 'O formirovanii Otdela TsK KPSS po rabote s zagranichnymi kadrami i vyezdam za granitsu" [On the Formation of the CPSU CC Department for Work with Foreign-Based Cadres and Travel Abroad], CPSU Politburo resolution, 15 March 1973, in RGANI, F. 3, Op. 72, D. 1147, L. 81.

52. See, for example, the series of problems discussed in "TsK KPSS" (CPSU CC), 14 April 1973, in RGANI, F. 5, Op. 66, D. 217, Ll. 4–27.

53. After the Soviet Union disintegrated, several former officials who had worked in or with the CPSU Defense Industry Department wrote first-hand accounts, some of which shed valuable light on the department's functions and bureaucratic role. See, for example, "Yubileinoe interv'yu s Igorem Nikolaevichem Bukreevym" [Anniversary Interview with Igor Nikolaevich Bukreev], *Informatsionnoe obshchestvo* (Moscow) 6 (2009): 30–39; Yurii Mironenko, "Inzhenerno-bronetankovye priklyucheniya, ili komicheskie momenty dramaticheskih situatsii" [Armored Tank Engineering Adventures, or Comic Moments of Dramatic Events], in *Zapiski multimaternogo studenta*, ed. Gennadii Stolyarov (Vol'sk, 2008), ch. 9 (esp. the section titled "Naedine s 'Ivanom Groznym'"); and Colonel-General Yu. V. Votintsev, "Neizvestnye voiska ischevnuvshei sverkhderzhavy" [(Unknown Forces of a Disappearing Superpower], *Voenno-istoricheskii zhurnal* (Moscow), no. 8 (August 1993), no. 9 (September 1993), no. 10 (October 1993), and no. 11 (November 1993), 54–67, 16–31, 19–27, and 12–27, respectively. The files of the CPSU Defense Industry Department were off-limits from April 1993 until August 2015 but are now accessible at RGANI, covering the years through the mid-1970s. (The files for later years are now being re-declassified.)

54. Mironenko, "Naedine s 'Ivanom Groznym,'" 8–9.

55. The records of the CPSU Propaganda Department, stored in Fond 5 at RGANI, are available for the whole Brezhnev period. The files are a gold mine of material about the different aspects of Soviet national security policy mentioned here.

56. "TsK KPSS," Memorandum No. 24996 (Top Secret) from A. Yakovlev and E. Mamedov to the CPSU secretariat, 6 September 1968, in RGANI, F. 5, Op.

60, D. 19, Ll. 200–206; and "Spravka o realizatsii predlozhenii po sovershenstvovaniyu informatsionno-ideologicheskoi raboty v svyazi s sobytiyami v Chekhoslovakii," [(Memorandum about the Implementation of Proposals for Overhauling Informational-Ideological Work in Connection with the Events in Czechoslovakia], Memorandum no. 35 (Top Secret) from A. Yakovlev to the CPSU secretariat, 2 January 1969, in RGANI, F. 5, Op. 60, D. 19, Ll. 207–209.

57. See, for example, "O preobrazovanii korrespondentskogo punkta Agentstva pechati 'Novosti' v Respublike Venesuela v byuro Agentstva pechati 'Novosti' v Respublike Venesuela" [On the Transformation of the Correspondent Station of the Novosti Press Agency in the Republic of Venezuela into a Bureau of the Novosti Press Agency in the Republic of Venezuela], Memorandum no. 7734 (Top Secret) from B. I. Stukalin, head of the CPSU Propaganda Department, and K. N. Brutents, deputy head of the CPSU International Department, to the CPSU secretariat, 14 January 1983, in RGANI, F. 4, Op. 28, D. 528, Ll. 96–99; "O dopolnitel'nykh propagandistskikh merakh v svyazi s obostreniem politicheskogo krizisa v YuAR" [On Additional Propaganda Measures in Connection with the Deepening of the Political Crisis in South Africa], Memorandum no. 931 (Top Secret) from L. M. Zamyatin, head of the CPSU Department of Foreign Policy Propaganda, A. N. Yakovlev, deputy head of the CPSU Propaganda Department, and R. A. Ul'yanovskii, deputy head of the CPSU International Department, to the CPSU Politburo, 3 October 1985, in RGANI, F. 4, Op. 28, D. 1364, Ll. 78–89; and "Ob uchrezhdenii byuro Agentstva pechati 'Novosti' v Respublike Panama" [On the Establishment of a Novosti Press Agency Bureau in the Republic of Panama], Memorandum no. 44757 (Top Secret) from A. N. Yakovlev, deputy head of the CPSU Propaganda Department, V. V. Zagladin, deputy head of the CPSU International Department, and L. M. Zamyatin, head of the CPSU International Department, to the CPSU Politburo, 10 November 1985, in RGANI, F. 4, Op. 28, D. 1375, Ll. 14–19.

58. For an exposition by one of the most skilled propagandists of the Brezhnev era, see G. A. Arbatov, *Ideologicheskaya bor'ba v sovremennykh mezhdunarodnykh otnosheniyakh: Doktrina, metody i organizatsiya vneshnepoliticheskoi propagandy imperializma* [Ideological Struggle in Contemporary International Relations: Doctrine, Methods, and Organization of the Foreign Policy Propaganda of Imperialism] (Moscow, 1970). On the origins of the Soviet propaganda state, see Peter Kenez, *The Birth of the Propaganda State: Soviet Methods of Mass Mobilization, 1917–1929* (New York, 1985).

59. See, for example, Mark Kramer, "The Role of the CPSU International Department in Soviet Foreign Relations and National Security Policy," *Soviet Studies* 42, no. 3 (July 1990): 429–446; idem, "The Demise of the Soviet Bloc," in *Imposing, Maintaining, and Tearing Open the Iron Curtain: East-Central Europe and the Cold War, 1945–1990*, ed. Mark Kramer and Vít Smetana (Lanham, MD, 2014), 367–435; Jeff Checkel, "Ideas, Institutions, and the Gorbachev Foreign Policy Revolution," *World Politics* 45, no. 2 (January 1993): 271–300; Douglas W. Blum, "The Soviet Foreign Policy Belief System: Beliefs, Politics, and Foreign Policy Outcomes," *International Studies Quarterly* 37, no. 4 (December 1993): 373–394; and Vernon Aspaturian, "Gor-

bachev's 'New Political Thinking' and Foreign Policy," in *Gorbachev's New Thinking and Third World Conflicts*, ed. Jiří Valenta and Frank Cibula (New Brunswick, 1990), 3–44.

Bibliography

Almquist, Peter. *Red Forge: Soviet Military Industry Since 1965*. Cambridge, MA: MIT Press, 1992.

Anderson, Richard D. *Public Politics in an Authoritarian State: Making Foreign Policy During the Brezhnev Years*. Ithaca, NY: Cornell University Press, 1993.

Andrew, Christopher, and Vasili Mitrokhin. *The Sword and the Shield: The Mitrokhin Archive and the Secret History of the KGB*. New York: Basic Books, 1999.

Arbatov, Georgi. *Ideologicheskaia bor'ba v sovremennykh mezhdunarodnykh otnosheniiakh: Doktrina, metody i organizatsiia vneshnepoliticheskoi propagandy imperializma* [Ideological Struggle in Contemporary International Relations: Doctrine, Methods, and Organization of the Foreign Policy Propaganda of Imperialism]. Moscow: Politizdat, 1970.

Aspaturian, Vernon. "Gorbachev's 'New Political Thinking' and Foreign Policy." In *Gorbachev's New Thinking and Third World Conflicts*, ed. Jiří Valenta and Frank Cibula, 3–44. New Brunswick, NJ: Transaction Publisher, 1990.

———, ed. *Process and Power in Soviet Foreign Policy*. Boston: Little, Brown and Company, 1971.

Blum, Douglas W. "The Soviet Foreign Policy Belief System: Beliefs, Politics, and Foreign Policy Outcomes." *International Studies Quarterly* 37, no. 4 (December 1993): 373–394.

Bystrova, I. V. *Sovetskii voenno-promyshlennyi kompleks: Problemy stanovleniya i razvitiya. 1930–1980-e gody* [The Soviet Military-Industrial Complex: Problems of Establishment and Development]. Moscow: Institut rossiiskoi istorii RAN, 2006.

Chazov, E. I. *Khorovod smertei: Brezhnev, Andropov, Chernenko* [Procession of Deaths: Brezhnev, Andropov, Chernenko]. Moscow: Algoritm, 2014.

———. *Zdorov'e i vlast': Vospominaniya "kremlevskogo vracha"* [Health and Power: Memoirs of the "Kremlin Doctor"]. Moscow: Novosti, 1992.

Checkel, Jeff. "Ideas, Institutions, and the Gorbachev Foreign Policy Revolution." *World Politics* 45, no. 2 (January 1993): 271–300.

Crump, Thomas. *Brezhnev and the Decline of the Soviet Union*. New York: Routledge, 2014.

Dawisha, Karen. *The Kremlin and the Prague Spring*. Berkeley: University of California Press, 1984.

Evangelista, Matthew A. "Norms, Heresthetics, and the End of the Cold War." *Journal of Cold War Studies* 3, no. 1 (winter 2001): 5–35.

Gelman, Harry. *The Brezhnev Politburo and the Decline of Détente*. Ithaca, NY: Cornell University Press, 1984.

Grishin, Viktor. *Ot Khrushcheva do Gorbacheva: Politicheskie portrety pyati gensekov i A. N. Kosygina* [From Khrushchev to Gorbachev: Political Portraits of Five General Secretaries and of A. N. Kosygin]. Moscow: ASPOL, 1996.

Gromyko, Anatolii. *Andrei Gromyko—Polet ego strely: Vospominaniya i razmyshleniya syna* [Andrei Gromyko—The Flight of His Arrow: A Son's Recollections and Reflections]. Moscow: Nauchnaya zhizn', 2009.

Ivkin, V. I., ed. *Gosudarstvennaya vlast' SSSR: Vysshie organy vlasti i upravleniya i ikh rukovoditeli, 1923–1991—Istoriko-biograficheskii spravochnik* [State Power of the USSR: The Highest Organs of Power and Control and Their Leaders]. Moscow: ROSSPEN, 1999.

Johnston, Laurie. "Shelepin Ends British Visit after Protests." *Times* (London), 3 April 1975, 33.

Karlsson, Håkan. "The Defense Council of the USSR." *Cooperation and Conflict* 23, no. 1 (1988): 69–83.

Keeble, Curtis, ed. *The Soviet State: The Domestic Roots of Soviet Foreign Policy*. Boulder, CO: Westview Press, 1987.

Kenez, Peter. *The Birth of the Propaganda State: Soviet Methods of Mass Mobilization, 1917–1929*. New York: Cambridge University Press, 1985.

Kramer, Mark. "Archival Research in Moscow: Progress and Pitfalls." *Cold War International History Project Bulletin* 3, no. 1 (fall 1993): 18–39.

———. "The CPSU International Department: Comments and Observations," in Sergei Grigoriev et al., *The International Department of the CPSU Central Committee: Its Functions and Role in Soviet Foreign Policymaking and Its Rise and Fall following the Major Reorganization of the Central Party Apparatus under Gorbachev*, 99–127. Cambridge, MA: John F. Kennedy School of Government, Harvard University, 1995.

———. "The Demise of the Soviet Bloc." In *Imposing, Maintaining, and Tearing Open the Iron Curtain: East-Central Europe and the Cold War, 1945–1990*, ed. Mark Kramer and Vít Smetana, 367–435. Lanham, MD: Rowman & Littlefield, 2014.

———. "The Kremlin, the Prague Spring, and the Brezhnev Doctrine." In *Promises of 1968: Crisis, Illusion, and Utopia*, ed. Vladimir Tismaneanu. Budapest: Central European University Press, 2010, 276–362.

———. "The Role of the CPSU International Department in Soviet Foreign Relations and National Security Policy." *Soviet Studies* 42, no. 3 (July 1990): 429–446.

———. *Soviet Deliberations during the Polish Crisis, 1980–1981*. CWIHP Special Working Paper no. 1. Washington, DC: Woodrow Wilson Center, Cold War International History Project, April 1999.

———. "The Soviet Union, the Warsaw Pact, and the Polish Crisis of 1980–1981." In *The Solidarity Movement and Perspectives on the Last Decade of the Cold War*, ed. Lee Trepanier, Spasimir Domaradzki, and Jaclyn Stanke, 27–67. Krakow: Oficyna Wydawnicza, 2010.

Kux, Dennis. "Soviet Active Measures: Overview and Assessment." *Parameters* 15, no.4 (fall 1985): 19–28.

"Leglo li stat' ministrom: Spetsial'nye korrespondenty peredayut iz Kramlya" [Is It Easy to Become a Minister? Special Correspondent's Report from the Kremlin]. *Izvestiya* (Moscow), 5 July 1989, 2.

"Masshtab otvetsvennosti: Beseda chlena Politbyuro TsK KPSS, ministra inostrannykh del SSSR E. A. Shevardnadze so spetsial'nym korrespondentom 'Izvestiya'" [Scale of Responsibility: Conversation of the CPSU CC Politburo Member and USSR Minister of Foreign Affairs E. A. Shevardnadze with the Special Correspondent of "Izvestiya"]. *Izvestiya* (Moscow), 22 March 1989, 5.

Mesyats, S. A. *Istoriya vysshikh organov KPSS* [History of the CPSU's Highest Organs]. Moscow: Auditorium, 2000.

Mironenko, Yurii. "Inzhenerno-bronetankovye priklyucheniya, ili komicheskie momenty dramaticheskih situatsii" [Armored Tank Engineering Adventures, or Comic Moments of Dramatic Events]. In *Zapiski multimaternogo studenta*, ed. Gennadii Stolyarov, ch. 9. Vol'sk: Voenmekh, 2008.

"Na Sovete oborony" [At the Defense Council]. *Pravda* (Moscow), 27 November 1989, 2.

"Novyi impul's" [New Impulse]. *Pravda* (Moscow), 29 March 1989, 4.

Odom, William. *The Collapse of the Soviet Military*. New Haven: Yale University Press, 1998.

Ogarkov, Marshal N. V., ed. *Voennyi entsiklopedicheskii slovar* [Military Encyclopedic Dictionary]. Moscow: Voenizdat, 1983.

"Otdely, komissii, instituty RKP(b.) — VKP(b.) — KPSS" [Departments, Commissions, and Institutes of the RKP(b), the VKP(b), and the CPSU]. In *Spravochnik po istorii Kommunisticheskoi partii i Sovetskogo Soyuza, 1898–1991 gg.* [Handbook on the History of the Communist Party and of the Soviet Union], 57–71. Moscow: ROSSPEN, 2005.

Primakov, Evgenii. *Konfidentsial'no: Blizhnii vostok na stsene i za kulisami. Vtoraya polovina XX–nachalo XXI veka* [Confidentially: The Middle East on Stage and Behind the Curtains. Second Half of the 20th–Beginning of 21st centuries]. Revised and expanded edition. Moscow: Rossiiskaya gazeta, 2012.

Rakhmanin, O. V. *K istorii otnoshenii Rossii-SSSR s Kitaem v XX veke: Obzor i analiz osnovnykh sobytii* [On the History of Relations between Russia/the USSR and China in the 20th Century: A Survey and Analysis of Basic Events]. 3rd edition. Moscow: Pamyatniki istoricheskoi mysli, 2002.

Russian Ministry of Foreign Affairs. *Sovetsko-amerikanskie otnosheniya: Gody razryadki, 1969–1976* [Soviet-American Relations: Years of Détente, 1969–1976]. Vol. 1, Bk. 1, *Yanvar'–mai 1972* [January–May 1972]. Moscow: MID RF, 2007.

———. *Sovetsko-amerikanskie otnosheniya: Gody razryadki, 1969–1976* [Soviet-American Relations: Years of Détente, 1969–1976]. Vol. 1, Bk. 2, *1969–mai 1972* [1969–May 1972]. Moscow: MID RF, 2006.

Ryabov, L. P. *Moi XX vek: Zapiski byvshego sekretarya TsK KPSS* [My 20th century: Notes of a Former CPSU CC Secretary]. Moscow: Russkii biograficheskii institut, 2000.

Rybas, Svyatoslav. *Gromyko: Voina, mir i diplomatiya* [Gromyko: War, Peace, and Diplomacy]. Moscow: Molodaya gvardiya, 2011.

Savranskaya, Svetlana, and William Taubman, "Soviet Foreign Policy, 1962–1975." In *The Cambridge History of the Cold War*. Vol. 2, *Crises and Détente*, ed. Melvyn P. Leffler and Odd Arne Westad, 134–157. New York: Cambridge University Press, 2010.

"S"ezd narodnykh deputatov: Stenograficheskii otchet" [Congress of People's Deputies: Stenographic Account]. *Izvestiya* (Moscow), 8 June 1989, 5.

Tompson, William J. *The Soviet Union under Brezhnev*. New York: Routledge, 2003.

U.S. Central Intelligence Agency. Directorate of Intelligence, Office of Political Research. *The Soviet Foreign Policy Apparatus*. PR-76 10037C, in CIA Electronic Reading Room, https://www.cia.gov/library/readingroom/home.

———. *The Soviet Weapons Industry: An Overview*. DI 86–10016, September 1986.

U.S. Department of State. *Soviet Active Measures: Forgery, Disinformation, Political Operations*. Special Report No. 88. Washington, DC: U.S. Government Printing Office, October 1981.

———. *Soviet-American Relations: The Détente Years, 1969–1972*. Washington, DC: U.S. Government Printing Office, 2007.

Valenta, Jiří. *Soviet Intervention in Czechoslovakia, 1968: Anatomy of a Decision*. Baltimore: Johns Hopkins University Press, 1979.

"'Versiyu o zagovore pridumali v TsK'" ["Allegations of a Conspiracy Were Concocted in the CC"] (Interview with Nikolai Egorychev). *Kommersant'-vlast'* (Moscow) 25 (2 July 2002): 50.

Votintsev, Colonel-General Yu. V. "Neizvestnye voiska ischevnuvshei sverkhderzhavy" [Unknown Forces of a Disappearing Superpower]. *Voenno-istoricheskii zhurnal* (Moscow) no. 8 (August 1993): 54–67; no. 9 (September 1993): 16–31; no. 10 (October 1993): 19–27; and no. 11 (November 1993): 12–27.

Wehling, Fred. *Irresolute Princes: Kremlin Decision Making in Middle East Crises, 1967–1973*. New York: St. Martin's Press, 1997.

"Yakov Ryabov o Borise El'tsine i Dmitrii Ustinove" [Yakov Ryabov on Boris Yeltsin and Dmitrii Ustinov]. *Rossiiskii kto est' kto: Zhurnal biografii*, no. 4 (July–August 1999): 9–13; and no. 5 (September–October 1999): 30–34.

"Yubileinoe interv'yu s Igorem Nikolaevichem Bukreevym" [Anniversary Interview with Igor Nikolaevich Bukreev]. *Informatsionnoe obshchestvo* 6 (2009): 30–39.

Zubok, Vladislav. *A Failed Empire: The Soviet Union in the Cold War from Stalin to Gorbachev*. Chapel Hill: University of North Carolina Press, 2007.

13

ERICH HONECKER—
THE "LEADING REPRESENTATIVE"
A Generational Perspective

Martin Sabrow

The biographies of communist Party officials do not draw a lot of public interest. In this chapter, I would argue that this lack of interest leads to a careless misapprehension. The main reason for this indifference is that the communist staging of leadership appears to be impersonal and focused strictly towards the aims of the leading party. However, life stories of confidence and doubt, rebellion and submission, career threats and assertions of power may be uncovered behind the façade that concealed them. Honecker's rise to political power was also wedded to a large number of self-written CVs and biographical questionnaires with which the "leading comrades" in the SED attempted to reassure their claims as the GDR's avant-garde, and to conceal their own biographical vulnerabilities.

Catherine Epstein, in a very insightful study, shows that the life stories of those "veteran communists" who were active before 1933 represent the collective biography of communism in the twentieth century.[1] Their life experience covered all the phases and breaks during the time communism fought for power from 1917 through 1991. In the same way as members of the founding generation of the German Democratic Republic (GDR) were influenced by their youth in the Weimar Republic and their fight against Hitler, after the end of World War II these "old communists" created a "new world" and secured their power over four decades, up to the final crisis of the socialist experiment at the end of the 1980s.

Combining all these aspects, we could say that the astonishingly long-lasting stability of communist societies and their startlingly sudden breakdown during the period from 1989 to 1990 cannot be separated from the persistence of this powerful generation of "old communists," nor can it be sufficiently explained without including the biographies of their leaders in a generational perspective. This assertion includes one of the youngest representatives of the veteran generation of communists: Erich Honecker. That he holds a very controversial place in the collective memory is well known. The ambivalence of retrospective judgment corresponds with Honecker's own ambivalence as a political protagonist. His political style of bureaucratized routine-leadership was based on his own concept of normality and normalization, in sharp contrast to Ulbricht's demonstratively conflict-laden self-legitimization. Honecker's style was characterized by the dichotomy between—or better, the companionship of—liberalization and repression, youthful freshness and old-man stubbornness, cultural relaxation and political rigidity, strictly maintaining ideological norms and an unbiased attitude in dealing with class enemies, such as the social democrats Chancellor Helmut Schmidt and Herbert Wehner—a former communist—or even the conservatives Chancellor Helmut Kohl or Franz Josef Strauß, the longtime prime minister of Bavaria (and for decades the personification of the capitalist enemy in the socialist GDR).

After the war, Honecker began his political career as a communist hardliner who loyally supported Ulbricht during the power struggles of the 1950s, organized the erection of the Berlin Wall in 1961, and who finally opposed his mentor when Ulbricht attempted to revive the socialist utopia by initiating various reforms. However, the same party official who in 1965 had kicked off a cultural ice age when he held a keynote speech on the GDR as a "clean state" in the Central Committee's so-called *Kahlschlagplenum* (clean sweep plenum)[2] presented himself as a promoter of the renovation of the GDR in his first few years in office and argued against the existence of any taboos in arts and literature, as long as the fundamental positions of socialism were not disputed.

How can this ambiguity be explained? An approach that focuses on psychological issues and on Honecker's allegedly peculiar mentality obviously does not meet the problem adequately—it cannot sufficiently solve the puzzle of Honecker's ambivalence. No biographer has yet tried to deliver a psychological explanation, and contemporaries and biographers usually do not give an explanation, contenting themselves with an unhelpful allusion to the sheer personal mediocrity of Erich Honecker. Helmut Schmidt, for example, on the death of his East German counterpart commented, "Never have I understood how this mediocre man may have held himself at the top of the politburo for such a long time."[3] In the same manner, biographers such as Jan Lorenzen simply point to the astonishing enigma, the mystery of a double-bound personality: "It may be this hidden paradox of Honecker's spirit that makes this biography so exciting."[4]

A more convincing direction may be found by an approach that embeds Honecker's biography into a comprehensive generational context. Erich Honecker never concealed the fact that he was born in Saarland, far in the western parts of Germany. The only two chapters of his 1980 autobiography written personally or dictated by Honecker are laden with admiration for his homeland. In 1987, during his delicate and somewhat tricky visit to the Federal Republic, he even took an explicitly private detour to the places of his childhood, where he visited his parents' grave together with his sister, who invited him for coffee in their parents' home in Wiebelskirchen.

For a communist official who worshipped proletarian internationalism, Honecker's emotional reference to his homeland was remarkable. The Communist Party officials Nikita Khrushchev and Leonid Brezhnev never bothered to refer to their Ukrainian descent, nor did Władysław Gomułka to his Galician origins. In contrast, Honecker's devotion to his homeland showed credibility and the cohesion of his biographical continuity, which never required him to break with his background and the values and certainties that he had acquired from early on. These beliefs outranked the inappropriateness of a West German birthplace, which Honecker's hidden opponents in the politburo tried to take advantage of in denunciatory reports to Moscow in the 1980s.[5] What concerned them most was Honecker's attitude towards the Federal Republic of Germany (FRG). Honecker did not take a class-orientated position at the FRG stands at the Leipzig spring fair. He allowed color photographs of his birthplace, his street, and other curiosities from Wiebelskirchen to be presented at the Saarland stands at the Leipzig fair. He also received two books about his homeland, and without hiding his emotion he thanked the trusty bosses of the Saar region. His detractors in the politburo concluded, "This means a major offensive on his emotional sphere. That is exactly the paradox . . . that a confirmed, inveterate West German stands at the spearhead of the GDR."[6]

More important than the geographical location of Honecker's hometown was its political situation. Honecker wrote about it: "In the national election in 1912, the year I was born, the Social Democrat candidate obtained a majority. From then on the constituency was called the "red village."[7] The Saarland town of Wiebelskirchen—where the Communist Party became stronger than the Social Democrats during the Weimar period—was the place where Erich Honecker was politically socialized, and by his own account, he descended from a pro-Communism proletarian family. At the age of six, his father taught him about the success of the *Novemberrevolution* (German Revolution 1918–19), the assassination of Rosa Luxemburg and Karl Liebknecht, and about the Russian revolution and its leader Lenin.[8]

After the end of the World War I, Honecker's home town Neunkirchen and the neighboring Wiebelskirchen, where he spent his childhood, had indeed become regional centers of a "left-proletarian" milieu,[9] which across party boundaries generated a world that was an alternative to the Catholic and bourgeois society at the River Saar. Erich Honecker, like three of his siblings, had his first institutional political experience in his family's political milieu at the *Jung-Spartakus-Bund* (Young Spartacus League) in 1922. In 1926 he joined the *Kommunistischer Jugendverband Deutschlands* (Young Communist League of Germany) and became its local leader in 1929, one year before joining the Communist Party.

After returning from his studies at the International Lenin School in Moscow in 1931, Honecker first advanced to the position of political leader of the Saar region's Young Communist's League, and in 1933 became a member of its Central Committee. He was temporarily arrested in 1934 while doing his youth work illegally after the National Socialists seized power), and again in 1935 after struggling with Herbert Wehner against Saarland joining the German Reich. The *Volksgerichtshof* (people's court) sentenced Honecker to ten years in the prison in Görden, Brandenburg, from where he was liberated by the Red Army at the end of the war.

When reporting back to Ulbricht's staff in May 1945, he was able to present an impeccable biography in the numerous questionnaires the Communist Party obliged everyone to fill out in order to screen their cadres. As he had been a prisoner in Brandenburg, he did not belong to the KPD's (*Kommunistische Partei Deutschlands,* or German Communist Party) so-called Moscow faction, yet as early as 1930 he had been captivated by Ernst Thälmann's legendary charisma[10] when he served as his bodyguard during a communist youth meeting. He even met Stalin twice in Moscow the following year, and again in 1949, the memory of which he treasured his entire life: "I have seen Stalin! It was the most important affair I ever have experienced!"[11]

The historic experience of the "GDR's first political generation,"[12] those who had been born prior to World War I, was defined by strong similarities. The communist veterans gained their identity as an "ingroup"[13] mainly through their differentiation: synchronously, from other milieus of the same generation, and diachronically, from the later (re)construction or building generation (*Aufbaugeneration*). The motifs central to their generation were not only that they had experienced emotional distress, poverty, and denied a childhood after the war, but also that they cherished the value of practiced solidarity and accepted guidance from fatherly role models; knew the cruelty and violence of political conflicts, including partisan thinking; had experienced the suffering of persecution and repression; exhibited self-assertion in the face of betrayal and personal weakness; and finally maintained the hope of redemption and ultimately a commitment to a radical and relentless change in society. They were characterized by their hardened behavior, fixed enemies, and the "habitualized inability to trust other groups or generations."[14] In 1945, the "generation of skeptical patriarchs"[15] set out to build a society whose people had previously been their enemies, or who had at least been indifferent toward them. The never-ending distrust of their own people is one of the fundamental characteristics of the "old communists." In their younger years, they had tried to construct their new Germany by implementing a politics of irreconcilability, which sometimes bordered on hate.[16] They opposed the idea of voluntarily giving up their power until their very last breaths.

There was no way out of this hermeticism. Neither inner emotions nor criticism from the outside were able to break open the worldview of the communist founding generation who defined criticism as a betrayal by their comrades or an attack by their enemies, and at the same time they aimed to suppress any autonomous political ideas in their people. The thinking of Honecker's generational "in-group" left no space for independent action by people deemed to be easily seduced and whose one break from civilization to barbarism had become the founding generation's lifelong trauma.

Honecker, up until the end of his life, imagined himself a conservative revolutionary of the left, whose compass was aligned with the inevitable course of history. His understanding of political responsibility was based on mistrust of his own people, alternatively interpreting the articulation of free will either as welcome affirmation, helpful orientation, or as a political threat, but never accepting the people's judgment of him: "The people's masses can easily be manipulated . . . . Without clear leadership by a Marxist Party this will not work! It is the evidence that we have come to through the centuries, that 'freedom is comprehending the imperative!'"[17] This is consistent with Honecker's interpretation of the 1989 people's uprising as a mere delusion: "'We are the people'? Fine, but I love the people. But which people is it? A manipulated people or one whose actions are based on reason? . . . Is it an enlightened people, a mature people? Or is it a people that follows the Pied Piper, the rat hunter?"[18]

Honecker's lack of appreciation of unguided social statements of will was not initially inspired by insights after he was forced from power; it was actually part of the basic mental equipment of a communist veteran who in 1933 had witnessed the collective enthusiasm for the Nazi's rise to power, and two years later the overwhelming vote of the Saarland people in favor of annexation to the *Reich*. In 1945, having only recently been installed as a youth functionary, Honecker did conjure the necessary "transformation of the younger generation" and exemplified "our task to eliminate any chauvinistic rubbish in the brains and hearts of our youth."[19]

Despite Honecker's harsh and supposed stubborn reaction to the emancipation of the East German people from the prison of this world order, he still proved flexible within the boundaries of his generationally and biographically hardened mental horizons. The same dictator who in the final crisis had ordered not to lament the civilians who had fled the country was in retrospect perfectly aware of the fact that the socialist experiment had not accomplished the production of the social acceptance necessary to succeed.[20] Despite (together with his entourage) blindly leading the country into doom, after his triumphant visit to the West German capital of Bonn in 1987, Honecker justified his remaining in power by proclaiming that he had planned to "set a few more highlights in foreign policy."[21] Up until his collapse during a Warsaw Pact conference in the summer of 1989, he had presented himself to be in great health, in contrast to the exhausted condition that in retrospect appears to characterize the image of the SED leaders in their decline. The participants of the *Freie Deutsche Jugend* (FDJ), the GDR youth organization, faced a witty secretary general who even spoke freely in his closing speech at their Pentecost meeting on 13 May 1989.[22]

The impression given by the media of Honecker having become a stubborn old man who had to be told that his time was over by his younger political ally in Moscow can lead us to forget that Honecker had submitted his political decisions to the opposite promise of youthfully breaking up obsolescent structures eighteen years previously. At the eighth party convention in June 1971, he presented a program designed to do everything to sustain the wellbeing of the people, thus reinforcing the concept of real existing socialism as a communist problem-solving agency that had shifted the "intention of socialism" away from the utopia of salvation and toward pragmatic problem-solving, based on values such as objectivity and feasibility.[23]

Honecker therefore resorted to the hands-on mentality he was familiar with from his Saarland socialization and onto which he held until his very last days in office. He returned documents that were presented to him for revision very quickly and with only the most necessary annotations, and he developed a management style that was open to individual decision-making, preferring quick and concrete decisions over general guidelines, but this led to him being overwhelmed with having to pay attention to a large number of minor problems and inquiries.[24] The character of the politburo meetings changed as well: under Ulbricht conflicts had been sorted out in protracted, occasionally threatening controversies, while now they followed an agenda that was worked through soberly and methodically and without bitter outbursts and strong debates.[25]

At the same time, Honecker cultivated a youthful image of himself that was habitually connected with the FDJ youth organization that he had led for ten years as its founding father. "His appearance is fresh and unaffected, which is why he will always be accepted by the youth," a party report stated in the summer of 1946.[26] Honecker tried to underline his casual style by often wearing a straw hat—even decades later—and by rubbing shoulders with the crowds, which distinguished him from his predecessor, Ulbricht.

The return to collective leadership, which Honecker announced in 1971, was intended to replace Ulbricht's dictatorial style and emphasized the reduction of hierarchies. Other members of the inner circle, especially the younger generation, such as Egon Krenz and Günter Schabowski, were to learn that this generational style of politics made way for a rigidity that turned Honecker from a consensus-oriented moderator into an autocratic leader. Honecker, however, still preserved the self-image of being the "youthful patriarch" whose arm did not need to be twisted to join the Wiebelskirchen Shawm Orchestra or to accept Udo Lindenberg's gift of a leather jacket and a guitar. Even as late as May 1989, he happily enjoyed the procession of flag-waving FDJ demonstrators and refused to understand when the prime minister of North Rhine-Westphalia at that time, Johannes Rau (who was later to become the federal president), asked him why the atmosphere in his country was so bad. His answer was naïve and convinced at the same time: "Mr. Rau, you are wrong. The unity of the masses and the party has never been as strong as today. The people back the party."[27]

Thus, extreme rigidity and pragmatic flexibility do not represent an inexplicable contradiction in Honecker's political life or personal character, and they do not fit the life history and system-historical timeline that parallels the advancing inflexibility of the aging dictator with the increasing stagnation of socialism in power. In fact, they are connected by forming an identity that led Honecker to take the side of the conservatives in the Stalin era and enabled him to advance in the communist power machinery without being affected by ideological struggles. In the 1970s, this wide range of political flexibility allowed Honecker to become the leading representative of a communist routine leadership that continued to believe in Joseph Stalin's thinking and yet could simultaneously communicate with the alternative world of Franz Josef Strauß and Herbert Wehner. In the end, however, even this link between the ideological rigidity and political pragmatism became an anachronism and, in the course of a decreasing bloc polarity, fell victim to far-reaching communication between the Eastern and Western hemispheres, a fact that Honecker himself did not seem to have understood up to the end of his life.

What, then, does Erich Honecker represent in a generational biographical perspective? To begin with, it is the life story of a communist official who recognized a guiding principle in clinging to the experience of his generation and his milieu, and who formed an identity of the self and a perception of the world across all epochal breaks until the end of his life. All the supporters of the communist concept based their self-assured and unswerving assertion against all opposition on their biographical consciousness of continuity. This attitude rendered them at the same time helpless in the face of the challenge of the socialist experiment, a challenge that did not occur in the traditional pattern of friend or enemy, but rather as a gradual decline of their values and a slow erosion of their mental order. Erich Honecker, however, combined this biographical continuity with the flexibility of a communist worrier, problem solver, troubleshooter, and an appeaser, who saw himself as a representative of a pragmatic politics of balances, and who was not afraid of unconventional approaches. In this tension between rigidity and flexibility, Honecker was the leading representative of a regime that gradually moved away from the idea of world conquest to that of merely securing its existence, and one which after long years of stability was to finally pay abruptly with a swift dissolution.

Martin Sabrow is professor of recent and contemporary history at Humboldt-University Berlin and director of the Centre of Contemporary History Potsdam. His current publications include *Der Rathenaumord. Rekonstruktion einer Verschwörung gegen die Republik von Weimar* (1994); *Herr und Hanswurst. Die Tragödie des Hofgelehrten Jacob Paul von Gundling* (2001); *Das Diktat des Konsenses. Geschichtswissenschaft in der DDR 1949–1969* (2001); *Erinnerungsorte der DDR* (2009); *1989 und die Rolle der Gewalt* (2012); *Die Zeit der Zeitgeschichte* (2012); ed. with Th. Lindenberger, *German Zeitgeschichte. Konturen eines Forschungsfeldes* (2016); and *Erich Honecker. Das Leben davor 1912–1945* (2016).

Notes

1. Catherine Epstein, *The Last Revolutionaries: German Communists and Their Century*. (Cambridge, 2003), 3.
2. Wolfgang Engler, "Strafgericht über die Moderne—Das 11. Plenum im historischen Rückblick" [Tribunal on modernity—The 11th plenum under historical review], in *Kahlschlag. Das 11. Plenum des ZK der SED 1965. Studien und Dokumente* [Demolition. The 11th plenum of the SED Central Committee 1965. Studies and documents], ed. Günter Agde, (Berlin, 2000), 16–36; Monika Kaiser, *Machtwechsel von Ulbricht zu Honecker. Funktionsmechanismen der SED-Diktatur in Konfliktsituationen 1962 bis 1972* [Change of government from Ulbricht to Honecker. How the SED dictatorship worked in conflict situations 1962–1972] (Berlin, 1977), 200–231; Norbert F. Pötzl, *Erich Honecker. Eine deutsche Biographie* [Erich Honecker. A German life] (Stuttgart, 2003), 83; Monika Kaiser, *Machtwechsel von Ulbricht zu Honecker. Funktionsmechanismen der SED-Diktatur in Konfliktsituationen 1962 bis 1972* [Change of government from Ulbricht to Honecker. How the SED dictatorship worked in conflict situations 1962–1972] (Berlin, 1977), 200–231.
3. Helmut Schmidt, *Weggefährten. Erinnerungen und Reflexionen* [Companions. Memories and reflections] (Berlin, 1996), 505.
4. Jan N. Lorenzen, *Erich Honecker. Eine Biographie* [Erich Honecker. A biography] (Reinbek near Hamburg, 2001), 10.
5. This paragraph refers to the original German by Werner Krolikowski, who informed his Moscow contact partners in a conspiratorial message in spring 1983, "Das besonders Besorgniserregende ist die Haltung von EH zur BRD. Auf der Leipziger Frühjahrsmesse hat EH auf den Messeständen der BRD keine klassenmäßige Position bezogen. . . . Außerdem bekam er 2 Heimatbücher geschenkt. Voller 'Rührung' bedankte er sich bei den saarländischen Konzernbossen dafür und erklärte: 'Das sei ja ein Großangriff auf seine Gefühlswelt.' . . . Es ist eben ein Paradoxum [*sic*], daß ein eingefleischter Westdeutscher an der Spitze der DDR steht" [The most disturbing aspect is the attitude of EH toward the FRG. At the Leipzig Spring Fair, EH did not occupy a class position on the FRG show. . . . In addition, he received two books from home. He expressed his gratitude to the Saarland group for this and declared, "This is a big attack on his emotional world." . . . It is just a paradox that a West German man is at the head of the GDR]. Notiz von Werner Krolikowski zur inneren Lage in der DDR am 30. März 1983 [Note from Werner Krolikowski on the internal situation in the GDR on 30 March 1983], in Peter Przybylski, *Tatort Politbüro. Die Akte Honecker* [Scene of crime politburo. The Honecker file] (Berlin, 1991), 352.
6. Ibid.
7. Erich Honecker, *Aus meinem Leben* [From my life] (Oxford, 1981), 4.
8. Stiftung Archiv der Partei und Massenorganisationen—Bundesarchiv (hereafter SAPMO BArch), NY 4167, 650, Staatliches Komitee für Rundfunk, Mitschrift einer RIAS-Sendung vom 21.8.1977.

9. Klaus-Michael Mallmann and Horst Steffens, *Lohn der Mühen. Geschichte der Bergarbeiter an der Saar* [Reward for hard work. History of the miners around the Saar] (Munich, 1989), 137.
10. Honecker, *Aus meinem Leben*, 60.
11. "Wir sahen Stalin" [We saw Stalin], *Junge Welt*, 28 December 1949, 1; "Zur Kategorie der Verzauberung als rauschhafter Form der charismatischen Beziehung" [About the category of enchantment as a glittering kind of charismatic relationship], in Martin Sabrow, "Der führende Repräsentant. Erich Honecker in generationsbiografischer Perspektive" [The leading representative. Erich Honecker in a generational perspective], *Zeithistorische Forschungen. Studies in Contemporary History* 1 (2013): 66–81; Erhard Stölting, "Die charismatische Suggestion und die Medien" [Charismatic suggestion and the media], *ZeitRäume. Potsdamer Almanach 2006*, ed. Martin Sabrow (Berlin, 2007), 183–192.
12. Wolfgang Engler, *Die Ostdeutschen. Kunde von einem verlorenen Land* [The East Germans. Tidings of a lost country] (Berlin, 1999). See also Mary Fulbrook. "Generationen und Kohorten in der DDR. Protagonisten und Widersacher des DDR-Systems aus der Perspektive biographischer Daten" [Generations and cohorts in the GDR. Protagonists and opponents inside the GDR system from the perspective of biographical data], in *Die DDR aus generationengeschichtlicher Perspektive. Eine Inventur* [The GDR from a perspective of biographical history. An inventory], ed. Annegret Schüle, Thomas Ahbe, and Rainer Gries (Leipzig 2006), 124.
13. Heinz Bude, "Die 'Wir-Schichten' der Generation" [The "we-classes" of the generation], *Berliner Journal für Soziologie* 7 (1997): 197–204.
14. Thomas Ahbe and Rainer Gries, "Gesellschaftsgeschichte als Generationsgeschichte. Theoretische und methodologische Überlegungen am Beispiel DDR" [History of society as a history of generations. Theoretical and methodological considerations based on the GDR], in *Die DDR aus generationengeschichtlicher Perspektive*, ed. Annegret Schüle, Thomas Ahbe, and Thomas Rainer Gries (Leipzig, 2006), 492–499, note 28.
15. Ibid.
16. On the communist "politics of hatred," see Richard Bessel, "Hatred after War: Emotion and the Postwar History of East Germany," *History and Memory* 17 (2005): 195–216.
17. Reinhold Andert and Wolfgang Herzberg, *Der Sturz. Erich Honecker im Kreuzverhör* [The fall. Erich Honecker under cross-examination] (Berlin, 1990), 420.
18. Ibid., 419.
19. Erich Honecker, "Neues Leben—Neue Jugend" [New Life—New Youth], *Deutsche Volkszeitung*, 7 July 1945, quoted by Erich Honecker, *Zur Jugendpolitik der SED. Reden und Aufsätze von 1945 bis zur Gegenwart. Erster Band* [On the youth policies of the SED. Speeches and essays from 1945 to the present. Vol. 1] (East Berlin, 1985), 7.
20. "Es steht völlig außer Frage, daß wir in den 40 Jahren nicht nur Erfolge erzielt haben, sondern daß eine beträchtliche Zahl von Bürgern die DDR nicht mehr bewußt als ihr Vaterland verstand" [There is no question that

we not only achieved successes in the last forty years, but a significant number of citizens no longer consciously considered the GDR as their homeland], Erich Honecker, interview in Moscow, summer 1991, *Moabiter Notizen* [Moabit notes], 86, note 62.
21. Reinhold Andert and Wolfgang Herzberg, *Nach dem Sturz. Gespräche mit Erich Honecker* [After the fall. Conversations with Erich Honecker] (Leipzig, 2001), 50.
22. Henrik Eberle, *Anmerkungen zu Honecker* [Notes about Honecker] (Berlin, 2000), 114.
23. "Es darf bei uns nicht einreißen, den sogenannten 1000 kleinen Dingen nicht die ihnen gebührende Beachtung zu schenken. Fortschritte in der Versorgung der Bevölkerung, vor allem Stabilität und Kontinuität, würden eine wesentliche Verbesserung des täglichen Lebens bedeuten und viele Anlässe für Reibungen und Verärgerungen aus der Welt schaffen" [It must not become a habit to neglect the so-called 1000 small things. Improvements in provisions for the population, especially stability and continuity, would mean a substantial improvement in everyday life and would eliminate lots of reasons for friction and annoyance]. From "Die weltverändernde Lehre des Marxismus-Leninismus war, ist und bleibt der zuverlässige Kompaß des Wirkens unserer Partei" [The world-changing doctrine of Marxism-Leninism was, is and will remain the reliable compass for our party], in Erich Honecker, *Revolutionäre Theorie und geschichtliche Erfahrungen in der Politik der SED* [Revolutionary theory and historical experience in the politics of the SED] (East Berlin, 1987), 22; Alexander Schalck-Golodkowski emphasizes that Honecker took petitions more seriously than politbüro decisions. Alexander Schalck-Golodkowski, *Deutsch-deutsche Erinnerungen* [German-German memories] (Reinbek near Hamburg, 2000), 270; For Honecker's detailed consideration with statistics of petitions and indications for shortages of supplies, see Eberle, *Anmerkungen zu Honecker*, 188–191.
24. Henrik Eberle and Denise Wesenberg, eds., "Eine Blütenlese bieten" [A collection of bizarre examples], in *Einverstanden, E. H. Parteiinterne Hausmitteilungen, Briefe, Akten und Intrigen aus der Honecker-Zeit* [Agreed, E. H. internal party memos, letters, files and intrigues from the Honecker period] (Berlin, 1999).
25. See also the article "Politbüro" in Andreas Herbst, Gerd-Rüdiger Stephan, and Jürgen Winkler, eds., *Die SED. Geschichte, Organisation, Politik. Ein Handbuch* [The SED. History, organization, politics. A handbook] (Berlin, 1997), 515–517; from a participants perspective see Günter Schabowski, *Das Politbüro. Ende eines Mythos* [The politbüro. End of a myth] (Reinbek near Hamburg, 1990), 20–21.
26. SAPMO BArch, DY 30, IV 2/11v/5344, Otto Meier, Charakteristik des Vorsitzenden der FDJ Erich Honecker, 6.8.1946 [Characteristics of the chairman of the Free German Youth Erich Honecker].
27. "'Er hielt sich für den Größten.' Wie Erich Honecker die Deutsche Demokratische Republik in den Abgrund geführt hat" ["He thought he was the greatest." How Erich Honecker led the GDR to ruin], *Spiegel*, 3 August 1992, 25.

Bibliography

Ahbe, Thomas, and Rainer Gries. "Gesellschaftsgeschichte als Generationengeschichte. Theoretische und methodologische Überlegungen am Beispiel DDR" [History of society as a history of generations. Theoretical and methodological considerations based on the GDR]. In *Die DDR aus generationengeschichtlicher Perspektive. Eine Inventur* [The GDR from a perspective of biographical history. An inventory], ed. Annegret Schüle, Thomas Ahbe, and Rainer Gries, 492–499. Leipzig: Leipziger Universitätsverlag, 2006.
Andert, Reinhold, and Wolfgang Herzberg. *Der Sturz. Erich Honecker im Kreuzverhör* [The fall. Erich Honecker under cross-examination]. Berlin: Aufbau-Verlag, 1990.
———. *Nach dem Sturz. Gespräche mit Erich Honecker* [After the fall. Conversations with Erich Honecker]. Leipzig: Faber & Faber, 2001.
Bessel, Richard. "Hatred after War: Emotion and the Postwar History of East Germany." *History and Memory* 17 (2005): 195–216.
Bude, Heinz. "Die 'Wir-Schichten' der Generation" [The "we-classes" of the generation]. *Berliner Journal für Soziologie* 7 (1997): 197–204.
Eberle, Henrik. *Anmerkungen zu Honecker* [Notes about Honecker]. Berlin: Schwarzkopf & Schwarzkopf, 2000.
Eberle, Henrik, and Denise Wesenberg, eds. *Einverstanden, E. H. Parteiinterne Hausmitteilungen, Briefe, Akten und Intrigen aus der Honecker-Zeit* [Agreed, E. H. internal party memos, letters, files and intrigues from the Honecker period]. Berlin: Schwarzkopf & Schwarzkopf, 1999.
Engler, Wolfgang. *Die Ostdeutschen. Kunde von einem verlorenen Land* [The East Germans. Tidings of a lost country]. Berlin: Aufbau-Verlag 1999.
———. "Strafgericht über die Moderne—Das 11. Plenum im historischen Rückblick" [Tribunal on modernity—The 11th plenum in historical review]. In *Kahlschlag. Das 11. Plenum des ZK der SED 1965. Studien und Dokumente* (2. erw. Aufl) [Demolition. The 11th plenum of the SED central committee 1965. Studies and documents (2nd extended edition)], ed. Günter Agde, 16–36. Berlin: Aufbau Verlag, 2000.
Epstein, Catherine. *The Last Revolutionaries: German Communists and their Century*. Cambridge: Harvard University Press, 2003.
"Er hielt sich für den Größten." Wie Erich Honecker die Deutsche Demokratische Republik in den Abgrund geführt hat ["He thought he was the greatest." How Erich Honecker led the GDR to ruin]. *Spiegel*, 3 August 1992: 25–27. Accessed 2 June 2016, http://www.spiegel.de/spiegel/print/d-9282914.html.
Fulbrook, Mary. "Generationen und Kohorten in der DDR. Protagonisten und Widersacher des DDR-Systems aus der Perspektive biographischer Daten" [Generations and cohorts in the GDR. Protagonists and opponents inside the GDR system from the perspective of biographical data]. In *Die DDR aus generationengeschichtlicher Perspektive. Eine Inventur* [The GDR from a perspective of biographical history. An inventory], ed. Annegret Schüle, Thomas Ahbe, and Rainer Gries, 113–130. Leipzig: Univeritätsverlag Leipzig, 2006.

Herbst, Andreas, Gerd-Rüdiger Stephan, and Jürgen Winkler, eds. *Die SED. Geschichte, Organisation, Politik. Ein Handbuch* [The SED. History, organization, politics. A handbook]. Berlin: Dietz-Verlag, 1997.
Honecker, Erich. *Aus meinem Leben* [From my life]. East Berlin: Dietz-Verlag, 1980.
———. *Moabiter Notizen* [Moabit notes]. Berlin: Edition Ost 1994.
———. *Revolutionäre Theorie und geschichtliche Erfahrungen in der Politik der SED* [Revolutionary theory and historical experience of the politics of the SED]. East Berlin: Dietz-Verlag 1987.
———. *Zur Jugendpolitik der SED. Reden und Aufsätze von 1945 bis zur Gegenwart. Erster Band* [On the youth policies of the SED. Speeches and essays from 1945 to present. Vol. 1]. East Berlin: Neues Leben, 1985.
Kaiser, Monika. *Machtwechsel von Ulbricht zu Honecker: Funktionsmechanismen der SED-Diktatur in Konfliktsituationen 1962 bis 1972* [Change of government from Ulbricht to Honecker. How the SED dictatorship worked in situations of conflicts]. Berlin: Akademie Verlag, 1997.
Lorenzen, Jan N. *Erich Honecker. Eine Biographie* [Erich Honecker. A biography]. Reinbeck near Hamburg: Rowohlt, 2001.
Mallmann, Klaus-Michael, and Horst Steffens. *Lohn der Mühen. Geschichte der Bergarbeiter an der Saar* [Reward for hard work. History of the miners around the Saar]. Munich: C. H. Beck, 1989.
Pötzl, Norbert F. *Erich Honecker. Eine deutsche Biographie* [Erich Honecker. A German biography]. Stuttgart: DVA, 2003.
Przybylski, Peter. *Tatort Politbüro. Die Akte Honecker* [Scene of crime politburo. The Honecker file]. Berlin: Rowohlt 1991.
Schabowski, Günther. *Das Politbüro. Ende eines Mythos* [The politburo. End of a myth]. Reinbek near Hamburg: Rowohlt, 1990.
Sabrow, Martin. "Der führende Repräsentant. Erich Honecker in generationsbiografischer Perspektive" [The leading representative. Erich Honecker in a generational perspective]. In *Zeithistorische Forschungen. Studies in Contemporary History 1* (2013), 66–81.
Schalck-Golodkowski, Alexander. *Deutsch-deutsche Erinnerungen* [German-German memories]. Reinbek near Hamburg: Rowohlt, 2000.
Schmidt, Helmut. *Weggefährten. Erinnerungen und Reflexionen* [Companions. Memories and reflections]. Berlin: Siedler, 1996.
Stölting, Erhard. "Die charismatische Suggestion und die Medien" [Charismatic suggestion and the media]. In *ZeitRäume. Potsdamer Almanach 2006*, ed. Martin Sabrow, 183–192. Berlin: Transit, 2007.
"Wir sahen Stalin" [We saw Stalin]. *Junge Welt,* 28 December 1949, 1.

14

INSIDE THE SYSTEM
The CPSU Central Committee, Mikhail Gorbachev's *Komanda*, and the End of Communist Rule in Russia

Jan C. Behrends

During the last decades of its existence, the Communist Party of the Soviet Union (CPSU) was an extraordinarily complex organization. Like the country it ruled, the Communist Party was enormous.[1] Its cells reached from the Polish border to the Far East, from the Baltic countries to the republics of Central Asia. This geographical and cultural diversity divided the party internally. The CPSU of Russia was not the CPSU of the Baltics; nor was it that of Central Asia. It was an imperial institution that, behind a facade of uniformity, embodied the USSR's diversity.

Yet it was not only size that mattered: the CPSU had a complicated history. It was a power structure in its seventh decade,[2] but even in the 1970s and 1980s, it was still shaped by its Stalinist past. Stalin had redesigned the Soviet power structure during the Great Terror; the Second World War, too, played its role in molding the party.[3] Those who held powerful posts under Leonid Brezhnev were survivors of an era that, though it seemed distant, still influenced the present. While society had developed and new generations had come of age after Stalin, there were certain Soviet institutions—the party, the army and the secret police—that proved more resistant to change.[4] They kept reproducing the system: de-Stalinization ended the terror and mass violence, but it failed to transform political culture at the heart of the Soviet state.

Leonid Brezhnev's doctrine of "the stability of cadres" meant that the fear and uncertainty that preoccupied elites under Stalin gradually disappeared.[5] By the 1970s, the *nomenklatura* no longer feared persecution or arrest. The struggle for survival of Stalin's days became a struggle for status. This limited meritocratic elements in the system. More than ever, personal relations and common background (*sviazi*) mattered most. Careers were built on loyalty and geography rather than policy.[6] Regional networks with local bosses ruled the vast USSR. Meanwhile, the political machine that was the CPSU continued to function according to its own set of rules; it was left untouched by campaigns for "socialist legality." Behind closed doors, in the grand edifices of the party apparatus, traits of Stalinism prevailed. After Stalin's death, there were some attempts to rebuild the party as an institution. Nikita Khrushchev tried to invigorate it politically and ideologically. But overall, he failed to make it a forum for discussion and debate rather than a patronage network where loyalty, personal trust, and male bonding remained keys to advance careers. Moscow was the epicenter of this system. The Central Committee (CC) at *Staraia Ploshchad'* (Old square) in the Soviet capital was the *sanctum sanctorum* of Soviet communism.[7] Although Moscow lost some of its dominance of the other Soviet republics after Stalin's death, the CC remained the most powerful political apparatus in the empire. The party bureaucracy expanded during the 1960s, and it continued to be the focus of attention for those at the empire's periphery.

Using memoirs and other egodocuments, this essay explores traits of the political culture of the Central Committee during the last two decades of Soviet communism.[8] It examines those who served at *Staraia Ploshchad'* during this decade, those who started their careers under Khrushchev and Brezhnev and reached the corridors of power under Gorbachev. This is not so much an analysis of the fateful policy decisions of those years as it is an inquiry into the Communist Party as social organism and cultural cosmos.[9] My investigation deals with the cultural history of politics in late socialism.[10] What was the meaning of the party during those years? What were the rules of the political game played within the CC? How did the informal rules at *Staraia Ploshchad'* shape the reformers? Finally, how and when did party culture change during the 1980s, and why?

Hidden Plurality and Tedium: The Center of Power and Soviet Society in Late Socialism

The negative image of the Brezhnev-era apparatchik is still remembered in the post-Soviet world and beyond: the gray and saggy suit, the odd glasses, the slurred speech, the greed, as well as the lack of cultural sophistication (*kul'turnost'*) and formal education. Iconic were also dull speeches in thick party newspeak and the awarding of (usually undeserved) medals and prizes to themselves. Brezhnev himself can be seen as the archetype of the late socialist functionary. The general secretary shared, and perhaps best represented, the characteristics and mediocrity of the generation of *vydvizhentsy* (social climbers) that had moved up the ladder after Stalin's Great Terror. Of course, to better understand the political culture of the CPSU, we need to move beyond this cliché. But it is useful to note that the stereotype of the dull apparatchik already existed—not only in the West, but also in the Soviet Union—while such types were still in power. Crucially, there were several generations of gray men—few women held responsible positions in the higher echelons of power; most were assistants, translators, or secretaries—and there were various shades of gray. These gray men had their own distinct culture: the political game of the USSR.

However, the metaphor of the gray apparatchik can be quite misleading. Despite the greyish facade, a colorful spectrum of political ideas existed within the Communist Party.[11] From red to brown to the yellow colors of the Russian Empire, the monolith had long ceased to be ideologically monolithic. In part, these varying currents stemmed from the fact that the CPSU was the only (legal) political organization in the country. During the decades after Stalin's death, the party became home to different ideas and positions. While all nominally supported Leninism and party orthodoxy, different groups favored different policies and had clashing visions for the future of the Soviet project. They also disagreed about the party's past: some were nostalgic for Stalin's firm leadership, but others favored further liberalization and condemned terror and mass violence. Both views coexisted, rather uneasily, within the same apparatus.[12] Insiders noted these internal divisions long before the Gorbachev era made them publicly visible.

In the 1970s, the Soviet dissident Andrei Amalrik wrote a survey of ideological currents within the party. Amalrik claimed that three conservative factions existed: "neo-Stalinist Marxism," "neo-Stalinist nationalism," and neo-Slavophiles, whom Amalrik dubbed "romantic conservatives."[13] Amalrik saw ideology-tsar Mikhail Suslov as the leader of the Marxist camp. He named long-serving head of the Moscow party (1967–1985) Viktor Grishin as a representative of the nationalist current.[14] According to Amalrik, these were the main currents of Russian "conservatism" in the CPSU.[15] Political conservatives and Slavophiles also existed outside of the CPSU—in the cultural sphere, for example—and they were often promoted and protected by influential party bureaucrats sympathetic to their views.[16] This conservative camp with its various subgroups, all well-represented in the Central Committee, was firmly established.

In opposition were the more "liberal" elements in Soviet society and, indeed, within the party leadership. These functionaries had been impressed by the twentieth party congress and the possibilities opened by Khrushchev's "thaw."[17] Later on they became supporters of Gorbachev's project of perestroika. As with Soviet conservatism, these more unorthodox views existed both inside and outside the CPSU. In contrast to conservative currents, however, the adherents of "liberal Marxism"—as Amalrik dubbed them—had to keep their heads down. After the Prague Spring, Brezhnev became more hardline and tended to favor the party's neo-Stalinists.[18] Thus, before 1985, the "liberal" current was considered dangerous, subversive, and against the party line. Some of its main proponents, such as Aleksandr Yakovlev, lost their powerful jobs because of their views.[19] Yakovlev was fired from the Central Committee's propaganda department in 1973 for criticizing nationalism and anti-Semitism in the Soviet Union. He was subsequently ordered to serve as ambassador to Canada, a dead-end diplomatic job, for more than a decade before Mikhail Gorbachev organized his return to Moscow in 1985 and made him his ideology-tsar.

Nevertheless, beliefs in liberal Marxism as well as liberalism and liberal values were common in dissident circles.[20] In the early 1970s, Amalrik considered Andrei Sakharov to be the main representative of liberal thought in the USSR, but he also perceived that there were many more closet liberals in the corridors of power, including "Party functionaries and industrial managers. However, this is, so to speak, the invisible part of the iceberg."[21] They certainly learned to hide their views during the later years of Brezhnev's rule. Most understood that being perceived as "liberal" was poisonous for a career in government. During perestroika, these functionaries' views would come to the surface.

Generally, the CPSU in late socialism was politically more diverse than in previous decades. This reflected broader trends in Soviet society and, in a broader sense, a new epoch of Soviet history. In addition, the traditional divide of the Russian intelligentsia between "Westerners" and Slavophiles reemerged, distorted, within the Communist Party. Certainly the attitudes of functionaries toward the West tended to determine their political positions. But these divisions could also be found in Soviet society at large, especially in its Russian center.[22] The party no longer had a monopoly on politics. It only enjoyed a monopoly on political power. On the liberal as well as on the conservative side, ideological boundaries did not correspond to the official party boundaries anymore. Political views found among the dissident intelligentsia could easily be found in the party, albeit covertly.

Of course, these currents of thought were hardly visible before perestroika. The gray facade of Soviet politics hid them from public view. Only thick journals, samizdat publications, émigré literature and, last but not least, reading in between the lines of official publications could reveal the limited pluralism of late Soviet socialism.

"Our people on the whole are good, besides, the authority complex has not completely disappeared from the Russian soul"[23]: Observations on the Political Culture of the Central Committee under Brezhnev

During late socialism, the Central Committee political culture was peculiar. Although it was arguably the most powerful political body in the USSR, it was not mentioned in the Soviet constitution. It constituted the more or less hidden brain and power center of the empire. After Stalin's death, the CC expanded its personnel and hired a cohort of young experts. Under Khrushchev, the party reestablished supremacy over the secret police and the army. This process expanded its power. Yet especially with the older cohort, Stalinist mentalities and structures remained. Those who started their political careers before 1953 continued to dominate the government into the 1970s and 1980s. What is more, the exact role of the Central Committee in the political game is hard to establish. Its influence was probably much greater than its appearance suggested. Many decrees adopted by Soviet ministries had their origins in the Central Committee. Decisions about cadres—essential to the Soviet system—were made at *Staraia Ploshchad'*. Other realms of Soviet society, mass media, culture, and ethnic relations—not to mention the international communist movement and foreign relations—were also within the committee's scope of authority. The politburo and its secretariat may have been the highest decision-making bodies, but even the party leadership depended on the expertise of the CC's bureaucracy.

In his memoirs, Georgi Arbatov gives some insight from the point of view of a "liberal" hired in 1964.[24] He remarks on the extraordinary power he wielded just by showing his CC party card. He could enter practically any government agency as a representative of the country's supreme authority. Soviet managers, even those in more elevated positions, treated him with respect, servility, and even fear. While Arbatov claimed that his initial salary was only slightly above average, it kept rising, and his job carried many privileges. These included monetary bonuses, access to the USSR's prime holiday locations, and exclusive health care at party hospitals. In an economy of shortages, CC staff was shielded from deficit. They could dine at the exquisite Kremlin cafeteria and buy the country's finest delicacies—including caviar, fish, and foreign fruits—for low prices. While ordinary Soviet citizens had to spend a large percentage of their income on food, and much of their time standing in line or "organizing" consumer goods, members of the CC enjoyed access to exclusive food and housing. In a country with an endemic housing shortage dating back to the 1920s, these apparatchiks received both private apartments in Moscow and dachas in the countryside. These privileges were granted according to rank; the party apparatus was a hierarchical world in the strictest sense. Yet parallel to this official order of the *nomenklatura* existed the informal network of patron-client relationships. Mikhail Gorbachev remembered, "The hierarchy of vassals and chiefs of principalities was in fact the way the country was run.... It was a caste system based on mutual protection."[25]

Georgi Arbatov describes the Central Committee apparatus of the Brezhnev years as divided by generations that enjoyed different lifestyles. There was an older generation that had risen to the top under Stalin; for a young apparatchik like Arbatov, who joined the CC in the 1960s, these people lacked culture and intellect. They were mainly interested in defending their power and status. The new generation, however, was divided within itself. Some younger CC employees were career party workers who had risen through the Komsomol and were keen to climb the ladder. Others, like Georgi Arbatov, Aleksandr Yakovlev, and Anatoly Chernyaev, who were better-educated experts that had come of age during late Stalinism and the Khrushchev "thaw," had more interest in the West and the world outside the USSR, and were not as devoted to the orthodox worldviews and lifestyles of the older generation.[26] As poverty and shortages were the norm for most in the Soviet Union, all party bureaucrats were constantly threatened by the loss of their material privileges, personal power, and the prestige they enjoyed as members of the top rank. This explains why they learned to maneuver cautiously. To avoid open conflict or controversy was—from Stalin's time onwards—an unwritten rule for all apparatchiks, regardless of political background or generation. They had much to lose and they knew it.

At the top of the Soviet power pyramid, opposing ideologies did not necessarily result in different political styles. While there may have been certain cultural markers of those more "liberal" and those more "Stalinist," it sometimes proved quite difficult to figure out where someone stood. Personal information was often hard to obtain because of the lack of open discussion and the culture of secrecy. It was a matter of trust to talk politics in the center of power, and trust was a scarce resource. From what we know, many were hesitant to openly convey their convictions. Talking openly was not an asset in a world of male networks struggling for power.

These specific male relationships that structured the CC may be illustrated by an anecdote from the career of Mikhail Gorbachev. After his studies in Moscow, Gorbachev was sent back to his native Stavropol, where he started work at the *Komsomol*.[27] He soon began working for the

CPSU and eventually became the local party chief, a powerful position in Soviet politics. Gorbachev explained his position: "First secretaries were the mainstay of the regime. . . . The prestige of a first secretary in his domain was comparable to that of a Tsarist governor."[28] It is also well-established that Gorbachev came to Moscow as a protégé of KGB boss Yurii Andropov. Despite his KGB-background, Andropov enjoyed a reputation of being somewhat more open to political dialogue than other leaders of his generation.[29] The two men often met while the ailing Andropov was resting at the spas of the Northern Caucasus, the area Gorbachev ruled. They spent time together, sometimes with their families, and Gorbachev came to consider the mighty Muscovite a "friend." To Andropov, he was a promising local functionary whose career he chose to promote. By the end of the 1970s, Andropov was Gorbachev's sponsor and paved his way to Moscow, where Gorbachev became the Central Committee's secretary of agriculture in 1978. The patron had opened the door to the center of Soviet power for his apprentice.

His party career hitherto limited to Stavropol, Gorbachev found the transition to Moscow life difficult. In Stavropol he had been the *khoziain*, or pater familias, who laid down the rules. In a few weeks he went from being the most powerful man in Stravopol Krai to a newcomer who had to reinvent himself and build his own network in the capital. Once a chieftain, he was now a novice. In his memoirs, Gorbachev recounts how stressful his arrival was, both politically and socially. He admits that he and his wife initially suffered from a lack of social life as they had few acquaintances in Moscow. In any event, the new job did not provide much spare time. Daily routine in the Central Committee was strenuous and often boring. CC workers spent long, tedious hours at *Staraia Ploshchad'* before returning to their apartments or dachas, where their wives awaited them.

Gorbachev was also rudely awakened to Moscow's culture of suspicion and secrecy. Apparatchiks were not usually expected to meet each other in private. Gorbachev recounts how Brezhnev would only invite an exclusive circle of colleagues to his home—Gromyko, Ustinov, Andropov, and Kirilenko.[30] It was a sign of special closeness and privilege to invite someone to a private meeting with the *gensek* (general secretary).[31] In the closed world of the CC any and every meeting was political—even a barbecue at the dacha. Since fear of treachery and intrigue loomed large, a special group would very likely be seen as conspiratorial, especially if it was meeting in private. Gorbachev did not initially understand these unwritten rules of the CC. He complained that Andropov—his sponsor and "friend"—did not once invite him to his house. Puzzled, Gorbachev decided to take the initiative and invite Andropov over. This led to the elder teaching the younger a lesson about privacy, friendship, and politics in the Central Committee. Gorbachev remembers the following dialogue between patron and client:

> Our dachas were next door to each other, and one day in the summer I telephoned Andropov. "Today we are arranging a meal in Stavropol style and, as in the good old days, we invite you and Tatyana Filippovna over." "Yes, those were the days, but I have to decline your invitation, Mikhail," Andropov answered in a calm, quiet voice. "Why?" I asked. "Because, tomorrow, there would be all kinds of loose talk—who, where, why, what was said?" "What are you saying, Yuri Vladimirovich?" I tried, quite sincerely, to suggest that it was not so. "No, that's the way it really is. While we were still on our way to you, Leonid Ilyich would hear about it. I say this, Mikhail, first and foremost for your own sake."[32]

The senior Chekist drew the borders of sociability tightly. Why were these unwritten rules so rigid? There are at least two general reasons for this lack of trust that precluded personal friendships or even informal gatherings. First, the *kto kogo* (who whom) of Bolshevik politics never stopped. The whole idea of a private meeting, as Andropov pointed out to Gorbachev, was absurd. At the top of the pyramid, everyday life and leisure time were just as political as time in the office. To be chosen to go hunting with Brezhnev was a sign of political privilege. Second, any person in the CPSU leadership had reason to be suspicious of such meetings. The powerbrokers of the CC had to be mindful of machinations and intrigues because there were hardly any clear procedures for removing people from office, except the death of the incumbent. Who was close to whom? Who would conspire with whom? Against whom? Being forced to ask these questions was part of working at the Central Committee. Of course, personal connections and informal practices are important in any political setting, but they were an essential, if not the critical, factor in Soviet politics because standardized power transitions and term limits were absent.[33] Even the lists of candidates for deputy to the Supreme Soviet, or for the CC itself, were drawn up somewhere in an inner circle. The unanimous public voting at party congresses or sessions of the Central Committee only rubber-stamped what had been agreed upon behind closed doors. It is for this reason that any clandestine meeting could be significant. In the diaries of Anatoly Chernyaev, whose chronicle runs from 1972 to the fall of the USSR in 1991, there are many pages where he closely observes who gets invited to which office, who attends what meetings and who is excluded. This was not just Chernyaev venting his spleen, nor curiosity. He was monitoring the political situation at *Staraia Ploshchad'*.

Every member of the politburo had his team of subordinates around him, but, at least under Brezhnev, these teams could not openly compete. While the "stability of cadres" certainly meant that apparatchiks no longer had to fear for their lives and even their jobs were pretty secure, they still had to act carefully. In order to advance in this "stable" setting, one had to watch others closely. For the most part, there were no more major conspiracies. The older generation certainly remembered the times of Stalin though, and they knew things could work in a different way. Even younger officials recalled the repeated, eventually successful, attempts to remove Khrushchev from office.[34] As such, the idea of a coup had not disappeared and it resurfaced at the end of perestroika. It was a party tradition just waiting to be revived at the convenient moment. Conspiracy was one way to accelerate or to stop change. Even the election of a new *gensek*, such as that after Brezhnev's death in November 1982, involved a great deal of informal preparation. A consensus had to be reached behind closed doors *before* there could be a formal vote in the politburo. An experienced Soviet politician, Andropov understood the workings of these shadowy politics. He had to turn his disciple's invitation down because going to the Gorbachev's dacha for dinner might have sent the wrong signal to Brezhnev and to his rivals.

What does this episode reveal about the political culture under Brezhnev at *Staraia Ploshchad'*? For one, loyalty was expected from every apparatchik: to his mentor, his team, his department, and, of course, to the general secretary, who was still the *vozhd'* (leader). There could be some subtle changes of position and political infighting, but, on the whole, the system demanded consensus, calm, and predictability. Any unusual move or conflict could easily turn into a scandal and make waves for everybody. Andropov intended to avoid this; he knew Gorbachev was firmly on his team, and he did not need any visible confirmation of his loyalty. At the same time, he was keen to be seen as a loyal player in the inner circle around the ailing Brezhnev.

In addition to personal ties, symbols and gestures also mattered at the top of the Soviet pyramid. Under Leonid Brezhnev and his successor, Andropov, these could be of equal importance to policy. The existing hierarchies had to be confirmed through acts of recognition. Again, violations of the unwritten protocol could cause irritation. Anatoly Chernyaev's notes are a valuable source on this subject. In January 1985, he discussed an episode involving his boss, Boris Ponomarev, who had been close to the party's ideology tsar, Mikhail Suslov. A veteran Bolshevik and head of the Central Committee's international department since 1955, Ponomarev had just celebrated his eightieth birthday. He was in charge of oversight of the international communist movement and may be seen as a prime example of the "stability of cadres": the ultimate insider at *Staraia Ploshchad'*, Chernyaev had served under Ponomarev for decades and could hardly imagine it being any other way. Yet, the latter's birthday celebration in 1985 was overshadowed by a breach of protocol. While other senior members of the Central Committee had long since received their second gold star—the "Hero of Socialist Labor" medal, with which Ponomarev had already been decorated once in 1975—on this occasion he was awarded only the less prestigious "Order of Lenin" (a medal he received six times during his long career). Chernyaev noted how the old Bolshevik was puzzled by this decision, which made him worry about his international reputation: "How will the Communist movement take it? How will our fraternal states, which awarded me their highest orders, understand this? How will the peace-loving public react to this fact?" Chernyaev asked him right away, "Do you know how it was done?" The answer: "No, I do not know anything."[35] Even to such veteran comrades as Boris Ponomarev, the inner workings of the system could be enigmatic. Clearly, he feared this was a signal that others would read. The golden star's absence at his eightieth birthday might endanger his status more than any concrete policy decision. In the end, his staff organized a small celebration, which Chernyaev hoped would help his boss overcome his bitterness.

Of course, one could argue that Chernyaev described this episode in such detail only because no other important events occurred at the time. To an outside observer, the whole affair seems petty. It also exposes how far-removed life at the palace was from the lives of ordinary citizens. But it proves that within the political culture of late socialism, symbols were vitally important. They helped to determine a person's status; that is why Brezhnev himself had so many medals (and so many telephones). Every decoration and each phone line cemented his status. What today seems banal—bordering on the ridiculous—had a distinct meaning within the framework of Soviet communism. Functionaries such as Boris Panomorev were creatures of the system, for they knew no other. The fact that the younger Chernyaev observed this charade with skepticism underlined the limits of the old order.

While some understood that the political culture of the CC was flawed, the status quo continued virtually unchanged until the self-proclaimed game-changer, Gorbachev, took office. How did things evolve under his leadership? After all, his election to the position of general secretary had still followed the traditional scheme: Informal deals among the top players secured him the office. Nevertheless, in the spring of 1985, Chernyaev expected change. He saw the election of the new *gensek* as a sign of hope: "People are tired of social stagnation, of the demonstration of official stupidity, when a leader is turned into an honored puppet, through which, however, some people wield great influence on the course of events." He was also optimistic: "He has great resources. The new personnel of the party apparatus and the real intelligentsia will support him."[36] Clearly, Chernyaev hoped for a new type of leadership from the new *vozhd'*, and as a consequence of the new leadership, for change in the policies and political culture of the Communist Party.

"Net, tak dal'she zhit' nel'zia"—"We cannot go on living like this"[37]: Change and Continuity in Central Committee Party Culture before and during Perestroika

Mikhail Gorbachev was from the party's flesh and blood. He had never held a job outside the realm of Soviet party politics. Still, he implemented reforms that dissidents such as Andrei Amalrik had deemed impossible. Amalrik wrote in 1969, "Any fundamental change would require such a drastic shake-up in personnel from top to bottom that, understandably, those who personify the regime would never embark on it. To save the regime at the cost of firing themselves would seem too exorbitant and unfair a price to pay."[38] This was, however, exactly the course Gorbachev embarked upon. He ended Brezhnev's "stability of cadres" by reintroducing the purge to the Communist Party.

The need for a purge to consolidate his rule was one of the many paradoxes Gorbachev encountered while trying to overhaul the party. He wanted reform, but had to use authoritarian means to enforce change. In a manner unthinkable for anybody but the *gensek*, he began to interfere with the party's internal structure and in the tradition of nineteenth-century Russian reformers, he ruthlessly imposed his policies from above. At the beginning, Gorbachev was still convinced he could turn the party into a vanguard supporting his changes. In order to get his agenda started, he had to use the extraordinary powers and the charisma at the disposal of the general secretary's office. Amalrik had rightly anticipated intense opposition to reform: Gorbachev was up against the *zheleznobetonnaia sistema* (iron-concrete system) that had developed over the decades. It took him some time to grasp that reform-minded functionaries were in the minority. From 1988 onwards, the *gensek* therefore tried to reform the country's political system in opposition to, not in concert with, the party machine.

In his postscript to the year 1985, Chernyaev stated that Gorbachev had changed the political atmosphere in the USSR. Chernyaev's view was that change certainly outweighed continuity. The long, sluggish period of Brezhnev's rule had come to an end, and Gorbachev was fighting for a different future. Even so, the USSR's established political culture did not disappear, and some weapons from the old arsenal of Bolshevik politics even made a comeback.

During the early 1980s, some in the Central Committee perceived that the Soviet system was in crisis. Without doubt, Gorbachev was not the only one who thought that reform was needed to save the system. Low productivity, cynicism, alcoholism, a loss of faith in the Soviet project, and the widening economic and military gap with the West were recognized as signs of political and moral crisis. As always in such situations, the new *gensek* was expected to save the day. Gorbachev started by replacing personnel in the CC. This opened up fresh opportunities for newcomers at the expense of many careers that had begun under Stalin. Those old-timers perceived as incompatible with the new course—such as foreign minister Andrei Gromyko, Moscow party-boss Viktor Grishin, or Ponomarev—quickly lost their positions. "Liberal" functionaries, such as Aleksandr Yakovlev (who spearheaded many of Gorbachev's reform initiatives), were invited back to the central party apparatus. These adjustments represented the most significant realignment of Soviet politics since the Stalin era. Indeed, Gorbachev's decisions on personnel came close to the "revolution from the top" that Chernyaev was hoping for.[39] Changes in the political culture, however, were bound to take more time.

One consequence of Gorbachev's reform was that divisions within the CC suddenly became visible—first internally and eventually publicly. Until 1987, the general secretary could push his decisions through using the power of his office. During the course of 1987, however, an opposition began to form within the party.[40] The doctrine of party unanimity, introduced by Lenin in 1921, slowly began to vanish. It also became clear to Gorbachev's team that the party branch in Moscow, as well as the branches in the outer republics, were stubbornly undermining the new course. The core of the party remained conservative, ready to defend its privileges and the old order. Even in the CC, the reformers were in the minority. The influential head of the organizational department, Yegor Ligachev, turned out to be a staunch defender of the status quo. The reformers had hoped that some changes at the top would suffice to set the CPSU on course. Facing opposition, Gorbachev and his entourage began to understand around 1987 that they had underestimated the amount of resistance their policies would provoke from within the party. Some functionaries distanced themselves from the reform camp in dismay. Chernyaev viewed only Yakovlev, foreign minister Eduard Shevardnadze, and Prime Minister Nikolai Ryzhkov as firm supporters of the general secretary. The anti-reform camp rallied around Ligachev.[41] At the same time, the new Moscow party boss, Boris Yeltsin—who had been a provincial chieftain like Gorbachev before his promotion to Moscow—began offering a populist alternative to Gorbachev's rule.[42] Taking advantage of the chaotic liberalization of Soviet society, Yeltsin questioned the party's overall performance (the deteriorating standard of living became a political issue), challenged its ideology, and attacked the privilege of the *nomenklatura*. To put it simply: he made up his own rules and no longer played his role in Moscow according to the Soviet script. He severed the bonds of loyalty to the party leadership and became his own patron.

Yeltsin turned out to be a politician who tried to advance his position by breaking the unwritten rules. He managed to gain popular approval from Muscovites, and his frequent attacks on the privileged party elite caused irritation within the apparatus. Yeltsin tried to use his charismatic appeal to forge new bonds with the people rather than build a network within the elite. Yet Yeltsin went too far when he publicly attacked Gorbachev—who had brought him to Moscow in the first place—at a Central Committee plenum.[43] He attacked his own patron and the *gensek*, Gorbachev. Yeltsin broke the taboo on openly voicing dissent against higher party leaders. He violated the consensus of what could be criticized even during the third year of perestroika. Evidently, an open assault on the party leader was still impermissible. In his criticism, Yeltsin claimed that change was too slow and that Gorbachev himself was deeply entrenched in the old ways. He argued that the general secretary was building his own "cult of personality," implying that even the reform camp was still tied to the Stalinist ways. Gorbachev and the rest of the party proved Yeltsin right. He was not only forced to resign at the end of 1987, but also publicly ridiculed and humiliated. The orchestrated campaign against Yeltsin was worthy of the old days. By putting him on medication, dragging him before a tribunal, shouting him down, insulting him and making him confess his guilt, the party showed the Stalinism that still ran through its veins. Yet something had changed: Yeltsin's political persona was destroyed, but he was still allowed to remain in the capital and would eventually be able to make a comeback. Had an attack like this been made on any of Gorbachev's predecessors, such a lenient sentence would have been unthinkable.

As we have seen, some of the taboos of Soviet politics were broken during 1987. Unanimity was no longer paramount. The policies of the general secretary could now be attacked in public, from the conservative side, as well as by populists like Yeltsin. Soon the liberal intelligentsia would also make itself heard. Gorbachev, in a way, fell victim to the liberalization he had initiated. In asking for open discussion, he facilitated the rise of an opposition. Nevertheless, his opponents had to maneuver carefully, as Yeltsin's example made clear. In early 1988, Ligachev chose not to attack the *gensek* himself, but instead released a letter by the obscure Leningrad lecturer Nina Andreeva to the now somewhat open press.[44] He chose a time when Gorbachev was out of the country. The letter, which called for a return to the old order, initially received much praise from inside the party apparatus. When Gorbachev returned home, he went on a passionate counteroffensive. In the end, Ligachev's attack backfired, but his *modus operandi* probably saved his position in the politburo. He ended up distancing himself from the campaign against perestroika that he himself had initiated. However, it did not escape Gorbachev's team that Nina Andreeva's letter had enjoyed substantial popularity with much of Moscow's officialdom. She became an icon of resistance to perestroika.

The affairs involving Ligachev and Yeltsin underlined two important changes in the political culture of the CC and the Soviet Union at large that occurred during perestroika. First, one could oppose the general secretary's policies without being politically doomed. Second, it was now possible to build a political base not only within, but also against the party. Yeltsin was the first person from the party apparatus that dared to take this step. But his move reflected a larger trend: while glasnost and perestroika progressed, the legitimacy of the Communist Party crumbled. Gorbachev and his *komanda* (team) understood this. In this light, the election of the Congress of People's Deputies at the beginning of 1989 was not just a step toward the USSR's democratization. It was also a step away from the party, an attempt to marginalize its entrenched, privileged elite and create a new playing field where reformers would dominate and Communist orthodoxy could be freely criticized. Though they were, perhaps, consistent with the spirit of glasnost, these moves toward open public debate and political contest created new problems for Gorbachev. The general secretary could now be publicly attacked from all sides. It was only a matter of time before his authority within the party and the USSR began to crumble. And the composition of the congress showed that the conservative camp could also organize electoral success.

The year 1989 not only saw Mikhail Gorbachev well established as the star on the international stage, but was also the year in which his popularity turned to disrespect in the USSR. In the fateful months of 1989, Gorbachev not only lost his power base, the party; he lost control of the political game. The man who had come of age in the ranks of the CPSU and had learned how to maneuver behind the closed doors of party buildings was not made for open political contest. This was also true for the other members of his entourage. Leaving the party to Ligachev and the provincial bigwigs, in 1988 Gorbachev's close associates had chosen to mostly abandon the brand of secretive Soviet politics they had lived and breathed their entire lives. They created new political and social institutions—a parliament and a public sphere—whose dynamic and open nature they failed to understand. Gorbachev's promotion to president of the USSR was needed to build an authoritarian counterweight to the pluralism his tenure as general secretary had created. Even so, the attempt to create a government of enlightened experts failed. Gorbachev and his team found the political forces they had unleashed more and more difficult to control.

At the very time when Gorbachev tried to use the Soviet state as a power base against his party, that state had begun to disintegrate at its peripheries. In 1990, he was the leader of an empire that had lost its position in Eastern and Central Europe and was starting to lose control over its own outer republics. Gorbachev had turned against the party structures, but had failed to build a new political base. Fatefully, Gorbachev no longer had the requisite influence to reform the centers of power that still existed: the Ministries of Defense and Interior, and the KGB. They continued to exist and, in the long run, proved to be the winners in this political game. The general secretary had managed to discredit the party, but he had not touched other core instruments of authoritarianism; this allowed the Soviet Army and the KGB to make institutional comebacks in the 1990s. By creating the presidency, he established the office that his successor, Boris Yeltsin, would turn into the base of a new Russian autocracy.

The CC itself was cut off from power and lost its function after the putsch in the summer of 1991.[45] Gorbachev himself slipped from power as the USSR disintegrated and Yeltsin's team took over the core of the state—the budget, the army, and the Security Services—in the fall of 1991. A study that examines the career of CC employees in post-Soviet Russia remains lacking. While Yeltsin briefly outlawed the Communist Party after the putsch, he and his team certainly needed the expertise of those who knew how Russia was governed, and the seat of administrative power remained: the new president chose to locate his administration at the former CC building at *Staraia Ploshchad'*.

Some Conclusions

The question of how Soviet party culture changed in this period has one obvious answer: it ended in August 1991, when Boris Yeltsin suspended the CPSU. That was one unintended result of the coup, as well as of the momentous reforms initiated by Gorbachev. The empire that the Communist Party had ruled for seven decades—the Soviet Union—survived the party for another couple of months. It is noteworthy that the office of the president, which Gorbachev had established, persisted in Russia. The center of authoritarian power, once in the party, gravitated to the Presidential Administration of the Russian Federation. It surely is no coincidence that the presidential administration is today located at *Staraia Ploshchad'*—the former seat of the Central Committee. Under Vladimir Putin, it is once again the most powerful institution in the country, which carries more weight than the government or the Duma.

Mikhail Gorbachev's attempt to create a parliament as a forum for debate and a counterweight to bureaucracy failed. Today's Russian Duma is once again the same type of rubber-stamp assembly that the Supreme Soviet had been in the USSR. The authoritarian tradition proved hard to replace, and "stability"—as in Brezhnev's times—is once again a catchword to justify autocratic structures. Public debate had irritated both Gorbachev and Yeltsin, but they deemed it necessary to modernize the USSR and, after its collapse, Russia. Under Vladimir Putin's rule, public discussion is limited to a small number of newspapers, the radio station *Ekho Moskvy*, and the internet. The state news networks' fixation on Putin resembles the Soviet-era cult of the *gensek* as *vozhd'*.[46] Meanwhile, the regime has once again lost the liberal intelligentsia that now forms the core of an opposition movement.[47] As in Brezhnev's days, the party of power (*vlast'*) stands in opposition to educated society (*obshchestvennost'*). Through propaganda, social benefits, and repression, it tries to keep the population acquiescent.

Apart from general observations on political culture in Russia, one may ask, what was left of the party? Well, there is still the Communist Party of Russia, led by Gennady Zyuganov.[48] But while it has become a haven for nostalgia and a hotbed of Stalinist nationalism, it has never returned to power. This is what distinguishes it from the CPSU: it is not a power machine. Rather, it is the faltering voice of those who have been left on the margins of the new Russia. Increasingly, it has had to play its assigned role in scripted post-Soviet politics.[49] Its political ideas derive from the Stalinist-nationalist current in the former CPSU. Interestingly, Zyuganov's party confirms one of Andrei Amalrik's predictions from the 1970s: in the event of an ideological competition between Stalinist nationalists and moderates, the Stalinists would ultimately prevail.

As Russia's Communist Party is now on the sidelines of political life, we must look elsewhere for the legacy of the CPSU's political culture. Overall, it is fair to say that the lack of trust that characterized interpersonal relations in the CPSU is still present in Russian politics. Mistrust, especially against people one does not know personally, remains the core of Russian governance and, indeed, society. At the same time, personal relations are still more important than political performance or formal qualifications for any given position. Like Brezhnev, who favored men from Dnepropetrovsk, Putin likes to promote men from his native St. Petersburg or from the Secret Services.[50] Sponsorship and personal loyalty are still crucial elements of political culture among Russian elites. There is still much we do not know about the inner machinations of the Yeltsin and Putin administrations, but we know that they consist of different teams that compete against each other, of male networks striving for the attention of the leader and for more power and wealth. Intrigue, conspiracy, and blackmail are significant as well, but, as in Soviet times, it is costly to be publicly identified with an oppositional current.[51] Most power games are played out behind the scenes; what the public sees is just the tip of the political iceberg. Under Putin, an informal politburo controls the higher echelons of power.[52] The Russian population is presented with the results of these inner struggles and is left to wonder why certain decisions were made, why certain policies were adopted, and why certain things were said. Neither the party machine nor communism survived either ideologically or structurally, yet equivalent institutions have emerged that support the autocratic and authoritarian political system. The Russian elite in the Kremlin and at *Staraia Ploshchad'* is still playing a political game that bears many similarities to the Soviet past.

Jan C. Behrends is a research fellow at the Centre for Contemporary History (ZZF) in Potsdam. He teaches East European history at Humboldt University Berlin. Recent publications include (ed.) *The Return to War and Violence: Case Studies on the USSR, Russia and Yugoslavia (1979–2014)* (2017), as well as (ed. with Thomas Lindenberger and Nikolaus Katzer) *100 Jahre Roter Oktober. Zur Weltgeschichte der Russischen Revolution* (2017).

Notes

I would like to acknowledge the assistance of Philip Decker, New York, in editing this essay.
1. On the history of the Soviet Communist Party, see, e.g., Leonard Shapiro, *The Communist Party of the Soviet Union* (London, 1960); A. B. Bezborodov,

ed., *Istoriia kommunisticheskoi partii Sovetskogo Soiuza* [History of the Soviet Communist Party] (Moscow, 2013). On the party's political and social history, see the sections in Manfred Hildermeier, *Geschichte der Sowjetunion. Aufstieg und Niedergang des ersten sozialistischen Staates* [History of the Soviet Union. Rise and downfall of the first socialist state] (Munich, 1998). For a party history in portraits, see Roy Medvedev, *All Stalin's Men* (Oxford, 1983); Dmitrii Volkogonov, *Sem' vozhdei. Galereia liderov SSSR* [Seven leaders. A gallery of the leaders of the USSR], 2 vols. (Moscow, 1995). On the last years of the CPSU, see Philip G. Roeder, *Red Sunset: The Failure of Soviet Politics* (Princeton NJ, 1992); Graeme Gill, *The Collapse of the Single Party System: The Disintegration of the Communist Party of the Soviet Union* (Cambridge, 1994); David Krotz with Fred Weir, *Revolution from Above: The Demise of the Soviet System* (London, 1997); Gordon M. Hahn, *Russia's Revolution from Above, 1985–2000: Reform, Transition, and Revolution in the Fall of the Soviet Communist Regime, 1985–2000* (New Brunswick, 2002); Jonathan Harris, *Subverting the System: Gorbachev's Reform of the Party's Apparat* (Lanham, MD, 2004); Atsushi Ogushi, *The Demise of the Soviet Communist Party* (London, 2008). On the communist movement and its interaction with the USSR, see Silvio Pons, *The Global Revolution: A History of International Communism* (Oxford, 2014).
2. For an overview of the CPSU's structure, see Ronald J. Hill and Peter Frank, *The Soviet Communist Party* (Winchester, MA, 1986).
3. For a history of the party leadership under Stalin, see Oleg Khlevniuk, *Master of the House. Stalin and His Inner Circle* (New Haven, CT, 2009). For late Stalinism, see Yoram Gorlizki and Oleg Khlevniuk, *Cold Peace: Stalin and the Soviet Ruling Circle* (Oxford, 2004); Sheila Fitzpatrick, *On Stalin's Team: The Years of Living Dangerously in Soviet Politics* (Princeton, NJ, 2015). For a recent biography of Stalin, see Oleg Khlevniuk, *Stalin: New Biography of a Dictator* (New Haven, 2015).
4. See Jan C. Behrends, "War, Violence and the Military during Late Socialism and Transition," *Nationalities Papers* 43 (2015): 47–66.
5. On Soviet elites, see Evan Mawdsley and Steven White, *The Soviet Elite from Lenin to Gorbachev: The Central Committee and its Members, 1917–1991* (Oxford, 2000); on the post-Soviet era, see David Lane and Cameron Ross, *The Transition from Communism to Capitalism: Ruling Elites from Gorbachev to Yeltsin* (New York, 1999).
6. The party was part of a larger trend in Soviet society as described by Alena Ledeneva, *Russia's Economy of Favors: Blat, Networking and Informal Exchange* (Cambridge, 1998).
7. For an account of the Soviet CC during late socialism, see Jerry F. Hough and Merle Fainsod, *How the Soviet Union Is Governed* (Cambridge, MA, 1979), 409–448. For an overview of its members, see A. D. Chernev, *229 kremlevskikh vozhdei. Politbiuro, Orgbiuro, Sekretariat CK Kommunisticheskoi partii v licakh i cifrakh* [229 Kremlin leaders. Politburo, orgburo, CC secretariat of the Communist Party in persons and numbers] (Moscow, 1996).
8. Memoirs and other accounts of political life in the Central Committee include Mikhail Gorbachev, *Memoirs* (London, 1996); Eduard Schewardnadse, *Die Zukunft gehört der Freiheit* [The future belongs to freedom] (Reinbek near

Hamburg, 1991); Boris Yeltsin, *Against the Grain: An Autobiography* (London, 1990); Yegor Ligachev, *Inside Gorbachev's Kremlin: The Memoirs of Yegor Ligachev* (New York, 1993); Georgi Arbatov, *The System: An Insider's Life in Soviet Politics* (New York, 1992); Vadim Medvedev, *V komande Gorbacheva. Vzgliad iznutri* [On Gorbachev's Team. A View from the Inside] (Moscow, 1994); Valery Boldin, *Ten Years that Shook the World: The Gorbachev Era as Witnessed by his Chief of Staff* (New York, 1994); Anatoly S. Chernyaev, *My Six Years with Gorbachev* (University Park, 2000); Raisa Gorbacheva, *Ia nadeius'* . . . [I hope . . .] (Moscow, 1991); N. I. Ryzhkov, *Perestroika: istoriia preddatel'stv* [Perestroika: A history of treason] (Moscow, 1992); Idem, *Ia iz partii po imeni "Rossiia"* [I am from the party called "Russia"] (Moscow, 1995). Of special significance are Anatoly Chernyaev's published diaries that cover the years 1972–1991, Anatoly S. Chernyaev, *Sovmestnyi iskhod: dnevnik dvukh epokh (1972–1991)* [Collective exit. A diary of two eras (1972–1991)] (Moscow, 2008). For further evidence on the CPSU in the Gorbachev era, see also Svetlana Savranskaya, Thomas Blanton, and Vladislav Zubok, *Masterpieces of History: The Peaceful End of the Cold War in Europe* (Budapest, 2010); M. S. Gorbachev, ed., *Gody trudnykh reshenii* [Years of difficult decisions] (Moscow, 1992); Anatoly S. Chernyaev, ed., *V Politbiuro CK KPSS . . . Po zapisiam Anatoliia Cherniaeva, Vadima Medvedeva, Georgiia Shakhnazarova (1985–1991)* [In the CPSU politburo . . . according to notes of Anatoly Chernyaev, Vadim Medvedev, Georgy Shakhnazarov (1985–1991)] (Moscow, 2006); Aleksandr Iakovlev, *Perestroika 1985–1991* (Moscow, 2008); idem: *Izbrannye interv'iu, 1992–2005* [Selected interviews, 1992–2005] (Moscow, 2009). For ideological texts on perestroika, see Abel Aganbegyan, ed., *Perestroika 1989* (London, 1989). For interviews with some of the protagonists, see Stephen F. Cohen and Katrina van den Heuvel, eds., *Voices of Glasnost: Interviews with Gorbachev's Reformers* (New York, 1989).

9. For the political history of perestroika and for different views on Mikhail Gorbachev, cf. Jonathan Steele, *Eternal Russia: Yeltsin, Gorbachev, and the Mirage of Democracy* (Cambridge, MA, 1994); Mikhail Geller, *Utopiia u vlasti: kniga tret'ia. Sed'moi sekretar'. Blesk i nishcheta Mikhaila Gorbacheva* [Utopia in power: The seventh secretary. Mikhail Gorbachev's glory and misery] (Moscow, 1996); Archie Brown, *The Gorbachev Factor* (Oxford, 1997); Martin McCauley, *Gorbachev* (London, 1998); Anthony D'Agostino, *Gorbachev's Revolution, 1985–1991* (Basingstoke, 1998); Archie Brown, *Seven Years that Changed the World: Perestroika in Perspective* (Oxford, 2007); Timothy J. Colton, *Yeltsin: A Life* (New York, 2008); William Taubman, *Gorbachev. His Life and Times* (New York, 2017) from a comparative perspective, see George W. Breslauer, *Gorbachev and Yeltsin as Leaders* (Cambridge, 2002); Mark Kramer, "The Demise of the Soviet Bloc," in *Imposing, Maintaining, and Tearing Open the Iron Curtain: East-Central Europe and the Cold War, 1945–1990*, ed. Mark Kramer and Vít Smetana (Lanham, MD, 2014), 367–435.

10. My perspective on political history is inspired by Thomas Mergel, "Überlegungen zu einer Kulturgeschichte der Politik" [Thoughts about a cultural history of politics), *Geschichte und Gesellschaft* 28 (2002): 574–606. See also idem, "Kulturgeschichte der Politik" [Cultural history of poli-

tics], *Docupedia–Zeitgeschichte,* 22 October 2012. http://docupedia.de/zg/ Kulturgeschichte_der_Politik_Version_2.0_Thomas_Mergel?oldid=84783.

11. For sociological data on Soviet party elites in late socialism, see Hildermeier, *Geschichte der Sowjetunion* [History of the Soviet Union], 826–857.
12. The Soviet memory of Stalinism is explored in Polly Jones, *Myth, Memory, Trauma: Rethinking the Stalinist Past in the Soviet Union, 1953–1970* (New Haven, 2013).
13. Andrei Amalrik, "Ideologies in Soviet Society," in *Will the Soviet Union Survive Until 1984?,* ed. idem (New York, 1980), 174–187.
14. On Russian nationalism within the official power structure, see also Yithak M. Brudny, *Reinventing Russia: Russian Nationalism and the Soviet State, 1953–1991* (Cambridge, MA, 1998); Nikolai Mitrokhin, *Russkaia Partiia: Dvizhenie russkikh natsionalistov v SSSR, 1953–1985 gody* [The Russian party. The movement of Russian nationalists in the USSR, 1953–1985] (Moscow, 2003). On Suslov, see also Medvedev, *All Stalin's Men,* 61–81.
15. Amalrik, *Ideologies,* 181. The ideological tendencies in the national branches outside Russia cannot be discussed in this essay. Certainly nationalist tendencies existed in many republics. In Central Asia the party was often characterized by clan structures.
16. Robert Horvath, *The Legacy of Soviet Dissent: Dissidents, Democratization, and the Rise of Nationalism in Russia* (New York, 2005).
17. William Taubman, *Khrushchev: The Man and His Era* (New York, 2003), 236–269. See also Jurii Aksiutin, *Chrushchevskaia "ottepel'." Obshchestvennye nastroeniia v SSSR v 1953–1964 gg.* [Khrushchev's "thaw." Public perceptions in the USSR 1953–1964] (Moscow, 2010).
18. From a "liberal" point of view, see the recollections of Georgi Arbatov, *The System: An Insider's Account of Soviet Politics* (New York, 1992), 104–142.
19. For an account of Yakovlev's views on Soviet politics, see Yakovlev, *Izbrannye interv'iu* [Selected interviews] (Moscow, 2009). See also his impressive account of Soviet party history, *A Century of Violence in Soviet Russia* (New Haven, 2002).
20. See, e.g., Gennady Gorelik, *The World of Andrei Sakharov: A Russian Physicist's Path to Freedom* (Oxford, 2005); Emma Giligan, *Defending Human Rights in Russia: Sergey Kovalyov, Dissident and Human Rights Commissioner, 1969–2003* (London, 2004).
21. Amalrik, *Ideologies,* 182.
22. On views within the intelligentsia, see Dietrich Beyrau, *Intelligenz und Dissens. Die russischen Bildungsschichten in der Sowjetunion, 1917–1985* [Intelligentsia and dissent. Russian educated classes in the USSR, 1917–1985] (Göttingen, 1993).
23. Chernyaev, *Sovmestnyi iskhod,* 595–596.
24. Arbatov, *The System,* 62–93.
25. Mikhail Gorbachev and Zdeněk Mlynář, *Conversations with Gorbachev: On Perestroika, the Prague Spring and the Crossroads of Socialism,* trans. George Shriver, with a Foreword by Archie Brown (New York, 2002), 48.
26. The memoirs and diaries of the more educated and Western-oriented apparatchiks also offer the more interesting insights into the political culture

of the CC. This might be the case because they could imagine a different political order while some of their colleagues just took the existing system for granted.
27. On Gorbachev's tenure in Stavropol, see Dalos, *Gorbatschow*, 23–54.
28. Gorbachev, *Memoirs*, 84. For a case study of local secretaries in late Soviet socialism, see Yoram Gorlizki, "Too Much Trust: Regional Leader and Local Political Networks under Brezhnev," in *Slavic Review* 69, no. 3 (2010): 676–700.
29. See Arbatov, *The System*, 62–93. On Yurii Andropov, see Dmitrii Volkogonov, *Sem' vozhdei. Galereia liderov SSSR* [Seven leaders. A gallery of the leaders of the USSR], vol. 2 (Moscow, 1996), 111–194.
30. Volkogonov, *Sem' vozhdei*, vol. 2, 121.
31. This had already been the case under Stalin. During the late 1940s and early 1950s, Stalin invited his inner circle to his Moscow dacha for politics and entertainment. To no longer be invited to these informal gatherings—like Molotov and Mikoyan in 1952—was a clear sign one was out of favor and possibly in personal danger. See Khlevniuk, *Stalin*, 142–149. For detailed descriptions of these gatherings and their political as well as social functions, see Nikita Khrushchev, *Khrushchev Remembers: The Glasnost Tapes* (Boston, 1990).
32. Ibid., 122.
33. The same was true to a certain degree for Soviet society in general. See Ledeneva, *Russia's Economy of Favours*.
34. For this putsch, see Taubman, *Khrushchev*, 578–619.
35. Chernyaev, *Sovmestnyi iskhod*, 594.
36. Chernyaev, *Sovmestnyi iskhod*, 11 March 1985, 608–610.
37. Quote attributed to Mikhail Gorbachev by his wife on the eve of his election as general secretary: Raisa Gorbacheva, *Ia nadeius'. . .* [I hope . . .] (Moscow, 1991), 13, but also a widespread feeling in the USSR at this time.
38. Amalrik, *Will the Soviet Union Survive*, 44.
39. Chernyaev, *Sovmestnyi iskhod*, 13 March 1985, 610.
40. See Chernyaev, *My Six Years with Gorbachev*, 97–134.
41. Ligachev, *Inside Gorbachev's Kremlin*, 83–145.
42. On Yeltsin, see Leon Aron, *Yeltsin: A Revolutionary Life* (New York, 2000); Timothy J. Colton, *Yeltsin: A Life* (New York, 2008).
43. For detailed accounts of the affair, see Aron, *Yeltsin: A Revolutionary Life*, 202–217, and Colton, *Yeltsin: A Life*, 129–150.
44. See Dalos, *Gorbatschow*, 170–176, for a detailed account.
45. Ignac Lozo, *Avgustovskii putch 1991 goda. Kak eto bylo* [The August coup of 1991. How it really was] (Moscow, 2014). See also Serhii Plokhy, *The Last Empire: The Final Days of the Soviet Union* (London, 2014). The most impressive inside account is Chernyaev, *Sovmestnyi iskhod*, 969–1046, who gives a comprehensive account of Yeltsin's counter-putsch and of the last days of Gorbachev's power.
46. For the specifics of Putin's cult, see Helena Goscilo, ed., *Putin as Celebrity and Cultural Icon* (London, 2013); Anna Arutunyan, *The Putin Mystique: Inside Russia's Power Cult* (Newbold on Stour, 2014).

47. Mischa Gabowitsch, *Putin kaputt?! Russlands neue Protestkultur* [Putin broken?! Russia's new protest culture] (Berlin, 2013).
48. Luke March, *The Communist Party in Post-Soviet Russia* (Manchester, 2002).
49. See Andrew Wilson, *Virtual Politics: Faking Democracy in the Post-Soviet World* (New Haven, 2005).
50. On Russia's political system under Putin, see Lilia Shevtsova, *Putin's Russia* (Washington, DC, 2005); Fiona Hill and Clifford G. Gaddy, *Mr. Putin: Operative in the Kremlin* (Washington, DC, 2015); Vladimir Gel'man, *Authoritarian Russia: Analyzing Post-Soviet Regime Changes* (Pittsburgh, 2015); Steven Lee Myers, *The New Tsar: The Rise and Reign of Vladimir Putin* (New York, 2015).
51. On blackmail and intrigue in post-Soviet politics, see Alena Ledeneva, *How Russia Really Works: The Informal Practices that Shaped Post-Soviet Politics and Business* (Ithaca, NY, 2006), 58–90.
52. Mikhail Zygar, *"Vsia kremlevskaia rat'." Kratkaia istoriia sovremennoi Rossii* ["All the Kremlin's knights." A short history of contemporary Russia] (Moscow, 2016).

Bibliography

Aganbegyan, Abel, ed. *Perestroika 1989*. London: Bantam Press, 1989.
Aksiutin, Jurii. *Chrushchevskaia "ottepel'." Obshchestvennye nastroeniia v SSSR v 1953–1964 gg.* [Khrushchev's "thaw." Public perceptions in the USSR 1953–1964]. Moscow: ROSSPEN, 2010.
Amalrik, Andrei. "Ideologies in Soviet Society." In *Will the Soviet Union Survive until 1984?* ed. Andrei Amalrik, 174–187. New York: Harper Colophon Books, 1980.
Arbatov, Georgi. *The System: An Insider's Life in Soviet Politics*. New York: Times Books, 1992.
Aron, Leon. *Yeltsin: A Revolutionary Life*. New York: St. Martin's Press, 2000.
Arutunyan, Anna. *The Putin Mystique: Inside Russia's Power Cult*. Newbold on Stour: Skyscraper Publications, 2014.
Behrends, Jan C. "War, Violence and the Military during Late Socialism and Transition." *Nationalities Papers* 43 (2015): 47–66.
Beyrau, Dietrich., ed. *Intelligenz und Dissens. Die russischen Bildungsschichten in der Sowjetunion, 1917–1985* [Intelligentsia and dissent. Russian educated classes in the USSR, 1917–1985]. Göttingen: Vandenhoeck und Ruprecht, 1993.
Bezborodov, Aleksandr B., ed. *Istoriia kommunisticheskoi partii Sovetskogo Soiuza* [History of the Soviet Communist Party]. Moscow: ROSSPEN, 2013.
Boldin, Valery. *Ten Years that Shook the World: The Gorbachev Era as Witnessed by his Chief of Staff*. New York: Basic Books, 1994.
Breslauer, George W. *Gorbachev and Yeltsin as Leaders*. Cambridge: Cambridge University Press, 2002.
Brown, Archie. *The Gorbachev Factor*. Oxford: Oxford University Press, 1997.
———. *Seven Years that Changed the World: Perestroika in Perspective*. Oxford: Oxford University Press, 2007.

Brudny, Yitzhak M. *Reinventing Russia: Russian Nationalism and the Soviet State, 1953–1991.* Cambridge, MA: Harvard University Press, 1998.
Chernev, Anatolii D. *229 kremlevskikh vozhdei. Politbiuro, Orgbiuro, Sekretariat CK Kommunisticheskoi partii v licakh i cifrakh* [229 Kremlin leaders. Politburo, orgburo, CC secretariat of the Communist Party in persons and numbers]. Moscow: Rodina, 1996.
Chernyaev, Anatoly S. *My Six Years with Gorbachev.* Transl. and ed. by Robert D. English and Elizabeth Tucker. University Park: Pennsylvania State University Press, 2000.
———, ed. *V Politbiuro CK KPSS . . . Po zapisiam Anatoliia Cherniaeva, Vadima Medvedeva, Georgiia Shakhnazarova, 1985–1991* [In the CPSU politburo . . . according to notes of Anatoly Chernyaev, Vadim Medvedev, Georgy Shakhnazarov, 1985–1991]. Moscow: Gorbachev-Fond, 2006.
———. *Sovmestnyi iskhod: dnevnik dvukh epokh (1972–1991)* [Collective exit. A diary of two eras (1972–1991)]. Moscow: ROSSPEN, 2008.
Cohen, Stephen F., and Katrina van den Heuvel, eds. *Voices of Glasnost: Interviews with Gorbachev's Reformers.* New York: Norton, 1989.
Colton, Timothy J. *Yeltsin: A Life.* New York: Basic Books, 2008.
Dalos, György. *Gorbatschow. Mensch und Macht.* München: Ch. Beck, 2011.
Fitzpatrick, Sheila. *On Stalin's Team: The Years of Living Dangerously in Soviet Politics.* Princeton: Princeton University Press, 2015.
Gabowitsch, Mischa. *Putin kaputt?! Russlands neue Protestkultur* [Putin broken?! Russia's new protest culture]. Berlin: Suhrkamp, 2013.
Geller, Mikhail. *Utopiia u vlasti. Sed'moi sekretar'. Blesk i nishcheta Mikhaila Gorbacheva,* vol. 3 [Utopia in power. The seventh secretary. Mikhail Gorbachev's glory and misery]. Moscow: MIK, 1996.
Gel'man, Vladimir. *Authoritarian Russia: Analyzing Post-Soviet Regime Changes.* Pittsburgh: University of Pittsburg Press, 2015.
Gill, Graeme. *The Collapse of the Single Party System: The Disintegration of the Communist Party of the Soviet Union.* Cambridge: Cambridge University Press, 1994.
Gilligan, Emma. *Defending Human Rights in Russia: Sergey Kovalyov, Dissident and Human Rights Commissioner, 1969–2003.* London: Routledge, 2004.
Gorbachev, Mikhail. *Memoirs.* London: Doubleday, 1996.
———, ed. *Gody trudnykh reshenii* [Years of difficult decisions]. Moscow: Al'faprint, 1992.
Gorbachev, Mikhail, and Zdeněk Mlynář. *Conversations with Gorbachev: On Perestroika, the Prague Spring and the Crossroads of Socialism.* Trans. George Shriver, with a Foreword by Archie Brown. New York: Columbia University Press, 2002.
Gorbacheva, Raisa. *Ia nadeius' . . .* [I hope . . .]. Moscow: Novosti, 1991.
Gorelik, Gennady. *The World of Andrei Sakharov: A Russian Physicist's Path to Freedom.* Oxford: Oxford University Press, 2005.
Gorlitzki, Yoram. "Too Much Trust: Regional Party Leaders and Local Political Networks under Brezhnev." *Slavic Review* 69, no. 3 (2010): 676–700.
Gorlitzki, Yoram, and Oleg Khlevniuk. *Cold Peace: Stalin and the Soviet Ruling Circle, 1945–53.* Oxford: Oxford University Press, 2004.

Goscilo, Helena, ed. *Putin as Celebrity and Cultural Icon.* London: Routledge, 2013.
Hahn, Gordon M. *Russia's Revolution from Above, 1985–2000: Reform, Transition, and Revolution in the Fall of the Soviet Communist Regime, 1985–2000.* New Brunswick: Transaction Publishers, 2002.
Harris, Jonathan. *Subverting the System: Gorbachev's Reform of the Party's Apparat.* Lanham, MD: Rowman & Littlefield, 2004.
Hildermeier, Manfred. *Geschichte der Sowjetunion. Aufstieg und Niedergang des ersten sozialistischen Staates* [History of the Soviet Union. Rise and downfall of the first socialist state]. Munich: C. H. Beck, 1998.
Hill, Fiona, and Clifford G. Gaddy. *Mr. Putin: Operative in the Kremlin.* Washington, DC: Brookings Institution Press, 2015.
Hill, Ronald J., and Peter Frank. *The Soviet Communist Party.* Winchester, MA: Allen & Unwin, 1986.
Horvath, Robert. *The Legacy of Soviet Dissent: Dissidents, Democratization, and the Rise of Nationalism in Russia.* London: Routledge, 2005.
Hough, Jerry F., and Merle Fainsod. *How the Soviet Union is Governed.* Cambridge, MA: Harvard University Press, 1979.
Jones, Polly. *Myth, Memory, Trauma: Rethinking the Stalinist Past in the Soviet Union, 1953–1970.* New Haven: Yale University Press, 2013.
Khlevniuk, Oleg. *Master of the House: Stalin and His Inner Circle.* New Haven: Yale University Press, 2009.
———. *Stalin: New Biography of a Dictator.* New Haven: Yale University Press, 2015.
Khrushchev, Nikita. *Khrushchev Remembers: The Glasnost Tapes.* Boston: Little, Brown and Co., 1990.
Kramer, Mark. "The Demise of the Soviet Bloc." In *Imposing, Maintaining, and Tearing Open the Iron Curtain: East-Central Europe and the Cold War, 1945–1990,* ed. Mark Kramer and Vít Smetana, 367–435. Lanham, MD: Rowman & Littlefield, 2014.
Krotz, David, with Fred Weir. *Revolution from Above: The Demise of the Soviet System.* London: Routledge, 1997.
Lane, David, and Cameron Ross. *The Transition from Communism to Capitalism: Ruling Elites from Gorbachev to Yeltsin.* New York: Macmillan, 1999.
Ledeneva, Alena. *Russia's Economy of Favours: Blat, Networking, and Informal Exchange.* Cambridge: Cambridge University Press, 1998.
———. *How Russia Really Works: The Informal Practices that Shaped Post-Soviet Politics and Business.* Ithaca, NY: Cornell University Press, 2006.
Ligachev, Yegor. *Inside Gorbachev's Kremlin: The Memoirs of Yegor Ligachev.* New York: Pantheon Books, 1993.
Lozo, Ignac. *Avgustovskii putch 1991 goda. Kak eto bylo* [The August coup of 1991. How it really was]. Moscow: ROSSPEN, 2014.
March, Luke. *The Communist Party in Post-Soviet Russia.* Manchester: Manchester University Press, 2002.
Mawdsely, Evan, and Steven White. *The Soviet Elite from Lenin to Gorbachev: The Central Committee and its Members, 1917–1991.* Oxford: Oxford University Press, 2000.

Medvedev, Roy. *All Stalin's Men*. Oxford: Blackwell, 1983.
Medvedev, Vadim. *V komande Gorbacheva. Vzgliad iznutri* [On Gorbachev's Team. A View from the Inside]. Moscow: Bylina, 1994.
Mergel, Thomas. "Kulturgeschichte der Politik" [Cultural history of politics]. Docupedia-Zeitgeschichte, 22 October 2012. http://docupedia.de/zg/Kulturgeschichte_der_Politik_Version_2.0_Thomas_Mergel?oldid=84783.
———. "Überlegungen zu einer Kulturgeschichte der Politik" [Thoughts about a cultural history of politics]." *Geschichte und Gesellschaft* 28 (2002): 574–606.
Mitrokhin, Nikolay. *Russkaia Partiia: dvizhenie russkikh natsionalistov v SSSR, 1953–1985 gody* [The Russian party. The movement of Russian nationalists in the USSR, 1953–1985]. Moscow: Novoe literaturnoe obozrenie, 2003.
Myers, Steven Lee. *The New Tsar: The Rise and Reign of Vladimir Putin*. New York: Random House, 2015.
Ogushi, Atsushi. *The Demise of the Soviet Communist Party*. London: Routledge, 2008.
Plokhy, Serhii. *The Last Empire: The Final Days of the Soviet Union*. London: Oneworld Publications, 2014.
Pons, Silvio. *The Global Revolution: A History of International Communism, 1917–1991*. Oxford: Oxford University Press, 2014.
Roeder, Philip G. *Red Sunset: The Failure of Soviet Politics*. Princeton: Princeton University Press, 1992.
Ryzhkov, Nikolai I. *Ia iz partii po imeni "Rossiia"* [I am from the party called "Russia"]. Moscow: Obozrevatel', 1995.
———. *Perestroika: istoriia predatel'stv* [Perestroika: A history of treason]. Moscow: Novosti, 1992.
Savranskaya, Svetlana, Thomas Blanton, and Vladislav Zubok, ed. *Masterpieces of History: The Peaceful End of the Cold War in Europe*. Budapest: Central European University Press, 2010.
Schapiro, Leonard. *The Communist Party of the Soviet Union*. New York: Random House, 1960.
Schewardnadse, Eduard. *Die Zukunft gehört der Freiheit* [The future belongs to freedom]. Reinbek near Hamburg: Rowohlt, 1991.
Shevtsova, Lilia. *Putin's Russia*. Washington, DC: Carnegie Endowment for International Peace, 2005.
Steele, Jonathan. *Eternal Russia: Yeltsin, Gorbachev, and the Mirage of Democracy*. Cambridge, MA: Harvard University Press, 1994.
Taubman, William. *Khrushchev: The Man and His Era*. New York: Free Press, 2003.
Taubman, William. *Gorbachev. His Life and Times*. New York: W. W. Norton, 2017.
Volkogonov, Dmitrii. *Sem' vozhdei. Galereia liderov SSSR* [Seven leaders. A gallery of the leaders of the USSR]. 2 vols. Moscow: Novosti, 1995.
Wilson, Andrew. *Virtual Politics: Faking Democracy in the Post-Soviet World*. New Haven: Yale University Press, 2005.
Yakovlev, Aleksandr. *A Century of Violence in Soviet Russia*. New Haven: Yale University Press, 2002.
———. *Izbrannye interv'iu, 1992–2005* [Selected interviews, 1992–2005]. Moscow: Mezhdunarodnyi Fond Demokratija, 2009.

———. *Perestroika 1985–1991*. Moscow: Mezhdunarodnyi Fond Demokratija, 2008.
Yeltsin, Boris. *Against the Grain: An Autobiography*. London: Cape, 1990.
Zygar, Mikhail. *"Vsia kremlevskaia rat'." Kratkaia istoria sovremennoi Rossii* ["All the Kremlin's knights." A short history of contemporary Russia]. Moscow: Intelektal'naia literatura, 2016.

15

THE IRONIES OF MEMBERSHIP
The Ruling Communist Party in Comparative Perspective
Padraic Kenney

We are at a very good moment in time for the study of the ruling Communist parties of Eastern Europe. Twenty-five years after the regimes they ruled have crumbled, they have become quite foreign, their cultural practices and mindsets exotic to anyone who did not live through them. Indeed, there are now historians of the Communist era who have written dissertations and books, and acquired positions at universities, who have no adult memories whatsoever of the Communist era, let alone of that mass institution at the center of that vanished political landscape. While of course that distance often enough allows for fantastical ideas about these parties and their members to circulate—that they were utterly foreign, for example—it should also allow us to approach them with equanimity and some analytical rigor, too. That is one of the signal achievements of the conference that has led to this book.

Thinking about how to explain this peculiar institution, I am struck by the similarity to the institution that studies it: namely, the academic conference. Has not each of us had the experience of telling a family member, "I'm spending a weekend in a conference room talking about Communist parties," or "I've been appointed to a committee to work on the strategic plan for my unit," and encountering a look of utter incomprehension? They ask, "What exactly is it that you do for a living?" Indeed, the world of a scholar, both on the extraordinary occasions and in the day-to-day, is quite alien to outsiders.

We are, I would argue, in a similar situation when we attempt to understand this strange world of people who went to work carrying their briefcases every day to the Central Committee building to have meetings and conferences, to listen to speeches on "the international situation," to plan party congresses, and all the rest. Without exaggerating too much, we might start by admitting that such a white-collar, knowledge-based hierarchy is not entirely unfamiliar.

A second general point to make as we study Communist parties is that their longevity requires us to take their world seriously. A dominant theme in this book is parties with a great deal of stability, whether at the intermediate or local levels. These are places where people make their careers. Of course, to this we can juxtapose glimpses of parties in decline or crumbling, or responding to some major crisis. What is really striking, though, is how late the party generally remains stable and active. Our retrospective angle tends to blind us to this: that is, scholarship on East European communism tends to project backwards from the 1980s, when with our excellent hindsight it is pretty much clear that the end was coming—the end of the gerontocracy at least, if not of the Communist system. And a word on the gerontocracy: while the last decade of Communist rule provided many macabre stories of doddering, indeed senile, leaders—Kádár, Brezhnev, Honecker, Ceauşescu, etc.—these men were once much younger, and their party was too. Todor Zhivkov was an old man indeed when Bulgarian communism fell apart around him, but he was only forty-two when he ascended to the position of general secretary in 1954.

Party dynamism became party inertia, eventually, but the party continued to act in a manner that was very much alive, and this continued activity is very much part of the story. Thus, for example, we see the SED preparing and performing a party document exchange in September 1989.[1] The Polish Communist Party (PZPR) in Poland was also conducting a questionnaire at approximately the same time.[2] A sardonic laugh at their expense, noting that they little understood their imminent doom, does not gain us much understanding. As we learn from these examples, the Communist parties were actually still vibrant organizations, and their members surely experienced them in this way.

It would be fruitful to consider comparisons across the Soviet bloc, as Archie Brown and Jack Gray did in their classic edited volume of 1977.[3] However, this strikes me as a second-order task, only after we have tried to understand—anew, from a distance—what a ruling communist party (RCP) was, how it operated, and what it meant to be a member. So how can we generalize about Communist parties? What I outline in the following are some basic party features that have emerged from the contributions in this volume in respect to their political and organizational culture. I will then suggest some key variables that should be considered in further study, with the hope that they might assist the reader in drawing together the cases in this volume and also inspire further directions of research.

Commonalities

First, all of these parties were agents of revolutionary transformation. For older Communists, revolution is a life experience,[4] yet for later generations it remains a touchstone. The idea of revolution, as well as its representation, remains long after that period of upheaval is past. The party still talks about bringing about revolutionary change in society. In December 1989, a month before the PZPR was dissolved, I was working in the PZPR archive in Wrocław. They didn't have a space for their first-ever foreign researcher, so I occupied a desk in an office with a number of secretaries. They kept the building's intercom on, allowing me to listen in, one day, to what must have been the last meeting of the province's party committee (the minutes of whose very first meetings, four decades earlier, I was then reading). I didn't follow the discussion, but at the meeting's close the assembled comrades stood to mumble along to "The Internationale." Irony cannot get us very far in interpreting moments like this. We should rather ask what revolution, class struggle, labor and capital, and agitation meant to these men and women. We should also remember that when they met comrades from other countries, whether those in the bloc, from (what was then called) the Third World, or from capitalist countries, these themes would resonate even more strongly.

We should not be daunted by the prospect of understanding the ideological code, for I don't believe we ourselves need to master it. We simply need to think about this part of their mental toolkit. Even as in some ways the wielding of state power may have looked like that elsewhere in the world, this fundamental difference remains to the very end of the party's existence.

Second, the Communist Party possesses a moral code. Morality is absolutely central to the Communist worldview, going back at least to Lenin's concept of the "vanguard party," whose members assume a leadership role above the proletariat. Many leaders no doubt came to understand superiority as a product of their leadership (and thus corruption could be easily excused), but moral qualities also enabled leadership. Consider, for example, how many Communist leaders have been perceived or portrayed as ascetics.[5] At the bottom, meanwhile, Communist parties often expelled members for drunkenness or other acts or behaviors that were not illegal. However, all levels of Communist parties are united by a belief in a moral-political order, not unlike that shared by members of a large and socially disparate nobility: this is why we are the elite, we possess this code because we are elite, and therefore we should act in accordance with it.

RCPs were always trapped by a contradiction: on the one hand, the ambitious plans to recast the land, the economy, and political culture required that large numbers of people be brought into the fold. On the other, these goals required dedication and sacrifice, and so the party was wary of those who simply aped the rituals and mouthed the tenets. They were concerned, in other words, with character. As Edward Cohn shows in his contribution in this volume, increasingly detailed moral codes emerged in the post-Stalin Communist Party of the Soviet Union (CPSU); in part codifying things that of course were already there, like the imperative that party members should not drink, etc. I would suggest that even when the ideological code had faded, leaving only the shell that Havel called post-totalitarian, this need for a moral center remained. While a shared moral code is not necessary to rule a state, it is a shared feature of Communist regimes and a shared experience of party members across the region. This, factor, too, needs to be approached without irony, taking it as it is.

A third feature is more widely studied. As has long been recognized, the Communist Party (like any ruling party) provides an avenue for social advance. This means that it can be experienced in a way entirely divorced from ideology. However we might view the party and its aims, we should at least consider the possibility that for some members it was simply an organization one joined for reasons related to one's own life paths. The same could be said of just about any social organization, of course. We need to be careful not to domesticate the party too much, making it seem like a mere networking organization performing a necessary function in society. Rather, we should keep in focus the hybrid social nature of the party, at once class-based and universal in aspiration. Party activists or leaders therefore strived to call everything "working class," not simply because they were trying to fudge things, but because they had these dual goals of being both universal and class-based. A universal party is open to everyone, while a class-based, morally grounded party is not. The Communist Party, in any country in the Soviet bloc, was both.

So far I have focused on the individual experience of the party, but the next two points refocus our attention on the place the party had in Communist sociopolitical systems. The fourth commonality shared by RCPs is a paternal relationship to society, which of course can also be a maternal relationship in some respects. The party's moral code enables it to teach lessons to, or discipline, society. It simply knows what is best and provides for society accordingly. This relationship can be most strongly seen at the moments of normalization that followed major unrest, as in 1956, 1968, or 1981.[6] At these times, the party both metes out exemplary punishment to those who have transgressed, and offers security and home comforts to the rest. Another way in which this appears is in the nationalist rhetoric employed by regimes, about which more below.

Finally, to continue this familial exploration, the Communist Party's "older-brother relationship," or fostering relationship, to the state seems to me still to require further research. Communist parties left state functions—such as the distribution of goods and the administration of power—to state bodies staffed, at the top at least, by party members. This entailed a certain duplicity, but an uneven duplicity. Sometimes it is advantageous to claim a place in the spotlight (for example, by exhorting the state to distribute goods, or helping the state to distribute goods). At other times, it is better to give the impression that all is in the hands of state organs (like the police or courts), eliding the way that they are shaped by the party. Relationships between RCPs and the apparatus of the states in which they governed have not yet received the sustained attention that is needed. As scholars have gone on to focus on postcommunist issues, this neglect has grown. However, many of the essays in this volume point a way toward better understanding this relationship.

Variety and Difference among the Fraternal Parties

Beyond these five common features, a number of important variables are worth our attention. Exploring each of them allows us to move beyond the party as an organization and to consider it as an organic part of the society where it ruled. This initial exploration assumes that we are considering the parties in their heyday, between the crises of 1956 and the decline that began in the early 1980s; the questions would be quite different in a discussion of the Stalinist era or of the last years.

First, how can we categorize the modes of the party's presence in society and in the state? What kinds of authority or legitimacy does it have, and how does it deploy that legitimacy? I will say something about nationalism in a moment; here I am thinking more about whether the party can draw upon already existing forms of party politics, such as that of interwar populist or socialist parties. Based on these forms, how effectively can the party mobilize sectors of society? Another way to ask these questions is by reference to the state. What theory of governance do party leaders have at different times? Do they think of governing through the so-called transmission belts, thus according importance to peasant groups, women's groups, and trade unions? Is governing something carried out by the state? Or does the party see itself essentially as governing? These positions vary over time: thus, for example, moments of crisis may induce the party to take the helm or to pull back as state forces of order take center stage. The latter process was evident in Poland in 1981–82; the former seems more characteristic of 1968. As the contributions of this volume show, some variation can be observed across the region as well—for example, between the cases of the Socialist Unity Party of Germany (SED) and the PZPR—but it will take some further investigations to place the parties along some kind of spectrum.

This leads me to my second variable, the party's engagement with repressive structures and/or its militarization. The Communist Party was not only a repressive apparatus, and we should also consider the relationship between it and the structures of force that are ostensibly controlled by the state. Much research has been done in recent years on this issue, and we can certainly see some variation. As mentioned above, an extreme case in that respect was 1980s Poland, where Jaruzelski had control of the repressive structures, although on the other hand it has been said that, beginning in 1980, the PZPR in a sense ebbed away, and that martial law was a defeat for the party. Whether or not this interpretation is accurate, it reminds us that we often assume some kind of a tension between the party and the repressive structures, presuming of course that they are not the same. Another aspect of this tension is that the party sometimes deploys its own repressive forces, though only rarely in Eastern Europe do we have a hint of anything remotely like the Chinese Cultural Revolution. When, and amid what kinds of crises, does an RCP unleash its members in this way, and in what social situations? Historians of the party need to move beyond the cataloging of regime repression to consider the lines of authority that wielded that repression, as well as the constraints that limited it.

A third line of comparison is the nature of the leader and of the leader principle in general. Here the scholarship on Eastern Europe has not advanced much beyond the two poles of study of the particular leaders on the one hand, and assumptions about their interchangeability on the other (as in references to the RCPs as gerontocracies). The same however, can be said about study of dictatorships in general. Only in the last few years have scholars begun to look more closely at the conduct of politics in dictatorships.[7] We should be investigating the level of cohesion around leaders, and their ability not just to bring with them a clique into the corridors of power, but also to create a clear sense of community. We can then ask how much of this is a result of party structure and/or ideology, how much (if any) can be traced to national culture, and how much depends on the personality of an individual party leader.

A particular contribution of this volume is the strikingly original prosopographical research on party membership. The party, in these studies, is made up of clans headed by regional bosses, and membership of the party is often close to hereditary. Michel Christian's comparison of data from Nauen in the German Democratic Republic (GDR) and Kutná Hora in Czechoslovakia reveals interesting variety in this regard. Now we must ask, which case is more typical of RCPs? Is the Czechoslovak case, in which new members tended to come from the families of party members, more typical? Or can the model Christian finds in the GDR, in which the path to the party is through mass organizations, be found in other countries? Finally, what factors would lead to one model or the other? A reader of John Connelly's classic comparative study would not, I think, expect Czechoslovak Communists to become clannish two decades later—so what has happened?[8]

Earlier, I suggested some broad common ideas shared by members of RCPs. Now I propose a few ways of differentiating them. How important, first, are ideas, not ideology, to the party? Most countries had one or more theoretical journals, as well as institutes of Marxism-Leninism. We know something about how much particular ideas, such as market socialism, were discussed in individual countries, but rather less about the discourse of ideas in general. What did "orthodoxy" mean in the discourse of a party? What did "pluralism" mean? Once again, I plead here for scholarship without an ironic lens: our understanding of pluralism is vastly greater than that of a typical party functionary, I am sure. I wonder, however, whether an understanding of the deviation acceptable in the 1970s—that allowed, for example, a Mieczysław Rakowski or an Imre Pozsgay to consider themselves fully members of the party—could help us see the success of opposition in the 1980s differently.

The party embrace of "national and historical traditions" is a related theme. The role of national traditions in Communist societies has been a major focus of scholarship for decades.[9] Nevertheless, that investigation needs to turn inward to look at how the party itself deployed national experience within its ranks. The parties also had their own histories, their own traumas that could unite or divide them. They had different experiences in the interwar years, suffered different levels of repression at home and in the Soviet Union, and embarked upon different kinds of resistance during World War II. Most adult party members in 1970 would have some experience of the war, of course. A colleague of mine once pointed out that the tragedy, if you will, of the Communist regimes in Eastern Europe was that they did not have World War II in the sense that the Soviet Union did, as a basic experience that had the potential to integrate party and society. In relation to society as a whole, that is true enough: only in Yugoslavia and Albania (exceptions which prove the rule) could society give significant credit to the Communists for their resistance to the Nazis. Within the parties themselves, how was the war experience shared and used? Each Communist Party faced one or more crises of rule, through intraparty struggles, anticommunist opposition, or both. I have already referred to the ability of the party to maintain rule after such challenges, but one can also examine internal mechanisms for coming to terms with these crises and assimilating them into the party psyche.

The last variable is at the same time the most amorphous. Coming full circle back to the party's relationship to society, we should ask what levels of stigma or prestige are associated with party membership. Leaving aside the party's outward show of moral certitude and superiority, and the role of the party in the workplace and in other institutions, what does it really mean to be a member of the party, in one's neighborhood, or on one's football team, or at the seaside? When and where do party members feel proud of being a member of this selective organization? We cannot take it for granted that most members were either indifferent to their party or afraid of the consequences of not being a member. Some might feel pride because they identified with the sociopolitical project, and others because they knew they were benefiting from membership. At other times, party membership comes with a stigma attached, and the party member does not affix the party pin to their lapel and avoids exhorting neighbors to come out for an election or a May Day rally. Perhaps this shame was dominant only in a very few situations in Poland, Czechoslovakia, and Hungary after their respective crises. On the other hand, consider the queue on an East European city street for some scarce goods: does the party member proudly exercise his or her prestige to move to the front, or quietly join the end of the queue? There is so much more to know about the relationship between the party and the whole of society, anywhere in Eastern Europe.

Inspired by the essays in this volume, I would like to suggest a research agenda for the study of Communist parties in Eastern Europe. A significant and very promising direction in historiography now is the history of emotions. While this direction emerged from the field of cultural studies, where it purported to show the constructed nature and uncertainty of emotional categories, historians more recently have used emotion as a way to understand social experiences of the past. Indeed, it is useful to recognize that human actions are not only the product of rational calculation along economic or political lines. As in so many other areas, the study of emotion in Communist history begins with Sheila Fitzpatrick, whose 2004 article explored the tension between "official" Soviet emotions and private ones.[10] We might also reach back to Czesław Miłosz's essay on "Ketman" in *The Captive Mind*.[11] Turning from Communist society as a whole to the narrower world of the party, I do not try to improve upon this work, but instead want to suggest three emotional pathways that might prove fruitful in understanding that world.

The first of these is joy, or perhaps rather euphoria: the enthusiasm that draws people to the party, or at least did so at one time in the revolutionary period, for some people whom we call "enthusiasts." I strongly suspect that this emotion was always, or at least through the 1970s, readily accessible to most party members. It was a possible emotion, inextricably associated with the party and its goal to remake the world, and to make it better. Perhaps representations of enthusiasm are most often present in a staged form, in parades and celebrations, yet as such this emotional experience is one that can be recaptured. It lies just out of reach, a feeling to which one can aspire. The easy comparison is to the exaltation experienced by churchgoers (and envied by those who are not), but one could just as easily point to the spirit of pioneers and the longing that later generations feel. To the extent that these emotions can be recuperated, they are I think always present in the culture of the RCP.

Inextricably linked to the ecstasy and enthusiasm of party membership is an opposite emotional set: disappointment, sorrow, and sometimes anger. These are as essential a part of the revolutionary community, precisely because of the utopian aspirations of the party. Seeking to remake the world, they must fall short. The enemies are still too powerful or wily; the people are not ready; mundane problems stand in the way of achieving communism in one's lifetime. Even as the fire of revolution still flickers, and no one dares propose turning back, frustration yields to disappointment. Because revolutions cannot quite achieve everything they want to achieve, being a member of a party that enacts revolution means one is always experiencing disappointment and sorrow, and sometimes anger at those who are preventing you from achieving these things. As with the positive emotions, these negative feelings are not evident at all times; still, even the most pragmatic member of an RCP confronts the problem of revolutionary time and the question of the ever-receding future.[12]

The final stance in the mental repertoire of the Communist Party member is not an emotion, but rather a critical distancing from emotion. I have made several pleas to the historian so far to avoid the ironic stance, but now acknowledge its importance in the emotional life of the party member. The ability to concede the smaller shortcomings or idiocies of the system while suggesting that they cannot be helped or do not negate larger values is an essential tool for the conscious supporter of so-called developed socialism. It is an attitude that enables the party member to deal with his/her conflicting emotions in a manner adequate to the circumstances and conditions of party life after 1956. The films of intellectuals such as Krzysztof Kieślowski, Andrzej Wajda, or Krzysztof Zanussi in the seventies are masterpieces of irony precisely in that they show people managing their "partyness." Their characters both rise above the tensions inherent in the party and yet remain in it by deploying irony: thus they are able to occupy two places at once. This stance may be adopted not only by intellectuals, but also by top-level functionaries: this, at least, is the evidence of memoirs (like those of Mieczysław Rakowski) and of fictional representation. Think of the relationship in Kieślowski's *Blind Chance* (*Przypadek*, 1981), for example, between the young protagonist, Witek, played by Bogusław Linda, and his party patron in the first part of the film, played by Tadeusz Łomnicki. Witek's patron, Werner, at several points offers him a subtle ironic commentary — a raised eyebrow, a shake of the head — on party responsibilities or rituals. Providing distance, these gestures also reinforce hierarchy. This is precisely what takes place in the Andropov-Gorbachev conversation in Jan Behrends's contribution in this volume: Andropov is entirely aware of the absurdity of refusing an invitation to dinner, but he offers his protégé a commentary on the reasons for his decline that both underscores a power difference while confirming membership in a community whose rules these are. That irony may to some extent characterize any political structure, but I suggest it is especially important in the RCP, where the tension between that which draws one in, between power and inertia, dreams and realities, is so powerful.

One of the more biting opposition slogans from late Communist Poland was *"Program Partii programem Partii"*: "The program of the party is [merely] the program of the party." This mocked the party slogan at the time of the Tenth Party Congress in 1986, which was "The program of the party is the program of the nation." It is interesting because in the 1980s we rarely see any acknowledgement of the continued existence of a party with a program. This slogan captures a fundamental challenge to any study of the RCPs: sorry, but in the end, who cares about some party document? It's only their program, a document from an enclosed little world, and studying it tells us nothing about the actual world — not to mention anything about the imminent collapse of that world.

The lesson of the contributions collected here is that the Communist parties merit serious study if we are to make sense of the regimes. Party history is the stuff of political culture; even their programs are part of that picture. We certainly need to understand the people who produced them, the meetings at which they are discussed, and the ways in which they were read and implemented. In short, we can't understand the Communist system without taking a deep breath and steeling ourselves and examining documents that are often just achingly dull, and building the stories of people whose world has completely lost its sheen. Insight into that political culture will take us beyond a deeper understanding of the Communist system as well as offering new approaches to postcommunism.

Padraic Kenney is professor of history and international studies at Indiana University. He is the author or coeditor of eight books, including *Dance in Chains: Political Incarceration in the Modern World* (2017). Previously, a series of books—in particular *A Carnival of Revolution: Central Europe, 1989* (2002) and *The Burdens of Freedom: Eastern Europe Since 1989* (2006)—examined the fall of communism across Central Europe and elsewhere. His work has been translated into seven languages. In 2016, he served as president of the Association for Slavic, East European, and Eurasian Studies (ASEEES).

Notes

1. See Sabine Pannen's contribution in this volume.
2. See Krzysztof Dąbek's contribution in this volume.
3. Archie Brown and Jack Gray, eds., *Political Culture and Political Change in Communist States* (New York, 1977).
4. See, e.g., Catherine Epstein, *The Last Revolutionaries: German Communists and Their Century* (Harvard, 2003).
5. See Padraic Kenney, "The Gender of Resistance in Communist Poland," *The American Historical Review* 104, no. 2 (April 1999): 405 (note 22) and 413.
6. Grzegorz Ekiert, *The State Against Society: Political Crises and their Aftermath in Eastern Europe* (Princeton, 1996).
7. See, e.g., Milan W. Svolik, *The Politics of Authoritarian Rule* (Cambridge, 2012).
8. John Connelly, *Captive University: The Sovietization of East German, Czech, and Polish Higher Education, 1945–1956* (Chapel Hill, NC: 2000).
9. Katherine Verdery, *National Ideology under Socialism: Identity and Cultural Politics in Ceaușescu's Romania* (Berkeley, 1991); Marcin Zaremba, *Komunizm, legitymacja, nacjonalizm. Nacjonalistyczna legitymizacja wladzy komuni-*

stycznej w Polsce [Communism, legitimation, and nationalism. Nationalist legitimation of Communist power in Poland] (Warsaw, 2001).
10. Sheila Fitzpatrick, "Happiness and Toska: An Essay in the History of Emotions in Pre-war Soviet Russia," *Australian Journal of Politics & History* 50, no. 3 (2004): 357–371.
11. Czesław Miłosz, *The Captive Mind* (New York, 1981), 54–81; Miłosz uses the term, which originates as a concept in Islam, to mean the practice of publicly affirming one's allegiance to the ideological system while maintaining different beliefs in private.
12. On the question of revolutionary time, see Stephen Hanson, *Time and Revolution: Marxism and the Design of Soviet Institutions* (Chapel Hill, NC, 1996).

Bibliography

Brown, Archie, and Jack Gray, eds. *Political Culture and Political Change in Communist States*. New York: Holmes & Meier, 1977.

Connelly, John. *Captive University: The Sovietization of East German, Czech, and Polish Higher Education, 1945–1956*. Chapel Hill, NC: Chapel Hill Press, 2000.

Ekiert, Grzegorz. *The State against Society: Political Crises and their Aftermath in Eastern Europe*. Princeton: Princeton University Press, 1996.

Epstein, Catherine. *The Last Revolutionaries: German Communists and their Century*. Cambridge: Harvard University Press, 2003.

Fitzpatrick, Sheila. "Happiness and Toska: An Essay in the History of Emotions in Pre-war Soviet Russia." *Australian Journal of Politics & History* 50, no. 3 (2004): 357–371.

Hanson, Stephan. *Time and Revolution: Marxism and the Design of Soviet Institutions*. Chapel Hill, NC: Chapel Hill Press, 1996.

Kenney, Padraic. "The Gender of Resistance in Communist Poland." *The American Historical Review* 104, no. 2 (April 1999): 399–425.

Kieślowski, Krzysztof. *Przypadek* [Blind chance], directed by Krzysztof Kieślowski. Łódź: Wytwornia Filmów Fabularnych, 1981. Film.

Miłosz, Czesław. *The Captive Mind*. New York: Secker & Warburg, 1981.

Svolik, Milan W. *The Politics of Authoritarian Rule*. Cambridge: Cambridge University Press, 2012.

Verdery, Katherine. *National Ideology under Socialism: Identity and Cultural Politics in Ceauşescu's Romania*. Berkeley: University of California Press, 1991.

Zaremba, Marcin. *Komunizm, legitymacja, nacjonalizm. Nacjonalistyczna legitymizacja władzy komunistycznej w Polsce* [Communism, legitimation, and nationalism. Nationalist legitimation of Communist power in Poland]. Warsaw: Trio, 2001.

Index

A
Albania, 359
Amalrik, Andrei A., 328–29, 336, 341
Andreeva, Nina, 339
Andropov, Yurii V., 113, 174, 283, 297–99, 301n5, 332–34, 361
Arbatov, Georgi A., 330–31
Aristov, Averkii B., 172
Austria, 244

B
Babiuch, Edward, 263, 271
Bad Salzungen, 213
Balkans, 154n1
Baltic Republics, 185n10, 187n40, 326
Baltic Sea, 154n1
Barcikowski, Kazimierz, 263
Baskakov, Sergei A., 171, 174
Bautzen, 245
Bavaria, 314
Behrens, Friedrich, 147
Belorussian SSR, 185n10, 187n40
Benary, Arne, 147
Beria, Lavrentii, 168, 184n4
    Berlin, 227n1East, 64, 76–78, 84, 190–91, 193, 195, 197, 200, 203, 205n4, 213, 216–18, 238–39, 244–45, 247–48, 251–54, 256nn38–39, 314
    West, 80–81, 203
Black Earth Belt, 185n10, 185n12, 187n39
Bochnia, 274
Böhme, Irene, 74
Bohnsdorf (Berlin), 193
Borna, 78, 89n22
Borning, Walter, 194, 201
Borowski, Czesław, 134
Brandenburg an der Havel, 11, 73, 75, 80, 82–83, 85, 87n3, 87n5, 90n30, 90n37, 91n51, 98, 214, 215–20, 224–27, 227n1, 229n16, 230n23, 231n26, 231nn30–33, 232nn35–36, 232–33nn39–47, 316
Bratislava, 52
Bratkowski, Stefan, 279n13
Brezhnev, Leonid I., 12, 38, 173, 184, 198, 202, 281–92, 297–99, 300n2, 301n5, 302n16, 303nn20–21, 303n27, 304n37, 315, 326–27, 329–30, 332–37, 341–42, 353
Brigades of Socialist Work, 64
Brown, Archie, 353
Bruk, Franz, 245
Brzesko, 274
Buchheim, Walter, 244
Bulgaria, 69n35, 265, 353
Bydgoszcz, 276

C
Cambodia, 294
Caucasus, 185n10, 187nn39–40
Ceaușescu, Nicolae, 353
Central Asian Republics, 95, 185n10, 187n40
Central Bohemia, 62, 67n12, 145, 155
Central Committee (CC)
    of the CPCS, 46, 49, 53, 55, 57–59, 67n11
    of the CPSU, 11, 26, 42n35, 111, 168–83, 184n1, 185n6, 186n19, 186n21, 205n7, 286, 288–90, 293, 295, 305n43, 306n45, 326–41, 343nn7–8, 345n26
        Cadres Abroad Department, 293, 295
        Defense Industry Department, 293, 295, 307n53
        Department for Ties with Workers' and Communist

Parties of Socialist
Countries, 293–95
Department for Work with
Cadres Abroad and for
Foreign Travel, 295
Department of Foreign
Policy Propaganda,
296–97
International Department
of the CPSU (ID), 293–94,
297
Propaganda and Agitation
Department, 175, 296
of the PZPR, 124, 126, 129,
131–32, 134–36, 259, 264–65,
267–71, 273–75, 270
of the SED, 11–12, 74, 76–78,
84–85, 88n11, 111, 190–204,
204n3, 205n7, 205n9, 205n11,
206n19, 207n29, 207n35,
208n42, 208n49, 217, 230n17,
245, 247–50, 253, 255n17, 314
Central Europe, 9, 340
Charité (hospital in East Berlin),
190–91, 195, 199, 204, 205n4
Cheliabinsk, 173, 177
Chernenko, Konstantin U., 298–99,
301n5
Chernyaev, Anatoly S., 331, 333–36,
334n8
China, 155, 157n16, 282–83, 294, 296
Churaev, Viktor M., 172–73, 179
Communist International
(Comintern), 193, 294
Communist Party of Czechoslovakia
(CPCS), 2, 7–8, 17n42, 46–50, 52–
66, 67n7, 68n14, 68n25, 70n53
Communist Party of the Soviet
Union (CPSU), 2, 6–8, 11, 13, 14n1,
17n36, 23, 25, 34, 49, 88n10, 88n15,
98, 111, 115, 118n7, 168–69, 171,
175, 182–83, 244, 281–98, 301nn5–
6, 301n10, 305n43, 306nn44–45,
307n53, 326, 328–29, 332–33, 337,
339, 341–42, 342n1, 343n2, 343n8,
355
Congress of People's Deputies, 339
Connelly, John, 358

Consultative Council (Rada
Konsultacyjna), 127
Copenhagen, 287
Cottbus, 244
Crimea Regions, 185n10
Cuba, 155, 292, 294
Cyrankiewicz, Józef, 274
Czarzasty, Zygmunt, 132, 134
Czech Lands, 51–52, 57, 61
Czechoslovakia (ČSSR), 2, 46, 57,
62, 65, 146–48, 153, 154n1, 158n19,
159n24, 192, 296, 358–59
Czechoslovakian Women's League,
64–65
Czechoslovakian-Soviet Friendship,
64
Częstochowa, 265

D
Dahrendorf, Ralf, 278n3
Defense Council (USSR), 282, 284–
85, 292, 302nn12–13, 302n16
Democratic Party (Stronnictwo
Demokratyczny), 129
Denmark, 287
De-Stalinization, 10, 25–26, 38,
125–26, 326
Djilas, Milovan, 4, 6, 17n40, 66
Dnepropetrovsk, 342
Dobson, Miriam, 32, 35, 37
Donetsk, 182
Doronin, Pavel, 176, 177
Drapich, Wit, 271, 279n19
Dresden, 195, 245, 247
Dubček, Alexander, 48
Duma, 341

E
East Central Europe (ECE), 2–3, 6,
11–13, 143–45, 149–50, 153, 154n1,
155n3, 157n16
East Germany. See German
Democratic Republic
Eastern Europe, 1, 2, 54, 58, 185n10,
283, 295, 300n2, 340, 352, 357, 359
Efremov, Mikhail T., 173
Egorychev, Nikolai G., 286–8, 291,
303n20, 303n24

366 • Index

Elias, Norbert, 249
Enyutin, Georgii I., 173
Epstein, Catherine, 313
Erfurt, 245, 247

F
Federal Republic of Germany (FRG). See West Germany
Foucault, Michel, 124
France, 77
Frankfurt/Oder, 244
Freie Deutsche Jugend (East German Communist Youth Organization), 106, 115, 218, 227n3, 244, 247, 253, 318–319
Freier Deutscher Gewerkschaftsbund (FDGB) (Free German Confederation of Trade Unions), 106, 150, 227n3
Friszke, Andrzej, 127
Fröhlich, Paul, 244–47, 253
Funke, Otto, 245
Furtseva, Ekaterina A., 179

G
Galicia, 315
Gera, 245
Geremek, Bronislaw, 124
German Democratic Republic (GDR), 3, 10, 13, 72–74, 77, 81–82, 85, 87n3, 96, 99–100, 107–108, 112, 115, 117, 145–48, 150, 153, 154n1, 157n13, 190, 193, 195–96, 198–99, 201, 203, 207n35, 214–15, 218, 220, 222, 227, 229n15, 237, 239, 313–15, 321n5, 358
German Women's League, 65
Gesellschaft für Sport und Technik (GST) (Sport and Technology Association in East Germany), 65, 106, 119n14
Gierek, Edward, 127, 151–52, 264–65, 273, 277
Glasnost, 86, 113, 339
Glende, Gisela, 202
Glende, Günter, 202
Goffman, Erving, 242, 262
Golčův Jeníkov, 54

Gomułka, Władysław, 260–62, 264, 276, 315
Gorbachev, Mikhail S., 10, 113, 125, 169, 187n30, 282, 284, 298–99, 302n13, 326–29, 331–41, 344n9, 346n27, 346n37, 346n45, 361
Görden, 316
Gorky, 173, 180
Górnicki, Wiesław, 131
Götzl, Eduard, 245
Gräf, Hugo, 192
Gray, Jack, 353
Great Britain, 192, 288
Grechko, Andrei A., 283, 290
Grishin, Viktor V., 286, 291, 328, 337
Gromov, Evgenii I., 172
Gromyko, Andrei A., 283, 293, 297, 299, 305n43, 332, 337
Grünau (Berlin), 84
Grünau (Leipzig), 252
Grüneberg, Gerhard, 244

H
Hager, Kurt, 197–98, 207n35, 249
Halle/Saale, 10, 245, 247–48
Havel, Václav, 355
Herger, Wolfgang, 202
Hering, Werner, 196–99, 207nn33–35, 208n40
Hirschmann, Albert, 66
Hoffmann, David, 23
Honecker, Erich, 81, 115, 195, 198, 201–2, 208n50, 217, 253, 313–20, 323n23, 353
Humboldt University Berlin, 77, 193, 205n4
Hungary, 13, 56, 69n35, 145–46, 148, 150–53, 154n1, 172, 359
Husák, Gustáv, 49, 58

I
Infratest Institute, 96, 99–104, 106–7, 110–11, 113–14, 116–17
International Lenin School Moscow, 316
Israel, 286
Ivanovo, 173

J

Janion, Maria, 267, 279
Jaroszewicz, Piotr, 271
Jaruzelski, Wojciech, 124, 127–29, 131, 136, 152, 269
Jędrychowski, Stefan, 261
Jowitt, Ken, 128
Jung-Spartakus-Bund (Young Spartacus League), 316

K

Kádár, János, 151–52, 353
Kalmyk, 174, 179
Kalmyk, Nikolai I., 181–82
Kapitanov, Ivan V., 172–73, 182
Kaplan, Karel, 58
Karelo-Finish SSR, 185n10
Karkoszka, Alojzy, 267, 270–71
Karl Marx University Leipzig, 114
Karl-Marx-Stadt (Chemnitz), 244
Katowice, 273
Katushev, Konstantin F., 294
Kazakhstan, 185n10, 187n40
Kędzierzyn, 261
Keldysh, Mstislav V., 283
Kępa, Józef, 270
KGB (Committee for State Security), 172, 184n4, 283, 285, 294–97, 332, 340
Kharkhodin, Oleg, 37
Kharkov, 172, 173
Khrushchev, Nikita S., 6, 23–27, 29–32, 37–39, 41n14, 41n20, 41nn23–24, 41n29, 85, 111–12, 168–70, 172–74, 176–78, 180–82, 184, 185n6, 186n27, 187n30, 187n38, 187n41, 282, 285, 287, 298, 315, 327, 328, 330–33, 334
Kiefert, Hans, 245, 247
Kieślowski, Krzysztof, 361
Kirilenko, Andrei P., 298, 332
Kiszczak, Czesław, 124
Klasa Józef, 270
Kociołek, Stanisław, 261
Kohl, Helmut, 314
Kommunistischer Jugendverband Deutschlands (Young Communist League of Germany), 316
Komsomol, 5, 172–73, 178, 183, 185n10, 187n40, 287, 331
Kosygin, Alexei N., 298
Kowal, Paweł, 124
Kozlov, Frol R., 24–25
KPD (Kommunistische Partei Deutschlands / Communist Party of Germany), 244–45, 316
Krakow, 271–72, 274–75, 279nn18–19
Kraśko, Wincenty, 273
Kremlin, 330, 342
Krolikowski, Werner, 321n5
Kuibyshev, 173
Kutná Hora, 62–65, 67n12, 68n14, 70n53, 70n55, 358

L

Laos, 294
LaPierre, Brian, 32, 37
Lehmann, Helmut, 196, 207n26
Leipzig, 114, 195, 226, 240–50, 252–53, 255n6, 256n19, 256n30, 256n38, 257n40, 315, 321n5
Lenin, Wladimir I., 316, 335, 337, 354
Leningrad (St. Petersburg), 178, 339, 342
Leonhard, Wolfgang, 193
Liashko, Aleksandr P., 182
Liebknecht, Karl, 316
Ligachev, Yegor K., 337–40
Linda, Bogusław, 361
Lindenberg, Udo, 319
Łódź, 134, 276
Loga-Sowiński, Ignacy, 261
Łomnicki, Tadeusz, 361
Lorenzen, Jan, 314
Łukaszewicz, Jerzy, 270
Luxemburg, Rosa, 316

M

Magdeburg, 244–45
Magnitogorsk, 10, 87n3
Main Intelligence Directorate (GRU), 283, 297
Maków, 268
Malin, Vladimir M., 174

Marxism-Leninism, 9, 13, 200, 323n23, 358
Matern, Jenny, 196, 207n27, 207n29
Mecklenburg, 245
Mecklinger, Ludwig, 197–99, 208n40
Mělník, 56, 67n12
Mewis, Karl, 245, 247
Mexico, 193
Miass, 177–78
Michnik, Adam, 124
Middle East, 282, 288, 300n2
Mijal, Kazimierz, 263
Mikoyan, Anastas I., 171, 304n32, 346n31
Miller, Leszek, 135–36
Miłosz, Czesław, 360, 363n11
Ministry of Communications (USSR), 296
Ministry of Defense (USSR), 292–93, 295–96
Ministry of Foreign Affairs (MID) (USSR), 293, 297, 305n43, 306n44
Mink, Georges, 127
Mitrokhin, Nikolai A., 174, 205n7
Mittag, Günter, 194, 198
Moczar, Mieczysław, 261
Moldova, 185n10
Molotov, Vyacheslav M., 293, 346n31
Mongolia, 294
Moravia, 52, 145, 155
Mordovia, 35
Moscow, 7, 17n36, 172–75, 177–79, 192, 245, 282, 286–87, 289, 291, 300n2, 315–16, 318, 321n5, 322n20, 327, 331–32, 337–39
Motyka, Lucjan, 270, 274
Müller, Helmut, 245
Mylarshchikov, Vladimir P., 170
Mysiadło, 264

N

National Socialist Worker's Party of Germany (NSDAP), 194, 206nn18–19, 239
Nauen, 64–65, 70n55, 358
Neubrandenburg, 245

Neues Deutschland (ND) (SED Party Newspaper), 79, 114, 243
Neumann, Alfred, 244
North Atlantic Treaty Organization (NATO), 112
North Korea, 292, 294
North Rhine-Westphalia, 319

O

obkom (oblast party committee), 172–75, 177–79, 181–82, 186n27, 187n29
oblispolkom (local Soviet executive organ), 181
Oelßner, Alfred, 193
Oleksy, Józef, 132
Olszowski, Stefan, 128, 263
Onyszkiewicz, Janusz, 271
Oranienburg, 228n6
Orzechowski, Marian, 125
Osęka, Piotr, 261

P

Pannhause, Gerhard, 219
Party of Democratic Socialism (PDS) (successor of the SED), 117, 229n16
Pękala, Jerzy, 271, 279n18
People's Commissariat for Internal Affairs (NKVD), 2
Perestroika, 10, 86, 123–25, 329, 334, 336, 338–39, 344n9
Perm (Molotov, 1940–1957), 171, 173–74
Petrovichev, Nikolai A., 173
Pigalev, Petr F., 173–74
Pisnik, Alois, 244–45
Plenikowsky, Anton, 193
Podgórecki, Adam, 268
Podgornyi, Nikolai V., 298
Poland, 3, 13, 96, 125–26, 145–46, 150–53, 154n1, 198, 259–60, 278n9, 283, 295–96, 305n43, 353, 357, 359
Polekhin, Mikhail A., 173, 181
Polikarpov, Dmitrii A., 174
Polish Socialist Party (PPS), 128, 136, 263, 275

Polish United Workers' Party
  (PZPR), 2, 7–8, 10, 12, 14n1, 123,
  126–31, 133–37, 259, 264, 269, 271,
  273, 353–54, 357
Polish Workers' Party (PPR), 128, 263
Politburo
  of the CPCS (Presidium), 46
  of the CPSU, 2, 11, 168–69, 171,
    175 282–95, 297–98, 301n5,
    301n10, 330, 334, 339, 342
    Presidium, 178–79
  of the PZPR, 128, 261, 267
  of the SED, 11, 191–92, 194,
    196–97, 199, 202, 204n3, 217,
    247–49, 252, 256n25, 314–15,
    319
Ponomarev, Boris N., 174, 294, 299,
  334–35, 337
Ponomarev, Mikhail A., 174, 179
Poplevkin, Trofim T., 182
Portitz (Leipzig), 246
Potsdam, 73, 216, 218, 224, 227n1,
  228n6, 230n21, 231n25, 231n33,
  232n38, 232n41, 233nn42–43,
  233n47, 245
Poznan, 10, 264
Pozsgay, Imre, 358
Prague, 10, 49, 52, 67n11
Prague Spring, 13, 60, 111, 148, 150,
  329
Presidium. See Politburo
Primakov, Evgenii M., 287
Primary Party Organization (PPO),
  24–25, 34, 39, 53, 56, 62, 72, 74–78,
  80, 85
Primorsk, 173, 178
Putin, Vladimir V., 282, 341–42,
  346n46, 347n50

Q
Quandt, Bernhard, 244

R
Racibórz, 261
Rakhmanin, Oleg B., 294, 307n50
Rakowski, Mieczysław, 124, 128, 131,
  269, 361

Rau, Johannes, 319
Red Cross, 64, 195
Revoluční odborové hnutí (ROH)
  (Revolutionary Trade Union
  Movement), 150
Reykowski, Jaussz, 132
Riazan, 176–77, 186n23
Riesman, David, 276, 279n20
Riesner, Hans, 245
Rostock, 245, 247
Rozsypal, Kurt, 147
Rusakov, Konstantin V., 294
Russia, 154n1, 282, 326, 340–41,
  345n15
Ryabov, Yakov P., 283, 301n6
Rybicki, Zygmunt, 271, 279n17
Ryzhkov, Nikolai I., 338

S
Saarland, 315–16, 318, 321n5
Saxony, 78
Schabowski, Günter, 319
Scherzer, Landolf, 213–14
Schilling, Günter, 223–24
Schirmer, Gregor, 199, 208n44
Schmidt, Helmut, 314
Schumann, Horst, 248, 252–53,
  256n29, 257n40
Schürer, Gerhard, 252, 256n39
Schwedt, 87n3
Schwerin, 244
Sefrin, Max, 197, 207nn33–34
Seidel, Karl, 191, 195, 198–99, 201–4,
  206n21
Semichastnyi, Vladimir E., 172–73
Serbin, Ivan D., 295
Serov, Ivan A., 172
Shelepin, Alexander N., 172–73, 278,
  288–89, 291, 304nn28–29
Shelest, Petro Y., 182, 289, 291
Shevardnadze, Eduard A., 285, 299,
  338
Shikin, Iosif V., 173
Shvernik, N. M., 25–26
Sindermann, Horst, 248
Slovakia, 52, 57, 61–62, 145
Słupsk, 132

Smirnov, Leonid V., 283
Smolensk, 175–77, 181
Social Democratic Party of Germany (SPD), 112, 115
Socialist Unity Party of Germany (SED), 2, 7–9, 11–13, 14n1, 53, 57, 64–65, 70n47, 72–74, 76–78, 87n5, 95–108, 110–118, 190–194, 196–198, 200, 206n22, 207n27, 213–27, 230n20, 237–51, 253–54, 255n6, 255n17, 256n26, 313, 318, 353, 357
Solidarność, 123, 129–31, 152, 198
Soviet General Staff, 201–2, 283, 285, 292
Soviet Union (USSR), 3, 13, 23, 26, 28, 31, 34, 37, 40, 47, 56, 64, 85, 87n3, 96, 113, 115, 154n1, 158n19, 168–70, 176, 179, 192, 198, 206n22, 212, 265, 282–81, 283–92, 296–99, 302n12, 305n43, 307n53, 326, 328–31, 333, 336–37, 339–41, 342n1, 346n37, 355, 358–59
Sovmin (the Council of Ministers, the Soviet government), 173, 178
Sovnarkhoz (regional economic council), 169, 179
Spain, 193
SPK (Staatliche Plankommission / State Plan Commission), 250, 252
Stahlmann, Richard, 193
Stalin, Joseph V., 2, 13, 26, 29, 31, 33, 168, 176, 208n50, 282, 291, 294, 298, 316, 320, 326–28, 331, 334, 337, 343n3, 346n31
Stalingrad, 194
Stalinism, 2, 13, 15n10, 39, 126, 135, 146, 327, 331, 338, 343n3, 345n12
Staniszkis, Jadwiga, 128
Stasi (East German Ministry of State Security), 79–80, 82–84, 96, 98, 110–16, 119n17, 147, 190, 197, 199–200, 202–3, 204n1, 208n47, 209n55, 220–21, 237
State Planning Committee (USSR), 283
Stavropol, 179, 187n30, 331–33, 346n27
Steffen, Max, 245

Stief, Albert, 244
Stoph, Willi, 251
Strauß, Franz Josef, 314, 320
Suhl, 245
Supreme Military Council (later renamed Military Council), 285
Supreme Soviet (USSR), 178, 187n29, 284–85, 290, 302n13, 333, 341
Suslov, Mikhail A., 283, 291–92, 294–95, 298, 301n5, 328, 334, 345n14
Svazarm, 64–65
Świda-Ziemba, Hanna, 260–61
Świrgon, Waldemar, 134
Szelényi, Iván S., 47, 66
Szlachcic, Franciszek, 263, 265, 270
Szydlak, Jan, 265

T

Tarkowski, Jacek, 269–70
Tejchma, Józef, 263, 269
Thälmann, Ernst, 316
Thiemann, Klaus, 199
Titov, Vitalii N., 172
Treiman, Donald J., 47
Tula, 180

U

Ukraine, 171–73, 183, 185n10, 187n40, 289
Ukrainian Communist Party (UkrCP), 289
Ulbricht, Walter, 148, 150, 195, 207n27, 207n29, 243, 247, 251, 314, 316, 319
Ulyanovskii, Rostislav A., 294
United People's Party (ZSL), 125–26, 129–30, 136
United States of America (USA), 77, 282, 286, 288–93, 298
Ural Regions, 185n10, 187n39
Ustinov, Dimitrii F., 283, 285–86, 293, 296–98, 301n6, 332

V

Vietnam, 154n1, 289–92, 294
Vladimir, 174
Volkskammer (East German Parliament), 224

Voronovskii, Nikolai A., 181
Voslensky, Michael S., 6

W
Wajda, Andrzej, 361
Walicki, Andrzej, 260
Wambutt, Horst, 201, 203, 205n62, 209n56
Wandlitz, 217
Warsaw, 264–65, 268, 273, 275
Warsaw Pact, 291–95, 299, 318
Weber, Max, 7, 156n7
Weber, Rudolf, 194, 206n17
Wehner, Herbert, 314, 316, 320
Weimar Republic, 313, 315
West Germany, 74, 77, 80–82, 84, 96, 101, 108, 203, 315, 321n5
Western Europe, 136
Wiebelskirchen, 315–16, 319
Williams, Kieran, 58
Wrocław, 354
Wyschka, Arthur, 192, 205n12

Y
Yakovlev, Aleksandr N., 296, 329, 337, 345n19
Yeltsin, Boris N., 338–42, 346n42, 346n45
Yugoslavia, 359
Yurchak, Alexei V., 74

Z
Zaikov, Lev N., 284, 302n13
Zamyatin, Leonid M., 296, 308n57
Zanussi, Krzysztof, 361
Zaporozhie, 173
Zetkin, Clara, 196
Zetkin, Max, 196, 206n24
Zhezlov, Nikolai I., 179, 187n30
Zhivkov, Todor, 353
Žleby, 54
Zuckermann, Leo, 193
Zyuganov, Gennady A., 341

www.ingramcontent.com/pod-product-compliance
Lightning Source LLC
Chambersburg PA
CBHW072142100526
44589CB00015B/2043